Thomas McKean
The Shaping of an American Republicanism

Thomas McKean and his son, Thomas McKean, Jr., a Charles Willson Peale painting. Courtesy Philadelphia Museum of Art: Bequest of Phebe Warren McKean Downs

Thomas McKean

The Shaping of an American Republicanism

G.S. Rowe

COLORADO ASSOCIATED UNIVERSITY PRESS
BOULDER

Copyright ©1978 by Colorado Associated University Press
Boulder, Colorado 80302
International Standard Book Number: 0-87081-100-2
Library of Congress Catalog Card Number: 77-94085
Printed in the United States of America
Designed by Dave Comstock

For my mother and father

Contents

Preface	ix
1. Ambivalent Legacies	1
2. Delaware Lawyer	14
3. Liberty Under Attack	31
4. Conspiracy	48
5. The Birth of a Republic	64
6. The Shape of Republicanism	84
7. Establishing the Courts	101
8. The Origins of a Moderate, Independent Judiciary	121
9. "A Valuable Acquisition in Congress"	142
10. The Changing Nature of Representation	164
11. New Directions	178
12. The Achievement of an Independent Judiciary	202
13. The Trials of Reform	227
14. Federalist	241
15. Republican	264
16. "The Democratic Judge"	288
17. Republican Governor	307
18. Republicanism Under Attack	332
19. The Move to Impeach	360
20. Look Back in Wonder	390
Notes	407
Bibliography	475
Index	485

Preface

One of the most creative and profitable means of understanding the historical developments in America between 1750 and 1815 is provided by a study of the changes in the peculiar cluster of attitudes and beliefs that historians have come to call "republicanism."[1] It has only been in the past two decades that historical studies have described in some detail the salient characteristics of republicanism and begun to chart the many changes it underwent during and after the Revolution. In its incipient stages republicanism did not demand allegiance to a specific form of government. It was primarily concerned with the proper character of society, with the principles underlying good government. It was a common set of political and social attitudes and assumptions, often reenforced by religious ideas, which shaped or helped to shape every segment of American society. Derived from a mixture of English dissenting thought, values inherited from the age of Puritanism, the study of ancient republics, Enlightenment abstractions, and the realities of the American environment, republicanism emerged as a unique libertarian heritage with a notable capacity for transforming itself.[2]

Politically, republicanism in colonial America came to suggest a general suspicion of government which in application resulted in a political system of limiting and dividing power that went beyond anything found in the Mother Country.[3] It was in part because of their successes in restraining power that Americans were able to foster the hope that good government was achievable, that man's quest for greater liberty could be successful. The social dimensions of republican thought embraced a concern for serving society in a virtuous and productive manner and placing the well-being of society above one's own personal desires and ambition, if need be. Understandably, a certain ambivalence towards prosperity was implicit in early republican thought, for there was an almost imperceptible line of demarcation between receiving fair and ample compensation for one's labors, and becoming obsessed with material gain. It was acknowledged that too great a reliance upon wealth and material rewards led to excesses, to an unproductive lifestyle, to a physical and moral flabbiness which undermined a person's will and capacity to resist the inevitable encroachments upon one's liberties.

With the imperial crises in the 1760s came impressive shifts in American republicanism. Conscious that republican values, like republics, tended to fade and disappear as a result of individual and collective failures, a softening of the commitment of the many to defend liberty against the few seeking the enlargement of their power and influence, Americans came to view the constitutional readjustments proposed by the British ministry as a deliberate and provocative conspiracy against their rights. They came to believe that to retreat one step, to permit one ancient right to be sacrificed to the ambition and design of the British ministry would prove fatal to all American liberties. A good many Americans were persuaded by 1774 that corruption within England had proven deleterious to historical rights and values there; they were determined that no such erosion of rights and privileges would occur in America— even if that ultimately necessitated severing ties with the Mother Country.[4]

America's declaration of independence in July 1776 established a republic for American republicans. It also prompted in Americans an even greater concern with private and public social and moral regeneration. Americans understood that a republic was only as strong and vital as its people. History proved that the lives of republics were exceedingly brief; invariably they had collapsed from within as their peoples failed to remain vigilant and virtuous and determined to defend their prerogatives and privileges. Understandably, great emphasis was placed on religion and education to instruct the American people in republican virtue. As Professor Gordon Wood and others have demonstrated, Americans became almost paranoid in their anxiety to maintain the high standards they deemed essential to the well-being of their republican experiment.[5]

Under the impact of revolutionary developments American republican thought was transformed and in the process it in turn transformed American society. Americans were moved to critically reassess such institutions as slavery, the law, established religion, office-holding practices, and their own deferential society. More and more they insisted that a person be judged less on "artificial distinctions" based on inheritance or false influence than on his own personal qualities and capacities. A person's commitment to republican values, to American independence, industry and virtue—many would add simplicity and frugality—came to loom ever larger in the political realities of the early republic. From this new set of social assumptions emerged a radically new political ideology which itself promoted changes in style and practices in the political community. Legal, social, and political systems felt the impact as Americans sought to give republicanism concrete and permanent form. Words like "rights," "consent," "democracy," and "representation" took on vastly new connotations.[6]

Unfortunately, honest men differed greatly in their political interpretations and hopes for republicanism. Despite the direction it gave to people's lives, in large measure republican ideology remained vague and indefinite. Thoughtful Americans conceded that a republic might mean "anything, everything, nothing." After 1776 people generally agreed that a republican government was the best form of government devised by man, that liberty was a natural right of man, and that a major goal of good government should be to guarantee the peoples' liberties. They also concurred that good government was based on the consent of the governed and was by definition limited government. But opinion as to how those areas of agreement were to be translated into the everyday practice of governing a community or nation differed markedly from person to person. *How much* liberty should man have? *How* could government best secure liberties? *How much* consent should the governed have? In what *form*? *How limited* should government be? Just *how* simple and frugal must a good republican be? Those questions and a good many others divided men. As Professor John Howe has shown, because the stakes were so high and because their sense of history persuaded them that they were likely to fail whatever their solutions to these problems, good Americans fell to quarreling—often violently so.[7] As late as 1815 the success of America's republican experiment by no means seemed assured.

The history of the United States between 1750 and 1815 is the story of Americans defining and redefining republicanism, and struggling to institutionalize their conclusions. No man fought more zealously to define and shape republicanism than Thomas McKean, and no man opposed more vigorously those who failed to share his own particular brand of republican ideology. His contemporaries readily acknowledged that he was "one of the first persons in Pennsylvania to perceive the soundness of republican principles, and...one of the most firm to maintain, defend, and diffuse them."[8] Yet McKean's republicanism, like that of most Americans, remained for the most part unarticulated; it was a vague, almost unconscious appreciation that certain values and practices were essential to a stable, progressive, enlightened and free society, amounting to a general set of principles to be applied to situations as they arose. Few men were in a better position to assess the political and social currents in America or to shape the course of events— and thus the configurations of Pennsylvania's republicanism— than McKean, with his impressive political and legal influence.

At one time or other McKean's official titles included president of the Pennsylvania Provincial Conference (1776), president of Delaware (1777), chief justice (1777-79) and governor (1799-1808) of Pennsylvania, and president of the Continental Congress (1781). He attended the Stamp Act Congress, provided inspired leadership to Delaware's struggle for independence, headed one of Pennsylvania's most aggressive and powerful extralegal committees in the early years of the Revolution, signed both the Declaration of Independence and the Articles of Confederation, commanded a battalion of Pennsylvania Associators, was one of the two most important figures in Delaware's constitutional convention (1776), and served eight years in the Continental Congress during its most crucial history. He also played a prominent role in Pennsylvania's ratification convention (1787) and in creating its second state constitution (1789-90).

As chief justice of Pennsylvania he ruled on some of the most significant and explosive cases in the early republic, and in the process established a body of law which shaped the early history of Pennsylvania and the United States. He more than any other man was responsible for the creation of an independent state judiciary in Pennsylvania.

This work is not an attempt to write the definitive account of American republicanism and its transformation between 1750 and 1815. Nor is it an attempt to produce a full-scale biography of McKean. Its goals are more modest; it seeks to explore McKean's impact on American republican ideals and practices between 1750 and 1815, and how, in turn, McKean was shaped by republican values and assumptions.

Sections of this book draw upon five articles, "'A Valuable Acquisition in Congress': Thomas McKean, Delegate from Delaware to the Continental Congress, 1774-1783," *Pennsylvania History*, XXXVIII (July 1971), 225-64; "Thomas McKean and the Coming of the Revolution," *Pennsylvania Magazine of History and Biography*, XCVI (January 1972), 3-47; "The Legal Career of Thomas McKean, 1750-1775," *Delaware History*, XVI (April 1974), 22-46; "The Travail of John McKinly, First President of Delaware," *Delaware History*, XVII (Spring-Summer 1976), 21-36; and "Outlawry in Pennsylvania, 1782-1788, and the Achievment of an Independent State Judiciary," *The American Journal of Legal History* XX (July 1976), 227-44, which are used by permission of the respective editors.

Many debts have been incurred in the process of writing this book. Professors John C. Miller, George H. Knoles, Carl N. Degler, and the late David M. Potter, all of Stanford University, offered valuable criticism when the work was in dissertation form. Professor Dayton D. McKean of Boulder, Colorado read a preliminary draft and graciously provided helpful editorial assistance while refraining from seeking to influence my treatment of McKean. A good many scholars, some of whom I have never met or communicated with, helped me more than my footnotes suggest, including Robert Brunhouse, Harold B. Hancock, Elizabeth K. Henderson, Sanford W. Higginbotham, Harry M. Tinkcom, David Hawke, Henry J. Young, Thomas R. Meehan, and John M. Munroe. I have also benefitted from the encouragement or aid provided by C.A. Weslager, Jack Marietta, Scott Rosenberg, and Gregory Smith.

The staffs of the Historical Society of Pennsylvania, the Library Company of Philadelphia, the Historical Society of Delaware, the State Archives in Dover, the New York Historical Society, the Department of Records in Philadelphia, the Chester County Historical Society, and the Division of Public Records in Harrisburg were particularly helpful. I owe special debts to Peter J. Parker of the Historical Society of Pennsylvania, Dorothy Lapp of the Chester County Historical Society, Ward J. Childs, III, Department of Records, Philadelphia, and Martha Simonetti, of the Division of Public Records, Harrisburg. No one has been more helpful in the face of unending requests for aid than Lucille Schweers and Jeanne McMahon of the University of Northern Colorado's James Michener Library.

My greatest debt of course is to my family. My wife, Mary, has done more than her share of typing and proofreading. Jennifer and Justin have endured their father's preoccupation with McKean and eighteenth-century America with a mixture of amusement and tolerance. To my parents who have been unfailingly supportive in all that I have done, I have dedicated this book with love.

UNIVERSITY OF NORTHERN COLORADO
GREELEY, COLORADO

G. S. ROWE

1. Ambivalent Legacies

As the clerk of the Delaware supreme court called for silence in the crowded New Castle courthouse, two young men rose to approach the bench. The younger of the two, identified in his petition as "Thomas McKean of New Castle, Gentleman," stood before Chief Justice Ryves Holt and associate justices, John Vining and William Till, seeking admittance to the Delaware bar. Doubtless his petition employed what had become customary language to confirm that he had "for some time Past been studying the Law, and [had] now a Desire of being admitted an Attorney in this worshipful Court." Though the justices were charged by law to discover whether applicants to the bar were "of an honest disposition...and Learned in the Law," no formal interrogation of McKean ensued. Associate Justice William Till merely administered an oath of allegiance and a second oath committing the young aspirant to an honest pursuit of his profession. Thus on October 7, 1754, at the age of twenty, Thomas McKean unceremoniously began a career in the law which spanned four decades, and opened to him some of the most prestigious offices in the early republic.[1]

Like most young men from Pennsylvania and Delaware drawn to the bar in the mid-eighteenth century, McKean came from a "reputable" family. The McKeans had been part of the stream of Scotch-Irish immigrants which poured into America after 1720. These impatient, grim, often irascible refugees from Ulster, part of a second wave of Presbyterian immigration, looked to escape the economic and religious grievances that they had borne for generations. Famine, the uncertainty of land tenure, rent-racking, and forced tithing combined unhappily with laws marking off Presbyterians as inferior citizens to drive them to the New World. At first in small numbers and then by the hundreds and thousands, they poured into Delaware, substantially reordering the demographic profile of those lowland counties. The great majority eventually found their way into the rolling uplands of the Pennsylvania backcountry, particularly into the western portion of Chester County and the eastern valley of the Susquehanna, leaving a chain of Presbyterian churches and communities in their wake.[2]

Thomas McKean's grandmother, Susanna McKean,* settled with her family in 1725 on a three-hundred-acre "plantation" in Chester County, Pennsylvania, a few miles southeast of the New London crossroads. She prospered and when she died in 1731 she left the bulk of her estate to her younger sons, William and Thomas, each receiving two hundred acres of her estate with "all improvements."[3] Not the least of the benefits which Susanna McKean passed on to her two sons was the locale of the McKean farm. Chester County was already remarkable for its large and munificent farms. Its accessibility to water and markets together with its rich soil and extended growing season made Chester County an ideal commercial farming area. If the sons profited greatly from saleable surpluses, as did a large percentage of their neighbors, their success can not now be measured with precision. However, it is worth noting that their two-hundred-acre farms were located in a county where farms

---

* The family's name is often spelled McCain, McCaine, McCane, McKean, M'Kean. It will be spelled McKean throughout this work.

averaged one hundred and thirty acres, and where a farm of seventy-five acres sufficed to support a family of five comfortably.[4]

Nonetheless, within a decade of their mother's death Thomas and William McKean were seeking new horizons. Both became innkeepers in 1741, Thomas moving north to Tredyffrin Township where he purchased a tavern and a tract of land nineteen miles from Philadelphia on the road from Lancaster, William seeking a license for a tavern at Half-Way House, in present day Chatham, London Grove Township. Four years later William McKean relocated in Cochranville, Londonderry Township, when the opportunity arose to succeed the late James Logan as tavern keeper there.[5]

Among the McKean's neighbors in New London were the Finneys, a family which, like the McKeans, had originated in Scotland before migrating to northern Ireland and then to Pennsylvania. In 1731 William McKean married Letitia ("Letty"), the fourth of Robert Finney's seven children, and Thomas McKean, the subject of this book, was born March 19, 1734. Eight years later, in August, Letty McKean died at the age of thirty-three, leaving her husband with four children, all under the age of ten. In 1745 William McKean married Ann, James Logan's widow, who had six children of her own.[6]

All who came to know the mature Thomas McKean—and recorded their impressions—found him stubborn, contentious, and impulsive. A nephew who knew him intimately observed that he "had no patience to bear contradiction...but kind forbearance and apparent acquiescence from others, although they could not cure, would avert any evil consequences." A longtime political associate of McKean's, Charles Biddle, spoke for many when he recalled that McKean was "a very violent man who had no command of his temper, but spoke whatever he thought on all occasions." According to his nephew, McKean's relatives and persons "who esteemed and loved him most" viewed his irascibility and combativeness as a "constitutional infirmity."[7]

Those who knew McKean's father and grandmother could have little quarrel with that assessment. Within a year of the purchase of her farm Susanna McKean had "complain[ed] heavily" to the proprietary agent that a tract of land adjacent to her property which had purportedly been promised to her earlier, and which cut her off from an area called "the Barrens," was being surveyed for one Gabriel Alexander. Susanna McKean insisted that Alexander had no right to the land "by grant or purchase." Unwilling to await an administrative or legal clarification, she boldly claimed and sowed the disputed acreage. She already had three hundred acres "of good Land that was surveyed...to Ye best advantage," groused Isaac Taylor, a knowledgeable surveyor himself and the man whose son had surveyed the land for Alexander; for her to seek the piece of land claimed by poor Alexander was "really unaccountable." Despite Taylor's observation and the efforts by more than a dozen neighbors who argued that "Alexander lived in this neighborhood odds of six years...and we...never knew him to defraud no manner of person, or wrong any man," Susanna McKean enlarged her estate at Alexander's expense. All that is known about Susanna McKean suggests that the stubbornness and aggressiveness that she exhibited in defying Alexander and those supporting his claims were in keeping with her general character.[8]

William McKean exhibited a similar pushiness and contentiousness but without the same success. When he sought a renewal of his tavern license in 1743 several persons in the vicinity petitioned local officials to deny him such a renewal, maintaining that he "hath in and for some time past kept or permitted a very ill conduct and practice in and about his aforesaid house in permitting or suffering people to swear, curs, fight and be drunk." Such practices, the petition went on, "must needs be vary afruntive & provoking to almighty God ...and [are] of...truble to all Sober & well inclin'd people." The permit was renewed only after McKean persuaded the magistrates that he would "behave better for time to come."[9]

Still, his troubles mounted. In 1746 and again the following year, he traveled to Chester on command of the orphan's court which was intent on guaranteeing that he was administering James Logan's estate in a suitable fashion, one that would ensure Logan's children their rightful heritage. By 1749 William McKean's trips to Chester were prompted by a more serious matter. He had been drawn into an awkward situation growing out of poor luck, his own unbridled ambition, a series of unfortunate land transactions and, beyond that, egregious miscalculations in choosing business associates. The specific maneuverings surrounding the many financial and legal developments remain so intricate and obscure as to be almost impossible to piece together with any real confidence. First he lost his tavern license. Then, when sued for debt he mounted his own offensive by initiating a number of protracted and rancorous countersuits. In the February and November terms, 1749, he lost two suits for debt, one to a Simon Hadley, a second of £20 to a Joseph McDowell. He had acted as his own counsel in an earlier legal dispute but aware by 1750 that he was out of his depth, he secured the legal services of David Finney, his nephew who lived in Delaware. These unfortunate legal contests burdened him for the next two decades.[10]

Thomas McKean's later contemporaries were very conscious of the paradoxes in his behavior and character. Indeed, it is remarkable how frequently the very people who described him as violent, contentious, and stubborn, in the next breath conceded his more admirable qualities. Charles Biddle, for all his harsh criticism of McKean, confessed he "had a high esteem for him," and in the end labeled him "a very honest man." Similarly, McKean's nephew, Thomas McKean Thompson, having provided some severe strictures on McKean's conduct and character, added that he was "kind and effectionate," a man of "sterling integrity," "paternal kindness," "affectionate beneficence." The biformity of McKean's character is attested to by an endless variety of contemporary comments, and not a few of McKean's acquaintances were as quick to attribute his more admirable characteristics to his family and early life as they were to find the sources of his failings there.[11]

The McKeans and the Scotch-Irish Presbyterians who comprised their neighbors and closest friends took inordinate pride in what David Finney called his family's "strictest honor and virtue." They strove to inculcate their children with these values in their schools as well as in the more informal setting of the family. When Thomas McKean was nine years old his father enrolled him and his older brother, Robert, in Francis Alison's New London Academy, established for "the Promotion of Learning, where all Persons may be instructed in the Languages and some other Parts of Polite Literature." Overseen by the local Presbyterian synod, the school was soon acknowledged "the most celebrated in the Province." Of particular interest to fathers in Chester and surrounding counties was the fact that their sons could obtain their education from Alison "without any Expense whatsoever."[12]

The guiding force and genius of the New London Academy clearly was Alison himself.[13] Mercurial in temperament, adamant in his political and religious convictions, yet often warm and sympathetic to his students and their needs, Alison was a gifted teacher whose "natural genius and powers of mind, appeared to every observer great and excellent, beyond the common race of learned men." The daily curriculum that Thomas and his classmates experienced was strongly reminiscent of the classicist program Alison himself had received at the University of Edinburgh. Each student received a strong dose of belle lettres and moral and natural philosphy in addition to the traditional Greek and Latin. There was also a strong emphasis on English grammar and composition which Alison taught by employing the *Guardian* and the *Spectator* as models. Each morning students received "the greatest advantage" from Alison's "critical examination" of their themes and other assignments, generally prepared in Latin as well as English. Contemporaries remarked on the adult McKean's "comprehension of mind in taking notes embracing substance, without omitting anything material," a skill which doubtless owed much to these early daily exercises.[14]

Certainly after 1746, and perhaps before, McKean and his schoolmates were introduced by Alison to the works of Francis Hutcheson, a central figure in the Scottish Enlightenment, with whom Alison had studied briefly at the University of Glasgow. Alison seems to have accepted Hutcheson's moral philosophy totally, and he frequently had his students make abridgements of Hutcheson's *Short Introduction to Moral Philosophy* where Hutcheson maintained that virtue and happiness were closely related, that any society to be happy and progressive must cultivate virtue above all else. He also believed "the end of all political unions is the general good of those thus united, and this good must be subordinated to the more extensive interests of mankind." Hutcheson argued that if a mother country should seek to change its relationship to its colonies by force, or if what had begun as a safe, mild union should degenerate into a "severe and absolute one," resistance on the part of the colonies was justified. Growth of the colony or its increased prosperity might also change the relationship. "There is something so unnatural," he wrote, "in supposing a large society, sufficient for all the good purposes of an independent political union, remaining subject to the direction and government of a distant body of men who know not sufficiently the circumstances and exigencies of this society."[15]

Alison added his own philosophy of revolution and change to Hutcheson's curriculum. "When ye Public liberty & safety cannot be otherwise secured," he told his charges, "it is lawful and honorable to make strong efforts for a change of government." "The divine right of Governors is a dream of court flatterers," he continued, "the rights of ye People are divine as well as those of Princes; Nay more divine as Princes were constituted for ye Good of ye People." McKean and his classmates diligently recorded these sentiments in their notebooks. How often McKean was to reflect upon these ideas in his later years is open to conjecture; it is clear enough that many of these ideas became part of his life.[16]

Alison "did not look with a careless glance on public affairs." He sought the same intense commitment to public service from his students that he himself constantly exhibited. He sought to create leaders, for he believed "We should all willingly bear an equal share of Public burdens & we should not expect that any man should undergo great hardships for the public safety & defense than we are willing to share ourselves according to our rights & privileges." In view of man's proven propensity to limit rather than to broaden his freedoms, it was essential that leaders be both virtuous and enlightened. "Liberty," he insisted, "is a most tender plant that thrives in a very few soils; neglected it soon withers and is lost; but is scarce ever recovered." Alison was convinced that "farmers' sons must furnish ministers & magistrates for all our frontier inhabitants: or they must Sink into Ignorance, licentiousness, & all their hurtful consequences."[17]

The New London Academy was ideally located to achieve Alison's purposes. Believing that the cities had "grown exceedingly expensive" and convinced that "few farmers are or will ever be able to give their sons a learned education in . . . cities," Alison saw New London as a perfect spot. As he pointed out to Ezra Stiles, of New Haven, "Parents feel that their children when [in the cities], by bad example are prompted to live above their abilities & future incomes." Besides, one living in cities could not "advance the interests of learning, as in the country." Rural schools were surrounded by "few, frugal & industrious people" and were situated where there were "cheap accomodations to be had" and, more important, "few temptations to luxury." The spare, disciplined Alison was persuaded that it was "in the schools of poverty . . . that great men could only be found, as in ancient Greece and Rome." In poverty and hardship one found courage, discipline, commitment. A new land, a hard land, demanded tough, resourceful, pious and virtuous leaders, Alison told his students. Luxury led to dissipation and dissipation led inexorably to moral and physical flabbiness. Young men who sought luxury and ease were "the most useless drones and the most contemptable burdens of the earth."[18]

Alison succeeded. There were no "useless drones" in his first class. Besides Thomas, there was his brother Robert who went on to become a prominent clergyman and the first president of the Medical Society of New Jersey; Charles Thomson, later a fine classical scholar and the secretary of the Continental Congress during its entire history; George Read, who would sign the Declaration of Independence and become a United States senator from Delaware as well as chief justice of the Supreme Court from that state; Hugh Williamson, a physician, scientist, and representative from North Carolina to the Constitutional Convention in 1787; Mathew Wilson, clergyman and physician in Delaware and an ardent patriot in the conflict with Great Britain; John Ewing, subsequently a professor of natural philosphy at the College of Philadelphia, and pastor of the First Presbyterian Church in Philadelphia; John Cochran, who later gained fame as director general of hospitals during the Revolution; James Latta, moderator of the General Assembly of the Presbyterian Church and founder of an academy at Chestnut Level; and Paul Jackson, who would succeed Alison as master of Latin at the Academy of Philadelphia. Hugh Williamson's

George Read, signed by Rembrandt Peale. Courtesy of Historical Society of Delaware

observation that Alison "never failed to emplant a love of civil and religious liberty in every heart of his pupils" is amply borne out by their subsequent careers.[19]

In 1750 McKean left the New London school to study law in Delaware with his cousin, David Finney. It is unlikely that Alison, with his commitment to sacrifice and service, played a part in turning the lad towards the law. Alison had not been among those warning young men of "such temptations and dangers as are in the law way," or pointing out that the term "lawyer" was often used synonymously with "liar," but doubtless he agreed with Poor Richard's caustic observation that "A Countryman between two lawyers is like a fish between two cats."[20]

Nonetheless Thomas McKean could not have been unaware of virulent anti-lawyer traditions in Pennsylvania and Delaware, or the charges that the practice of the profession was antithetical to a republican society. It was said that one should not look to lawyers for public leadership, for they were "generally pricking fellows, and maintainers of false suits, and accustomed to let out their tongues and talents for hire, to call good evil, and evil, good, to defend guilt and declaim against innocence, just according as they are paid." The Pennsylvanian James Allen, himself a lawyer, admitted the temptations to do evil. "The further I engage in law matters I find it necessary to put a guard on my virtue," he wrote in his diary, ". . . being habituated to exercise one's ingenuity in inventing arguments on the wrong side, at least warps the Judgment, & will in time corrupt the heart, unless constantly opposed by an active virtuous principle."[21]

But McKean was equally aware, as were most young men, that the persistent and often vicious condemnation of the craft failed to obscure its social, political, and financial rewards. Lawyers might be characterized as "sharp, contentious . . . and unnecessary," and some lads might protest that they would prefer to "be brought up in a Profession in which there was a possibility of being honest," but the law was, without a doubt, the quickest avenue to wealth and prestige open to a young man in mid-century America. The obvious success of men like Tench Francis and John Moland in Philadelphia whom McKean often witnessed plying their profession in Chester courts, was not lost on young men like himself. Nor, doubtless, was the implication of Richard Peters' concession that John Ross, an attorney who assiduously worked the Philadelphia, Chester and Delaware courts, was "successful beyond his merits."[22]

McKean may have been encouraged to join the bar by the enthusiasm of George Read, who in the previous year had left Alison's to study law under the direction of John Moland. But no doubt he was persuaded also by the unique opportunity afforded by the Finneys, for his cousin, David, was an attorney in the courts of the Lower Counties, and his uncle, John Finney, was an active and influential member of the New Castle bench.[23] The boredom and hardships of the apprentice system were often mitigated only by the personality of the master, and McKean was fortunate in having a man like David Finney as his preceptor. Finney was said to be "kind and cheerful. . . his benevolence unbounded."[24]

Finney's contributions to McKean's education went far beyond benevolent instruction, however. Finney had "a good law-library." And he had influence. With the aid of his father he arranged to have McKean commissioned a clerk to the prothonotary of the New Castle court of common pleas, an office which introduced McKean to the language and form of the law. Because the prothonotary of the courts of common pleas was also the register for the court of chancery in each county, McKean soon acquired the skills and forms associated with that post. His experience and knowledge of the law broadened still further when, at the age of eighteen, he was commissioned deputy prothonotary and register for the probate of wills for New Castle County. These offices advanced his legal education more effectively than any apprentice program confined to a practitioner's office ever could have.[25]

Much of McKean's most valuable legal education took place in the various courthouses where Finney practiced law. Here he had the opportunity to meet the principal lawyers, judges and citizens of each court district and to participate, however modestly, in the legal process. It was equally rewarding to observe older practitioners like Tench Francis, John Moland, John Ross, and by 1754, talented newcomers such as Joseph Galloway, Thomas Otway, John Price, David Henderson, and George Read. The impressive success of Read in attracting clients in his first year before the Chester courts must have been reassuring to McKean who, early in 1754, was nearing the end of his apprenticeship. The records show that inexperienced men could and did challenge the old guard in the Chester courts and attract their share of the legal business.[26]

McKean had added reason to observe closely the practice of Finney after 1752, for Finney argued a number of critical cases before the Chester court in behalf of McKean's own father whose legal woes were mounting. Between 1751 and 1754 four men won verdicts ranging from £18 to £34 against William McKean. Despite winning substantial sums of money himself in two instances, McKean was unable to collect and his "goods and chattels" were twice seized by the sheriff. It was probably to aid his brother that in 1751, William McKean's brother Thomas advertised his Tredyffrin Tavern for sale despite its "good credit and good business." Persons familiar with the McKeans in these years continued to judge them a "reputable" family but William McKean's fortunes by 1754 were visibly on the decline.[27]

Four years with David Finney did more than merely provide Thomas McKean with the skills essential for success at the bar. McKean's association with the Finneys introduced him to grand homes, impressive connections, wide influence, and the material rewards of gentry status. Though he clung tenaciously to the values promulgated by Alison and thereafter exhibited the same naked ambition and contentious personality that characterized his father and grandmother, he turned his back irrevocably on the crude and often violent life he had known in New London.[28] He possessed the size and the sturdy constitution—as well as the impulsive reactions—that one associates with frontiersmen, but he was neither particularly sympathetic to nor comfortable with frontier types and their life-style.[29] McKean never thereafter publicly admitted his humble beginnings; indeed, he fought so transparently to obscure them that his later political enemies quickly recognized his vulnerability on the subject.[30]

The law called for McKean to establish clearly his proficiency and suitability for the law before the justices of the Delaware supreme court, but McKean knew, as did Finney, that such exams were generally perfunctory. Faced with crowded dockets and all-night sessions, the justices were not anxious to initiate comprehensive examinations of lads coming before them seeking admittance to the bar. Their own limited formal training added to their reluctance to pursue lengthy interrogations. Fortunately, as in McKean's case, the justices were usually well acquainted with the aspirant's talents and promise, the quality of his apprenticeship, and the ability and station of his sponsor long before the novice approached the bench with a formal petition to enter the bar. When McKean and Finney approached the bench on October 7, 1754 to request McKean's admittance to the bar, the verdict was already in.

2. Delaware Lawyer

The legal circle which McKean joined in October 1754 was undergoing slow, subtle, but potentially far-reaching changes. The number of unauthorized and meagerly trained lawyers continuing to serve their own personal interests and those of others coming before Delaware courts suggests that the community's demand for legal services still outstripped the ability of formally trained personnel to meet it. It also signaled the community's continuing reluctance to rely exclusively on professionals for their legal needs. Delaware attorneys, like practitioners in other colonies faced with a similar phenomena, resisted the proliferation of lay lawyers. Practitioners protested that "great Inconveniences have arisen to Gentlemen of the law from the Bar & Council Table being taken up by Persons who have no claim to a seat thereon," and urged that judges act to restrain these legal interlopers. A practicing attorney in Pennsylvania courts presented himself to the court of oyer and terminer in Sussex County in

1756, unencumbered by letters of recommendation or sponsors, and "prayed for to be admitted an attorney & take the oath." The records show he was "accordingly admitted & sworn an attorney & took the oath." But increasingly pressure was applied to deny practice before the courts to local legal aspirants without a four-year apprenticeship, or without requisite experience as a clerk in one of Delaware's courts.[1]

By the 1750s greater attention was also being paid to the conduct of lawyers plying their trade before Delaware justices. The law provided by that time that when "attorneys misbehave they shall suffer such penalties and Suspensions as Attorneys at Law in Great Britain are liable to in such cases." Occasionally, local attorneys were openly rebuked and restrained from practicing. John Neill, a Sussex attorney active in Delaware and Maryland courts, was tried on a forgery charge emanating from one of his cases and exonerated by a jury. The presiding judge nonetheless suspended him from practicing in the courts of the Three Lower Counties, telling him "Yet certain it is That you have been guilty of an Act & Practice unworthy of a Person who bears the name of an Attorney at Law."[2] In its own unspectacular way the Delaware bench and bar were groping toward a greater self-consciousness and a more demanding level of performance from its members.

Still, the bar in the Lower Counties was distinguished neither by its numbers nor talent. It continued to be, in fact, a mere appendage of the Pennsylvania legal community. If the records can be trusted at all there were probably less than a dozen formally trained Delawareans practicing law in 1754, although several were the beneficiaries of European training.[3] Knowledgeable observers of the Delaware courts were hard pressed to name a single lawyer of quality. The fact that one local attorney could be described as "erroneous in his principles" and "immoral in his practice" might disturb members of the Delaware bench and bar, but it was not calculated to elicit much attention from a community which often viewed the courts as "dens where greedy lions are." The Irish of New Castle flatly alleged that "they [had] no chance for common justice" in the county courts.[4]

Judges, too, were maligned for their personal and professional deficiencies. The Assembly felt compelled to pass legislation restraining individuals who by their over-zealous criticism were thought to undermine justice and the dignity of the courts. Delawareans outside the legal community were resigned to the backwardness of their province in matters of the bench and bar and were seemingly content to have their professionally undermanned courts monopolized by lay judges, and by attorneys from Maryland, New Jersey, and Pennsylvania. But the 1750s were an important transition in the development of a local bar.[5] As resourceful and talented men like George Read, John Dickinson, fresh from England, and Thomas McKean profited greatly from their labors at the bar, other ambitious and capable lads were drawn to the craft. As more capable sorts turned to the law and became more sophisticated in their knowledge of the law, their profits increased commensurately, and they drew still larger numbers to the bar. McKean proved to be an important part of this ineluctable cycle in Delaware.

McKean's first year of practice was a remarkably successful one if his claim of having earned four hundred pounds in Pennsylvania currency is to be believed.[6] Given the stringent statute limitations on legal fees then current in Delaware, his earnings reflect an exceedingly busy year for a novice, an accomplishment doubly impressive in view of Delaware's small population and limited commercial activity. Nor was New Castle, the focus of his efforts, seemingly a prosperous and promising town in 1754. As the "ancientest Town" and the seat of the government, New Castle was crowded during "Publick Times." In less exciting or less hectic times, however, inhabitants and visitors alike conceded that the town "waxes poorer & poorer, and Falls into Contempt more and more." "The truth is," admitted one inhabitant," [New Castle] is in ruinous condition, without trade & meanly inhabited." In 1753 John Moland sought to dissuade his student, George Read, from centering his practice in New Castle, arguing that the "county was poor, and not able to support more of the fraternity than were in it already."[7]

Still, young lawyers like Read and McKean, recognized as two of the most talented of the newcomers to enter the Delaware bar, could boast that, with some effort, a decent, even attractive living could be wrung from opportunities in New Castle and its surrounding areas. Even without the commercially oriented law that sustained many a lawyer in Philadelphia, Delaware attorneys found work enough. Delaware's farmers, artisans and small tradesmen proved to be as litigious as any Philadelphia merchant. But whereas Philadelphia-based lawyers could often associate with one or two merchants for the bulk of their business and secure high fees in the process, Delaware lawyers, like those in the smaller communities of Pennsylvania, relied for their financial success on the quantity of their business. McKean drew on the substantial Irish population which looked to anyone sympathetic to their plight before the courts of the Lower Counties. He could also make substantial sums by handling the legal details of naturalization for the many emigrants pouring into the Delaware counties.[8]

Apparently not all of McKean's contemporaries at the bar viewed his "considerable practice" with equanimity. Late in his life he remembered that his rapid rise had elicited a great deal of envy "not only among the Juniors but also . . . some of the seniors of the Profession." He assures the reader of his autobiographical sketch that the envy and enmity of his colleagues proved nothing more than "an additional spur" to his industry; that he continued indefatigable in his quest for legal learning and an expanded practice. His account of his reaction to the jealousy of his colleagues probably offers us more about McKean's personality than he cared to convey. If his colleagues' envy did prove to be an additional incentive for him, it was not the last time that he was to pursue a course of action as much because of, as in spite of, the opposition it fomented.[9]

In all probability the enmity of McKean's contemporaries, so indelibly impressed upon his mind sixty years after the event, stemmed as much from his general conduct in this period as from the sudden professional success he enjoyed. In the early Fall of 1754 McKean, twenty years old and still an apprentice lawyer, cavalierly disregarded a Delaware tradition which placed a premium on mature, established men in high public office, challenging more experienced candidates in a contest for the sheriff's office of New Castle County. He did so by ignoring a second long-standing tradition in Delaware politics, that men did not publicly court public posts. To campaign indirectly, to allow friends, relatives, and sympathizers to disseminate the word that a candidate would accept a post, or agree to run because of public demand was one thing; actively to solicit or publicly seek the office for its own sake was quite another.[10]

McKean brashly advertised in the Pennsylvania *Gazette* for five consecutive weeks prior to the October 1754 elections, soliciting votes of the "Free holders and others, electors of the County." His explanation that he was seeking their votes in a manner "pursuant to a practice in a neighboring province" could not have measurably aided his cause in a community bitterly conscious of its subservient relationship to Pennsylvania. No other candidate saw fit to court similar notoriety. Evidence of his degree of success through this gambit is lacking; the records merely indicate that political veterans John McKinly and William Golden were the two top vote getters, and Golden was eventually appointed to the post.[11]

So far as can be discovered McKean never again advertised his candidacy for public office. He thereafter insisted—and often with considerable adamance—that he had never once pursued office; the people, he maintained, had always sought him out for public service, often to his own discomfort and financial loss. The capriciousness of competitive popular politics was brought home to McKean early and he never forgot it.[12]

The political developments—and family rivalries—in New Castle County during this period which encouraged such rash self-promotion by McKean in opposition to the more established Golden and McKinly despite a traditional suspicion of young, untested men, is untraceable. Nonetheless the incident reveals with abundant force the strength of McKean's ambition and boldness. It reveals, too, something of his weakness, his impetuosity, his tendency to miscalculate political opportunities and to misread the political climate.[13]

McKean's self-assuredness, so visible in his early challenge for the sheriff's office, apparently stood him in good stead in his law practice. He attracted several men of influence who saw in his ability and boldness a safeguard and promotion of their own interests. But unless the pattern changed appreciably in the third and fourth years of his practice, the Finneys' varied interests were especially vital to McKean's success from the first. The frequent litigation emanating from the Finneys' considerable property and interests afforded him a steady source of business. Available court dockets establish that David Finney continued to pursue his own practice after McKean joined the bar, but he did so less aggressively than before. At least some of his clientele turned to McKean.

McKean's practice expanded rapidly. In 1755 he gained admittance to the bar of Chester County where he successfully joined the dogfight for business in the busy courts of the bustling market town of Chester. Thomas Otway, John Price, John Moland, Joseph Galloway, and George Read were among the busiest of the lawyers when McKean began his practice in Chester's courts, but within two years he was competitive.[14]

A crucial part of McKean's business in Chester centered around his efforts to disentangle his father from a myriad of continuing legal troubles. In May 1753 William McKean, still represented by David Finney, won a verdict of £50, plus court costs, but was unable to collect in the face of the defendant's pecuniary status. In the following year he lost three separate verdicts and again saw his "goods and chattels" seized by the local sheriff. The articles failed to be sold at public vendue only "for want of buyers."[15]

The orphans' court and attorneys and guardians for Logan's children were still anxious about William McKean's ability or willingness to protect the youngsters' share of their father's estate. Their concern was exacerbated when, in 1751, Ann Logan died and the execution of the estate was thrust more completely in William McKean's hands. Logan's oldest son and namesake seemed particularly concerned with what he considered to be the senior McKean's eagerness to exploit and control a plot of land deeded to his father.[16] It was into this legal jungle that Thomas McKean stepped in the fall of 1755, replacing David Finney as his father's principal legal counsel.

In one of the very first cases in which he pleaded for his father, McKean faced John Moland, stentorian-voiced leader of the Philadelphia bar—and won. Unfortunately for William McKean he continued to win judgments only in those cases where the defendants were without funds or resources, or were able and eager to battle him through an interminable series of costly appeals. He won a substantial judgment against one Morrial Allen in 1755 in a case which lingered on in the

Chester courts for more than five years. Earlier he had won a verdict against a Lillis Caldwell; the McKeans were still suing the Caldwells in 1761 in an effort to receive even a portion of what was coming to them.[17]

There were some important side effects for the young McKean in all this. Simon Hadley, who won a judgment of £24 against McKean's father in 1750, sought out Thomas McKean as his own attorney in 1756. McKean readily accepted and argued persuasively in Hadley's behalf in several cases. By 1758 McKean's successes in the courts of Chester County and in the Lower Counties prompted him to expand his practice into the courts of Philadelphia, including the Supreme Court there.[18]

Much of McKean's success in the law stemmed from his good fortune on the circuit.[19] Still, Delaware lawyers quickly learned that the political advantages of the circuit often outweighed the financial rewards. As the majority of legal and judicial figures were also prominent in provincial politics, the circuit provided unparalleled opportunities for resourceful young men like McKean to lay the foundation for political preference. It was here that one established his capacity, formed the necessary connections with influential people, did all those things McKean failed to do properly before his precipitous try for the sheriff's office in 1754. McKean's success before the Sussex courts, for instance, had much to do with his being named by John Ross deputy prosecutor for the Crown in Sussex County in 1756. McKean profited from the office's impressive fees for two years before resigning.[20]

McKean made tentative plans late in 1757 to seek additional legal proficiency and prestige by attending the Middle Temple in London. Whether he was influenced by the example of John Dickinson, recently returned from schooling abroad and a close friend of his brother Robert or by his own brother's experience in London,[21] or whether he merely succumbed to the increasing interest in the Inns which developed in America after 1750, is not clear. But that he was intent on attending the Middle Temple is demonstrable. He went so far as to buy several law books, including a copy of Kebel's *Reports,* which he inscribed, "Thomas McKean of the Middle Temple." Whatever his original plans, he did not study abroad.

Instead he sought admission as a special student—a *specialiter*—which allowed him to bypass residency and examinations at the Temple, by paying £ 4-14-6 for entrance fees and the cost of his certificate. In all likelihood McKean arranged to go to London, then for some reason, perhaps his involvement in the local militia company formed in 1757, or his father's deepening legal embroilments and financial losses, he was forced to abandon his original intentions.[22]

Expanding personal opportunities also may have played a role in McKean's failure to attend the Middle Temple. He was still a deputy prosecutor for Sussex County, and the chance to plead cases for the crown and to profit from each of the cases he prosecuted meant a substantial increment to his income. The opportunity to curry favor with the Proprietary interests no doubt proved equally alluring. And political preferment was not long in forthcoming. In October 1757, due largely to the efforts of Benjamin Chew, one of the more powerful voices in Proprietary circles and Speaker of the Delaware Assembly, McKean was chosen to be clerk of the Delaware legislature. He was unanimously voted a second term in October 1758. He added the fees attached to that office to his already substantial income.[23]

Still, his overriding interest remained his law practice. He diligently sought to increase his clientele and to build his reputation beyond the borders of Delaware. His case load in these years, so far as it can be reconstructed on the basis of fragmented materials, centered on the prosaic needs of an agrarian community: he collected a debt from Jonathan Stout for Job Wolford of Hunterdon County, New Jersey; he helped Nathaniel Wilds recover money due on a bond from Patrick Connor; he assisted Dr. James Boggs in a contestment will suit; he acted as an agent for Phillip Keaney who offered a £ 15 reward for the return of Violet, a "very active" and "rather artful" female runaway slave with three small children. He handled hundreds of such cases. A nephew who commented upon McKean's early success ascribed McKean's ability to attract clients to his absolute honesty, his rigid sense of righteousness.[24]

Disputes and acrimony among individuals in the three lower counties might increase his dockets but as a civic leader he toiled diligently towards a virtuous and tranquil society. And, as one would expect of a student of Alison's, McKean looked first to education in the struggle against lawlessness and dissipation. Of particular interest to him was the welfare of Alison's Academy. He contributed time and money to that institution and when, in 1763, the school was moved to Newark, Delaware, he joined a small group of interested citizens, among them his former classmates John Ewing, Matthew Wilson, and Charles Thomson, to oversee the school in its fight for survival. Later, in 1769, he was formally named, along with Alison, Ewing, Wilson, Thomson, and notable Pennsylvanians William and Andrew Allen, as a trustee of the Newark Academy.[25]

It was largely because of his untiring efforts in the interests of free public education in the Lower Counties and Pennsylvania that the College of Philadelphia conferred on him an honorary M.A. degree. The trustees of the college had determined that it might be of some service to the college to confer honorary degrees on several gentlemen of Pennsylvania and the neighboring colonies "who were of distinguished character for their usefulness and Learning." The faculty granted McKean the degree on May 17, 1763 before a "vast audience" which included Benjamin Franklin, the man most instrumental in the college's growth and survival. Throughout his lifetime McKean bore witness to the impact of Alison's priorities on his own career, for in whatever political capacity he subsequently functioned, he pressed for an expansion of free public education.[26]

Though he ultimately settled permanently in Philadelphia, asserting that the opportunities in Delaware were "too limited," he seemed content enough with the potential of the Lower Counties in the 1760s, and with good cause. In the face of serious competition for clients from such entrenched practitioners as Benjamin Chew, John Dickinson, Read, George Ross and Joseph Galloway, and from talented local newcomers Nicholas Van Dyke, Alexander Porter, and David Thompson, McKean managed to hold his own. Indeed, by the mid-1760s he had apparently captured an impressive portion of the legal business in New Castle County and not a little in the other counties, especially Sussex. The Supreme Court records for these years have not survived but the various county court dockets unmistakenly point up his eminence. If the names in the court dockets reveal anything, they suggest that the heart of his clientele came from Irish and Presbyterian elements. A few clients were Quakers; a surprising number were women.[27]

It would appear from the records that four men besides McKean engrossed most of the business coming before the New Castle courts by 1768: Read, Alexander, Porter, Nicholas Van Dyke, and David Thompson, all of whom had joined the bar after 1750. From the clerk's marginal notations in these dockets it is easy to apprehend McKean's larger case load vis-a-vis his competitors. In the May term of the 1768 common pleas court, McKean was the identifiable counsel in nearly twice as many cases as his nearest competitor, George Read. David Thompson was a distant third. This pattern seemed to carry over into other terms. In a single court term McKean was also designated by the court "a specially constituted" counsel in some seventeen instances; again, almost twice as many as his closest rival.[28]

The county court sessions not only provided the Delaware lawyer with an opportunity to ply his trade but often to protect his own business interests as well. Cases involving suits by lawyers or suits against lawyers were commonplace, and for obvious reasons. In Delaware as in other colonies the law was a vehicle for rapid social and professional differentiation and the improved status that normally accrues to such specialized knowledge and skills. And money, at least in this instance, followed status. It was not chance that dictated that many of the largest landholders and most prosperous men in colonial Delaware were attached to that colony's bar. This connection between wealth and the legal bar was clearly appreciated by the population at large—and widely resented. The charge was frequently made that lawyers, once established, put on airs and expressed sentiments often critical of the middle and lower stations of society—lawyers like McKean "whose ancestors, two generations ago, were upon an equality with some of the meanest of us."[29]

Lawyers increasingly came to dominate the county court sessions in Delaware, monopolizing both sides of the counsel table. The economic interests of men like Read, Porter, John Vining, Van Dyke, and McKean padded the courts' dockets, dominated the justices' attention, and provided a quarterly showcase for these aggressive, acquisitive men. Not infrequently

McKean was called upon to defend a colleague at the bar in a land case or a suit centering on disputed commercial transactions. He defended young Nicholas Van Dyke and David Thompson in a session of the 1768 term, for instance, and in return had Thompson prosecute his own ejectment action against one of his tenants who failed to fulfill a contract. In a single court session McKean opposed Thompson and Van Dyke in separate actions, associated with each of them to argue against clients represented by Read and others, acted as a counsel for Van Dyke in a suit, before having Thompson prosecute a case against William Golden—sometime sheriff of New Castle County—in which he himself was a party.

The litigious bent of the McKean family also contributed to the increase of case dockets in many a county court in the 1760s, and often inadvertently produced in these sessions the semblance of a tempestuous family gathering. William McKean continued to be plagued by legal woes in Chester and his offspring and their relatives made life interesting for the justices of Delaware's courts. In seeking to guarantee what they felt to be their interests, the Delaware McKeans forced local attorneys into a number of complicated alliances. Thus, spectators to the May term of the 1768 New Castle court of common pleas saw Thomas McKean in separate actions defend his younger brother William against Benjamin Noxon and William Pugh; his brother-in-law, John Thompson; his cousin, David Finney; and his uncle, John Finney, in property settlements. They also saw him pleading the cause of several litigants pressing individual suits against his cousin and uncle.

McKean's steadily growing importance as a legal figure can be seen in part in the increasing status of his clientele. The requisite tax lists that would throw light on the social and economic status of McKean's clients have not survived, but the status of some is clear enough. Not only was he approached for legal services by such eminent members of the Delaware gentry as James Latimer, Thomas Dunn, John McKinly, George Munro, Benjamin Noxon, and Thomas Duff, but he became involved in the Delaware concerns of leading Pennsylvanians, among them Richard Peters, Henry Drinker, Benjamin Chew, Abel James and Samuel Purviance.[30] These legal contacts often ripened into friendships paving the way for political advancement.

It will be remembered that Chew had been responsible for McKean's securing the clerkship of the Assembly in 1757, while Peters drew John Penn's attention to McKean as a political advisor and was among those responsible for his being named a justice of the peace in 1765 and retaining him in that position in the next decade.[31]

McKean steadily improved his status and reputation in Pennsylvania's legal community in the decade before the Revolution, continuing to plead his father's business and that of other clients in Chester courts, and representing a number of Chester County residents before the Supreme Court of that province. John Dickinson, more prominent in Pennsylvania than McKean, was sufficiently impressed with McKean's skills to welcome his help in a number of cases before that high court. Perhaps more significant is the fact that men like Joseph Reed and Miers Fisher, popular younger members of the Philadelphia bar but not as close to McKean as was Dickinson, also sought out his services and worked with him on important cases. Knowledgeable observers considered McKean by 1770 second only to Benjamin Chew in his legal accomplishments.[32]

Through the practice of law McKean thus advanced his social and political standing in Delaware, and at the same time accumulated rather extensive land holdings. Two years after opening his practice in Delaware his first transaction of what was to become a continuous and methodical enlargement of his estate was recorded in the New Castle land office. Not infrequently McKean purchased plots of land sold at public vendue as a result of court cases which he himself argued. But his interest in land was not confined to this type of purchase. He bought and sold small and medium-sized tracts in Pennsylvania and Delaware until his death in 1817, at which time his will described parcels totaling over ten thousand acres.

The greatest portion of his estate at his death was accumulated after the American Revolution. Predictably the size of his purchases increased with his reputation, his position in the community and his income. In 1763 he purchased "Chatham," lost earlier by his father. Four years later he purchased 805 acres in Cumberland County, Pennsylvania, one of his largest holdings to that time. He must have derived great satisfaction in 1769 from his purchase at public vendue of 143 acres belonging to his father's old nemesis, Andrew Caldwell of Chester County. Between 1757 and 1775 he paid out sums ranging from £10 to over £200 for real estate, a continuous outlay which underscores his penchant for accumulating acreage as well as his substantial income. By 1768 he and George Munro, a physician and sometime member of the Assembly, were lending large sums of money to individuals willing to put up attractive parcels of land as collateral.[33]

McKean played a conspicuous role in the expansion and upgrading of the Delaware bar, if only by example. His pursuit of excellence epitomized the standards increasingly demanded of practitioners before the bench and his growing wealth and life-style attracted talented young men to the bar in the 1760s and 1770s. So, too, did the increasing availability of legal materials. The accessibility of Blackstone's *Commentaries* by 1773 prompted a great many young men to turn to the law. Charles Inglis, a man intimately familiar with the Lower Counties, remarked that Blackstone's work rendered the study of law so "easy & agreeable . . . that numbers of Young Gentlemen at the Universities chuse to study the Law instead of going into Orders." Talented young Delawareans like Nicholas Van Dyke, Alexander Porter, David Thompson, Alexander Montgomery, David Hall, and John Parke were among those who turned to the law during this period.[34]

In view of his reputation and prospects it is not surprising that McKean married well. In July 1763, then twenty-nine, he married Mary Borden, nineteen, the eldest daughter of Joseph Borden of Bordentown, New Jersey. Borden, proprietor of a boat and stage line connecting Philadelphia with New York and New Jersey, came from a family prominent in colonial affairs for over a century and had himself held important local and provincial cffices in the colony. In 1763 he was a respected member of the New Jersey Assembly whose ambition was to dominate the public transportation facilities in the middle colonies.[35]

McKean's concern for the guarantee of liberties in no way diminished with wealth and status as Alison had warned it might. In fact, in 1770 McKean found himself in the middle of one of the most celebrated cases in pre-revolutionary Delaware, defending clients in Sussex County who believed themselves faced with a conspiracy to deny them their constitutional rights.

The origin of the case was a longtime rivalry between John Clowes, Jr., a sometime member of the Assembly, and Boaz Manlove, a leader of the Sussex court party, two headstrong personalities who coveted the sheriff's post in that county. It opened officially in September 1767 when the Sussex County grand jury, headed by Clowes, called Manlove to appear before it to answer for his conduct in the case of one William Walls, Jr. Manlove, convinced that he was innocent of any wrongdoing, and that the grand jury's call was merely a political ploy instigated by Clowes to embarrass him, chose to ignore the summons. It was only in the face of a threatened contempt citation from the grand jury that Manlove agreed to appear before a magistrate during the April 1768 term to explain his actions.

The grand jury, still headed by Clowes, listened intently to Manlove's proffered explanation of his dealings with Walls, before indicting him for "false swearing."[36] Manlove's supporters, particularly his brother Manuel and Levin Crapper, a local judge and an acknowledged leader of the Sussex delegation in the Assembly, rushed to his aid. By soliciting a number of people to convince the justices of the court that the grand jury's actions were inaugurated in political jealousy and represented the opinions of Clowes more than any other, the Manlove-Crapper faction successfully frustrated Clowes and the grand jurors. The court, manned by justices sympathetic to Manlove's politics, refused to act upon the grand jury's charges.

Disgruntled, the members of the grand jury took the occasion of the November term to read a remonstrance highly critical of the court's previous reticence. It was a bold move, for the justices of the court included several pro-Manlove men and a number of influential members of the Delaware Assembly, including Benjamin Burton, John Wiltbank, Thomas Robinson, and Levin Crapper. The grand jury's boldness was matched by the court's stubbornness. Members of the grand jury who signed the remonstrance were found in contempt of court and fined. At least twelve of the jurors, including Clowes, refused to pay the fines and were jailed. Though the imprisoned jurors were popular with a substantial element of Sussex society, they soon found themselves unable to secure their release or find adequate counsel. Delaware lawyers shied away from the volatile Clowes who, enraged over the turn of events, continued to fight his battles in the Philadelphia newspapers and repeatedly asserted his determination to fight the case to the highest court.[37]

Early in 1770 McKean agreed to take over the Clowes case. He quickly secured writs of habeas corpus for the jurors, and began preparations to defend Clowes at his trial scheduled for May 1770. The court party, eager to defend the justices' action, hired three attorneys.

On May 8 McKean pleaded Clowes' cause in the Lewes courthouse before a large audience. The case proved to be "a cause of great expectation and attended by many of the people who very universally applauded Mr. McKean of New Castle, for his virtue and resolution in defending their cause, when others refused it, thro' fear of the court." Clowes by this time had become known as the "John Wilkes of Sussex," a reference to the celebrated Englishman whose struggles with Parliament and the British courts were recorded daily in the Pennsylvania newspapers. Clowes' supporters saw no exaggeration in the parallel, for in Sussex as in England the question had become one of popular rights versus arbitrary and capricious power.[38]

McKean began by arguing that the remonstrance or petition of the grand jury—the source of Clowes' judicial woes—was no libel against the court but rather a legitimate effort on the part of the grand jury to point out mistakes of the court. Even if the document were technically a contempt it was not a designed contempt. If the court did deem it a contempt—"contrary to the scope and plain construction of the words," McKean thought—the punishment was still out of proportion to the deed. To fine and imprison the offenders a full three months after the supposed affront was contrary to many laws and cases. McKean cited a variety of cases calling for a judgment to be "flagrante crimine." He challenged the opposition to cite a single case—"the infamous Star-Chamber not excepted"—which would justify the denial of a jury trial by peers in a similar instance.

"To allow the present decision to stand would encourage justices to be judges, jurors, witnesses, and informers, and thus enable them to put half the fines in their own pockets," according to McKean. This would be an ugly precedent indeed. He concluded by contending that the act of assembly upon which the court professed to found their judgment was entirely mistaken as to its true meaning and was "unhappily misapplied."[39]

Any of the reasons he had raised was justification for the discharge of the prisoner, McKean insisted, and he called for the court to grant Clowes his freedom. The Pennsylvania *Journal,* clearly in Clowes' corner, commented that "Mr. McKean in the debate shewed a clear knowledge of the constitution, and tho' he treated the inferior court with great candor and politeness, he undeniably proved his points to the satisfaction of the audience, the interested only excepted."

Following two days of deliberation, Justices Caesar Rodney and Richard McWilliams voted to uphold the inferior court's action but David Hall, whose son and namesake was a law clerk and apprentice in McKean's office, angrily dissented and read his minority opinion in open court—to the delight of the gallery.[40]

McKean and members of the Sussex County country party were naturally disappointed in the court's ruling, but they were outraged by the elections the following October, in which Boaz Manlove returned as sheriff in a general sweep of the court party. Ironically, Clowes was one of the few successful country party candidates, being returned to the Assembly for another term. Other losses rankled, however. Being on the short end of a two-to-one vote in court was one thing, being blatantly robbed of an election was quite another. Clowes and his followers insisted that one Isaac Smith had introduced "about 80 votes more than there were voters... in order to support the sinking credit of the court party." If McKean and those with whom he sympathized were not convinced before the election that the "young squires" and "Grand Monarchs" of Sussex were conspiring to destroy all opposition to them— and to trample the rights of their enemies in the process—they surely were convinced afterwards.[41]

David Hall, Jr. Courtesy of Delaware Archives, Hall of Records, Dover, Delaware

3. Liberty Under Attack

When John Clowes and supporters of the Sussex County country party took their accusations of election day chicanery to the assembly for redress in October 1770, they found McKean anxious to promote their cause. Recognized as a skilled legislator and one of the most active of the assemblymen, McKean was beginning his eighth year in that body in 1770.

When McKean had first entered the legislature in October 1762 at the the age of twenty-eight he had discovered eleven of his seventeen colleagues were either lawyers or experienced members of the judicial hierarchy. Four others became justices within two years while retaining their assembly seats.[1] The dual public exposure enjoyed by these men undoubtedly contributed to their entrenchment in both branches of government. The continuous reinforcement of identification between political and social authority was a salient feature of life in colonial Delaware. A rough correlation existed between leadership, status and property. But mere wealth, even a combination of wealth and ability, did not assure office. Frequently, as in the case of McKean, men of outstanding ability and connections, along with sufficient wealth and leisure time, had to give way to more established, experienced men. Once a man demonstrated ability and was elected however, the political and social milieu virtually guaranteed him a long tenure and promoted his ambition. Only under extraordinary circumstances did lesser leaders, or the voters, challenge the right of the higher gentry to rule their lives.

Even the most cursory perusal of the names representing the three counties in the colonial assembly between 1762 and 1770, and on the bench in the same years, reveals the conservatism present in that society, and the deferential nature of its political and judicial life. Eight, namely William Armstrong, John Vining, Caesar Rodney, Jacob Kollock, Jr., Benjamin Burton, Levin Crapper, David Hall, and Evan Rice were elected every year; three others missed only one year. The usual refrain following each October's election was "the Old Assembly continues." Legal practice might furnish a number of social, political, and economic advantages for a man like McKean, but in the final analysis other institutions than the courts determined how quickly he would wield power—and for how long.[2]

Yet there were factors within the political matrix which could blunt as well as embolden such ambition. If the political system virtually assured a man a long tenure once elected, divisive economic, geographical, social, and religious forces often created blind opposition, and a conservatism based on isolation and ignorance responded only grudgingly to new personnel and new ideas. Family rivalries and widespread political chicanery were added hazards for the novice or reformer in Delaware politics. Those who were politically articulate, while craving harmony and homogeneity, accepted the reality of contending factions and frequently pursued their political convictions with an enthusiasm bordering on the frenetic.[3]

New Castle County, compared to Kent or Sussex, enjoyed greater commercial or social ties with Philadelphia and a more heterogeneous social and religious society, thus drawing new personalities and innovative ideas. But even here a strong Anglican mercantile faction and landed aristocracy dominated the political, social, and economic life in the 1760s. As an assemblyman, McKean came to know these facts of life, to utilize them on occasion, and struggle against them in most instances. Yet the extraordinary hold that McKean maintained on his New Castle constituency was of lasting importance in his career. Remaining a member of the Delaware Assembly from New Castle County, save for one year, until 1779, McKean did so without always actively campaigning for the seat. On two occasions he requested the people of New Castle to choose someone else to fill the post but saw his protestations ignored.[4]

In his first year as an assemblyman, McKean exhibited none of the trepidation or caution of a novice among his more experienced colleagues. He brashly called upon his associates to correct their negligence in maintaining the Assembly's official records and involved himself deeply in matters of the courts and justice. Of crucial concern to him was a bill requiring the Supreme Court to hold its sessions permanently in New Castle County. McKean was disturbed as were many of his constituents by the fact that the court, hampered by an aging and overworked bench, had met locally only sporadically of late. The judicial needs of the three counties were changing more rapidly than the court's capacity to meet and serve them, and even in the face of recent legislation to improve the court's efficiency, the justices continued to provide inadequate service. Still, a large part of McKean's concern stemmed from a consideration of the prestige and convenience that would accrue to his constituents if the court were stationed permanently in the northernmost county. His bill, appealing as it did to historic intercounty rivalries, was doomed from the start.[5]

At any rate, McKean's role in the 1762 Assembly had been noteworthy. He successfully drafted a bill for the better regulation of the levy courts, and he was a principal figure in collecting and printing valuable land records which were rapidly deteriorating in scattered depositories, some as far away as New York. Of interest to local lawyers was the printing of the minutes and laws of the Assembly. Apart from Benjamin Chew's edition of the laws, published in 1752, little of a systematic nature had been done when McKean joined the redoubtable Caesar Rodney of Kent to accomplish both publications. The two revised the laws and saw to it that they were printed and distributed along with an edition of the *Votes and Proceedings* of the 1762 Assembly.[6] These efforts by McKean to preserve valuable records for subsequent legislators and lawyers presaged a lifelong concern for the raw materials of law and history.[7]

After 1763, when the British ministry instituted measures to produce more revenue and to enforce existing imperial legislation, McKean assumed an active role in Delaware's reaction against these measures. He was aggressive and eager; his sound law practice provided resources and leisure time for greater public service. He and his fellow assemblymen found their antagonism to imperial exigencies confused, however, by developments in Pennsylvania. There, Benjamin Franklin and his political allies were working to bring about a royal takeover of the province. Despite militant opposition provided by John Dickinson and the Presbyterian-dominated Proprietary party, the Pennsylvania Assembly agreed in May to a petition favoring the change of government. The Lower Counties, their destiny tied closely to events in Pennsylvania, saw little value in the proposed scheme. In August, taking its cue from Benjamin Chew—the Proprietary "prime minister" who traveled to New Castle to offer "advice"—the Delaware Assembly voiced its opposition to the Pennsylvania petition. Delawareans wanted it on record that they were no more enthralled with the changes sought by the Pennsylvania Assembly than they were with those being pursued by the revitalized British Ministry. As a member of the Committee of Correspondence, McKean was one of those charged with delivering these sentiments to the proper authorities.[8]

The opportunity for Delaware to unite more actively with other colonies in protesting British legislation came in June 1765 following the passage of the Stamp Act. At that time the Massachusetts House of Assembly issued a call for a general congress to be held in New York in October to protest the Act. Pursuit of a zealous policy by McKean and other Delaware assemblymen was inhibited, however, by Delaware's small size and its concomitant dependence on neighboring colonies.

Caesar Rodney, signed by Rembrandt Peale. Courtesy of Historical Society of Delaware

It was incapable of pursuing a bold and unilateral policy even had it wished to do so, which clearly it did not. In such circumstances it was Delaware's lot to follow rather than to lead. At any rate, the legislature was not in session. Only the Proprietary governor, John Penn, was empowered to call an extraordinary session, and it soon became evident that he had no such inclination.

McKean was among those who devised a ploy by which Delaware could select representatives to the Stamp Act Congress without convening the Assembly.[9] And he was elected, along with Caesar Rodney of Kent and Jacob Kollock of Sussex, to attend the intercolonial assembly. The fact that New Castle County's "instructions" to the delegates proved to be more militant than those from either Kent or Sussex Counties was attributable in large measure to McKean's efforts.[10]

When news of the passage of the Stamp Act reached Delaware a lively debate ensued over the need to summon an American congress. During the debate the Proprietary governor raised McKean to two very prestigious posts, naming him justice of the peace for the New Castle court of common pleas and quarter sessions and of the orphans' court for the same county. He also designated McKean the sole notary and tabellion for the Lower Counties, a lucrative post which drew a variety of fees.[11]

Why the Proprietors saw fit to reward McKean, a leader in Delaware's "country party," at this particular time is open to question. It is unlikely McKean's advancement was designed to encourage in him a cautious approach toward either the Stamp Act or the intercolonial congress; Proprietary interests were as unhappy with the Stamp Act as was the general population. Rather it may have been to help solidify the Presbyterian elements behind the Proprietary party in its struggle against Franklin's efforts to turn Pennsylvania into a royal province. The Penns, by wooing Presbyterian and German elements through a judicious use of their patronage, hoped to cement them to their party. During 1765 John Penn turned over a large number of justice of the peace offices to Presbyterians, so many in fact that he elicited from one opposition leader the admission that the Proprietors "have remarkably caressed these people." Political appointments of Presbyterians in Delaware

Liberty Under Attack 37

were as appreciated in the Presbyterian communities as were those in Pennsylvania. The growing politicization of the Presbyterians was a boon to men like McKean. As the Presbyterians increased in numbers in both Delaware and Pennsylvania, and became more articulate, McKean for one began to reap the political rewards.[12]

If, as a bonus, the Penns chose a man who would effectively promote Delaware's opposition to the Stamp Act, an act which the Proprietors blamed chiefly on Franklin, they chose wisely. McKean and Rodney joined with twenty-five delegates from eight other colonies on October 7, after having spent nearly a week in New York taking stock of local opinion. Rodney was sufficiently impressed with the delegates to write that the Congress was "An Assembly of the greatest ability I ever Yet saw." McKean did not share Rodney's exuberance. On the contrary, he soon concluded that the delegates, at least the great majority of them, were a moderate lot. "Indeed," he later remarked, "some of the members seemed as timid as if engaged in a traitorous conspiracy." His actions within the Congress suggest that his observation in this instance was not merely the product of historical hindsight.[13]

The first real order of business, that of choosing a chairman, clarified the divisions anticipated by McKean. The choice of speaker was quickly narrowed to a contest between two Massachusetts delegates, James Otis and Timothy Ruggles. McKean considered Otis "to be the boldest and best speaker" and supported his candidacy in a losing cause. Ruggles' victory was the result of a single vote, according to McKean, the margin of victory being provided by the large and moderate New York delegation. The success of the moderates in electing Ruggles, a man handpicked by Governor Francis Bernard to bring much-needed caution and conservatism to the Massachusetts delegation, convinced McKean, as it doubtless convinced others, that no truly radical pronouncements would be forthcoming from this Congress. It also persuaded McKean to insist hereafter on equality in voting among the several colonies.[14]

Even with the general tone of the Congress' work seemingly assured, the specific task facing the delegates proved to be an elusive one. For twelve days they strove to clarify the "rights and Privileges of the American Colonies." In truth, the identification and cataloging of American rights and privileges was not the stumbling block; most Americans could acquiesce in the final list of "fundamental rights" which the Congress drew up. The dilemma was expressed by Rodney when he told his brother Thomas that the representatives felt "duty Bound to Assert the Rights & Privileges of the Colonies" and at the same time "Carefully to avoid any Infringement of the prerogatives of the Crown and the Power of Parliament." For McKean and his associates this was the rub. Should a specific acknowledgment of Parliament's powers be stated? Would such a statement be detrimental or prejudicial to the colonists' case?[15]

To recognize Parliament's right to regulate trade, some argued, might be construed as an admission that taxes such as those levied under the Sugar Act were legitimate. Such taxes were in fact the central issue, for it was almost impossible to distinguish between taxes levied for revenue and for purposes of trade regulation. The divided delegates, unable to resolve the dilemma after extensive debate, eventually side-stepped the issue. They made clear that "no taxes should be imposed on them, but with their own consent, given personally, or by their immediate representatives," and that the "act for granting and applying certain stamp duties, and other duties in the British colonies...have a manifest tendency to subvert the rights and liberties of the colonists."

No mention was made of Parliament's specific powers to tax for reasons other than to raise revenue. This omission was significant. It meant that Congress neither acknowledged nor disavowed Parliament's right to regulate trade. It merely proclaimed—and rather ambiguously at that—that "his Majesty's Subjects in these Colonies...owe all due Subordination to that August Body, the Parliament of Great Britain."[16] Only through such a vague and open-ended pronouncement could some semblance of consensus be achieved among the disputing delegates. Even then the resolutions were not unanimously supported, nor, it seems, universally understood among the congressmen responsible for them. Did they mean to imply that Parliament had no right to levy taxes of any kind? Or that Parliament could levy external taxes which fell within the scope of its regulatory powers but could not impose internal taxes for revenue?

Two of the delegates, Robert Ogden of New Jersey and Timothy Ruggles, were convinced that the final congressional resolutions did deny Parliament's right to tax, implicitly at least. Each was perturbed by the Congress' failure to include in its pronouncements an unmistakeable recognition of Parliament's right to tax the Colonies. Until such a clear acknowledgement was forthcoming, neither would acquiesce in the final draft. McKean, disgruntled by the reluctance of his fellow delegates, lashed out at those refusing to sign the finished product of the Congress' labors. He was never comfortable in the face of opposition, but even more than opposition he abhorred timidity.

McKean's anger and frustration centered in part on Ruggles, whom he had distrusted from the first. When Ruggles announced his reluctance to sign, McKean demanded that he make known the reasons for his misgivings. When the chairman responded somewhat evasively, McKean continued to badger him until Ruggles shouted that to sign was "against his conscience." At this point McKean, or so he later remembered, "rung the charge so loud" that the seventy-two year old Ruggles cried out, "Young gentleman, you shall hear from me." Although McKean later reported that the "Plain language was given by Him and accepted in the presence of the whole corps," a personal confrontation was averted. McKean boasted to John Adams in later years that Ruggles evaded the duel by "departing the next morning before day, without an adieu to any of his brethren."[17]

Ruggles' precipitous departure did not wholly allay McKean's anger toward those repudiating the congress' work by refusing to affix their signature to the completed resolutions. His attention shifted to Robert Ogden who first bitterly opposed the calling of such a congress, then, having been persuaded to attend, shared Ruggles' concern over the omission of a specific acknowledgment of Parliament's power. Ogden argued rather lamely that repeal of the Stamp Act could be achieved more readily if the individual colonies worked independently of each other rather than antagonizing English ministers by proposing a program such as the Congress offered.[18]

Aware that his argument did not impress the majority of his colleagues in New York, and fearful that he would become a target of abuse once the Congress adjourned, Ogden looked to Joseph Borden, his New Jersey colleague, for aid. He sought a pledge from Borden that he would remain silent concerning Ogden's conduct at least until the New Jersey delegation had returned home for some time. Moreover, at least according to McKean's later account, Ogden pleaded with Borden to seek a similar pledge of silence from his son-in-law: Borden agreed to try, but he was successful only in securing from McKean a promise not to initiate any discussion of the matter. McKean made it plain, however, that if anyone should ask him the names of those not signing the congressional resolutions he would not hesitate to reveal them.

As he no doubt anticipated, the question of who had refused to sign the resolutions was put to the delegates almost immediately upon adjournment. True to his word, McKean provided the names. As a result, knowledge of Ogden's perfidy quickly spread among ardent Whigs and he was burned in effigy "in almost every town in the Jerseys," stripped of his speakership in the New Jersey Assembly, and eventually forced to resign his Assembly seat. Clearly his "moderation"—some Whigs uncharitably defined it as cowardice—was unpalatable both to his Assembly colleagues and to the majority of his constituents. It is perhaps understandable that the angry and chagrined Ogden came to regard McKean as the chief source of his personal humiliation, and he made little effort to conceal his feelings about McKean's actions.

According to McKean's account of the affair—and it rings true in view of his later career which can be documented more surely—he promptly accepted the challenge and visited Burlington, New Jersey, to give Ogden every opportunity to confront him. McKean made a point of speaking with the governor and generally made himself conspicuous for two days "without hearing any menaces whatsoever." Satisfied that his honor was unstained, he returned to Delaware.[19]

While participation in the Stamp Act Congress and its immediate aftermath provided McKean with an intercolonial arena in which to exhibit his uncontrollable temper, it afforded him a more attractive opportunity as well—to discuss the legal and constitutional issues dividing the American people with some of the most knowledgeable men in colonial America.

It helped him to assess the sentiment outside Delaware, and to clarify the positions he was later to espouse in the Continental Congresses. It forced him to sort out his priorities and assumptions, and to determine how far he was prepared to go in defending them. Once having concluded to his own satisfaction that under no circumstances could the King or Parliament tax Americans for revenue or exact any kind of gift from the Colonies, he never wavered from that position.

When McKean returned to Delaware from the New York Congress he was realist enough to appreciate that what he and his colleagues had accomplished only partially represented colonial resistance to the Stamp Act: more telling and strident responses were coming—and had been coming—from local communities. The issue was not what theoretical arguments colonials could muster against the Act in an intercolonial congress, but whether, in the final analysis, the British law would be obeyed.[20]

By October 24 it was clear that the Stamp Act would not achieve the revenue expected of it. Throughout the Colonies local mobs and militant associations threatened ships' masters who brought the stamps and officials who distributed them, ensuring that no stamps would be available on November 1, the day the Act was to take effect. The basic question of whether or not Americans would obey the law was unresolved. So long as the ports and courts remained closed, and newspapers were unpublished, the majority of Americans could consider themselves at least technically within the law. A refusal to carry out functions requiring stamps was generally agreed the wisest, most reasonable and judicious course of action pending a formal repeal of the vexatious Act. To those convinced the law was blatantly unconstitutional such adherence to the niceties smacked of hypocrisy. One writer asked, "What signify all our arguments against the Stamp Act, if we by it, in any instance, are turned out of or stopped in our ordinary way of transacting our affairs?" McKean, for one, concurred.[21]

Legislation adversely affecting colonial commerce naturally struck a severe economic blow to American lawyers. The American bar itself was threatened by Stamp Act taxation on the traditional use of court documents, giving colonial lawyers cause to hasten a repeal of the Act. Their opposition was no doubt increased by arguments like that of an English writer, trading on the widespread animosity towards lawyers in colonial America, that the Stamp Act would tend to destroy "that nest of small pettyfogging attorneys whose business it was to create disturbances and law suits, and live by the plunder."[22]

But it was one thing for lawyers like McKean to oppose the Act, to formulate constitutional arguments decrying its illegality, and to refuse to purchase the obnoxious stamps; it was quite another to carry on business as usual in defiance of the law. As an attorney recently appointed to the New Castle bench, McKean found himself in the winter of 1765 wrestling with the issue on two levels. Closed and silent courts might satisfy a number of political strategists and a few debtors, but individuals who counseled total resistance to arbitrary and capricious laws, and those Delawareans fearful of anarchy should the courts fail to function, called for the courts to remain active. McKean's ultimate decision, like those of other Delaware justices and attorneys, had to take into account at once his own professional aspirations and Delaware's historic abhorrence of precipitous and unilateral actions.[23]

McKean got little real help by way of example in this matter from the larger and most sophisticated bars in Pennsylvania, Maryland, and New Jersey. Pennsylvania attorneys, meeting to determine a course of action, argued the merits of several proposals, including one from Joseph Galloway and an enebriated John Ross against proceeding without stamps, before committing themselves to inaction "till some other Government had sett us the Example."[24] Lawyers in New Jersey formally, and in some cases eloquently, opposed the Stamp Act but were at the same time unwilling to conduct business as usual in local courts. Popular leaders in that province, recognizing the important position occupied by lawyers in that society, pressed hard for continuing business without stamps, but to no avail. Many throughout the Middle Colonies complained that local lawyers were "snoring over the Liberties and Properties of their fellow Subjects in the most supine Indolence." Judges, too, for reasons of their own, were unwilling to take the initiative.[25]

In this instance, at least, Delaware's attorneys and justices proved to be more forward than their neighbors. Circumstantial evidence suggests that McKean was in the vanguard of those most ardently pushing for the opening of Delaware courts in the winter of 1765-66. He later remembered that in the November 1765 and February 1766 terms, as a justice of the courts of common pleas he had enlisted his colleagues' help in conducting business without the hated stamps. Indeed, he was somewhat pleased to discover that he "had influence enough to have justice administered upon unstamped paper." There is little evidence besides his own words to substantiate his claim for the November term; confirming dockets have not survived. Newspapers of the period make no mention of McKean's court in the fall of 1765.[26]

If McKean in his later years was correct only in regard to the February 1766 court term, he seemingly took more personal credit than he deserved. The New Castle county courts did open in February, but they did so under the goad of public opinion, not solely on McKean's initiative. On February 7, 1766, before word reached the Colonies of the repeal of the Stamp Act, a conference consisting of New Castle justices, clerks, and lawyers, having been pressured and persuaded by the freemen of the county, resolved to open the courts of quarter sessions and common pleas. It is safe to assume that McKean played a critical role, probably in league with George Read, the other dominant figure in New Castle's bar, in marshaling public opinion before such a conference, and maneuver the committee to acknowledge the public weal once the conference got under way.

Contributing to the conference's resolve was the determination of the New Castle grand jury to "absolutely refuse to qualify, unless the business of the pleas was carried on as usual." Inasmuch as the main function of the grand jury centered around criminal cases, which were not adversely affected by the Stamp Act, this was an interesting development. The grand jury's insistence on opening the civil courts before dealing with criminal matters was recognized in legal circles as a political move. The populace of New Castle viewed the action as "a Noble example... to other courts and grand juries." Only Rhode Island, New Hampshire and Maryland courts joined Delaware in opening their courts prior to the news of the Stamp Act's repeal.[27]

After completing his February term as county judge "without regard to the Stamp Act" McKean stepped down from the bench to resume his legal practice. His willingness—even eagerness—to oppose the Stamp Act to its logical conclusion in no way distinguished him from most of his Delaware contemporaries. Delaware suffered no sharpened political divisions as a result of the Stamp Act controversy as did Massachusetts, Pennsylvania, Connecticut, and, to a lesser extent, Virginia. A number of Delawareans might quarrel with McKean's methods, or fear and resent his impetuosity at times, but his opposition to the act was widely supported.[28]

That McKean was no revolutionary at this juncture but was content, like the majority of his contemporaries, to express his opposition within the existing political structure, is evident from his activities in the 1766 Assembly. Even before the Stamp Act Congress had concluded its work a committee of the Assembly drew up a petition which, while expressing its conviction that "no Person or Persons have any Right to raise or levy Money upon, or exact any Kind of Gift from the Inhabitants under any other Colour or Pretext of Power whatsoever," was nonetheless profuse in its expressions of continued loyalty to the Crown.

Lest this petition be thought incompatible with McKean's radicalism at the Congress and after, as an attempt by more conservative assemblymen to counterweight the activities of McKean and Rodney at New York, McKean's subsequent actions prove otherwise. He proposed that a second resolution be sent with the first, expressing Delaware's gratitude for the repeal of the Act, the news of which had reached the Lower Counties by that time. Written jointly by what was rapidly becoming a Delaware triumvirate—Read, Rodney, and McKean—the second resolution proclaimed the authors' "unfeigned zeal" for the King's person and government, and asserted they could not "help Glorying in being subjects of a King, that has made the Preservation of the Civil and Religious Rights of his Government, and the Safety, Ease and Prosperity of his People, his chiefest Care." They made no mention of Parliament's powers. Still, Dennys DeBerdt, a London merchant who acted as an agent for the Lower Counties, later reported that a delighted King had read Delaware's declaration twice.[29]

McKean's expressions of loyalty in the 1766 Assembly following the repeal of the Stamp Act did not preclude a continuing vigilance of American liberties, however. He remained a member of Delaware's Committee of Correspondence and it was he, reacting to the previous year's passage of the Townshend duties, who in October 1768 pressed the Assembly to consider opposing the duties. He saw them as a deliberate contrivance by the ministry to establish precedents for later economic and constitutional encroachments upon American rights. The apparent reasonableness of the taxes convinced him that the British had so designed them in order to minimize opposition to them. Failure to mount decisive opposition would threaten the colonial constitutional position in the event of additional taxes.[30]

A Committee of the House, responding to McKean's urging, found that the duties tended to deprive the colonists of their right to tax themselves, and were, consequently, "Pernicious to American freedom." Accordingly, the Committee suggested that still another petition seeking redress be sent to the King. The resultant petition, written by Read, Rodney and McKean, declared that unless Delawareans opposed the Townshend legislation "Our Assemblies will be no longer the Representatives of a free People, but deprived of the Right of Exercising their own Judgments in Consulting the Good and prosperity of their own constituents."[31]

To broaden and deepen Delaware's opposition to the Townshend duties McKean joined all "the Principal freeholders of New Castle County" on August 26, 1769, to follow the lead of other colonies in entering a compact to support a boycott agreement, and to publicize those persons failing to adhere to this understanding.[32]

By 1770 McKean had earned something of an ambivalent reputation in the assembly. He was unquestionably an important figure, certainly more conspicuous in the assembly records than most of his colleagues. But he wielded none of the everyday power and influence of a George Read, a Thomas Robinson, a Caesar Rodney, or even a William Armstrong or Evan Rice. He remained part of a minority faction—the country party. Much of his failure in challenging the influence of men like Rodney,

Read, Robinson and Rice was due to religious factors and the lingering prejudice towards the Scotch-Irish in Delaware. Scotch-Irish Presbyterians for all their social progress and political involvement in the governing apparatus of the Lower Counties, continued to be viewed with suspicion and contempt by the older, more established citizenry.

Much of McKean's failure was also personal. He was an articulate public speaker able to delineate an issue and mark out the options available to those who wished to act. Still, in private he lacked the subtlety or imagination to create strategy or the patience to maneuver and persuade those whose help he needed for the success of his cause. He was impulsive, he longed to act, to attack. He had little tolerance for anyone failing to share his convictions and perceptions or his enthusiasm for quick, decisive action. Too often he determined his position quickly, girded for battle, made his cause a personal vendetta, all before more prudent men had assessed the problem, weighed the alternatives, and devised a workable strategem. The Rodneys and Reads, with their superior backgrounds and political-social strength, sought to ally with McKean on critical issues not just because he was a benefit to any campaign—and he was that—but also because they knew he was no man to have opposing you. Friends learned early that the key to dealing with McKean was to restrain his excesses while allowing free reign to his talents.

At no time were McKean's strengths and weaknesses as an assemblyman more evident than in his 1770 response to the appeal by Clowes' followers for an Assembly investigation of fraud in the October elections, and a determination as to whether another election should therefore be held. McKean knew the Sussex country party was pressuring for more than a new election: it wanted the Assembly to look into allegations that the Crapper-Manlove junto was savagely repressing political opposition. He could not escape the impression shared by Clowes' followers that "the spleen of the court party" had been methodically directed against those whom they "resented [for their] freedom in reproving vices, and [for] appearing to countenance men borne down by an arbitrary power, in [the] late violent attempt on our excellent constitution." One young man had been accused of riot when his only crime seemed to be his authorship of a song favoring the late grand jury headed by Clowes.³³

The first round of the struggle took place in November 1770 when McKean and several allies—in all probability John Haslet, Alexander Porter, James Latimer, and John Evans—won a motion to investigate the rumored corruption. It was McKean who pressed the House to examine Levin Crapper and to take additional testimony from the successful Assembly candidates, including Benjamin Burton, Thomas Robinson, and Burton Waples. It was also McKean who insisted that the House question Manlove, Isaac Smith and a half dozen other election officials. He tried valiantly to push the House into "ascertain[ing] & determin[ing] the Number of Votes given . . . in the late Election." Finally, he argued that the Assembly should declare that "the Return of the Sheriff & six Freeholders at the late Election . . . was untrue."

Despite McKean's most diligent efforts little was accomplished. The Assembly attempted only half-heartedly to probe political activities in the southern county. It refused to call for another election and failed to agree on the degree of complicity of Manlove and Smith. When the chips were down, the Sussex and Kent delegations, with ample help from George Read, had strength enough to turn the attention of the Assembly to other matters. McKean and a small coterie of assemblymen might fume and complain of the inequities, but to little effect. Until they could marshal the votes to frustrate Manlove and his allies in the legislature their role would remain that of a vocal but impotent minority. McKean knew, as did his friends in the Assembly, that should the threats to the liberties of the people of Sussex and the American people generally become more pronounced, this condition would be intolerable.³⁴

4. Conspiracy

McKean was disturbed by developments in Sussex and the Assembly but he could not have been surprised by them. Francis Alison had expounded at length upon Man's natural inclination to reduce other men's liberties, and his own familiarity with Delaware politics had prepared him for electioneering corruption, if on a lesser scale. McKean was disturbed as well by the propensity of the British ministry to challenge and diminish American rights. But he remained persuaded that the recent actions of the ministry were aberrations, the product of a few misguided and willful men; it was not a policy in which most Englishmen acquiesced. McKean acknowledged that Americans still had much to gain from their connection with Great Britain.

Office and status for a fortunate few were clearly among the primary benefits McKean had in mind. In the Fall of 1771 he sought and received the Collector of Customs post for New Castle, a much sought-after office with a sizeable salary and fees attached to it. Apparently he sought the office in conjunction with his brother-in-law, Francis Hopkinson, who had married Ann Borden in 1768 and since that time had dabbled in law and trade. By 1771 Hopkinson was badly in need of revenue following business reverses and he sailed to England hoping to obtain a lucrative office. When the customs post opened in New Castle upon the death of the incumbent, McKean and Hopkinson moved to secure the commission, Hopkinson focusing his efforts in England among his influential friends. Seemingly it was understood between them that McKean would hold the post temporarily, then as a deputy to Hopkinson.

McKean received the appointment on September 10 and took the oath of office before George Read three days later. According to his papers he was to hold office "til an appointment shall be made by the commission [of customs]."[1] Why he sought the customs post and why British officials conveyed it upon a man who had so ardently denounced British customs policies and practices remains a mystery. Unquestionably the revenue attached to the office played a part in McKean's decision. And he may have thought that it would be an advantage to the Whig cause if such offices were in the hands of patriots. Certainly the history of American shipping to 1763 revealed the benefits of having customs officials whose allegiances were not exclusively to their English superiors or to the English government. Perhaps for their part the customs commissioners in Boston thought—as suggested by McKean's later enemies—to buy him off and thus neutralize his zeal for the Whig cause. It may be that they simply gave the post to the man whose reputation for energy and thoroughness was recognized by all. There is little question that current conditions and the incompetency of the previous incumbent required a resourceful and meticulous successor to be named.[2]

The precise relationship between McKean and Hopkinson in this whole arrangement also remains a mystery. Hopkinson was appointed to the office on May 1, 1772. There is no evidence to suggest that McKean acted as his deputy after that date. Nor is there evidence that he carried out the duties of that office during the nine months between his own appointment in September 1771 and that of Hopkinson's.[3] Later political detractors would argue that McKean did serve and in fact had been nudged away from his earlier whiggism by the impressive fees associated with the customs post. For his part McKean never admitted serving. He had ample opportunity in the gubernatorial campaign of 1799 to answer those who charged him with selling out to the British and he did not. He provided no detail on his efforts in the customs post either to carry out the laws or to subvert the objectives of the various British tax laws, but he did acknowledge that he had received the commission.

Although most Americans resented the rigid enforcement of the customs laws and did not look with favor upon customs officials, apparently no political stigma was attached to McKean's actions—whether or not he served—for the Assembly chose him speaker of the House in October 1772. McKean later told John Adams that he was chosen unanimously ". . .when, of all members present, there were but six, including myself who were esteemed Whigs."[4]

The British reaction to the burning of the *Gaspee* in the coastal waters off Rhode Island in 1772 produced in Delaware a renewed sense of urgency over imperial affairs. As speaker of the Delaware Assembly McKean was the recipient of resolves from Virginia, Rhode Island, and Massachusetts imploring Delaware's support in their protest against recent British actions. When he presented the resolves to his associates in October 1773 he urged their endorsement. But the unanimity and good humor that prevailed in earlier sessions was not evident in 1773; McKean's efforts to instigate policies similar to those voted in Massachusetts, Rhode Island and Virginia were met with coolness. Sentiment was changing within the Lower Counties.[5]

The nature and direction of this change within the Delaware political community during these years are not easy to evaluate on the basis of meager source material. There are indications, albeit tenuous ones, that constant discussion of rights and privileges contributed not only to a growing tension between the Assembly and the Proprietary governor but stimulated a movement to question the franchise requirements, and to push for greater popular power. The power wielded by the New Castle Committee of Inspection in 1769-70 profoundly affected those Delawareans drawn into political issues for the first time and newly aware of the influence they might exercise through organized effort. As early as March 1770 the Kent physician Charles Ridgely, disturbed by the drift of sentiment, argued "it would be very well to say in so many precise words, what a Free-hold is." Ridgely himself had no doubt what constituted a freehold but many of Delaware's "Construers of Laws, & the Bulk of the People" did not, or chose to obscure the obvious.[6]

By October 1773 McKean's growing realization of Britain's systematic provocation of the Colonies led him to change his approach. In a move seemingly borne more of strategy than ideology he deliberately sought to mobilize a more vocal citizenry to lend impetus to the Whig cause, to prod the Assembly into a semblance of enthusiasm for the Virginia, Rhode Island and Massachusetts resolves, and to do it in open session. Animated by a desire to utilize the ardent public sentiment found in New Castle, McKean strove to open the traditionally closed Assembly doors to the public. Supporting McKean were John Evans, John McKinly, Alexander Porter, James Latimer, all of New Castle County, and John Haslet of Kent. Only George Read of the New Castle delegation supported the opposition, and only Haslet of Kent broke the solid Kent and Sussex bloc. Charles Ridgely was absent, but there is nothing in his history to suggest that he would have supported McKean and the New Castle delegation in this affair. McKean was reduced to insisting that those opposed to public Assembly deliberations be officially named in the Assembly's minutes.[7]

The stark outline provided by Delaware's *Votes and Proceedings* for the 1773 session offers few guidelines to what must have been an important struggle behind the scenes. One can only surmise what happened between the Assembly's negative response on Friday, October 22, to McKean's motion to read and discuss the Virginia, Rhode Island, and Massachusetts resolves, and the Assembly's positive, almost eager response to George Read's similar proposal the following day. In all likelihood it was agreed "out of doors" that the Delaware Committee of Correspondence called for by the resolves be enlarged and staffed by conservative assemblymen.

Thus assured that involvement in imperial matters would be more restrained than if governed by Rodney, McKean and Read, the Assembly subsequently agreed to McKean's proposal that the Assembly officially commend the measures taken by the committees of correspondence in the three colonies as "very Salutary and highly necessary at this Time, when the Rights and Liberties of all appear to be systematically invaded." It then unanimously named a committee of correspondence which included Read, Rodney, McKean, John McKinly, and Thomas Robinson. The inclusion of the powerful Thomas Robinson to offset the cautious John McKinly, however loyal McKinly may have been to McKean of late, could have done nothing to boost McKean's morale.[8]

The shadow of John Clowes continued to hang over this Assembly. Clowes, still fuming over what he considered shabby treatment at the hands of the Sussex court, petitioned the Assembly to reconsider his case. A solid bloc of Kent and Sussex delegates again moved to frustrate McKean, who ardently supported Clowes' petition. The fact that the same blocs appeared in the Assembly's reaction to the Clowes' case as in the previous questions suggests that the parties were rapidly solidifying. McKean did not win any converts to his cause when he pressed to have members Benjamin Burton, John Wiltbank, Thomas Robinson, and Levin Crapper absent themselves from the House during any debate over Clowes' criticism of the quarter sessions court which had imprisoned him. All had supported the "tyrannic, despotic administration" in Sussex, and all had been justices of that court. Opponents might sniff at Clowes as a pale reflection of John Wilkes and denigrate his cause, but Clowes' friends saw the parallel between Clowes and Wilkes to be a remarkably apt one. Clowes, like Wilkes, was a victim of a conspiracy against his liberties and must be defended lest all men lose their rights. Nothing came of McKean's insistence, however, Read and his supporters easily voted down McKean's request and dismissed Clowes' petition.[9]

If further evidence of a ministerial design to reduce American rights was needed, it came for McKean early in 1774. The imposition of the coercive acts on the people of Boston which, among other things, seriously restricted the historic governmental processes in the Massachusetts Bay Colony, particularly incensed him. He became a leading member of a committee established by the freeholders of New Castle County on May 29, 1774 to aid the people of Boston. He also sought to

Thomas Robinson, owned by Mrs. Thomas Robinson. Courtesy of Historical Society of Delaware

array public opinion behind another official protest to England. On June 17, 1774, signing himself "A Freeman," he appealed to the people of New Castle to meet at the courthouse twelve days later to consider the proper mode of procuring relief for their "brethren" in Boston.

His appeal dwelt at length on the most recent violations of American rights in Boston and New York. He emphasized that though the depressing developments in New England were "unbelievable," they were "no phantoms arising from a heated brain." They were all too real and must be dealt with with some alacrity. He concluded by asking, "Shall the people of this large and wealthy county, heretofore the foremost on many occasions . . . to oppose all attempts to deprive them of their personal security and private property, be now inactive and silent?"[10]

On Wednesday, June 29, "upwards of five hundred" people met on the New Castle common to discuss the call for relief of Boston. Always a powerful and persuasive speaker, McKean was chosen unanimously to chair the debate. He opened the deliberations with a lengthy address reviewing the original compacts made by the several monarchs with the first settlers of America on behalf of Great Britain, and the constitutional rights of the colonies as freemen and English subjects. All in all, it was a lawyer's brief, a legalistic look at imperial relations prior to 1765. Warming to his task, he showed unequivocably that the erosion of colonial rights had been constant and methodical since the recent war. Indeed, the violations of those original compacts had become the hallmark of British policies in recent years. He concluded with a discussion of the unfortunate circumstances in Boston, where the hand of tyranny was seen in its most virulent form.

The gathering responded by passing seven resolutions prepared in advance by McKean and other popular leaders. Among the resolutions was one urging a subscription for the relief of Boston. The crowd also delegated Caesar Rodney, speaker of the Delaware Assembly (now adjourned), to call upon assemblymen to meet in New Castle no later than the first of August to consider further action. It named a New Castle committee of thirteen, headed by McKean, to oversee that county's response to developments. George Read recorded that "not a sign of dissent appeared."[11]

The lack of enthusiasm exhibited by Sussex and Kent for a positive program of resistance convinced McKean of the need to expand his activities. On July 28 he traveled to Sussex to argue for a firm, united policy in Delaware. At Lewes, before one of the largest popular meetings held in the Lower Counties to that time, McKean led the arguments that New Castle's proposals were reasonable and judicious. He enumerated colonial rights and inveighed against recent British "lawless usurpations of those liberties." The impact of rhetoric and ideas emanating from other colonies, especially Massachusetts Bay Colony, was evident in his Lewes address. His initial reaction to the *Gaspee* incident and to later events in Boston had been to denounce the "systematic" usurpations of American liberties. Now for the first time he publicly ascribed to a small coterie of disloyal Americans, English ministers, and members of Parliament deliberate stratagems to subvert American rights. "For about ten years past," he insisted, "the conduct of the British Ministry, and a majority of Parliament seems to be one continual plan to rob us of our dearest liberties." As a result, McKean concluded, Americans had "gradually lost [their] free constitution." He attributed the "present undeserved frowns of the parent state" to the "base calumnies, wicked insinuations and most false misrepresentations of the Bernards, Hutchinsons, [and] Olivers."

McKean readily conceded that most Americans wished to remain loyal. He was too aware of sentiment in Delaware to proclaim otherwise. Despite numerous infringements upon their liberties and the methodical attack upon their rights, the majority of Delawareans persisted in their love of Great Britain and her institutions. He reminded British officials that less devoted subjects would surely have rebelled long before.

But even these loyal subjects were losing patience with the thrust of recent British policy. McKean discussed in detail twenty-seven grievances shared by all Americans, ranging from burdensome economic restrictions to the conferring of honors on unworthy individuals, "a dreadful catalogue indeed." "If *America* be enslaved," McKean warned, "the freedom of *Britain* will not long survive." But Americans must not wait for the British ministry to awaken to its own foolishness, he declared. Americans must act. They must eliminate those conditions in the Colonies—luxury, irreligion, and African slavery, for example—that were "so dishonourable" to Americans and "so provoking to the most benevolent Parent of the Universe." McKean pleaded meanwhile for support from the people of Delaware for a general congress, even if such a congress proposed a non-importation agreement to jar the ministry into reversing its current program. Unquestionably anticipating such a move, McKean named a boycott of British products as an effective ploy in forcing England to recognize the American position. "American virtue" had played a major role in achieving the repeal of the Stamp Act, he told his listeners, and it would stand them in good stead during the current crisis.[12]

Read, Rodney and McKean were elected to represent the Lower Counties in the upcoming Philadelphia congress, but not before opposition to the principle of naming delegates to the Congress was overcome. Despite reluctance on the part of Thomas Robinson of Sussex (and probably a number of his closest political allies in the Assembly) to dignify such a congress by appointing delegates to it, instructions to delegates were drawn and formalized. The document proclaimed Delaware's continued allegiance to the King together with the hope that "Great Britain and the colonies would remain bound together by mutual respect, for ever," and reiterated the belief that Delawareans ought to have and enjoy all the liberties, privileges and immunities of free men and natural born subjects of Great Britain, including the right to be taxed only by their own consent and the right of a fair trial in their own courts before their own peers. To this end the delegates were instructed to "prevail with the Deputies from the other Colonies to frame decent and becoming Petitions to His most gracious Majesty and both Houses of Parliament for the redress of all our grievances." McKean failed in his efforts to include explicit support for economic restrictions against Great Britain.[13]

In September 1774 McKean could look back upon two rather painful, hectic years. Minority status in the Assembly during a period when local affairs predominated was tolerable, if not always satisfactory. As the Assembly began to grapple with critical imperial issues after 1773, however, and to consider strategems for the protection of the people's lives, liberties, and property, minority status became intolerable. Fortunately his eminence and influence had grown in the past year. The death or retirement of such powerful Assembly voices as William Armstrong and Evan Rice catapulted him forward. Imperial exigencies played their role in promoting, his political ascendancy and encouraging his already impressive amibition.

On the personal level, McKean suffered the loss of his wife, who died on March 13, 1773, two weeks after giving birth to their sixth child.[14] His many civic and professional responsibilities, and his efforts to push an often reluctant Delaware into the mainstream of colonial dissent, occupied an inordinate amount of his time. His legal obligations kept him away from home for long stretches of time. The task of being both mother and father to his children, even with the help of servants and relatives, fell heavily upon his shoulders.

Yet McKean managed a successful courtship during the eighteen months between Mary McKean's death and the opening of the First Continental Congress. On September 3, 1774, three days before taking his seat in the Congress, he married Sarah Armitage, twenty-eight, the youngest of nine children born to James and Francis Armitage of New Castle. Mrs. Armitage was the half sister of Hannah Armitage Alison, wife of McKean's former instructor at New London. Exhibiting the type of dedication to his public life that Sarah (Sally) could only later fully appreciate, McKean spent his honeymoon attending the Continental Congress.[15]

McKean was forty years old and at the height of his physical and mental powers when, on September 6, the Congress met at Carpenters' Hall in Philadelphia.[16] His association with those members of Congress noted for their "forwardness and zeal" began early. He was among the first to welcome the Massachusetts delegation on its arrival in Philadelphia, and to caution John Adams against assuming too precipitous a policy of American resistance in the early going, at least on a public level. He was a frequent dining companion of Adams and others sympathetic to his political sentiments thereafter. On August 29 he joined Adams and a group of public figures who gathered at the City Tavern to discuss the problems and strategy facing the Congress, and to discuss law, a profession shared by an inordinate number of the members. It was McKean, well aware of the pivotal role played by lawyers in the recent resistance to Great Britain, who pointed out to Adams that of the fifty-six congressmen, twenty-two were practicing attorneys.[17]

The number of contacts McKean had with Adams was not unusual; several men who later opposed Adams' views saw more of him than did McKean in these weeks. What is important is the impact made by Adams upon McKean's thinking and strategy. Adams exhibited none of the timidity that was anathema to McKean. He was a pusher, a doer; he refused to permit the initiative to fall to others. McKean was attracted as well to Adams' particular brand of republicanism, with its emphasis on personal virtue, simplicity, discipline and commitment to sacrifice in the interests of freedom. Even before the Congress began, McKean's compatibility with Adams and other leaders of the "Eastern bloc," and southerners like Richard Henry Lee who supported them, was firmly established.[18]

The Congress was in session until October 26. McKean participated in the writing of the Declaration of Rights and Resolves which the members had agreed upon by mid-October, and he concurred with the Congress' efforts to send a series of addresses to various parts of the Empire to explain the American actions and the basis for their concerns. He also ardently supported the Congress' resolve on October 20: first, that each colony create an "Association" whereby the populace would agree not to import or export materials from England; then, to encourage local committees to see that transgressors would be "publicly known, and universally condemned as the enemies of American Liberty."[19] From what can be gathered from the records of the Congress, neither Rodney nor Read found any difficulty in accepting these measures.

McKean broke ranks with his Delaware colleagues late in September, however, when they supported Joseph Galloway's Plan of Union, an attempt to disengage conservatives and moderates from congressional programs thought by the Pennsylvania and New York delegations to inflame rather than reduce tensions between the two peoples. On September 28, with solid support from New York's James Duane and his associates in the New York delegation, Galloway proposed the Plan, whereby a continental legislature would grapple with the Colonies' internal problems and needs while Parliament and the King would hold full sway over external or imperial matters. A president-general, appointed by the King, would preside over this American council made up of representatives from each colony. It was argued that such a proposal was more compatible with the charge of the Congress—to seek means of reconciliation—than were the measures so far enacted, most of which would undoubtedly exacerbate the feelings on both sides of the Atlantic.

New Yorkers James Duane and John Jay, and Edward Rutledge of South Carolina lent their impressive weight to Galloway's plan, arguing that such a union was a workable and rational basis for a renewal of the harmony which had characterized the relationship between the Colonies and England prior to 1764. Patrick Henry and Richard Henry Lee maintained, on the other hand, that such a union would irreversibly alter the relationship not only among colonies but between the Colonies and the mother country, and that it was an arrangement susceptible to manipulation by powerful men. They argued, too, that the delegates did not have the authority to consent to such a political union.

The following day, September 29, saw a feverish period of lobbying by the Plan's opponents and proponents. Circumstantial evidence suggests that when the vote finally was taken, McKean did not support Galloway's proposal; rather he joined with those voting to kill the Plan by having it tabled, a strategy which succeeded by a narrow 6-5 margin. Apparently Rodney and Read supported the Plan, for Delaware was among the five colonies opposing the tabling motion. This critical vote began a pattern within the Delaware delegation of increasing isolation of McKean from Read—and to a lesser extent, from Rodney.[20]

Despite the differences of opinion over the probable efficacy of the Galloway proposal, the three Lower Counties' delegates were seemingly satisfied with the proceedings and programs of the Congress when it adjourned on October 26. Although Delawareans sympathetic to their views sought to implement congressional directives through the creation of local committees, large numbers of Delawareans were angry and disillusioned. Concerned lest the policies instituted by the Congress lead to war with England, or to civil insurrection at home, the discontented elements rapidly made their disaffection known. Even before the Congress adjourned moves were under way to repudiate congressional pronouncements if they should reflect too militant and uncompromising a position. Assemblymen Charles Ridgely and Thomas Robinson no longer attempted to hide their suspicions of congressionally induced developments, and their distrust of men like McKean who enthusiastically endorsed them.[21]

Religious factors seriously aggravated political conditions in Delaware. The ties between England and the Anglican Church were acknowledged by friend and foe alike. McKean was well aware of potential Anglican conservative reaction in his own county. He remained convinced until his death that the religious question was of paramount importance in Delaware's reaction to British measures after 1774. The ministers of the Society for the Propagation of the Gospel, he later wrote, "told their hearers, many of whom, especially in Sussex, were illiterate, ignorant and bigoted, that [opposition to England on the part of the Presbyterians] was a plan of the Presbyterians to get their religion established!" The truth of the matter, according to McKean, was that "the Anglican clergy realized that if opposition to England degenerated into open rebellion, and if America became an independent state or nation, their salary, between 50 and 60 pounds, would necessarily cease.... It was in their interest, therefore, to oppose the revolution, and they did oppose it, though with as much secrecy as practical," he concluded.[22]

McKean's virulent condemnation of the policies of the Anglican Church is fascinating in view of his family history. McKean's first wife, Mary Borden, had been a devout Anglican and wholeheartedly endorsed McKean's decision to name his second son after his brother Robert, who had been ordained an Anglican priest in April 1757. Upon his return from his ordination in London Robert became an Anglican missionary in New Jersey and a prominent member of the Anglican leadership there. Until his death in 1767 he remained an avid proponent of installing an American bishop in the Colonies.

That McKean loved his brother and was more intimate with him than with his other brothers and sisters is clear; how he reconciled his feelings towards his brother with his antipathy towards the political and ecclesiastical policies of his brother's church is not so clear.[23]

The unanimity of the Presbyterians in espousing the colonial cause was duly noted by Anglicans. Anthony Serle, a visitor from England, was adamant by 1775 that "Presbyterianism is really at the Bottom of this Whole Conspiracy, has supplied it with Vigor, and will never rest, till something is decided upon it." Although "civil liberty was the ostensible object, the bait that was flung out to catch the populace at large and engage them in rebellion," contended Charles Inglis, an Anglican observer intimately familiar with Delaware politics, "yet it is now past all doubt that the abolition of the Church of England was one of the principal springs of the dissenting leaders' conduct and hence the unanimity of the dissenters in this business." He looked upon the Continental Congress merely as a political tool in a Presbyterian conspiracy, a view shared by many Delawareans.[24]

No one was more pleased by the violent condemnation of the British policies on the part of the Presbyterians than McKean, and no political figure in Delaware profited more by their increasing politicization. Presbyterians were not alone in their denunciation of recent British acts but clearly it was they who spearheaded moves for a tough line against England. After observing the Presbyterian response to the Stamp Act, Joseph Galloway had remarked that the Presbyterians "if I may judge from all their late conduct, seem to look on this as a favorable opportunity of establishing their Republican Principles and of throwing off all connexion with their Mother Country." His observation regarding Pennsylvania Presbyterians was equally valid for those in Delaware. And their zeal by 1775 had, if anything, increased: McKean's New Castle pastor, Joseph Montgomery, inveighed against British measures and supported the possibility of a defensive war. Delaware Presbyterians increasingly looked to McKean as the spokesman for their cause.[25]

If the news of the unrest in Delaware's counties during this period did nothing to instill confidence in McKean, the actions of the local Assembly did. He returned to New Castle on

Sunday, March 12, to report on congressional activities and to push for their acceptance. The receptivity of the Kent and Sussex delegates to the blandishments of McKean and others was apparently markedly increased when an inspection party from the King's schooner *Diana* boarded a Delaware shallop on March 7, savagely beat the captain and ransacked the vessel. It was only a week later, on March 15, that the Assembly "unanimously" approved the conduct of its congressional representatives, and reappointed McKean, Read, and Rodney to represent Delaware in the Congress scheduled for May 10. The final designation of unanimity which appears in the journals more accurately reflects a traditional dislike of publicly acknowledging divisions within the Assembly than it reflects the reality of the circumstances. Behind that final determination of unanimity lay serious divisions—despite southern representatives' unhappiness over the *Diana* affair.[26]

The instructions subsequently drawn up to guide the delegates in the next Congress cautioned them to "studiously avoid...everything disrespectful or offensive to our most gracious Sovereign, or in any Measure invasive of his just rights and prerogatives." Still, they were to insist on their traditional rights. McKean, tied to these instructions for his conduct in the Congress, nevertheless spent his full tenure in that body as a permanent resident of Philadelphia.[27]

McKean viewed his move to Philadelphia simply one of convenience. He had begun to shift his interests more fully to Philadelphia after his first wife's death. His nephew, Thomas McKean Thompson, thought that McKean was motivated by a desire to increase his law practice. McKean himself once told John Dickinson that his move was prompted by the fact that his "most valuable and valued acquaintances & friends resided there," but it seems obvious that he was frustrated somewhat by Delaware's limited opportunity and saw his political and professional ambition better served in cosmospolitan Philadelphia. McKean was disturbed by the implications of the current conspiracy being pursued by the British government but he was pragmatic enough to appreciate that the rapidly changing political climate caused by the Americans' growing awareness of the ministry's aims, offered a variety of opportunities for himself.[28]

Still, McKean had no intention of truncating his Delaware career. He continued to foster economic, legal, and social interests there, and he held onto his political posts in that province.

5. The Birth of a Republic

Although the personnel of the Second Continental Congress which met on May 10, 1775, did not differ markedly from that of its predecessor, the tasks facing the delegates were very dissimilar. Bloodshed had already taken place at Lexington. The North ministry had declared Massachusetts to be in rebellion and had declared itself ready to send troops to punish the errant people of the Bay Colony. Parliament approved the Restraining Act on March 9, 1775, proclaiming that all colonies save New York, North Carolina, Georgia, and Delaware, must henceforth confine their commerce to British ports or her dependencies. With war now existing in actual if not official form, McKean and his fellow delegates were called upon at once to encourage military preparations in their own provinces, to raise a national army, and to continue the delicate and often frustrating reconciliation efforts.

McKean was eminently prepared and qualified for the new mood and talents demanded by this Congress. If sheer attention to detail, long hours of work and the proper attitude could guarantee success, success would be his. In the thirteen months between the beginning of the Second Congress and its declaration separating the Colonies from England, McKean found himself chairing five committees and being a party to thirty-three others. The problems and responsibilities associated with such prestigious committees as Accounts and Claims, Qualifications, Treasury, and the Secret Committee became his.[1]

He not only devoted an extraordinary amount of time to ferreting out those resisting Congress' will, but he became a conduit for persons with information on Tory behavior. It was he who joined Thomas Willing of Pennsylvania in pressing Congress to intervene in a dispute between settlers from Pennsylvania and Connecticut in the disputed Wyoming valley, a disagreement which threatened to undermine colonial solidarity, and he continued to play a prominent role in congressional efforts after that date to minimize the deepening problems between those settlers of the sister states. By December he was secretary of the prestigious Secret Committee and throwing himself into the problems of that agency, particularly its efforts to supply a successful Canadian expedition.[2]

Though his many congressional assignments were clearly a burden to him, he thrived under the mounting status and influence they brought him. When he wrote in the beginning of 1776 that he was "almost worn down... owing to the multiplicity of business" it was as much to convey his status in Congress as to detail his physical or mental well-being.[3]

Meanwhile, the question of a viable commercial policy, which had raged for months, surfaced again in October to plague Congress. The first Congress had established a non-importation policy and had determined that a non-exportation policy should also be implemented in the following November if no adequate remedy to colonial ills was forthcoming by that time. No accord was reached by the deadline and, on September 10, 1775, the non-exportation agreement went into effect. What had appeared to be a viable policy the year before, however, now looked to be counterproductive in view of the pressing need for foreign trade and munitions.

Spokesmen for the Middle Colonies proposed that the four colonies—New York, North Carolina, Georgia, and Delaware—

exempted by the Restraining Act, whose ports had been closed only through the efforts of Whigs in each of those colonies be reopened to commerce. These "favored" colonies it was pointed out, could provide limited trade and thus relieve the other colonies of an economic stranglehold and in the process provide much-needed ammunition and war materiel. Proponents of the Eastern or New England bloc were unkind enough to suggest that the representatives of the favored colonies—especially businessmen in New York—were more interested in gaining profits than in securing an effective response to British wrongs. New England representatives and southern allies like Christopher Gadsden and Richard Henry Lee were intent upon a wholesale attack upon British commercial legislation and to this end they insisted on acting in concert. To allow four colonies commercial privileges would be deleterious to colonial unity in the long run, they complained. Either all colonial ports should be closed, or all should be opened.

McKean agreed. On October 12 he urged that the favored colonies, including his own Delaware, put themselves on an equal footing with their sister colonies. He had listened impatiently to the argumentation of New York's James Duane, John Jay, and Robert Livingston, and of Pennsylvania's Thomas Willing, as each sought to define the advantages to the colonial cause from permitting the four colonies to resume limited trading under congressional supervision. He now argued that the ministry had insidiously calculated to divide the Colonies through exempting the four colonies in the Restraining Act. Such duplicity and manipulation would continue, McKean assured his colleagues. When it was to the ministry's advantage the exemptions would be terminated. McKean suspected that just such a move would be forthcoming soon. It was therefore in the Colonies' interest to assume the initiative by taking that decisive step first. All ports must be closed by their own hands.

He told the middle bloc that a decision on the part of the four favored colonies to close their ports by their own volition would eliminate any desire on the part of these colonies to prolong the current difficulties in an effort to solidify their trade monopoly. Such unanimity would also serve to convince the British ministry that there were no weak links in the colonial armor and thus perhaps increase the possibility of a quicker reconciliation between the imperial cousins. He was not at this minute ready to throw open all ports, he admitted to the New England delegates, but if the proposed Canadian expedition should prove to be successful, he would then favor such a move.[4]

The Congress, tired and irritated from nearly a month of constant debate and faced with a deadlock, voted on November 1 to continue the status quo. With Rodney and Read absent during much of the debate and during the critical November 1 vote, McKean was able to ally Delaware with the more radical New England bloc. Or more accurately, he kept Delaware out of what many thought to be her natural alliance, with John Dickinson's middle group strategy.[5]

It was clear by November 1775 that if McKean did in fact favor reconciliation as he claimed, it was not the reconciliation envisioned by the majority of the middle bloc delegates. And despite his obvious play to the men of moderation in his October 12 speech, persons both within and without Congress judged McKean now to be firmly in the New England or radical camp. Read was solidly committed to the moderation of Dickinson and his New York allies, and despite an occasional independent foray, so still was Rodney. McKean was a different story. One observer, "very much acquainted with the principal characters of the present day," considered McKean already "hearty" for independence.[6]

Whether or not McKean had determined by November that independence was the only reasonable course to pursue under the circumstances, he certainly did not forsee the type of reconciliation hoped for by his good friend John Dickinson, despite Dickinson's continued efforts to bring him around. On September 23, before the debates on commercial policy had flared anew, McKean had taken a long and thoughtful walk with John Adams and two delegates from Maryland, William Paca and Thomas Johnson. The men had "walked, a long Time... backward and forward, in the Statehouse Yard," debating with considerable animation the question of Parliament's authority over the Colonies. Adams for once was silent except for an occasional probing question in an effort to define another's views. Paca's position was that Parliament

Thomas McKean, painted by Charles Willson Peale. Courtesy Independence National Historical Park Collection

while having no right to tax the colonies for revenue, did have authority to regulate trade. McKean would brook no such distinctions. He had "no Idea of any Right or Authority in Parliament."[7]

Despite his impressive congressional assignments it was in the military and political developments outside Congress that McKean's growing power and influence was most obvious. Cognizant of the claim of many Pennsylvania Whigs that by 1775 the most serious efforts to press for a vigorous resistance to British encroachments stemmed from the many extra-legal committees dissatisfied with the Assembly's caution, he quickly aligned himself with those groups critically compromising the legislature's position. In April 1775 he joined the Associators, enrolling as a private in Captain John Little's Company of the Second Battalion, a unit comprised of men "eighteen years & upward who are able and willing to bear arms" from the Middle Ward of Philadelphia. In his new political and military organizations he discovered the warmest advocates of "forwardness" to be Scotch-Irish Presbyterians like himself.[8]

Despite his enthusiasm for military service he was somewhat ambivalent toward those with whom he associated in the Second Battalion. Associators were often artisans, laborers, journeymen and apprentices who, denied significant political and personal expression in the regular political apparatus, looked to the military associations as an alternative. Their strident demands for a greater voice in the body politic made a good many Whigs—including McKean—a bit uncomfortable. Still, he wanted as strong a military as Pennsylvania could achieve. When the Congress passed an act "against Apprentices, small debtors and Infants enlisting," he initially worked to have it reconsidered. It was only when John Adams convinced him that "an army of Farmers and Traders" would be more effective that he changed his mind.[9]

When the August congressional recess rolled around, he took the opportunity to join the Committee of Inspection and Observation, a rapidly growing and increasingly powerful political organ in Philadelphia affairs. On the eighteenth of that month, he was appointed one of its chairmen, along with Joseph Reed, George Clymer, and Samuel Meredith. Prominent among the committee's concerns in August was the failure of local Quakers to participate in the political and military preparations instigated by concerned Whigs, and their efforts to elude fines imposed on persons unwilling to engage their time. When, on October 27, 1775, the Philadelphia Quakers petitioned the Assembly to exempt them from all military preparations and earnestly entreated that body to "guard against any Proposal or Attempt to deprive us and others of the full Enjoyment of Liberty or Conscience," it was McKean who helped draft a reply, and it was he, along with George Clymer, who, presented the counter-memorial to the Assembly.[10]

The memorial, delivered personally to the Assembly by Clymer and McKean, asserted that the Quaker position "bears an Aspect unfriendly to the Liberties of America and maintains Principles destructive to all Society and Government." If the Friends of Liberty succeed in "the present Glorious Struggle" the memorial pointed out, the Quakers and their posterity, even though they have not contributed a single penny or a moment of their time, will "enjoy all the Advantages derived from it." On the other hand, if the Friends of Liberty fail, the Quakers not only will not suffer, the petition argued, they will in fact be rewarded. Moreover, by their reluctance to participate militarily the Quakers were failing to adhere to Man's "Original Compact and Agreement" to defend themselves and their communities against those who "attempt unlawfully to deprive them of their just Rights and Liberties." At the bottom of the Quakers' reluctance to resist England, according to McKean, was their fear of losing political control of Philadelphia. McKean was rapidly perceiving the contest between Great Britain and the Colonies as a Holy War; those who were not for you were against you, and must take the consequences.[11]

As part of the leadership corps McKean was eager for such a move when in February 1776 the Philadelphia Committee of Inspection and Observation sought to challenge more blatantly the Assembly's role in Pennsylvania politics by calling for a province-wide convention on April 2, ostensibly to seek the true will of the people. Forged initially to implement the resolves of the first Congress, the Committee of Inspection and Observation had grown from forty-three members to one hundred and had expanded its influence commensurately.

It was clearly more radical than the Assembly and did not hesitate to usurp powers once confined to the Assembly and to the local courts.[12]

A mixture of shock and confusion naturally greeted the Committee's move, many Whigs sharing Joseph Shippen's fear that "such a Step would certainly be productive of the greatest Confusion Anarchy & Disunion." It was widely accepted that the plan aimed at forcing Pennsylvania to accept the idea of independence was, in the words of one observer, the work of "violent wrong-headed People of the inferior classes" who outvoted "the few Gentlemen belonging to the committee."[13]

But McKean was one gentleman who was willing to contribute personally to the dismantling of the legitimate colonial government if by his actions he could secure an agency more responsive to recent congressional moves, and a more equitable political representation in Pennsylvania. His acquiescence in the rapid blurring of lines between legal and extra-legal agencies was rooted more in a desire for effective colonial action in the imperial dispute than in any hope or anticipation of a widespread internal social revolution. McKean was no leveler. He remained more old fashioned than his comments on representative democracy and popular sovereignty implied.[14]

In early March a temporary halt to the idea of a convention was secured through the strenuous efforts of moderate Whigs who wrung from the Assembly an agreement to expand its numbers and to provide thirteen new seats for the backcountry. On May 1 an election was held to fill the additional Assembly seats, including those from the city. To their chagrin the more radical elements failed to carry the hotly contested election. The failure of the more zealous Whigs either to dominate the Assembly or supplant it as the principal voice in the province, convinced militant Pennsylvanians like McKean that unless a new impetus was quickly discovered, whatever momentum their movement might have attained to that point would be lost.

So, Dickinson and his followers, buffeted in congressional debate, began to view the Pennsylvania Assembly as a last bastion against the more impetuous voices for radicalism and independence. Militant Pennsylvanians on the other hand, rebuffed in the Assembly, now looked more eagerly than ever to the resources of Congress. Congress thus began to play a somewhat different role in Pennsylvania society. McKean, as an influential member of Congress and a man intimately connected by this time to the radical cause in Philadelphia, became an important liaison between radicals outside the Congress and the "violents" within. Christopher Marshall, James Cannon, Thomas Young, all zealous for an independent America, and all relatively new to the role of political leadership, conferred with him at critical moments. The meetings accelerated after the May 1 defeat and it is clear that the details of just how Congress would step into the void were being slowly ironed out.[15]

McKean was buoyant when Congress provided the necessary momentum desired by Pennsylvania popular leaders. On May 10 Congress adopted John Adams' resolution to the effect that "respective Assemblies and conventions of the United Colonies [should] where no government sufficient to the exigencies of their affairs have been hitherto established...adopt such government as shall...best conduce to the happiness and safety of the constituents in Particular and America in general." The resolve itself could be innocent enough—John Dickinson supported it by contending that it clearly had no reference to Pennsylvania's government—but it was broadened considerably five days later when Congress, under the goad of Adams and Lee, added a preamble which established that it was "absolutely irreconcilable to reason and good Conscience, for the people of these colonies now to take the Oaths and affirmations necessary for the support of any government under the crown."[16]

McKean listened as congressional opponents protested that taken together the resolve and the preamble fell "little short of Independence." Dickinson, convinced that the issue was closed after the May 10 resolve, had retired to his farm in Delaware for a few days and it was left to the Carlisle lawyer, James Wilson, to shoulder the burden of opposing the May 15 preamble for the moderates. Despite a fervent and at times eloquent plea by Wilson and additional arguments by New York's James Duane not to accept the new introduction to the resolve, the preamble passed, either six to four, or seven to four.

Delaware's congressional position on the May 15 preamble is difficult to assess. It has been widely assumed that Delaware joined with New York, North Carolina, and New Jersey in voting against the resolution.[17] There seems to be no question that George Read voted against the preamble. But for Delaware to vote against it as a delegation either McKean or Rodney had to join Read, and both left strong sentiments favoring it. According to John Adams, McKean supported his preamble on the floor of Congress, playing upon the fears engendered by the news that the King had dispatched foreign mercenaries to the American shores. McKean, Adams reported, warned his colleagues not to doubt that foreign mercenaries were coming to destroy them. There were now two distinct governments facing each other, McKean argued, and unless Americans supported the May 10-15 resolves, "We shall Loose [sic] our Liberties Properties and Lives Too."[18] Such an impassioned speech could hardly have been followed by a negative vote.

Rodney remarked to his brother several days after the critical vote that "Continuing to Swear Allegiance to the power that is Cutting our Throats is certainly absurd." He also observed that "Cool considerate Men think it [the preamble] is a declaration of Independence." But that he voted for the preamble on the 15th seems unlikely.[19]

Men of all political persuasions in Pennsylvania understood that the resolves ultimately meant a convention of the people, one that would, as James Allen expressed it, "consist of the most fiery independents [who] will have the whole executive and legislative authority in their hands." Another of the Allens, Andrew, ascribed Congress' interference in Pennsylvania affairs to a "deep laid plot...to blow up the Constitution and Government of the Province which has hitherto been a Barrier against their dark Designs." Moderate Whigs, once willing and eager to encourage opposition to England, now found themselves bemoaning the precarious position of "their old tottering constitution."[20]

McKean apparently was not the least disturbed by the turn of events. In concert with other popular leaders, he did not even wait to observe the Assembly's reaction to the congressional moves. In the evening of the same day that Congress accepted the preamble, May 15, he chaired a meeting at the Philosophical Hall "where was debated the resolve... respecting the taking up and forming new Governments in the different colonies." On the following day he joined with those who met and voted to call a convention "with speed," and to insist on the Assembly ceasing to act until the sense of the province could be determined in the province-wide convention. He also concurred with those calling for still another public meeting on May 20 to discuss further the rapidly changing political conditions.[21]

On May 20, the very day that the Pennsylvania Assembly convened in a desperate effort to retain some semblance of control, McKean met with more than four thousand people to debate further the congressional resolves and their implications for Pennsylvania. Without mentioning Dickinson by name McKean attacked the basis of Dickinson's recent strategy. It was Dickinson who had pressed the Assembly in the preceding November to write instructions specifically denying to Pennsylvania's congressional delegates the right to consider independence as a reasonable option. It was a calculated effort to embolden the Assemblies at least of New York, New Jersey, and Delaware. Now McKean lashed out at the Pennsylvania Assembly's unwillingness to reassess its position even in the face of being petitioned by the people to that end. No longer could faith be placed in members of that body, McKean contended, in light of its indifference to the people's will. In short, it was exactly Dickinson's policy of stiffening Middle Colony defiance of congressional initiatives through the boldness of the Pennsylvania Assembly that should render the legislature suspect in the eyes of the people.[22]

As chairman of the city Committee of Inspection and Observation, McKean signed and probably drafted a memorial to the Assembly reminding it that it had withdrawn from its union with Congress as a consequence of its refusal to change its congressional directives to allow for a vote on independence, and its reluctance to accept dutifully the May 10-15 resolve. According to McKean the Assembly had no right to restrain its delegates in this matter; it had lost this right because it did not "contain a fully and equal representation of the province." It was not "the legitimate agency of power."[23]

To continue its assault on the Assembly, the Committee on June 3 sent a memorial to the justices of the quarter sessions for the City and Liberties of Philadelphia, asking them to terminate the authority of the courts until such time as a new government could be framed upon the true will of the people. McKean delivered the message personally to the court personnel. As a lawyer he could not escape mixed emotions as he contemplated the implications of his political efforts, for the success of the Committee's pressure to bring the courts—all courts—to a virtual standstill was attested to by the subsequent observation by the Pennsylvania lawyer, Joseph Reed, to the effect that the "Courts are stopp'd[;] consequently no Business done in my Profession." When McKean joined other radical Whigs to grind the Supreme Court to a stop he had several cases pending before it. Indeed, the lawyer McKean appeared in court right up to that moment when McKean the Patriot put a stop to it.[24]

Despite the inexorable logic of attacking the courts once the legitimacy of the Assembly had been questioned, McKean's willingness to truncate the judicial processes is a bit surprising. Perhaps he believed, as his memorial to the justices suggested, that the delay occasioned by the courts' closing would be of small, if any injury to the present suitors, that a new government and new courts would quickly be forthcoming.[25] But he could not have failed to perceive the rising fear of anarchy among a great many Pennsylvanians and those familiar with political conditions in that province. Nor could he have been unaware of the political consequences to his cause from such growing fears. Even among McKean's closest political associates in Congress there was an increasing uneasiness that the Whigs, in mobilizing support for their cause, had unleased political forces which now threatened some of their most cherished assumptions concerning power and authority. Even before its attack on the Assembly and the courts, McKean's own committee had contributed to the growing sense of anarchy among some Pennsylvanians by its systematic punishment and intimidation of those it deemed inimical to America. In fact, its contribution was two-fold, for the Committee had also awakened among its members, some heretofore politically inarticulate, a new sense of importance and power.²⁶

To halt the courts and measurably contribute to the growing sense of chaos was a critical move, perhaps more startling in its symbolic significance for the common man than the Committee's assault upon the legislature. It was a step into the unknown. One might seek to continue control over the Committee—and thus guide the current policies down reasonably safe channels—by maintaining respectable types in the critical leadership roles, or one might even replace the current Assembly with similarly respectable but more responsive types. One might even—despite some observers' complaints that the Associators were ungovernable—guide the militia through resourceful and astute leadership and thus blunt or curb the Associators' more democratic proclivities. But to destroy the courts was to eliminate a real as well as a psychological barrier to disorder. Still, McKean deemed the risk essential in order to achieve his longstanding objectives: a more equitable representation in the Pennsylvania Assembly, and a more effective colonial response to the endless series of exasperating provocations on the part of the British ministry.

One way to insure the continuation of committee leadership, and thus see that elements from below did not assume too great a voice, was to mobilize the army safely behind the current leaders. This necessitated a masterful balancing act on the part of a number of the leaders, including McKean, for they had to assume a position advanced enough to satisfy the yearnings of the Associators even while seeking to protect and maintain various privileges and responsibilities in their own hands. In the first week in June Timothy Matlack took the first step in arraying the power of the Associators behind the current Whig program when he encouraged officers of his Fifth Battalion to ratify the work of the Committee. Not to be outdone, the Committee of Privates insisted that the entire battalion meet as a body to endorse the measures of Congress and voice its approval of the Committee. Other battalions quickly followed suit.²⁷

For his part, McKean, now a colonel,²⁸ reported to the people of Philadelphia on the enthusiasm of his Fourth Battalion, stressing its "hearty approbation" of the measures so far pursued by Congress and the Philadelphia Committee of Inspection and Observation. When, on June 10, McKean asked his battalion "whether they wished the Province of Pennsylvania to be a free and independent state and united with the other twelve colonies represented in Congress" the affirmation was unanimous. McKean was quick to assure the public that "no arguments or persuasions were urged for or against the... proposition; and all present, amounting to upwards of four hundred, shewed their hearty approbation of the whole transaction by three huzzas," a somewhat more sanguine version than that provided by one by-stander. But Benjamin Rush, the brilliant Philadelphia physician and political activist, was by this time elated enough with events to write that "our cause prospers in every county in the province," and he attributed much of the Whigs' success to McKean, telling his wife that the true Whigs were relying "chiefly upon Colonel McKean and a few more of us for the salvation of the province."[29]

Even before they heard the disturbing news of the passage of the May 10-15 Resolve, many Delawareans were openly espousing the British cause. As early as January 1776 many of the "Principle [sic] gentlemen" of Delaware were actively assisting British naval personnel in the Delaware River and seeking advice from them on how best to blunt the revolutionaries in their province. Despite his greater proximity to events in Philadelphia during this critical period, McKean remained one of Delaware's principal liaisons with the national government, and it was he who reported to Congress the deteriorating conditions in Sussex County when, on June 13, Tories openly challenged congressional authority and seriously disconcerted the local Assembly.[30]

It was McKean, too, who placed before the Delaware Assembly on June 14 an official copy of the May 10-15 Resolve, and urged its acceptance. Despite the opposition of large majorities in Kent and Sussex counties, and divisions within the Assembly itself over the measure, the Assembly nonetheless approved the resolution "unanimously." Though McKean apparently pleaded eloquently and persuasively in the resolution's behalf, much of the credit for the Assembly's receptivity to his blandishments belongs to Rodney, who used his considerable acumen and influence to convince the members that unless they cooperated, and thus maintained a semblance of control over the situation, Delaware would soon be witnessing the same type of push for a convention that Pennsylvania was currently experiencing.[31]

At any rate, McKean was elated with the Assembly's decision on June 15 to suspend the Proprietary government and to continue to execute the functions of the government in the name of the counties of New Castle, Kent, and Sussex upon Delaware. He was also satisfied with the Assembly's new instructions for its congressional delegates, the wording of which, while not explicitly directing a vote for independence should Richard Henry Lee's June 7 resolution come up for a formal vote, allowed sufficient latitude for such a move. He hastened to Philadelphia on June 16 to share with John Adams the fact that he now had "full powers" to vote for independence.[32]

On the day that he presented the May 10-15 Resolve to the Delaware Assembly and pleaded for its acceptance, the Committee of Inspection and Observation for the City and Liberties of Philadelphia elected McKean and twenty-four others to the forthcoming provincial conference. Four days later 108 delegates representing twelve committees throughout Pennsylvania were brought together at Carpenters' Hall to establish the ground rules for a constituent convention. As chairman of the host organization McKean opened the meeting by reviewing the maze of events and motives which prompted the gathering. He repeated the now familiar charges against the Assembly, stressing its unrepresentative—and thus illegal—make-up, and identified the course of events which had brought the colonies into direct conflict with the parent country.[33]

The conference quickly elected McKean president.[34] The presidency of such conferences, like the chairmanship of public meetings, was generally reserved for very popular figures, for men whose ideas most closely approximated the consensus of those present, or for men whose sense of fairness was acknowledged by men of all political persuasions. At times it was reserved for men whose gifts in commanding large gatherings, or whose ability to bring order and decorum out of restless, often turbulent crowds, was firmly established. McKean owed his presidency of the conference—and later similar posts—less to his popularity than to his attractiveness as a spokesman, and his ability to convey a sense of fairness and efficiency. In this instance he also owed it to his recent effectiveness as a leader of Philadelphia's largest committee.[35]

Ironically, McKean assumed the titular leadership of the conference not at the moment his views were most thoroughly representative of those in attendance, but when they were rapidly becoming incompatible with—or at least too limited for—the ultimate aims of the majority of the conference members. The conference's subsequent actions and policies indicate clearly that the impetus and momentum were swinging to those people desirous of going far beyond what McKean sought to achieve through the current struggle with Great Britain. McKean remained one of the ostensible leaders of the conference, and he continued to help draft and sign the addresses emanating from it. But he no longer represented the true direction of that body. It was a problem faced by a number of men other than McKean.[36] To demand more equitable representation in the Pennsylvania Assembly, or to insist on an Assembly truly responsive to the Whig cause was one thing, but to advocate radical innovation, to seriously rend the political and social fabric, was something for which McKean was not prepared.

Recognition by McKean of the extent of his alienation from those now directing the destinies of Pennsylvania's politics, or at least a public indication of it, came later. Not until the following September, when he had occasion to read the constitution produced by the constitutional convention which he had done so much to create did he fully sense his disagreements with his co-leaders.

Meanwhile, between June 18 and June 25 he worked with his usual diligence with the leaders of the conference to lay the groundwork for the constituent convention. After a visit from representatives of the various Associator groups who decried their own lack of political voice, the conference voted to broaden the electorate to include all those who were residents, twenty-one, and tax-payers. Significantly, however, the conference was careful to eliminate much of their opposition by excluding from the suffrage any individual who had been termed an enemy of American liberties by a committee of inspection, or by a committee of safety. Anyone could qualify for election to the forthcoming convention if he were qualified to vote, had resided for one year in the area from which he was elected, would acquiesce in an oath declaring his allegiance to the new government, and oppose any attempt to restrict the religious principles and practices of "any of the good people of this Province as heretofore enjoyed." He also must profess "faith in God, the son, and in the Holy Spirit and acknowledge the holy scriptures of the old and new testament to be given by divine inspiration."[37]

In his capacity as president of the conference McKean notified the people of Pennsylvania on June 22 that in obedience to the power derived from the people the conference had fixed July 8 for the critical elections to choose those who would attend the convention. "Divine Providence is about to grant you a favour which few people have ever enjoyed before," McKean's proclamation declared, "the privilege of chusing Deputies to form a Government under which you are to live." The significance of this new responsibility, and the gravity of the situation now confronting Pennsylvania, was impressed upon the people's minds. They were encouraged to choose those who were "distinguished for wisdom, integrity and a firm attachment to the liberties of this province as well as to the liberties of the United Colonies in general," an admonition no doubt included to comfort men like McKean. The proclamation also established that further allegiance to the Crown would be looked upon as treason. It was the conference's will that Congress declare the Colonies independent of Great Britain.[38]

The conference call for independence was wholly in line with McKean's thinking. The three weeks' postponement of congressional debate over Richard Henry Lee's resolution calling for separation from Great Britain was to McKean merely delaying the inevitable, although he recognized, as did most delegates, that if unanimity were a prime concern, a delay was necessary. Thomas Jefferson's draft of a declaration of independence was read aloud and routinely tabled by Congress on June 28, to permit the delegates a final weekend of contemplation and manipulation before voting on it. A vote on

The Birth of a Republic

independence itself would of course have to precede further consideration of Jefferson's document.

On the first of July McKean discovered that the situation was still unresolved. By the time Secretary Charles Thomson called for Delaware's vote in the informal poll of the committee of the whole, five colonies had already declared their support for the Lee Resolution, Pennsylvania had voted 4-3 against it, and New York, still without instructions, had been forced to abstain. Delaware split its vote, Read opposing the motion, McKean supporting it. Though Maryland, Virginia, North Carolina, and Georgia followed with "ayes," South Carolina joined Pennsylvania in opposition. Following a hurried discussion it was decided to delay a formal vote until the following day. In the meantime perhaps the recalcitrant members could be persuaded to reverse their votes and New York might finally receive instructions to act. Eager to guarantee Delaware's support for the resolution on independence, McKean hastily sent for Caesar Rodney, absent in Kent.[39]

McKean met the fatigued Rodney at the State House door on the afternoon of the second, and the two men joined their rain-soaked colleagues moving into the building for the critical vote. It was quickly evident to McKean as to others that the sentiment of the group had changed markedly from the previous evening. Dickinson was noticeably absent from the Pennsylvania delegation, as was Robert Morris who shared Dickinson's opposition. On this day, when Thomson called upon Delaware in the roll call, all colonies save New York had fallen into line, Pennsylvania by a narrow 3-2 margin. New York was again forced to abstain for want of instructions. McKean's hopes for his own colony were realized when Rodney joined him in supporting the resolution against Read's negative. All other colonies to the South fell quickly into line. Thomson handed the final tally to President John Hancock who announced the results to the delegates: the colonies had unanimously declared their separation from the Mother Country.[40]

The coincidence of having three members of a single class from Francis Alison's New London Academy participating in the roll call on America's independence could not have been lost on Thomson, Read, or McKean. A little over two decades before, each had read and pondered Francis Hutcheson's views on colonies and the colonial relationship to the Mother Country, and had listened to Alison's almost daily exhortation in favor of broadening the rights and liberties of the people in defiance of tyrannical princes. Now on July 2 they had no choice but to deal with the practical application of those views and theories. Even George Read's refusal to be pressured into a move he thought precipitous was consistent with Alison's appreciation of courageous, independent action.

McKean spent the third and fourth of July listening to the debate over the exact wording of Jefferson's document establishing the rationale for the Colonies' action, attending committee meetings on military questions, and catching up on a variety of minor details before the Congress. He then joined others on the fourth informally accepting the Unanimous Declaration of the Thirteen Colonies, and it was over.[41]

The vote to sever America's ties with Great Britain was not taken lightly by anyone connected with it. But if the decision to declare America independent created in George Read a sense of disquietude and in Dickinson a foreboding of doom, it brought only exhileration to McKean.[42] If many Americans saw in the congressional vote on July second only the last of a series of unwarranted and precipitous acts, to McKean it was the culmination of a cautious and logical development rendered necessary by continuing British intransigence. Many delegates reflected their constituents' fears that rebellion would elicit a demand for power and place by "new men." McKean thought the cause worth the risk; indeed, prompted by fairness. As one of the "new men" he could not have thought otherwise. But he believed that the new equality he had helped to stimulate by his activities and public pronouncements need not destroy the subordination so essential for an orderly, progressive society. The equality he sought was that sought by most Americans, an equality not of condition but of opportunity.[43]

For many observers of Congress' action in the first week of July, it was a time of bewilderment over the loss of a way of life familiar to them, a termination of a fruitful and, until recently, mutually satisfactory partnership. For McKean it marked a beginning. Though the search for offices and honors had not originally prompted his revolutionary activities, he had become aware by 1775 that conditions in Pennsylvania offered avenues for advancement that only the British had been able to provide before. He was aware, too, that the creation of the American republic was of such transcendant importance that it would effect Americans and non-Americans alike for generations to come. In the last days of his tumultuous life, some forty years after he and Rodney cast their votes for separation to push Delaware out of the British Empire, McKean's complicity in that act still burned bright in his memory. To the day of his death he considered it a pivotal event in his life—and in the history of mankind.[44]

6. The Shape of Republicanism

The immediate problems of giving concrete legal and constitutional form to America's—and Pennsylvania's—republican experiment fell to shoulders other than McKean's in the days and months following the congressional vote to separate from Great Britain. He was not among the ninety-six men elected to meet on July 15 to create a new Pennsylvania government. He could not have attended had he been selected. Even before he had affixed his signature to the Declaration of Independence his attention was turned to military developments.[1]

On Thursday, July 5, he chaired a meeting of congressional delegates and military leaders from Pennsylvania, New Jersey, and New York called to contemplate uniform strategy for the defense of the Middle Colonies, and to correlate the efforts of Congress in military matters with those of state authorities. Of crucial concern to those at the meeting was the overall strategy of defending New York, then under threat from the massive British armaments directed by General Howe. Since

June 3 George Washington had been pressing for the formulation of a Flying Camp of ten thousand men from New Jersey, Maryland, Delaware, New York, and Pennsylvania to secure New York and thus to blunt an obvious desire on the part of the British to drive a wedge between New England and the Middle Colonies. The Flying Camp would protect New York by securing New Jersey. It would also deny to the British easy travel across New Jersey to Philadelphia if New York should fall. A spot near Perth Amboy was thought to be an ideal locale for the Flying Camp.

Because the Flying Camp had not yet materialized by July 5, McKean's committee agreed to send all of Pennsylvania's militia units to New Jersey except for those units in Westmoreland, Bedford, and Northumberland Counties. McKean thus found himself in the next two weeks scurrying around, not only reviewing the mobilization of the militia units but overseeing the preparation of his own battalion as well. By July 23 he and his battalion had arrived in Perth Amboy "in full parade with 360 odd men . . . officers included."[2]

He wrote his wife on the 26th that he was "within about 600 yards of the Enemy, hundreds of whom [he had] seen everyday since [his] arrival." Two days earlier he was standing near a battery of two four pounders when he spotted a shallop sailing close along the enemy's shore. After he ordered the shallop several times to bring to and it failed to heed his commands, he ordered it fired upon. Unfortunately rain, high winds and darkness prevented a concerted attack upon the enemy vessel and amidst flashes of lightning the Americans watched the shallop round the island to a man-of-war and the matter ended. "These were the first guns I ever ordered to be fired against human beings," McKean told his wife, "if I may be allowed to call the Enemies of Mankind such."

On Thursday there had been a similar incident. When five shallops had sailed along the same area, the Americans fired several four pounders at the vessels. This time the British responded by bombarding Amboy for almost an hour, killing one and wounding two. McKean found himself in the midst of the long-range duel. He told Sally that some twenty cannon balls fell close to him which frightened his horse and made him "not a little scared myself (being the first time I ever heard a cannon ball)." A horse near him ("about the width of market street away from me"), had been shot through the neck. He estimated that the British had expended nearly sixty shots, mostly four- to ten-pounders, in a little less than an hour.³

But life in camp was far from a regimen of unrelieved excitement and confrontations with the enemy. If McKean ever harbored visions of military glory he rapidly discarded them. He must have quickly sensed how unfit he was to command the Associators, whom he later described as "some of the most rude, turbulent, impudent, lazy, dirty fellows...that I have every beheld." Apparently they were no happier with him. In later years, during a bitter gubernatorial contest in which McKean was involved, one witness to his military exploits remembered that "from his tyrannical, arbitrary, imposing conduct upon the soldiery, not a single man in his Battalion either loved, feared or respected him." They deemed him a "base, tyrannical, overbearing coward." Even making allowances for campaign rhetoric, it is clear that McKean's efforts at Perth Amboy were less than successful. Nonetheless his experiences with the Associators made an indelible impression on him. Life at Perth Amboy evoked in McKean neither sympathy nor understanding for army life nor soldiers generally. He continued to exalt the militia as the foundation of the republic—certainly it was more acceptable to him than a standing army—but after Perth Amboy he found himself more comfortable with that presumption in theory than in application.⁴

His military experience also convinced him that his contributions to the shaping of events would have to come in the legal or political arenas. When drastic changes in the military conditions and the continuing desertion of Associators made apparent to all that the camp had been a mistake, McKean reported to the Philadelphia Committee of Safety that he had "not above an hundred effective men remaining." With a sigh of relief he resigned his commission. Earlier he had written his wife that he "really wish[ed] to be rid of all public employments" for he was "injuring [his] fortune and [his] health rather too much." But news from Caesar Rodney that the convention charged with writing a new state constitution, scheduled for August 29, would be "undoubtedly the most important assembly that Ever was chose" in Delaware, reawakened his desire to serve. News from his wife that his enemies in New Castle were conspiring to see that he was not chosen for the convention also whet his appetite for renewing the political struggles. He need not have worried about his New Castle constituency; it easily elected him to the convention.[5]

McKean returned to Philadelphia on Sunday, August 25, for a brief reunion with his family. Then, with his eldest son Joseph ("Josie") he hastened on to New Castle, where he arrived on Tuesday, August 27. Before departing Philadelphia, McKean hurriedly conferred with the troubled Rodney. Each recognized the chronic inability of Delaware to maintain a full complement of congressional delegates in Philadelphia and concurred that the convention should change the rules governing the congressional delegates by vesting the power of voting in one representative. Implicit in their assumption was the fact that if that one man were an aggressive Whig, Delaware in the future as in the past could be represented by a delegation far more liberal and patriotic than the population it represented. Still, while agreeing with such a move in theory, McKean hesitated to push the issue too far. As he patiently explained to Rodney, he was "so aversed to and determined against the convention taking upon them or concerning with, the least Iota Except the barely frameing a plan of Government" that he was determined never to consent to their appointing delegates or even altering their power, "lest they should afterward be inclined to hold it out as a president [sic] for their takeing upon them other matters." And he, for one, thought it perfectly clear that his enemies within the convention would seek not only to provide a new state constitution but to overthrow the more militant Whigs as well.

He confessed to Rodney that he was tired of attending Congress and wanted desperately to be relieved of his official duties in Philadelphia, but he was determined that the Tories and Timid Whigs should not turn him nor any other zealous Whig out of office. Should such an attempt be made he was resolved to "try the strength of the County with them Even at the risk of the Court House." McKean sought to assure the anxious Rodney that he would use whatever power and resources he possessed to see that the convention focused exclusively on framing a new government.[6]

That McKean had definite ideas concerning the form of government most conducive to the happiness of Delaware whiggery can not be doubted. Prior to his appearance in New Castle he had drafted a constitution to place before the convention. Late in his life McKean described how he had gone "to New Castle, joined the Convention for framing a constitution for the future government of the state of Delaware...and produced a constitution which [he] wrote in a tavern, without a book or any Assistance."[7] He did have a draft in hand when the convention began. His later remarks suggest, too, that he was intent on having it accepted without amendment. Taking the initiative in such matters had worked successfully in numerous county meetings, and he saw no reason why it should not work again. The problem facing McKean and those allying with him was to convince the convention to accept the draft without crippling amendments or radical changes; unfortunately for McKean developments both before and during the convention rendered it impossible for him to succeed in such a ploy.

His stint in the army had kept him out of the political maneuverings preceding the elections, as well as strategy work done between the fall elections and the convention. He had no chance to elaborate upon his own position or animadvert that of his opponents. Equally important considering his interest in Sussex county and his alliance with numerous warm Whigs there, McKean had no opportunity to support those who sought to control the Sussex delegation.

Consequently, when the convention met on the morning of September 27, Sussex presented two lists of electors to the convention. One, favored by the Sussex Committee of Inspection and Observation, listed such ardent Whigs as John Dagsworthy, John Clowes and David Hall; it was opposed by the second, headed by the more conservative Dr. James Rench, Isaac Bradley, William Polk, and Jacob Moore. For three days the question of which list to accept as the legal electors preoccupied the delegates. At a critical juncture of the convention, on the morning of Friday, September 30, just after Hall,

Clowes, Dagsworthy, and their colleagues on the first ticket were rejected in favor of the list headed by James Rench and Jacob Moore, and before the convention turned its attention to choosing a president, McKean was called away, as was his brother-in-law and political ally, John Thompson.[8]

McKean's sister, Dorothea McKean Thompson, her son, Thomas McKean Thompson, and McKean's son, Josie, now twelve, were seriously ill at the Thompson's home in Red Lion Hundred. News of the illnesses reached McKean and Thompson late on the twenty-ninth but they apparently decided to attend the morning session, perhaps in anticipation of supporting the Clowes ticket and voting on the convention's presidency before going home to their sick families. Josie was better by September 2 but McKean's sister's condition steadily deteriorated over the week-end and she died early that morning.[9]

It was September 6 before McKean returned to the convention. His brother-in-law returned September 12, then only for sporadic duty. Fortunately for McKean the convention had not begun the formal process of writing or considering the new constitution. It had turned its attention to its military obligations to the Congress and to preparation of a Declaration of Rights and Fundamental Rules of this State. The lost time was critical nonetheless. The convention deliberately postponed the important business of framing a new government until McKean's return.[10] But if George Read was not the most influential delegate when the convention started, he certainly was by September 6. That meant the convention was largely in the hands of those McKean called Timid Whigs.

On September 2 McKean had been added to the committee working on a Declaration of Rights; he was subsequently among the twelve delegates charged with framing a constitution for the state. Of this last committee six were from New Castle, three each from Sussex and Kent. New Castle's advantage in numbers was offset, at least in McKean's view, by the fact that few of the New Castle delegates had been close allies of his in the last several years. Only John Evans, Nicholas Van Dyke and John Thompson had been aligned with his position after 1774 and Van Dyke was absent during most of the convention. Relative newcomers to the New Castle delegation like Abraham Robinson, Richard Cantwell, and John Lea were unknown quantities. Strong voices from the other counties, notably Richard Bassett, Jacob Moore, and Charles Ridgely looked to Read rather than McKean for leadership.[11]

McKean later claimed much of the credit for the final results, choosing to ignore a good deal of contemporary evidence disputing his claims. Read admitted to Rodney on September 17 that the declaration of rights was not "an object of much curiosity, it is made of Y^e Pennsylvania & Maryland Draughts." Also according to Read, "Y^e Plan of Government" had been drawn up after it had "undergone such daily amend^{t}s y^t it coul'd have been little satisfactory to have known ye 1st State of it." McKean, himself, in a letter two days later commented to the effect that his original draft had recently undergone a number of amendments.[12]

The Constitution, approved on the twentieth, was not to be submitted to the people for ratification. It was to go into effect with the election of the legislators. The plan provided for a two-house assembly, the upper house to be called the Legislative Council, the lower house the House of Assembly. Each county would elect three men to the upper house on alternate years for three-year terms, and seven members annually for the Assembly. No change was called for in the franchise provisions; anyone who was a freeholder owning fifty acres of land, with at least twelve clear and improved, or worth fifty pounds, could vote. The executive was to be chosen by the Assembly for a three-year term. He would be assisted by a Privy Council consisting of two men elected by the House and two by the Council. There was no significant departure from the old judicial structure.[13]

In spite of its moderation the Constitution elicited some surprising responses. McKean bemoaned the fact that his original draft had called for a "discreet, modest & respectable Magistrate and useful Member of Society" but the convention had amended it to read a "very powerful & dangerous man,"—an almost irrational response in light of the final provisions of the constitution. Thomas Rodney thought the constitution contained "drastic changes" and railed that it gave complete sovereignty to the people. John Haslet complained that the Tory-dominated convention had "done as little as possible, & modeled their new government as like the old as maybe."

He assumed that "the hand of McK[ean] was in it." Opinions of the Constitution seemed to be formed on the basis of personalities involved as much as on serious consideration of its parts.[14]

The heat of opinion, if the outbursts of McKean and his friends are any indication, was engendered not so much by the form of government as its purpose and who would control it. Rodney and McKean were particularly concerned lest the Tory element dominate the new government, manipulate the elections to their advantage, and place their sympathizers in the important offices, particularly the Council of Safety and the congressional delegation. If successful, these "Tories" could then pursue the Revolution in their own fashion and at their own speed, thus jeopardizing the Whig cause. Equally important, these timid Whigs, or Tories, could dominate the power and offices of the local government. The question of patronage and power was never far from the minds of those laboring in New Castle.

McKean surmised that the Kent and Sussex delegations, with the support of George Read, were intent on eliminating as many solid Whigs as possible from active participation. Article 29, which declared in part that "no Clergyman or Preacher of the Gospel of any Denomination shall be capable of holding any Civil Office in the State, or of being a Member of either of the Branches of the Legislature," he thought an undisguised attack upon Presbyterian clergymen like Joseph Montgomery, his own minister in New Castle, who were the backbone of the Whig cause in Delaware.

McKean's most explosive attack was provoked by Richard Bassett's and Charles Ridgely's attempt to change the Assembly's permanent meeting place from New Castle to Dover. He accused them of trying to increase their own popularity in Kent before the next elections. He was already upset by the fact that Ridgely and Bassett had previously carried a motion to establish October 21 as the day of the important Assembly elections, which would eliminate the ardent whigs serving in the military. Bassett and Ridgely pushed their meeting place issue late in the evening of September 18 to take advantage of the absence of Richard Cantwell, Alexander Porter, and John Lea from the New Castle delegation. McKean and John Evans sought desperately to postpone consideration "till the morning . . . as it was late and many members absent," but except for Jacob Moore, John Wiltbank, and Phillip Kollock, the Kent and Sussex delegations held firm. As a last resort McKean leaped to his feet and shouted at President Read that he "could not with honor, nor in conscious, sit any longer in such an Assembly." He snatched his hat and bolted from the room followed by Nicholas Van Dyke, John Jones, and Abraham Robinson, all of New Castle. Before John Evans and John Thompson could follow, the meeting was adjourned in confusion.

It was a short-lived "victory." The votes to pass the offending provisions were still ranged against McKean and his supporters. when the convention met on the morning of September 19. His final move to expunge the article denying clergymen participation in the government lost overwhelmingly, 20-5; only Porter, Thompson, Van Dyke and Evans joined McKean. The provisions for time and place of the next elections were then quickly passed and McKean was reduced to grumbling about the iniquity of it all.[15]

After completing a number of military matters and charging local authorities to begin preparations for the upcoming elections, the convention adjourned Saturday evening, September 21. McKean left almost immediately for Philadelphia. He did not return to Delaware until October 30th, even though he learned meanwhile of his election to the Delaware Assembly. Upon his arrival in the Delaware counties he found himself surrounded by those he deemed only "lukewarm" to the patriotic cause. Moderates or outright Tories held the speakerships of both houses, and Rodney had not been returned from Kent. Ardent Whigs such as John Haslet and Nicholas Van Dyke were preoccupied with military developments and could offer no political assistance. McKean's worst forebodings were confirmed on November 7 when he was passed over as a delegate to the Continental Congress. Replacing Rodney and McKean in Philadelphia were John Dickinson and John Evans, both more cautious and conservative than McKean. Read, who had been hesitant to accept the concept of independence and who had led the more conservative forces within the constitutional convention, was re-elected.[16]

McKean found conditions in Pennsylvania no better. The Pennsylvania constitutional convention that he had done so much to promote published the results of its labors on September 10. Precisely when McKean, busy arguing the final draft of the Delaware constitution, read the Pennsylvania version is unknown. But he was not happy with what he read.[17]

The Pennsylvania constitution was in his opinion a disaster. The Delaware constitution contained provisions he thought unwise, and he was disturbed with the general direction of some of its articles, but all in all it was a moderate document, one that, given the right people to oversee its functioning, could be effective. The new Pennsylvania constitution seemed beyond redemption. His disenchantment with the product of the convention he had done so much to bring about had at least one immediate effect: it drove him back into a close personal alliance with his longtime friend, John Dickinson.[18]

Opposition to the new government was well under way by the time McKean returned to Philadelphia. On October 17 a meeting was held at the Philosophical Hall to organize and implement that opposition. Those attending (circumstantial evidence suggests that McKean was among them) took an oath that their "sole intention in giving opposition to the constitution formed by the late convention, [was] to provide a free and good government, to be established in Pennsylvania, on the authority of the people." They pledged not to "directly or indirectly do any act or thing prejudicial to the independence of this state, or of the United States."

The meeting, chaired by John Bayard, produced some thirty-two articles describing the weaknesses or errors of the new constitution, running the gamut from its form to its substance. A mass meeting was called for October 21 to discuss the new government further in open session.[19]

McKean and Dickinson were the principal speakers opposing the new government. Arguing against his former colleagues James Cannon, Timothy Matlack, Thomas Young, and James Smith, who supported it, McKean and Dickinson lashed out at a variety of weaknesses inherent in the new structure. No record remains of McKean's specific criticism but he doubtless repeated much of the argument already voiced in the October 17 meeting. The major criticism leveled at the supporters of the constitution was that the convention had gone beyond its powers and had established a government which "unnecessarily deviated from all resemblance to the former government of this state." The government it created differed from "every government that has lately been established in America on the authority of the people." McKean, whose experience with his Associators had reduced his enthusiasm for some of the new ideas and advocates of the Revolution, concurred that the people of Pennsylvania did not seek nor would they accept such "strange innovations" as those proposed by the convention.[20]

The resolutions of the October 17 meeting—probably voiced by McKean and Dickinson on the 21st and 22nd—specifically disapproved of a single legislature with power to remove judges from office without trial for misbehavior. Other objections were made: that executives were dependent on a single legislative body from whom they received a salary and must be elected; that no court of appeals had been created, and such a court was necessary in light of the Supreme Court's power to try cases in the first instance and eventually rule upon them; that there was thus no effective mode of settling errors. Power to amend lay, not with the Assembly, but with a Council of Censors to be revived only every seven years. Finally, the oaths demanded by the new government were unreasonable and "unprecedented on this continent," Some objected that the new constitution had not been, nor would it be, submitted formally to the people for approval. It is highly unlikely that McKean included this last criticism in his attacks; there is certainly no indication he was unhappy with Delaware's decision to bypass a formal popular vote on accepting the constitution.[21]

The public meeting at the State House did not terminate the debate over the new government. The festering acrimony continued to rage in the newspapers, the coffee houses, and in private drawing rooms. Congress assailed the factious elements and sought to promote unanimity and vigor in a program that would concentrate Pennsylvanian venom on the British threatening to take possession of the city. Proponents of the new constitution—labelled Constitutionalists—pleaded for amnesty in the verbal war, arguing that "an enemy is at our gates and an enemy is within our doors.... Without government, laws and civil magistrates, we can neither draw forth our military strength to oppose one, nor exact our civil power to suppress the other."[22]

Despite his almost visceral dislike of the new constitution McKean was eager to do what he could to head off both calamities. The dissolution of the Committee of Inspection and Observation in September had so encouraged Tories within the city that on November 25 a committee of safety met at the Indian Queen Tavern to effect some remedy. McKean was chosen to chair the gathering of more than seventy people. As a result of testimony before McKean's "court" several persons, including Joseph Stansbury, were "convicted" and spent time in jail. Stansbury might complain that his only "crime" was singing "God Save the King" in his home, and denounce the illegality of the proceedings, but McKean and his supporters remained satisfied that republicanism may sanction coercive action and intimidation by public and quasi-public agencies against disloyal individuals in the interest of the common good.[23]

McKean's involvement in these quasi-judicial activities brought him into contact with Constitutionalists eager to initiate effective anti-Tory controls, whether through the more formal state agencies or through a continuing reliance on extra-legal committees. He was anxious to lend his talents to the process of destroying the British and weeding out those Americans giving aid and comfort to the enemy. Whether or not he antiticpated the results, the Constitutionalists came to appreciate the need for more moderate support in general, and the worth and talents of McKean in particular.[24]

Obviously a large portion of those opposing the state government shared neither McKean's enthusiasm nor his strategy. Despite persistent congressional pleas for the people of Pennsylvania to cease their bickering and submit "to the exertion of an authority which is indispensably essential," they persisted in their labors to bring down the government. One such scheme involved a boycott of offices; by depriving the new order of much-needed talent and experience, the constitution's opponents hoped to render the government stillborn. Lawyers were in the vanguard of those endorsing such "a deliberate sabotage." Robert Morris, George Clymer and James Wilson, with others, "hoped that the Gentlemen of the Bar [would] agree not to act under the present government." By March 1777 Jasper Yeates of Lancaster could write that "the posts of mere trust go abegging. No one can be found . . . to accept them."[25]

Opposition by the legal profession staggered the new government, for without its cooperation and experience no court system could function; without a functioning court system no government could exist for long. Of critical importance to the proponents of the new government was the chief justice's chair. On March 20, 1777, the Supreme Executive Council agreed to offer the post to Joseph Reed, even though Reed had earlier advised his friends to accept no posts in the new government. Reed deliberated for four months. On July 23 the Council, desperate for a commitment, urged him to decide one way or the other. "Criminals confined for Capital Charges press for Trial or bailment, in many of the Counties, the inferior Courts of Common Pleas cannot well proceed without the upper court, with wch. they are systematically connected," the Council wrote Reed, "nor can the benefit of habeas corpus be properly enjoyed. . . . The damage done to the administration by the present decrepit condition of the body politic is extensive & mischievous," they confessed. On that same day Reed bowed to pressure from his friends and refused the post.[26]

During much of the time that Pennsylvanians argued the merits of their new government, and Reed pondered the wisdom of accepting the chief justiceship under the new constitution, McKean was in Delaware. The threat of an English takeover of Philadelphia in December had impelled him to move his family out of harm's way. Between January and March McKean attended the Delaware Assembly and actively sought to strengthen its political and military powers. Most matters coming before the Delaware legislature at this time revolved around the state's preparation for war and the need to maintain civil order in the face of serious cleavages within its political community. In April McKean joined the Second Militia Battalion commanded by Samuel Patterson, formed in White Clay Hundred, New Castle County. He also helped to sort out Delaware's financial obligations to the national

Joseph Reed, painted by Charles Willson Peale. Courtesy Independence National Historical Park Collection

government and to put its own currency and bills of credit on a firm footing. Why the legislature did not again name him a delegate to Congress is something of a mystery.[27]

It did elect him speaker in the spring of 1777. Men like George Read were quick to admit that while they disagreed with McKean's politics, he got things done. When McKean was not there to give impetus and direction, matters stalled in the Assembly. As speaker he prodded the Assembly to revise the militia structure to produce a more effective fighting force. The Assembly passed a militia law in May but to little effect. The president of the state complained that counterfeiting was increasing and that "sundry base and sordid persons inhabitants of the County of Sussex . . . do carry on a criminal intercourse and traffic with the crews of the enemy's ships of war." Rewards for stopping or significantly reducing this activity had little result. McKean judged the sources of this ineffectiveness to be the timidity of President John McKinly and the reluctance of the legislature to act decisively. There were not enough true Whigs in Delaware, he concluded; Assembly members might elect him speaker but they failed to bestir themselves at his urging to do what was needed.[28]

Despite his unhappiness with the Assembly's slothfulness, McKean seemed content to remain in Delaware.[29] His ostensible reason for relocating his family in Newark—the threat of an English invasion of Philadelphia—was not the whole story. Philadelphia held little appeal with its political exacerbation, its widening political divisions. He established a temporary law office in Newark and found that he had clients enough to keep him occupied. He also continued his interests in public education in Delaware and remained an active member of the board of trustees of the Newark Academy. In the spring he was doing much of the paperwork for the Academy.[30]

McKean thus did not engage in much of the conflict over Pennsylvania's constitution, nor did he become involved in various schemes, including boycotting state offices, to bring it down. He did not write stinging letters to the local press criticizing the constitutional provisions. When in May the president of the Supreme Executive Council, Thomas Wharton, and the Board of War were called upon to schedule another convention to alter, amend, or confirm the Constitution—a move to counter "weakness and languour... apparent in every part of the government," McKean ignored the call. From November 1776 to July 1777 he reduced his contacts with Philadelphia and refused to add to the political wrangling. While Joseph Reed kept state officials waiting for an answer to their offer of the chief justiceship, McKean seemed content to provide a modicum of leadership to the state, to practice law occasionally, and oversee the summer harvests on his numerous estates.[31]

All this changed in July. Five days after Joseph Reed refused the chief justiceship, George Bryan, Timothy Matlack and other Constitutionalist leaders offered the post to McKean. Though several of his closest friends advised him against accepting the offer, McKean determined to take the position. "To prevent the least suspicion that I was against any government but such as I framed myself, and that I wanted to embroil the state and occasion disaffection to the common cause... which had been liberally propagated," he wrote John Dickinson, he had accepted the post. He accepted, too, "to evidence that I had nothing in view but to promote the happiness of my country... (tho manifestly against my interests) to imitate the Great Lord Hale, when pressed to the like by Cromwell, and was for the same and better reason prevailed with to accept it."[32] He was also moved to believe, as he told Dickinson, that the supporters of the constitution would provide for another convention to reform the new government whenever conditions allowed.

Historians have tended to dismiss McKean's letter to Dickinson. Portraying McKean as a vain office seeker, quite willing to forsake principle for profit and honors, a man adept at trimming his political convictions to suit the political climate, they have been virtually unanimous in attributing to him selfish motives for accepting the chief justiceship.[33]

But McKean did believe that a convention would be called.[34] And there was more to his decision than a desire to placate his vanity, though that unquestionably influenced his decision. McKean detested the British by this time; he was incapable of moderation or timidity in view of the political and military developments of the last two years. He had plunged into almost every effort to resist the British and to retard Tory Activism. To sacrifice Pennsylvania Republicanism because of petty bickering, to blunt the Whig cause over a disagreement of constitutional frailities seemed preposterious to him. Few who came to know his commitment to the Whig cause and the sacrifices he made in time, health, and family tranquility would suggest that he grasped the chief justiceship as a sinecure, or as a mere sop to his ambition.

No one knew better than McKean that America's quest for independence was a matter of life or death; that his own life would soon be forfeit should America not win its current struggle.[35] That knowledge, reinforced by the educational legacy of Francis Alison, along with professional ambition and recent political experience, served to stimulate his interest in office and influence. Recent economic, political and constitutional pressures in the Middle Colonies had served to mobilize an increasing number of urban and rural Delawareans and Pennsylvanians. Revolutionary rhetoric had added its own impetus to the politicization of those elements of society heretofore denied a meaningful voice in the body politic. An impressive portion of the traditional elite had broken under the current strains and now clung tenaciously to Loyalism. Members of the older elite who supported the American cause now looked to an uneasy combination with men like McKean who represented the newer gentry to steer Americans toward "republican" rather than "democratic" institutions and ideals.

McKean recognized that to play a pivotal role in guaranteeing that the current republican experiment survived and developed along lines pleasing to him, he would need political leverage. It was imperative, he thought, that the leadership remain secure in the hands of men "distinguished for wisdom [and] integrity." Political and constitutional developments both in Pennsylvania and Delaware in the previous year underscored how critical it was to reverse current trends. When McKean formally took the oath of office on September 1, 1777, the revolutionary movement in Pennsylvania took on an even more pronounced Presbyterian flavor.[36]

7. Establishing the Courts

The first Assembly to meet under the new Pennsylvania government took steps in January 1777 to promote much needed law and order. An act was passed identifying the various courts and their personnel, and providing for the reconsideration of all cases suspended in the courts when the judicial system had ground to a halt in the preceding Summer. The same act declared that all British and provincial statutes as well as the English Common Law heretofore binding in Pennsylvania would again be in force after February 11, 1777, except for that portion of law rendered obsolete by the current political revolution.[1]

Despite these well-meaning efforts little of a substantive nature had been accomplished when McKean became chief justice in July. Only weeks before McKean assumed his post, James Allen had recorded in his diary that "Not one of the Laws of the Assembly are regarded...No courts open... [and] no justice [is] administered." On July 21, however, the

Philadelphia city court opened at the courthouse "amidst a great crowd of citizens" and a grand jury "composed of reputable and worthy citizens" returned twenty-one true bills. The Pennsylvania *Gazette* reported that the "whole business of the court... was conducted with the utmost good order and decorum."[2]

But the boycott of the government by conservatives remained sufficiently complete to keep most county courts inoperative. Justice of the peace posts went abegging. Supporters of the boycott scheme rightfully perceived that if the county courts remained closed, courts of oyer and terminer and the Supreme Court would be stillborn. Without courts there could be no effective government; the radicals would ultimately be forced to call another convention to produce a more reasonable and effective constitution.[3]

By July, in addition to the normal civil and criminal demands upon the county courts, there were the added actions emanating from the rebellion, cases of treason, misprison of treason, counterfeiting, and confiscation. Pressure by the citizenry to act on these matters—and more—and a growing uneasiness on the part of established lawyers that in the face of their boycott newcomers might "run off with all the business" ultimately helped to break the log jam and reopen a number of the courts, as did the energetic steps taken by members of the Supreme Executive Council.[4] Under the goad of Vice President George Bryan the Council moved to punish, often by executive fiat, those hindering the workings of the court.[5]

By August Lancaster's courts were reported functioning. Late in that month the Chester courts of quarter sessions and common pleas were open. By early September the quarter sessions and common pleas for the city and county of Philadelphia began without incident. Bedford County followed in October, Sunbury in November. By the end of the year most of the county courts were holding sessions, at least on a limited basis.[6]

As odious as the courts were as symbols of the new government, suspected Tories had their reasons for wanting the courts to exercise more authority. For James Allen the contest by mid-1777 had been reduced to "those that Plunder and those that are Plundered." With ample justification he complained that anyone disinclined towards independence suffered daily at the hands of local Whigs, houses were broken into, property confiscated and people imprisoned "without any colour of authority by private persons." He argued that the whole dispensation of justice had ended up in the hands of the field officers of the several city and county battalions, the result in part of a January 1776 congressional resolution urging state legislatures and various local committees to suppress Tory activities "by the most speedy and effectual measures."[7]

With the adoption of the new state government in September 1776, the legal basis for the prosecution of Tories theoretically shifted from Congress to the state. This proved beneficial in several respects, for Pennsylvania posed problems for those seeking to define treason and Toryism not found in other states nor fully appreciated by the members of Congress. The presence of Quakers and other non-combatants made it essential in any definition of treason to distinguish between active adherence to the British cause and mere refusal to participate in matters of a military nature.[8]

Pennsylvania's initial response had come on September 5, 1776, when the convention determined that on February 11, 1777, the Common Law of England, including its provisions on treason, hitherto binding in Pennsylvania, was to remain in force unless it conflicted with specific acts passed by either the revolutionary committees or the new Assembly. The new legislature in January negated the September ordinance of treason and sedition and clarified for the court the issues of treason and misprision. It listed seven types of activities thought to constitute high treason. Anyone convicted of accepting a commission from the enemy, levying war, joining or persuading others to join the enemy, providing the enemy with arms or materiel, carrying on a traitorous combination, or supplying vital information to the British, faced disinheritance and death with forfeiture of all property excepting any income the justices of the Supreme Court might designate for the welfare of the offender's wife and children, or for the children exclusively.

Misprision of treason was defined as knowing of and concealing such activities, or knowingly assisting a traitor. Persons guilty of such acts were to forfeit one-third of their estate, and to be imprisoned for any term not exceeding the duration of the war.[9]

Besides the treason and misprision ordinances, the new government had at its disposal such weapons as acts of attainder and confiscation to curb the inveterate Toryism. As rancor and acrimony mounted in Pennsylvania, subversion was prosecuted also under charges of piracy, larceny, burglary, counterfeiting, and robbery. Complicating matters was the fact that the court would hear cases predating the new government as well as those arising from prosecutions under ordinances effective after September 1776.

McKean's court was in a unique position to define the limits and powers of the new state government, its courts and its personnel. In the process of delineating the powers of the state government it could not fail to clarify the relationship of the court to the executive and legislative branches of the state government, or to congressional authorities. If it succeeded in being a resourceful, independent court, it could also determine the scope and tone of repression in revolutionary Pennsylvania. The irony in all this was that before McKean could establish the vigor and independence of his court, he would have to wrest the initiative from many of the extralegal political committees with which he had labored so assiduously in the past. The question of who would enforce the laws of the new government was not a foregone conclusion in July 1777.

To help marshal the power and resources of the Supreme Court, McKean could turn to associate justices John Evans and William A. Atlee. Atlee, a man of "very gentlemanly deportment," had read law with the Lancaster lawyer Edward Shippen before joining the bar in 1758. When trouble with England began Atlee became a member of the Committee of Safety in Lancaster and a commissary of prisoners. It was hoped that Atlee's candidacy for the Supreme Court in August 1777 would pacify Pennsylvania's conservatives and encourage them to support the new government.

John Evans, like Atlee a mild-mannered and essentially conservative man, was the oldest of the three justices, some six years older than McKean. After studying law following a classical education, he was admitted in 1749 to the Chester bar, where he developed a substantial practice. He became involved in the Pennsylvania committee system at the outset of the imperial troubles, and was a prominent member of the State

Supreme Executive Council when he was nominated for the Supreme Court in August 1777.[10]

As chief justice McKean's first serious encounter with the issue of loyalty brought him into direct conflict with his own government. The disagreement presaged an incompatibility between McKean and the Supreme Executive Council that was to become more marked with each passing year. Highly visible Tories and Timid Whigs had come in for severe scrutiny by state authorities as early as the fall of 1775, especially the Quakers, who by their refusal to accept Continental currency—which they claimed to be "currency... emitted for the purpose of war"—had drawn the ire of state officials and Congress. As the war intensified, animosity towards the pacifistic Quakers deepened. Some prominent Quakers, anticipating trouble, went into exile. Still, by summer 1777 Congress was urging that Pennsylvania apprehend those remaining who were "notoriously disaffected" and search their homes for "fire arms, swords and bayonets." A congressional resolve identified eleven Friends as harboring views contrary to the best interests of the United States and pressed Pennsylvania officials to deal promptly and effectively with them.[11]

The state responded by calling upon David Rittenhouse, William Bradford, Sharp Delaney and Charles Willson Peale, among others, to list persons inimical to the Whig cause. The lists eventually included McKean's sometime associate, Miers Fisher, and twenty-eight others deemed "dangerous to the community." They were subsequently arrested and confined. On September 3, acting through Israel Pemberton, John Hunt, and Samuel Pleasants, the Quakers petitioned for release, claiming that the order to seize and hold them was "arbitrary, unjust and illegal."[12]

Their appeals fell on deaf ears. State officials, particularly the Supreme Executive Council, convinced that these Friends were a threat to the legitimacy and efficacy of the new government, yet aware that they were not guilty of treason and therefore could not be charged, determined to hide the problem as best they could. On September 9 the Supreme Executive Council charged the Quakers with being "persons who have uniformly manifested by their general conduct and conversation, a disposition highly inimical to the cause of America," and ordered them exiled to Staughton in Virginia. Even as the Quakers marched into exile their representatives asked McKean for writs of habeas corpus.[13]

On the basis that the only authority for their arrest and exile seemed to be a letter from Vice-president George Bryan to the town major, Lewis Nicola, McKean awarded the writs to the Quakers. McKean had worked zealously with Council and congressional members eager to prosecute and exile the Quakers. He was well aware of widespread antipathy towards persons posted by state authorities and no doubt understood Bryan's desire to obscure an embarrassment to the government. But he believed the Quakers were legally justified in their requests for recourse in this instance. The Habeas Corpus Act was an integral part of the Pennsylvania legal code, he later told John Adams by way of explaining his actions, and an invaluable protection for the individual. He issued the writs fully aware "how apt many are to disapprove of proceedings that are disagreeable, without duly reflecting upon their propriety and necessity." Still, his readiness to justify his actions to Adams, and through him his friends in Congress, suggests that McKean was not innocent of protecting his political flanks.[14]

For his efforts McKean was passionately upbraided by Whigs both in the state and in Congress. Those who had earlier viewed McKean as a mere tool of the new government, obsequious in return for honors, were disillusioned and outraged by his actions. The Assembly wasted little time in negating his writs. Meeting hastily on Sunday, September 14, it ordered that the policy of exile should be speedily carried out. It ignored the writs issued by the chief justice and suspended all further writs of habeas corpus emanating from his court. In an effort to conform to the legal niceties it provided that the Quakers then in Reading should be released—then immediately rearrested. McKean's writs and the Assembly's orders reached the Quakers and their guards at Reading simultaneously.[15]

When Alexander Nesbitt, overseeing the forced exile for the state, ignored the chief justice's writs in favor of carrying out the Assembly's orders, he received assurances from the Council that he had "acted right." He was told that while the "Council are not well informed how Mr. Chief Justice came to issue

Writs of Habeas Corpus for the Prisoners...the Assembly had put the matter out of debate."[16]

But not entirely. On Thursday, September 18, Quaker representatives sought another writ for the exiles. McKean was reduced to protesting his helplessness in the matter and, according to one source, made "many professions of his disapprobation of the unprecedented measure [of the Council]." 'He assured the Friends that were it in his power he would grant them a hearing, but at least for the time being the Council had effectively prevented him from doing so. As it was, he would take no payment for the earlier writs. Robert Morton, a young Philadelphia Tory, observed the exchange between the Friends and McKean and concluded that the chief justice's actions were "worthy of immitation."[17]

More disruptive to McKean's efforts to oversee the development of his judiciary than the quarrel with the Council were events in Delaware. On September 13 John McKinly, Delaware president, was captured by the British and confined aboard a man-of-war. Under normal conditions the powers of McKinly's office would have fallen to George Read as speaker of the Legislative Council, but Read, in Philadelphia attending Congress and reluctant to return to occupied Delaware, proved unavailable. As a result, the office fell to McKean, speaker of the Assembly, who was then in Chester.[18]

McKean assumed command on September 20 "with no other view but to do all I can in the worst of times, to save my country," he told Caesar Rodney. He found, in his own words, a "state without a head, without a shilling, public records & papers in possession of the enemy, together with their capital & principal trading town." He also found the militia "dispirited and dispersed, and many of them fled out of the state for safety." He soon discovered that those who remained were often "disaffected." He did what he could. He moved the capital to Newark out of reach of the British, ordered the militia, or what was left of it, into readiness, named Caesar Rodney major general, and summarily promoted Samuel Patterson and others he considered trustworthy. He won authority to borrow on the state's credit three thousand pounds, from Congress or from any persons willing to loan the money.

He issued a proclamation for an election of assemblymen in New Castle County so that a new government could be assembled in Newark.[19]

He had no opportunity to make major reforms. The British controlled the coastal towns, their soldiers and agents made repeated forays into the interior to disrupt the local government and bedevil state officials. But what McKean did do he accomplished with his usual diligence and abrasiveness. Those who conceded the need for quick and arbitrary rallying of good Whigs were gratified by his willingness to lead. Others were less so. He was charged with being as hostile and unfeeling toward loyal Delawareans as he was toward the British and their sympathizers. He was charged, too with grasping the presidency primarily to foster his reputation and to solidify power in the hands of his friends. His cavalier disregard for those he termed Timid Whigs—most of whom were political followers of John McKinly and George Read—formed the basis of these last charges.

McKean bitterly denied that he sought personal gain. "Every friend . . . indeed every man of common sense," he wrote to Rodney, "must know that Nothing under heaven but the life of my country & of the virtuous part of the Delaware State, could have induced me to have undertaken the command." He reminded his detractors that he could just as well have remained in peace and honor in Pennsylvania and "taken care of his own property & domestic without censure from any one." But he had forsaken domestic safety and happiness to step forth to aid Delaware, "a poor & distressed state." Those who charged him with seeking honors and offices were misinformed: the command was for only a few weeks, hopefully, and another person would succeed him "who might either disconcert every plan he should propose or adopt, or reap the honor of it." In the meantime he was "hunted like a fox by the enemy."[20]

Although the term of McKean's presidency was short—Read took over the reins of government in mid-October after spending more than a month in the Jerseys—McKean was satisfied that he had done what he could to keep Whig hopes alive.[21] By November he had left Delaware for Lancaster, tired and still angry over his treatment at the hands of Read and his followers. He threw himself into the duties of chief justice with characteristic abandon, lashing out at those refusing to take oaths of allegiance to the state government and clamping the lid on activities of any he considered disloyal to the Whig cause. The young Lancaster lawyer, Edward Burd, who watched McKean's activities that November, reported that "Chief Justice McKean...behaves in the most violent & imperious manner.... He is governed by his Passions," adding facetiously, "an excellent Quality in a Chief Justice." Tired and frustrated as McKean was, when Delaware a month later elected to return him to the Continental Congress, he accepted. "I thought it my duty," he wrote, "though I confess, I am almost tired of serving my country as much at my own expense."[22]

After securing crude but serviceable lodging for his family in Paxton, a small village out of the reach of the British northeast of Harris' Ferry, McKean traveled south on January 29 to York, where Congress had retreated in September. There he tried to share his time with Congress and his court. John Bayard, speaker of the Pennsylvania Assembly meeting in Lancaster, also demanded his time. Bayard told him early in February that the House was concerned at the failure of the courts of oyer and terminer to open and relieve the county courts of their crowded dockets. "There are great numbers confined in their several jails charged with the highest crimes which call for immediate & exemplary Punishment," McKean was informed. McKean was also needed to help the Assembly with several major bills which "require[d] [his] Advice & Assistance." Of special concern to legislators, and to McKean, was further legal definition of treasonous activities within the state.[23]

McKean worked closely with the Pennsylvania Assembly from March 9th until the 17th. One of the most pressing bills, necessitated by General Howe's occupation of Philadelphia and written with the aid and advice of the chief justice, required a special pass for civilians to move through American lines, and that white males eighteen and over take an oath of allegiance by June 1. Anyone failing to take the oath could be designated a non-juror and lose his rights in the courts. Non-jurors would be prohibited from accepting any legacy, deed, or gift, or engaging in trade, commerce, surgery, medicine, pharmacy, law, or education. They were to pay double the tax rate, and those exiled would forfeit their estates to the state. Their real estate was to be treated as if they had died intestate, except that all natural heirs who were non-jurors were to be disinherited. The stringent law, passed on April 1, remained in effect until the following December.[24]

The first week in April McKean began the oyer and terminer proceedings for the state. On Tuesday, April 8, he arrived in Lancaster at noon and was escorted into town "by a number of Gentlemen of the Law, Justices of the Peace... besides the officers." He was pleased with the reception; it augered well for the new court in trying times. He wrote his wife, in Paxton that "matters have been conducted equal to my most sanguine hopes, indeed everything is as I would wish it." He took the occasion in Lancaster to deliver a charge to the grand jury which one observer described as "elegant and spirited... suitable to the times."[25]

As he would in subsequent courts, McKean made the most of his address to explain the war for independence and to share his understanding of America's republican goals. He admitted that "to dissolve all connections with Great Britain was like the separation of soul and body," but the colonists had had no choice: "securing the safety, liberty, and happiness of every individual in the community and affording an asylum to the lovers of liberty in every part of the globe [had become] the objects of contention." Americans had come to accept that "all men are... equal with respects to civil power and civil obedience; and [that] all authority... must be originally derived from the people." Compelled by these assumptions, the American states had "formed new governments for themselves, the wisdom and policy of... which," McKean predicted, "will be the admiration of future ages."

These decisions, McKean went on, had not been without their price. Disagreements among Americans had arisen; indeed, bitter accusations and denuciations still abounded. He conceded that in Pennsylvania "these sentiments [had] been expressed, not gently and amicably, but with heat and unbecoming reflection on both sides." He wished this acrimony stopped. "Away with these uncharitable opinions," he advised, "We all mean the same thing, the happiness of the community."

He told the jurors that "There can not be perfection in this imperfect State" and warned that those who refrained from participating in the government because it fell short of their hopes were being unreasonable. He urged those disenchanted with the present constitution to serve the state as he did until that document could be amended, a prospect he anticipated as soon as the British should evacuate Philadelphia. He concluded by asking the jurors to be steadfast but compassionate. He implored them "in all doubtful cases to incline rather to acquital than criminations," for, as he pointed out, it was "safer to err in acquiting than in punishing."[26]

Despite notable exceptions, however, the courts of Pennsylvania functioned neither smoothly nor efficiently in most counties as McKean worked "double-tides" in York. Persons had been appointed to local courts whose only qualification was loyalty to the new government. Large numbers of experienced and talented lawyers still refused to lend their loyalty or their talents to the state. Without an adequate number of lawyers and judicial officials some courts remained closed even when "the people [were] ansious [sic] to have Business done." Attorney General Jonathan Dickinson Sergeant reported from Reading that "Business suffers, & the Cause, too, for Want of a Man of Character & Abilities to act in the Courts."[27]

McKean was acutely conscious of his inability to be everywhere at once. A series of criminal outrages and Indian attacks in Bedford County drew his attention there in late May but congressional and judicial responsibilities elsewhere made it impossible for him to attend that county. Equally frustrating was the court's inability to function efficiently even when those charged with crimes came before it. McKean was provoked to complain to Vice-President George Bryan on May 21 that a certain James Bracken, named in an attainder issued by the Supreme Executive Council, had been brought before him "without any testimony or evidence whatsoever against him." McKean found himself in an untenable position: to try the man under the existing circumstances "may be a reflexion on the justice of this State," but to release him might free a man "uniformly inimical" to the American cause.[28]

Fortunately, the evacuation of Philadelphia by the British late in June 1778 enabled the McKeans to celebrate there the second anniversary of America's independence. When McKean met with other members of Congress at the State House on July 2 he was profoundly conscious of the enfeebled condition of his court and the fact that Whigs were returning from exile with more than celebration on their minds. Personal violence abounded. There were old scores to settle—and a few new ones. McKean described the city as "suspicious." He judged the inhabitants of Philadelphia to be either "afraid of one another, or the Whigs cannot yet believe that their friends have the government of the City."[29]

Local committees and the Supreme Executive Council were soon busy identifying traitors —those who had stayed, profited, and aided the enemy while loyal Whigs like McKean were suffering hardships in the hinterlands. William Lewis, the ambling cigar-smoking Chester County lawyer soon to be a giant of the Philadelphia bar, complained that a client, Peter Deshong, had turned himself over to the court and had entered into security for his appearance in order to abide by a writ only to find himself pursued by "a Party of Men, armed with Clubs, who were in search of him for ye avowed Purpose of Revenge." Lewis pleaded with the Council to issue a proclamation "setting forth, that as the Civil Authority is now reestablished in this City, those who have offended ag^t the Laws of the Land will be called to answer, and punished according to their Demerits; and therefore forbidding the taking of Private Revenge." Unless such action was taken, and unless the Council and the courts acted promptly to assume control of the situation, "Bloodshed and Oppression" would continue, Lewis argued, for his client "is not the only Instance of Many of taking Revenge out of the Course of regular Proceedings."[30]

Nothing would have pleased McKean more than to set up at once a formidable and efficient judicial system to neutralize the impromptu extralegal harassment of Tories. At some point, he felt, it became dangerous to orderly government for people to circumvent the governmental agencies that they themselves had created. But the extralegal responses would have to continue until such time as his courts proved effective. As early as July 7 McKean reported that nearly forty persons attainted by the Council had turned themselves over to his court to stand trial. He sat every day in the upstairs chambers of the City Hall processing such cases, gathering information wherever he could concerning the relative merits of each one and interviewing a steady stream of visitors pleading their own cases or those of friends or loved ones. Such visitors were soon convinced that the interview with the chief justice was critical to their fate or the fate of those for whom they pleaded. A few went so far as to suggest that only through an obsequious deference to McKean could they escape, or at least have their punishment meaningfully reduced.[31]

Tench Coxe could lend some credence to that belief. Coxe, a young Philadelphia merchant with impressive family connections, had remained in Philadelphia during the British occupation and carried on business as usual. On May 21, 1778, he had been named along with a number of others "adjudged guilty of High Treason." Two days after he was attainted by the Supreme Executive Council he had taken the oath of allegiance to Pennsylvania, but the popular mood in Philadelphia in July was to scorn that type of pragmatic patriotism. He would have to face McKean in that upstairs chamber of the City Hall. The interview with the chief justice had gone amazingly well. Coxe could write his cousin William Tilghman on July 13 that McKean's "behaviour was much more friendly than I could have expected, & genteel." Coxe was forced to give bond for an impending trial, but he left McKean's office convinced that the charges against him would ultimately be dismissed. It was later observed that McKean, who was distantly related to Coxe by marriage, was the "man who saved him, whose influence protected him."[32]

Coxe was not the only person saved by McKean's personal intervention. Elizabeth Graeme Ferguson, granddaughter of a Proprietary governor and eldest daughter of one of Philadelphia's most prominent physicians, sought McKean's aid when her husband, Henry Hugh Ferguson, had his property confiscated after being attainted in May 1778. She insisted that travel problems and communication failures accounted for her husband's inability to turn himself into state authorities in time to ward off the attainder, and that she should not lose her portion of the estate because of his legal difficulties.

Though distressed by her grasp of "the facts," McKean allowed her to secure at least most of her furniture and personal effects until there should be a final disposition of her case—even though the Supreme Executive Council seemed intent on denying her everything.

McKean was also among those who privately defended Edward Shippen, Benedict Arnold's father-in-law, when many sought his incarceration or exile. Even McKean's enemies later conceded that "many who had mistaken the path of true honor in forsaking their country to serve a tyrant were by his private generosity rescued from public vengence, and the inexorable law."[33]

That might be, but Grace Galloway was one of many who thought the price too high. The wife of the notorious Tory, Joseph Galloway, she had received an estate in an inheritance from her father, Laurence Grouden. When her husband was formally attainted in March 1778 he fled to England, leaving his wife behind. In accordance with the law in such matters, the state seized the Galloway property, including those portions which had been willed to Mrs. Galloway by her father, and sold it at public vendue. Her friend Benjamin Chew, the ex-chief justice of Pennsylvania, told her that McKean held the key to whatever success she might enjoy in retrieving her land; without McKean's acquiescence nothing would happen to her estates. Nicholas Waln and Abel James, acquaintances, also emplored her to "throw a remonstrance in to Maceean." She remained convinced that McKean "ought to do Justice without being Petitioned," and lost her estate in the end, she concluded, "for No other reason but because I did not pay him a Compliment."[34]

By the third week in September 1778 forty-five bills for treason alone had been sent to the grand jury; twelve were ignored, the remainder were to stand trial.[35] This was to be the first real opportunity for the McKean court to pass judgment on the question of loyalty, and to determine the extent of the repression that Pennsylvania would experience. The earlier courts of oyer and terminer held in Lancaster and Chester Counties had been mere prologue. Because he was clearly the dominant figure on the bench, more forceful, persuasive and learned than either Atlee or Evans, McKean

Establishing the Courts

held in his hands the power to determine in large measure the scope and tempo of the repression in his state.

One of those charged with treason in September 1778 was Abraham Carlisle. A prosperous, elderly Quaker carpenter, Carlisle was charged with having falsely and traitorously taken a commission from General Howe to guard the city gates during the British occupation, and with "falsely and traitorously prepar[ing], order[ing], wag[ing], and levy[ing] a public and cruel war against [the] Commonwealth." His alleged treasonous activities, besides his gatekeeping, included seizure of salt from Whigs and supplying vital information to the enemy. Defending Carlisle were George Ross, the learned and brilliant James Wilson, and the astute, theatrical William Lewis.[36]

The trial, which began on September 24 and took place in the College of Philadelphia, revolved around the Commonwealth's ability to establish an overt act of treason. The defense's strategy became clear almost immediately as Wilson argued that no adequate proof had been offered by Joseph Reed and Jonathan Dickinson Sergeant, who pleaded the state's case, to prove beyond a shadow of doubt that Carlisle had ever accepted a commission from the enemy. A commission must be produced, Wilson argued, or irrefutable proof offered of an overt act, very strictly defined. Anything less did not meet the standards of English law, particularly as defined in the statute of 25 Edward III (1351).

The defense also asserted that Carlisle had never levied war against Pennsylvania as charged. Wilson and Ross stressed that an overt act must be proved; merely to present a number of very general actions suggesting treason was insufficient. Had he ever taken armed action against the state? Against its people? The defense offered a dozen witnesses who recalled acts of charity and leniency on the part of Carlisle during his tenure as a city guard. The state on the other hand paraded witnesses of its own to prove that the defendant had acted as a guard at one of the northern entrances to the city and had encouraged a spy to report on the movements of the Continental Army.

McKean held that if the Commonwealth established that Carlisle had taken a commission to serve as a guard the defendant was guilty; proof that he had merely issued passes, while acceptable, fell short of proving conclusively that

Carlisle held a commission. McKean also upheld Wilson's objection that the seizure of salt was not admissable as evidence of Carlisle's having accepted such a commission. But having conceded a number of points to the defense, McKean, in his final charge to the jury, backed off a bit to favor the broader definition of treason posed by the prosecution. He ruled that not all details and evidence must appear in the indictment; diverse acts may be laid to the same indictment, and the charge of levying war against the state could be justified by proof of a number of small acts which show a person's adherence and allegiance to a foreign power.

The jury deliberated for almost twenty-four hours before returning a verdict of guilty. An appeal was filed immediately, and attorneys for the respective sides met on October 5 to argue before McKean four points mentioned by the defense in its petition of appeal. Wilson, Ross and Lewis argued that the indictment had been "vague and uncertain," that the formal charges were not drawn with "sufficient precision." Despite Wilson's learned appeal and Lewis' articulate and passionate insistence that the State's case was neither "pullain" nor "cul-lear," their efforts were non-availing. McKean and the court found for the State.[37]

Meanwhile, three defendants who followed Carlisle before the September court of oyer and terminer, Joshua Molder, John Taylor, and a man named Malin, fared better. All three were acquitted. In the Molder case McKean conceded a number of points by Ross, Wilson, and Lewis and ruled that every person accused or indicted of high treason should have a copy of the entire indictment a reasonable time in advance of the trial. He held that a defendant should receive a copy of the panel of jurors who were to try him at least one day before the trial. In the Malin case McKean's charge to the jury favored the defense, especially its contention that words alone did not constitute treason; an overt act must be proved before conviction of treason was warranted. In the face of the Council's often frantic—and, some argued, irresponsible—prosecution of opponents of their government, McKean's rulings in the Molder and Malin cases were critical. They sought to mitigate many of the evils inherent in the current system.[38]

The second conviction came in the more highly publicized John Roberts case. Roberts, an elderly Quaker miller, was charged with ridiculing the American cause, predicting that the British would eventually vanquish the American rebellion, and attempting to persuade individuals to enlist in the British army. Some witnesses maintained that he had threatened to have a loyal American hanged as a traitor; others that he had proposed to lead a troop of British horse to the rescue of the Quaker leader, Israel Pemberton. The critical question in this case was whether or not a person must actually succeed in persuading an individual to enlist before his act was treasonable. Witnesses admitted that Roberts' attempts had been unsuccessful, although through no fault of his own.

McKean held that the legislative act on which the indictment was based meant to imply success in an act of persuasion. Therefore he determined that proof of an actual enlistment must be obtained before conviction was possible. It was at this point that the prosecution, again directed by the persistent and meticulously-prepared Joseph Reed and Jonathan Dickinson Sergeant, equally intense and urbane, introduced Roberts' own confession of his deeds. Reed and Sergeant submitted that the confession clearly proved the defendant's treasonable designs.

Ross and Wilson protested that Pennsylvania law prohibited the admission of a confession in trials of treason. No precedent existed, they argued, for using such a confession to convict in a treason case; only after a treasonable act had been firmly established by at least two witnesses could such a confession be used, and then only to corroborate what had already been confirmed by at least two witnesses. The court, through McKean, ruled that a confession after the fact, though not competent alone to supply the want of two witnesses, was still acceptable as a means of corroboration. If two witnesses could be found to establish an overt act, the material could then be introduced to confirm the testimony. The mandatory witnesses were produced to substantiate the prosecution's claims.

More than a dozen witnesses testified for the defense that Roberts had actively helped loyal Americans and prisoners of the British. One witness maintained that on a number of occasions the old Quaker had reaffirmed his interest in remaining absolutely neutral and had in fact told him where the journal of the Continental Congress was hidden from the British. Despite this impressive array of evidence in Roberts' favor, the jury found him guilty. The sentence of death was pronounced against him by McKean.[39]

McKean's sentencing of Roberts for high treason was widely publicized, deliberately so on the part of the Council, with verbatim text appearing in newspapers throughout Pennsylvania and beyond. In his comments to John Roberts before sentencing him to die for his crimes, McKean reminded the old miller that he had had all the indulgences and advantages that the law would allow. But "treason is a crime of the most dangerous and fatal consequences to society," McKean told him. "It is of a most malignant nature; it is a crimson colour and of a scarlet dye." What punishment must one desire, asked the chief justice, "who joins with the enemy of his country, and endeavors the total destruction of the lives, liberties and property of all his fellow citizens, who willingly aids a cause which has been complicated with the horrid and crying sin of murdering thousands, who were not only innocent, but meritorious; and aggravated by burning some of them alive and starving others to death?"

To a silent courtroom McKean conceded that among Roberts' acts were acts of "humanity, charity, and benevolence, but the acts did not negate his greater crimes." Finally McKean implored Roberts to "reflect upon his past conduct, to be incessant in prayers and to seek the conversation, advice and prayers of pious and good men." He then sentenced him to die by hanging.[40]

A veritable deluge of petitions requesting amnesty for Abraham Carlisle and John Roberts poured into the Council. Significantly, among them were petitions from the chief justice and his associate justices asking that the Council use its constitutional powers to pardon the condemned. McKean's Uncle Thomas, still living in Chester County, and McKean's former teacher, Francis Alison, were among those seeking mercy for the convicted men.[41]

McKean's appeal in the interests of Roberts, coming as it did immediately after his harsh pronouncement of the condemned man's deeds, can best be understood in terms of

McKean's view of the court's role in society. Retribution must be tempered with mercy and tolerance. A conviction must lead to the betterment of society, and if that could be achieved through the threat of the court's awful power rather than the actual punishment, so much the better. The court, therefore, must be able to save as well as to destroy, to offer hope as well as despair. It was a policy that he and his associates on the bench employed throughout the Revolution, and it contributed heavily to the fact that Pennsylvania did not in the final analysis have a repressive judicial system. Pennsylvania's judicial response to the revolutionary years was tempered with reason and charity.[42]

Unfortunately for Roberts and Carlisle, the petitions—even those from the justices of the Supreme Court—came to nothing. Both were executed for their crimes on November 4, 1778. Joseph Reed alone of those associated directly with the cases expressed complete satisfaction with their deaths. Mercy should not be extended to either Carlisle or Roberts, Reed argued, the stakes were too high. "New characters are emerging from security like insects after a storm," he wrote Nathaniel Greene, "treason, disaffection to the interests of America, and even assistance to the British interest, is called openly only error of judgment, which candour and liberality of sentiment will overlook.... We could not for shame have made an example of a poor rogue after forgiving the rich," he concluded to Greene.[43]

For his part in the trials of Roberts and Carlisle McKean was portrayed as a bloodthirsty chief justice, a hanging judge. Forgotten were his pleas to the Council for mercy and his earlier admonitions to juries to be compassionate. His grim assessment of Robert's behavior convinced contemporaries, as it has convinced historians since, that hysteria was rampant in Pennsylvania in 1778, and that McKean was a harsh and single-minded judge. Perhaps no other single act of McKean's judicial career made a comparable imprint on the minds of contemporaries or historians. It was certainly one of the most visible and public of his deeds. But the fact remains, similar charges were not uncommon in the middle colonies both before and during the American Revolution. And it was equally common for judges to follow such colorful and grim pronouncements with pardons or significantly reduced sentences.[44] The impact of McKean's charge resulted largely from its more personalized, less ritualized character.

Those frustrated by the court's power, and those opposing the current state government, came to view the judicial branch as the symbol of their discontent and McKean the personification of their discomfiture. Tory satirists had a field day with the roles of Reed and McKean in the September trials. But the picture is overdrawn as Professors Meehan and Young have shown. Of the forty-five bills brought to the grand jury, the jury indicted twenty-three to stand trial. Only Roberts and Carlisle of those twenty-three were judged to be guilty. In the great majority of cases McKean conceded the defense's demand for irrefutable proof before a conviction was encouraged. In several instances the court freed men on mere technicalities. It is true that McKean on later occasions used his position on the bench to vent his personal and political prejudices, and to display his arrogance and terrible temper, but his conduct in the September term of the oyer and terminer proceedings was marked by fairness as well as by personal and professional restraint.[45]

For McKean, who equated a republic with the rule of law, the oyer and terminer proceedings in the fall of 1778, and those that followed, bode well. By the early months of 1779 the superior courts of Pennsylvania had seemingly gained a will of their own. Though the judicial support system on the county level remained incomplete and often inadequate to the tasks confronting it, the superior courts so laboriously established and tested late in 1778 ground ineluctably on. Evidence was relentlessly gathered, writs methodically issued, dockets compiled, juries enpanneled, and verdicts rendered.

8. The Origins of a Moderate, Independent Judiciary

Revolutionary exigencies in Pennsylvania in 1779 continued to encourage a largely ad hoc response on the part of the new state government to problems confronting it. One observer remarked that the "Assembly was employed as usual in inventing new oppressions for the disaffected." Yet in a telling afterthought he observed, "if the laws were executed, it would be impossible to live amongst them." But the judiciary, small and flexible, was able to act more promptly and more decisively than either the Council or the Assembly. It thus drew to itself a multitude of functions which in more normal times would have remained with other branches of government. As president Joseph Reed and the Council joined with members of the Assembly to draw the court into a wider range of problems—often into areas where the court itself sought no initiative—the court's power was correspondingly enhanced.[1]

McKean had little need to seek the enlargement of his duties. He found it increasingly difficult to find time for congressional work, although he attended Congress whenever his judicial duties allowed it. The Council continued to bombard him with requests to look into suspicious activities. He remained the principal conduit for private individuals reporting the disloyal activities of their fellow citizens. Nor was there any let-up in the numbers of persons attainted or charged with crimes, or wishing to exonerate persons charged, who flocked to McKean's chambers to plead their cases. The Assembly, too, often had occasion to call on his services, and he to call on it.

Despite the often mutual reinforcement of the efforts of the Supreme Executive Council and the Supreme Court, important differences of temper and policy persisted between the Constitutionalists and Reed on the one hand and McKean on the other. When several defendants were acquitted of charges of treason in the Newton oyer and terminer proceedings in October 1778, and two notorious Tories, Samuel Garriques and James Stevens, were acquitted the following April, Reed complained that "Too easy an Ear has been given by the Ministers of Justice to the application of those who are disaffected to their Country & that from a Fear of the Imputation of Rigour or giving Offense, the contrary Error of extreme Compassion...has taken place." Even while conceding that the court's actions were laudable in some instances, and in others "excusable," he felt that the overall impact of the judicial leniency "had a tendency to weaken Government & encourage the political Sinners of the State." The Whig diarist, Christopher Marshall, upon hearing of the acquittal of Garriques and Stevens observed bitterly that "their behavior had been so atrocious while the enemy were in the city" he was not surprised that "the honest inhabitants of Philadelphia were much displeased" by the verdict.[2]

McKean's handling of the Samuel Fisher case further antagonized Reed and other Constitutionalist leaders. The charge brought against Fisher, a Philadelphia Quaker, in March 1779 emanated from a letter he had written to his brother, Jabez in New York containing sentiments the Council considered detrimental to the patriot cause. Having secured the offending letter, the Council turned it over to McKean for his advice and action. Convinced that the letter did contain suspicious opinions, McKean summoned Fisher to his home to answer charges. On March 31, 1779, Fisher, along with his brother Miers and a friend, Samuel Smith, went to McKean's residence to answer his accusers.

After preliminary wrangling between Fisher and McKean, the chief justice informed Fisher that the best policy for him would be to give bail and enter into a personal recognizance. Failure to comply with this procedure could result in a jail term that could last the duration of the war. Andrew Doz, who had entered the meeting, offered to put up bail. Fisher resisted, however, even after John Ewing, a Presbyterian minister who had also come into the meeting, told him "in a soft tone...that the Security was not demanded under the new law, but by the Old Laws of Pennsylvania." When McKean eventually allowed Fisher to go home rather than sending him to jail, Fisher erroneously concluded that McKean thought him innocent.[3]

State officials, notably Joseph Reed and Timothy Matlack, were uncomfortable with Fisher's freedom and insisted that either bail be given or Fisher be committed to the gaol. The gaol it was. Fisher remained incarcerated, with some personal comforts, until 1781, and produced an interesting personal record of the court's activities during that time. He inadvertently left a substantial record of McKean's insistence—and success—in issuing writs of habeas corpus to those desiring them—even in the face of Council opposition.[4]

Reed judged the court to be failing on at least three levels. It continued to show too much leniency towards persons suspected of treasonous activities or sentiments, and proved itself too independent of both Council and the Assembly in crucial moments. Moreover, it had not yet fully controlled and disciplined the inferior courts which frequently indulged in unwarranted and precipitous actions embarrassing to the state. The lingering failure of the superior courts beyond Philadelphia to function as effectively as those within the city encouraged justices of the peace in outlying districts to "assume a Jurisdiction only invested in the Justices of the Supreme Court." This was especially true in matters involving the army. Officers complained to Reed that "great Inconveniences & injury" were brought about when the justices of the peace undertook, as they frequently did, to judge the "expiration of the terms of Service of the Soldiery... often upon the loosest & most uncertain Evidence." Reed, burdened by complaints from outraged officers, pressed McKean to expand the effectiveness of his courts and to "caution [the justices of the peace] against this Interference."[5]

Though he left no written evidence of it, McKean himself doubtless sensed the court's shortcomings; several of his deepest hopes remained unfulfilled. There was little evidence by 1780 that the court had appreciably reduced disorder and mayhem in the backcountry. Tory sympathizers and local banditti still roamed at will in certain counties. Treason cases continued to fill the dockets. Even among good Whigs murder, rape, and arson abounded, stark testimony to the courts' failure to "civilize" the newly settled areas. And McKean took the "civilizing" aspect of his role seriously.[6]

McKean's inaction disappointed the Constitutionalists on still another issue. In March the more radical elements in the Assembly pushed for extending the policy of confiscation into the vast Penn domain. Under this policy the state punished persons loyal to the British cause by confiscating their estates, which brought much needed money into the state coffers and promised a fundamental revolution in American society by redistributing land and shifting the basis of political power to the common man. The change from provincial government under the Crown to an independent state had brought into question the future of lands originally held under the Penns' charter, thus complicating confiscation policies. By February 1779 the radicals, secure in their position, determined to clarify their policy on these lands.

Experimentation was inescapable. The new state government could not accept the status quo of huge tracts of land held untaxed by individuals owing allegiance to the Proprietors. Even those patented and improved lands from which the Proprietors had exacted quit-rents had to be reassessed in light of current exigencies. The Assembly, largely at the urging of President Reed, first took up the issue of the Penns' lands on March 2, when a committee was formed to "examine into the claims of the late Proprietors, and report wherein they are incompatible with the Happiness, Liberty and Welfare of the good People of this State." The committee was also charged with preparing "suitable Resolutions for remedying the Evils arising from the said Claims" in such a manner, form and substance as may "be the most conformable to the Rights of the People."

Eventually six questions were posed. Did the Crown have the authority in the first instance to convey lands described in the original charter? Were the grants outright or in trust? To what extent were concessions to be confirmed to the first purpose purchasers? Did the right exist to reserve a tenth of the land and the quit-rents? Did the proper appropriations of the latter rest with the Proprietors? What effect did the change of government have upon the preemption rights of the Proprietors?

Doubtless Reed had discussed the general question of the Penns' lands with McKean, and McKean himself must surely have anticipated the issue. In either case it is understandable that the Council sought McKean's answers only two days after he formally received the questions. General discussions had not given Reed a clear view of McKean's thinking, however. Had Reed anticipated his chief justice's responses, clearly he would not have sought his official advice.

The effect of McKean's subsequent ruling was to uphold the Proprietary claims. In a statement he urged to be read in a legal rather than a political light, McKean found that the King did have full discretion to convey the lands to the Penns. Only on the fifth point, in which he ruled that the Penns had no right of preemption to unsold lands in the future, and that all lands lying within the boundaries of the state belonged to Pennsylvania, did he tell the Constitutionalists what they wanted to hear. It is not surprising, then, that the Constitutionalist-dominated Assembly declined to heed McKean's legal findings. Brushing them aside, no doubt with embarrassment on Reed's part, the Assembly made its own determination of the Penn legacy. For nine months it wrestled with the details, but from the first it was evident that state authorities viewed the lands as only a trusteeship conferred on William Penn by Charles II through the Charter of 1681. Revolutionary exigencies necessitated the transfer of that trusteeship to the state.

The resultant Divesting Act of November 27, 1779, was passed over the vehement protestations of ex-Governor

John Penn, who insisted that the lands were being confiscated without regard to due process, and that the Act was "injurious and repugnant to every rule of justice and equity." The Act allowed to the heirs of the Penns only the manors and private estates clearly defined as theirs. McKean's opinion upholding much of the Penns' claims may have influenced the Assembly's subsequent decision to offer some compensation to the Penns and their heirs. The Assembly, "not without remembrances of the enterprising spirit which distinguished the founder of Pennsylvania, and mindful of the expectations and dependence of his descendants," granted the Proprietors £130,000 sterling for the loss of lands and their annual income from quit-rents.[7]

Republicans deplored the policies pursued by McKean. They accused him of being insensitive to the feelings of the Quakers and running roughshod over the niceties of the law to secure convictions of those suspected of disaffection. They were displeased, too, with his apparent hostility towards officers of the Continental line. When McKean acquiesced in the state's move to expropriate the old College charter, he made additional enemies in the Republican camp.

Several factors drew the attention of the radicals in the Council and Assembly to the College of Philadelphia in 1779. The first was the Tory leaning of the faculty and trustees, their slowness for example to take the state loyalty oath. Secondly, the Episcopalian caste of the faculty displeased the Presbyterians among Pennsylvania's revolutionary forces. Early in 1778 the Assembly passed an act depriving the trustees of all power for a limited time. Later in the same year a second act required trustees, provost, and teachers of any college or academy to take the loyalty oath in order to continue in their professions. Even though most of them had complied by the Summer of 1778, much antagonism remained.

McKean was present in the Assembly room on September 10 when the future of the College was debated. James Wilson and William Lewis, with very little time to prepare their case, argued for the retention of the College charter in its present form. In an obvious effort to gain time they urged the Assembly to seek the opinion of the Supreme Court before framing any bill altering the charter. The ploy got nowhere. It is unlikely that either Wilson or Lewis expected much else; both knew that McKean was basically in sympathy with the proponents of change in the College's role and emphasis. Their desire for increased Presbyterian influence and a reformed educational basis struck a responsive chord in McKean. He offered no help or encouragement to Wilson or Lewis or to those for whom they spoke.[8]

An act of November 1779 abolished the College under its former leaders and created the University of Pennsylvania. The bill guaranteed £1500 additional income, required the oath of loyalty from trustees and faculty, and provided that the Assembly ratify all trustee appointments. Six officers of the state, including the president of the Supreme Executive Council, were to sit on the board. By virtue of his position as chief justice, McKean was one of those selected. He proved to be an effective and conscientious trustee.[9]

The most pungent criticism of the bench continued to come from within the government. Though Tories and Republicans viewed Reed and McKean as close associates and the twin pillars of the Constitutionalist party, Reed remained disturbed over the court's role in the Revolution and McKean's performance as chief justice. Hostility between the two men was exacerbated by events growing out of economic and political discontent in Philadelphia late in October. Frustrated citizens, including large numbers of German militiamen, were intent on ridding the city of Tories and Tory sympathizers. Among the militiamen's targets were Republican leaders planning to stand for the Assembly in the forthcoming elections. They could not tolerate persons in their Assembly who they considered disloyal and destructive to their own political and economic happiness.

On October 2 a Committee of Privates publicly asked all militiamen to attend a mass meeting on October 4 at Burn's Tavern. On the day of the meeting a handbill was circulated calling upon loyal militiamen to "fall upon a plan, to drive from the city, all disaffected persons, and those who supported them." Despite bitter quarrelling over what strategem would be the most productive, the mass meeting broke up around noon and the people began to march through the streets looking to seize "disaffected" citizens. Eventually the crowd of perhaps two hundred "captured" four men and forced them to march through the streets "with the Drum after them, beating the Rogue's March."

At the same time some three dozen Republicans paraded in front of the City Tavern. When they saw the militia approaching, they moved into Walnut Street and drifted into James Wilson's house on the corner of Walnut and Third. As the militia passed the Wilson house a shot rang out. A riot ensued, with members of the militia seeking to break into the house. Several persons were killed in the skirmish and many wounded. Authorities jumped to the conclusion that the fault for the altercation rested primarily with the militia, and several soldiers were jailed. Their comrades, who viewed the incarceration as a blatant example of the government's inability to appreciate their grievances, were infuriated. German militiamen from the county advanced on the city proclaiming a desire for revenge. Only the nimble efforts of Joseph Reed and a small band of government officials managed to turn them back.[10]

At ten o'clock on October 4 Timothy Matlack, secretary of the Supreme Executive Council, sent McKean an urgent letter to inform him that a "very great riot" had occurred which "has been attended with bloodshed," and President Reed requested that McKean return to the city "immediately." Matlack stressed that the chief justice's presence in the city was "highly necessary on this melancholy occasion." While the immediate threat of riot seemed over, the jailing of the German militiamen and the continued threats to Wilson and Robert Morris presaged further trouble. Matlack judged the people to be "heated to an extreme degree."

Matlack's letter reached McKean two days later in Lancaster where he and William A. Atlee were attempting to hold court without the third member of the judicial team, John Evans, who was ill. The two conferred at once on the implications of Matlack's missive, weighing the importance of the current docket in Lancaster, and elsewhere, against the aid they might be able to supply the beleaguered government in Philadelphia—and, one suspects, against the danger in returning to the city. Certainly the distance between Philadelphia and Lancaster did not preclude the judges' fairly rapid return. However, their decision was to remain in Lancaster to deal with the judicial exigencies there. McKean wrote their decision to Reed on the seventh stressing that Atlee fully concurred with the choice.

Reed was stunned by McKean's response. Angered by the turn of events in the city and the reluctance of his chief justice to come to his aid, and violently ill with fever, Reed pressed his vice-president, George Bryan, to insist that the justices return to Philadelphia "immediately, business of the present circuit notwithstanding." By the tenth, however, Reed's fever had broken and the mood of the city had changed sufficiently to warrant a more relaxed approach. On that day Bryan informed the judges that "the public good is greatly restored" and they were no longer needed. Whether Bryan or Reed seriously thought the judges would return is problematical; by giving them orders not to come they were, to a degree, reasserting their authority. But the incident did nothing to help the strained relationship between Reed and McKean. When Reed was reelected president in November, partly in recognition of the manner in which he had handled the "Fort Wilson" affair, and McKean joined others at the courthouse to celebrate his second inauguration, the relationship between the two men had noticeably cooled.[11]

The year 1780 began much as the preceding year for McKean and his court. Both continued to be viewed with equanimity, suspicion, or contempt, depending on the political persuasion of the observer. McKean did convert a few former critics. T.H. Hartley of Lancaster who observed McKean on the bench for the first time in the late months of 1779, was surprised to find him an impressive and reasonable judge. Hartley, who had been prepared for the worst, told his associate Jasper Yeates that "the Chief Justice appears to most advantage upon the bench... and he is by no means a... tyrant." He concluded that McKean had "some merit as a judge... nay, I might say a great deal."[12]

Others were less impressed. The Friends remained among those most disillusioned with McKean and his court. The first group to incite McKean's opposition to Council policy in the matter of writs of habeas corpus, and the most likely one to profit from an independent court willing to issue such writs, the Friends persisted in opposing McKean whenever they could.

To acknowledge McKean's power and authority meant to acknowledge the legitimacy of the current state government—and this they refused to do. Moreover, McKean's role in the September 1778 oyer and terminer term had eroded whatever goodwill in Quaker circles he had achieved by issuing habeas corpus writs in the fall of 1777.

With considerable justification Quakers criticized McKean for personally abusing Friends coming before his court. They accused him of "endeavouring as it were to crush and root out from the very earth...an innocent harmless people."[13] As alarming to the Friends as McKean's vindictiveness was his seemingly mindless harassment of individual Quakers. They were particularly outraged over what they considered to be McKean's irrational treatment of John Elmslie and Daniel Dawson, indicted for contempt of authority in refusing to serve as constables. John Elmslie, who had hired a man to serve in his stead, sought to defend himself by establishing that the same action had been sanctioned by an earlier court in 1770. Despite Elmslie's persistence in giving the court details of this earlier arrangement, McKean refused to admit the testimony, finally having to shout down the defendant. Daniel Dawson, "seeing how it had gone with his Companion...had little to say," according to one witness.

Neither Elmslie nor Dawson argued their strongest defense: that the state's own law requiring an oath of all office holders disqualified them from serving as constables. Whether this was an oversight by the accused, who refused legal counsel, or a deliberate act on their part, is not revealed by the records. That it was deliberate may be inferred from the fact that other Quakers present were very much aware of the irony of the state's actions. Whatever their reason for remaining silent on this point, Elmslie and Dawson doubtless recognized that to call the court's attention to the law in this instance would be fruitless. Neither the court nor the jury seemed troubled by their predicament.

It took the jury an hour to decide on their guilt. Prior to the verdict McKean "spoke sharply against them, as being obstinately disaffected & that he supposed they wanted or expected to have a leaf in the book of Sufferings." The chief justice's observation that though the law permitted him to fine each to the total of £ 200 he would be moderate in fining each of them £ 50 and court costs, placated the Quakers—defendants and observers alike—not one whit.[14]

This case and similar ones earned McKean the undying enmity of the Friends.[15] Such verdicts and gratuitous observations reflecting unfavorably on the character of the Friends prompted a longtime Quaker friend of McKean's, Warner Mifflin, to write him a long and passionate letter. He wished not only to "clear the Society of some groundless charges thou threw out against us," but to ease the chief justice towards a complete re-evaluation of his actions. He hoped that despite his recent conduct in the courts McKean "retained something of that friendship that [he] formerly manifested towards [Mifflin], and the respect [McKean] had expressed to [Mifflin's] wife and mother." Mifflin warned the chief justice that he had to recognize that what the Quakers do they do because of their conscience. "You have made a just stir in this land about liberty," the Friend told McKean, "and we can not help taking notice as I lately have of the kind that is brought forth, the tree being...known by its fruits." Much of the new liberty had turned out to be "licentious liberty, even a liberty to endeavor to crush piety and virtue....I am more concerned for you under whom my friends suffer," Mifflin wrote, "than I am for them....Can you have any the least hope that the interposition of an Almighty power will be in your favor, when you are making decrees and putting them in execution that whosoever will not fall down to the image you have set up shall be cast into the fiery furnace?" McKean must have read these sentiments in a cold fury. The echoes of John Roberts' trial had come resounding back.[16]

The nature of the Revolution and the shape of state politics by 1780 still forced McKean's courts to respond in a piecemeal fashion. As a result, the court's record remained episodic and inconsistent. It was challenged almost daily by the Council and to a lesser extent by the Assembly, as well as by local committees or, as in the "Fort Wilson" affair, by rioters who tried to take the law into their own hands.

These failings and limitations notwithstanding, McKean had some reason for optimism. With each passing day the division of powers within the government of Pennsylvania became more pronounced, the executive, legislative and judicial branches were clearly defined. As the court's competence—or at least acknowledged territoriality—in local and state matters slowly expanded, the Assembly and Council were able to give more attention to purely legislative and executive affairs. This development was haphazard and was played out in a political arena rife with machinations, personal animosities and, at times, violence. Yet the enhancement of the court went inexorably on, a trend in large measure attributable to the personality of the chief justice.[17]

McKean's insistence upon proper protocol and the trappings of the court impressed all who saw it, even those who considered him too imperial. McKean demanded deference to himself and his fellow judges and that the dignity of the court be upheld. Any who showed disrespect for the court and its personnel came to rue such actions. McKean made the courts respectable—and respected. The thief who robbed his home in February 1780 was one of the few people in Philadelphia who did not appreciate the impressive personal and institutional power wielded by McKean.[18]

While McKean could not always control a disruption such as the Fort Wilson debacle, he could, and increasingly did, control the routine of the courts and force a greater volume of cases into the confines of the court's jurisdiction. He was helped to some degree by the people of Pennsylvania, particularly those within Philadelphia, who were increasingly receptive to organized and legitimate judicial responses to everyday problems. Paradoxically, even as impromptu committees had sprung up to deal with economic and social dislocations in the summer of 1779 there were now serious reactions against such ad hoc "justice." With notable exceptions the people came to view the court's judicial procedures and routine as a welcome relief from often rudderless extralegal procedures. McKean's court might be severe, and too often it was slow, but it was generally predictable. In part because of the slowing revolutionary momentum and in part because of McKean's continuing effort to institutionalize the judicial processes, legal responses extended to issues and areas heretofore left to extralegal committees.[19]

In the early months of 1780 there arose several excellent opportunities for the McKean court to shape further the course of the Revolution in Pennsylvania. Many of the cases involving confiscation, for instance, were ripe for adjudication. From the beginning the confiscation policy of the state government had been fraught with legal and administrative difficulties. Forfeiture of estates was often rendered difficult when the original deeds were not surrendered, or when, despite confiscation and the sale of certain lands, the original holder continued to devise the lands to others. The state attempted to protect those purchasers of forfeited estates by assuming responsibility for the payment of private claims for debt against the estates of traitors. It also defended purchasers of forfeited estates against ejectment suits brought by the original occupants or those who had inherited portions of the forfeited estates. If an ejectment suit was upheld by the courts, the state agreed to reimburse the purchaser. These guarantees did little to reduce the legal entanglements resulting from confiscation and sale procedures.

In April 1780 the court turned its attention to the case of James' Claims in the hope of clarifying some of the legal issues surrounding confiscated lands. Sitting on the bench for the first time in his capacity as fourth judge was George Bryan, appointed in that same month. Bryan, perhaps as responsible as any man for the selection of McKean as the state's chief justice in 1777, had spent earlier years in the Council as vice-president of the state. Now on the bench he gave the court a more radical tinge than it had heretofore exhibited.

In the case of James' Claims, Abel James, a longtime acquaintance of McKean's and a sometimes legal associate before the Revolution, maintained that he had rightful claim to the estate of one John Parrock, who had lost his estate through an attainder. Parrock had originally received the estate from his sister, Sarah Parrock, whose will decreed that at his death the estate was to pass automatically to his children. If he were childless or if his children did not survive until their twenty-first birthday, the estate was to go instead to Abel James. Parrock, however, was attainted for treason, and his estate was confiscated by the state and sold at public auction. James, speaking through his attorney, William Lewis, argued that the seizure of the lands from Parrock passed the estate out of Parrock's possession, and since he had no children at that time, the estate, as stipulated by Sarah Parrock's will, should pass to James, not to the state. It was Lewis' contention—and he was by this time recognized as an expert on Pennsylvania's treason legislation and its implications—that the state could not impose itself between Parrock and James' legal claims.

The court, following a lengthy examination of the case, dismissed Lewis' arguments and found for the state. McKean and the justices held that Parrock held the lands for his natural life only, but the estate was meant to go ultimately and inexorably to his children. This fact established a limitation upon James' claims; indeed, Parrock had no children at the point of the state's expropriation of the estate, but James could not presume that this condition would remain. The state's claim—based on a March 29, 1779 law—was upheld. The decision did not stop James from continuing to resist the state and advancing his claims, but it did put the court squarely behind the state confiscation policy in this and in similar cases.[20]

But neither McKean's inclination nor Bryan's presence on the bench guaranteed to the state a rubber-stamp court. By the winter of 1780 McKean was still battling to assert the supremacy and independence of the court. He found an occasion to remind the state of his goal in the case of Joseph Griswold.

In December 1780 Griswold was arrested and jailed on suspicion of treason by an order of the Council. He applied for a writ of habeas corpus which McKean promptly granted. Upon learning of his action, the Council ordered Griswold rearrested. The Council was upset over the need to redo what it had originally done, and pressed McKean to wait upon the Council and to explain the developments of the case.[21]

On December 12 McKean responded by asking that the Council "reflect a moment on the tendency of this proceeding.... If a judge is obliged to satisfy the Council on the propriety of his judgment, or to consult their opinion, in any one case," McKean warned, "he must be under the like obligation in every one." He for one would have nothing

George Bryan. Courtesy City Archives, Philadelphia

to do with that kind of relationship. He maintained that he could not see how or where the line would hereafter be drawn between the two agencies of government, if such a precedent were set. Such action, he argued would only compromise the nature of the judiciary and the integrity of the judges. He ended by assuring the Council that "a precedent of the kind . . . shall never be introduced by me."

He was open to consultation, but he told Reed that any meeting between the chief justice and the Council must not be "in a formal manner, but in a private and friendly way." That is, if consultation was desirable and could be done in an informal manner, such meetings would be welcomed by him. If, however, such meetings were designed to indicate a subservience to the Council on the part of either McKean or the court, he would have none of it. He protested that his conduct in the Griswold case "was . . . only strictly conformable to the law and [his] duty." He added that while he had no reluctance to meet informally with the Council, he had "not been able to walk, nay scarcely to stir, since last Friday, owing to a violent cold or rhematism in [his] loins." The disability, though not feigned, was convenient.

His missive earned a terse reply from Reed. The president emphatically denied that the Council's intent in the Griswold case had been to encroach upon the prerogatives of the judiciary. Reed, a successful lawyer himself and a onetime nominee for the chief justiceship, declared that the independence of the justices was not the central issue here at all. He seemed genuinely surprised that McKean should interpret the Council's actions in such a light. What was at stake, according to Reed, was the desire on the part of the Council to confer with judges on important matters "so as to provide for the publick safety, and in future prevent Interferences of Authority which only weaken Government & increase the Insolence of the disaffected." Reed complained that he had not been forewarned of McKean's actions, and he was impatient with having to rearrest Griswold and duplicate the Council's earlier actions. The issue here was not the independence of the judges but better and more efficient communication between two state agencies. Reed left little doubt that the Council was voiding the writ issued by McKean to Griswold and would void future writs issued under similar circumstances.

There was also no mistaking whom Reed blamed for the confusion surrounding the Griswold case and who he thought held the potential for exacerbation of judicial-executive friction. "If further discharges are made & if any consequences prejudicial to the public ensue, we shall deem ourselves entirely exonerated from any Blame," Reed told his chief justice, "& if Harmony of the executive power is disturbed, we shall hold ourselves equally innocent."[22]

McKean feigned surprise that his letter to Reed should have offended the Council, or should have been interpreted as a challenge to the members of the Council. "I wrote as an independent Judge," he told the Council, "& expressed my sense of his duty in decent & respectful language." He reminded Reed and members of the Council that Griswold's application for a writ of habeas corpus had been in proper form. There had been no legal grounds for refusing it. The issuance of the writ had been communicated to the attorney general, an act which he insisted he had done out of courtesy to the Council. He was not required to do so.

The situation quickly solidified. Reed remained disturbed by McKean's insistence upon a strict adherence to the law at the expense of revolutionary developments and the needs of the Council. For Reed, only a close association of the judiciary and executive powers could guarantee the pursuance of an effective revolutionary state policy. He remained adamant that the present circumstances did not warrant McKean's concern—or obsession—with the independence of the judiciary.

McKean, on the other hand, saw that if the courts were to enjoy freedom from domination they must achieve that freedom under the most severe conditions. Any court could be independent in times of peace and tranquility. His correspondence with the Council left little doubt that neither the public clamor over Griswold's release nor the Council's strictures against his actions would force him to deviate from the issuance of writs when legalities demanded it. Reed recognized McKean's obstinacy in this matter. "As you seem still to mistake the Intention of the Council for a control of your judicial Freedom," he wrote McKean in an effort to end the issue ". . . there is no necessity to enlarge farther upon a disagreeable subject." The Council was not happy with McKean, but by December it was fully cognizant of his position—and his determination to uphold it.[23]

McKean was a confident, secure man by 1781. Not only did he exhibit a more positive approach in the Congress during the months of 1781 but also in the courts where he took several decisive steps to cap his policy of moderation towards the opponents of the state. One of his most charitable decisions came in the April session of the Supreme Court in the case of *Respublica* v. *Chapman*. Samuel Chapman, born and reared in Bucks County, Pennsylvania, left the state on December 26, 1776, a few months after the creation of the new state government. He subsequently joined the British, was captured at sea and taken to Massachusetts as a prisoner of war. When authorities in Pennsylvania learned of his capture, they successfully gained his extradition on the claim that he had been attainted by Pennsylvania on June 15, 1778, and he had not complied with that writ of attainter.

The issue before the Supreme Court in April 1781 was whether or not Samuel Chapman was a citizen of Pennsylvania and thus subject to state law and the jurisdiction of its courts. Chapman's counsel contended that Chapman left Pennsylvania during a period when the old government had callapsed and the new was not yet fully established and functioning. Thus no government existed to give him the protection of its laws or to receive his allegiance in return. His counsel was quick to point out that Chapman had absented himself from Pennsylvania a month before the new state government had enacted its first law and was therefore at liberty to accept, reject, or absent himself from the government in this critical period. The crux of the argument advanced by Chapman's attorney was that the act of January 28, 1776, passed to revive the laws, recognized that the laws were not in force from May 14, 1776, to February 11, 1777, and the state therefore could not prosecute individuals for disobeying laws during that hiatus.

William Bradford, the Princeton educated attorney general who had taken office following Jonathan Dickinson Sergeant's resignation on November 20, 1780, denied this interpretation. He held that when Chapman left Pennsylvania on December 26,

Pennsylvania was a commonwealth and Chapman owed it allegiance. The substance of Bradford's argument was that a government existed from the time of the May congressional resolves in 1776 through February 11, 1777, and beyond. The power had been transferred from Great Britain to the Congress of the United States through the people acting in extralegal committees. The new state government created by the state constitution of 1776 merely accepted the sovereignty hitherto exercised by the revolutionary committees. Chapman had withheld his loyalties to that legitimate state government, indeed had acted against its behalf, and must now pay the penalty for his actions.

McKean upheld the arguments of Chapman's attorney. He accepted the contention that a government independent of Great Britain existed before the constitution of 1776, and that when the new state government was formed sovereignty remained unbroken, merely being transmitted from the revolutionary bodies to the state authorities. As a state government existed prior to March 4, 1777, and a constitution was operative in October 1776, a person could commit treason against any or all of these governmental bodies. Besides, a specific act against a specific governmental body was not necessary for commission of a crime, for treason was a crime known to the common law.

Having found the prosecution's case to this point feasible and legally correct, McKean turned to accept critical portions of the defense argument. He found that the law of January 28, which provided that laws originally created under the power of the Crown now had as their source of power the new state government, was faultily conceived. The January legislation had suspended current statutes to accomodate the revolutionary conditions between May 14, 1776, and February 10, 1777. The treason legislation of February 11 therefore marked the point after which treason could be committed against the present government. Chapman was found innocent.[24]

McKean's pronouncement in the Chapman case represented a great stride towards fixing moderation as a state policy. He had earlier expressed similar views to Reed, but those were unofficial and lacked the sanction of the state judiciary.[25] The Chapman decision recognized what many sought to deny: the confusion and mixed allegiances of many citizens in Pennsylvania during the early years of what was essentially a civil war. The decision exacted allegiance only of those who remained in Pennsylvania after the establishment of a new state government and the enactment of specific legislation by that government. McKean thought that prior to February 11, 1777 an individual was free to oppose Whig policies or exile himself to territory more compatible with his political sentiments. If a person remained in Pennsylvania after the creation of the constitution of 1776, he owed allegiance to that government and to the legislation it enacted. Acts designed to harm or destroy it were acts of treason. A great many Pennsylvanians profited from his leniency in this matter.[26]

A few months later the court took still another step towards protecting citizens against an overly zealous state government in *Respublica* v. *Buffington.* The state sought an execution warrant from the Supreme Court against Joshua Buffington, a Chester County yeoman, attainted in October 1780. The writ of attainer issued by the Supreme Executive Council, dated October 2, 1780, called for "Joshua Buffington, Now, or Late, of the township of East Bradford, Yeoman," to turn himself in or face the ultimate consequences, by November 13, 1780. The state had subsequently taken Buffington prisoner and now sought to carry out the writ by having the court confirm that Buffington was the man named. It argued simply that the said Buffington had lived in Chester County from 1776 to 1780 as a yeoman, and that he was the only Joshua Buffington in Chester County, a sufficient identification to satisfy the writ.

William Lewis and Jared Ingersoll, counsels for Buffington, argued that the writ to be legal and binding must be exact, that there was no room for the smallest error. And the present writ did contain errors. They drew the court's attention to the fact that their client had moved to Delaware several weeks before the state's writ of attainder was issued. Moreover, Buffington, during his long tenure in Chester County, had never resided in East Bradford Township. His home had been in West Bradford. These discrepancies were sufficient to render the writ inoperative. He was indeed Joshua Buffington, perhaps the only Joshua Buffington in Chester County, but the writ contained errors, Lewis and Ingersoll insisted, and these errors rendered it invalid. The court agreed with the defense. In his charge to the jury McKean so clearly accepted the argument presented in Buffington's behalf that the jury had little trouble finding for Buffington.[27]

McKean never lost sight of the historic vulnerability of republics to contention and dissipation from within, and by 1781 he was persuaded that a republic of law would serve as a bulwark against internal dissension and decay. He had concluded, however, that before a republic of law could be guaranteed the courts must be independent—and moderate.

9. "A Valuable Acquisition in Congress"

By 1781 McKean recognized that if he was to play a pivotal role in shaping the course of the Revolution it would be as the chief justice of Pennsylvania, not as a congressman from Delaware. He continued to be lauded by his friends for his contributions in Congress and acknowledged by others to be a formidable foe in congressional matters but he was sorely disappointed in the congressional record to date and in his inability to provide effective and sustained leadership.

When McKean had arrived in York late in January 1778 he found President Henry Laurens complaining that the "extraordinary and immeasurable" workload continued to "fall heavily upon a very few members from 17 to 12 who faithfully attend their duties at the expense of domestic happiness and the improvement of their private estates." Laurens had welcomed McKean warmly and had acknowledged him to be "a valuable acquisition in Congress." In the next two months McKean found himself serving on thirteen committees and chairing six additional ones.[1]

Yet even in the bleakness and isolation of York there had been some surprising accomplishments. In April McKean's spirits had revived when the French finally signed a treaty guaranteeing the Americans financial and military aid. McKean was convinced the French king was "the most wise, most just and most magnanimous Prince not only in the World at present but to be found in history." He was also encouraged when Lord Howe and General Clinton officially recognized the status of Congress by correctly addressing a missive to "Henry Laurens Esquire President of Congress at Yorktown," in the first week in June: the British were belatedly showing some respect for the American cause.

The decision of the British ministry to send three peace commissioners to join with Howe and Clinton to negotiate a peace settlement with the Americans, however, failed to impress McKean. He saw little chance that the peace commissioners would agree to the one thing that seemed inescapable: American independence. And he held in contempt those who would render the Revolution stillborn in 1778 by responding sympathetically to the overtures of Lord Howe and his commissioners.[2]

McKean had good reason to be suspicious of the commissioners' motives and maneuvering. One of the commissioners, George Johnstone, brought with him a letter to McKean from Joseph Reed's brother-in-law, Dennys DeBerdt. Written "in very flattering terms," the letter implied that Johnstone's peace mission could be greatly facilitated by "Gentlemen of such abilities" as, among others, McKean. Several such letters were received by prominent Americans. More than a month before the letters were formally turned over to Congress on June 15, McKean made plain his own attitude toward the commissioners' aims. "I am determined never to give up on the independence of the United States after so much expence of blood and treasure whilst I have a breath to draw," he had written Caesar Rodney. "I shall neither be allured nor intimidated into it." When congress stood firm, forcing the commissioners to treat with it as they would an independent nation, McKean rejoiced that he had "lived to see the day, when, instead of 'Americans licking the dust from the feet of a British Minister,' the tables are turned."[3]

Some important advances in Congress had been made in terms of policy and administration also. Though pessimistic over Congress' myriad problems in 1778, McKean never lost faith that a reformation of sorts could be achieved. "Peculation, neglect of duty, avarice, and insolence in most departments abound," he wrote Read in April, "but, with the favor of God, I shall contribute my part to drag forth and punish the culprits, though some of them are high in rank and characters I did not suspect." His desire to stimulate moral regeneration in Congress as in society at large led him to inquire into the workings of several congressional departments, including the corruption-ridden clothier general and quartermaster. His efforts toward these reforms continued after Congress returned to Philadelphia; in June 1780 he chaired a committee to investigate the quartermaster's office. The committee condemned the inefficiencies in that office and the personnel serving it.[4]

McKean was instrumental in establishing a congressional court to arbitrate admiralty appeals, and in strengthening the regular army by allocating federally financed half-pay life pensions for officers. Unfortunately, his ardor for reform far outran his capacity or opportunity to effect it. What with his judicial obligations and congressional workload, a concerted reform effort on his part was impossible. He could only appear, do what he could under the circumstances, and go home again. Significant reforms within Congress, when they did occur, were largely the successes of others.[5]

Any delegate who, like McKean, was committed to a redefinition of congressional powers and reformation of its internal structure could not fail to appreciate the implications of the Articles of Confederation to those goals and to the nature of the American union. McKean's favorable opinion of the Articles was not shared by the Delaware government, however, despite its interest in his enthusiasm for reform elsewhere. McKean had been assigned to the original committee established on June 12, 1776, to consider the best form of government to be permanently instituted among the new states, but he had not participated in the important maneuvering preceding the adoption of the final plan in November 1777. It is impossible to ascertain his response to John

Dickinson's earliest drafts or to the subsequent changes wrought in that draft under the goad of North Carolina's Thomas Burke. It is clear that he was content for the most part with the form of the Articles in the spring of 1778 even though Delaware, fearful that the confederation would work against its interests, withheld permission for him to sign.

Read had written McKean on March 4, 1778, expressing deep concern that unless limits were placed on lands claimable by the larger states, smaller states like Delaware would have no opportunity to share in western lands. He foresaw the smaller states eventually being taxed to protect and settle those lands. Somehow Delaware must share in these lands and utilize them to pay off its war debts and its soldiers. In raising the issue Read was articulating what troubled many Delawareans of all political persuasions.[6]

McKean sought to allay Delawareans' fears concerning the Articles. He confessed to some minor reservations of his own but he doubted that Congress would consider further changes in the Articles at this stage. He said Read's concerns were of quite another nature. The time for serious objections, McKean pointed out, would have been in late 1776 or early 1777, when Delaware had seen fit to remove himself and Rodney, substituting less energetic and persuasive men, as representatives to Congress—an observation that could have done nothing to improve Read's temper.

Not personally involved in western land speculation nor close to those who were, McKean saw no danger to smaller states from the landed states. He told Read that if a state like Virginia increased its size two things could happen, neither injurious to Delaware: the enlarged state would simply assume greater tax burdens as it grew, or the people within that area could seek to create new, smaller states. In any case, Delaware would have the right to apply for townships in Virginia to satisfy her troops.[7]

It was not until the following February that Delaware—still persuaded that the Articles were "unequal and disadvantageous to this State"—reluctantly changed its instructions to permit him to sign on the 22nd of that month. When the final deadlock among the states had been broken on January 2, 1781, and Maryland signed to complete the confederation, McKean described it as "an auspicious event...one calculated to commence a new era." The celebration at the McKean residence must have been impressive; certainly the wine flowed freely. When one guest, Thomas Rodney, sat down to write his wife following the affair, he was tipsy enough to address her as "sir." Despite McKean's celebration of the confederation, he warned Thomas Collins, speaker of the Delaware Assembly, that it would "require considerable improvements to bring it to perfection."[8]

McKean and the Delaware government had failed to see eye to eye on still another matter which surfaced in the spring of 1778: the fate of President John McKinly, captured by the British in September 1777. Zealous Whigs charged that McKinly's ascendancy to the highest executive office in the state had been the result of his ties with the "Dionysian faction," led by Read, which they described as largely "Court Sycophants" from the Sussex delegation swept into office by use of widespread political intimidation in October 1776. As President McKinly had done little to persuade his detractors that he could provide the proper momentum for the Whig cause. One radical noted uncharitably that McKinly's capture by the British "had so little the appearance of accident, that many people suspected design."[9]

Already troubled by the cautious conservatism of McKinly and Read over the issue of independence, and their seeming tolerance of Tory behavior among Delawareans, and embittered by their control of the state government and the patronage attached to it, McKean was predisposed by February 1778 to exact some revenge. If he needed additional motive to move against Read and McKinly in the early months of 1778, he found it in McKinly's alleged association with Tories Thomas Robinson and Boaz Manlove, both of whom had played pivotal roles in the earlier harassment and imprisonment of John Clowes. To learn that McKinly was consorting with the men he had so valiantly spoken against only a few years before was apparently the last straw for McKean.

On February 12 McKean penned the first of two critical letters to Read, the only such letters the two men ever exchanged. In the first, McKean implicitly contrasted his own willingness to serve the state under the most trying times with

Read's eagerness to reduce his own official duties. In the second he explicitly suggested that most of Delaware's troubles stemmed in large measure from the decision of the Read-dominated government in October 1776 to curb the influence of McKean and Rodney.[10]

Political realities and his own respect for George Read dictated that McKean limit his "attack" to a few intemperate letters. McKinly, on the other hand, was more vulnerable. McKean could use his considerable influence in York to see that Congress did not entertain a move for McKinly to be exchanged for a British prisoner for some time. McKean knew that McKinly's continued incarceration would solve two problems at once: it would punish McKinly for his unfortunate choice of comrades, and it would deprive McKean's political opponents in Delaware of one of their chief spokesmen. McKean therefore initiated a subtle policy of obstruction. By March the state government conceded that there was little immediate hope of McKinly's release. By July McKinly was complaining bitterly of "the neglect which has been shown by those from whom I had reason to expect some more attention." There can be little doubt that he alluded principally to McKean.[11]

McKean continued his policy of obstructing McKinly's release until the last week in August. Then, prompted by a letter from Caesar Rodney, the changing political environment in Delaware, and his own sense of strategy, he helped to defeat a congressional move on September 14 to restrain McKinly from returning to British lines until, as a quid pro quo, Hugh Wallace, a Tory currently seeking to ignore his parole obligations, surrendered to American authorities. McKean on that same day resisted successfully a motion to substitute one William Thompson for McKinly in an exchange for William Franklin, the ex-Governor of New Jersey. Finally, by a 9-3 vote, with McKean among the majority, Congress agreed to the exchange of McKinly for Franklin.[12]

William Thompson, captured by the British during Benedict Arnold's Canadian campaign in 1776 and paroled to Pennsylvania, had watched the exchange of McKinly with growing disgust. Eager to return to action and discouraged with Congress' willingness to arrange exchanges for others he considered less deserving, he came to view McKean as the primary source of his discomfort. Thompson and McKean finally ran into each other in the Philadelphia Coffee House on November 18, 1778. Details of the meeting are highly charged and contradictory, but a general picture of what followed can be pieced together from a variety of witnesses. McKean was sitting in a booth with Justices Evans and Atlee and the Commissary of Prisoners, Thomas Bradford, discussing a new list of prisoners to be exchanged by General Clinton. Brigadier General Thompson, who had just come from the Indian Queen Tavern where he had told a companion, George Noarth, of his intention "to whip [McKean] whenever [he] met him, unless Mr. McKean would fight him as a Gentleman which [he] believe him too great a coward to do," entered the Coffee House to find McKean and his party in deep discussion.[13]

Knowing Thompson to be on Bradford's list, McKean called the brigadier general to his table. Eyewitnesses agreed that McKean approached Thompson in good humor, apparently under the impression that the news of a possible release would be well received by Thompson. He was mistaken. Thompson began to pour out his bitterness against McKean as those in McKean's box wandered off in an effort to give the men some privacy. McKean later reported, as did Atlee, still nearby, that Thompson called McKean a rascal and a villain and Congress a pack of damned rascals. It was said also that Thompson used "other low expressions" in describing McKean and Congress.

Thompson also told McKean of his resentment at the treatment meted out to him by McKean as chief justice. He alluded to an incident in Carlisle the previous April when McKean had requested the brigadier general to come to his lodgings to answer a charge brought by an army officer that Thompson's servant was a deserter. Thompson now informed McKean that his letter had been insulting and abrasive; it was a summons, not a polite letter. McKean contended that his message to Thompson had been nothing more than a polite note designed to permit Thompson to explain matters informally to the army official. When Thompson reiterated that the summons had been insulting McKean demanded that he produce the document so that the issue might be settled. Thompson shouted that he no longer had the offending letter for "he had wip'd his arse with it."

With that McKean told Thompson that "he was no Gentleman." Witnesses generally agreed that at this point Thompson advanced on the chief justice, put his hand on McKean's shoulder and asked pointedly, "Are *you* a Gentleman?" To which McKean replied that he was Thompson's "superior," that Thompson "was nothing but a bully and a brute." Thomas Bradford, outside of McKean's booth now but within earshot, reported that a small scuffle ensued, McKean saying "aye, strike me if you dare, I will make your heart ake if you do," to which Thompson replied "Damn you, I will make your bones ake first." Calmer heads prevailed, however, and the two men were separated.

After the encounter McKean left little doubt that Thompson would rue his impetuous and uncivil behavior. As good as his word, he reported the incident to Congress the next day. Claiming Thompson's behavior "to be a gross insult to Congress," and "to have a tendency to destroy the freedom of voting in Congress," he placed the ugly issue directly on the congressional doorstep.[14]

On November 23 congressional hearings were held to determine the facts of the case. Almost two dozen witnesses were called by both sides. The critical question was whether or not Thompson had inveighed against Congress in uncivil terms and called into question the honor of that body, as McKean charged. Thompson, supported by a score of witnesses from the Coffee House, insisted that his pejorative comments had been directed against McKean the chief justice, not McKean a member of Congress. Whether or not McKean sincerely believed that the honor of Congress had been besmirched, or that the legitimacy of its voting had been compromised, he placed an unwelcomed burden on Congress, already seriously overworked.

Neither McKean nor Thompson gained by the congressional hearings. Most witnesses failed to confirm either claim in total, and the characters of both men emerged tarnished. Thompson strove to extricate himself by writing a memorial reviewing at length his complaints against McKean as an individual and as chief justice of Pennsylvania. He charged McKean with having accused him "with the mean & infamous Crime of Harbouring Deserters." This from a man who, according to Thompson, refused to enter a local tavern because he did not want "to sit down with a parcel of upstart Continental Officers." Thompson readily admitted calling McKean "a Rascal and a Villain," but he again vehemently denied that any of his aspersions had been directed towards Congress or congressmen.

Thompson's memorial gave fresh offense. President Henry Laurens, already disturbed over the quarrels wracking Congress and angry over the lack of deference shown to Congress by individuals, was outraged. He wrote to the president of South Carolina on December 16 that Thompson had "insulted Congress by an Apologetic letter, denying that he had called [Congress] Rascals, but acknowledging the application of the term Rascal to the Honorable Mr. McKean." Laurens and those who shared his unhappiness had the satisfaction of seeing Congress vote the brigadier general guilty of a breach of privilege. But it bode ill, Laurens thought, that Thompson remained "in favor with a party in Congress who seemed determined to support him at the expense of the honor of Congress."[15]

Eager to maintain its dignity yet perplexed whether to judge Thompson's conduct as a challenge to McKean the congressmen or McKean the chief justice of a sovereign state, Congress fell to quarrelling. The debate continued into the last weeks in December despite complaints by members that the issue had consumed too much time already. The hearings and the debate which followed caused friction between heretofore friendly congressmen and strained relations between state and congressional authorities. Finally, on December 24 Congress voted to accept Thompson's apology—a vote in which McKean concurred—and put the matter behind it.[16]

The matter was far from closed, however. Five days after he escaped Congress' wrath, Thompson published a full account of the situation as he viewed it in the Pennsylvania *Packet*. For the benefit of the "honest soldier" and the "candid citizen" he reviewed once again the particulars of the dispute with McKean and Congress, concluding that "Chief Justice McKean has, in an affair which does not relate to his conduct in Congress, and which is of a private nature, behaved like a lyar, a rascal, and a coward." He reiterated his earlier allegations that

McKean was reluctant to enter a local tavern because he did not wish to associate with Continental officers, and hinted that McKean's actions against him were thus not only personal but derived from a general disapproval of the army and its officers.[17]

Two days later, the Pennsylvania Supreme Executive Council entered the fray. Noting the "acrimonious remarks" by Thompson, the Council ordered its congressional representatives to supply the Council with the proceedings relating to Thompson, and any other evidence pertinent to a final judgment on Thompson's conduct toward Pennsylvania officials. A week later, having digested the gist of Thompson's *Packet* letter, the Council determined that "the interests & the honor of the State are deeply affected by such charges" and announced its intention to find out "if McKean should be removed from office or if reparation should be made to him and the state." On January 6, 1779, it voted to bring Thompson before the Council the following morning "to give the Board such information and satisfaction in the Premises, as the interests of the State in such cases require." Thompson refused to attend.[18]

In the meantime McKean answered Thompson in the *Packet*. He said although Thompson was "beneath [his] contempt," and "merit[ed] little attention," the people of Pennsylvania had a right to know the facts in order to judge for themselves whether or not the conduct of their chief justice warranted disapproval. He reviewed his conduct step by step. He had not mistreated Thompson or used his official position to abuse him but had gone out of his way to "render him what little service lay in my way," because of a "regard for some of his connections." Here McKean doubtless referred to the fact that Thompson was George Read's brother-in-law. He concluded by announcing that he would "take no farther notice of the low, vile epithets contained in this publication, than to inform the Author and Printer, that both are equally criminal and punishable." The message was clear to Thompson and the Printer, John Dunlap. McKean was going to sue.[19]

Despite his promise to "take no farther notice" of Thompson's accusations, on February 2 McKean again brought the issue before the public. He wrote that he had waited four weeks for Thompson to explain to him or the public his constant references to a "private affair." He directed much of his vitriol to Thompson's allegation that he had "refused going into a room in a tavern...where...a number of...officers were." "The Malicious design of this invented tale is obvious," McKean raged, "and it has been circulated by his partisans, I am told, with great industry among the Gentlemen of the Army." McKean claimed the story was without foundation.[20]

John McKinly, a central figure in the unfolding drama but a passive onlooker to this point, also had his say, informing both men on February 15 that he had been twice abused. First he had been unfairly treated in the developments leading to his exchange, then he had watched his position misrepresented in the pages of the *Packet*. He wished both men—and the readers of the *Packet*—to know that he felt himself to be the victim of something of a conspiracy during his captivity. He was especially critical of McKean's account of his feelings. It was true that he had been convinced that his exchange had been "obstructed and delayed," but he had never thought it was "out of favour to the Brigadier." He gave the impression that he had recognized from the outset that his delay had been the result of McKean's lukewarm advocacy of his cause.[21]

And so the matter rested—except for legal repercussions. McKean's suit against Thompson and Dunlap was not settled until the spring of 1781 when he was awarded more than £5,700 in damages. When he "released the damages," asserting "he only wanted to see the law and the facts settled," friends saw in the gesture confirmation of McKean's disinterestness.[22] But the Thompson affair proved more about the chief justice and his brand of republicanism than was conceded in the observation by his friends. It showed how open McKean was to charges that he was unsympathetic to the army and that he seldom hesitated to wield his considerable official power and influence to protect—and, indeed, to enlarge—his private interests. Equally important, the Thompson affair clearly identified his growing concern with the propensity of citizens publicly to criticize their officials, and his unwillingness to countenance it when such criticism was directed towards him.

Not unexpectedly, McKean was drawn into the growing party spirit and rancor within Congress in 1779, suffering the

Thomas McKean, signed Rembrandt Peale. Courtesy of Historical Society of Delaware

accompanying personal abuse. Now he became a central figure in a drama involving American representatives abroad that had been unfolding for the past two years and would continue to plague Congress for a number of years to come. The conflict had its origins in 1776 when Congress, responding to sectional rivalries among its members, appointed Arthur Lee of Virginia, Benjamin Franklin of Pennsylvania, and Silas Deane of Connecticut to its foreign posts. The three men soon fell to quarrelling over public issues. At the bottom was the question of whether the aid secured by America from France was a gift or a loan. Deane maintained that the materiel was loaned, Lee that it was offered without thought of repayment. This fundamental disagreement was soon broadened by a series of personal charges and counter-charges. Lee charged that Deane was more intent on securing profits for himself and a small coterie of friends than protecting legitimate New England—or American—interests. Although a Southerner, Lee, with his close ties with the Adamses, found considerable support from the New England or "Eastern bloc" within Congress. Deane's most ardent advocates were to be found in the Middle and Southern states.[23]

When Deane was recalled in 1777 and replaced by John Adams, a favorite of the Eastern bloc, friends of Deane bitterly protested that the wrong man had been recalled. They interpreted the appointment of Adams and two others, William Lee of Virginia (to Vienna and Berlin) and Ralph Izard of South Carolina (to Tuscany) to have been inspired by Eastern bloc prejudices. Lee and Izard might be Southerners, it was argued, but they were personally and ideologically sympathetic to the Lees and the Adamses. Only Franklin found support in both camps, and he too had occasional harsh words with Arthur Lee. So it was that Franklin was named sole American representative to France on September 14, 1778.

The conflict took a decided turn for the worse when in 1778 Deane pleaded for an investigation of his conduct by his congressional colleagues. Frustrated by Congress' unwillingness to provide the exacting type of investigation he sought, Deane determined in December 1778 to appeal over Congress' head to the people.

His public criticism of congressional troubles and divisions led on December 9 to the resignation of Henry Laurens. Troubles mounted when Thomas Paine, secretary to the Committee on Foreign Affairs, wrote a piece under the pseudonym "Common Sense" supporting Arthur Lee's position. He suggested that official congressional correspondence and documentation supported Lee's basic contention that French aid prior to the Alliance of 1778 had indeed been offered with no thought of compensation. Enraged at such a public disclosure to the embarrassment of his government, French Minister Conrad Alexandre Gerard pressed Congress for an official denial of Paine's assertions.[24]

A wide-ranging congressional investigation of its representatives followed. A committee of thirteen, formed to evaluate the total conduct of the foreign ministers, recommended in April that all foreign representatives be summarily recalled. Between April and June a series of critical congressional votes was taken on these recommendations. The first vote, on April 22, was on the question of Franklin's recall.[25]

McKean, who had been absent since February for judicial duties but kept informed through personal contacts, appeared in Congress that day to support Franklin. Gouveneur Morris, heading a scheme to oust Franklin, was so startled by McKean's sudden appearance that he moved to postpone the vote. Morris' assumption that McKean would vote the Adams-Lee line—that is, support the retention of Franklin—was well founded. McKean had been in on the origins of the diplomatic corps dispute and involved in its ramifications. Two of McKean's closest friends in Congress were John Adams and Richard Henry Lee. As a member of both the Secret Committee which in 1775 initiated many of America's foreign contacts, and the committee later formed to investigate the actions of American commissioners abroad, McKean understood the issues and personalities involved. His congressional voting pattern closely paralleled those of such radicals as William Whipple, Samuel Holten, Richard Henry Lee, and Samuel Adams, all core members in the Lee-Adams faction.[26]

It was clear, then, by his sudden arrival in Congress on April 22, that McKean was there to support Franklin in the interests of the Lee-Adams party. It would be misleading, however, to assume that McKean was blindly bound to any faction or group in Congress in 1779 or early 1780. Given his personality and personal predilections it is unlikely that he would have consistently supported any one bloc even if his attendance had been regular. Neither in his judicial nor congressional capacities is there evidence of consistent partisan posture despite the vigor with which he often supported individual partisan measures. For example he did not share the Eastern bloc's earlier enthusiasm for compromising Washington's position or removing him, or for opposing measures granting half-pay for life to officers of the Continental Line; nor did he share the Eastern bloc's rampant Francophobia.

The clues to just why the Lee-Adams faction should be anxious to save Franklin's diplomatic skin while leaders of the Deane group sought his dismissal can be discerned in the maneuverings of the Committee of Thirteen, charged to produce a recommendation on the foreign ministers. McKean was appointed to this committee in January 1779. Initially the membership included a slight edge for those partisans of Lee, for in its original make-up William Whipple, William Ellery, Oliver Ellsworth, James Searle, Henry Laurens, and McKean gave them a solid six votes. The swing man on the committee appeared to be Elbridge Gerry, a firm supporter of New England's interests but never a rabid advocate of the Lee-Adams bloc. McKean's absence from critical meetings between January and April, coupled with Ellsworth's absence after February 19, permitted the Deane group of James Duane, John Fell, William Paca, Richard Smith, Thomas Burke, and Edward Langworthy to dominate the committee and thus control its deliberations and, ultimately, its conclusions.

While the specific strategy of the Deane supporters within the committee is more obvious than the motivation behind it, it is demonstrable that they sought to recall all foreign ministers, probably under the impression that to ensure the recall of the Lees and Izard they would have to sacrifice Franklin as well. Gouveneur Morris apparently saw in Franklin's dismissal an opportunity for himself in some foreign post. But whatever the motives behind the strategem, the Deane group was ready to sacrifice Franklin to secure the dismissal of the repugnant Lees and Izard. They maneuvered the voting so as to isolate John Adams from the remaining foreign agents on the premise that as long as Adams was included the New England members would reject any across-the-board dismissals. By April the Lee group had recognized the ploy and tried to frustrate it, using congressional reluctance to remove Adams and Franklin as protection for the more vulnerable Lees and Izard. Out of the manuevering and manipulation in April came a plan to treat each case individually. Franklin's fate was to be determined first.

It was at this point that McKean arrived abruptly in Congress, and Morris, recognizing the implications of his arrival, moved unsuccessfully to postpone the vote until McKean was preoccupied elsewhere.[27] As anticipated, McKean cast his vote to retain Franklin in his diplomatic post. Despite his political differences with Franklin and his lack of personal fervor for the man, McKean was intent on maintaining the status quo in terms of America's foreign representatives. He had been uneasy for some time; he had watched the "virtuous band" in Congress (as he characterized the founders of independence) slowly dwindle, replaced by inferior and less dedicated men. Opponents of the "virtuous" remnant had lately been pursuing a strategy he could not quite comprehend. They were apparently set upon turning member against member, McKean wrote, Congress against the states. Every artifice was being employed to instill prejudice against America's foreign ministers and commissioners, particularly the Lees. He correctly saw that the Deane faction planned to recall "without exception." It was McKean's vote which saved Franklin.[28]

McKean had always been reluctant to publicize Congress' dissension over foreign matters: his vote on April 22 was in part to maintain a modicum of secrecy regarding these problems, and in part to allay French fears that America was increasingly receptive to overtures from Great Britain. To McKean, a radical shift in foreign personnel at this juncture would give credence to false reports that Congress was considering a re-evaluation of its relationship to France. He intended to do whatever he could to avoid such changes.[29]

That McKean had no real enthusiasm for Franklin as a diplomat despite his April 22 vote is clear in subsequent events.

In June 1781 Congress considered establishing an American commission to negotiate peace with England, should the occasion arise. The French wanted a commission favorably inclined toward their interests. Gerard's successor, Chevalier Anne de la Luzerne, made Congress aware of French dissatisfaction with John Adams as commissioner to handle the critical negotiations. Luzerne wanted Adams removed or at least neutralized by the addition of commissioners more receptive to French interests. The French asked for Franklin. Congress eventually bent to the French will and named four commissioners, including Franklin, in addition to John Adams. McKean resisted Franklin's appointment throughout. When a motion was made to put both Franklin and Jefferson on the delegation, McKean tried to have only Jefferson named. He lost, and his feelings toward Franklin were apparent to all.[30]

To his dismay, McKean was unable to lend support to Arthur Lee when voting took place on that minister's recall. He was away on circuit that day, May 3, and his absence proved critical. There is only circumstantial evidence to suggest that leaders of the Deane faction waited until he was on circuit to raise the question of Lee's removal, but it was painfully clear to McKean that such a strategy was under way and he was helpless in the face of it. Four states, including New York, Maryland, Virginia, and North Carolina supported the move to recall Lee while four others, New Hampshire, Connecticut, Massachusetts, and New Jersey voted against it. The remaining four states voting were divided, Rhode Island, South Carolina, Pennsylvania and Delaware. For Delaware, Dickinson's vote to recall Lee was cancelled by Van Dyke's to support him. Thus, McKean's vote not only would have thrown Delaware into the nay column but would have provided the margin of Lee's victory. As it was the vote ended divided.[31]

Arthur Lee's embarrassment over the outcome of the vote was of no small concern to McKean. He expressed the hope that those delegates who had opposed Lee's interests would be removed by their states from Congress. McKean in consoling the Lees tried to leave no misunderstanding in their minds as to his own role in the matter. "When I reflect upon the assiduity, the zeal, the fidelity, the abilities and patriotism of Doctor A. Lee," he wrote Richard Henry Lee, "I cannot help deploring his fate and reprobating the ingratitude of Congress itself." He assured Arthur Lee of his "many unshaken friends remaining" within the national government. He described his own inability to stave off the May 3 vote and his frustrations over the scheme to postpone it until he was preoccupied elsewhere.[32]

It was of some concern to McKean in 1779 that those who opposed republican virtue (as he, Arthur Lee, John Adams, Samuel Adams and others of the Eastern bloc defined it) had made inroads in matters of economic policy as well as in the field of foreign policy. The deteriorating economic conditions in 1779 encouraged persons intent on speculation and profits even as they cheated the "true patriot." What was at stake here, in McKean's eyes, was not short-range economic policy but the long-range nature of American republicanism; it was a struggle to determine whether avarice or virtue would become the dominant feature of the American republic.

McKean watched with an increasing sense of helplessness as Congress fumbled through one financial disaster after another. A January 1779 resolution had substituted new bills of emission totaling over fifty million dollars for old bills of credit. February had seen over ten million dollars worth of new bills emitted and April another five million—this in the face of Congress' persistent inability to get a large portion of the old bills of credit out of circulation. The financial deterioration in Congress was closely paralleled by progressive economic dislocation in Pennsylvania.

By summer 1779 McKean had concluded that only an immediate infusion of money could defray expenses on state and national levels. If citizens like himself failed to sacrifice what they could to bolster their sagging governments' financial posture, he told his wife, state and national government alike might collapse. The proliferation of extralegal committees in Philadelphia designed to stop the rampant inflation and currency manipulation—and to bypass McKean's court if necessary to that end—was ample proof that the possibility of collapse was very real.[33]

To bring some order into congressional finances McKean attempted to raise funds for Congress by advertising his lands for sale. When that proved ineffective he successfully moved that Congress pledge itself to a policy of currency limitation.[34] Because "it is inexpedient to derive the supplies for a continuance of the war from emissions of bills of credit." he told his colleagues on September 1, Congress should "on no account whatever, emit more bills of credit than to make the whole amount of such bills two hundred million dollars." Nor should it "emit the forty million necessary to compleat that [current] sum, provided a sufficient supply of money for the public exigencies can be obtained by other means." Only the Virginia delegation opposed his move.[35]

On the state level he participated in a mass meeting held on May 25 to protest the continuing manipulation of currency and worsening inflation in Philadelphia. McKean was appalled that throughout Pennsylvania men should be "making a fortune on speculation, engrossing and the use of public money." He backed away from the issue, however, when it became apparent that the committees formed to enforce the meeting's objectives, and the private activity spawned by the meeting, directly challenged his court. He stayed away from a second meeting, telling his wife he hoped "good may ensue from it" but confessing he had "some apprehension to the contrary." Thereafter he confined his efforts to pledging large sums of his own money (although he suffered economic reverses himself) to Pennsylvania's share of provisions for the Continental Line, and offered advice on how the state might best utilize the expropriated Penns' lands.[36] McKean's efforts had no great effect on the state's willingness to contribute more or Congress' success in obtaining private donations and foreign loans. By 1781 little had been achieved in those areas.

Meanwhile, even before Maryland signed the Articles thus completing the Confederation, Congress had begun to move toward an executive-oriented operation. A committee to study reorganization was commissioned on August 29, 1780, and by January 1781 had brought forth a resolution to establish a single secretary for foreign affairs. Other agencies were then created: departments of war, treasury, and marine. Conservatives, or Nationalists as they came to be labeled, saw in the grim realities of 1780 and 1781 an opportunity to use the nation's deepening financial woes to secure basic political reorganization. Fiscal reform, a vital part of their program, was aimed at reconstructing the union to the satisfaction of the commercial interests. The central figure in this development was, of course, Robert Morris, a longtime target of Pennsylvania Constitutionalists.[37]

McKean concurred in the need for efficiency through reorganization, but in the early months of 1781 he was seriously troubled lest such changes lead to wrong policies giving power to the wrong men. He endorsed most of the Nationalist program; he sympathized with efforts toward a more effective army, an excise tax, pensions for officers, and wholesale departmental reforms. Nonetheless, he looked with disfavor on the increasing shadow cast by Morris and his particular brand of republican ideology.

A letter from his congressional friend William Houston argued that though his own "mind labour [ed] under a load of anxiety respecting the settlement of the Power of the Superintendent of Finance" he hoped that McKean would share his conviction that "those powers or similar ones, must be vested in some one Person." McKean may have shared Houston's assessment that "Stagnation must soon take place and Ruin cannot be far Off" without serious remedial steps by Congress such as those offered by Morris. Still he hesitated. As he told Samuel Adams, "There are amongst us who are so fond of having a great and powerful Man to look up to that, tho' they may not like the name of King, seem anxious to confer kingly powers, under the title of Dictator, Superintendent of Finances, or some such."[38]

Power per se did not frighten McKean. He had coveted and wielded considerable power and influence himself. What he feared was power exercised by those he distrusted or disliked, or for reasons he felt inadequate or dangerous to America's republicanism. Typically, he accepted the concept of a department of marine but assiduously sought to prevent it from falling under Morris' authority.[39]

It was in July 1781, when "the most trifling thing [could] not be done in any department but through Mr. Morris," that the presidency of the Continental Congress was offered to McKean. The incumbent, Samuel Huntington of Connecticut, had asked to be excused because of failing health and the press of personal business. The office was subsequently declined by several members before Congress finally brushed aside McKean's hopes of retirement and prevailed upon him on July 10 to accept the post. At least one cynical observer commented that "the Chair went a begging & many refus'd the dignity; but that must be oweing to a consciousness of their unworthiness—an objection which can by no means apply to the present case." Contemporaries—like later historians—were quick to ascribe McKean's acceptance of the post to vanity; they failed to appreciate his willingness to serve and to sacrifice when others declined.[40]

McKean's hesitancy in accepting the post was sincere; as late as July 8 he did not want the office. Anyone familiar with his appreciation of honors and offices must concede that he surely found the offer enticing. His personal papers establish that despite the prestige and fame it would bring him, however, he did not court the presidency. He took on the duties July 10 only after exacting a promise that he would be allowed to step down in time for the October circuit. He would serve his country for four months, providing he be relieved after that.[41]

One of the first to congratulate him was George Washington, who complained that McKean's predecessor had too often left him "in the dark in matters which essentially concerned the public welfare; and which, if known, might be influential in the Government of my conduct in the Military line." Washington need not have worried about the new president's interest in his affairs, as he soon discovered. McKean established a systematic correspondence with the commander-in-chief and did not confine his comments to matters of public welfare or political concerns. He passed along rumors, military information based on reliable—and some not so reliable—sources, discussed strategy for the American army, and tried on several occasions to outguess the British leadership.[42]

The months McKean spent as president of Congress were exhausting ones for a man already overburdened. He later confessed that it was the most tiring and physically difficult period of his life, an observation that says a good deal, considering his efforts as Delaware's president in September 1777 and his tenure at York during which he was both congressman and judge, and target for British marauders.

McKean tackled his duties with the abandon he gave to any task. As he had written to Dickinson earlier, "What I attempt to do I do with all my Mite."[43]

Yet McKean's presidency was notable neither for its innovation nor its long-range impact on the office. He may have wished to challenge Morris' sway over Congress but there is no evidence he used whatever prestige and power his office had—and it was minimal—to that end. Nor is it likely in view of developments that much support for such a program would have been forthcoming. If his tenure differed markedly from his predecessor's it was in his dedication to the minutiae associated with the office and in his capacity for organization. As noted, he outdid his predecessor in providing General Washington with information; his efforts to correlate state and national strategems, despite some tentative steps in that direction, came to very little. Neither through his presidency nor his many congressional committee assignments did McKean significantly shape the administrative history of Congress. He did seek to revive the flagging American spirit. In almost every letter he commented that America was "at the eve of great events." If optimism would do it, McKean would turn the tide.[44]

In this instance at least he proved prophetic. Washington and his troops, ably aided and abetted by the French, succeeded in choking off the British at Yorktown in October and forcing the surrender of Cornwallis and his entire army. The news of the capitulation reached McKean early on October 22. The official celebration took place two days later and McKean, as president of Congress, became the recipient of official visits from local dignitaries, members of Congress, the Pennsylvania Assembly, and officials of France offering congratulations.

Later, when the victorious French troops marched through Philadelphia, McKean reviewed them dressed, according to his neighbor and friend Peter Du Ponceau, in a black velvet suit, sword by his side. When the captured flags were brought to the city, it was McKean who received them. His letters to General Washington and to the French government remarking on the victory at Yorktown were fulsome in their praise.[45]

McKean stepped down from the presidency of the Continental Congress on November 3, 1781.[46]

10. The Changing Nature of Representation

McKean's rewards for serving as president of Congress were few: exhaustion, an honorary degree from the College of New Jersey, and a bruised reputation.[1] Throughout his tenure as president of Congress he suffered a series of scathing public attacks on his plural office holding. The announcement of his ascendancy to the presidency prompted several anonymous correspondents to take up the controversy over pluralism that had festered since 1779. "Tenax," writing in the *Freeman's Journal,* reminded the people of the Assembly's February 1779 vote against McKean's pluralism,[2] and argued that the state constitution had very wisely guarded not only against the corruption of sinecure but against the excessive growth of power in the hands of a single man, or a few men, by providing that a man should hold no more than one post at a time. Article 23 of the Constitution which provided that the judges of the Pennsylvania Supreme Court "shall not be allowed to sit as members in the continental congress, executive council, or general assembly, nor...hold any other office civil or military," was hotly debated. "Legality" protested that the Article clearly prohibited McKean from serving in both capacities, and asked, "Is it not his duty, as a patriot, to resign his seat in Congress and on the bench, equally tainted with impassible illegality?"³

McKean's friends wasted no time in striking out at his critics. "A Citizen of Philadelphia" argued that the government of Pennsylvania and those who had looked to McKean as its chief justice were aware he was a delegate from Delaware to the Congress. He thought it would be "very unkind and niggardly to deny the services of our able citizens to our neighbors, when they need and solicit them." Moreover, the writer felt that it was silly to assume that because a man functioned for another state that his position or effectiveness was seriously impaired at home. He concluded by suggesting that rather than a bane for Pennsylvania, McKean's position as president of Congress was "certainly a great honor and may be an important advantage to this state." "Senator" concurred. He at least wished to give McKean the benefit of the doubt. To "affirm that one person cannot do the duties of president, member of Congress and chief justice at the same time, is prejudging the gentleman who now holds them," he wrote. "It remains to be seen if he can."⁴

Overall, McKean received little encouragement in the public press. Much of the support he did engender was expressed to him privately. William A. Atlee urged McKean to stay on in both stations. "I can see advantages resulting from [your presidency] to the Confederacy & must congratulate the Union on their acquisition," he wrote, "but my own state in her seats of Justice must suffer, if deprived of those virtues & abilities which made her Courts & her Judges respectable." He seemed eager to retain McKean on the court if only for the help he would bring in squeezing from the Assembly more decent salaries. John Evans, too, was fulsome in his praise of McKean and encouraged him to ignore criticism of his pluralism. He assured his fellow justice that the opposition came from "little invious [sic] minds who have their own supposed greatness ultimately in view, but who have neither ability nor popularity"; McKean could take comfort, according to Evans, in the knowledge that he had the unqualified "approbation of the disinterested & virtuous people."⁵

McKean himself publicly lashed out at "Tenax" and "Legality," calling them "puppies" who bark at "any great... object." Noting that both authors "seemed to have little learning, and the latter ["Legality"] cannot write English," McKean was persuaded that their attacks were rooted in "envy or malice." In vigorous albeit strained argument, he observed of the Assembly's earlier [1779] vote, that "though every man is obliged to know the laws of the country he resides in, and to square his conduct by them, yet no man is legally bound to know or take notice of any resolve, vote or minute of the house of assembly, unless duly served with a properly authenticated copy." He conceded that a chief justice of Pennsylvania could not also be a representative in Congress from Pennsylvania, but Article 23 did not preclude, or mean to preclude, that judge from being a member of Congress, of Council, or assembly from *another* state. At least publicly he rejected any thought of reducing his commitment to Congress in the face of such criticism. He reminded his detractors that his being a judge while sitting in Congress as a representative from Delaware was nothing new; everyone knew his position in 1777. Nor did his current conduct constitute either misbehavior or maladministration of office. Any talk of impeachment was both irresponsible and futile. As he had no intention of resigning either of his posts, the issue, at least so far as he was concerned, was closed.⁶

If he thought his pronouncements would end the matter, he was sorely disappointed. His comments merely fed the flames. "Tenax" responded to McKean's slurs on his education by reminding the judge that the laws were for men "of but little learning as well as for the wise and great." He accused him of being more technical than accurate in his explanation of Article 23, and he suggested that McKean's interpretation left open the possibility that he could hold an office under one of the European states while retaining his judicial seat. He asked the citizens of Pennsylvania whether Congress was "so poor in worthy men, that they can find no other president?" Can the state of Delaware find no other delegate? Can Pennsylvania find no other judge? Are we reduced to this distress in America, he asked? Though "Tenax" would have denied it, the answer to at least the first two seemed to be a conclusive no.[7]

Despite Thomas Rodney's sound advice to ignore the "boisterous clamor . . . until like the foaming sea beating against the rock it subsides by itself," McKean could remain neither passive nor silent. He was not persuaded by Rodney's insistence that the accusations would leave "no unfavorable impression on anyone's mind not already prejudiced against you," or that "active men will always have enemies"—even though these were two of his own favorite homilies.[8]

On August 22, 1781, McKean, this time signing his own name, stripped the mask from those who had attacked him behind pseudonyms. He identified "Tenax" as Jonathan Dickinson Sergeant, his former attorney general, observing that in his last "pretty piece" Sergeant claimed to be a painter. McKean would leave it to Sergeant "to finish his own portrait." "Legality" and "most if not all the others" were said to be William Clajon, a Frenchman who "has never taken the oath of allegiance to the Commonwealth" and a man who "receives fifty-six dollars a month from congress as secretary to General Gates as interpreter of the northern department," a position which was in fact a sinecure, for those were "stations for which he does no duty."[9]

Constitutionalists were frequently unhappy with McKean's propensity to pursue an independent course and to challenge the assumptions of his own government as he did in the matters of habeas corpus and the Penns' lands. There were those who viewed his essential moderation in the oyer and terminer proceedings late in 1778 and into 1780 as equally disturbing. Some argued that his dual roles diverted his attention from critical issues, that his commitment to his congressional duties in York, while admirable, had prevented him from sufficiently stimulating county courts to prosecute Tories in the critical first months of 1778.

Criticism in Pennsylvania to McKean's dual roles stemmed as much from constitutional grounds as from political or personal considerations. Those most responsible for the creation of the Pennsylvania Constitution of 1776, and those most ardent in support of it in 1779, found themselves in something of a quandary, for as advocates of a one-man, one-office ratio and the concept of rotation in office as essential for a truly democratic government, they were faced with a flagrant violation of those principles by a man who had been a vital factor in their success. McKean's acceptance of the chief justiceship in July 1777, when prominent men were seeking to render the government stillborn, had given a substantial boost to radical hopes for survival.

Ironically, those in opposition—the Republicans—conceded the right of a public figure to more than one public office, and they lent their support to the harassed chief justice. Some of course acted out of spite, in an effort to embarrass the Constitutionalists. Others—and they seemed to have been in the majority—acted out of a conviction that McKean, for all his personal faults, was a sound chief justice and had carried out his plural functions reasonably and effectively. To admit less would have been to undermine their belief that good men should hold office, as many offices as they could accumulate. Pennsylvanians were thus treated to the spectacle of the supporters of the Constitution fulminating against their own chief justice and their political enemies rallying to his defense.

If some Pennsylvanians seemed eager for McKean to reduce the number of his offices, Delaware Whigs harbored no such sentiments. The opposition to him in Delaware was minor and based largely on local considerations rather than on any concern with his Pennsylvania connections. Some antipathy was personal and dated from the period preceding the imperial crisis; some was in response to his eagerness after 1765 to push the Colonies into a strong position against the Mother Country. Provoked by his early commitment to the more radical Whigs' program, particularly in Congress between 1774 and 1776, and stung by his opposition in Delaware's constitutional convention late in 1776, conservatives sought to strip him of his political power. The very conservative and Tory elements never reconciled themselves to McKean serving them, but moderate Delawareans—men like George Read and John Dickinson—recognized McKean's value to the state and resigned themselves to it.

With good cause. In spite of his "irregular" attendance in Congress after 1777 due to commitments in Pennsylvania, in contrast to his Delaware colleagues he was a conscientious congressman, frequently serving at the cost of health and family tranquility. In his absences Delaware more often than not went unrepresented in the national government. Of the 478 congressional votes recorded for Delaware between 1778 and 1783 McKean participated in 343, or 74.7 percent; in 40.4 percent of Delaware's votes in the same period he cast the only vote attributed to his state. In 1780 and 1781 alone, of the 119 votes cast by Delaware delegates 90 were single votes and he cast 75 of those. He participated in 104 of the 119 votes recorded. The rewards—at least the measurable ones—were minimal. Late in 1780 he begged John Dickinson that the Assembly relieve him of duties or at least provide a substitute whenever the judiciary or his obligations as a trustee of the University of Pennsylvania called him elsewhere. He reminded Dickinson that Delaware had failed to compensate him by a single farthing since January 1779.[10]

Three weeks before McKean stepped down from the presidency of Congress Nicholas Van Dyke announced that once out of Congress he could no longer spend his personal fortune in travel, rent, entertainments, and other profitless burdens incumbent upon a congressman in Philadelphia. Van Dyke and Caesar Rodney knew McKean wanted to quit his congressional post. Rodney's confession that there were no talented men to replace McKean, and Van Dyke's decision to quit virtually assured McKean that Delawareans would call on him again to represent them.[11]

Actually, Delaware Whigs pressed McKean to hold down three posts; they insisted he was needed in their legislature. McKean announced publicly his desire to give up his Assembly post in September 1777, but zealous Whigs would have none of it. In January 1778 Samuel Patterson wrote to McKean in York urging him to return to Delaware; the legislators had sat for twenty days and "did little or no business." According to Patterson, only McKean knew "how to steer through the Story that is in this unhappy State." A few months later Caesar Rodney wrote to say that "Most [of the Assemblymen] are new members...They want a Pen...They want you."[12]

Despite McKean's intense desire to resign in August 1778, Whig leaders continued to look to him for leadership in

Delaware. "I will push McKean," Samuel Patterson told Caesar Rodney during a discussion on how to make the legislature effective, "he will not refuse." McKean's New Castle constituents swept aside his protestations and re-elected him in October. Thomas Rodney told him that his election "more than compensate [s] for our losses here [in Kent]." "Unless you come down," he warned McKean, the Assembly "will be... at a loss for a person of sufficient knowledge in business to direct them."[13]

It was not until September 1779 that McKean took decisive steps to resign from the Delaware Assembly. This time he traveled to New Castle during the October elections and pleaded in person for the people of that county to release him from service. He was not reelected to the Assembly; his congressional duties, however continued.[14]

One finds in McKean's presidential correspondence a persistent exhortation for Americans to have faith that the nation was "then at the eve of great events." Yet it would appear that few in Delaware shared his optimism, even after the American success at Yorktown. Conditions in Delaware seemed, if anything, to be deteriorating and relations with Congress worsening. The promise of an energetic government, the end of anarchy and the creation of the aggressive and disciplined militia anticipated in the leadership of Caesar Rodney had by 1781 gone largely unfulfilled. The people of Delaware were still subject to frequent depredations by Tories as well as by marauders from Pennsylvania and Maryland. The judicial system, particularly at the county level, was clearly unable to cope with current exigencies.

Discontent in Delaware gave rise in late 1781 to increasing conservatism. While it is not clear that the state government was becoming more responsive to the wishes of the people by 1781 or that the people had moved the representatives towards a closer adherence to their will, there did exist a ragged correlation between the temper of the people and the Assembly. George Read and his followers, always more cautious and restrained in responding to events of the Revolution than was the Rodney-Van Dyke-McKean coalition, seized upon deepening discontent to effect a change in the state government. They successfully backed for the presidency John Dickinson, whose semi-retirement from state politics and casual attendance in the Continental Congress had spared him the enmities accruing to more active public figures. Dickinson took office November 13, 1781, ten days after McKean resigned the presidency of Congress.

Thomas Rodney pressed for more states-conscious delegates in Philadelphia. He was concerned about the changing climate in Delaware and growing nationalistic stress in Congress. His anxiety was not apparently caused by anything McKean had done in office, although McKean had been Delaware's sole representative after August 20, but rather by conviction that any concerted effort to strengthen the national government would damage the interests of Delaware. Despite minor disagreements, usually involving strategy, McKean's politics seemed to please Rodney. Rodney had been one of McKean's chief supporters for the presidency of Congress in July; in fact, he claimed sole credit for McKean's appointment.

Dickinson shared Rodney's desire for a more effective state government and a stronger congressional delegation but he had very different long-range goals. Whereas Rodney would bolster the state's power for that end alone, Dickinson viewed such strengthening as a first step toward insuring an American union. Dickinson argued that until the individual state governments were vigorous and capable the American union would remain enfeebled. Central to his program was a desire to wed Delaware to the Continental Congress, a congress hopefully revitalized and centralized.[15]

He advocated that four men rather than the usual three be chosen, and that they should be a different breed. Largely at his urging, Delaware chose Dickinson's brother Philemon and Samuel Wharton, Caesar Rodney, and McKean as congressional delegates on February 2, 1782. Instructions were drawn up to guide the new delegates along more comprehensive and restrictive lines than previously. These instructions were a ploy by Dickinson and his supporters to tie the delegates more closely to the Dickinson government; they were not, as some historians have suggested, an outgrowth of a revolutionary desire for faithful adherence of congressional representatives to the aspirations of the majority.[16]

The more zealous Delaware Whigs condemned Dickinson's "new system" and raged against the naming of men like Philemon Dickinson and Samuel Wharton to the congressional posts. Wharton, according to the embittered Thomas Rodney, had "no Knowledge of or connection with the affairs of this State, and perhaps hardly an acquaintance in it except with G[eorge] Read."[17] The choice of Wharton and Dickinson was in fact consistent with Dickinson's national emphasis. In this light it is interesting to speculate on the motives behind the retention of McKean in Philadelphia by the Dickinson-Read faction. Was his selection—and that of Caesar Rodney—merely a sop to the opposition, an effort to reduce factionalism within the state? Were McKean's views by this time consistent with those of the new leader? Was he included simply because he lived in Philadelphia so could continue to serve the state?

McKean had recently expressed some criticism of Rodney's administration, particularly with regard to continuing judicial paralysis, but the Rodneys had remained blissfully uncritical of McKean and it is unlikely that McKean's drift from allegiance to Caesar Rodney was so noticeable as to ally him with Dickinson's politics. After all, Rodney himself was named as a delegate. It is possible that both McKean and Rodney were seen as token delegates. Both were reluctant to serve; by naming two such distinguished members of the opposition, both of whom would probably spend very little time in Congress, the Dickinson faction could have the best of both worlds.[18]

McKean continued to be an ideal representative from Delaware's point of view. Many of the disagreements between himself and Dickinson had by 1781 dissolved.[19] Even during his alignment with the Lee-Adams faction McKean had remained basically conservative in matters of personal and property rights. Two influences had moved him toward closer alliance with the Morris group in Congress and the Dickinson faction in Delaware. The first was his increasingly federal or centralist perspective, gained in handling a multiplicity of issues during his long tenure in the Congress. The second was his growing appreciation of the financial emergency and its implications to the war effort after 1779. Still, McKean's conservatism was hardly the deciding issue. His integrity and fidelity to Delaware had never been questioned by Read or

Dickinson, for whom he often covered in the Congress in spite of their hearty opposition to his policies and methods.

McKean's loyalty to Dickinson was unaffected by jabs at the Delaware president by "Valerius" for his pluralism and power-seeking in one state while frustrated in another.[20] McKean had heard it all before. "Valerius'" accusations that the state adhered to "foreign" representatives. did affect McKean's career, however. In February 1783 Delaware terminated McKean's congressional career by naming only local men as delegates.[21]

Delaware delegates were neither good Delawareans nor good democrats, the anonymous critic had written. "Look at your delegation, compare it with the great original cause of the present war." Admittedly the records and reputations of Philemon Dickinson and Samuel Wharton did little to invalidate such accusations.[22] John Dickinson's abrupt resignation from the presidency of Delaware on November 4, brought home "Valerius'" questions concerning representatives whose loyalty lay in another state or in their own reputations and special interests. Dickinson's eagerness to seek the presidency of Pennsylvania with Republican support gave Delawareans the impression that he had cavalierly used them for political advancement. They were not anxious to be taken in again, either by the state government or the state's delegation to Philadelphia.[23]

McKean had read attacks on his pluralism year after year and did not resist when Delaware first tied him more closely to the state then terminated his congressional duties so that "locals" might serve; but he accepted in theory neither the criticisms of pluralism nor the basis for Delaware's actions. He persisted in his beliefs in traditional pluralism and representation.

Though McKean's last official connection with Delaware was severed in 1783, he did not hesitate to interfere in Delaware government matters after that date. In 1790 he plunged into a controversy between his old friend Thomas Rodney and the Assembly over an alleged debt the Rodney estate owed the State of Delaware dating back to Revolutionary days. McKean sought to save his friend on a private level but accomplished little. He offered Rodney and his son, Caesar Augustus, free advice, commiseration, and little more. Rodney

Caesar A. Rodney. Courtesy of Delaware Archives, Hall of Records, Dover, Delaware

went to jail and remained there until 1792; much of his estate was lost. By then McKean, painfully aware that he was impotent to help, withdrew from the matter. A prime reason for his decision to back off was his failure to enlist the New Castle delegation in the Assembly behind the Rodneys' interests as he had promised to do.[24]

Friendship and political considerations both prompted McKean's efforts to aid the Rodneys. He wanted to strike out at former opponents who in his opinion now perpetrated injustices upon his friends, and for the past several years he had been embroiled with Delaware officials over the status of Delaware lands. In 1789 Edmund Physick, agent for Proprietary claims, returned to the United States to negotiate the settlement of Penns' lands in Delaware. Evidence reveals that Physick expected to secure the services of George Read and McKean in resolving the land issue, but after conferences with both it was apparent that Read could not or would not work toward the Penns' interests. McKean was willing to aid Physick.[25]

When Delaware sought permission from Physick in 1789 to cultivate portions of the New Castle Common, McKean proposed that negotiations include a wider range of settlements. Physick and McKean were granted plenary powers by the Penns for the settlement of rents and lands in Delaware. As the agents they offered the governor of Delaware first opportunity to the state to purchase the lands under review. On learning these startling developments the people of Delaware reacted much as did their representatives: they demanded that the Assembly purge the state dockets of feudal claims and quit-rents. The Assembly responded with resolutions prohibiting McKean and Physick from acting, asserting its prerogative in matters of state lands.[26]

Those offended by McKean's role as agent tried to discredit him by suggesting the Penns paid him five hundred pounds a year; he was accused of selling his loyalties for hard money. McKean replied that he had not received nor had he been promised compensation. He had only wanted to see the issue settled quickly and amicably between parties who both trusted him. His answer did not preclude receiving compensation at a later date and indeed he did receive a substantial sum.[27]

Meanwhile Physick and McKean retaliated to the Assembly's resolutions by publishing *A Calm Appeal to the People of Delaware* wherein they reviewed the legalities and history of the Penns' claims and offered to let the Supreme Court of the United States arbitrate the difficulty. The *Calm Appeal* also hinted that one remedy, to repeal the Assembly resolutions, "could be achieved only through the election of new and more sympathetic representatives." A political fact conceded by all, the observation bordered nonetheless on tampering with the internal affairs of an independent state. To have made such a suggestion to the people of Delaware while in office as chief justice of Pennsylvania's Supreme Court was for McKean an act of incredible insensitivity. His rationale was based on the conviction that the Assembly's prohibitive action was in violation of the Treaty of Peace and the state and federal constitutions; he judged the action to be a bill of attainder and an ex post facto law. Delaware authorities were unimpressed with his argumentation; they confiscated the Penns' lands and offered no indemnity to the Penns' heirs.[28]

Failure to fulfill his purpose in this matter, as in the Thomas Rodney case, was particularly galling to McKean. He seemed genuinely shocked at Delaware's abrupt and abrasive response. In July 1792 he reviewed his activities for his old friend John Dickinson, still convinced that his proposals and conduct as an agent for the Penns had been "generous." There was no reason, he argued, that the whole of the lands could not be sold at public auction, "either by the entirety or by counties, or by parcels to the highest bidders." He thought the Delaware Assembly of 1775 would have accepted such an offer had one been proferred, and reminded Dickinson that he himself owned "about a thousand acres . . . and [his] relatives a great deal more in New Castle," subject to the same terms.[29]

McKean's willingness to "represent" the people and interests of Delaware after 1783, either in his private capacity as friend of Thomas Rodney or as agent for the Penns, produced moderate grumbling among Delaware assemblymen and citizens privy to his actions. In the end nothing much came of these activities, but his tenacious adherence to time-worn views of pluralism and representation was to have a profoundly unsalutary effect on his later political career. If he found it easy to concur in theory with the growing assumption that representatives were merely the "tools" of the people rather than their rulers, he found it impossible in his own case to act on that premise.

11. New Directions

McKean's professional career had changed along with political changes in Delaware. His shifting political and judicial perspectives, and the evolving demands upon his court during the Confederation, further affected his profession. He discovered that the cessation of hostilities with Great Britain did not end the challenges to his court or guarantee increased popularity for himself or his court.

He did not pursue a deliberately conservative, counter-revolutionary path as chief justice after 1782 but it was clear to court observers that his decisions did not always enhance the position of his government nor comfort those zealous Constitutionalists who hoped that the Revolution would destroy the stranglehold of English law as well as English power and influence.

The question of just how much English law should be retained as relevant for Pennsylvanians would not be argued publicly for several more decades. But how much English law had been transferred to the American colonies? How much of it was workable now that America was separated from the Mother Country? These were questions among lawyers and legislators and the subject of a number of important cases. One such case, *Morris's Lessee* v. *Vanderen,* came before the McKean court in April 1782.

In this case the plaintiff sought to recover through an ejectment a plot of land on the west side of Second Street in Philadelphia. To substantiate his claim he offered the court a variety of documents, among them a draft from the surveyor general's office naming the original purchasers from whom he derived his claim, a survey copied from the surveyor's book, and several personal letters; he produced a probate of a will and a deed, both executed in England but recorded in Pennsylvania. Finally he offered a deed executed in England, recognized in Pennsylvania but never officially recorded. A number of witnesses stood ready to verify his legal claims.

The defendant's counsel maintained that the plaintiff should provide the actual deeds which were then still extant and that the survey which the plaintiff had copied did not in fact exist. Counsel also pointed out that a probate of wills was not evidence in land cases. What the case boiled down to was to determine whether or not certain British statutes, notably those dealing with embracery and a statute of limitations, were in force in Pennsylvania.

To McKean it was beyond debate that not all English statutes were in force or ever had been in force in Pennsylvania. Sir William Jones, attorney general under Charles II, had determined in a 1681 decision that unless British statutes had been specifically directed toward the Colonies, or accepted by action of their local Assemblies, the statutes were not in force in America.[1] McKean believed that such statutes could be transferred by practice and custom, however, seriously complicating the task of identifying with precision just what law had crossed the Atlantic. McKean also assumed that the common law of England had always been in force in Pennsylvania whenever it proved adaptable to the circumstances of the new country. But as a lawyer with considerable practice in Pennsylvania

McKean knew, as did the current crop of attorneys, that it was almost impossible to define with any exactitude just what that meant in terms of specific cases.

The ultimate significance of *Morris's Lessee* v. *Vanderen* was McKean's definition of precisely what part of English law continued to impinge upon the lives of Pennsylvanians. He concluded that the statute on limitations had always been in effect in Pennsylvania but the statute on embracery had not.[2]

The following September McKean wrestled again with the workability of English law when, in *Respublica* v. *Mesca,* four Italians were charged with the murder of a ship's captain. Defended by Jared Ingersoll and a Mr. Swift, the defendants sought to challenge the jury system and gain an award of a tales de medietate linguae, based on a statute from 28 Edward 3. 13. Basically, what the defendants' lawyers wanted was a jury at least partially comprised of their countrymen, or if the state could not provide such a jury to have the case dismissed. Ingersoll and Swift argued that statute 28 Edward 3. 13 had been in force in Pennsylvania prior to the Revolution and "sound policy justified its continuance." To substantiate their claims they called on one Thomas Clifford, who testified that when in February 1764 a German named William Frederick Ottenreed was arrested for burglarizing his home the state granted to Ottenreed a "moiety of foreigners on his jury."

The prosecution did not deny that certain English laws and practices had been and continued to be part of Pennsylvania law. The attorney general did deny that this particular statute, this mode of trial, was part of Pennsylvania's inheritance from Great Britain; neither the legislature nor the courts had declared it part of the rule of law, according to William Bradford. Moreover, a trial per medietatem linguae had never been granted to local Indians or to Blacks. Such a system might even be detrimental, denying to foreigners the protection of Pennsylvania's guarantee of a jury and counsel. To assume that the practice was part of the system on the basis of only one case, and that case based on the recollection of one man, was unwarranted, Bradford held.

McKean, impressed with the arguments on both sides and their "full consideration of the subject," had "little difficulty" in pronouncing the court's decision. The statute of 28 Edward

3. 13 was in force in colonial Pennsylvania, and the legislation emanating from the Assembly in 1776 made clear its transference to the post-revolutionary period. That was clear enough. What was less clear was whether that statute also pertained to supreme court rulings. The first legislature under the Commonwealth had ruled that "such of the statutes as have been in force in the late Province of Pennsylvania, should remain in force, till altered by the Legislature." Whether the legislature also meant "to comprehend likewise, such statutes, as had been extended by the judgment of the supreme court, or received there in usuage, seemed to be, in some degree, less certain." Many statutes for "near a century" had been practiced in the late Province although never formally accepted, and they had been in force in Pennsylvania, at least this was implicit in a British statute passed in 1754 enabling legatees to be witnesses to wills and testaments.

On the grounds that a precedent had been established, McKean ruled that the court was bound on this occasion to grant a trial per medietatem linguae. He said that without a precedent he would have been reluctant to grant it, however. He thought the practice pernicious to freedom and lectured the court's observers on the advantages of American customs and legal safeguards. At no time did the McKean court entertain the denial of English law in Revolutionary America or advocate the wholesale replacement of British precedents by an American common law. But it admitted the superiority of some particular American law and customs on more than one occasion.[3]

If the more extreme Constitutionalists would have liked McKean to use his judicial weight to chart a new course for Pennsylvania law and were frustrated by his independence and judicial conservatism, most were willing to use his name and influence whenever possible to achieve their ends. In the fall of 1782 when Constitutionalists' hopes of maintaining power in the Council and elsewhere appeared slim, they suggested McKean be proposed for Council from Chester County with the idea that, if successful, he would then easily be elected president. McKean could then secure for Joseph Reed the vacated chief justiceship, a move that would assure Reed, who had been outside the sphere of power for over a year, a return to prominence.

The rationale for rallying around McKean as bearer of the party's fortunes was sound enough. The chief opposition would come from John Dickinson, whose successful career as Delaware's president had encouraged Pennsylvania's Republicans to press him to return to Pennsylvania politics as president of the Council. McKean, like Dickinson, was basically conservative, a man who had retained even in the face of repeated newspaper attacks some semblance of non-partisanship. Moreover, McKean was one of the most visible men in Pennsylvania; his contacts were many, and his influence undisputed.[4]

McKean was not altogether pleased with the ploy for several reasons. The possibility of a head-on confrontation with his friend Dickinson once both were in the Council had its drawbacks. Further, in October 1782 McKean was serving the last months of his term as Delaware's congressional representative and those who protested his holding the chief justice post while serving in Congress would be no less angered by his holding the presidency of the state while retaining his congressional office. Joseph Reed, who had much to gain from McKean's election in Chester, was certain that McKean was not doing all he could to assure the success of his election.[5]

The strategem of the Constitutionalists was quickly perceived by the Republicans. "Quidnunc," writing in the unfriendly *Independent Gazetteer,* asked if the good people of Chester were going to "rob the state of Pennsylvania of an upright and impartial judge, and Congress of a useful member?" He also asked if it was true that "the Independent Electors of Chester County can not find a person in that extensive county, qualified to fill the office of Counsellor" without relying upon McKean. "Anti-Quibbler" affected not to be concerned if Chester voters should elect McKean to the Council but he reminded them that McKean would possibly be succeeded on the bench by the abrasive Reed.[6]

McKean's chances for election were not enhanced by the furor of several court cases in late September and early October. He was again embroiled in the old question of pluralism, and in confrontation with the army, issues calculated to embarrass him personally and politically. During the September 1782 oyer and terminer court term, McKean fined one Colonel Francis Nichols £50 for assaulting Joseph Gardner, a member of the Supreme Executive Council. Eleazer Oswald, the fiery editor of the *Independent Gazetteer,* considered the fine exorbitant, reflecting the chief justice's irrational treatment of army personnel. The incident occurred on the eve of the Chester election; the two developments were discussed side by side in the *Gazetteer.*[7]

McKean lost the contest, whether by reason of such embarrassments or his personality and record on the bench. Whatever the cause, the voters of Chester chose to return John McDowell.[8] McKean was no doubt discomfited, but Joseph Reed was bitter and turned his anger and frustration on McKean. Never close, the two were now estranged. McKean sought to assuage Reed by nominating him to replace Robert R. Livingston in the foreign department, but the gesture only deepened Reed's bitterness. "Mr. McKean had an opportunity to have obliged me," Reed told George Bryan two months after the election, "but as he did not make use of that, I presume this is by way of compensation." He was determined to quash the nomination; he had no desire to be reduced to "one of Morris' underlings" in Congress.[9]

On April 16, 1783, Sheriff William Will announced to the citizens of Philadelphia that hostilities between Great Britain and America had ceased. For McKean the prospect of leisure time and tranquility promised by peace and the termination of his congressional term failed to materialize. As the fall months passed, McKean found himself once more in an imbroglio which assumed political as well as judicial dimensions.

The incident had its origins when a local election official, John Cling (or Kling), requested Colonel Thomas Proctor to show his certificate of oath of allegiance to the state. Proctor, an impulsive and turbulent man, deemed such a request an insult in light of his meritorious army record. The colonel berated Cling; then, upon meeting him the next day, struck him. Cling brought charges of assault against him and on November 24 the grand jury handed down an indictment against Colonel Proctor.

Unrepentant throughout his trial, Proctor asserted that he had "chastised [Cling] according to his deserts." McKean lectured Proctor on his conduct, reportedly saying, "You Gentlemen of the army hold your head too high, but I will teach you how to behave.... I will bring you down, we shall be overrun else." He fined the Colonel £ 80.

Oswald, already incensed over McKean's recent treatment of Francis Nichols for his assault on Joseph Gardner, lashed out at McKean in an October 1 article signed "A Friend of the Army," in which he criticized McKean, calling his conduct of both trials "unmerciful," "ungenerous," even "improper." He asked McKean if he had "acquired an intuitive knowledge, an infallible rule by which you can perfectly comprehend the merits of every case from hearing one side only."[10]

"The Tatler" discussed the characteristics of Judge Jeffries, drawing a parallel between Jeffries' "strong and ungovernable passions [and] generally insolent" behavior in office and McKean's reputation. "Mathematicus" asked pointedly, "if to flagellate a Counsellor costs £ 50 and to chastise an insolent, unworthy officer cost £ 80 ... what sum is required to correct the vilest Hostler, garbed in black?"[11]

Almost apoplectic over what he deemed a libel against him in the "A Friend of the Army" article, McKean sent for Oswald on October 12, reprimanded him, and ordered him to post a surety for £ 750 guaranteeing his future good behavior. As combative as the chief justice, the editor retaliated by accelerating his newspaper attacks against McKean and the court. On October 15 he described his confrontation with McKean for his readers, republished the offending article by "A Friend of the Army," and added a number of others highly critical of the chief justice. The irate justice again called him before the court to answer for his conduct. Specifically, McKean wished to know the author of "A Friend of the Army." Oswald refused to provide the information and was placed on bail for £ 1000. Undaunted, Oswald suggested to his readers that the chief justice was incapable of understanding the benefits derived by the people of Pennsylvania from the army and furthermore accused McKean of speculating in distressed soldier certificates. If McKean was not committed to bringing Oswald down before this accusation appeared in print, he certainly was afterward.[12]

Oswald's attack on McKean and the courts, and McKean's personal response to Oswald, provoked an onslaught of articles dealing with a free press and the rights of individuals as guaranteed by the state constitution. If McKean's surveillance

Eleazer Oswald. Courtesy of City Archives, Philadelphia

of the local press was deemed unwarranted and, indeed, destructive by many, it did serve to stimulate important public debates of issues and values crucial to the survival of a republic. Throughout October and November barrage after barrage was leveled at McKean. "Wilkes" wrote that the press should be "completely free and unrestrained." If indeed the press occasionally went beyond good taste and propriety it was a small price to pay for freedom. The public should be willing to tolerate "partial evil for universal good." He reminded the people of Pennsylvania that men in high office had been historically unfriendly to a free press. "Koster" went still further, pointing out that Oswald's rights were guaranteed by Sections 12 and 35 of the state constitution. Thus, to attack Oswald was in this instance to attack the state's fundamental law and the freedoms it guaranteed. "Junius Wilkes" also supported Oswald: men in high offices should be accountable to the people and only through an energetic press could such an accountability be guaranteed or secured. The constitution recognized the right of anyone to treat and examine the conduct of government, and thus seditious libel in this instance was not applicable. Moreover, if McKean felt unduly accused he could always take advantage of a free press to argue the merits of his conduct.[13]

Such opinions reflected the belief that Oswald was being punished for telling the truth. When it became clear that McKean was determined to seek an indictment against the editor for "publishing a false, scandalous, and malicious libel," public furor mounted. "Candid" thought that the truth should be an adequate defense for such charges; he stressed that "even mistakes in matters of fact, not proceeding from design, and malice" ought to be ignored by the courts, for the "best men, with the best intentions, may err, and too much severity towards such mistakes would render this boasted privilege a nullity." He pinpointed the source of Oswald's present sense of injustice and McKean's overzealousness in Pennsylvania's indiscriminate borrowings from English law. "Candid" called for a commission to select English laws more suitable to Pennsylvania and exclude the rest. He suggested the first to go should be the English laws of libel.[14]

On the day the grand jury met to consider bills to indict Oswald, "A Hint to Grand Juries" appeared in the *Gazetteer* warning the jury to acquaint themselves with questions of libel and to consider deeply the implications of a guilty verdict against Oswald. This was not the fight of a single man, the article maintained, it was the fight of all citizens for their liberties. The grand jury, doubtless influenced by Oswald's charge that McKean would sacrifice libertarian principles to establish a strong seditious libel law, refused to bring in a true bill.[15]

McKean and Bryan did not accept the jury's vote of ignoramus but sent them back with a reprimand to reconsider. Such a practice was not unusual in Pennsylvania courts; in this case the jury, stung by the attitude of the judges and the tone of their reprimand, produced a memorial expressing displeasure at the court and justifying their conduct. McKean brushed aside the memorial and dismissed the jurors. The grand jury memorial was printed in full in the *Gazetteer*.

McKean had evidently wanted to force the grand jury to bring forth a bill and then let the court and a petty jury decide the issue. He believed the grand jury refused to indict for political reasons, and were swayed by Oswald's propaganda in the *Gazetteer* into thinking him innocent. But the jury's task was not to determine guilt or innocence; it was to decide whether there was sufficient evidence for a trial. As subsequent events were to make clear, McKean was also chary of permitting grand juries—or petty juries, for that matter—wide latitude in interpreting the law. The courts or the legislature should determine the course of the law, according to McKean, not local juries subject to transitory political passions and personal pettiness.[16]

Sides were quickly drawn in the local press. "Civis," "Cicero," and "A By Stander" all attacked McKean and the court, "Cicero" repeating Oswald's opinion that McKean was another Jeffries.[17] McKean and Bryan were quick to respond: they described the historical development of the grand jury system and showed how its powers and duties were clearly violated by the actions of the current jury. Bryan, more liberal than McKean, emphasized that the jury as a tool of the court and subservient to it should have responded to the witnesses provided by it. The court was obligated to correct the grand jury whenever it erred, as it certainly had in this instance, according to Bryan. McKean, disturbed by the increasing propensity of citizens—and juries—openly and uncivilly to challenge their superiors in the press and to criticize the workings of the government, took a similar tact. He also pointed out the illegality of the jury's efforts to procure witnesses other than those provided by the court. "There is respect due to a Grand Jury," he wrote, "but there is a greater respect due to the highest court of criminal jurisdiction in that state."[18]

The Oswald case gave Francis Hopkinson an excellent opportunity to vent his spleen against McKean in particular and the court in general. Personally incompatible, repelled by McKean's arrogance, jealous of his power and influence, and resentful of McKean's purchase of his sister's magnificent house following its confiscation by the state,[19] Hopkinson had become McKean's most bitter and persistent critic. So intent was he on ridiculing McKean and Bryan in this instance that his talent for humor often failed. Still, he was frequently able to make his points with a skill matched by few of his contemporaries. Bryan's actions in the Oswald matter he dismissed as the result of inadequate training. McKean's behavior was more dangerous: it was the product of a flawed personality and unrepublican principles.[20]

McKean's circuit duties provided some escape from the Philadelphia press, but even the judicial circuit brought McKean and his "legal cavalcade" (as William Bradford called those who accompanied him on the rounds of the county court houses) unexpected experiences during this period. Constant through the years, however, were the long and tedious routes sometimes amounting to 150 miles between towns, and rain, hail, wind or snow. Once, late in 1783, the judicial entourage ran into a combination of all four on their way to Washington County. Occasions to dine and socialize with the "great Folks of [each] county" were sometimes offset by periods of boredom, fatigue and inadequate lodging. Or weary justices might find the dockets empty, or experience long delays through the night perhaps, as the court awaited the jury's verdict. "I have seduced the grave judges into so many Schemes of Amusement," William Bradford wrote his financee from the circuit in 1784, "that one might suppose I was striving to forget you." On still another occasion he reported that he had talked with McKean, "until the Chief dozed in his chair."[21]

Yet McKean looked forward to the circuit, attracted in part by its welcome change of pace. "My health requires a ride in to the country," he once wrote George Washington on the eve of a circuit, "and my mind some relaxation." He was attracted, too, by the extraordinary legal demands and circumstances found on the circuit. There the novel became routine, the extraordinary, commonplace. In the West Branch Valley, an area between Lycoming and Pine Creeks along the west branch of the Susquehanna, McKean spent a fascinating afternoon learning from an old Dutch settler the particulars of the local "fair play" law which had governed the "Fair Play Republic" prior to the coming of the McKean court. Late in 1783 in Washington County he found himself overseeing the trial of one James Goffney charged with stealing with force and arms "one pair of silver-plated-spurs of the value of Seven shillings & six Pence." The victim? William A. Atlee. The principal witness? William Atlee. Goffney discovered soon enough that his choice of victim had been a poor one.[22]

The grim realities of backcountry life were not for the squeemish. McKean became no stranger to the raucous, coarse and often violent life beyond Philadelphia. Every court term brought before the courts the full play of dissipation, brutality, desperation, and fear continually unfolding on the frontier. Elizabeth Wilderness burned in the left hand for brutally slashing to death her husband, father of her eight children; the Negro York, servant of Chester's Michael Ege, executed for "ravishing a white woman"; Patrick McSherry, Jr., tried for hacking John Weigert to death with a sickle; John McDonald tried for murdering Laurence Kreamer's wife and son and burning Kreamer's home. Stories of desperation. The execution of Elizabeth Wilson for snuffing out the lives of her bastard twin sons. Margaret Angle, spinster, charged with murdering her "new born male bastard." Margaret Lour and Elizabeth Veiner, both single women, accused of murdering Miss Lour's bastard child. Licentiousness and hate. The stark and earthy testimony of any number of buggery, sodomy, rape, and fornication cases. And, occasionally, compassion. The freeing of blacks accused of murder, rape, arson in hostile communities. McKean heard and saw it all.[23]

The judicial circuit riders went deeper into the frontier country as it developed during and following the war. McKean was impressed with the politeness and sensibilities of some of them, but he wrote Sally from Washington County in 1783 that "the far greater number of both the Justices and Jurors, whom we have seen, are yet but in the middle stages state of Civilization." He judged the war to have badly "retarded their improvement." Three years later conditions had somewhat improved. He could write that "the People appeared to be greatly reformed in their manners; those whom we have conversed with, who are not a few, are as decent & orderly as any persons in the oldest settled counties in Pennsylvania." He was impressed that the people "paid as much attention and respect to the Judges in every way practicable as in any part of the State."[24]

Discernible in all this, and more important than McKean's sensitivity to the deference paid him and the court, was the process by which the backcountry was wedded to the state government in Philadelphia. McKean was a link in this process, for in demanding respect for the court he was demanding respect for the will and authority of the state. He and other judges were an important communication link, too, between the state capital and the local courthouses, between state political figures and local justices of the peace.

The court and the chief justice had their detractors in western courts, however. Many westerners disapproved of court decisions they considered unresponsive to frontier conditions and needs; being a litigious people, they criticized the expense and delay inherent in the system, for example four judges sitting on a single jury trial; even two was to them exorbitant. The elitism of the court and the lawyers attached to it came in for critical commentary as well.[25]

Westerners were particularly outraged by the unresponsiveness of the court to peculiar frontier conditions. At no time did the court seem so oblivious to the wishes of the community or incapable of flexibility in the face of extraordinary circumstances than in the case of the Indian,

Mamachtaga, heard by McKean and Bryan in the fall of 1785.[26] Mamachtaga ("the hurricane"), said to be "the most violent and Bloody Catliff of the Delaware Tribe," was charged with murdering (while in a drunken rage) one John Smith, a sometime day laborer for Hugh Henry Brackenridge. Even though after killing Smith and wounding two others Mamachtaga sobered up enough to appreciate the gravity of his crime, he allowed himself to be turned over to the authorities in Pittsburgh to stand trial.

The community threatened to lynch the Indian and rough up those intent on protecting him, including his attorney (and McKean's long-time friend), Hugh Henry Brackenridge. Fearful that Mamachtaga might be acquitted by "the crooks of the law," the Washington County militia attempted to wrest the prisoner from local authorities and to "Tommihawk" him, but without success. Nonetheless, community leaders were understandably shaken by these events and pleaded with state officials to hasten the circuit judges to Pittsburgh so that decorum and justice could prevail.

Had the issue not been so serious and the outcome so tragic, the proceedings of the court which followed the arrival of Bryan and McKean would have been comical. Mamachtaga obviously understood little of what was happening to him. He paid Brackenridge his fee in the form of one beaver pelt; in doing so he believed he was making full restitution for his crime. His confusion deepened when the court permitted him the right to challenge jurors and when the role of the judges was explained to him. Impressed with the dignity of the two justices dressed in their scarlet robes, Mamachtaga concluded that McKean was God and Bryan the Saviour of Man.

Bryan appeared to be more sympathetic to the Indian's case than McKean. He thought that at least half the jurors should be "foreigners." They need not be Indians to satisfy the law concerning medietatem linquae, he concluded, for such a law "did not require that the aliens be of the nation to which the accused belonged." He remembered a Chester case where an Indian charged with rape was granted such a trial, but in that instance six Indians had been found to serve as jurors. McKean, choosing to interpret narrowly his own ruling in the Mesca case, did not trouble himself with such legal protection for the Indian.

Hugh Henry Brackenridge. Courtesy of City Archives, Philadelphia

The outcome of the case, tried on November 2, 1785, was never in doubt once McKean and Bryan deprived Brackenridge of his only valid argument by ruling against drunkenness as a defense. The jury found the Indian guilty without ever leaving the jury box. The dubious distinction of being the first man hanged in Hanna Town thus went to an unfortunate Indian caught between the values of the two societies in which he lived.[27]

McKean found himself embroiled in an even more sensitive case during the last months of 1785 and the early months of 1786. George Washington had purchased land in Fayette and Washington Counties in 1768 through the offices of one William Crawford, who obtained the land directly from the Indians. Although Washington added to these tracts periodically, he attempted only the most minimal improvements and eventually squatters moved in to work the land. Washington maintained that the squatters "knew the land had been surveyed for [him]; that it was always called [his]." In 1784 he demanded either that they leave or pay rents and formally lease the land. When they refused all his options, he went for help to Thomas Smith, a Philadelphia lawyer recognized for his ability in land cases.

The question of land titles was understandably a sensitive issue in the west. With this in mind, and eager to impress his famous client with his prowess, Smith set out to guarantee the success of Washington's case. An important foundation was laid when, in a case preceding Washington's, Smith won a precedent favorable to Washington's ejectments. In the earlier case the defendant claimed by improvements only, but Smith's objections to having the improvements entered as evidence was upheld by McKean. The plaintiff then produced an order and survey and won his case. The jury, with no evidence on which to judge the defendant's claims, did not even leave the room before returning a verdict for the plaintiff. Smith correctly perceived that McKean's ruling would "produce very important Effects on the Property of that County, and . . . shake the confidence of [Washington's] opponents."

The trial of *Washington v. James Scott, et al.*, argued October 24 to 26, ended as expected, in a victory for Washington. Brackenridge for the settlers argued that Washington's purchases were illegal, having been acquired from the Indians at a time when neither Pennsylvania nor Virginia recognized such sales. He also argued that the settlers, not Washington, had improved the land. The settlers should not have to pay rents or lease lands made valuable by their own efforts, he insisted. It seemed a simple, effective, and from the western point of view, altogether logical and irrefutable stance. Throughout most of Pennsylvania's history it had been customary to give first consideration to actual improvements rather than to the holder of a paper claim. It was also not unusual in colonial cases at least for juries to ignore judges' instructions on the law and decide the law by themselves in both civil and criminal cases.

But here the court cut Brackenridge's eloquence short. No evidence of improvements was allowed and the jury apparently did not act upon its historical right to determine the law in the face of McKean's intransigence. The result was a rather quick disposition of the claims of all thirteen families. It is not clear whether McKean's rule forbidding improvements as evidence applied to claims emanating from the Purchase of 1768 or all purchases. What is demonstrable is that McKean clung to the rule for another nine years. And he did so in the face of opposition from westerners and many of Pennsylvania's lawyers. Brackenridge thought McKean's experience as a Delaware lawyer with that colony's emphasis on paper titles had denied him the opportunity to fully appreciate Pennsylvania's practice of settlement title. He hurried to the Assembly following the trial and successfully persuaded its members to pass an "Actual Settlers Bill," suspending McKean's ruling temporarily in the Purchase of 1768 only.[28]

The thirteen families involved and their western neighbors could not but resent a chief justice and a court capable of ruling against them under the circumstances. This decision no doubt contributed to the animosity manifest for the court in the frontier regions.

One area of the Pennsylvania backcountry presenting McKean's court with particularly deep-rooted and seemingly insoluable problems was in the vicinity of Wyoming, a settlement located on the Susquehanna River a few miles northeast of Wilkes-Barre. The dispute centered around conflicting land titles there between Pennsylvanians and claimants from

Connecticut. Settlers from Connecticut had been encouraged to seek lands there as early as 1750 by various land companies, including the Susquehannah Land Company, which eventually absorbed all the others. Connecticut did not aggressively support her settlers in the Wyoming region until 1771. By then, as McKean was only later to fully appreciate, Connecticut law and custom there were taken for granted. The dispute between settlers from the two colonies flared up in 1775, but was smoothed over in the interests of a solid colonial front against Great Britain. In 1775 McKean was among those congressmen most eager to effect a truce between the warring factions in order to preserve the always fragile colonial unity.[29]

Following the ratification of the Articles of Confederation in 1781, Pennsylvania claimants to land in the Wyoming region petitioned Congress to name a commission to arbitrate their dispute with the Connecticut settlers as provided for in Article IX. McKean, in his capacity as congressman, welcomed Congress' intervention and advocated a congressionally imposed settlement. When Connecticut representatives moved to stall the creation of a congressional commission, McKean opposed them.[30]

In November 1782 a court of commissioners established by Congress held that "the State of Connecticut has no right to the lands in controversy," and that "the jurisdiction and preemption of all territory lying within the charter boundary of Pennsylvania, and now claimed by the State of Connecticut, do of right belong to the State of Pennsylvania." That of course left the question of individual land claims unresolved, but the commission urged that the state of Pennsylvania adopt conciliatory and humane actions regarding the Connecticut claimants.[31]

McKean learned soon enough, as did all concerned, that the findings of the congressional court of commissioners did not end the controversy between Connecticut and Pennsylvania or even reduce the tensions in the disputed areas. Spurred by the court's findings, Pennsylvania settlers (Pennamites) became more aggressive, frequently employing force and violence to have their way. To McKean fell a large share of the task of establishing Pennsylvania law and authority in the troubled Wyoming area.

Prior to the fall of 1783 McKean's attention had been drawn to the Wyoming region primarily by Indian depredations, or by reported Tory activity.[32] One observer described the area as "a strange divided Quarter—Whig, Tory, Yankee, Pennamite Dutch Irish and English influence are strangely blended." Late in 1783 and again in the spring of 1784 Pennamites resorted to force to oust the Yankees from "their" lands. These outrages, spurred by the Connecticut claimants' refusal to accept proferred one-year leases or compensatory lands elsewhere, led to retaliation on the part of the Yankees. Throughout the months of June and July 1784 McKean found himself busily investigating "this very disagreeable Business" and providing the Council with his findings.

The court eventually secured the indictments of more than fifty persons for "Riot and false imprisonment of divers Inhabitants at Wyoming." McKean reported to President John Dickinson that the justices had not yet determined who had been the "first or the greatest aggressors in this Extraordinary violation of order and good Government," but they were confident that the trial in Sunbury, some miles downriver from the Wyoming settlement, would establish the facts. What he learned could hardly have comforted him, however, for the recriminations had moved beyond the respective combatants and had drawn into the brutality and violence innocent bystanders, including women and children of both camps. He learned, too, that his court and laws were among the targets of the Connecticut claimants who complained that Pennsylvania law was a poor substitute for the law they had once known. One claimant expressed the prevailing view when he "damned the laws of Pennsylvania and them that made them."[33]

Depositions of the imprisoned Connecticut claimants also contained complaints that Pennsylvania courts were not functioning fast enough, fair enough or effectively enough. Twenty-seven petitioners muttered about being "confined in two Rooms, in Irons, and nothing to live upon but one pound of Bread a Day" during a long wait for the court to sit. The Wyoming litigants raged that not only did local persons rob and brutalize them and the state militia disarm them, but the court put them under extraordinary "heavy Bonds for [their] Appearance at the . . . Supreme Court."[34]

The response of the McKean court in the fall and winter of 1784 did nothing to change such opinions of the courts. At

Sunbury the grand jury brought true bills against a number of Connecticut claimants for riot, robbery and assault and battery. At court proceedings in Easton, eleven Yankees accused of murder were acquitted, but the court assessed the costs and "laid them under large Bonds with Surety for their good Behavior." To men already burdened with financial woes, the court's assessment seemed patently unfair.[35]

Schemes and counter-schemes continued to wreak that troubled region now part of the newly formed Luzerne County (lying to the south of Wilkes-Barre) following 1785, and to involve McKean in activities there. When rumors coursed through Philadelphia that John Franklin, member of the Susquehannah Company and acknowledged leader of the extremists among the Connecticut settlers, hoped to join forces with Colonel Ethan Allen of Vermont to establish an independent state out of the Wyoming lands, McKean's aid was sought to abort the ploy. William Montgomery, a member of the Council of Censors, wrote McKean in May 1786 that the issue in Wyoming was no longer merely a "Land Jobbing Quarrel... no longer a private Quarrel, it is now a serious Governmental concern." He urged Pennsylvania to "assert her supremacy as fully [in this controversy] as she did her Independence in the late Revolution." He relayed to McKean what current information he had regarding the scheme of John Franklin and Colonel Allen and pressed the chief justice to use the opportunities of his circuits to "remove the scruples of Gentlemen about interesting themselves in the Controversy, as supposing it rather a debate about private property than otherwise."[36]

The alarms voiced by Montgomery and others regarding the possibility of the dismemberment of Pennsylvania were not realized. Though Allen entertained a move to "spedily [sic] repair to Wyoming with a small detachment of Green Mountain Boys to vindicate... the right of soil of those [Connecticut] proprietors," in the end his ambitions came to nothing. By 1787 the main activities in Wyoming centered around a bitter quarrel among the Connecticut claimants over who should lead them and to what strategy they should adhere. John Franklin, who had survived several challenges to his leadership prior to 1787, found himself in that year facing the most formidable attack yet on his position. Timothy Pickering sought to mobilize the settlers of the region behind his own moderate strategy and leadership. A New Englander and a holder of Wyoming lands under a Connecticut title (yet no member of the Susquehannah Company), Pickering worked to wed the settlers to a policy of accomodation with Pennsylvania. He asked that they proclaim their allegiance to the state, forego the extralegal arrangements that had previously served as their local government, and accept the county elections and officials called for by Pennsylvania authorities in Luzerne County. He assured them that the Pennsylvania Assembly would deal fairly with their individual claims and that they need not fear Pennsylvania claimants initiating a rash of ejectment suits in Pennsylvania courts should they follow his lead.[37]

Support for Pickering's claims seemed to have been provided by the Pennsylvania Assembly in March 1786, when it passed the Confirming Act recognizing the right of the Connecticut settlers to lands "occupied or acquired" by actual settlers and assigned to them before the Trenton decree of 1782. Settlers denied their lands by the operation of Pennsylvania law were to be compensated by receiving equivalent grants elsewhere. To confirm their Pennsylvania titles the settlers had only to present their claims to a body of commissioners, of which Pickering was one, within eight months.[38]

McKean, a bystander in much of the interplay between state officials and events in Luzerne, could take comfort in May with Pickering's success in establishing state courts in Wilkes-Barre. Pickering reported on May 29 that officials there had "opened & held the first courts here this day in perfect tranquility." Two other pieces of information in his reports, however, bode ill for the tranquility and acceptance McKean sought. John Franklin was not then in the settlement, and already rumors were rife that the Pennsylvania Assembly would bow to the opposition elicited by the Confirming Act and repeal it. McKean's hopes for tranquility dimmed as did Pickering's in the following months when Franklin returned to foment more disorder. Though elected "the first and only representative for the County of Luzerne" to the Pennsylvania Assembly, John Franklin did not attend and continued in his efforts to undermine Pennsylvania authority in the region. Moderate settlers, most of whom by July had signed a pledge of allegiance to

Pennsylvania, charged that Franklin's absence from the Assembly deprived them of representation and undermined the jurisdiction of Pennsylvania in their lands.[39]

On August 31, McKean ordered the sheriff of Luzerne County to bring John Franklin before him or one of the other justices of the Supreme Court to answer charges "and to be further dealt with according to law." McKean had learned—and by August 31 had "good reason to believe"—that John Franklin was "a pernicious & seditious man, and a person of a disquiet mind" who "contriving, practicing and maliciously & turbulently intend our peace & tranquility, to molest and disturb." He was charged specifically with denying Pennsylvania's jurisdication over the county, and inciting and encouraging inhabitants of the county to disobey Pennsylvania laws and to resist its government.[40]

The county grand jury, perhaps encouraged by McKean's order for his arrest, brought in their own charges against Franklin, finding two bills against him "for breaches of the peace & feloniously stealing and carrying away another man's grain & hay." More critical were the growing charges that he still conspired to dismember Pennsylvania by establishing an independent state out of the county, this time in league with sympathizers in New York. On September 25, 1787, the Council issued a proclamation for his arrest along with three others for misprision of treason. He was seized and jailed in Philadelphia. Shays' Rebellion in Massachusetts provided an ugly backdrop to the charges against John Franklin and convinced many that Pennsylvania could afford no repetition of such chaos. Pickering at least thought that Franklin was clearly guilty and that McKean, whom he considered "an old & able lawyer" whose "law knowledge is rather superior to that of any lawyer in the county of Luzerne" would see the case clearly. Pickering reported that the chief justice had seen "many depositions and proofs of [Franklin's] treasonable practices...in the possession of the executive council."[41]

John Franklin proved to be as disruptive in jail as he had been when free. Almost immediately the question of his bail created friction among legislators, as well as between court and Council. Though his initial application to the Assembly for bail was regarded with favor by the committee to which it was conveyed, the Assembly adamantly refused to allow his freedom. The judges determined to look into the matter of bail themselves and after a full discussion decided on April 16, 1788, to grant the bail "on account of the peculiar circumstances of his case, tho' accused of treason." Foregoing standard procedure, the judges allowed Franklin's £ 2000 bail to be provided by "as many freeholders" as the officials in Luzerne "shall be satisfied are worth two thousand pounds altogether, in that sum." This last decision was the result of a direct plea on the part of Franklin to McKean wherein he stated "the difficulty which would probably take place in procuring any two persons at Luzerne . . . who would be adjudged equal to the Sum Required."

Even so, Franklin remained incarcerated. When friends of his met with McKean early in June to determine why nothing had been done regarding his release, McKean maintained that the issue at this point was out of his hands; members of the Council were apparently preventing his release. When on June 8 a member of the Council finally visited Franklin in jail, the councilor began by arguing that the matter "rested entirely with [McKean] and insisted that the Council had nothing to do in the affair." Under Franklin's questioning, however, he confessed it was his own opinion that the security demanded of Franklin by the court was deemed by Council members to be "insufficient." He himself believed that "not any ten of the Wyoming settlers were worth £ 200 much more £ 2000 [,] that the Whole of the settlers were a pack of thieves from Connecticut who had Robbed others of their Property and now presumed to call it their own."

Some judged the lenient bail demanded by McKean's court to be a ploy to free Franklin quickly so that he might foment still more opposition to the state. Others, alarmed at the state's unwillingness to free him despite the court's agreement to bail him, viewed his continued incarceration as a deliberately spiteful policy against the leaders of the Connecticut forces, a policy seemingly confirmed by the Assembly's decision in March 1788 to suspend the Confirming Act of the year before.[42]

Whatever McKean's sympathy for John Franklin in the matter of his bail, his patience with Franklin's Connecticut supporters was severely strained when, on June 26, a body of men dressed as Indians kidnapped Timothy Pickering under the belief that Pickering had written to ask that bail be denied Franklin. Though Pickering did not suffer unduly at his captor's hands, and parted on amicable terms with them after nineteen days of captivity, the court viewed the "outrageous Assault battery and imprisonment of Colonel Pickering... as a Riot," and ordered the offenders to stand trial on the charge. McKean considered the kidnapping "certainly one of the most audacious and atrocious nature."[43]

McKean tried the "rioters" on Monday, November 6. In the end the accused "on account of the poverty & because misled by the old men, [were] mildly dealt with." But McKean took the occasion to warn them that they had been "guilty of High treason, and that in any country in Europe they would all be hanged, and it was to the mildness of the government of Pennsylvania they were indebted for the light punishment now ordered." John Franklin's plea for a delay in his trial was granted and he was returned to his Philadelphia jail cell.[44]

McKean was pleased that the courts in Luzerne continued to function and to administer justice even in the face of that region's turbulent history and continued provocations. He informed Pickering that the proceedings against the rioters had gone so smoothly that he was prepared to "make a particular representation thereof to the Assembly." But if McKean believed that the proceedings in Wilkes-Barre ushered in a period of tranquility or guaranteed the absence of a Shays' Rebellion in Pennsylvania, he put the best face on developments. A solution to the Wyoming question appeared no nearer in 1788 than it had been in 1785.[45]

McKean's judicial experience on Pennsylvania's western frontier could not fail to impress upon him that the American republic—and America's republican ideology—would be shaped in large measure by the character and aspirations of those often turbulent and ill-disciplined frontiersmen. Just how crucially they would shape his own political career and his own republican ideology did not become apparent for another decade.

12. The Achievement of an Independent Judiciary

Much of the criticism directed toward McKean and his court after 1782 had nothing to do with intracolonial squabbles, the question of libel, or the role of grand juries. It was directed toward the alleged insensitivity and growing callousness of the courts in matters of loyalism. With hostilities brought to a close, many Pennsylvanians felt that it was time for the courts to be less aggressive in meting out harsh punishments, both to those persons suspected of being inimical to the American cause and to those unfortunate patriots driven by wartime conditions to the commission of crimes. There seemed spectacular examples to support the contention of those who looked upon the court as excessively cruel and harsh.[1]

Wartime criminal activities by members of the Doan families and their associates prompted the Pennsylvania Supreme Court in September 1782, to institute outlawry proceedings. The Doans had been openly sympathetic to the British during the early months of the war. When Whig neighbors in Plumstead

Township, Bucks County, warned that the Doan menfolk must either voluntarily join the patriot cause or face impressment into the American military, the Doans answered by running away or joining the British army. Eventually, however, many of the Doans joined with other dissidents to harass state officials and persons loyal to the American cause. They especially preyed upon state and local tax and payroll personnel. By the late stages of the war they were roaming at will over much of Bucks, Westmoreland, Fayette, and Washington counties as well as throughout several neighboring states and, it was said, attracting an unusual number of renegade Indians and Blacks to their movement.[2]

Prior to August 1782 Pennsylvania authorities confined themselves to confiscating the lands of those Doans known to have actively joined the British. State leaders did not fully appreciate the degree to which the Doans and their companions were implicated in the many crimes being committed in Bucks County despite their efforts to ferret out information on some unidentified "very bold and Daring...Villains" responsible for a series of robberies there against state and county officers. Recognition of the partial scope of the Doans' involvement came with the capture of Jesse and Solomon Vickers in the summer of 1782. When it became evident to McKean and Associate Justice George Bryan that the Vickers knew a good deal about the criminal activities in Bucks and surrounding counties, they pressed the state Supreme Executive Council to grant the two men pardons in exchange for testimony against members of the band remaining free.[3]

The strategy succeeded. Largely on the basis of the Vickers' confessions in August the Supreme Court in September instituted the process of outlawry against two of the Doans' most resourceful lieutenants, Caleb and John Paul, for their part in robbing Bucks County magistrate Joseph Hart. In subsequent oyer and terminer terms additional outlawry proceedings were initiated by McKean against Abraham Doan for robbing tax collectors Phillip Smith, Nicholas Hole, James Snodgrass and John Baron; Moses Doan for his part in robbing Snodgrass, Hole and Nicholas Grover; Levi Doan for the crimes against Snodgrass and Smith; and Aaron Doan for robbing Hole, Hart, and Job Barton. The crimes against Grover and Smith led to the outlawry of Mablon and Joseph Doan, Sr., while the robberies of Baron, Hart and Barton resulted in outlawry proceedings against George Sinclair and Robert Steele. Writs of capias were eventually awarded as well against Jeremiah Cooper, Amos White, and Edward and Henry Connard for their participation in a variety of robberies. The writs were returnable April 10, 1783. None of those posted in the September and October terms voluntarily surrendered to the court by April, however, and sentences of outlawry were accordingly pronounced against them.[4]

Outlawry had had a long history in England, first as a declaration of war by the state against an offending member, then as a regular means of compelling submission to the authority of the state. It was, according to Pollock and Maitland, the state's "ultimate weapon" against a member of society. At least in felony and treason cases, proceedings began with presentation of a bill of indictment, then were followed by the issuance of a writ of capias ad respondendum, and, if the accused could not be located by the sheriff of the county in which the action was initiated or if he refused to surrender, by a writ of exigent. Should the accused remain free after the sheriff demanded his surrender at five successive county court sessions, a pronouncement of outlawry was decreed.[5] In medieval times outlawry put the offending person beyond the pale of the law and made it incumbent upon every man to seek him out, to "ravage his land, to burn his house, to hunt him down like a wild beast." Until 1329 the outlaw might be killed with impunity and his lands forfeited to the state.[6]

By the eighteenth century the process in England had become somewhat less harsh. Although outlawry continued to be recognized as a necessary instrument of the criminal process to enforce appearances before the courts, the means of escaping its ultimate punishment were gradually multiplied. Provisions came into being concerning the number of times and in what places the writs of capias must be posted before a person was duly outlawed. It became the practice to reverse outlawries if the accuracy in the return of an outlawry was not beyond question. It was not unusual by the early eighteenth century for such cases to flounder on the basis of a single misspelled word. In 1718 the Pennsylvania provincial assembly revised its legal code under the prod of Governor William Keith. In "An Act for the advancement of justice and more certain administration thereof," this early eighteenth-century version of outlawry proceedings was identified as being part of the laws of the province. Despite its early arrival, however, there is no evidence of a judicial outlawry being employed in Pennsylvania prior to 1782.[7]

Altogether seventeen men were outlawed on more than sixty charges throughout the period 1782 to 1784.[8] The Court's sudden willingness to award writs of outlawry came as something of a surprise to the legal community. Although acts of conditional attainder had been used extensively by the Assembly and the Supreme Executive Council during the war—against more than five hundred persons—judicial attainders had not been employed. Even during the critical years from 1777 to 1779, when the state witnessed the most concentrated attacks upon its viability and legitimacy, the Court had not seen fit to embrace outlawry as part of its arsenal.[9] If the Court viewed the process of outlawry in this instance merely as the swiftest and simplest means of compelling the Doans and their accomplices to surrender and stand trial—sound legal ground—it badly miscalculated the response of the Doan gang—and in the ultimate sense, that of the public.

Some Pennsylvanians saw in the Court's choice of legal weapons in 1782-84 ample verification of their suspicions regarding the growing harshness of McKean and his court. But judicial attainders, despite the emotionalism attached to their use, included, as we have seen, a variety of safeguards by the mid-eighteenth century and therefore were often less harsh in application than the conditional attainders widely utilized by the Assembly and Council.[10] It was also charged that McKean viewed outlawry as a political weapon, an accusation doubtless stemming in part from the political nature of much of the Doans' activities, and in part from the fact that in October 1782 McKean, as described above, was put forward as a candidate for the Council from Chester County by the Constitutionalists. Presumably McKean's dramatic response to the banditti in Bucks County was meant to impress Chester

County voters suffering similar depredations at the hands of a collection of unidentified individuals.[11]

Despite the sustained efforts of the Supreme Court in pursuing the outlaws and a renewed interest on the part of the Council in confiscating Doan lands late in 1783, most of the Doans and their accomplices remained free and unrepentant.[12] Throughout the summer of 1783 they continued to intimidate citizens of Bucks County who sought to aid the state in its efforts to capture persons implicated by the Vickers' confessions. In August, Joseph Hart, himself the victim of one of the Doans' earlier robberies, petitioned the Assembly, "setting forth apprehensions entertained by a number of . . . inhabitants in consequence of an advertisement set up by [outlaws] threatening to put in execution their villainous intentions of destroying and burning the persons and property of the good citizens in that neighborhood."[13]

The Assembly responded on September 8 with "an Act to encourage the speedy apprehending and bringing to justice diverse robbers, burglars and felons." Though Hart's petition did not list those he suspected of being behind the threats to the citizenry of Bucks County, the Assembly, on the basis of the court's earlier findings and supplemental information provided by representatives from Bucks County, named thirteen men "duly attainted by Outlawry, in the Supreme Court," and five accomplices against whom it considered it had "good cause to suspect and charge."

The act provided that anyone turning any of the accused over to the sheriff of any county would receive £300. If any of those named in the bill turned in two or more of their friends, and those colleagues were subsequently convicted, the turncoat would be paid £100 and receive a pardon from the state. Anyone convicted of buying stolen goods from those listed, or associating with them in a friendly manner, would face death without benefit of clergy, as well as suffer the loss of dowry and forfeiture of lands and goods. Provisions were made for the families of private citizens killed in any attempt to capture the Doans, or for those injured in such activity.[14]

The Doans remained defiant. In that same month a Bucks County posse surrounded a house temporarily occupied by Moses and Levi Doan and their cousin, Abraham. In the ensuing shootout Moses Doan was killed. Somehow the other two escaped the encirclement. A note discovered on the person of the dead man threatened to kill state officials, including members of the Court presumably, if the state persevered in its efforts to convict and execute members of the band. "For every Refugee you put to Death Wee will put Ten to Death," the note read. "We Are Not Your Subjects Neither will Wee Ever Bee." It was signed "The Royal Refugees."[15]

The ability of the "Royal Refugees" to carry out their threats was not lost on state officials, or on the public. Two of the Doans and three of their accomplices were captured late in 1783. Yet Joseph Doan, Sr., Mablon Doan, and Thomas Bulla, who were turned in by persons seeking state rewards, were able to escape with the aid of other members of the gang. The people of Bucks County might be placated by the fact that the state recaptured and convicted Joseph Doan, Sr., in the following spring, and convicted Joseph Doan, Jr., and one Nathaniel Holsey in April 1784, but disturbing signs remained. The banditti remaining free seemed, if anything, to be expanding both their activities and their range, and several of those captured were freed when proceedings had to be quashed because of irregularities. By June, commissioners in Washington County were forced to muster the militia in order to frustrate the Doans there. The inhabitants of Bucks County antagonistic to the Doans were reduced to petitioning the Council for the commutation of the death sentence pronounced against Joseph Doan, Jr., in the hopes that he would agree to testify against others.[16]

Little discussion regarding the use of outlawry by the Supreme Court occurred among officials of the state prior to September 1782. For that matter, little notice of it was taken by the Pennsylvania press, a fact of no small wonder in light of the nearly frenetic efforts by certain Philadelphia editors—like Eleazer Oswald—to criticize and embarrass McKean. It was only with the capture of Aaron Doan in August 1784 that the issue of outlawry proceedings became a political and constitutional one. Doan was brought before McKean on September 24 to be formally identified as the person charged in the October 1782 capias with robbing Joseph Hart of £656·13·4 on October 27, 1781. The ardent efforts of William Lewis and

Sampson Levy, Doan's attorneys, to quash the writ on various technicalities and errors, were overruled and execution was awarded against Doan on October 9.[17]

As president of the Pennsylvania Supreme Executive Council, John Dickinson was charged with seeing that the warrant for Doan's execution was carried out. This he refused to do. Supported by a majority of the Council, Dickinson pressed for a complete reassessment of the Doan proceedings. The case of Aaron Doan had come to weigh heavily upon his conscience; he entertained serious reservations both as to the legality of the proceedings and the deleterious effects of such action on the liberties of the people of the state. On November 22, in a letter reflecting his anxiety, Dickinson raised—or rather re-raised—those issues first explored in September by Lewis and Levy.

Dickinson's move (in the view of one biographer the most noble act of his illustrious career) was a deliberate attempt to provoke an intragovernmental dialogue embracing the legal and constitutional questions implicit in the Doan action. He articulated the concern increasingly evident in public and private discussions of the case. A month earlier the politician James Irwin had pressed Justice Bryan to clarify for him and others the Court's thinking in the matter of the outlawries. Of critical concern to Irwin was the difference between an execution based on legislative or executive acts of attainder implemented by judicial proceedings, and one based solely on judicial proceedings. Irwin and others were disturbed, as was Dickinson, by the fact that there seemed no clear-cut Pennsylvania precedent for the present action against Doan.

Bryan's subsequent conversations with McKean and the court prothonotary, Edward Burd—reported to Irwin by Bryan—led to a discussion of the David Dawson case. Dawson of West Caln, Chester County, had been executed for treason in 1780 under a proclamation of the Council and judicial proceedings. The judges considered the Dawson case very much like the Doan action "tho' not so clear as to the proceedings." Doan's case was "at common law, the mode of demanding only being an act of assembly." If Irwin had been convinced by the judges' fine distinctions, Dickinson had not.[18]

Dickinson and members of the Council had "attentively considered" the transcript of the Doan case and "it appear[ed] to [them], a case of a novel and extraordinary nature, which, once established as a precedent, may greatly affect the lives, liberties and fortunes" of the people of Pennsylvania. Dickinson asked the justices of the Supreme Court to comment on nine broad questions he deemed pertinent to any decision on the Council's part to see that the Court's warrant for Doan's execution be carried out. He wished to know whether the proceedings were based on common law, on the Pennsylvania statute of 1718 designed to implement common law practices in outlawry, on a recent act of the Pennsylvania Assembly, or on one of Parliament. He also desired to know if there were precedents in modern English history for the practice of outlawry, especially when it involved judicial proceedings alone as in the current instance. Was there a precedent in Pennsylvania history, Dickinson asked? Was such a precedent consistent with the state constitution's stress on trial by jury as one of the principal safeguards of human liberty? Did the Court feel that Doan's statement to the effect that he was in New York at the time the writ of capias was awarded against him altered the complexion of his case? Could the Council issue a specific warrant for death by hanging, or simply leave the issue of the punishment to the discretion of the sheriff?[19]

Dickinson's move shocked the justices. McKean, who had seriously considered stepping down from his judicial post the previous summer but had changed his mind and accepted an appointment in July for a second seven-year term, viewed Dickinson's efforts as a serious threat to the independence of his court that he had labored so diligently to achieve.[20]

Even as Dickinson mulled over the implications of the Doan case in November 1784, and drafted his challenge to the Supreme Court, the Court's confidence and strength were being manifested to the people of Pennsylvania. The opportunity to exhibit its independence in this instance was provided by the celebrated Marbois-Longchamps affair. Charles Julian de Longchamps, a French citizen, migrated to Philadelphia in 1783 and took the oath of allegiance sometime in the following year. He courted a local Quaker girl over the vehement protestations of her guardians, who were outraged at his criminal activities, both proved and alleged, and suspicious of his claims of high birth. When the two young people were married the angry guardians financed a newspaper campaign calling into question Longchamps' titles and reputation.

On May 17, 1784, Longchamps turned to Francis Barbe de Marbois, consul general of France and secretary to the French embassy in Philadelphia serving under the French Minister Charles de la Luzerne, to aid him in establishing his claims of high birth. Frustrated by Marbois' unwillingness to render him aid or to take seriously his claims to titles, Longchamps had strong words with the secretary and "insolently" threatened him. An unsigned, threatening letter received by Marbois two days later was judged to be from the disaffected Longchamps. That same day, May 19, when the two men met on Front Street near the Coffee House, additional hot words were exchanged and Longchamps struck Marbois with his cane. Learning of the circumstances of the altercation from Marbois, Luzerne formally requested that the Pennsylvania Supreme Executive Council see that Longchamps, "a Frenchman without character," be apprehended and turned over to French authorities for punishment. He thought it was "of the greatest Importance for the security of all those who shall reside here in a public character that an outrage of this kind be severely punished."[21]

Dickinson quickly assured the minister that he "highly resent[ed] the outrages" mentioned in the minister's letter, and that the state would take "every step which the Laws of the State will permit for the reparation of these excesses." The following day he added the assurances that Justice George Bryan, who had recently returned from the circuit, had been directed to issue a warrant for the apprehension of Longchamps and to give proper direction for its immediate execution. Dickinson was able to announce on May 22 that Longchamps had been arrested and bailed.[22]

A temporary embarrassment arose when Longchamps broke bail and escaped from his home while the sheriff waited for him to change his clothes. Marbois expressed his disappointment to Dickinson that "there was a very ill placed confidence, a most unwarrantable neglect on the side of officers of the state when they suffered a man guilty of so heinous a crime so easily to run away from the hand of Justice." But Longchamps was quickly recaptured, and the focus of all concerned turned to the complex legal questions involved in Luzerne's request that the Pennsylvania authorities hold Longchamps until he could be returned to France for punishment. Even as the state insured his personal appearance Dickinson was not so sure that either the state constitution or the laws of Pennsylvania authorized state authorities to deliver him up to French officials. Somehow the case had to be dispatched consistent with the "honor of the State and the Law of nations." Dickinson was not unmindful that the state's response was being watched closely by members of Congress who viewed the attack as an ugly precedent.[23]

On June 2 Dickinson sought the advice of McKean's court on whether or not the state could seize Longchamps and incarcerate him at the instigation of the French embassy until he could be returned to France for trial. He stressed his own conviction that the "Consequences of the insults offered to Mr. Marbois...are likely in a very high degree to affect the honor of this commonwealth [and]...if the offender is not imprisoned...the ministers of France & the United Netherlands will with their attendants immediately depart from this State." Dickinson knew of what he spoke. O.J. Van Berkel, minister of United Netherlands, as outraged as was Marbois, had threatened Dickinson that his delegation would depart the city if a reasonable solution was not quickly forthcoming. Van Berkel, sharing Luzerne's belief that the attack upon Marbois was an attack upon all members of the diplomatic corps, urged Congress to proclaim the law of nations to be an integral part of the law of each of the states.[24]

Dickinson's letter reached McKean and his associates Atlee and Rush at Sunbury, where they were engaged in an oyer and terminer proceeding. The judges were forced to consider the legal dilemma posed by Dickinson without recourse to their law books (there was little room for books among the justices' duffle on the circuit). The justices concluded after some consultation that the Council could not detain Longchamps, as he had by then been released on a properly requested writ of habeas corpus. In addition they determined that the Council had no power to seize him for deliverance to the French authorities. They agreed to move the oyer and terminer court scheduled for Philadelphia from the twenty-eighth to the twenty-fourth so as to deal with the case as quickly as possible.

The opinion of the judges and their willingness to move up the oyer and terminer proceedings hardly solved Dickinson's immediate dilemma. He was under increasing pressure from Luzerne to turn over the errant Longchamps, and from the Dutch consul, who continued his threat to resign and return home if Longchamps were not turned over to the French authorities. Pressure from another source appeared when supporters of Longchamps, including the talented lawyer Peter S. DuPonceau, argued the case in the local press.[25]

McKean and justices Atlee and Rush had gained some appreciation of the seriousness of the affair from Dickinson's letter, but it was not until they returned to Philadelphia that they perceived the full scope of the storm and controversy aroused by the case.

To guarantee that the state's position was argued persuasively Dickinson encouraged James Wilson to assist Attorney General William Bradford in the prosecution. To Jonathan Dickinson Sergeant, one-time attorney general, fell the task of defending Longchamps against the state's charges. The first charge was that Longchamps had threatened and menaced bodily harm to Marbois; the second was that he had unlawfully struck Marbois in opposition to the law of nations and the peace and safety of the United States and of Pennsylvania. Sergeant insisted that the words uttered by Longchamps during the first meeting between the two men were too ambiguous to be construed as evidence of menaces of corporal harm. It was a maxim in law, he reminded the Court, that words should be taken in their mildest form or sense. Sergeant denied that international law was involved. Reparation sought and the remedy offered was confined to Pennsylvania law. There was also reason to question the propriety of the second charge inasmuch as it was not sufficiently proved that Longchamps was the aggressor. He pointed to one witness who testified that Marbois had struck the first blow.

The prosecution stressed the need to "protect and secure the persons and privileges of ambassadors; the connection between the law of nations and the municiple law, and the effect which the decision in this case must have upon the honor of Pennsylvania." No national court existed to exercise jurisdiction in the matter. No state statute was pertinent to the case. Pennsylvania had to prosecute and to do so on the basis of the only applicable law in this instance, international law. Only a verdict that left no doubt that the law of nations was an integral part of Pennsylvania state law would insure respect of the world at large.

After "minutely recapitulating the evidence and applying it to the charge in the indictments" for the jury, McKean addressed the jury. Fully aware of his own role in this precedent-setting case, he reminded the jurors that this was "a case of the first impression in the United States." He stressed that the case must be determined on the principles of the law of nations as the prosecution contended, and if the alleged act did take place, there could be no doubt that those laws had been violated. The jury initially returned a verdict of guilty on the second count only but McKean urged them to reconsider the evidence and a verdict of guilty on both counts was subsequently returned.

At this point Dickinson and the Council requested that sentencing be postponed until the determination of several pressing questions which remained. Dickinson wished to know if Longchamps could now be delivered up to the French. He also pressed for a ruling on whether or not Longchamps could be given a sentence to end when the French were fully satisfied. Finally he asked if the Council could now take steps to see Longchamps imprisoned. These questions were debated in open court on July 10 and 12 with members of the Council arguing the affirmative and negative of each question. McKean and Bryan, who heard the arguments, dismissed most of the assumptions implicit in Dickinson's questions. They denied that the Council had the power to deliver the defendant to the French or to acquiesce in any determination of the sentence by the French. They held that "punishment must be inflicted in the same county where criminals were tried and convicted" and that the sentence must be "certain and definite in all respects."

For two months McKean weighed the question of Longchamps' sentence. When he walked to the courthouse on

October 7, 1784, to deliver his decision, Philadelphia's political society watched with unfeigned interest. Opposition to a court decision turning Longchamps over to the French had mounted even as the conservatives more aggressively asserted that Longchamps' punishment must be meted out by French authorities. Luzerne and the popular Marbois made no bones about their own wishes in the matter. Resisting the pressure from all sides, McKean determined that though Longchamps could not be turned over to the French he would be punished by Pennsylvania courts. He was to be imprisoned until July 4, 1786, a period of just under two years, to pay a fine of one hundred crowns, and to provide a £1000 recognizance and two £500 securities for good behavior for seven years. Radicals happy with McKean's decision to protect Longchamps from French authorities were at the same time deeply chagrined at the severity of the sentence. Conservatives, satisfied with the sentence, lamented the Court's failure to accede to French wishes.

Nor was France placated. Her ministers continued for over a year to demand that Pennsylvania surrender Longhcamps for a trial in France. When members of Congress expressed concern that the Longchamps issue was "a cloud which threatened a degree of coolness between the court of France and these United States," Congress passed a resolution pressing the states to institute laws punishing any person who by attack or abuse on foreign ministers or their servants endangered the dignity of sovereign powers.[26]

Though McKean made few friends with his decision in the Longchamps affair, it proved to be one of his finer hours. His leadership was everywhere manifest during the conduct of the trial. His manner gave assurance that the Court would function regardless of the turmoil around it and the pressure applied to it, whether the pressure came from sources inside his own government or out. If persons viewed the Court as a political tool of the administration before the Longchamps affair, few did afterwards.

It seems clear that McKean's efforts and those of his associate justices in behalf of an independent court had in practice been largely achieved by 1784. There were unmistakeable signs that members of the Assembly had come to appreciate that fact. A disruptive salary dispute, long smoldering between the

Assembly and the justices in the high Court was settled in favor of the justices late in 1784 when Constitutionalists in the Assembly granted the judges a pay raise and sought to provide "fixed and permanent salaries." More important, Republicans increasingly recognized that to compromise the Court by continuing to manipulate the judicial salary schedule would be politically damaging. Both parties came to perceive that the public did not want the Court to be made a political football.[27]

It is not surprising, then, considering the progress of the Court into the winter of 1784, that McKean would view John Dickinson's November 22 letter, like the December, 1780, correspondence with Joseph Reed, as a stark and dangerous challenge to his court. To ignore Dickinson's acquiesced or attempted interference would undermine the emerging ideal of a judiciary that governed by law and hence undermine the judiciary itself. Dickinson's message contained more than questions regarding the Court's proceedings in the Doan case; it was replete with insinuations of judicial insensitivity and procedural errors. That the president was goading the Court to reconsider its policies and procedures and to discover a means of quietly reversing itself in the Doan outlawry was not lost on the justices.

Moreover, Dickinson's challenge to the Court in this instance identified an ironic tension between himself and his longtime friend McKean which transcended the immediate issues of the outlawry proceedings. McKean, long associated with the radical forces in Pennsylvania, is seen here in search of a republic of law. For him, America's republican experiment could be safely constructed only on a foundation of a strong, independent judiciary, and laws secure from any tampering by capricious men and transient passions. The chief justice admitted freely—and repeatedly—that he abhorred "innovations, especially in the administration of justice . . . and . . . would avoid tampering . . . as with edge tools." His concern extended to juries intent on expressing their own interpretation of the law in their verdicts.[28] On the other hand, Dickinson, spokesman for Philadelphia's conservative element and an arch foe of the democratic thrust in the state, emerges as an advocate of the right of the people to make and directly control the context of their laws. Here he champions jury trials by which local veniremen might mitigate the inequity of the law and resist practices inconsistent with America's new republicanism.[29]

Lawyer that he was, Dickinson framed his letter as he would a legal brief to urge that the Doan outlawry be reversed and to provide a variety of specific legal illustrations why such a reversal was justified. A close examination of the transcript, the capias, and the returns had persuaded him that a number of technical violations had occurred, any one of which would warrant the outlawry being set aside. The original capias had directed the sheriff to return to the Supreme Court; instead he had returned to the court of oyer and terminer and general gaol delivery. Admittedly, the same judges sat in both courts but the title was different and the sheriff's action thus represented a violation of the writ of capias, according to Dickinson. The sheriff's return also indicated that he had not called upon Doan by proclamation to "answer to the Commonwealth" as the capias had directed. The act of 1718 required that the sheriff make the proclamation of outlawry himself, but the returns in this instance established that he had only seen to it that such proclamations were made. Dickinson argued that the ambiguities in the wording and the "defects in the proceedings" surrounding the writ and returns called aloud for judicial redress.[30]

The justices did not respond until January 15, 1785. Then, prodded by McKean, they made it clear, as McKean previously made clear to Reed, that they were under no obligations to answer Dickinson's inquiries. "Judges do not hold themselves bound to assign any reasons for their judgment," the justices wrote, "and when they do give reason, it is always *in public*." Dickinson was cautioned against construing their present correspondence as a precedent. It was merely a courtesy on their part, one that could easily be ignored in the future. But, in the interest of clarifying the issues raised by the president, they proceeded to answer his questions.

The justices began by pointing out the obvious: outlawry had been a legitimate instrument of the law for centuries, and they could think of no instance where any question of law, upon a writ of error to reverse an outlawry in a criminal case, had ever undergone a serious litigation before that of John Wilkes in 1770. The current proceedings were based wholly on the 1718 Pennsylvania law, as Dickinson surmised. The "histories of the times" and the "periodical publications" in England seldom listed executions of capital offenders, so the judges were unable to answer with any certainty whether or not men had been executed upon judicial proceedings alone prior to the American Declaration of Independence. Nor did they know of a single instance where anyone in Pennsylvania had been executed under judicial proceedings alone. Still, there were indications based on a comment by Blackstone that a sizeable number of English precedents existed, and the execution of David Dawson in November 1780 was "a case of like nature" in Pennsylvania. They sketched in the details of Dawson's case for the edification of the president.

It was the opinion of the justices that the Doan case in particular and outlawry in general were fully compatible with the state constitution; the accused were not denied a jury trial by the state but rather by their own actions. Their failure to surrender themselves to the proper authorities determined their fate in this respect. The justices rejected—and cited precedents for rejecting—the many "defects" catalogued by Dickinson and reminded him that his arguments had been ably anticipated by Doan's counsel, fully explored in open session in September 1784, and answered by the Court.

Because the justices could find no valid reason to reverse the proceedings, they would not do so. "It is a breach of duty to reverse a good as it would be to affirm a bad outlawry," Dickinson was told. "The mischief goes farther than an unrighteous sentence in the particular case; for, to reverse without an error is to abolish that part of the law."

The Court left no doubt as to its position. If the law was repugnant to members of the Council they could urge the legislature to alter or abolish it. The Council could, if it so desired, intercede with mercy in the defendant's behalf. It had the constitutional prerogative to pardon Doan or to reprieve him. The Court could neither alter the law nor grant a change in sentence; the separation of powers doctrine forbid it.[31]

Unpersuaded by the terse reply from the Court, or unwilling to be convinced, Dickinson doggedly withheld the death warrant. It was he who urged the Council on March 28 to consider the implications of the Doan case formally to determine if they should grant a pardon. James Irvine, John Boyd, John McDowell, Jonathan Hoge, John Neville, and John Whitehill concurred with Dickinson that a pardon should be awarded. Charles Biddle joined with George Wall, Jr., and James McLene in resisting such a move. The same majority then concluded that the Council could not legally issue a warrant for Doan's death in view of the irregularities in the case.[32]

Dickinson did not issue the pardon as was his constitutional prerogative. Instead, on March 29, he wrote to the Assembly reiterating his concern and that of the majority of the Council over the Court's handling of the Doan matter. Informing the Assembly that the absence of a court of appeal with power to issue a writ of error and the Council's conviction that it could not legally issue a death warrant necessitated the case being turned over to the legislature for a proper disposition, Dickinson dropped the matter in the Assembly's lap. He appended a long letter wherein he repeated and amplified on the arguments for a reversal that he had first sent to the justices in November.[33]

Dickinson's decision to send the matter to the Assembly was an additional shock to the justices. Their own role and those of the Assembly and Council seemed clear enough to them. Dickinson's efforts to pry from the Assembly what amounted to a writ of error seemed to them a travesty of the separation of powers doctrine. Bryan complained that "Scarcely ever was there more contempt or Dissatisfaction shown" to the Court.[34]

On the same day that it received Dickinson's message the Assembly appointed a committee consisting of John Clark (Bucks County), George Woods (Bedford), and Robert Whitehill (Cumberland) to consider it and to recommend a proper response. The committee's report, first read on April 4, was adopted without significant revision three days later. The assembly found that the Court had acted according to its duty and the law. So far as the Assembly could determine, the Court had thoughtfully weighed all relevant arguments, carefully surveyed the known history of the banditti, consulted the options available to it offered by the legal code, and in the end concluded reasonably that it had little choice but to outlaw Aaron Doan.

The same sensitivity to the laws and constitutional processes had not characterized the Council's actions, according to the Assembly report. The Council was not entrusted by the constitution or custom to declare what the law was. It was seeking to give a judicial determination in this instance, the committee found, and it had no right to do so. The Council had only three options open to it: it could reprieve Doan, or pardon him, or issue the warrant for his execution. The Assembly accepted the committee's recommendation to reject any idea of reversing the outlawry by an act of Assembly or in any way interferring further in the case. The Constitutionalist-dominated Assembly may have reaped a good deal of political satisfaction from brusquely dismissing the pleas of the Republican Council, but members seemed genuinely provoked by the constitutional implications of Dickinson's strategy.[35]

Despite his personal disappointment, Dickinson chose to abide by the legislators' will. He made no effort to push for an absolute pardon. Doan was still incarcerated—despite a series of petitions from him to the Council—when Dickinson left office in October 1785. It was not until May 17, 1787, when Benjamin Franklin was president and there had been a complete turnover in the Council personnel that it responded favorably to the latest petition from Doan and pardoned him on the stipulation that he would leave the United States forever. Happy to accomodate the Council, Doan initially retreated into New Jersey, where for a brief period he slipped back into a life of crime before escaping to Canada.[36]

Meanwhile, largely because of the confrontation between the Court, the Council, and the Assembly over the Doan proceedings, the constitutional niceties were scrupulously observed in the case of Robert Steele, apprehended and brought before McKean in September 1785. Steele's counsel sought to show that the writ of capias awarded against him failed to accurately describe Steele's person, situation or residence, but to no avail. When the Court granted a warrant for Steele's execution, the Council made no effort to seek legislative redress. This, despite the fact that members harbored many of the same concerns over the Steele case that the previous Council had expressed in the Doan matter. It did, however, grant Steele a pardon after a lengthy discussion—a move in which McKean and the other justices concurred.[37]

Yet the issue of the Doans and their accomplices and its constitutional ramifications for McKean's court were far from over. Throughout 1785 and into 1788 the prosecution of minor figures of the gang and those named as accessories continued. Several, like James and Jacob Paul, escaped conviction in June 1785, when witnesses at Newton failed to testify. But Sarah, wife of Thomas Bulla, was convicted of being an accessory after the fact, and Joseph Doan, Jr., continued to run afoul of the law. Henry Wynkoop of Chester, troubled by recurring robberies and convinced that many of those involved were the same who had been implicated in the earlier outlawries, reported to McKean in March 1786 that it "look[ed] as if another Doan . . . generation had arose."[38]

The final act of the constitutional drama was played out in 1788 when Levi and Abraham Doan were finally captured and brought before McKean in the Supreme Court for identification. They were quickly established to be the men charged in the 1782 writs of capias and the Court pronounced their sentence of death. Despite the lessons seemingly learned in the struggle between the Assembly and the Council three years before, a concerted movement developed to secure jury trials for the condemned men. Perhaps the groundwork laid by Dickinson in 1784-85 was evident in the movement. Perhaps, too, with the coming of a new federal constitution an era had ended; the Revolutionary War seemed a long way off. In all likelihood the widespread push in Pennsylvania for legal reform—heartily endorsed by such diverse personalities as Benjamin Franklin, Dickinson, McKean, and Bryan—made a move to secure trials for the Doans seem only logical.

Those seeking a reversal of the Doans' outlawries not only protested that a jury trial was every person's right, but that the Doans were essentially charged with what amounted to political crimes. Persons "residing in and near the township of Plumstead" petitioned the Council for a jury trial for the two Doans, declaring that "if nothing appears against them but what is alleged in the outlawry, that you would in mercy be pleased to spare their lives." Numerous prominent and influential figures, including Sharp Delaney, United States Senator Robert Morris, and Bishop William White, added their signatures to those seeking mercy.[39]

Public cries for pardons or a commutation of their sentence were also heard. A writer identified only as "Trial by Jury" attributed the sins of the Doans in part to the confusion of allegiances in the early stages of the war and in part to a revolution which deprived them of a "virtuous education." Interestingly enough, he also blamed the state for much of the Doans' activities, particularly the confiscation of the father's property which "exposed them in early life without home or friend." He attacked McKean's court as well, arguing that "the depredations which [the Doans] committed afterwards were the natural consequence of the outlawry." He judged that only a few high officials wanted death for the two men, that "nine out of ten citizens" favored commutation of their sentences.[40]

"Z" also favored leniency for the Doans. He reminded Philadelphians that for a state intent on making its laws more humane and with rehabilitating its criminals, the execution of the Doans represented a gigantic step backwards. He joined with those recommending a pardon, exile, or hard labor as viable alternatives to the death penalty.[41]

Understandably Levi and Abraham Doan added their own voices to those seeking mercy. Initially they conceded that while the facts of the Court's case were essentially correct, the charge that they had acted against the state government out of love for Great Britain was false. They had been young and impressionable and had been seduced by older, designing men. In a later petition they maintained that they had been "unacquainted with the Nature and operation of Outlawry, or that such a process had been had against them." Both versions were challenged by a group of Bucks County residents who had been subjected to the Doans' earlier reign of terror. They demanded guarantees from the state that it would carry out the executions expeditiously and close the matter once and for all. They condemned any effort by either the Council or the Assembly to help the two terrorists.[42]

McKean and his associates on the bench were unmoved by the private and public moves to save the Doans. When the

Council, on July 23, requested the Court's opinion as to whether or not there was anything favorable to be said for the Doans, McKean and Bryan answered in the negative and tersely referred the Council to the January 1785 letter to Dickinson. Knowledge of the criminal activities currently being carried out in New Jersey by Aaron Doan, pardoned the previous year, did nothing to soften the Court's position. The fate of the Doans—scheduled to die on September 24—now lay with the Council. What it chose to do concerning the awards of execution was not now the Court's formal business.[43]

When their numerous petitions elicited no interest from members of the Council, the Doans turned on September 19 to the legislature, "praying [its] interposition in order to restore them to the inestimable privilege of trial by jury." Despite the obvious parallel between what the Doans sought and what Dickinson had earlier sought from the Assembly, a committee comprised of Thomas Fitzsimons (City of Philadelphia), John Chapman (Bucks County), and William Findley (Westmoreland County) was formed to consider a response.

Ironically enough, the Assembly did not turn its attention to the fate of the Doans until September 22 because of an attempt by Eleazer Oswald to impeach three of the four justices of the Supreme Court, including McKean. One member of the committee assigned to consider the Doans' petition, Thomas Fitzsimons, prepared a bill on the twenty-second designed to restore to the men the privilege of trial by jury, but the move was vehemently opposed by William Findley, who judged the bill to be corrosive to the Court's independence.

Still, Fitzsimons received able support from William Lewis, who had argued several of the outlawry cases before the Supreme Court, including Aaron Doan's. Lewis personally had little doubt that "from the concurrent voice of the people" the Doans deserved to die. He readily admitted that outlawry proceedings were of "great antiquity; depend[ing] not only on the act of our assembly, but on the common and statute law of England." But, as he pointed out to his colleagues in the Assembly, the proceedings differed markedly in the two countries. England, for instance, demanded five proclamations to guarantee the accused a longer period to learn of his

William Lewis. Courtesy of Mrs. Edmund L. Dana

outlawry and to act to avoid its terrible consequences. Should it be said, he asked, that the rights of the subject are more tenaciously guaranteed in that country than they are in "the assylum of injured liberty?"

Conceding that the outlawry process was necessary and an acknowledged tool of the Court, Lewis asked only that it be refined somewhat in Pennsylvania. He cited examples of how the wording in the Pennsylvania statute allowed a man who simply left home to be posted. He illustrated how if one man were indicted for robbery and another outlawed for the same crime, the second man was punished more severely. Should a man denied a trial deserve the harsher punishment? Lewis asked. He urged the legislature to redress this inequity. In the meantime, he argued, a committee should be appointed to confer with the Council on the possibility of obtaining a six-day delay in the Doans' execution to permit the Assembly time to deliberate on their case more fully.[44]

The committee favored by Lewis was appointed only after a lengthy and bitter debate. James McLene, who as a councilor in 1784 had opposed efforts to save Aaron Doan, sought to stall the move to appoint the committee, warning his colleagues that they were interferring in a judicial matter. This was the second such instance of meddling on the part of the Assembly, he reminded them, and he believed "in all cases it was improper," as the Assembly itself had established three years before. William Findley, who had earlier resisted Fitzsimons' bill to guarantee to the Doans a jury trial, was originally named a member of the committee charged with meeting the Council, but he begged off, asserting that he concurred wholeheartedly with McLene that the Assembly had no power to meddle in the Court's constitutional prerogatives. He wished to be no part of a committee prepared for such tampering. Despite the staunch opposition of McLene, Findley and others, however, the Assembly pressed on. David Rittenhouse was subsequently appointed in Findley's stead and the committee waited upon the Council.[45]

To the dismay of the Assembly committee, the Council refused to meet with it. It may be, as one scholar has observed, that the Council's refusal was prompted exclusively by political considerations. But the Assembly debate established that a body of assemblymen was genuinely troubled by the baleful implications of the legislative move to review the judicial proceedings and to tamper with the sentence of the Court, and while members of the Council left few records of their individual sentiments in rejecting the committee's overtures, they were not unaware of the Assembly's 1785 pronouncement. Nor were they oblivious to the constitutional implications of their own actions. Indeed, Charles Biddle was persuaded that the legislature's actions in 1788 forced the Council to treat the issue as a constitutional question, a development which Biddle thought "proved fatal" to the Doans, who died with "great firmness" on the twenty-fourth, as scheduled.[46]

In one respect McKean's use of outlawry in 1782-84 was an historical aberration. No Pennsylvanian before 1782 and none who was not associated with the Doans' activities in some way after that date ever suffered the process of outlawry during the course of the first state constitution. Yet, in another respect, the proceedings in the Doan affair were not abberational at all. Indeed, those proceedings raised a central legal issue for the post-Revolution generation: whether the content of American law should be determined in accordance with abstract, objective principles generated from non-political sources, or whether the law should be directly and immediately responsive to the will of the people. On one side in the Doan affair stood men like Dickinson and Lewis contending that either legislators as representatives of the people or the people themselves sitting on juries ought to apply the law of outlawry to the cases at hand and thereby determine the substantive content of that law. On the other side stood McKean and other members of the Pennsylvania Supreme Court, together with their supporters in the legislative and executive branches, arguing that the scope of outlawry should be determined by precedents received from as far back as the Middle Ages. Time and again in this debate, all three branches of the government were forced to define and defend their constitutional prerogatives. From the debate, which was often confused and exacerbated by personal jealousies and political scheming, there emerged in Pennsylvania a clearer appreciation and articulation of the separation of powers doctrine.

The Court withstood every challenge.⁴⁷ The foundations of an independent judiciary so painstakingly prepared by McKean during the war years were buttressed after 1784 by the ultimate acceptance and explicit acknowledgment—however grudging—of the Court's powers on the part of the Council and Assembly.⁴⁸ In the end, the Assembly and Council fell to quarreling over which body had the right to determine a pardon or reprieve for the Doans, a right never claimed by the Court. Both explicitly conceded the Court's jurisdiction in matters of procedures and sentencing. Challenges to the Court would arise after 1788, but they invariably centered on alleged abuses of the Court's prerogatives and powers; they did not deny the legitimacy of the Court's determining, apart from politics, the meaning of the law.

13. The Trials of Reform

Despite McKean's unwillingness to bend the system for the unfortunate Mamachtaga or for the thirteen families on Washington's lands—and his lack of sympathy for the Doans in the outlawry proceedings—he was intensely interested in promoting legal and penal reform. By nature a reformer, he was driven by an almost Puritanical zeal to improve society, as seen in his support of the Adams-Lee bloc, during the Revolution, in their quest for a society free of corruption, ostentatious consumption, and avarice. His enthusiasm for congressional reform was an expression of his concern for a persistent regeneration of society. Eschewing radical innovation, he was no social revolutionary: he was a conservative man who would root out of society inefficiency, brutality, and corruption. Nowhere do we see any intent to destroy existing institutions or to seriously jeopardize traditional rights and privileges.

Of a more superficial nature was his insisting that the judges be robed in scarlet, "of a very fine light Broadcloth," in keeping with his desire to "anglicize" the Court's appearance as well as its procedures. McKean believed that a sense of awe would thus be created, which he thought essential to judicial stability in revolutionary times. His fellow justices seemed less interested than he in the robes, at least, and the scheme seems to have fallen into disuse rather quickly.[1]

Not surprisingly McKean's impetuosity and combativeness as a judge sometimes proved counter-productive to his reforms. In more than one instance his conduct triggered attempts to reform the Court and the laws of Pennsylvania in directions against him, including public suggestions that major reform should begin with his removal from office. Typical in this respect was his over-reaction to the conduct of John Nicholson, the state comptroller, in 1785. Late in that year, Timothy Matlack, for years secretary to the province, sought to settle accounts with the Commonwealth. After investigating the books thoroughly, the comptroller determined that Matlack was in debt to the state to the tune of £2,043·0·8, and demanded that Matlack settle the account fully and quickly. Matlack took his case to the Supreme Court, where a special jury subsequently determined that, rather than Matlack owing the Commonwealth over £2,000, the Commonwealth in fact owed Matlack £75·12·6, a decision in keeping with the chief justice's assessment of the facts. Nicholson "politely express[ed] himself" that the jury's ruling stemmed from "an abberation [sic] *from the truth,* in the chief justice's charge." He wrote two letters to the Council complaining that McKean's charge and the jury's subsequent findings had rendered an injustice to his accounting and to the state. McKean sought to curb Nicholson's tongue. "I was induced to administer a little moderate correction to [Nicholson] with hopes of curing him of his petulancy," he recalled to a friend, "but I find he is incorrigible." He added (obviously in reference to Nicholson's letters) that he was "now constrained to make some strictures on this second performance."

For McKean the issue was simple enough. If his charge had contained an error, Nicholson should have made that the basis of his letter. But to allege that there had been "an abberation [sic] from truth" was untenable: "such language is not used in the courts, nor among Gentlemen." Secondly, the comptroller had intimated that nothing ought to have been allowed to Matlack for militia commissions, but the legislature and jury had thought otherwise. If the jury determined that the salary was not adequate, they had the power to rule on that point. Finally, Nicholson had argued that McKean had told the jury that "the Comptroller received fees in his office." He denied saying it and added that he doubted whether Nicholson really believed that he had said it. "For this allegation, I must rather credit his good invention, that debit his bad memory," McKean told Charles Biddle.[2]

As for Nicholson's desire to bring the whole issue before the Assembly, perhaps in an impeachment case, McKean was sanguine. He admitted to Biddle that Nicholson was "welcome to the fame he may acquire by having a contest with the Judges of the Supreme Court." But McKean had earlier related to Benjamin Franklin, now president of the state, that Nicholson knew better than to criticize the courts to the Supreme Executive Council "but upon an impeachment by the House of Assembly." He thought Nicholson's letter could be considered in no other light "than as an infamous libel upon the Supreme Court." Nicholson had "too frequently with impunity under the pretended colour of office, calumniated his Superiors; and in such language as vulgarity itself would blush at . . . . I hope this will be the last instance of it." McKean added ominously, "Even Ignorance when it is willful, becomes criminal."[3]

Like most internal disputes, the furor over the Nicholson-McKean controversy escaped the confines of the State House into the public awareness, reinforcing existing prejudices which occasionally surfaced in the press. Criticism was leveled not only at McKean but at the courts, especially the Supreme Court, for bringing people before the high courts without warrants, asking leading questions "calculated to convict and criminate [sic] the party." High judicial costs and fees came under fire, fees high enough, it was said, to constitute extortion. Courts bred lawyers, and lawyers came in for their share of vilification. They were too plentiful, it was argued; their numbers should be drastically reduced in Pennsylvania. They were also parasitic. "Lawyers find good times when people quarrel, scold, assault, strike and wrong one another, when wives and husbands run away from one another," a writer pointed out, "so they can get rich."⁴ A correspondent in the *Independent Gazetter* reported on an epitaph for a lawyer:

> God works wonders now and then;
> Here lies a lawyer and an Honest Man.

After some reflection he suggested the following addition:

> This is a meer law-Quibble, not a wonder;
> Here lies a Lawyer, and—his Client under.⁵

Some criticism of the Court stemmed from over-crowded dockets, expanding circuits, and exhausted judges. McKean's lament that he was "thoroughly tired" became a common refrain in his letters. But though he resisted those who would criticize or change either the structure or personnel of the courts, there is little doubt that his own irascibility gave ammunition to those who opposed him.⁶

McKean also resisted those in Pennsylvania who would substantially change the institution of slavery within the state. And slavery was a subject of some interest to Pennsylvanians in 1785. Five years earlier, in March 1780, the Assembly, acting at the instigation of Joseph Reed and George Bryan, had passed a law requiring adult slaves to be registered by their owners. The law also provided that adult slaves would remain slaves, but Blacks born after the passage of the act became free upon reaching the age of twenty-eight. The Abolition Society of Philadelphia aggressively promoted court cases centering on this legislation.

In the fall of 1785 the first of these cases came before the McKean court. Phillip Dalby, a resident of Virginia, visited Philadelphia in February 1785 on business and brought with him his slave, a young mulatto named Francis Belt. The Abolitionist Society, impressed by Belt's light complexion, persuaded the boy to use the Pennsylvania courts to seek his freedom. Dalby was served with a writ of habeas corpus compelling him to appear before Justice Bryan to answer questions concerning his slave's status, and after listening to preliminary arguments in his chambers, Bryan scheduled a session in

McKean's chambers for the following day. After long and passionate discussion between the two parties, McKean suggested throwing the case into a form of action *de Homine repleqiando,* and Dalby was ordered to appear before the court in April.[7]

George Washington, who learned of the "vexatious lawsuit" from Dalby, wrote Robert Morris in Philadelphia to express his outrage. "It would seem that this Society is not only acting repugnant to justice so far as its conduct concerns strangers," Washington wrote, "but, in my opinion extremely unpolitickly with respect to the State, the City in Particular, and without being able to accomplish their ends." He thought people with slaves would not visit Philadelphia if such actions did not cease.[8]

At the trial (delayed until October 1785) Thomas Mifflin, representing the angry Dalby, based his argument on the fact that the boy's mother and grandmother were and always had been slaves, that he had been legally purchased in Maryland, and that Maryland law recognized him as a slave. Pennsylvania must recognize the legitimacy of Maryland laws in governing Belt's status. Attorney General William Bradford and William Lewis of the Abolition Society defended Belt, charging that Pennsylvania law did not recognize slavery. They conceded that civil law might decree that issue follow the mother but common law ruled that issue followed the status of the father, and in this case the father had been free. They pointed out that a bastard ought to be free, that he who would gain nothing by inheritance ought to lose no part of his natural freedom by relation to his progenitors. In his charge to the jury McKean, after tracing the Biblical and historical development of slavery, defined the English form of villeinage with its recognition of issue following the father, and of bastards being free, but told the jury that villeinage had never been part of the inheritance of America. Slavery, however, was an inheritance, and America's "practice is so strongly authorized by the civil law, from which this sort of domestic slavery is derived, and is in itself so consistent with the precepts of nature, that we must now consider it as the law of the land." The charge is remarkable from several aspects. It contained sentiments so divergent from those held by Bryan that one marvels at McKean's power in controlling the Court's direction. It also demonstrates that McKean held minimal sympathy for the antislavery movement. His charge left the jury with little choice but to return a verdict for Dalby, the defendant.[9]

Like many of his fellow Scotch-Irish Presbyterians, McKean's personal and judicial life suggests a strong willingness to accept slavery at face value. He was not among those in Delaware in the early 1760s who sought to weaken slavery there. John Thompson and Zachariah Van Leuvenigh, McKean's brothers-in-law, owned a number of slaves, as did his younger brother William. McKean himself owned black servants; it is not clear whether all of his Blacks had servant status. In any case his study of history convinced him of the moral and legal right to own slaves. As a lawyer he frequently aided persons seeking to reclaim runaway slaves, and in cases thrust upon his court by the Abolition Society of Philadelphia, he invariably supported local laws regarding slavery and the sanctity of the contract for private property. He also accepted the widespread assumption that bastard children born of white, free fathers and Negro, unfree mothers, belonged with the mothers and were themselves slaves, as he ruled in the Dalby case. Only in the system of villeinage, once a form of slavery unique to England, could the child of such a union be considered free. In subsequent years McKean reaffirmed the feelings and assumptions expressed in *Dalby* v. *Belt.*

In the case of *Respublica* v. *Negro Betsy,* in June 1786 McKean not only supported the institution of slavery but expressed personal reservations about the free negro's ability to function in a free, white society. When an owner of slaves in Pennsylvania failed to comply with the March 1780 law to register his slaves, the Abolition Society instituted proceedings against him to free his slaves. The owner admitted his failure to comply and agreed to accept the consequences, but claimed the children of the freed slaves should remain his property. In the first trial, McKean and Bryan agreed that the children belonged to the slave owner, but as the court was short-handed, the justices decided to postpone their final ruling until the other justices could either concur or dissent. The second trial took place three years later, in September 1789. McKean's summation, representing his mature thinking on the subject, provides insight into his position on the Negro in American society. His thinking, in fact, dated back before the Dalby case, for in that decision he had indicated he had been reading in the subject of slavery for some time.[10]

McKean acknowledged that as this was the first case seriously to challenge the 1780 law, his decision would establish a precedent. Drifting from purely legal arguments, he observed that Blacks freed from bondage were not always well situated to survive in Pennsylvania's community. If the Negro Betsy

> were discharged from her Master, she would be incapable to take care of herself, and her parents are unable to educate her: she cannot suffer so much by living with a good master, as being with poor and ignorant parents, by a contrary judgment, she... would be little benefitted and her master, who hitherto has derived no advantage from her services, and has been subjected to considerable expenses for her food, clothing, and lodging, would be a great sufferer; so that the balance on this consideration seems, likewise, to preponderate on the side for which I have declared my opinion.[11]

The master was to keep his children, was the chief justice's opinion. In this second trial, however, Bryan, Rush, and Atlee dissented, and the children were subsequently freed.[12]

McKean's reluctance to aid Blacks was recognized beyond the courtroom. He was occasionally accused of agreeing too hastily to help owners in regaining runaway slaves. In 1787 one Scroggan of Maryland claimed his mulatto man ran away from him and escaped to Philadelphia, where he found work. Scroggan found him, assaulted him and, at pistol point, sought to force the mulatto to return to Maryland. Citizens of Philadelphia then stepped in and brought Scroggan before McKean. Scroggan contended that the mulatto was wanted in Maryland for a crime, that he had escaped bail and therefore should be returned at once. McKean ruled that, under the circumstances, neither bail nor records were required, and ordered the servant to be delivered up to Scroggan for the return trip to Maryland. Many Philadelphians were furious at this step, accusing McKean of neglecting to follow procedures in requiring from Scroggan a message from the Maryland governor requesting extradition. One writer publicly declared McKean's move to be a "deadly blow at the whole community."[13]

Even while he was being castigated for his conservatism in the area of slavery and antislavery legislation, McKean was roundly condemned for his liberalism in advocating penal reforms. As a judge McKean acted on the assumption that he was to conserve the law, not alter it; thus he was not disturbed during the Revolution by the paucity of Assembly statutes altering substantive law. But he had seen as many of the horrors of the Revolution and perhaps more of the domestic strife than most, and he was convinced of the need to mitigate some of the more severe punishments demanded by the law. In this respect he did not hesitate to abandon English precedents. The conviction that the laws must be revised and softened in keeping with an enlightened republic was widely shared among the justices of the Court by 1784, as it was by a large portion of the population.

McKean headed a petition signed by his fellow Supreme Court justices and the grand jury of the Philadelphia oyer and terminer court to press the Assembly to act on reforms in that year. Among the recommendations were those to eliminate the death penalty for crimes such as robbery and burglaries, and to maintain it only for such acts as treason and murder. It was hoped that torture would be discarded as a means of punishment. In place of the death penalty would be hard larbor, a policy by which social shame could be employed as a tool for rehabilitation. The Assembly took up the issue in the same year.[14]

With John Dickinson, McKean also discussed the possibilities of reform relating to the habeas corpus act, and the process of verifying land titles more efficiently. Both men expressed great interest in effecting some changes in these areas, but neither found time in the hustle and bustle of 1784-85 to accomplish either.[15] However, in several charges to juries McKean advocated the creation of a court of chancery. In "a learned and circumspect opinion" in *Wharton et al.* v. *Morris et al.*, tried in April 1785, for instance, McKean lamented the lack of a chancery court where equity powers could be exercised. He was aware that agitation for the creation of just such a tribunal had appeared prior to the Revolution, but the Assembly had forestalled it fearing such a court would diminish the governor's powers as chancellor. McKean was nonetheless persuaded that such a court was now essential. The lack of a chancery court had denied relief for those involved in cases of a breach of truth or cases of covenants with a penalty. He urged some reconsideration.[16]

It was his public advocacy of the penal reform bill that elicited the greatest storm of protest. By supporting an Assembly bill which called for criminals to clear the streets of Philadelphia and to receive up to one shilling nine pence per day for their work, he hoped, as did the Assembly, that both criminal and city would benefit. Agreeing that such a rehabilitation scheme was worth a try, he put his considerable weight behind the operation. He once wrote that "a wise and frugal government is more bent upon preventing than punishing crime" and that ". . .a penitentiary prison is a bad school for teaching good morals." About thirty convicts—called wheelbarrow men—were so employed throughout 1788 and into the early months of 1789, but with each passing month there was increasing pressure to put an end to the experiment. It was charged that the wheelbarrow men were using their time beyond prison walls to plan and execute crimes, and, indeed, five were ultimately convicted and executed for murders committed during their working hours. As one of the prime figures in the original scheme, McKean naturally drew to himself a large share of the adverse comment by citizens of Philadelphia who saw themselves victimized by the rehabilitation project.[17]

The instigator of much of McKean's discomfort continued to be his old nemesis, Francis Hopkinson. McKean could twist and turn, and chart any number of new headings, but the one constant in his life was the knowledge that Hopkinson would interpret his actions in the darkest colors. A good deal of Hopkinson's public criticism of the chief justice was admittedly petty[18] and irrational.[19] But it is equally true that much of it was legitimate.

It was not so much McKean's legal power Hopkinson resented as what he perceived to be his enormous political

Francis Hopkinson, owned by Robert Edge Pine. Courtesy of the Historical Society of Pennsylvania

influence. Hopkinson wrote to Jefferson in September 1785 to describe the "tight Struggle" looming in the October elections. "It is agreed by all that Dr. Franklin is to be President of the State & he seems willing to accept the Charge," wrote Hopkinson, "but in our Constitution, two or three leading members of the House drive the political Coach, the President is the Footman of the Chief Justice [who] rides in the Body of the Carriage—& the People run whooping & hollowing along side, choak'd with Dust & bespatt'd with Mire."[20]

Still, Hopkinson was not unmindful of McKean's impressive legal powers and the fact that, if anything, McKean's influence was increasing yearly. Of particular interest to Hopkinson in 1786 was the Assembly's new penal reform bill. He had his own reasons for fearing the passage of the law. He conceded the need for a more effective rehabilitation program and he favored mitigating some of the more severe punishments demanded by the law, but he insisted that the bill's major fault lay in the power it gave to the justices of the Supreme Court. The powers already wielded by the justices were much too extensive. McKean, according to Hopkinson, as well as being chief justice, was judge in the high court of errors and appeals, a judge in the court of admiralty sessions for the United States, a judge of the admiralty sessions for the state of Pennsylvania, and a trustee of the University of Pennsylvania.[21] McKean had, in addition, the power to decide the fate of all claims against estates forfeited to the Commonwealth and against the forfeiting persons. He had the power to perpetuate testimony, to care for persons and estates of lunatics, and to determine all matters pertaining to marriage and divorce. The justices also had control over defaced deeds and other official papers. The proposed law, Hopkinson warned, would substantially enhance McKean's power by providing that the justices of the Supreme Court could punish criminals according to their discretion up to fourteen years' hard service.

Hopkinson maintained such power was dangerous, especially when given to a small body like the Supreme Court. Power lodged in fairly large bodies such as the Assembly and the Supreme Executive Council, which changed personnel frequently, was less dangerous to the citizens of Pennsylvania than power in the Court, which shifted personnel infrequently.

The Court's exclusiveness, its homogeneity and stability, and the fact that the judges continued during good behavior, made it a threat to republicanism in Pennsylvania. By taking advantage of their friends in the Council, the judges could easily retain their powers. Moreover, when the judges' commissions expired the renewal process took place hurriedly and secretly, minimizing the efforts of those who would oppose the reissuing of the justices' commissions. The real threat to liberties in Pennsylvania, then, came not so much from the Assembly or the Council, but from the Supreme Court—and especially from the chief justice. Hopkinson called for the traditional insistence on judges who mechanically applied immutable rules and standard sentences. "Excessive power has a natural tendency to debauch the best disposition," Hopkinson write, "but when it falls into the hands of a proud, capricious, and ambitious man, its operation must be watched with a jealous eye."[22]

On August 28, 1786, just days before the Assembly was to give final consideration of the bill, Hopkinson wrote a second piece concerning the implications of the reforms included in it. He warned the legislators that "innovations are to be suspected and prudence dictates that novelties, under the guise of improvement, should be strictly scrutinized." Again he warned them and his readers of the dangers inherent in giving justices so much power. The consequence of the proposed legislation was, in his mind, to "transfer great power to apportion punishments to crimes from the sovereignty of the state, where it certainly ought to be, to two or three individuals where it certainly ought not to be." He provided several telling examples showing how two men committing the same offense under roughly the same circumstances might end up with rather dissimilar sentences. As long as McKean was chief justice Hopkinson wanted as little room as possible for judicial discretion. And as long as McKean was associated with reforms, Hopkinson wanted to be the first to bring those reforms to the attention of the public if they failed to pan out.[23]

Hopkinson's caution was justified: many reforms instigated by the Assembly did bring McKean and his court new powers and influence—some in fact made him uncomfortable, pushing the Court into questions such as slavery for which he had little enthusiasm. Divorce was another such question. Prior to

1785 divorces were granted in Pennsylvania by the Assembly and then only after the party had petitioned for it. Each case was determined on its own merits by a committee of the Assembly, a practice which led to frequent inconsistencies and hardships both for the petitioners and the Assemblymen. In September 1785 the Assembly passed a law giving the Supreme Court absolute jurisdiction over matters of alimony and divorce. Thereafter only extraordinary cases went to the Assembly. Before the ink on the bill was dry, John Brice asked the Court for a divorce from his wife, Sarah, whom he accused of being repeatedly unfaithful. Married in 1774, he had submitted to his wife's unfaithfulness from that point on. But by 1785 he had had enough. He pointed out that the tempestuous Mrs. Brice had earlier been convicted of adultery by McKean's court. McKean and the justices granted the divorce. Thereafter hardly a court session went by without McKean being plagued by a wide range of domestic squabbles.[24]

In 1788 McKean was called upon to exert his influence in quite another area. That year the Assembly passed a bill allowing stage plays in Philadelphia. By that time the Assembly was no longer under the absolute sway of the Quakers and the western Presbyterians, who agreed in their suspicion of plays. Members of the 1788 legislature did not share the view that the stage was the "great corruptor of mankind," or that "theatrical representations may be abused by indecent, vicious, and immoral performances...to the scandal of religion and virtue." ("Is it not notorious," one Quaker petition asked, that "fornication and adultery...are among the characteristics of the devoted pupils of the stage?") Despite opposition of legislators like Quaker George Logan, who argued that theatrical exhibitions undermined morality and the purity of republican manners, the bill passed, and provided that a board of review consisting of the president of the Council, the chief justice, and the president of the court of common pleas in Philadelphia be created to guard against plays that might transcend community standards or prove to be blatant threats to the good morals of the city. McKean was named to head the board, to oversee all productions, to clear inoffensive productions, and to levy fines up to £200 against those productions ignoring their licenses. Those who anticipated that McKean's rigid

Presbyterianism would seriously limit theatrical offerings were soon surprised. Edward Shippen and Thomas Mifflin, members of the board, took a more conservative position than McKean. They were, according to the Philadelphia lawyer William Rawle, "several times opposed to the latitude of opinion in the Chief Justice who thought a good double entrendre not objectionable."[25]

The personal hatred Hopkinson felt for McKean continued—even deepened in the following years—but his public attacks on McKean ceased by 1787. There were events—"great reforms"—that were ineluctibly drawing the two men into the same political circle and the personal, public attacks on McKean by Hopkinson were the first casuality of this new political alignment.[26]

14. Federalist

One important reform on which McKean and Hopkinson concurred—that of readjusting the constitutional arrangements of American republicanism—helped to break down old political blocs in Pennsylvania, and to provoke a rash of new political and constitutional issues which forged new alliances. Though some opposition materialized to an Assembly bill in 1786 to fund the vast debt owed by the United States to the citizens of Pennsylvania, leading members of both parties supported it. They quarreled over whether it was better to have the state or the federal government act, but they agreed that some action was essential. McKean, a holder of over five thousand dollars in depreciated certificates, was not a disinterested observer.[1]

Constitutionalists and Republicans by 1786 also shared a disappointment in Congress. The first widespread impulse for serious change in Pennsylvania came not from a concern with the distribution of powers within the state government, but from a dissatisfaction with the relationship of Pennsylvania to the other states in Congress. Transfixed by the spectre of power they could not control, whether exercised by the people or the aristocracy, and insistent upon limited government wedded to local interests as far as possible, the Constitutionalists were by 1786 willing to concede the failure of the general Congress in dealing with critical national problems. When in 1786 there was a proposal for a federal constitutional convention, in Pennsylvania at least there was "very little bustle...and little or no opposition."

Though he, too, was cautious, McKean was eager for some change. He had never been completely pleased with the basic organization of the state government, and still held firmly in 1786 the criticisms he had expressed in 1777. His adherence to the Constitutionalists during that period had been based more on a loyalty to the government employing him and a visceral antagonism to anyone critical of himself personally or his court, than on any deep-rooted acceptance of the Constitutionalist political and philosophical programs. As we have seen, in the first decade of his chief justiceship he opposed the Constitutionalists as often as he was sympathetic to their aims.[2] The great majority of complaints directed at the chief justice by the Republicans were aimed less at his basic political positions than at his personal failings or his powers.

If McKean needed any push toward a full commitment to change in the spring of 1787 it was provided by John Adams. On the advice of Adams, his bookseller sent McKean a number of volumes of Adams' *Defense of the Constitution of Government of the United States of America,* asking him to commit them to some local bookseller for sale. McKean turned them over to a dealer, but not before he had read deeply in Adams' work. He found himself agreeing almost completely with Adams' assumptions of the proper balance of power.

On April 30, 1787, he wrote Adams his thoughts on the upcoming political developments. He described "his entire approbation of [Adams'] system and concurrence in all the sentiments in [his] work." Despite his loyalty to Pennsylvania's present government he confessed that the proper constitutional balance had not yet been achieved. "The balance of the one, the few, and the many, is not well poised in this state," he wrote, "The legislature is too powerful for the executive and judicial branches of government. . . it can too easily make laws, and too easily alter or repeal them." He concluded that "we must have another branch, and a negative in the executive, stability in our laws, and permanency in our magistracy, before we shall be reputable, safe and happy." He confessed that in respect to the upcoming constitutional convention the "popular opinion is, that we should be very jealous of conferring power on any man or body of men. . . indeed we seem afraid to enable any one to do good lest he should do evil."

McKean himself was not wholly without suspicion. He was not willing to see wholesale changes wrought in the national government. "In general," he told Adams, "I dislike innovations, especially in the administration of justice; and I would avoid tampering with constitutions of government, as with edge-tools." Some changes in the structure and organization might be helpful, he admitted, but in the end a government was only as good as those controlling it.[3]

McKean was not elected to attend the Philadelphia constitutional convention—he placed very poorly in the race for delegates—but he had considerable contact with those who were chosen. Many of his friends who had served long and hard in the Continental Congress with him returned to Philadelphia to take up the chores of producing political changes. He dined with members of the convention so frequently that by August he could tell Atlee that "the Convention is still sitting. I am tired feasting with them." Whatever the information he learned from these friends prior to the public review of the new constitution, McKean was content with their changes and anxious to ratify their work.[4]

McKean recognized as did most Pennsylvanians that the vote for delegates to the Pennsylvania ratification convention would be close. Both sides argued ardently in the period between September 29 and November 6 to impress the people with their positions. McKean had judged the political divisions in the state to be dead even in April and he had no reason to assume that sentiment had shifted precipitously one way or the other after that date. Though by late October he was grousing over the fact that "those who have the least at stake and who know the least about government are the most busy," he still was optimistic that all states would ratify the

Constitution. He judged "the advantages they will derive from it so greatly preponderate over any disadvantage, that it is undoubtedly the interest of the Great Body of the People to embrace it."[5]

McKean, by then his sympathy for the new constitution known to all, was backed by the Federalists as a delegate. He won 1157 votes to join the Federalist slate, the highest vote going to George Latimer with 1215. When the ratifying convention met on November 21, 1787, McKean and forty-five other delegates were known to support the new constitution; twenty-three others had serious reservations as to its efficacy.[6]

McKean lost the presidency of the convention to Frederick Muhlenberg by a single vote.[7] In view of the criticism directed toward McKean by Hopkinson and others in the preceding years, and in view of the propensity of current historians to see McKean as a political trimmer, the election is significant. There is little hint in the vote to suggest that the Federalists were unhappy with McKean's presence, or viewed his acceptance by the convention with suspicion. By the same token there is little evidence to support the charge that the Constitutionalists viewed him as a turncoat. New issues had confused old alliances in Pennsylvania. Most viewed the Constitution as a new issue and the resulting divisions were accordingly novel and flexible.

When the convention began serious deliberations on the twenty-fourth, it became apparent that McKean and James Wilson, a political veteran of the Philadelphia Federal Constitutional Convention, were to carry the burden of the Federalist efforts. McKean did not wait long to assume the initiative. The fifty-three-year-old chief justice, after acknowledging that the convention was without precedent to guide it in ascertaining the proper mode of proceeding, moved that delegates adopt and ratify the government as agreed upon by the federal convention. He assured members that his motion was designed merely to focus their attention upon the primary task before them and should in no way be considered an effort to secure "an instantaneous decision of so important a question." Subsequent events suggest, however, that McKean might not have been wholly candid in his assurances.

Wilson, the only member of the body who had participated in the federal convention, submitted for the Assembly's enlightenment those principles which produced the new government. His arguments were designed less for those in attendance (it was clear to all that the Federalists had the requisite votes and there was little evidence that the opposition could be persuaded to change its stance) than for those beyond the walls of the convention. In an impressive and often eloquent presentation, the cool and deliberate Wilson sought to pacify those who viewed the new constitution as destructive to the values and political gains derived from the recent revolutionary struggle. He assured the minority that the benefits of democracy had been preserved, that the federal convention had been eager to maintain the benefits and to avoid the pitfalls of the balance of the three historic divisions of rule: monarchy, aristocracy and democracy.

Wilson's pronouncements were largely ignored by the anti-Federalists, who at this point were less interested in substantive arguments than in procedural considerations. John Smilie, the Fayette County representative, brushed aside Wilson's observations and directly attacked McKean's original motion which he deemed to be a subterfuge, "consistent with the system of precipitancy that had uniformly prevailed in respect to the important subject before the convention." Smilie saw only danger in the undue haste which characterized his opponent's machinations. He admitted the sensibility of "giving additional strength and energy to the Federal Head," but he cautioned the Assembly to "go coolly and circumstantially into the consideration of the business." He reminded the delegates that while strengthening the federal government was an admirable move they were not "obliged to accept any terms."

Ruffled by Smilie's remark, McKean reaffirmed that his motion was designed "not to preclude, but promote a free and ample discussion of the federal plan." Assuming his best judicial manner, he warned the convention that it had not been called to legislate, or to inquire into the powers of the late convention, or to alter or amend its work; "the present task [was] simply to ratify and confirm, or, upon due consideration, reject in the whole, the system of federal government." The minority should harbor no illusion that it had the power or the resources to rewrite the Constitution to its satisfaction. Nor was there any cause to deliberate at great length on each article for the purpose of considering alternatives. Theirs was the task of appreciating the overall structure, according to McKean, and either accepting or rejecting it.

Robert Whitehall of Cumberland County, as formidable an opponent to the Federalists as William Findley or John Smilie, was willing to grant the chief justice the benefit of the doubt as to his motives, but he nonetheless insisted that before the convention could vote, a microscopic examination must be made of the Constitution's individual provisions. This was especially essential, he maintained, since it was clear that delegates to the federal convention had exceeded their directives, which were to merely "revise" the Articles of Confederation.

The debate provoked by Whitehall's demand clarified the strategy of both sides. Federalists sought to gain quick acceptance of the plan while the momentum was theirs and thus influence the contests in other states. They saw no need for extended debate and delays. "Shall we," Wilson asked, "while we contemplate a great and magnificent edifice, condescend like a fly, with its microscopic eye, to scrutinize the imperfections of a single brick?" Anti-Federalists, wanting to use the convention to mobilize public opinion against the proposed constitution and to encourage opponents of the new government in neighboring states, knew they could best be served by delay involving examination of the document. "Shall we not Sir," Findley retorted to Wilson's simile, "when we are about to erect a large and expensive (for as far as it respects us, we are about to erect this mighty fabric of government in Pennsylvania) examine and compare [sic] the materials of which we mean to compose it, fitting and combining the parts with each other, and rejecting everything that is useless and rotten?"

The debates which followed established one critical point respecting McKean: his oral responses differed in form and tone from his written argumentation. The decorum and balance that marked his judicial decisions were absent; he seemed incapable in public debate to conducting a calm, moderate, and subtle exchange. To him face-to-face confrontation became

William Findley, painted by Rembrandt Peale. Courtesy of Independence National Historical Park Coll.

personal attack, an opportunity to exhibit his intellectual superiority, to defeat, and if possible humiliate his adversary. Out of sensitivity to opposition he exaggerated differences between himself and his opponents, and at times took positions that caricatured his more deliberate and moderate thinking, so that he spoke sharply and derogatorily to those for whom, prior to the convention, he had entertained respect, even affection.

Once he had embraced the new system, he embraced it thoroughly and enthusiastically. He dismissed his opponents' fear of the new system as irrational. He saw nothing in the new fabric, he told his colleagues, "to be the object of terror or apprehension." The powers granted to the new government were necessary to its existence, he argued, and to the political happiness of the people. The objections offered arise "from an evident perversion of its principles, and the presumption of a meaning which neither the framers of the system, nor the system itself ever meant." The adoption of this new framework would provide "what had been his constant wish—permanency in the government and stability in the laws."[8]

A careful reading of the proposed government convinced him that the requisite checks and balances were present. He dismissed those who feared excessive taxation, noting that "the greatest restraint upon excessive taxation arises from [the fact] that the same act by which a representative imposes a tax upon his constituents, extends to himself and all his connections." He shrugged off the argument of those who complained that the appellate jurisdiction of the Supreme Court impaired the concept of trial by jury. "It has been a subject of amazement to me," he confided, "that the verdict of a jury shall be without revision in all cases. . . . Juries are not infallible because they are twelve in number." He argued that a bill of rights was not necessary under the circumstances, "for in fact the whole plan of government is nothing more than a bill of rights." In brief, McKean saw no reason why the people at large nor the individual states should fear the proposed government.

The good will of those responsible for creating the new system was the most obvious safeguard of the people's rights. Though a good system of government was certainly a blessing,

McKean observed, no doubt thinking of his last ten years under the Constitution of 1776, "yet it is on the administration of the best system that the freedom, wealth and happiness of the people depend." Admitting what all doubtless believed, but found impolitic to articulate, McKean went on to say that "despotism, if wisely administered, is the best form of government invented by the ingenuity of men." He went on to suggest that "the people under absolute and limited monarchies, under aristocracies and mixed governments, are as contented and as prosperous as we are when there is virtue and wisdom by their rulers." "It is also true," he suggested, "that the best government may be so conducted as to produce misery and disgrace, and the worst so administered as to ensure some dignity and happiness to a nation." The current government had the double blessing of being a good system and administrated by responsible, sensible men.

Characteristically, it was McKean who became the central target of anti-Federalist vilification. He was accused of deliberately misquoting arguments from the federal convention in order to put the best possible light on the Constitution's provisions. Anti-Federalists were particularly incensed over what they considered his corruption of a George Mason comment to minimize the role of jury trials. They resented too his habit of treating their views "as trifling and contemptible, and this with a magisterial air." He retorted that their case could have been completed in no more than a few hours, that he found their arguments . . . "a mere sound, like the workings of small beer in a rebellious stomach." When the opposition press protested against the "indecent, supercilious carriage of its [the Constitution's] advocates towards its opponents," there was little doubt whom they had in mind.⁹

On December 12, 1787, the convention formally ratified the federal constitution, the second state to do so. The vote split along familiar lines, forty-six favoring its ratification, twenty-three opposing it.¹⁰ At least in his public statements McKean suggested that his motives for supporting a new government were many and complex. He told the convention that by drawing on the wisdom and assistance of all the states America would strengthen the government and the people of the United States. It would also "settle, establish and firmly perpetuate our independence, destroy the hopes of foreign countries who still seek our downfall, encourage allies who wish to join with us, induce foreign nations to enter treaties, invigorate commerce and encourage shipping, and generally reduce the willingness of other nations to insult or make war upon us." He told his colleagues that the new constitution had produced "the best system that the world has yet known."[11]

The fact that McKean was a holder of public securities doubtless played a role in his support of the new constitution. His holdings, amounting to $5,581 in securities which he funded in 1786 under the state assumption act, and an additional $1,772 in Continental office certificates, placed him somewhat above the average Pennsylvania holder in this respect. Yet neither in his public nor private correspondence did he emphasize the economic benefits which would accrue to individuals or groups from the new framework. Apparently economic considerations were not the prime determinant in how a delegate voted in Pennsylvania's ratification convention.[12]

McKean urged that Pennsylvania's ratification be celebrated in a manner commensurate with its historical importance. The delegates to the ratifying convention decided to meet at the courthouse to announce the ratification and to participate in a commemorating procession. There they were joined by state officials, the president and vice-president, assemblymen, various city dignitaries, and the faculty of the University of Pennsylvania. The procession wound its way to the courthouse where "a great gathering of people" listened to the announcement of ratification and Federalist cheers to the tune of cannon and bells.[13] Eleazer Oswald, his hatred of McKean still rampant, reported that "our friends, the majority, after dining together, enjoyed much happiness in the pleasure of the social bottle till late at night, when our worthy chief justice... was a little affected by the working of small beer, and so retired." His reference to small beer was not lost on anyone who had followed the convention's progress.[14]

Federalist exuberance at the courthouse and later at Epple's Tavern was not shared by all. Opposition to the federal government and its supporters intensified in the West. In Carlisle, a group of Federalists celebrating the ratification was rudely dispersed by a mob armed with staves and axe handles. When they tried on the following day to continue their celebration they were overwhelmed by a jeering crowd displaying effigies of James Wilson and McKean. The rioters "formed in order, had the effigies carried in front, preceded only by a noted Captain of the militia, who declared he was inspired from Heaven, paraded the streets, and with shouts and most dreadful exacrations committed them to the flames."[15] "The effigy of the Chief Justice was pretty Well Dressed, a good Coat but not black, a pretty good hat & wig & rifle," wrote John Montgomery, a Federalist who maintained his sense of humor in the face of poor treatment at the hands of the mob, "The fellow who gave the coat will repent of his Liberality before the end of the Winter." Those who knew McKean well could appreciate the dual meaning of Montgomery's observations.[16]

The Carlisle Federalists sent letters and affidavits to McKean requesting warrants against some twenty rioters. George Bryan, himself no sympathizer with the new constitution or McKean's new political orientation, found the business not only irksome but somewhat embarrassing. He noted that McKean, too, was uncomfortable over just what action to take. The chief justice tried to persuade Bryan or Atlee to issue the warrants, "alleging it was indelicate for him to act when he was ill-used."[17] Even when arrests were eventually secured on the basis of warrants issued by Atlee and Bryan, the sheriff's helplessness in the face of local opposition was evident to all. Militia units parading through town intimidated those charged with prosecuting the offenders of law and order. The question of what to do about conditions in Carlisle became a prime topic of conversation among Philadelphia's Federalists. It was argued by some that to do nothing would invite anarchy and disrespect for all government. Others maintained that the best policy would be to "bury . . . the whole in oblivion."[18]

McKean, for once, chose discretion. He moved to halt the prosecution in the interests of future peace and tranquility, anticipating the Assembly's decision to drop its investigation. McKean was not intimidated by threats of violence to himself if he should ever show his face in Carlisle. William Bradford wrote his wife in May to tell her that the chief justice had gone on to Carlisle and "the folks who burned him in Effigy [it is said] insinuated that he was afriad [sic] to visit Cumberland, but as soon as he announced his intention of going they have taken another turn & intend to come out and pay him the compliment of waiting on him into town."[19]

A factor in McKean's decision to withhold prosecution of Carlisle offenders was the fact that anti-Federalists there were talking about calling a state convention—one more responsive to the "will of the people,"—to negate the work of the previous one. Even if no such convention were called, McKean knew, further division within the state would most certainly imperil the Federalists' cause should they later challenge the state constitution and seek to bring it into line with the national government—a possibility a number of Federalists no doubt impressed upon McKean. Perhaps, too, like Benjamin Rush, McKean now realized that much of the opposition to their plan, and subsequent violence, was attributable to the haste and often overbearing manner in which they had carried out ratification.

By June 25, 1788, the necessary states had ratified the new government and on July 4 Philadelphia celebrated the Federalist victory. Rush wrote that "the constitution was carried by a great law officer [McKean] to denote the elevation of the government of law and justice above everything else." Had he been more inclined to add detail, he might have mentioned that McKean rode on a carriage over twenty feet long, its rear wheels eight feet in diameter, the front less than two feet smaller. On the carriage rode a replica of the federal eagle, a figure over thirteen feet long and thirteen feet high. On the eagle's breast was a crest marked by thirteen stars against a pale blue background, and thirteen red and white stripes. The silver-haired McKean, reminiscent of an old Roman senator, rode with his hand upon a staff bearing a replica of the Constitution. On the shaft appeared the words, THE PEOPLE, in golden letters.[20]

One wag ("Abigail Callicoe") was not impressed. In describing the parade, he wrote,

> Then there came the Chief Justice drest all in scarlet (like the whore of Babylon some said) with two other Judges behind, drest in the same manner, upon a

> monstrous high car.... The car was as high as the houses.... Some wondered how the judges got into the car, if by a ladder or upon the people's shoulders. The Chief Justice had a pole in his hand, upon which were painted the words "The People." I hope it does not mean that the people are to be knocked down with poles.[21]

Despite these and other unfriendly observations directed toward him, McKean could look upon the Federalist victory as a personal victory. He, along with Wilson, had been the main spokesman for the Federalist cause in Pennsylvania; the honors and acclamation, his prominence in the parade, were not only testimony to his position in Pennsylvania officialdom but to his important role in the convention. One wonders whether the fact that Francis Hopkinson had been a prime architect of the parade brought a wry smile to McKean's lips as he moved through the streets of Philadelphia.[22]

McKean was not to be insulated from Pennsylvania's tempestuous political life, however. Serious disagreements continued in Philadelphia regarding the proper role of the press in a free republican society, and the extent of legal change necessitated by the Revolution. Early in 1788 Eleazer Oswald had published a number of articles critical of Andrew Brown, a prominent Philadelphia Federalist. Asserting that the articles libeled him, Brown secured the services of William Lewis to sue Oswald if the editor did not make available to him the names of those correspondents responsible for the offending articles. Oswald conceded that "some of the pieces as is usual in political squabbles, and in times of high political ferment, [had] not been altogether purged from a proportion of invective and abuse," but he refused to name the correspondents. He thought Brown should preserve his temper, not take the matter to court.[23] When Oswald refused to divulge the names on the ostensible grounds that Brown's actions were politically motivated and supported by Federalists seeking to destroy his anti-Federalist *Gazetteer,* Brown prosecuted him. Bryan, who heard the preliminary arguments on whether or not Oswald should be held for bail, concluded that Oswald should not be held and permitted the editor to return to his paper, where the impulsive Oswald immediately discussed the case in the columns of the *Gazetteer*. He did not go easy on the Court or the chief justice.

Incensed that Oswald should treat a pending case in his columns and still rankled by Oswald's earlier barbs, McKean charged the editor with contempt of the Court and with libeling the Court and its justices. McKean told the Court that "libeling is a great crime, whatever sentiment may be entertained by those who live by it." He considered the heart of a libeler "is more dark and base than that of an assassin." Those like Oswald who sought "to assert that the judges are influenced by passion and prejudice, willfully [sought] to corrupt the source, and to dishonor the administration of justice." He fined the editor ten pounds and sentenced him to one month in jail, telling him that "your circumstances are small, but your offense is great." Either Oswald "would bend to the law, or the law shall bend to [him]." McKean left no doubt that it was his duty to see "that the former shall always be the case."

Throughout the proceedings Oswald complained that McKean was perverting the doctrine of libel, a doctrine "incompatible with law and liberty and at once destructive to the privileges of a free country." He argued that this British doctrine had gained no foothold in Pennsylvania and he pressed the people to resist any violation of freedom accorded the press by "any refined pretense which oppressive ingenuity or courtly study can invent." Oswald's attacks ultimately encouraged a rash of articles in Philadelphia newspapers critical of McKean's treatment of the press.

McKean knew, as did the mass of lawyers in Pennsylvania, that Oswald spoke with more hope than accuracy. The common law doctrine of libel was a recognized part of Pennsylvania law and the courts had upheld it time and again. As both Bryan and McKean emphasized, "there is nothing in the constitution of the state, respecting the liberty of the press, that has not been authorized by the constitution of [England] for near a century past." McKean was sensitive to the hope shared by most Americans that their laws and courts would serve republican values and promote the "contagion of liberty" given birth by the Revolution, but he was republican enough to recognize that libel eroded the very public support of government that was so vital to the success of a republic. If it took British laws and precedents to save American republicanism, McKean could live with the irony.

The obdurate Oswald, stung by his recent fine and imprisonment and still bitter over McKean's past treatment of him and his friends, and convinced that the public supported him, attempted to use the incident to destroy McKean and any justices concurring with him. Careful to exclude Bryan from his charges, Oswald sought the impeachment of McKean, Rush, and Atlee. To this end, he sent a memorial to the September 1788 Assembly in which he enumerated the failings of the three justices and elaborated on their alleged willingness to deny to citizens of Pennsylvania their constitutional guarantees. His hatred of McKean was such by this time, it was said, that only the public hanging of the chief justice would satisfy him.[24]

Oswald's memorial, calling "aloud for Legislative redress," came before the Assembly on September 5, when it was tabled until the twelfth. William Lewis was unsympathetic to the memorial's design and moved that the House sit as an inquest rather than forming a committee to investigate the charges. Since everyone was familiar with the facts of the case, he reasoned, it was simply a matter of determining if those facts contained an injustice and, if so, what remedy should be forthcoming. "If the Judges of the Supreme Court are guilty of violating and disregarding the Constitution and the laws of the State," he argued, "they ought to be immediately presented before the proper tribunal and punished." But he warned that the investigation was to determine innocence as well as culpability. If the justices were blameless the Assembly owed it to them to establish that fact and to quickly make its verdict known to the community.[25]

McKean was sanguine about the outcome. He seemed assured that his court would be upheld by the Assembly, and that Lewis in particular would do justice to the Court's position. He and Lewis had spent many an afternoon fencing with each other in the courtrooms of Pennsylvania and each greatly respected the other's legal acumen. McKean told Atlee that "a public investigation was [his] wish, tho' it gave too much countenance to such a seditious turbulent man." Still, he thought "Lewis [was] so well acquainted with every particular that there [would] be no occasion for anything other than that he should be heard." Plans were afoot to see that Lewis' speech on the question would be published "as soon as it shall have been delivered, in order to diffuse information & knowledge among the people."[26]

Though the House voted thirty-two to twenty-eight to deny Oswald counsel, William Findley, an assemblyman unfriendly to McKean, offered to provide whatever legal advice Oswald desired. Findley did not share Oswald's belief that impeachment of the justices was warranted, but he viewed the justices' recent actions as an unconstitutional exercise of judicial power and an alarming precedent. His arguments, though eloquent and heartfelt, failed to convince the majority, however, and the memorial died aborning. Criticism of McKean in the Oswald matter was widespread but the move to impeach him garnered little support.[27]

Even as his position was being reaffirmed by the Assembly, McKean was casting covetous eyes on a federal judicial office. The creation of the new government had caused much interest among Pennsylvanians in securing federal posts. The lure of office was always strong even in local politics and the prospect of federal posts with their superior prestige added to the age-old lure. In March 1789 John Bayard, a longtime friend and colleague, sought McKean's advice on how to gain office in the Washington administration. McKean provided a fairly elaborate scenario, including advice to make contact with President Washington by learning where and when he would be traveling, then giving profuse "general compliments to make Washington aware of him." Bayard was also to find out whom Washington principally consulted. "These you must make with as opportunities offer," McKean concluded. He was quick to deny that he himself had used such tactics, but he deemed them sound, nonetheless. "It is a new era, and an unknown administration," McKean told Bayard, "Yet you will have therefore to trust to the chapter of accidents in a great degree."[28]

McKean, always ambitious, was not altogether willing to trust to the chapter of accidents in his own case. On April 27, 1789, he wrote President Washington seeking a position on the federal judiciary, telling him, "I have an ambition to take a share in your Excellency's administration, and know of no line in which I can render so good service as in the judicial department." He was candid enough to admit that he thought the financial rewards would be attractive. He told of losing through depreciated Continental currency upwards to six thousand pounds of his own acquiring ("for I have been the maker of my own fortune") and he had a "wish to recoup in some honourable way, at least, a part of it for the sake of eight promising children." His decision to apply for the post had been a "sudden resolution" on his part. But he expressed pride in the fact that, although a good judge can not be popular, he had "reasons to believe that [his] integrity has never been called into question." He expressed pride that "no judgments of the Supreme Court since the Revolution has been reversed, or altered in a single iota." Thomas Rodney produced a letter extolling McKean's virtues, but it proved of no consequence. McKean received the same curt noncommittal reply from Washington as did hundreds of others, including James Wilson, who had also sought a federal judicial post.[29]

In the end, McKean seemed more disgruntled over the failure of Philadelphia's Federalists to support his quest for a federal post than he was over Washington's unwillingness to consider his application. His increasing disenchantment with Philadelphia's Federalist faction late in 1789 and throughout 1790-91 had its root in part in his disappointment over not securing the federal judgeship. Nonetheless, major areas of compatibility between McKean and Federalists remained. In the Federalists' attempt to control city politics and to insure the writing of a more conservative state constitution, McKean became a willing ally. His desire to have the federal government fund the domestic debt and thus to increase the value of his public paper drove him closer to Federalists, many of whom, like Matthew Clarkson and William Bingham, had been not only his political enemies but his social "superiors."

Late in August McKean was among the public creditors in Philadelphia who petitioned Congress to say that they had lost a great deal of money, and had taken considerable risks in purchasing public paper during the Revolution. They strongly urged Congress to fund the domestic debt at the earliest possible opportunity. McKean felt deeply enough about the memorial to go to New York on August 28, 1789, with

Charles Pettit to present it personally to Pennsylvania's congressmen George Clymer and Thomas Fitzsimons.[30]

In September 1789 Republicans in the Assembly issued an address over the protestations of the Constitutionalists calling for a convention to meet in November to revise the state constitution. The desire on the part of the Republicans to rid the state of its constitution was a long-standing one. What distinguished their current push was the skill with which they turned their opponents' republican ideology back in on them. They increasingly posed as advocates of the authority of the people, charging that the current unicameral government prevented the true principles of liberty from being realized. They scored their opponents for denying revolutionary principles, for resisting the people's constituent powers, for fearing to trust the people with their own power, and for assuming that the people were such stupid creatures as to be unable to choose proper men to make a successful constitution for them. Republicans insisted that the people of the state wished to call a convention to produce a new constitution and they were going to give it to them.[31]

McKean was among those chosen to participate in the revision of the current government. He thus joined James Wilson and William Lewis to form a rather impressive legal triumvirate in support of serious revision. The men elected along with Wilson, Lewis, and McKean were among "the most capable and talented body of Pennsylvanians that ever gathered together to perform a public function," according to observers. They also harbored little of the rancor and animosity that had characterized the ratification convention of two years before.[32]

A number of factors contributed to this new harmony. Those favoring a substantial revision of the state constitution had only a slim advantage in the new convention, a fact contributing to their caution and to general good will towards their political opponents. Yet it was clear that they could win despite their slim majority, and this created a feeling of magnanimity hitherto missing in their approach. The fact that many of the old issues separating men had become obsolete, and that there were new men in each faction, contributed to greater good will in both camps. By the same token, those who lacked ardor in seeking changes were not averse to some revision and most were resigned to a Federalist victory.

The convention met on November 27. McKean immediately moved to have the resolves of the General Assembly calling the convention constitute a preface to the minutes of the convention. When on December 1 the convention organized into a Committee of the Whole "to take into consideration whether and wherever, the constitution of the state required alternation or amendment," McKean was unanimously elected chairman. He served in that capacity until January 26 when he reported that "business of a public nature would force him to absent himself for a few days," and he received a leave of absence. When he returned on the twenty-ninth he said that "his health rendered it inconvenient for him to resume the chair." The convention voted "that the thanks of the committee be given to [him] for his able and *impartial* conduct, while chairman thereof.[33]

There seems to be more to McKean's decision to step down from the prestigious but neutral post as chairman of the Committee of the Whole. It is true that McKean had been allowed the unusual privilege of a floor member but his own sense of propriety in that post restrained him from taking undue advantage of his position. His restraint can be explained in part, too, by the fact that in the early going no real critical issue isolated him.[34]

He shared with his colleagues numerous areas of agreement. He agreed that the sovereignty of legitimate government was derived from the people, and that the will of the majority should determine the course of government. He also discovered great advantages in annual elections for most offices and a short residence for voters and candidates alike, both of which were of benefit to the newer settlers.[35] He agreed that the two primary functions of government were the safeguarding of its subjects' liberties and the protection of their property. All people deserved protection against arbitrary and unwise government. A government not beneficial to the needs of the people should not be tolerated; the Revolution itself had clearly established the legitimacy of those sentiments.

To guarantee the majority's rights to protect themselves he favored a reasonably widespread suffrage; he thought a freehold estate in the city or county of three pounds annual income or an estate of fifty pounds a reasonable requirement. He advocated a favorable cycle of elections and the powers and structure of the House of Representatives to secure the people's interest. In his acceptance of a single executive, a bicameral legislature, and a renovation of Pennsylvania's Bill of Rights, McKean found numerous political allies, as he did in his strong advocacy of free public education for Pennsylvania's young.[36]

But here the similarities with the majority of delegates ended. McKean's interpretation of government and his specific suggestions as to how it could be most effectively carried out quickly branded him as unrepresentative of the delegates and doubtless of the majority of Pennsylvanians. It was just these differences of opinion between himself and most of the delegates that probably motivated McKean to step down from his chairmanship in order to voice his views. He seemed to think that the delegates up to that time were more concerned with maintaining the harmony looked for in the elaborate arrangements worked out by Wilson and Findley than in truly thrashing out the best form of government for the people of Pennsylvania.[37]

He wished to stress the protection of minority rights and interests much more aggressively than did his colleagues. His statements leave little doubt that he viewed his own rights and interests with the minority, the elite. The path of the American Revolutionary struggle had by 1789 come down to a struggle between distinct and opposing social elements, what McKean identified as the "democratical" and "aristocratical" parties. More particularly it was a struggle to determine the proper relationship and emphasis between those two forces within a republican society. It was a matter of stress, of weight, not a clash of pure doctrines. The large property holders of Pennsylvania must have security, McKean protested; only a government capable of providing safeguards for both majority and minority interests deserved his support. His remarks confirmed that he felt the current emphasis favored the majority over the minority.[38]

For one thing, he looked for a bicameral legislature in the classical English form. He wanted a senate made up of landowners holding five hundred acres or owners of personal property valued to five hundred pounds. Senators would be elected by electors rather than by popular vote, to be proportioned by districts on the basis of wealth and population. He pressed for a tenure of six years rather than the four-year term favored by most delegates. In these matters he raised only minimal support. Even the conservative Alexander Graydon described McKean's senate proposals as "invidious and sordid."[39]

To achieve what he considered a better balance in the legislature he favored decreasing the size of the Lower House from sixty to forty-five. The essence of McKean's concern, however, was that the House had to be constructed on a different basis from the Senate. The majority was to be represented in the Lower House but the minority could look to the Senate for the protection of its interests. The Senate to succeed in this should be composed of the better, wiser, richer sort protected by a longer, more secure tenure. McKean apparently made an assumption not widely shared by political thinkers in late eighteenth-century America—that American society could still be divided into the ancient categories of the one, the few, and the many, an assumption he shared with his friend, John Adams.[40] Most agreed that there was a senatorial element in the community, but identifying it had proved to be elusive. American society was too flexible, mobile, and seamless for such divisions. He also pushed for a requirement that gubernatorial candidates possess clear real and personal property estimated at four thousand dollars at least six months prior to the election. He wanted, too, a requirement that 5/7 vote of the House and 6/7 vote in the Senate be mandatory for amendments to the Constitution. His was to be a small, compact, and highly filtered government.[41] He found little support for most of his ideas. William Lewis and Timothy Pickering were the only prominent Federalists who gave McKean any consistent backing.[42] Outside the convention, the prothonotary of the Supreme Court, Edward Burd, was pleased when little support developed for McKean's proposal to give the chief justice power to appoint all officers of the Court. He reported that William Lewis had "turned quite pale" upon discovering he could not rally any strength for the plan.[43]

McKean took his defeats philosophically, content that the points of agreement between himself and the majority far outnumbered areas of disagreement, or more characteristically, persuaded that his efforts at education had been blunted by myopic and misguided colleagues. He signed the ratification.[44]

While intent on charting a new federal constitutional course, McKean was concerned that the state's legal progress—and his role in it—would be lost. Thus, when his lawyer friend Alexander James Dallas suggested the need to collect and preserve records of the state court during the Revolution and post-Revolutionary years, McKean agreed to help him. As a longtime practicing lawyer he could attest to the inconvenience created by the absence of printed precedents.[45]

Dallas attempted to reconstruct the legal history of Pennsylvania insofar as it was possible through the decisions of its courts. He was able to retrieve from local attorneys barely thirty pages of cases relating to the provincial period. Most opinions had been lost or were never written down. Commonplace books had disappeared and many of the practitioners of the period were now dead. Much of the law of the early period had been oral law, and when practitioners died, became senile, or experienced fading memories, law too was lost. Opinions were often lacking even for the period of the Revolution.

With the help of McKean and several other lawyers and justices, Dallas compiled a fairly impressive record of cases after 1777. He published the decisions under the title, *Reports of Cases Ruled and Adjudged in the Courts of Pennsylvania before and since the Revolution.* The initial volume, published in 1790, was one of the first of its kind in America.[46] The first edition was dedicated to McKean, whose work comprised the largest part of the volumes. In his introduction Dallas noted that "a work of this nature is only to be esteemed, like a mirror, for the truth and accuracy with which its object is reflected; and I do nothing more on the occasion, than present you with your own portrait." The only praise Dallas coveted, according to the dedication, was "that of having preserved some resemblance to the original. . . . History must hereafter do justice to [McKean's] merits."[47]

Pleased with the results of Dallas' work and with his own role in it, McKean sent a copy of the *Reports* to the aged English jurist, William Murray, Lord Mansfield. Critics of McKean, had they known of his action, would not have been surprised at his choice of heroes. Mansfield, chief justice of England from 1756 to 1778, was unpopular in some American circles for his earlier opposition to American independence and his harsh rulings in a series of seditious libel cases in the 1770s. Opponents charged him with efforts to usurp proper legislative prerogatives, with persistently frustrating the jury system, and with being hostile to principles of personal liberty. McKean commented to Mansfield on the *Reports*, "It has novelty, tho' perhaps little else to recommend it.... You will find here the decisions of a native of Pennsylvania, the first Chief Justice of a new republic in America... and his endeavoring humbly to imitate your right example."[48]

A reading of the *Reports* convinced Mansfield that the cases did "credit to the Court, the bar and the reporter." He wrote McKean that they showed readiness in practice, liberality in Principle, strong reason and legal learning; their method too is clear and the language plain." This judgment seems consistent with the evidence, even now, from the perspective of the twentieth century.[49]

15. Republican

McKean's alliance with the Federalists did not last. If it had been a union of love on his part, it seemed nothing more than one of convenience for the inner circle of the city's Federalist politicians. He apparently viewed the association as both political and social, marking his arrival into Philadelphia's most exclusive elite. To be among the elite was a dream shared by others who, like McKean, had come to wealth and prominence during the Revolution. Their desire to curb the most blatant manifestations of democracy and to assume what they considered their rightful place in the community had combined with their admiration for the new federal and state constitutions to forge an impressive political coalition with the older, more established Federalists. The result was an impressive list of political victories: ratification of the federal constitution, the creation of a new state government, and control of the city's political machinery.[1]

There were tensions in this marriage from the first. Would-be elites found it next to impossible to breach the inner circles of Philadelphia's "society." One wag observed,

> There are several classes of company—the Cream, the *New Milk*, the *Skim Milk*, and the Canaille! In private parties and in public meetings, the distinctions here are accurately preserved. The Cream generally curdles into a small group on the most eligible situation in the room. The New Milk seems floating between the wish to coalesce with the Cream and to escape from the Skim Milk; and the Skim Milk, in a fluid kind of independence, laughs at the anxiety of the New Milk, and grows sour upon the arrogance of the Cream.[2]

Presbyterian McKean was very much the "new milk." It had been the Revolutionary upheaval in Pennsylvania that had opened to him a major political office—the chief justiceship. In the fall of 1780 he had persuaded the Assembly to allow him temporarily residence in the magnificent Jacob Duche mansion, confiscated by the state when Duche was judged to be a Tory. In May 1781, he was able to raise £ 7,750 "lawful money of Pennsylvania" to purchase the property at public vendue. The three-story brick mansion was said to be one of Philadelphia's most imposing residences, complete with coach house, stables, and four large lots. It was situated on the east side of Third Street and occupied the whole side of the square from Pine Street on the south to Union Street on the north, and for thirty feet in depth.[3]

By 1790 McKean's economic worth and political position encouraged a high degree of cooperation and intimacy between his family and the very best of Philadelphia society, as did his association with a variety of social and political organizations. He held membership in the American Philosophical Society (as a counselor), the Society for the Promotion of Agriculture, and The Order of the Cincinnati. In that year he helped to organize and subsequently was elected president of The Friends of Hibernia, a group dedicated to providing poor relief for emigrants from Ireland, and he continued to serve the University of Pennsylvania as a trustee.[4]

The McKeans were guests at many elite parties and balls in the city and, on occasion, held their own parties and dinners for prominent families. They associated with the Morrises, Binghams, McCalls, Chews, Rushes, Clymers and Dallases. Foreign ministers were frequent guests at the McKean's, and George Washington made a point of visiting them during his celebrated visit to Philadelphia in 1789. McKean's son, Joseph, now a Philadelphia lawyer, had been accepted by the prestigious, bluestocking First Troop of Philadelphia Cavalry in 1786, and his marriage to Sarah Miles, daughter of General Samuel Miles (Philadelphia merchant, trustee of the University, and prominent figure in Philadelphia's political life) attached the McKeans to a respected part of Philadelphia society. Letitia "Letty" McKean had also married well, for her union in June 1789 to George Buchanan, the son of General Andrew Buchanan, allied the McKeans with one of Baltimore's leading families. In December 1791, McKean's oldest daughter, Elizabeth, would marry Andrew Pettit, son of the prominent Philadelphia merchant and land speculator, Charles Pettit.

Yet McKean, like others described as "new milk," never really enjoyed full acceptance into the inner circle that he wanted, and expected. He did not belong to those organizations or the inner junto of merchants and politicians which distinguished the cream from the new milk. Nor did his children marry into the true inner circles of Philadelphia society, but attached themselves to families, like themselves, on the periphery. Indeed, McKean in 1790 enjoyed the same relationship to the most exclusive families in Philadelphia that he had enjoyed with the Anglican elite in New Castle prior to the Revolution. The McKeans were close to but not an integral part of the older, more polished, more established families. His personality, origins and religious-ethnic make-up all played parts in frustrating his social aspirations.[5]

Political differences also tended to separate those supporting the Constitution from the older, more deep-rooted conservatives in Philadelphia. Late in 1790 the coalition, so successful throughout the three previous years, began to come asunder. A number of Federalists who found the new federal constitution palatable now choked on Hamilton's funding proposals. McKean, who had staunchly supported a funding program in

1789, found himself nursing serious reservations about Hamilton's specific proposals in 1790. When, on July 9, 1790, a committee of public creditors met to discuss matters of funding and assumption McKean was still among the leaders, and he doubtless shared the conviction of most Philadelphians that the federal assumption of Pennsylvania's debt was a sine qua non for a satisfactory funding bill.[6] But his growing reservations concerning elements of Hamilton's program drove him to join those who met on December 15 to record and publish criticisms of the Funding Bill. Under the prodding of Charles Pettit the meeting pushed for a more ·equitable system. Demanded among other things was payment by the United States of special bills of credit issued between September 1777 and March 1788, which Hamilton had chosen not to take into account. Critics complained too that the certificates they currently held were superior in value to those offered by the Treasury in exchange. In addition they asserted that Hamilton's measures abridged in part debt provisions guaranteed by the Articles of Confederation. For all these reasons McKean and those who met with him now pressed for a congressional reassessment of Hamilton's funding bill.[7]

The memorial produced by the December meeting forced Hamilton and Congress to grapple with the criticisms leveled by Philadelphia's public security holders. A compromise of sorts eventually was worked into the Secretary of Treasury's Report on the Public Debt of January 1792, but as later events reveal it failed fully to satisfy McKean.[8]

So it was that McKean, critical of the federal government's efforts to establish an equitable funding bill, and disenchanted with the lack of tangible support from old-line Philadelphia Federalists, began to swing away from the old coalition. Like a number of "new men" unable to crash the inner circles or disappointed in the direction of Federalist policies, McKean began to weigh his political alternatives.

Pennsylvania's election laws provided no satisfactory means in 1792 to nominate federal representatives or presidential electors; out of the confusion over how such nominations should be obtained a more pronounced political bifurcation emerged. In the late spring the city's Federalist leaders proposed a series of open meetings in each county to draw up party tickets for the upcoming elections. Representatives from each county meeting were to gather at Lancaster late in August or early September to formulate the final tickets. Unhappy with these maneuvers, and wanting to establish the widest possible appeal for its own tickets, the opposition—led by the shrewd, corpulent Dr. James Hutchinson and the slender, sagacious Alexander Dallas—determined to form tickets which would include a number of moderate Federalists and to challenge the Federalist method of forming tickets. Both parties were desperate to read the political winds accurately and to apply the most attractive strategy for marshaling public support.[9]

Ultimately it was the aggressiveness of the Hutchinson-Dallas group that paid the largest dividends. When the Philadelphia Federalist junto held their meeting on July 25 publicly to propose its plan for drawing up tickets, Dallas and his followers were there to disrupt the proceedings. A second meeting two days later achieved little more than the first as it, too, was reduced to chaos by the Hutchinson-Dallas-led dissidents. Satisfied with the scuttling of the Federalists' meeting, the Dallas-Hutchinson faction announced that it would hold its own public meeting on July 30. So far as is known, up to this point McKean took no part in the activities of the dissidents.

The meeting called by the Republicans, as the Hutchinson-Dallas faction came to be known, attracted so many that it had to move from the Assembly room to the State House yard. McKean was named chairman, a choice encouraged by Dallas, who viewed McKean as effective bait in luring moderate Federalists into opposition. McKean's first act was to recognize Hutchinson, who launched into a harangue against the Federalists' strategy of nominating candidates. He claimed their public meetings would merely put a formal stamp of approval on decisions determined in secret earlier by a small and unrepresentative group of Federalist leaders. A more effective and equitable way to determine the true will of the people, Hutchinson declared, would be an extensive survey of public opinion conducted by a chain of committees of correspondence. To this end he carried a motion voiding all decisions made at the meeting of July 27, and a second motion naming a seven-man committee of correspondence. McKean was one of those chosen to this important committee, whose job ostensibly was to read the political pulse of the state.[10]

In an effort to recapture at least some of the momentum lost by the Republican tactics, the Federalists scheduled still another meeting for July 31. To their dismay the supporters of Hutchinson and Dallas again disrupted the proceedings. The dissidents nominated McKean as a candidate for the chairmanship in opposition to the Federalist choice, the Quaker Samuel Powel. The fact that a number of Federalists acquiesced in McKean's candidacy suggests that for all his involvement with various public issues, McKean was still viewed at this point in largely non-partisan terms. When neither McKean nor Powel could achieve a clear majority, however, both declined to serve. To the complete frustration of most of the Federalists, the next three polls failed to identify an acceptable chairman. Hoping to salvage something for their efforts, they withdrew to the other side of the State House yard to conduct a rump session. When their opponents refused to allow them peace even in this venture a small scale riot ensued. Like most of the Republican leaders, McKean vacated the State House yard before the more violent activities began.[11]

While the Federalist junto retreated to lick its wounds and to reassess its status, Republicans plunged ahead. On August 3, 1792, a circular signed by McKean, among others, was widely circulated throughout the state announcing that the "Correspondents" (as the Hutchinson-Dallas faction came to be labeled) were not delegated to deliberate upon elections, nor to admit or reject names of candidates, nor to declare the sense of the people or frame a ticket. "All that we are authorized to do (all that we have undertaken or mean to do on the present occasion)," the Correspondents made clear, "is to obtain a list of various characters, whom the citizens of every denomination and in every part of the State deem to be qualified." They explained they would submit their nominees without comment to the people.[12]

The circular was not completely candid regarding the procedures to be employed. This was no battle between the people and the aristocrats, between those truly seeking the will of the people and those desirous of thwarting that will. The Correspondents and the "Conferees" as their opponents were now

called, charged each other—and with abundant justification—
with fixing tickets in private and then appealing to the people
in an effort to delude the populace in assuming its opinion was
seriously solicited and weighed. The framing and circulation
of tickets became a favorite political activity in Pennsylvania;
aspiring candidates vied with each other in the art of bringing
their names before the people—all this to the background of a
battle in the press between the two factions and a third group
denouncing both and imploring the public to "exercise a free
and unbiased judgment" in writing their own tickets.[13]

The Philadelphia Committee of Correspondents, ostensibly
under the leadership of McKean, published its lists of candidates
on September 29, 1792. Although the lists purported to be the
product of an intensive canvass of the state's peoples, Dallas
and Hutchinson were clearly the framers of the tickets. Just
how privy McKean was to the machinations of Dallas, Hutchinson and others of the inner circle of Republican leaders is
difficult to assess. There is no evidence to suggest that he
played a significant role in identifying candidates or that they
looked to him for advice on political strategy. Men like
Hutchinson and Dallas recognized him as an asset to their
political aspirations. They willingly utilized his influence and
baldly played upon his ego in matters of public meetings and
the writing of political manifestos, but his participation in
their innermost counsels was limited. Throughout his career
McKean exhibited little talent for political intrigue and
organization.[14]

Opponents of McKean and the Correspondents attempted to
place the label "anti-Federalist" on their efforts, but such an
interpretation was more politically advantageous than accurate.
Despite McKean's flirtation with an opposition group, he
harbored no irrevocable disenchantment in 1792 with the
federal government or with President George Washington. He
ended up heading the opposition's ticket in Pennsylvania's
contest to name presidential electors, but neither the leadership
nor the membership of the Correspondents seriously opposed
Washington's candidacy in 1792, and there were only minor
disagreements over whom to support as vice-president. The
November 6 returns saw McKean garner the third highest vote
total, placing behind William Henry of Philadelphia and Joseph

Hiester of Berks County, both of whom were included on both Federalist and Republican tickets. McKean's total made him the highest vote-getter of the single-ticket men; he was the only one to succeed who was not represented on the Federalist ticket.[15]

Disagreements over the nature of the federal union and the proper balance between state and national powers accosted McKean in the courtroom as readily as they did in the papers and coffee houses of Philadelphia. One such example was the litigation over the sloop *Active,* certainly among the most complex and bizarre judicial proceedings in his career or in the history of Pennsylvania. The case had its origins during McKean's second year as chief justice and centered around conflicting claims over the spoils from the capture of the *Active,* bound for New York from Jamaica with a cargo of coffee and rum. The Pennsylvania brig *Convention* and the American privateer *Gerard* both claimed to have captured the *Active.* Complicating the case was an American sailor on board the *Active,* one Gideon Olmsted of Connecticut, who asserted that he had overpowered the British crew, with the help of three other sailors, before either the *Convention* or the *Gerard* gained possession of her. Olmsted thus claimed the spoils belonged rightfully to him.

The *Active* was brought into port on September 8, 1778, and the following day a Pennsylvania court was established to deal with her. On November 4, with George Ross presiding, the state's admiralty court began to hear the claims. Although Ross was clearly sympathetic to Olmsted's case, the jury's findings gave him no recourse but to divide the spoils into four equal parts among the State of Pennsylvania, the owners of the *Gerard* and *Convention,* and Olmsted. Olmsted appealed his case to Congress. Benedict Arnold, who was looking for a means of obtaining large sums of cash, agreed to subsidize Olmsted's appeals in exchange for a portion of the spoils should he be successful. To aid Olmsted in his legal battles, Arnold secured the services of lawyers James Wilson and William Lewis.

McKean was at that time president of the congressional court of appeals, which was assigned the task of looking into the Olmsted claims. When the court undertook the *Active* case in December 1778, McKean absented himself from the proceedings, however, arguing that his position in Pennsylvania necessitated such a move. The court eventually reversed the Pennsylvania decision and awarded the entire claim to Olmsted. Pennsylvania authorities reacted rather ambiguously to this congressional decision; they freely admitted that Congress had the final authority, and that the state would have to revise its admiralty laws accordingly, but they nonetheless maintained that the state had the power to establish jury trials and to deny appeals in such cases. They had done so in the *Active* case strictly in accordance with the instructions of Congress itself. Pennsylvania succeeded in reversing the congressional decision awarding the entire spoils to Olmsted; the state then sold the ship and distributed the profits as Ross had originally directed.

As a direct result of the complications of the *Active* proceedings, McKean, acting in his capacity as a member of Congress, urged on August 26, 1779, that a congressional committee be formed to design one or more supreme courts of appeal to act in all maritime cases. Though he was not part of the initial committee assigned on January 8, 1780, to pursue such a project, he was eventually named to a second committee for that purpose. As we have seen, he also chaired a committee drafting commissions for the prospective judges and three times was himself nominated for one of the judges.

In the meantime, selling the *Active* and the distribution of the funds in accordance with Ross' directives did not end the matter. Olmsted brought charges in the Lancaster County court of common pleas to gain the full share of the *Active's* worth as directed by Congress. Ross had by this time died but Olmsted sought to collect from his heirs. The Lancaster court found no derelection on the part of Ross in the matter, but it determined that Olmsted was entitled to the full sum as the Congress had found. The executors of the Ross estate predictably appealed in turn, and the case ultimately wound its way before McKean's supreme court in April 1792.

The case posed a number of interesting political and legal problems. Not only was it long and legally complicated, but indirectly it pitted the state against the federal government. The McKean court decided against Olmsted and his heirs, reversing the decision of the Lancaster court by denying that it ever had proper jurisdiction in the matter. McKean found that the determination in 1780 to establish the law of nations as the guiding force in the congressional court of appeals clearly indicated that prior to that date jury decisions were thought to govern a court's rulings. He therefore placed great emphasis on the original jury's findings which called for Olmsted to receive but a fourth of the spoils. But whereas Associate Justices Jasper Yeates and Edward Shippen wrote decisions from a markedly nationalistic position, McKean did not. Even though by 1792 McKean had become associated in the minds of many as an ardent nationalist his decision in the *Active* case indicated a willingness to accept considerable lattitude of action by the state. He had desired a stronger federal government in 1787, but by 1792 he shared a few of Hamilton's assumptions about a vigorous and pervasive central government.[16]

McKean's appreciation of the proper balance between state and federal government was put to the test in more practical terms when a series of riots and disorders broke out in Pennsylvania's western counties protesting Hamilton's excise bill, which had passed the House in January 1791. Westerners charged that the tax on whiskey provided by the bill hurt them on two levels: it taxed a primary source of their wealth and, according to some, severely compromised state sovereignty. It also placed an unusual burden on those in the West by issuing as well an equal tax on whiskey, which was worth considerably more in the East than in the West.[17]

Despite a federal proclamation on September 15, 1792, threatening westerners who were obstructing federal laws, the protests continued, and even increased in severity. President Washington termed the disturbances "unwarrantable proceedings... and subversive of good order." He thought them "of a nature dangerous to the very being of government" and announced the end of his government's "previous leniency."[18]

The state also sought to end the disorders. Governor Thomas Mifflin appealed to McKean to charge the grand juries of the several counties within their districts "to inquire into and present all offences of the nature to which the Proclamation refers." McKean accordingly took the occasion of the meeting of the Philadelphia grand jury on November 8 to convey the governor's message to the jurymen. Characteristically, he added his own strong views to those of his governor. "It is strange," he told the jurors, "that a people, but just rescued from the galling yoke of foreign bondage, having just got rid of a despotic government, will not submit to one free and equal.... What avails it to be exempt from the chains of a precarious tyranny," he asked, "if men still continue slaves to caprice of their own corrupt nature?" He found little justice in a cause whose leaders "quarrel with a Constitution and government purchased at the expense of much blood and treasure, and framed by themselves." He held little good will for men "who despise the rulers of their own choice and trample on laws of their own making."[19]

It was their bald defiance of law which prompted his strongest opposition to their cause. At the same time he sympathized with a number of their grievances: the federal government's promotion of eastern interests at the expense of the West; seeming government indifference to the need for protection against Indians; lack of government enthusiasm for securing navigational rights on the Mississippi River, and federal insensitivity to the antics of unscrupulous eastern land speculators. He also agreed with western complaints against the continued presence of the British in western posts and believed as westerners did that unless decisive measures were adopted soon the British would become more aggressive. Much of the government's response—or lack of it—smacked of a blatant pro-British policy and McKean was no friend of England.[20]

Though popular dissent occasionally boiled up in Allegheny and Washington counties throughout 1792 and 1793, a passive, almost circumspect attitude was maintained on the part of both state and federal authorities. The continuance of the county courts in the Monongahela country and the continuing visits by McKean and his legal entourage on the circuits belied the underlying anarchy and created a false sense of authority and command. The creation of Democratic societies such as the one founded in the Mingo Creek settlements in February 1794, which threatened to usurp the courts' prerogatives, bode ill, however.[21] Of greater concern to McKean and other state officials was the possibility that the unrest would become more intense. For the moment the opposition to the excise act and to federal excise officials reflected poorly on the federal courts. But such opposition, should it get out of hand, also held the potential of undermining McKean's own state courts, and, if permitted to become more widespread, of stimulating a federal response capable of going beyond mere overshadowing of state courts to compromising the very sovereignty of the state.

McKean's appreciation of western grievances notwithstanding, he continued to have little enthusiasm for their cause until July 25, 1794 when he learned that a mob had attacked the home of Allegheny County excise collector John Neville. Earlier, on June 5, the federal government had tried to reduce tensions in the western counties by enacting a law permitting western defendants in excise cases to be tried by state courts in the county where the irregularity was committed rather than being transported to Philadelphia to stand before a federal judge. Now this. To eliminate the disorders which threatened to become more general, President Washington called a conference of select federal and state officers for Saturday, August 2. McKean, Governor Mifflin, Secretary Dallas, and Attorney General Jared Ingersoll were to meet with President Washington and federal government officials Hamilton, Edmund Randolph, and William Bradford.[22]

President Washington had requested from James Wilson, associate justice of the United States Supreme Court, an opinion on whether or not the courts were capable of meeting the exigencies created by the excise disturbances; he told the conference that Wilson's conclusions would be crucial in the determination of policy. In the meantime, could the state give him assurances of its ability to cope with the current difficulties? Would the state consider taking some "preliminary measures?" The President's subsequent remarks made it clear that the federal government was willing to employ the Pennsylvania militia to put a quick end to western irregularities. Indeed, state officials were left with the impression that their federal counterparts were already predisposed to the use of military force and were merely using the present conference to secure the state's acquiecsence.[23]

Their reading was sound. Secretary of the Treasury Hamilton viewed the insurrection as a convenient opportunity to determine whether or not the federal government could maintain itself. Its ability to crush the insurrectionists and to do it with some dispatch would in large measure establish its long-range power and durability. The Pennsylvanian William Bradford, now Washington's attorney general, concurred; he saw the excise troubles as part of "a formed and regular plan for weakening and perhaps overthrowing the General Government." He, too, favored a quick military response. For that matter the entire cabinet on the eve of the August 2 conference was solidly aligned behind a policy of force.[24]

When the drift of Washington's August 2 maneuvering became unmistakable, McKean protested. He boldly asserted without qualification that "the judiciary power [was] equal to the task of quelling and punishing the riot and that the employment of a military force [was] equally unconstitutional and illegal." The state and McKean's court had faced riots and disorders on its western and northern frontiers for a decade. Experienced with perennial bandetti and the Wyoming dilemma, McKean hardly viewed the current disorders as an immediate and fatal threat to the union, however embarrassing and unpleasant they might be. State officers at the conference exhibited an understandable reluctance to approve any program which would reflect badly upon its own administration. McKean would have been out of character had he not also been nettled by Washington's reliance upon James Wilson to judge the efficacy of the Pennsylvania courts. He and Dallas well knew that the state courts were temporarily unable to bring the rioters to justice, but to have federal authorities stress this fact to justify their own program of force and to compromise state sovereignty in the process was unacceptable.[25]

McKean's observation concerning the illegality of any use of militia terminated the conference. His blunt statement, articulating the state's fixed opposition to the immediate use of force, pressured the cabinet into devising a new strategy. On August 4 Wilson reported his belief that the courts were for all intents and purposes inoperative in Allegheny and Washington counties, and that dissident forces there could not be brought to justice through judicial proceedings alone. His statement surprised no one. State officials refused to budge from their position that while perhaps the federal courts had failed, insufficient time had lapsed to determine the effectiveness of state action. Governor Mifflin told President Washington he would send state commissioners to the western counties to mediate the dispute. To a cabinet already unhappy with the state's recalcitrance the governor's announcement smacked of obstructionism. The effect of the state's position was to convince President Washington that one more effort at conciliation ought to be pursued; he agreed to send federal commissioners to a meeting of western representatives at Parkinson's Ferry on August 14.[26]

On August 6 Governor Mifflin appointed McKean and General William Irvine as state commissioners. "The conduct which it may be necessary to pursue, and the topics which it will be proper to discuss," he told them, "are generally submitted to your discretion." The commissioners were specifically empowered to promise pardons to persons who entered into agreements with the state to guarantee peace and tranquility and obedience to the law.[27]

When McKean and Irvine reached Pittsburgh on August 14 they were met by a pessimistic trio of federal commissioners. Bradford, who a month earlier had viewed western actions as a conspiracy to overthrow the government, had discovered nothing on his western trip to revise his opinion. Discussions with inhabitants in and near Pittsburgh had merely reinforced his convictions and convinced him the dissention was widespread. Western moderates, with little hope for protection from either federal or state courts, were intimidated into silence or ostensible acquiesence in the radical program of defiance. Both choices tended to encourage further resistance on the part of the general population.

If McKean harbored any hope that his presence or the threat of his court's powers would substantially reduce the militancy of the backcountry his illusions were soon dispelled. Like their federal counterparts, McKean and Irvine sensed almost immediately rampant hostility towards federal laws and those seeking to enforce them. Nothing encouraged them in the hope that Pennsylvania might reassert its authority over the region and thus alleviate the use of military force and all that such a policy implied for state-federal relations. Irvine, more experienced in dealing with the western mind than McKean, concluded that though "the Idea of a civil war is dreadful . . . I fear things are gone too far."[28]

The intransigence of the population at large was brought home to McKean and the commissioners with remarkable clarity on the very day of their arrival. Crowds gathered in the streets to raise a liberty pole in the presence of the commissioners to illustrate their disregard for the power and authority of the two governments. Encouraged by their initial success and flushed by the inaction of the chief justice, his associate justice, and the federal attorney general, several in the crowd tried to raise a six-striped flag as a mask of rebellion. After considerable debate and commotion they were persuaded to hoist the flag of the United States instead. Irvine wrote that night to Dallas that "nothing can be done."[29]

Still, McKean and Irvine did what they could. They talked at length with David Bradford, a leading lawyer in Washington County and one of the more vocal and militant of the insurgent leaders, trying to persuade him that his conduct could only lead to disaster, not only for himself and his followers, but for the state of Pennsylvania. They urged him to submit to state and federal terms of agreement and to encourage those who looked to him for leadership to do the same. He was warned his moderation in the upcoming Parkinson's Ferry conference was essential. Apparently the recalcitrant lawyer made no commitment one way or the other; McKean and Irvine were left with little hope of success in the forthcoming conference.

On August 20 representatives from the western counties met to discuss recent developments. For three days the commissioners and delegates sought an equitable solution to their problems. As a state commissioner McKean's position was by necessity less important than that of James Ross, Jasper Yeates, and William Bradford, the federal representatives, but he did what he could to bring the state's case to the insurgents. It was proposed that the conferees of the four counties "sign an instrument in writing" promising they would "at all times be obedient & submit to the laws of the State, and also of the United States of America," and commit themselves to a policy of recommending similar obedience from their followers. It was further proposed that the "Committee of Sixty" which served as the executive committee for the various county committees of safety, also submit satisfactory assurances to the state commissioners "of the same import and effect." For their part the state commissioners were authorized to promise that should the people of the western counties keep the peace until June 10, 1795, a full, free, and general pardon would be extended. The state terms were similar to those being offered by the federal commissioners.

McKean left no record of his reaction to the August 20 meeting, but if he shared the views of the majority of commissioners he was reasonably pleased with the outcome. The western committeemen had agreed, however reluctantly, to call a meeting of the standing committee for August 28 and to recommend submission to the commissioners' proposals. A letter penned by Irvine on the twentieth suggests that his pessimism had abated somewhat. The formal report submitted by McKean and Irvine to Governor Mifflin two days later suggests that the commissioners' belief in a systematic and well-organized conspiracy had been shaken. All knew that the meeting of the standing committee called for Brownsville on the twenty-eighth was critical, however.[30]

The gathering at Brownsville established at least one thing. McKean's efforts to persuade the lawyer David Bradford to pursue a moderate course had been ineffective. Bradford pressed for a quick vote on the issue, one that would establish beyond any doubt westerners' commitment to a policy of resistance until the unfair laws were repealed. Only the untiring efforts of James Edgar, a local Presbyterian divine, convinced the majority to delay a vote until all the arguments had been heard. On the following day Albert Gallatin, one of Fayette County's most illustrious citizens, and Hugh Henry Brackenridge argued the case for submission, while Bradford continued to plead for resistance. Fears of intimidation and retaliation were so great among the committeemen that only after an elaborate system to safeguard secrecy was agreed upon did a final tally take place. The standing committee voted thirty-four to twenty-three to accept the commissioners' proposals, and to submit the same to the people of their respective counties.[31]

The Brownsville vote encouraged McKean to believe a settlement was possible, but continuing disorders in the neighboring counties soon took the edge off his optimism. "We are extremely grieved," McKean wrote Mifflin, "that our communications can afford you so little hope of that happy termination to our Embassy which you have so much at heart, and had such good reason to expect." McKean put his feelings more bluntly in a letter to his attorney general, Jared Ingersoll, immediately following the Brownsville decision, when he expressed his belief that the American republic was rendered vulnerable by the activities of the Pennsylvanians in that the majority of people in the western region might opt "to become British subjects, to remove into the Indian country, or at all events, to detach themselves from the laws of the union." Even if they should not opt for such a drastic course, their recalcitrance threatened to destroy republicanism from within. Conditions in the West differed from anything he had encountered before, even in turbulent Wyoming. "A frenzy seemed to be diffused thro' the country," he told Ingersoll, "the still voice of reason [is] drown'd." He reported that "the wildest chimeras [seemed] to have taken possession of men's minds . . . one might think it was the work of magic, or owing to some physical cause." It was thus no easy task to bring reason to bear on the difficulties. "My errand here was a humane one," he wrote, "It was to remove desperation from conscious guilt, to calm ruffled minds and to induce the inhabitants of our counties to consult their own happiness. . . . It may be thought an easy task to convince men that it is for their benefit not to be hanged," he continued, ". . . but such [is] not the case."

McKean discovered that the wiser and better type of citizen needed little persuasion to turn away from a course of insurrection. But "the next class to them, and those placed a grade still lower" would "scarcely listen to anything of this import." He considered their "prejudices & passions had usurped the judgment seat of reason and for some time induced a belief that they could not be governed by the arm of truth & persuasion, but by military coercion only."[32] Still, his letter leaves the impression that he judged most of the recalcitrance to have abated by August 29.

McKean's disapproval of the westerners' conduct was reciprocated. Of the commissioners negotiating with the insurgents, McKean was viewed most unbending. Rumors circulated among the dissidents that he had demanded as part of a larger settlement the recall from the Pennsylvania Assembly of all protest leaders who held seats there. On September 3 a body of men attacked McKean and the commissioners in the Greensburgh home of Simon Drum. One irate participant attempted to engage McKean in a quarrel by accusing his servant of stealing his boots and spurs. Though the man's efforts to force his way into Drum's home to confront McKean failed when those in the house threatened to fire upon him, a crowd of drunken men soon surrounded the house and began throwing stones and shouting epithets. They dispersed only when Irvine threatened to shoot them if they didn't leave.[33]

The September 3 attack, and other exhibitions of rebellion against the commissioners' proposals, soon dissipated McKean's optimism. No clear-cut vote in favor of submission emerged from the referendum in the first week in September; indeed, the proliferation of mob activity and the widespread raising of liberty poles evoked a rising despair.

Perhaps the most telling evidence for McKean that the time had arrived for stronger measures was provided by the inhabitants of Cumberland County. McKean and Yeates, having heard of disorder in Carlisle, headed there from Drum's house on September 9. Dissidents in Carlisle had erected a number of liberty poles posted with seditious messages, even as they intimidated the general population. McKean and Yeates moved swiftly to punish the rioters, arresting several of the leaders and threatening to bring the state's powers to bear on the rest if tranquility was not preserved. Satisfied by September 11 that peace had been effectively restored and the power of the state reasserted at least temporarily, McKean and Yeates left for Philadelphia. Unknown to the judges, their assertion of the state's power in Carlisle had infuriated inhabitants of the surrounding countryside. Even as the judges left the borough, a band of over two hundred angry men were marching toward Carlisle to "be revenged on the judges."

The mob arrived in Carlisle on the evening of the eleventh, only to discover that the judges had left hours before. Angry and "disappointed in their main object," they erected a liberty pole near the courthouse, covered it with "seditious inscriptions" and shouted their frustration. They burned an effigy of McKean and fired "many vollies" before dispersing at daybreak, satisfied with their defiance of the authorities. News of their near fatal confrontation with the mob did not reach McKean and Yeates until they were safely beyond Cumberland County, but the details of the crowd's activities and intent did nothing to stimulate McKean's interest in encouraging the state to resist a general call-up of the militia. When McKean learned that President Washington had ordered the state to draw up its militia, he offered no protest.[34]

He played no part in the army's western swing or in the court trials that followed. He was content to remain silent in the face of the obvious: Hamilton had won.

Despite these developments and the disappointments they represented, McKean apparently determined that more concerted and partisan political activity on his part could wait. No pointed criticisms are to be found in his public or private statements during 1792-94. The characteristically partisan jabs at opponents so apparent in McKean's career, once he had determined his position and identified the "enemy," are nowhere to be found. He seemed to be watching, evaluating, mildly unhappy with a number of federal and state developments, but not yet convinced that a total and highly visible commitment to an opposition party was necessary.

He had shed many of the values he had clung to in the past. He mulled over a copy of the new Delaware state constitution sent him by Dickinson in July 1792, and managed to analyze it without undue regard for his own part in the creation of the dismantled government, or his political beliefs of those earlier years. He was pleased that executive powers had been strengthened at the expense of the Assembly. He thought Delawareans had little to fear from a governor who by law must be a longtime resident, chosen by the majority and limited in his term of office. The provision allowing the governor an effective veto would wisely permit the executive to curb the legislature and mitigate the more unseemly manifestations of unbridled democratic rule.[35]

He was able to view past events with greater equanimity. He worked closely with a number of his past "enemies," with John Penn in the matter of the Penns' lands, and with Benjamin Chew, once chief justice of Pennsylvania, then president of the state's high court of errors and appeals. He seemed receptive to permitting some Tories to return to the state, including the most notorious of the exiles, Joseph Galloway. At least, friends and relatives of the exiled Galloway intepreted private remarks and actions by McKean to mean that the state might be willing to reconsider his case. Lawyers for Galloway sought positive confirmation of the state's attitude, and Galloway wrote a long and passionate letter to McKean enlisting formal aid in his quest to return to America. Nothing came of it, however, and the embittered Galloway died in exile.³⁶

If a number of McKean's views had changed by 1793, or at least softened, one—his admiration for the French and their role in the American Revolution—remained steadfast. Like most Americans McKean saw in the early stages of the French Revolution a working out in France of the principles that had motivated Americans. He once told John Adams that it was not until the French King was decapitated (which he judged to be "not only a very atrocious but a most absurd act") that he "clearly perceive[d] *that* nation was incapable at *that* time of being ruled by a popular government." He had then, as he later wrote Adams, "lapse[d] into a kind of apathy with regard to the leaders of the different parties" in France. His memory was faulty in this instance however, for after news of Louis XVI's death reached him in March, McKean demonstrated continued enthusiasm and interest in the Revolution. The fact that the British were "searching, seizing & detaining [American] vessels, and taking by force [American] seamen" helped to keep him firmly in the pro-French party.³⁷

His course of action after April suggests that he concurred in the wisdom of President Washington's neutrality proclamation more readily than did many of his Republican colleagues. He assumed an uncharacteristically low profile in the proceedings surrounding the arrival of citizen Edmund Genêt in May. He was not among those in charge of preparations for the Frenchman's welcome, and while he did attend a bipartisan banquet at Oeller's Hotel in honor of Genêt on May 18, he made no speeches or other public appearances on behalf of either Genêt or the French Revolution.³⁸

Privately he remained a staunch friend of France. He joined and soon became president of the Society of Friends of the French Revolution. Though he left no record of his feelings in these months, in all likelihood he experienced, as did the majority of Philadelphia's Republicans, a growing disillusionment with the impetuous Citizen Genêt. Genêt's indiscretions and the embarrassment he caused friends and foes alike is a familiar story. But the failure of Genêt to live up to initial American expectations was not enough to destroy McKean's sympathy for the French or to shake his antipathy to the British. By the spring of 1794 he and his son Robert were prominent in public denunciations of British policies in America and abroad. They also were active in fund-raising for the American victims of British-induced piracy in Northern Africa.[39]

By 1795 McKean's break with the federal administration was complete. His association with Dallas, Beckley, and Hutchinson in political matters was by then open and patently partisan. His dissatisfaction with the national Federalists, prompted by Hamilton's failure to provide a satisfactory funding program, had further been nurtured by the federal government's policy toward the western insurrection and its seemingly pro-British attitude in foreign affairs. Historians who have discovered in McKean the ultimate political weathercock and who have described his association with the Republicans exclusively in terms of his willingness to accommodate himself to successful movements have done him a disservice, even while giving him more credit than he deserves. The political road McKean followed from Federalism to Republicanism was a much-traveled road. A large portion of the Republican party had come a similar way, propelled by similar concerns. His moves had been no more calculating or precipitous than most. To the charge that he unerringly chose the winners, one must answer that even by 1795 there was no assurance that the Republicans would become a dominant force in Pennsylvania politics.[40]

Nor was McKean an aberration among Republican party leaders. The party leadership was studded with men of similar social and political views. McKean was no more uncomfortable with the democratic rhetoric which distinguished his party's political pronouncements than were other Republican leaders who calculatingly utilized it to political advantage. What held Republicans together by 1795 was a broad appreciation of what republicanism involved, the foreign policy that could best achieve America's advantage, and an unrelieved desire for offices and honors.[41]

Conditions surrounding the acceptance of the Jay Treaty in the summer of 1795 added to McKean's disenchantment with the federal government. Even before the Senate ratified the treaty by a slim margin in June, rumors were coursing through Philadelphia that the treaty surrendered American rights in a pathetic effort to build a British-American understanding. When the resourceful and fiery editor of the *Aurora*, Benjamin Bache, surreptitiously obtained a copy of the treaty and published it on July 1, Republican apprehensions seemed confirmed. Jay's Treaty convinced those already suspicious of the administration's Anglophilism that American interests were being systematically sacrificed to the British, and that part of this policy involved a concerted effort to support the British against America's longtime ally, France. Propaganda that rolled out in support of the treaty failed to persuade McKean. He was as genuinely horrified as any Republican by the treaty's provisions.[42]

He joined other leaders of the Republican party on July 23 at a public rally to denounce the treaty and to draw up a memorial to President Washington pleading that he not sign the offensive document. The committee chosen by this meeting to draft the memorial included, among others, McKean, Blair McClenaghan, Charles Pettit, and John Swanwick. The importance of the memorial was twofold: it would be an effective device for calling the President's attention to the treaty's shortcomings, and by passing it around for signatures Republican leaders could "discover the names and number of the British adherents, Old Tories, and Aristocrats who modestly assume the title of Federalists and stile themselves the best friends of our beloved President."[43]

At a second meeting on July 25 the memorial was read and discussed. It was at this meeting that Blair McClenaghan incited the crowd to action by waving in his hand what the people took to be a copy of the treaty, and "mak[ing] a motion that every good citizen in this assembly kick this damned treaty to hell." A copy of the treaty was then attached to a long pole and a crowd estimated at three hundred persons paraded through the streets, eventually stopping before the homes of several prominent residents, including the British and French ministers, to burn copies of the treaty. Leaders like McKean and Dallas were hard pressed to disassociate themselves with these activities.⁴⁴

Republicans were eager to see Jay's Treaty become the central issue in the upcoming city and county elections. The fact that McKean did not become intimately involved in the everyday strategy and activity of the city and county elections or publicly support a list of candidates is revealing. The Republican hierarchy normally did not call upon him in the more mundane local contests. He remained a valuable figurehead, to be paraded out at critical moments, at large public gatherings where his talents as chairman were useful, or where his status as chief justice added a degree of respectability to a national project. How often McKean was chosen for such roles and how often he was able to garner substantial support for a cause has gone largely unappreciated. Dallas, Hutchinson, and John Beckley needed McKean every bit as much as he needed them.

The fact is McKean was much more avidly drawn to national concerns and elections than to local politics. In 1796 he was particularly eager to assume a prominent role in the national elections and Republicans in Pennsylvania were content to have him head their ticket of presidential electors. The critical issue in the election so far as McKean was concerned was the apostacy of his old friend, John Adams. Once a sound and honest Republican, Adams had seemingly become a confirmed and dangerous monarchist. The rage elicited from Adams by the opposition of old friends like McKean was deep and profound. Adams described the Pennsylvania ticket opposing his election as composed of "the lowest dreggs of the mob of Philadelphia," and referred to McKean as "a dangerous Democrat, a Jacobin, a Disorganizer, etc."⁴⁵

McKean's disappointment in Adams was equally intense. It was not McKean who had changed, but Adams. To hear McKean tell it, Adams now favored a hereditary presidency and senators chosen for life. He sought to consolidate the "federal government [and] to annihilate the state governments." To McKean, at least, his actions and pronouncements suggested such a drift. McKean's efforts to confront Adams to discuss his current opposition to his views were frustrated.⁴⁶

As Professor John R. Howe has demonstrated, the flexibility and fragility of republicanism account for many of the nearly hysterical charges and counter-charges leveled by various political figures in both parties in the 1796 elections. Within the broad context of republican thought there was room for so much diversity that no orthodoxy seemed possible. Yet the success of republican institutions relied so heavily upon individual virtue and honor, and history had dealt so harshly with earlier republics, that no American could take republicanism for granted. Indeed, it was essential for all citizens to be alert to oppose ideas and actions deleterious to republican values and institutions. To destroy republicanism or to allow its dissipation was to lose forever the opportunity opened by the Revolution, not only for Americans but for all mankind. Little wonder that men watched each other closely and viewed with unfeigned alarm those actions and doctrines that seemed to them unrepublican.[47]

McKean himself did not escape the charge of apostasy. The legitimacy of his place on the Republican ticket was called into question by Federalists who pointed to his "monarchist tendencies." John Fenno, the scurrilous editor of the *Gazette of the United States,* compared McKean unfavorably with the head of the Federalist ticket and asked pointedly, "Who is the plain, simple republican and who is the haughty, imperious monarchist?" This, and similar attacks, proved unavailing, however, and in a hotly contested election McKean and the Republicans prevailed. On December 7, 1796, McKean cast his ballot for Thomas Jefferson.[48]

16. "The Democratic Judge"

McKean's suspicions of American foreign policy, so evident in his response to Jay's Treaty and its immediate aftermath, were not allayed by the new administration. By 1797 McKean shared John Dickinson's belief that for France the least admirable facets of the Revolution had been overcome, and the French were once again attempting to pursue goals similar to those sought by Americans two decades before. Obstructing that country's legitimate aspirations, in McKean's view, were the European powers solidly aligned against it, countries pursuing it like jackals, slowly pushing it into a military republic for self-preservation. The American government with its decidedly pro-British policies was doing its part to frustrate and pervert the French cause. The possibility that these policies would subvert American republicanism as well seemed very real to McKean.[1]

The last days of the Washington administration had deeply troubled McKean. It had become increasingly astigmatic and partisan. Much of its failure, according to McKean, derived from the administration's adherence to Jay's Treaty. Washington's stubborn insistence that the treaty be accepted however flawed it was, even in the face of bitter and legitimate criticisms, bespoke an unhealthy arrogance. It appeared to McKean that following the controversy over the acceptance of the treaty the President had judged public men almost exclusively in terms of their position on the treaty issue. He wrote Dickinson in June 1797 that so far as he could tell Washington had appointed no one to office who had opposed or criticized the treaty.

Washington's post-treaty appointment policy had thus produced a pro-English administration blindly committed to thwarting any legitimate efforts at securing a reconciliation with France, according to McKean. He judged the current Congress also to be replete with individuals anxious to break "old ties with France." He thought such a policy would almost certainly lead to war; it would drive America slowly but inexorably "into the arms of the British" who, as the price of allegiance, would doubtless demand that American trade and commerce "conform to them." It would be "an intolerable" situation, one that could be circumvented only with immediate and effective realignment of American policy. For all his dire predictions, McKean remained hopeful that some type of "counter-current" could be mounted.[2]

McKean was in fact actively involved with John Dickinson in an effort to mount a "counter-current." For months he and Dickinson had mulled over foreign policy developments and the desirability of an effective public statement on the benefits of a pro-French foreign policy. Dickinson, in Delaware, had begun to put his thoughts on the subject down in a series of "letters." In the meantime he hoped that McKean would send him "any sort of useful information" regarding foreign developments or administration machinations. Of particular interest to Dickinson was information touching upon instructions to the current diplomatic personnel.[3]

Two months later McKean made his own foreign policy preferences known to all. On June 27 James Monroe arrived in Philadelphia, recalled by the Washington administration for his unneutral conduct as minister to France. A testimonial dinner for the returning minister at Oeller's Hotel on July 1

John Dickinson, signed by Rembrandt Peale. Courtesy of Historical Society of Delaware

provided McKean with a public forum from which to denigrate the government's current policies. Before an audience which included Jefferson and numerous senators and congressmen, McKean officially welcomed Monroe home. "After viewing *all* the evidence of your diplomatic transactions," McKean told the pleased Monroe, "we find, that you have uniformly endeavoured to fulfill the objects of your mission; to render your country and yourself agreeable to the Republic of France." He assured Monroe that against his laudable conduct "the machinations of the insidious, and the slanders of the profligate, can be of no avail."

Particularly irritating to McKean had been the government's handling of Monroe's assignment. "We have heard nothing, for which an American *Republican* ought to blush," he told his Oeller Hotel audience, and yet the government had neglected to protect Monroe's "honor from obloquy and reproach." The administration had not only misunderstood and deliberately misinterpreted Monroe's efforts but had in its own way encouraged his critics to speak out against his efforts, and thus undermined his effectiveness. McKean assured Monroe that his friends were many in Philadelphia.

McKean's performance at the Oeller Hotel did not go unnoticed by the press. William Cobbett ("Peter Porcupine") ridiculed the address, observing that McKean's references to "viewing all the evidence" of Monroe's diplomatic transactions smacked of a judge "addressing a thief, or *traitor.*" He drew attention to McKean's criticism of the barbs leveled against Monroe in his diplomatic capacity and his plea for protection of a diplomat's honor and integrity to point out McKean's own conduct in the Jay's Treaty controversy. He reminded his readers that the chief justice had been conspicuous by his presence at a meeting that led to violence against Jay's reputation and integrity, and against the dignity of several members of the city's diplomatic community.[4]

By October Dickinson, having completed several of his "letters," sent them to McKean with a request that McKean aid him in securing their publication in France. Because of family obligations and business demands, McKean was unable to reply until January 20, 1798, but in the meantime he had broached the issue of Dickinson's writings to Jefferson and had expended energy in a search for a sympathetic and reliable translator. For his part Jefferson had spoken "in very pleasing terms" about Dickinson and his sentiments.[5]

At McKean's urging the French consul general had also perused Dickinson's letters. He proved to be less than enthusiastic, judging the "favorable expressions toward the late King and Queen, and implied censure of those who had a share in their death, would not be well received in France at this time." McKean seemed not to have taken the consul general's criticism seriously. His quick review of Dickinson's work disclosed but a single reference to subjects alluded to by the French representative. The more he learned about the sentiment within Congress the more anxious he became to place Dickinson's sentiments before both the American and the French people. "I fear things are not right," he wrote Dickinson, and he readily agreed to provide a suitable preface for Dickinson's work.[6]

Dickinson's "The Letters of Fabius in 1788, On the Federal Constitution; and in 1797, On the Present Situation of Public Affairs" was published in Wilmington and widely circulated in Delaware and Pennsylvania. In this work Dickinson made clear his belief that the French were currently engaged in a "just war" in Europe. He viewed the French as a "brave, generous and humane" people and any victories won by them would be in the best interests of liberty. "Republics," he wrote, "have always had the high honor of being hated by monarchs." Thus opposition to the present French government was merely the continuation of an historical enmity which kings had always held for republics. If the French should lose, all republics would be "immediately annihilated." It was something for the American people to ponder.[7]

McKean's solution to this growing threat was to give American envoys powers adequate to restore the French Republic "to the same relationship" France had held with America at the commencement of the present hostilities with Great Britain. Only if this were done soon would the present troubles be "amicably settled." For his views he was satirized unmercifully as a "coward" and a "war-monger."[8]

The apprehension McKean and Dickinson shared over the drift of the administration's foreign policy and its internal ramifications continued to mount. So long as the Federalists pursued a foreign policy designed to cripple France there was little hope for a just and speedy resolution. "The rulers of our exterior relations appear to me to have been actuated by passion rather than true policy respecting the French Revolution," McKean complained to Dickinson. "That nation may have given us just cause for war, but I conceive it to be highly impolitic to wage one with them." America was in no position to wage a foreign war; a military confrontation would seriously, perhaps fatally, compromise America's strength and independence. He told Dickinson that "With so powerful and favored a people we should have submitted to some sacrafices [sic] and sufficient crimes we want the power to punish." He "would have preferred conciliatory measures, prepared for the worst, and trusted to the chapter of accidents for the rest."

The Federalist foreign policy, however myopic and dangerous, was at least legal, a faithful extension of the views of persons dominating the councils of government. The Alien and Sedition Acts, passed in June and July 1798 by an xenophobic Congress, were, in McKean's opinion, irrefutably unconstitutional. But their unconstitutionality aside, they were also "unnecessary, nay injurious and provoking, unaccompanied with any possible advantages to the United States." He was persuaded that "Trial by Jury and the Sovereignty of the respective States [would] be prostrated" by these "most extraordinary Acts of Congress."[9] If this were not enough, congressional measures passed on July 13 and 14 to support an expected war with France through a land tax were destructive to the peace and harmony of Pennsylvania's back country. Already there were disorders as persons in Bucks, Northampton, Montgomery, and Berks counties expressed their disapproval of the new tax legislation. Federalist policies seemed to promise war at home and abroad.

George Logan, a prominent Quaker and one-time member of the Pennsylvania Assembly, was determined to do something about the foreign problems facing the nation. To that end he proposed to visit France, to act as a sort of unofficial good will ambassador from the United States, to convey directly to the French the desire of the American people for peace and amity. When it became obvious that American envoys to France, rebuffed by Talleyrand and the Directory, were preparing to return home without a settlement, to perhaps effect a complete rupture between the two countries, Logan knew he had to persuade the Directory to reconsider its position. The alternative would be a capricious and crippling war.

Early in June Logan came to McKean for legal aid. He anticipated that when the goal of his mission was discovered by the Federalists they would attempt to destroy him by confiscating his estate. To eliminate this possibility he asked McKean to convey the power of attorney to his wife, a move which would permit her to oversee his affairs and, if necessary, to sell his property in a last-ditch effort to keep it out of Federalist hands.[10]

Although Logan had not mentioned his scheme to Jefferson on June 4, when he had requested a certificate of citizenship from the Vice President, he did reveal his hopes to McKean. He became aware of McKean's sympathy for his cause even before he finished sharing the details. McKean's enthusiasm was obvious. "Thank God," he told his friend, "that we possess one man who is capable and devoted enough to undertake the task." He offered a toast to Logan's success and furnished the Quaker with a simple statement of citizenship declaring him to be a native-born Pennsylvanian and a former member of the Pennsylvania legislature. Logan left for Europe aboard the *Iris* on June 12.[11]

The purpose of Logan's expedition was discovered soon enough. Before the month was out Federalist speculation centered on Logan's personal interference in the foreign policy of the two nations. Predictably, William Cobbett's roar of disapproval was the loudest. "Recollect that seditious Envoys from all the Republics that France has subjected first went to Paris and concerted measures with the despots; recollect the situation of this country at this moment, and tremble for its fate!" he wrote. He warned of impending disasters, suggesting that the terrors of the Revolution would soon come to America's shores, to the very streets of Philadelphia. "Take care: when your blood runs down the gutters," he told his readers, "don't say you weren't forewarned of the danger."

Other Federalist editors were equally quick to assume the worst of Logan's mission and to suggest that his visit to France was the harbinger of a move to introduce, as the *Philadelphia*

Gazette put it, "the genuine value of true and essential liberty by reorganizing our government, through the brutal operation of the bayonet and guillotine."[12]

The vehemence of the Federalist response did not surprise McKean. Nor was he particularly taken aback by the news that he was being accused of being an accessory to Logan's "crime." He wrote Dickinson on June 24 to tell him that Logan was suspected of going to France for treasonable purposes, and that he himself was being implicated. Federalists assumed that Logan must have been going for treasonable purposes, McKean told Dickinson, because Logan had settled his estate before leaving the country. "It is conjectured that the Doctor wishes to preserve peace," McKean wrote, "[and] this alone would be construed treason by some of our high toned Government men."[13]

For McKean, Logan's mission and the furor it elicited in Congress following his return, meant greater attention from Federalists and Republicans alike. To Federalists McKean represented the worst type of sycophant, a man naively undermining the American republic through a commitment to a blindly pro-French policy. He became, along with Logan and Jefferson, the butt of Federalist satire. On the other hand his brief but crucial association with Logan pleased Republicans intent on identifying those striving resourcefully for peace. His reputation as a "sound" Republican was, if anything, enhanced by his role in the Logan affair.[14]

In the meantime, McKean became embroiled in still another protracted battle over freedom of the press. The Spanish minister, Joseph Jaudennes, a close friend of the McKeans, had introduced his successor, the proud and fiery Don Carlos Martinez D'Yrujo, to the McKeans, and by 1797 Yrujo was in love with McKean's youngest (and favorite) daughter, Sarah (Sally). Yrujo became Spanish minister just in time to express his government's displeasure over the provisions of Jay's Treaty, which Spain claimed granted to the English rights the United States had no power to grant. In the following two years Yrujo became an outspoken critic of British policies and the American government's response to them.[15]

For his actions the arrogant and impetuous Yrujo found himself the target of abuse in several Pennsylvania newspapers.

Marchioness de Casa Yrujo (Sally McKean). A Gilbert Stuart painting, owned by Thomas R. McKean. Courtesy of Philadelphia Museum of Art

Benjamin Bache's *Aurora* gleefully harpooned Spain and its representatives, labeling the Spanish as "the most cowardly of the human race" and their army "the most ignorant soldiery of the infamous tyrant of Castille." Even more persistent vitriol came from the pen of Cobbett. Referring to Yrujo as "Don Yarico," "Peter Porcupine" described the Spanish minister as "half Don, half sans-culotte." "Ever since Spain has been governed by princes of the Bourbon family," Cobbett informed his readers, "the Spanish name has been disgraced in peace and in war." Currently the Spanish monarch was a mere puppet. "Every important measure has been directed by the crooked politics of France," Cobbett insisted.

Indeed, the Spanish King was not even a decent puppet; he was a nonentity. Cobbett wrote that "the degenerate prince that now sways the Spanish spectre, whom the French have kept on the throne merely as a trophy of their power, or as the butt of their insolence seems destitute not only of the dignity of a king but of the common virtue of a man." Yrujo was no better. "As the sovereign is at home," Cobbett argued, "so is the Minister abroad.... The one is governed like a dependent by the nod of the five despots at Paris; and the other by the direction of the French agents in America."[16]

Unlike many of Philadelphia's diplomatic personnel, Yrujo was unwilling to overlook the propensity of the American press for personal attacks. He undertook to prosecute "Peter Porcupine" for libel. As belligerant and as proud as his antagonist, Yrujo bitterly complained to the State Department and to the Secretary of State, Timothy Pickering. Although federal authorities were cool to his complaints, he did succeed in obtaining a warrant binding Cobbett over to Judge Richard Peters in the federal courts. Rapidly disillusioned with the lack of progress in his federal suit, however, Yrujo pushed to have the case transferred to the Pennsylvania state courts. Doubtless he knew from his close association with McKean that Pennsylvania's chief justice would be a more receptive judge than Peters in this instance.[17]

McKean was as incensed as any Republican over Cobbett's daily attacks upon the French and Spanish, and his constant extolling of British virtues. He was unhappy, too, with Cobbett's cavalier attitude toward his own career and activities.

Cobbett referred to him as "Mrs. McKean's husband," and accused him of "boozing and brawling" in a public house. Whether it was McKean's idea to have the Spanish minister bring his attack upon Cobbett into Pennsylvania's courts, or Yrujo's, is not clear. What is demonstrable is that both were intent on bringing Cobbett to his knees in the quickest possible way. On November 18, largely at McKean's urging, the state drew up a bill of indictment against Cobbett for "certain infamous and wicked libels" against the King of Spain, Chevalier Charles Martinez de Yrujo, and the Spanish Nation. He was charged with "tending to defame the... King, envoy and minister, and the subjects of the... King, to alienate their affection and regard from the Government and citizens of the United States of America... [and] to incite them to hatred, hostilities and war against the... United States."

A week later Cobbett was brought before an oyer and terminer court to await grand jury action on his indictment. Among the nine witnesses against Cobbett was McKean himself who left the bench to testify. Then, in his capacity as chief justice, McKean charged the jury to do its duty. To guard against their taking the case too lightly, he reviewed for them the history of libel, reminding them that "Libels, or *libelli famosi,* taken in the most extensive sense, signify any writings, pictures, or the like, of an *immoral* tendency." He drew the jury's attention to the current journalistic malaise in Philadelphia, to the fact that the "direct tendency of [the current] libels [was] the breach of the public peace, by stirring up the objects of them, their families and friends, to acts of revenge, and perhaps bloodshed." When such libels were leveled against public officials they "tend[ed] to scandalize the Government, by reflecting on those who are intrusted with the administration of public affairs."

Attacks against a government, or a group of government officials, posed a special problem, McKean informed the nineteen jurors. Most offenses where one or two individuals were concerned, or when specific names were used, were punishable either by indictment, information, or civil action. But when no one in particular was named, when the United States Congress, the courts or civil magistrates were the subject of abuse, proceedings were more difficult. Still, prosecution was not only possible, it was desirable. The instance at hand was just such a case, where criminal prosecution was a legitimate weapon at the disposal of the people's representatives. Personal reputations were at stake here as was the peace of the community. It was to every citizen's benefit that Cobbett be prosecuted. The jurors should also keep in mind that Cobbett had sought "to frustrate a conciliation with France and to provoke a war between sister states."

Nor should these proceedings be thought by jurors to restrict the freedom of the Pennsylvania press. It was a free press, McKean told the jury; neither the federal government nor the state placed any prior restraints on materials published. But the law clearly held that an editor was responsible for what he did with his freedom. Editors could print whatever material they wished, but if it proved to be libelous or seditious, they must pay the penalty exacted by law. The law afforded individuals and the community that remedy. And, according to McKean, it was high time that Pennsylvanians looked to that remedy. "Libeling has become a kind of national crime," he told the jurors, "and distinguishes us not only from the States around us, but from the whole civilized world." He told them that he, "impressed with the duties of [his] office," had tried to check the libelous trend by binding Cobbett, whose papers had been "licentious and virulent beyond all former example," to his good behavior. And he had done so strictly in accordance with the provisions of the law.

And yet, the jurors were informed, Cobbett had "perserver[ed] in his nefarious publications; he [had] ransacked our language for terms of reproach and insult." McKean directed the grand jurors to retire and to "inquire with zeal, hear with attention, deliberate with coolness, judge with impartiality, and decide with fortitude." It was McKean at his best, and his worst: forceful, impassioned, precise, articulate, too partisan, too personally involved.

The jury chose not to bring in a true bill. They were unhappy with McKean's overzealous promotion of the state's case, and sensitive to Cobbett's argument that the chief justice had been selective in his prosecution and had deliberately chosen to overlook journalistic abuse directed against his political enemies. The jurors therefore returned the bill *ignoramus*.[18]

On April 10, a month before George Logan consulted with McKean about his proposed mission to France, Sally McKean, converted to Catholicism, married the Spanish minister at the home of the Chevalier de Frere, Portugal's minister to the United States. Her father faithfully recorded Yrujo's full title in the McKean family Bible: "Don Carlos Martinez D'Yrujo, Knight of the Royal & Distinguished Order of Charles III, Envoy Extraordinary and Minister Plenipotentiary of his Catholic Majesty to the United States of America."[19]

Most Philadelphia newspapers ignored the marriage or reported it in a perfunctory manner. Cobbett alone exhibited no reluctance in editorializing on the event. For more than a year he published articles insulting the young couple. He printed a poem commenting on Yrujo's "Spanish imbecillity" for believing that his "Dulcinea" had "turned...Roman." The poem commented on the fact that while his marriage to Sally McKean had not brought any money to Yrujo it did guarantee him "Pontius Pilatus for [his] father-in-law and Protector." Stories followed illustrating the rudeness and profanation of Yrujo and Sally in their dealings with various neighbors.

Cobbett used the articles on the Yrujos as vehicles from which to strike out at the McKeans. Young Sally was said to be only slightly less temperamental and shrewish than her mother, who habitually destroyed the chief justice's wig while he was drunk. Cobbett complained that the McKeans scandalized Philadelphia society with their drunken domestic quarrels. The McKean boys were no better. Tommy McKean purportedly shocked a neighbor by loudly denouncing his mother as a "bitch."[20]

Whatever additional encouragement McKean needed to reinstitute legal proceedings against Cobbett was supplied by Cobbett's *The Democratic Judge,* a scathing denunciation of McKean's role in the previous November's oyer and terminer action against *Porcupine's Gazette.* While reporting in full the state's indictment against him and McKean's celebrated charge to the jury, *The Democratic Judge* systematically ridiculed McKean's efforts at harassment. It pointed out the chief justice's partisan behavior and laboriously provided readers with examples of Republican slanders and libels, all of which the judge had seen fit to ignore. The message was clear: scurrility was acceptable to McKean so long as it was not directed towards himself or his friends.[21]

McKean's ploy for silencing Peter Porcupine was to rescind his recognizance. In December 1798 the court employed a debt suit to determine whether Cobbett's recent actions constituted a breaking of his contract with the state guaranteeing his good behavior and whether or not he had thus forfeited his substantial bonds. Such a move effectively bypassed the need for a jury's judgment on whether the publications were in fact libelous. Cobbett and his attorneys, anxious to frustrate the state's tactics, claimed that Cobbett was still a citizen of Great Britain. As an alien his case should properly come before the federal circuit court, not the state court.[22]

Cobbett and his counsel also maintained that the very nature of the case necessitated federal jurisdiction. This was not a suit against a state; it was a suit instituted by a state against an alien and it fell within the powers and jurisdiction of the Supreme Court, which had original jurisdiction. Cobbett's counsel, time and again, insisted that Pennsylvania's action was merely an action of debt and thus was a simple civil suit.

If Cobbett's attempt to remove jurisdiction from the state courts to the federal courts were allowed, the state countered, it would "prostrate the authority of the individual states" and render states completely dependent on federal courts whenever an alien became involved in a bailable offense. Indeed, it would guarantee that state courts would have to turn all cases involving aliens over for federal disposal. To do so would be fatal. No court could survive long with its power to bind or bail persons so seriously compromised. The very nature of the federal system was thus at stake here. To rule favorably on Cobbett's petition seeking removal of the case to federal jurisdiction would do irreparable damage to the union.

The contention by Cobbett's attorney that the suit was a civil action was erroneous, according to the state. Because the action was not a suit of civil nature, it did not fall within the view of the Constitution or an act of Congress. While not strictly a criminal prosecution, it was a suit of a criminal nature. The state had charged that the party menaced the public peace. All the state had to do in support of its claim was to show that the defendant had committed an offense. Any offense effectively broke the defendant's contract with the state. The contract or recognizance, then, was a part of the criminal process of the law.

The court's decision was unanimous. In this instance, at least, the more conservative associate judges concurred with their chief justice in the state's efforts against the pro-Federalist *Porcupine's Gazette*. They held that Pennsylvania had jurisdiction in this action. They conceded, however, that the case brought by Cobbett was fraught with legal and constitutional questions of a very sensitive type. In fact, McKean, reading the court's opinion, prefaced his comments on the merit of Cobbett's petition with an observation on the structure of the American union. America's "system of government... differ[s] in form and spirit, from all other Governments.... It is as to some particulars *national,* in others *federal,* and in all the residue *territorial,* or in districts called *States.*" The Constitution had made clear a number of areas in which the state and federal governments were to share authority. It had granted some powers exclusively to the national government and others specifically to the state. But a federal system provided for a wide sharing of powers, and in some instances sovereignty was not altogether clear. Moreover, it was not always clear *who* was to determine the ultimate distribution of sovereignty. As the system then stood, however, McKean's court could see nothing which suggested that the Constitution gave exclusive powers to the Supreme Court of the United States to rule in any confrontations between a state and the national government.

Fortunately, Cobbett's action was not complicated. The jurisdiction of the state court was clear. Where an alien had a controversy with a state over a contract or other matters of a civil nature, the Supreme Court of the United States had uncontested sovereignty; it and not the circuit courts must rule in such cases. If Cobbett's action was a mere civil debt suit, as he contended it was, he must then direct his petition to removing the matter into the Supreme Court, not the circuit court as he had done. But the action against Cobbett was a criminal proceeding as the prosecution had argued, and neither the Constitution nor an Act of Congress granted to the Supreme

Court cognizance of such matters. As the state had reasonably maintained, the current action was a contract case but it involved criminality, crimes against the state and its people. The case must therefore be ruled upon by a state court. Cobbett's petition to remove the action to the circuit court was thus denied.[23]

Two years later William Cobbett lost his case against McKean. As a result of the court's decision Cobbett, personally responsible for much of the bail put up in the previous year to guarantee his good behavior, faced mounting financial woes. The one thousand dollars in sureties that Benjamin Davis and Richard North had signed for the editor were lost, as was his bail, when he lost his case. Cobbett's basis of financial support began to wither, and eventually this undermined his confidence and power. But if in 1798 Cobbett was injured it was not fatal; like a wounded animal Peter Porcupine continued to lash out at his detractors. Some of the most telling barbs ever directed at McKean came from Cobbett's pen a year after his motion to change courts was denied. It was clear even to Cobbett, however, that his days as a Philadelphia editor were numbered.[24]

Meanwhile domestic disagreements over the new federal taxes designed to support the expected war against the French, and quarrels over the Alien and Sedition Acts, intensified partisanship already generated in Congress and the local press by the Logan Mission and other foreign policy squabbles. As libel and slander cases increased in the state courts, federal prosecutions under the Sedition Act accelerated. If Federalist editors felt the heat of Pennsylvania's courts, Republican editors were terrorized by the federal judiciary. Public riots and a series of vicious personal confrontations jarred the populace's sensibilities. Philadelphia had become a turbulent and angry city.[25] Growing bitterness and division within Pennsylvania society largely shaped the gubernatorial contest in 1799. The contention and rancor clearly worked to McKean's political advantage. By early 1799 Republicans recognized the need for a governor who would assume a more aggressive and partisan stance than had the retiring incumbent, Thomas Mifflin, a gentle, tolerant man who had assumed few partisan positions while in office. The tenor of the times suggested that there was now little place for such a man in Pennsylvania politics.²⁶

In many respects McKean was an ideal gubernatorial candidate. No one was naive enough to deny that he had made more than his share of enemies during his twenty-two years on the bench, or that his support was suspect among Pennsylvanians who resented his decisions in land cases or his role in the Whiskey Rebellion or the Wyoming controversy. The inner circles of Republican power acknowledged the qualms of men like William Duane (editor of the Republican *Aurora*) and Dr. Michael Leib over McKean's devotion to true Republican principles, or at least to their definition of republicanism, which emphasized the more democratic tenets of the ideology. McKean's highly visible career would admittedly provide abundant material for the opposition, and there was no doubt in any Republican's mind that the Federalists would take full advantage of the opportunity.²⁷ Against these liabilities were great strengths, however. Few men were better known in the state than McKean, or were more knowledgeable about local government and its personnel. Even his detractors admitted that he had been an effective judge, and that he had been primarily responsible for the independence of the state judiciary. No one in Pennsylvania could claim more general experience on the executive, legislative, and judicial levels than the chief justice, or claim to have participated in more crucial conventions or decision-making bodies responsible for the destiny of the state. His reputation as a staunch defender of American liberties in the Revolution was secure. Those familiar with the everyday workings of the state administration acknowledged that McKean and Dallas had provided the real impetus in the face of Mifflin's growing alcoholism.²⁸

It was understood that McKean was willing to leave the bench to pursue the governor's chair, despite his protestations to the contrary. The demands of his judicial post had increased. Despite efforts on the part of the legislature to reduce the Philadelphia dockets of the Supreme Court, quarterly sessions had lengthened and the case load of the justices had swelled.²⁹ By 1799 the high court of errors and appeals was exacting its toll of McKean's time and energy, and, one senses, his pride. In this court McKean played a role subservient to Benjamin

Chew, its president and his predecessor as chief justice. This court reviewed decisions appealed from his Supreme Court, which could not have been comfortable to a man known for his pride in never having his verdict reversed.[30] Equally deflating probably was the competition offered by the federal courts, especially the United States Supreme Court, which held its proceedings in Philadelphia. Many of the more spectacular and novel cases which before 1790 automatically had been tried in McKean's courts, now fell under federal jurisdiction. Philadelphia lawyers looked to the federal courts to establish their reputations and to enhance their earning power. The third volume of Dallas' *Reports,* published in 1799, for example, reflected the changing status in Pennsylvania's judicial community by emphasizing federal cases almost to the exclusion of proceedings in the state courts.[31]

Other factors pushed McKean towards the gubernatorial chair. He could not withstand the physical demands of the circuit as he once could. And though he continued to wield impressive power both inside and outside the courtroom, he felt by 1799 that he had done all he could do in his judicial capacity.[32] In the end however it was his own ego and his belief that American republicanism stood on the brink of disaster that compelled him to seek the governorship of Pennsylvania. He had come to believe that he was perhaps the only man in the state capable of insuring the survival of republican values and institutions in the state.[33]

McKean was not the only possible candidate. Peter Muhlenberg had support among the state's Republicans, as did General William Irvine, George Logan (fresh from his European trip) and Alexander Dallas. Muhlenberg, Irvine and Logan had been effective state legislators and had served Pennsylvania in a number of critical offices. Dallas, who had gained a reputation as an efficient organizer during his tenure as Mifflin's secretary, was acknowledged as one of the most talented and shrewd of the Republican leaders. While he coveted the governorship, he was realist enough to know that he did not have the necessary support to win. As a close friend of McKean's anxious to hold on to his post as state secretary, Dallas recognized that McKean's election would not only serve the state well but would guarantee his secretaryship. For these reasons he became one of the most vocal and tireless of McKean's supporters.[34]

The final decision to nominate McKean as the party's candidate was made in Philadelphia on March 1. At that meeting it became evident that Irvine, Dallas, Logan and Muhlenberg could not compete with McKean's reputation and experience. Peter Muhlenberg did not want the post, and though he did not make this fact publicly known prior to the meeting, his reluctance was appreciated by party insiders. Ballots taken at the meeting showed "that the opinions of a large majority" were in favor of McKean, and he was accordingly designated as the Republican standard-bearer. A Committee of Correspondence, including unsuccessful candidates Muhlenberg, Irvine, and Dallas, as well as Michael Leib (who with Duane had preferred Muhlenberg to McKean), William Penrose, Tench Coxe, and Samuel Miles, father-in-law to Joseph McKean, was named to oversee McKean's campaign. Several of the committeemen, Muhlenberg and Dallas in particular, had already worked assiduously to assure McKean the nomination. Moreover, committeemen like Leib who had favored another candidate readily supported the chief justice once he was named the party's candidate. Republican leaders were hard-nosed political realists. They desperately wanted a Republican victory, and McKean could get votes, as his role in the 1796 presidential elector contest had proven. For good or ill, he was their candidate. Duane's *Aurora* quickly became McKean's most ardent defender.[35]

To the Federalist Cobbett, McKean's nomination meant only one thing: should McKean win, Cobbett would have to leave the state. He girded his loins for battle.[36]

17. Republican Governor

If McKean and the Republicans wished to make Pennsylvania's republicanism the central issue of the election, the Federalists were happy to oblige. They judged McKean a dubious Republican at best. They paraded McKean's voting record in the state constitutional convention of 1789-90 to point out to the public his aristocratic predisposition and to reveal conclusively that he shared few republican values. His unrepublican behavior on the bench was documented by a seemingly endless number of victims who had purportedly suffered at his hands. His callous disregard for the poor was described in detail. "Show me a poor man," they quoted him as saying, "and I will show you a rogue."[1]

A basic tenet of republicanism was an appreciation of America's uniqueness. According to McKean's Federalist detractors he remained, however, an uncompromising sycophant to France, a tool of the French and their American agents. His efforts against Jay's Treaty and in behalf of George Logan, and other examples were cited to prove his obsequiousness to French interests. Moreover, he was not averse to seeking help from the Irish when the need arose. He was charged with saying that, if necessary, "20,000 United Irishmen would land in America" to guarantee republican dominance. Presumably that would include the securing of his election.[2] In brief, held the Federalists, how could a man like McKean, so fiercely committed to foreigners and their aims, so willing to disregard his own religious principles, so eager to switch allegiances when faced with offers of office and honors, so congenitally incapable of treating the common citizen with respect and courtesy, produce a truly republican administration in Pennsylvania?

As expected, Cobbett led the attack. He reveled in exposing what he considered to be McKean's checkered and hypocritical careers, painting him as a political weathercock and an arbitrary and violent judge. He described McKean as a man desperate to conceal his rough origins by aggressive behavior, imperiousness, and unwarranted intimidation of those careless enough to cross him. Cobbett's McKean was a man devoid of principles, driven in part by avarice and in part by egomania from one political affiliation to another, from one lucrative public office to another. McKean's entire career smacked of ambition and vanity, according to Cobbett.

Cobbett struck directly at McKean's strong point, his reputation as a firm patriot. Little in McKean's background escaped the thorough Peter Porcupine, or those to whom he opened his columns. *Porcupine's Gazette* published letters purportedly from those intimate with McKean during the New Jersey campaign in the fall of 1776, testifying to McKean's incompetent—even traitorous—behavior. McKean was accused of profiting from the purchase of depreciated soldier certificates, supposedly acquired at from 1s 6d to 2s 6d per pound, and using the profits to purchase the Duche estate. "Are you a soldier or a sneaking sycophant?" asked *Porcupine's Gazette*. "Are you an honest speculator or a base coward?" Even McKean's pre-Revolution activities failed to meet Cobbett's standards. He asserted that in 1771 McKean had sold out his patriotism for the lucrative New Castle customs office. McKean's willingness—even eagerness—to accept the post and take an oath committing himself to a faithful compliance of

British laws was instructive. It illustrated how quickly McKean would disregard his principles for profits and offices. An examination of McKean's career after 1776 revealed similar weaknesses and inconsistencies.

If this were not enough, McKean was corrupt. During much of his time as chief justice, Cobbett warned his readers, McKean had taken advantage of the law requiring the various counties to pay the tavern expenses of the chief justice and his aides on the circuit. He had consistently run up exorbitant weekly bills; in 1790 alone his tavern bill had run as high as £74. When the law had been revised to provide the chief justice a four-dollar per diem so that he could attend to his own bills, the tavern accounts dropped appreciably. McKean's baseness on the circuit, at least of late, according to *Porcupine's Gazette,* extended to his using the circuit as an opportunity to canvass voters. Not only was McKean "soliciting the vote of the present citizens, but he [was] *absolutely making new ones!*" Cobbett asserted that the chief justice was indiscriminately giving the oath of citizenship to Irishmen in the various counties in a desperate effort to ensure his own election.

McKean's religious convictions were also scrutinized. Cobbett assailed McKean for seeking to mobilize the Irish vote by encouraging rumors to the effect that he was Catholic. *Porcupine's Gazette* dwelt with unfeigned fascination upon the marriage of Sally McKean to Yrujo, arguing that the Presbyterian McKean submitted willingly to the humiliation of his daughter's conversion to Catholicism simply in order to call himself the "father of a nobleman"—and collect Catholic votes in the process.[3]

Not surprisingly, the greatest part of the Republican effort was directed toward defending McKean's republicanism. Accusations against McKean's conduct and personality were dismissed as the product of political desperation. Republican committeemen commented favorably on his proposals for free public schools, and his commitment to the American cause in the Revolutionary years. They published accounts of the hectic events of July 1776 and McKean's pivotal role in them. McKean's opponent, it was said, "cannot be supposed to possess either the experience or to hold the respectable stand of Mr. McKean, whose service in the various stations of public confidence and responsibility from the first days of our Revolution to the present day, have been an unremitted career of public service, with an established and full title to integrity and patriotism." The citizenry was to rest assured that "Judge McKean is, as he was in 1775, a decided Republican." He was "one of the first persons in Pennsylvania to perceive the soundness of Republican principles, and . . . one of the most firm to maintain, defend, and diffuse them." McKean "cannot be forgotten by the lovers of their country, as long as Washington is held estimatable—the memory of Franklin revered—or liberty is thought dear to man,—with them he bore a part in a trying conflict, with them he risqued fame, fortune, and life," reported one fulsome Republican broadside.[4] If in the excitement of the rigorous campaign Republicans created a McKean more committed to their ideas and ideal than reality warranted, one could hardly fault him.

Republicans saw the real threat to republicanism in Federalist policies. They charged Federalists with fomenting distrust and division among the peoples of Pennsylvania for political gain, with striving to turn German against Irish, Irish against English. "No device is unemployed by [the Federalists], no tale too dull, nor falsehood too gross," Republicans complained, "At one place Judge McKean is a Roman Catholic, and therefore unfit to be trusted. At one time he is a Democrat who wishes to level all law and order, at another, a tyrant who wishes to substitute his will for law." "A Freeman" assured the people that the "aristocratic junto" was merely trying to divide and conquer. Not only were Federalists accusing McKean of various personal failings, changing the charges to fit their immediate audience, but they were also intimating that Quakers ought to support Logan and the Germans Muhlenberg "to confuse the issues and detract from McKean's vote."[5]

The sharpest Republican barbs were saved for the Federalist candidate, James Ross, a successful Pittsburgh lawyer. "Who is Ross?" asked a broadside. "An usurer who exacts seventy-five pounds for forty! A Land Jobber! A trimmer in the Senate who was constantly playing bo-peep that he might become a governor! A friend to alien and sedition laws! An advocate of exorbitant salaries!" McKean was described as "a devout Christian," "a steady patriot of 1776," "an experienced

Magistrate," and "a friend to the poor." Against him the Federalists had pitted "an avowed Deist," "a trimming politician of 1794," "a Monarchist," "a litigious attorney," and a "usurer." It was not surprising, concluded the Republicans, that Ross' support came primarily from "old tories," "inveterate Aristocrats," and "office holders or office hunters." The only thing which could possibly deprive McKean of the gubernatorial chair, the people were told, would be the failure of good Republicans to vote, or election chicanery by unscrupulous Federalists.[6]

McKean assumed a low public profile throughout the campaign and trusted the various state Republican committees to electioneer on his behalf. He did give a number of splendid dinner parties for the Republican faithful and sought to persuade those on the political fence, but overall his efforts were restrained. The mere fact that he was able to contain his impetuous temper and his harsh tongue was of inestimable help to his cause and to those who labored for him. McKean may have been content to restrain his impetuosity during the campaign, but his eldest son was not, as revealed in an incident provoked by troubles in Bucks, Berks, Northampton, and Montgomery counties. In March 1799 federal authorities had requested that Governor Mifflin call out the state militia to curb the activities of John Fries and his followers, still unhappy over the ramifications of the federal tax legislation passed the previous June. Eight troops of cavalry were among the forces subsequently sent into the troubled area the first week in April. The troops put down the "rebellion" with cold dispatch and affected a number of "arrests." Enraged by the developments, William Duane printed seven affidavits describing the excesses of the troops, and charged the militia with refusing the right of bail to captured suspects, illegally entering homes, and indiscriminately terrorizing the countryside. On May 15, thirty or more of the troopers, including Joseph McKean, visited Duane on the second floor of his printing office. Young McKean, who was pushed to the front of the group as spokesman, thrust a copy of the offending newspaper under the editor's nose and demanded to know who had written the outrageous lies concerning the soldiers' activities. Duane refused to say and reminded McKean that he was "leagued with [his father's] enemies." With that McKean struck the editor in the mouth and the group dragged the struggling Duane down the stairs into an alley where they continued to pummel him with a "cowskin." Fortunately for the senior McKean, Duane chose not to let young Joseph's violent behavior influence his own efforts on the father's behalf. Publicly Duane viewed Joseph McKean's actions as part of a Federalist plot to dupe him into embarrassing the father. Privately Duane was less sanguine; he instigated charges against members of the attacking party, including Joseph McKean.[7]

Despite this ugly altercation and the enthusiasm with which Federalists supported Ross against McKean, Republicans remained confident of victory. Caesar A. Rodney wrote his father as early as March 7 predicting that the "chief justice . . . will be the next governor of Pennsylvania. . . . The Whigs are in high spirits." As the election neared, those like Leib, Dallas, Coxe and Duane, who were the most responsible for managing McKean's campaign, predicted McKean would win by 5,700 votes in the process of carrying sixteen counties. They conceded nine counties and the city of Philadelphia to the Federalists and Ross.[8] Election results confirmed Republican predictions of victory if not their anticipated margin. Republicans rejoiced that they had not only elected a governor but had assured themselves a majority in the Lower House, where they enjoyed a forty-one to thirty-five edge. The one dark spot on the horizon for Republican hopes of dominating the state was the Federalist-controlled Senate. Considering the partisanship of the campaign, McKean could expect little compassion from this body of political enemies intent on refuting the lamentations of their more despondent colleagues concerning the future of Federalism in Pennsylvania. Federalists were hurt but not comatose.[9]

McKean responded in public and private letters to the resolutions expressing approval of his ascendency to the governor's chair. He assured a York County Republican committee that its confidence in his republicanism was not misplaced, and informed them that he "admire[d] [the] present democratic form of government, [was] warmly attached to it by choice and habit, and [would] at all times be zealous in its support." He told a Republican crowd in his native Chester County that he had "never spared to expose [his] person and property in procuring the independence of our Country, in framing & establishing wholesome constitutions for [their] government, and in securing equal rights and privileges for all." He declared his determination to continue along that path. Still, Cobbett was taking no chances; he packed his bags and left the state.[10]

Unfortunately, the partisanship that Republicans had looked for in McKean surfaced sooner than most party members anticipated. The first exhibition of his political myopia came in answer to a Republican committee which had expressed its pleasure in McKean's "firmness that neither cabal nor faction had been able to shake," and in his "old fashioned principles of right." After thanking the committee members for their gracious sentiments he suddenly lashed out at those who had opposed him, labeling them "Traitors, Refugees, Tories, French Aristocrats, British agents, and their corrupt dependants together with not a few apostate Whigs." Despite some rather awkward attempts to explain away his intemperate comments it seemed clear to all that the next three years would be tumultuous ones.[11]

McKean was inaugurated on December 17, 1799. When he addressed both houses of the Assembly on that day and called for a "continuance of that harmony, which happily subsisted between the Legislative and Executive Departments during the Administration of [his] patriotic Predecessor," the Federalist Senate sat unimpressed. His observation that the "present crisis in human affairs evidently demands the exercise of wisdom, moderation and fortitude from all who are employed in the business of government," had a hollow ring to those who were the object of his earlier obloquy. The Senate now seemed as eager to pick up the gauntlet as McKean had been, earlier, to throw it down. The senators responded to McKean's address in insulting language, suggesting that McKean should heed his own advice concerning moderation and conciliation. They professed to "lament the occasion which calls for this language; but animated by a Spirit of Republicanism[!] and disdaining the servility of courtly adulation," they felt "impelled" to use it.[12]

Despite the furor caused by his inaugural remarks, the sixty-five-year-old McKean was busy at his desk the day after his inauguration, thumbing through a spate of applications for executive pardons, and an already impressive collection of requests for patronage posts, and, with Dallas, William Findley, and other Republican leaders, analyzing the election returns and the possible use of patronage to cultivate support in areas where he and the party had not shown well. McKean had already given considerable thought to the state's judicial personnel and county leaders, but now he began a concerted review of possible appointees. As a consequence of his long career as a close observer of county governments and courts, and as a result of the campaign, he knew a number of office holders who would have to be dismissed. He began to draft a series of executive orders regarding the changing order.[13] His rigorous first day as governor typified what soon became a routine work day for him. In January 1800 he told his wife that he was still "fatigued with business." Six months later he confided to John Dickinson that "tho my situation in life is changed, my cares remain, I have never had greater employment for body & mind, than from the last six months, unless when I was president of Congress." He remained confident, however, that although his "duty was great," once over the immediate demands of the office he would "at least have as much leisure as when chief justice."[14]

McKean's first crisis as governor had its origins in the presidential election of 1800, specifically the state's inability to reach agreement on the means of choosing presidental electors. The law which had governed the state's choice of presidential electors in 1796 by general election had expired. Both parties privately conceded that a renewal of the law would virtually guarantee Republican domination. Predictably, Republicans were eager to have the law revived; on December 30, 1799, the Republican House voted thirty-eight to thirty-four to continue the earlier law. The Federalists were understandably determined to substitute a plan whereby the state vote would be taken by districts, a strategy which would insure them at least nine of the state's fifteen electors. Eleven days before the House had acted, the Federalist Senate voted fourteen to nine to oppose the revival of the election law. As a consequence of the non-agreement of the two houses, the dispute was transferred to a conference committee which ultimately proved unable to bring about a compromise. Not surprisingly, the obstinacy of the Senate nettled McKean, who was anxious to throw the weight of the state behind Republican candidates in 1800 and to humble the unyielding Senate in the process.

McKean did not perceive these developments as a mere political struggle; this was a private war between individual Federalists and himself. "The British or Tory party here seem determined to do everything they dare, and they are desperate to render me uneasy," he confided to his wife on the very day the Senate had formally resisted the continuation of the election law, "and I am determined to retaliate and treat them with deserved contempt." He went on to explain the present political alignment as he perceived it. "A Majority of the House of Representatives are Republicans and of course my Friends; a majority of the senators are otherwise, or at least Tools of those who are so, and of course my Enemies." Still, he reassured Sally that "As to the tempests & irritation in public station I have been so long habituated to them that they now make a weak impression upon me: the oldest sailor cannot bear the buffetings of the waves with more sang-froid than I can."[15]

With the two houses—and the conference committee—at loggerheads, the problem of presidential elections fell to McKean. No resolution of the difficulty would be forthcoming in the present session, and the next session would not convene until after the presidential election, in December. If Pennsylvania was to have a voice in the selection of the next president, the governor would have to call an extraordinary session. McKean first thought of calling a special session of the legislature for August. In a letter to Jefferson he explained conditions in Pennsylvania and his current thinking on constitutional options open to him. He left no doubt that he would not suffer an obstinate Senate to thwart the Republican will of the state, as such a development would mean that thirteen or fourteen willful men could frustrate the wishes of the general population. However, McKean was persuaded to forego the special session in August: it would be expensive and unprofitable, as there was little likelihood that either house would have substantially changed its mind by then. The October elections, which hopefully would redress the balance in the Senate, would offer the people an opportunity to choose the state's presidential electors by determining the strength in each house.[16]

To McKean's chagrin, and the Republicans', the October elections changed only the numbers; the stalemate continued. Despite several Federalist losses generally, the party clung to its hold on the Senate, this time by a margin of two votes. Four days after the election McKean called for a special session of the Assembly to meet November 5. On November 7 he addressed the joint session of the Assembly to plead for positive results. "To rescue Pennsylvania...from the stigma of exhibiting to her Sister States, a fatal example of discord and disorganization," an answer must quickly be found, he told the Assembly. The current alarming situation was "superior to the suggestions of party" and should persuade them to "disdain a contest about forms."[17] Twelve days later he prodded the still recalcitrant Senate, telling it that the absence of Pennsylvania's participation in the upcoming election would deliver the federal union a blow from which it might never recover. But federalist senators interpreted McKean's pleas as a bald attempt to secure a solution favorable to Republican interests and they had no desire to help him or his party. For his part McKean had begun to suspect that the thirteen Federalist senators did not want Pennsylvania to participate in the forthcoming presidential contest; they were merely using the ploy of a concurrent vote, clearly unacceptable to members of the House, to achieve that end. It was a suspicion shared by a growing number of Republicans, including McKean's aide and confidante, Alexander Dallas.[18]

The recognition by Republicans in mid-November that the contest between Jefferson and Adams would be uncomfortably close did nothing to reduce their sense of urgency. By the third week in November McKean had given up hope that Pennsylvania would cast electoral votes in 1800.[19]

Fortunately, as McKean told Jefferson on December 15, William Findley (now "a true Republican") had offered a plan which ultimately facilitated a compromise calling for each house to nominate eight electors. Fifteen of the sixteen nominees would then be chosen by a joint vote. McKean, by now convinced that a one-vote advantage would be better than no vote at all, hurriedly signed the compromise bill, and on

December 2, 1800, eight Republicans and seven Federalists were named. McKean waited only hours after the results were known to issue a proclamation ordering the electors to meet the following day in Lancaster to cast their ballots. As expected, the eight Republicans supported the Jefferson-Burr ticket, the seven Federalists, Adams and Pinckney.[20]

The story of the 1800 election is now a familiar one. Burr and Jefferson received seventy-three votes apiece, Adams sixty-five and Pinckney sixty-four and, as a result, the election was thrown into the House of Representatives. Following the election but before the House had begun its crucial voting, McKean shared with Jefferson his assessment of the current situation. McKean had concluded "from the explicit & honorable conduct of Mr. Burr there will be no competition on his part." Regretably, he had learned too "that envy, malice, despair and a delight in doing mischief" would prompt "the Anglo-Federalists" to frustrate the easy determination of the matter. The House had a duty to choose either Burr or Jefferson, but should characters "act[ing] the desperate part" work their will to see the will of the majority blunted, the candidates themselves must take the initiative. The two candidates could "agree between themselves by an instrument in writing... which of them shall act as President, which as Vice-President." Such a strategem would allow the constitutional choice of the people to be carried into effect. McKean assured Jefferson that in the event that "bad men dare traiteriously to destroy or embarrass [the] general Government & the Union," he conceived it his duty to "oppose them at every hazzard of life & fortune."[21]

It was not until February 17, after thirty-six ballots, that the House named Jefferson to succeed Adams. Writing to Jefferson on February 20, the day the news of his victory reached Philadelphia, McKean told the new president that "the bells of the Borough have been ringing ever since." He reported that the "two Houses of [Pennsylvania's] Legislature were electrofied [sic]." More important, the joyous news had forced McKean to revise his thinking of the last several weeks. He had written a long letter to Jefferson earlier, detailing his "intended operation in case of a certain unfortunate event in the decision of the House of Representatives." He now informed the president-elect that upon hearing of his victory he had consigned the letter "to the flames." He did not elaborate on its contents except to suggest mysteriously that the letter contained his "projected plan," which the Federalists would call "a bold stroke." His Republican friends had agreed to continue in session until after the fourth of March to aid in the deployment of his scheme should drastic action be necessary.[22]

It was not until March that McKean responded to Jefferson's urging to fill him in on the particulars contained in the destroyed letter. Pennsylvanians "would certainly have acquiesced" had Burr been elected president "by the representatives of a majority of the States," he told Jefferson, but they would never have accepted "any other person than one of the two elected by the Electors." Fearful that either the Senate or a joint venture on the part of the Senate and House would take advantage of the stalemate between Burr and Jefferson to name a third person—perhaps John Marshall—to the presidency, McKean had drafted a proclamation "enjoining obedience . . . on all officers civil & military, and the citizens of [Pennsylvania] to [Jefferson] as President and Mr. Burr as Vice President." After frantic consultation with Republican leaders, including George Logan, McKean had overseen the drafting of a resolution for adoption by the House (and a majority of the Senate) approving the proclamation. McKean had been prepared to call out the state militia, primed to move and armed with 20,000 muskets and several brass field pieces. Militia orders would have been to arrest any member of Congress acquiescing in the plot, or any "other person found in Pennsylvania who would have been concerned in the Treason," and the state would have prosecuted those involved. McKean expressed his happiness that the deployment of these plans had been unnecessary, "for otherwise the consequences might have been deplorable indeed."[23]

Correspondence between Jefferson and McKean began to allude to problems of patronage as both executives grappled with "the thirst for office" among their fellow Republicans. McKean sketched in some detail for Jefferson the moves only hinted at in his earlier outburst against the "Traitors, Refugees, Tories, French Aristocrats, British agents, and their corrupt dependants together with not a few apostate Whigs." Initially he had planned to restrict his removals to those who were incompetent or who had castigated him personally. A review of the personnel under his administration had convinced him that "a great many officers are unworthy of their station in any, but particularly in a Republican government." He was determined in his appointment procedures to give "a preference to a real Republican or Whigs, having equal talents & integrity, and to a friend before an enemy." He concluded that it was "at least imprudent to foster spies continually about one's self." To reduce the Federalists' ability to strike back at him, he remarked, "they must be shaven, for in their offices (like Sampson's locks of hair) their great strength lieth."[24]

In mid-1801 McKean was still pressing Jefferson to remove a number of Federalist office holders in Delaware so that good Republicans—and friends of his—like William Killen, Caesar A. Rodney, and David Hall, might be appointed in their stead. His friends' interests aside, one is left with the impression that the unreceptivity of the Delaware leaders to the proposals of McKean and Edmund Physick between 1789 and 1793 was very much in McKean's mind when he suggested the removals to Jefferson. But similar moves in Pennsylvania were also essential, he claimed. "It is out of the common order of nature," McKean told Jefferson, "to prefer enemies to friends...." A daggar ought not to be put into the hands of an assassin."[25]

McKean concurred with Jefferson that a cautious policy, one that would not antagonize the more moderate Federalists, was desirable. Yet his concurrence with Jefferson was seriously qualified by his lack of faith in Man. "From long and attentive experience," he told Jefferson, he had learned that "no measure your Excellency or myself can adopt will ever obtain their cordial approbation and that whenever a favorable opportunity shall occur they will exhibit their accustomed enmity." He warned the new president that his own party was not immune to the cancer of spoils. "Whenever any party are notoriously predominant they will split; that is in nature; it has been the case time immemorial, and will be so until mankind become wiser & better." "The Outs envy the Ins," he wrote, "The struggle in such a situation is only for the loaves & fishes."[26]

Those who knew him best predicted McKean's patronage program would differ from his predecessor's in at least two respects. The first had to do with the personality and experience of the new governor. The thoroughness McKean brought to the task of reviewing the personnel in the Mifflin regime was based on an intimate knowledge garnered over two decades of political and judicial involvement on both the state and local level. The second difference was a willingness to reward his friends and to chastise his enemies to a degree that was unknown in Mifflin's administration. If at first the Federalists thought, as William Irvine told McKean, that "although they have just lost the election they have to console themselves that it only requires a little attention by flattering the *Old Chief's* vanity to gain him to their side in a few months," he soon disappointed them.[27]

On December 18, the day after his inauguration, McKean ordered Dallas to issue a circular letter to some twenty-four office holders, mostly registers, recorders, and prothonotaries, dismissing them from their posts and informing them they need not reapply for their positions. Among those dismissed were George Bryan's old friend from Lancaster, John Hubley, William R. Atlee from Montgomery, and the highly sensitive Alexander Graydon, prothonotary in Dauphin County. He also sent notice to all office holders who held their posts by the governor's commission that they had three months to apply for a renewal of their commissions. Eventually he removed close to a hundred office holders. "I have been obliged, though no Herculus," he wrote Dickinson on June 23, "to cleanse the Augean Stables with little or no aid."[28]

When Federalists in the legislature complained of appointments and removals in McKean's first weeks, McKean answered them heatedly. He resented "the most opprobrious epithets on [his] arrangement of the subordinate offices of the state" and the "wicked designs" attributed to him. He told the Senators that they had "erred in the unqualified assertion, that 'a great number of respectable characters [had] been removed from office, against whom no other blame rests, than the exercise of their right, as freemen, in opposition to [his] wishes.'" He lectured them on the place of rotation in office in a republican government. He had selected and he would continue to select "for public stations, he told them, men who are tried and faithful friends to the genuine principles of our republican institutions."[29]

Still another significant difference between McKean's and Mifflin's approach to patronage as foreseen by political observers was McKean's willingness to provide for his kin, to pursue what has been termed as "patron-client" form of patronage. "I shall not be surprised if ere long we see a McKean at the head of every public department," Charles Ogden wrote in May 1800, "God Forbid!" Although Ogden's lament did not become literally true, the number of the governor's sons, cousins, sons-in-law, and nephews offered posts in his administration was impressive and grew more so with the passing of the years. Joseph accepted the post of register for the probate of wills for the city and county of Philadelphia on April 11, 1800, but resigned to become his father's attorney general, replacing Jared Ingersoll on May 10. McKean's nephew, Thomas McKean Thompson, replaced Alexander Dallas as secretary when Dallas resigned in April 1801. On March 8, 1800, McKean's son, Robert, thirty-four, was appointed auctioneer for the city of Philadelphia, a post he held until February 1801. Tommy McKean, now twenty-two, served as his father's private secretary for a spell before resigning to take a military commission. McKean eventually found offices for sons-in-law Andrew Pettit and George Buchanan, cousins Andrew and William Henderson, Thomas McKean Thompson's father-in-law, John Heusted, and his brother-in-law, William McKennan.[30]

McKean did not hesitate to ask Jefferson's aid in securing suitable federal posts for his family, telling the President in January 1801 that he had a son, Robert, "who [had] a liberal education tho' brought up a merchant" who deserved "a bigger office" than the auctioneership of Philadelphia. "It was all I could do for him," he told Jefferson, "He is the only person I am anxious about." If a vacancy should occur in the customs house "or any other department," McKean hoped that his son would receive consideration. In the following March McKean pleaded with Jefferson to request Yrujo's continuation as minister to the United States. "I love him as a child and never expect to see my daughter again after their departure for Europe," he told the President. Eighteen months after that first mention of Robert, McKean notified Jefferson of his son's death on June 8, 1802. At the same time the single-minded governor suggested that Robert's brother-in-law, Andrew Pettit, "a reputable gentleman and alderman" in Philadelphia would be an acceptable substitute, adding that he thought only "inveterate Tories, who an Angel could not please" would oppose the substitution. Life may end, but family responsibilities continue.[31]

Mindful that his western political fences needed mending, McKean scrupulously placated westerners through his patronage policies. John B.C. Lucas' appointment as associate judge of the court of common pleas in Allegheny County, and Hugh Henry Brackenridge's elevation to the Supreme Court were deliberate concessions to western office hunger. Less visible, but equally important, appointments were made at the justice of the peace and prothonotary level. McKean had power and would willingly wield it to help those who supported him, westerners noted.

Overall, McKean's policies of removal and appointment appear reasonable. If he removed some of his more ardent enemies within Federalist ranks, he also appointed and reappointed Federalists whose talents he respected. Edward Shippen received the chief justiceship despite strong pressure on the governor from members of his own party to look elsewhere for a more suitable candidate. Charles Biddle, Edward Burd, and Edwin A. Atlee were prominent Federalists named to lesser offices.

Even so, Federalists fiercely condemned McKean's removal policies. Stunned by his December 18 circular and its implications for their office holders, the Federalists initially resisted by not dutifully submitting their resignations. When this ploy did not appreciably slow down McKean's removals, they took their case to the public. They complained that "many of the Soldiers and Officers in our Revolutionary War, are to be dismissed from their present civil employment, without even an imputation of malconduct." Letters by ex-Federalist office holders appeared in local newspapers laying their cases before the people. Joseph Hopkinson, for example, complained that his political opposition to McKean, and McKean's hatred for his father, Francis, had accounted for his removal from office in the mayor's court. Some implied that such removals had led to extreme hardship. One Federalist doubtless spoke for many when he exclaimed that "McKean's driving is like the driving of John the son of Mimshe, for he driveth furiously."[32]

There were lessons to be learned here, and McKean anticipated that Federalist and Republican alike would be quick to grasp them. A man's removal from office need not be permanent. His removals were designed to rehabilitate as well as to injure or punish. McKean's attitude towards Joseph Hopkinson is instructive in this respect. On March 7, 1800, McKean had confided to Jefferson that he was preparing to remove Hopkinson—McKean called him his "graceless nephew"—and replace him with someone more loyal. Hopkinson need not despair of holding office under McKean, however; if he should "by proper concessions and reformation" put it in McKean's power, the governor "might after make him amends" by appointing him to some post of trust. It was up to Hopkinson to reassess his political priorities and loyalties. So it was with other Federalists. McKean would await their reformation.[33]

Even more galling to the Federalists than removal of their own was the type of men who replaced them. "McKean's administration has brought forward every scoundrel who can read and write into office or expectation of one," wrote one disillusioned Federalist in August 1800, "and the residue of Democratics, with the joy and ferocity of the damned, are enjoying their own hopes of preferment, and that of their friends, in proportion as they dismiss the fears of the gallows." Too typical, Federalists argued, was the case of Adamson Tannehill, appointed by McKean as justice of the peace in Pittsburgh, whom Federalists announced had been previously convicted for extortion. A disenchanted Federalist concluded that "a government under such an administration would be infinitely worse than no government at all."[34]

Initially, Republicans were delighted with McKean's actions. A correspondent in the *Aurora,* in apparent full agreement with the governor's politics, reminded the people of Pennsylvania that this administration did not practice rotation in office and "if McKean has erred...the error is not having carried the principle completely through." He deemed it a "bad policy...to meet an enemy with an unequal weapon." Another Republican justified McKean's removals, asking in effect, can the people blame McKean for getting rid of those "who if they were not the framers of the scurrility and Billingsgate, which was poured out against him and his family, yet either sung, said or whispered those lies?" Ross would have done the same thing were it in his power to do so, pointed out another Republican editorial, any man with the power would have done so. The *Aurora* at least, considered that most removals had been for lack of talents or skills.

Republicans scornfully answered Federalists complaining publicly of being removed. "Tacitus" responded to Joseph Hopkinson's accusations by going into some detail on Hopkinson's poor performance in office and concluded that there were quite legitimate reasons for his dismissal, reasons as apparent to his Federalist friends as to his Republican enemies. Joseph McKean answered Hopkinson's charges in the pages of the *Aurora* and concurred with "Tacitus" that "The order and regularity with which [Hopkinson] kept the offices of the mayor's court, and the orphan's court, did not entitle [him] to a renewal of [his] commissions." "To whom should offices during pleasure be given," asked Joseph McKean, "to the political and personal friends of the executive magistrate, or to his political and personal enemies?"[35]

But as Thomas McKean anticipated, many Republicans became dissatisfied with procedures that did not guarantee them offices. He was criticized for not removing more of the Federalists; disappointed office seekers complained that deserving Republicans were being ignored. Duane, initially an admirer of McKean's tactics, began to resent them. Content to praise the governor in public, Duane seethed in private over what he considered a slight against himself for, as he saw it, he had been a prime mover in McKean's election but had not shared sufficiently in the spoils, and neither had his friends.[36]

It was not unexpected that McKean should face some resistance to his program from the legislature. Less expected perhaps was the degree of Republican discontent which surfaced during his first term. On nonpartisan issues he had little difficulty initially. The legislature responded favorably to his call for an expansion of the state free public school system, especially his charge to establish immediate educational relief for the poor, and seemed to agree that election laws for both presidential electors and federal senators should be revised; the governor ought to have the power, furthermore, to oversee the construction of a canal between the Delaware and Schuylkill Rivers. Nor was there opposition to his call for a more concerted effort to collect and preserve state records. Partisan matters were a different story. When McKean requested a special appropriation to cover executive expenses not provided for in the general budget, Senate Federalists complained that McKean was a spendthrift.[37] They criticized him in December 1801 for failing to make a formal report of his appointment of George Logan to the Senate, judging his "oversight" to be a deliberate insult.

The Logan appointment revealed an inchoate divisiveness in Republican ranks that bode ill for the governor. On February 18, 1801, an election was held to replace William Bingham, whose term of office was to expire in coming months. Two Republicans, George Logan (still a close friend of McKean's) and Peter Muhlenberg, who had done so much for McKean in the recent gubernatorial contest, were the prime candidates. Each received forty-five votes on the first ballot and it was not until a Federalist changed his vote on the second ballot that Muhlenberg was declared the winner.[38] The hue and cry in the Republican press following the election stemmed less from disenchantment with Muhlenberg than with the fact that a sizeable number of Republicans had joined with Federalists to vote against Logan. The willingness of these Republicans to forgo party unanimity and combine with "the enemy" to defeat Logan, perhaps third only to Jefferson and McKean in being anathema to the Federalists, bordered on treason, according to Duane.[39]

Muhlenberg's election not only identified a rift in the Republican ranks; it posed a dilemma for McKean, who looked upon Muhlenberg as both an ally and a serious threat to his leadership in the party. Muhlenberg was so highly regarded in party circles that some thought he could have successfully challenged McKean for the gubernatorial nomination in 1799 had he sought the honor. Certainly, perhaps as early as 1802, he was conceded to be a logical successor to McKean. As a state senator Muhlenberg might make a successful challenge for party leadership in the upcoming election.[40] There was always the hope that Muhlenberg would decline public office as he had in the past. When he did not, but in fact won the senate seat, McKean favored a move—ostensibly to promote party tranquility—whereby Jefferson would name Muhlenberg to the lucrative supervisor of revenue post, and McKean would in turn choose Logan for the vacated senatorial seat. The difficulty would have appeared overcome when Jefferson did provide Muhlenberg with federal employment, and Logan accordingly became Pennsylvania senator-elect, had McKean not neglected to notify the legislature officially of his action, thereby incurring criticism.[41]

The same combination of Federalists and Republicans who scored McKean for his "insult" expressed dismay over McKean's failure in the same month to notify them of Thomas McKean Thompson's elevation to the secretaryship of the Commonwealth, necessitated by Dallas' resignation. Dallas' office holding had caused McKean a number of headaches. His resignation from the Secretaryship failed to placate Federalists and some Republicans were still disturbed by the fact that he continued to hold both state and federal posts: besides being recorder of the City of Philadelphia he acted as the federal United States attorney for the District of Pennsylvania. The House passed an Incompatability Act prohibiting Dallas from concurrently holding state and federal offices. It was a Republican, Nathaniel Boileau of Montgomery County, who initiated the act maintaining that Dallas' office holding violated the separation of powers. The Federalist Senate seized upon the opportunity to amend the bill to include another prominent Republican, Michael Leib, and the bill passed to the governor.

McKean watched these developments with a growing sense of *deja vu*. The basic argument against pluralism had never impressed him. His own career he thought ample repudiation of the argument that one man could not serve effectively in more than one official capacity. Moreover, the current fascination with Dallas' pluralism seemed a convenient way to censure his own conduct in naming Dallas to the recordership. On February 3, 1802, he vetoed the Incompatability Act, strenuously protesting that the bill was unwarranted and unfair. Only two men were involved, he told the Legislature, "What possible evil can arise to Pennsylvania from these two appointments?" He had received no signals that the people of the state were disturbed over the lack of separation between federal and state offices, no petitions or official complaints had reached his office. To sign the bill would imply that his appointment of Dallas had been "criminal." "The Tenure of such commissions," moreover, "ought not to depend on every gale that blows." The legislature ought not to vacate or impair a contract solemnly made between the Commonwealth and the individual.

The logic of McKean's argument escaped members of both houses. By an overwhelming vote of seventy-six to four the House overrode his veto. Party lines were also blurred in the Senate as that body followed suit, eighteen to seven.[42]

Dallas did not share McKean's hard feelings over the actions of the legislature. He resigned his state office without bitterness, telling the legislators that "a fair difference of opinion is not cause for animosity."[43]

Perhaps only in his acquiescence of the move to impeach the Federalist Judge Alexander Addison did McKean find universal support in his own party. Addison's failings, at least so Republicans argued, derived from his almost congenital Federalist prejudices and his insufferable—and unprofessional— behavior on the bench. A prime target of Addison's abuse had been his colleague on the bench, John B.C. Lucas, a staunch Republican and a McKean appointee. McKean encouraged Joseph McKean to do whatever he could to facilitate action against Addison.[44]

By far the most perplexing problem McKean encountered during his first term, the controversy over land titles in the Wyoming Valley, he inherited from his predecessor. His own role in the Wyoming discontent had been minimal since 1789, when his court had initiated proceedings against the indomitable John Franklin for treason. Subsequently the charges had been dropped. Most of the crucial activities relating to that fiercely contested area since that time had occurred in the state legislature as that body strove to resolve the differences between state interests and those of the Connecticut claimants. The one major legal case emanating from the difficulties—*Van Horne's Lessee* v. *Dorrance*—was not tried before McKean's court.[45]

When McKean became governor state officials were busy carrying out the provisions of the Compromise Act of 1799 whereby Connecticut settlers would pay for lands claimed by them on the basis of their land's worth, and interest-bearing state certificates would be provided to those Pennsylvania claimants agreeing to release their lands. McKean as governor faced the need to continue the implementation of the law and to reduce mutual distrust. Against a backdrop of Republican editorials critical of Connecticut's claims and Connecticut's continuing efforts in Congress to frustrate Pennsylvania's hold on the land, McKean named Thomas Cooper, John Steele, and William Wilson as commissioners to continue the state's negotiations with both claimants. Not surprisingly, even this perfunctory assignment exacted a political toll as Federalists promptly belittled his choices, maintaining that the three were Englishmen and asking how wise it was to assign "Old English Men" to negotiate with "New England Men." Despite the efforts of the *Aurora* to dismiss these criticisms as politically inspired and patently misleading, the question remained politically embarrassing.[46]

Reports submitted from the troubled area by the commissioners, and by Tench Coxe, secretary of the land office, confirmed that the Compromise Act had not affected a final settlement. Although Pennsylvania claimants, in conformity to the Compromise Act, had by December 1800 released some forty thousand acres, and a sizeable number of Connecticut settlers seemed receptive to carrying out their part of the agreement, there was also, as Coxe phrased it, "an unpleasing evidence that some of the New England leading men still keep up their exertions to prevent the restoration of [Luzerne] County to tranquility & prosperity." Coxe concurred with the commissioners' assessment that John Franklin, who continued to "openly maintain the validity of the Connecticut title," remained a formidable deterrent to an amicable settlement, and should be prosecuted.[47]

By the summer of 1801 McKean was concerned enough about the reports of continuing resistance to the provisions of the Intrusion and Compromise Acts to issue a proclamation reaffirming the state's determination to "forbid all future intrusions of lands within the limits of the . . . Counties of Wayne, Northampton, Luzerne, Lycoming, and Northumberland." It ordered all persons who had "intruded on any lands contrary to the provisions of the [Intrusion Act] . . . to withdraw peacefully." It also enjoined all state officials to prevent further intrusions and "to prosecute by legal means all who shall attempt such an intrusion." For all of McKean's good intentions, his proclamation seemed little more than a stale addition to the impressive list of acts and proclamations relating to the Wyoming Valley.[48]

McKean's Wyoming policy at the end of his first term was essentially what it had been at the beginning: a policy of watchful waiting. Unconvinced that it was necessary to employ the militia or encourage the arrest of the dissidents' leaders, yet apparently not persuaded that a total commitment to conciliation would prove to be as successful as Cooper and the commissioners implied, he straddled the fence, seemingly content with the gentle nudge implicit in his 1801 proclamation. When he did lose his temper it was not conditions in Wyoming that angered him so much as it was the legislature's failure to adequately support the Commissioners.[49] One thing must have been clear to him as his first three years in office came to an end: his administration had achieved no more success in Wyoming than had his predecessor's.

Opposition to McKean within his own party was embryonic and that within Federalist ranks unenthusiastic and disorganized when his first term neared its termination. A steady but perfunctory stream of criticism emanated from Federalist presses throughout McKean's three years in office decrying his arbitrariness, his vindictive and partisan patronage policies, and his unrepublican demeanor. Federalists mocked him, compared him unflatteringly to Jefferson. "Can Jefferson and McKean be both good Republicans, and be so unlike each other?" asked a correspondent in the *Lancaster Journal.* Another observer in the same paper concluded that Jefferson could "either approach the fame of a Washington, or sink into the contemtibleness of a McKean." Typical of the attacks leveled against McKean was the open letter to the governor purportedly from a young Republican who had supported him in 1799. "Your conduct, since you have been placed in the chair of state, short as your career this far has been, has blasted in the bud, every rising hope, [and] forced me to view you with the abhorrence of a tyrant," he wrote. Still, the barbs lacked the acidity of previous attacks. The Federalists could marshal neither the will nor the means to contest seriously McKean's re-election.[50]

Nonetheless some feeble efforts were made to deny McKean his party's nomination, then to frustrate his success once a candidate. Tentative approaches were made by Federalists to several prominent Republicans in the hope that the promise of Federalist support would entice them to oppose McKean, but these efforts failed to produce results. The death of Frederick Muhlenberg in June 1801 stripped the Federalist party of a candidate who might have carried a sizeable German vote and some Republican votes despite his earlier support of Jay's Treaty. Jasper Yeates was considered briefly, but in view of his inexperience in elective office he proved to be an unattractive candidate. As a result of these developments, Federalists were reduced to promoting rifts among Republicans. More realistic Federalists in Pittsburgh placed McKean at the head of their ticket in the hope of using his political coattails to secure lesser offices for Federalist candidates.[51]

Though there was little enthusiasm either on the part of party regulars or the candidate, a small group of Philadelphia Federalists did finally name a candidate at the last moment. On August 25, 1802, they officially turned again to James Ross.[52]

Some Republicans, particularly those representing the left wing—or Duane-Leib faction—of the party, were unhappy with McKean. At the heart of Duane's disenchantment was the governor's patronage policies. Duane and his ally Leib felt that neither they nor their friends had received sufficient reward for their efforts in McKean's behalf in 1799. Should McKean remove more of the "oppressors and persecutors," as Duane termed the Federalists remaining in office, party discontent would be substantially reduced. Several Republicans, including Samuel Bryan, Peter Muhlenberg, and George Logan, entertained interest in the gubernatorial nomination, if only fleetingly in some cases. McKean himself construed the rumors of their interest and that of others to be of sufficient weight to give a number of lavish dinners designed to solidify his position and to dissuade others from challenging him.[53]

There was little hint in all this that McKean took seriously Duane's disillusionment with his patronage distribution or Jefferson's gentle admonitions regarding the wisest patronage procedures to follow. But it hardly mattered. Republican options were few. Even those interested in seeking the nomination were hesitant to openly challenge a man like McKean who relished wielding power and would not hesitate to either reward his friends or punish those who opposed him. To challenge him openly—and unsuccessfully—might prove fatal to a man's political career. Those who wielded the greatest influence in party counsels—men like Dallas, Coxe, Leib and Logan—judged McKean to be as popular—and probably more so—in 1802 than he had been in 1799. Despite an impressive amount of maneuvering between various party leaders like Leib, Duane, and Logan for a more powerful voice in the party, no one mounted a serious challenge to McKean.[54] Thomas Leiper doubtless spoke for most Pennsylvanians—Federalists and Republicans—when he observed that "McKean has a fee simple in that office for ten years to come."[55]

The election confirmed Republican optimism. McKean carried 47,879 out of some 65,000 votes and in the process carried thirty-three out of the thirty-six counties. His margin of victory was more than a testimony to the disorganized state of the opposition party; it demonstrated the effectiveness of McKean's administrative and patronage policies. Even as he solidified his power and popularity in the areas he carried three years earlier, he made substantial gains in western and Federalist areas heretofore hostile to him. Despite some awkwardness and an occasional slip, McKean had done a competent job and the people knew it. In a few areas, such as eliminating corruption and inefficiency in several administrative offices (he had been the prime mover behind the reform of the Land Office and the removal of Daniel Brodhead, for instance) he had done an exceptional job, as even the Federalists conceded. No one denied he worked extremely hard at his job. The legislature observed with satisfaction that he dealt with their messages and bills promptly. If some observers saw in his victory a triumph of ideology rather than an endorsement of the man, McKean could be forgiven for interpreting the results as a celebration of his accomplishments.[56]

18. Republicanism Under Attack

Even in the face of his lop-sided victory and the general triumph of the Republican party in the October 1802 elections, McKean was not completely satisfied. Two malignancies continued to ravage Pennsylvanians in general and Philadelphians in particular, McKean told the legislators in his opening message on December 11. The first was the more obvious, the "malignant fever" which took its perennial toll of the city's inhabitants—close to three hundred in 1802. But a second and even more debilitating disease plagued the state's political institutions and ideals. That was the "fatal tendency of party feuds [to] . . . disturb and destroy the harmony of society." If the source of the yellow fever was still a matter of bitter debate among the city's physicians, McKean had no doubt as to the source of the current political evil. The press's "unparalleled licentiousness, in publishing seditious and infamous libels (leveling all distinctions between truth and falsehoods, between virtue and vice)," McKean told the legislators, "exposes our national character to contempt abroad, general distrust and disaffection at home and threatens finally to annihilate every benefit of this boasted medium of public information."

No one was exempt from the press's libels, according to McKean. He judged it high time that the representatives commit themselves to rescuing Pennsylvania from "a tyranny, by which the weak, the wicked, and the obscure are enabled to prey upon the fame, feeling, and the fortunes of very conspicuous members of the community." McKean hoped to attack the problem by "diffus[ing] the blessings of education among the poor." This, and invigorating the courts so that they could more quickly and efficiently enforce existing laws would be ample protection against this persistent and dangerous malady.

He concluded his inaugural remarks by insisting that the recent election returns proved that "the glorious spirit of the American Revolution [was] again active to perpetuate the blessings of a free republican government." Though the "early education and unfounded prejudices of some amongst us, inimical to a republican form of government . . . darkens our prospects, and impedes our political movements," he told the Assembly, "I do not despair of reconciling even those to our system, by using reason, persuasion, and lenient measures."[1]

An interesting prospect: McKean mellowed by an impressive personal victory. Still, there were signs that the old, stubborn McKean remained. Indeed, two days prior to his address to the General Assembly, he had vetoed the "Act for the recovery of debts not exceeding one hundred dollars," a bill designed to extend the powers of the justices of the peace and to create a system of arbitration as an integral part of the state's judicial proceedings. According to McKean, the bill, sponsored by a number of his own party, denied participants a jury trial and forced a too heavy reliance on untrained justices of the peace. By eliminating the role of the lawyer in an effort to reduce the cost of litigation in these small claims courts, and to simplify procedures for the convenience of the common man, the sponsors had "put to disadvantage" foreign born citizens or persons "untalented or fearful." Equally disturbing, McKean argued, the bill would actually increase the cost of litigation by encouraging a greater number of appeals to higher courts.[2]

The majority of regular Republicans and most Federalists concurred with McKean's assessment of the bill, but an important segment of the party was dismayed by his position. It believed that no serious improvement of the state's judicial system could take place until some fundamental assumptions were changed. The law had become too complicated and too expensive for the average citizen. By turning much of the litigation in smaller claims over to courts overseen by lay justices, and by encouraging a simple system of common sense arbitration, a substantial step toward eliminating the current evils would be taken. Merely to create more personnel for the present system, as McKean proposed, was to ignore the real flaws in the procedures. From the onset of his administration McKean had pressed for judicial reform. He was more eager for change in December 1802 than he had been three years before. But he wanted cautious, narrow reform. In 1787 he had told John Adams that he "dislike[d] innovation, especially in the administration of justice," and would "avoid tampering" with it "as with edge-tools," and he still felt that way.[3]

The division in Republican ranks over the proper course of judicial reform provided considerable amusement for the state's Federalists. They reminded Republicans that not only had their governor vetoed one of their party's most cherished judicial improvements, but in the previous February his son, Joseph, had joined Republican lawyers like Peter Stephen DuPonceau and Alexander Dallas in favoring retention of the Federal Judiciary Act of 1801, an act anathema to many Republicans, including Duane, who viewed it as a mere ploy to provide offices for Federalists, and as an unnecessary and costly creation of courts. To be reminded that the party was obviously working at cross purposes in questions of judicial reform was a political embarrassment for Republicans.[4]

McKean's veto of the "One Hundred Dollar Act," and the Senate's failure to override that veto on December 30, did little to dampen the ardor of those embarked on more thorough legal reforms. Early in 1803 the legislature sent to the governor a bill entitled, "An Act to provide for the adjustment of disputes and the Recovery of Debts within this Commonwealth," designed, like the previous bill, to extend the principle of arbitration in Pennsylvania courts. And, like the previous bill, its principal aims were to diminish both the cost and the complexity of the law. It too fell victim to McKean's veto on March 21. Observing the bill's "crude theories, fanciful alternatives, new projects and pleasing visions," McKean struck it down on the ground that it pitted rich against the poor, the learned against the ignorant. Like the preceding legislation it would overwork the justices of the peace and thus likely drive capable, learned men from these crucial positions. By promoting argument before the lay judges, the bill jeopardized the civil rights of various types. If one of the parties were trained in the law and the other were not, if one were learned and sophisticated and one were not, if one party were normal and the other deaf or a stammerer, justice could easily be subverted. "Innovations," McKean warned the legislators, "especially in the administration of justice, are dangerous.... It is always safer to borrow from former establishments, then to introduce plans entirely new." The objections contained in his December 9 veto pertained as well to this bill, "with more than double force, as this bill, if enacted into a law, would be more than doubly oppressive and injurious." The Senate failed to override the veto, voting thirteen to eleven to support the bill, far under the required two thirds.[5]

A month after McKean's veto of "An act for the adjustment of disputes and the Recovery of Debts within this Commonwealth," the legislature placed before him a bill entitled, "An act to extend the powers of the Justices of the Peace of the State," whereby a 1799 act extending the powers of the justices was revived. But the harder the General Assembly pushed for a radical departure from the old, tried system, the more McKean resisted. On December 8, 1803, he vetoed this bill, denouncing it as patently unconstitutional. Its failure to provide for jury trials "in a great variety of transactions" rendered it contrary to the state constitution and thus unacceptable. "An attack upon the trial by jury, in civil cases," McKean warned the legislators, "will afford to bad men, in worst times a ready pretext for undermining the trial by jury in criminal cases."[6]

By December 1803 McKean was visibly disturbed by the antics of the General Assembly. On the twenty-second of the month the House overrode his veto by a resounding seventy-five to four majority. Earlier, in March, he had found himself forced to reject a bill he considered highly beneficial and capable of saving a great deal of time and expense, because of the insertion into it of a provision giving to justices of the peace jurisdiction over cases involving amounts up to fifty dollars. Such a provision, in McKean's estimation, "conferr[ed] too much power on gentlemen of that character" and contravened the constitutional safeguard of a jury trial. He reminded the legislators that every objection that he had made to the previous bill on December 9, 1802, pertained to this bill; he begged them to read those strictures carefully. To his dismay both houses easily passed the bill over his veto.[7]

McKean's disagreements with the Assembly were not confined to judicial matters. On March 16, 1803, he had felt compelled to veto an "Act to alter or amend the act entitled 'an Act to regulate the general elections within this Commonwealth.'" His principle criticism revolved around the bill's shortening of the required time for aliens to achieve citizenship. He construed the law as providing insufficient time for aliens to "wean [themselves] from the prejudices and habits, as well as from the natural regard for their native soil." Prior to the Revolution the British had established a seven-year residency for citizenship and the last three American Congresses had agreed on five. For Pennsylvania to reduce the required period still further "without very striking and cogent reasons" was unwise. He had no reservations about the state's ability to permit aliens (with or without meeting residence requirements for citizenship) to elect or be elected into township or county offices, or to hold state appointments, yet he seriously doubted the state's power to give aliens the right to elect members of Congress, presidential electors, or even state legislators as they appointed federal senators.[8]

Throughout 1803 McKean grumbled about the lack of real talent in the General Assembly. "With the best intentions in the world," he told Jefferson in early February, "our legislators are attempting innovations, but as their Bills have been generally without limitations, and some of them appeared to be dangerous even for an experiment, I have been too frequently compelled to interpose my qualified negative." He yearned for "a few Gentlemen of Science in law, history, & Government" though he "despair[ed] of being so gratified." Twelve days later he wrote to his friend George Logan lamenting the fact that he was "without a friend capable of affording [him] any assistance." He would greatly appreciate "a free communication with an intelligent & good man." "We are here full of chimerical experiments," he told Logan, "and my knowledge acquired with great labor, study & reflection, and the advantages of a long & public life, cannot at times stop or check the giddy innovations attempted in our legislature."[9]

McKean's enthusiasm for punishing libel and for applying pressure on editors, despite his moderate comments in December 1802, drove still another wedge among Republicans. In February McKean had expressed to Jefferson his dismay at the "infamous & seditious libels, published almost daily in our newspapers." He thought that if they could not be prevented altogether, some checks at least could be thrown up by a "few prosecutions." He admitted that he had been considering such a move on his own but he had hesitated since "the President, Congress, and several of the principal officers of the United States have been frequently implicated." He deemed it judicious to consult Jefferson and to obtain his advice and consent before proceeding, but he was adamant that the current propensity for libeling was a national vice which "call[ed] aloud for redress."[10]

Days before receiving McKean's letter Jefferson had described his own hope that the press would be limited by the public's ability to distinguish between the abuse and the wholesome use of the press. But two weeks later he returned McKean's favor to express his agreement that the Federalists were abusing the press, seemingly intent on destroying its freedom by "pushing its licentiousness & its lying to such a degree of prostitution as to deprive it of all credit." He construed this to be a "dangerous state of things" and declared that the press "ought to be restored to its credibility if possible." He [judged] the restraints provided by the state's laws to be "sufficient for this if applied." Very ingeniously he informed McKean that he had long thought that "a few prosecutions of the most prominent offenders would have a wholesome effect in restoring the integrity of the presses." At the same time he warned that no "general prosecution" ought to be pursued, "for that would look like persecution." He suggested instead a "selected one." He sent along to McKean a paper judged by him "to offer as good an instance in every respect to make an example of." He knew McKean well enough to know he need say no more. The paper sent to McKean by Jefferson was undoubtedly Joseph Dennie's *Port Folio,* for a month before Jefferson's letter to McKean Dennie had attacked the President on very personal grounds, suggesting that "the circle of our President's felicities is greatly enlarged by the indulgence of Sally, the sable, and the aupicious arrival of Tom Paine, the pious." A week later there had been additional references to Jefferson's "tricks, with sooty Sal," an obvious allusion to Jefferson's relationship with his slave, Sally Hemings.[11]

Five months after the initial exchange between McKean and Jefferson concerning the problems of the press, Dennie was charged by state authorities with libeling. Choosing to ignore the more personal passages relating to Jefferson, state officials, prodded and directed by McKean, indicted Dennie on the basis of a passage in the April 23 *Port Folio* detailing the futility of democracy. The indictment, entered in the mayor's court in July but eventually removed to the Pennsylvania Supreme Court in its December term, began a long drawn-out litigation.[12] McKean's role in this affair, and it could be no secret that he was involved, made him few friends in the legislature. Not even the fact that his target in this instance was a Federalist comforted Republicans convinced that a free press was an integral part of a free society.

But then, McKean was exasperated with them, too. In December 1803 he told the legislators that "the spirit of litigation, the ruin of honest suitors, and the triumph of fraudulent debtors and others equally culpable, can no longer be disingenuously ascribed to the machinations of a profession, nor be regarded as the mere incidents of the law's delay." He intimated that the fault lay at the door of the legislature, a legislature more inclined toward foolish innovation than serious reform. He left no doubt that political capital gained by compromise with those most intent on careless innovation held no attraction for him. On a number of occasions McKean, despite reservations, accepted bills "as an additional evidence of the deference [he paid] to the opinion of the legislature, by preferring it to [his] own." But his willingness to exercise his veto on crucial issues had already deepened the suspicions of many in his own party regarding his fitness for the gubernatorial chair. Equally disturbing to Republicans was the fact that Federalists were beginning to openly praise his judicious use of the executive veto.[13]

McKean's reluctance to accede to the wishes of some Republicans to rid the state of its highest judicial personnel also eroded his political position among the state's Republicans. The proceedings against Alexander Addison, begun the previous year, brought no divisions within the party; McKean spoke for most Republicans when he expressed his belief that should Addison (whom he labeled the "transmontaine Golia[t]h of federalism" and "a remarkable political apostate") fall, "federalism would fall with him in the six western counties." By a strictly party vote of eighteen to four Addison was found guilty on January 26, 1803, and removed from office.

McKean's own conduct and his assessment of the proceedings cast doubt on the charge that the proceedings were blatantly partisan, however. His commitment to the courts and his sensitivity to any precedent which might undermine their authority guaranteed his opposition to any frivolous or merely partisan effort to impeach a judge, including Addison. McKean took some pains to determine where the pressure for the impeachment of Addison originated, and to identify those who viewed the subsequent proceedings with equanimity. He thought it significant that even some of Addison's most renowned friends and political allies, including James Ross, failed actively to support the judge. McKean's assessment seems sound: Federalist party leaders did not rally to Addison's cause; they considered his conduct indefensible for the most part and looked upon his cause as a political liability.[14]

For a man as sensitive to precedents as McKean, he seems not to have anticipated that the success against Addison would spawn additional charges against the state's judicial personnel. Yet McKean's response to a subsequent effort to remove judges demonstrates how fundamentally cautious he could be when it came to his courts. On February 28, 1803, a memorial from Thomas Passmore, a Philadelphia merchant, calling for the impeachment of Chief Justice Edward Shippen and two of his associate justices, Jasper Yeates and Thomas Smith—all Federalists—was introduced into the house.[15]

When, on March 13, 1804, a committee of the legislature brought in a report in support of Passmore's memorial and recommending that the judges be impeached, the House supported the resolution fifty-seven to twenty-four. Though the judges urged a speedy resolution of the matter one way or the other, nothing was done until January 1805. Complicating matters was the decision by Brackenridge on March 24, 1804, to request that he be included in the House charges against his associates. He notified the speaker of the House that he concurred fully in their actions and it was only chance that had deprived him of the opportunity to participate in the case. Infuriated by Brackenridge's action and its implied accusation of blind partisanship in the matter of the judges, the House prepared an address calling for Brackenridge's removal. Seven days after Brackenridge's letter reached the speaker of the House, the House approved the resolution fifty-three to twenty-two. The Senate approved it seventeen to two and it was sent along to McKean.

McKean was appalled by the legislature's actions. He was unalterably opposed to impeachment proceedings against the three Federalist judges or the removal of Brackenridge. Two of the judges, Shippen and Brackenridge, were his own appointees, and while he did not always concur with Yeates and Smith—indeed, on a number of occasions he had formally disagreed with them on points of law—he had worked closely with them for over ten years and he respected both. Brackenridge was a personal friend. McKean chose to make no formal recognition of the Assembly's address to him respecting Brackenridge's dismissal and he provided no encouragement for those bent on removing the judges. When a committee of the House approached him to urge his immediate removal of Brackenridge he angrily dismissed their arguments. He expressed his pleasure when the judges were subsequently acquitted.[16] Heartened he may have been, but his conduct cost him valuable support in Republican ranks. The *Aurora*, which had not actively supported those urging radical judicial reforms nor those eager to remove Addison, endorsed Passmore's action.

Himself the victim of judicial contempt citations, Duane had little sympathy for the courts, or for individuals like McKean who seemed blindly to support them. Though he kept his remarks uncharacteristically temperate, Duane criticized McKean for his failure to respond positively to the legislators' plea to remove Brackenridge.[17]

In only one area of judicial reform did McKean find his initiative supported by the majority of legislators. He diligently pursued the removal of incompetent and corrupt justices of the peace, responding promptly to citizen petitions identifying irresponsible personnel. Thomas McKean Thompson provided the General Assembly with a steady stream of complaints against justices who, on the basis of incoming petitions, McKean thought ought to be removed. He also supported legislation in January 1804 detailing the mode of taking testimony in cases of complaints against JPs. It was the type of judicial reform with which McKean was most comfortable. In his eyes it was not the system; rather it was the personnel—or the lack of it— which created most of the present difficulties.[18]

With each passing month these narrowly perceived reforms became less and less acceptable to a legislature bent upon substantial changes. Thomas Paine complained that McKean was "induced" to veto reforms "as a lawyer, for the benefit of the profession...not as a *magistrate,* for the benefit of the people." But radical Republicans were no longer satisfied with merely extending arbitration or diminishing the costs of legal procedures. Indeed, some came to question the basis of the law itself, asserting that British law failed to reflect the true goals and aspirations of the American people. Better to rid America of a law conceived in Europe by and for Europeans, and to replace it with an American common law. It was a theme repeatedly harped on by Nathaniel Boileau during the impeachment proceedings against the three Federalist judges. It was a theme increasingly attractive to Republican legislators.[19]

Criticism begat criticism. Lawyers, always viewed with a combination of distrust and envy, came in for an increasing share of abuse. It was asserted that lawyers had a vested interest in maintaining the *status quo,* that they were unmoving in their resistance to reforms which would diminish their lucrative practices. As early as 1802 Duane had written that "the present age is as much in danger from lawyers as the three last have been the victims of priests." By 1804 criticism of the bar had become both more virulent and widespread. McKean complained to Dickinson that there were not enough lawyers in the present legislature and few lawyers would consent to run; "such is the present prejudice against them . . . among the Common classes of men." He doubted that lawyers could be elected if they did seek office.[20] At least publicly McKean shrugged off criticism directed at him and plugged away at his official duties. He permitted a revised version of the "Hundred Dollar Act" to become law without his signature in March. Reintroduced into the House and passed in late February by an overwhelming majority, sixty-four to fourteen, then accepted by the Senate with amendments by an eighteen to three majority, McKean saw little hope in sustaining a veto. "Such is the inflation of the times," he told his youngest son, as he watched the bill become law without his official signature.[21]

Though this action and others intensified the antagonism between the governor and legislators, McKean sought in his opening address to the Assembly in December 1804 to put the best face on things. He lauded Pennsylvania's "prosperity," as well as its "institutions [which] offer ample encouragement to virtue and industry . . . and the inestimable blessings of liberty and order." He pointed to recent developments in the seventeen townships of Luzerne County which finally promised hope that conditions there could "soon be brought to a fair [and] satisfactory conclusion." Much progress had been accomplished in recent years, he told the legislators, they had merely to guarantee that "the good works of our ancestors should not be suffered to molder and decay." Which brought him inexorably to the subject of legal reform. Once again he expressed his conviction that "the imperfections of our legal code should be amended with a respectful, though steady hand," and warned that "the charms of novelty should not be permitted so far to facinate [sic] as to give to mere innovation the semblance of reform." Only by "dismiss[ing] the desultory passions and prejudices of the day," he informed them, could they achieve the needed revisions.[22]

None of this persuaded the majority of Republican Assemblymen. Already deep into several projects of legal reform that differed markedly from McKean's narrowly conceived reforms, they were anxious to polish the bills and to submit them to the governor. Equally significant, they were more intent on challenging any veto he might apply. They did not have long to wait. On March 29, 1805, McKean struck down "An Act regulating the administration of justice within this Commonwealth," a bill requiring that before litigation could go through the normal legal channels it must be submitted to compulsory arbitration. Much of his criticism of the bill could be found in his previous veto messages relating to judicial bills. However, this bill in his judgment also impaired state contracts by reducing the salaries of various judges, including the presidents of the several courts of common pleas. The state constitution prohibited such reductions of judicial salaries during a judge's tenure in office, McKean reminded them. He watched with relief as the House leadership failed to marshal sufficient votes to repass the bill.[23]

Four days earlier McKean had negated "An Act to alter the mode of appointing the Comptroller General and Register Generals" which he thought clearly violated Section 8 of the state constitution giving the governor the right to appoint all officers whose offices were established by the constitution or whose appointments were not otherwise provided for. For the legislature to usurp the power to appoint the comptroller general and the register generals was to encroach upon his powers as executive. He observed rather testily that the two offices in general had been appointed by the governor since 1790. To have done otherwise would have compromised the independence of both the legislative and executive branches. The executive was charged to see that the laws were faithfully carried out, and he could not continue to do so effectively unless he had the power to appoint officers for that purpose. On one level, he insisted, the issue was "a matter of perfect indifference" to him. But "having been a member of as many Congresses, conventions, Legislative Assemblies, and other public bodies, as perhaps, any Gentleman in the United States," had convinced him that "a large public body is not so well qualified to select the best characters for subordinate Offices, as a single person, responsible, unfettered, and independent." He did not veto this merely to protect his own power, he assured the legislature, but he held it a "sacred duty to transmit the Constitution... to [his] successor, unimpaired and unshackled, by any act of [his]." House Republicans succeeded in obtaining the necessary votes to override but the bill failed to pass the Senate.[24]

By 1805 McKean was totally disillusioned with the legislature's schemes. His earlier uneasiness over the propensity to experiment was not lessened by signs that they were now threatening the very foundations of republicanism within the state. Despite constant warnings on his part, the legislators persisted in advancing novel, dangerous, even unconstitutional changes in legal matters, and chipping away, either deliberately or inadvertently, at what he considered a wise and sound state constitution. The one bright spot was his discovery that the battles with the legislature had "revived the spirit & exertions of [his] prime of life." He would not be intimidated or pressured into accepting a course of action repulsive to him and perhaps fatal to republicanism. "One who had not been affected by the roaring of the British Lion," he told his namesake, cannot possibly be affrighted by the braying of Asses."[25]

Obviously the struggle between McKean and Republicans within the Assembly was not without its political price. Many westerners laid the blame for the failure to impeach Yeates, Smith, and Shippen directly at his doorstep. But the most obvious toll McKean paid for his unwillingness to sanction the reforms pushed by the county Republicans and, recently, by Duane and his city followers, was the *Aurora's* growing disenchantment with his administration. Only mildly disapproving of McKean's position at the beginning of his second term, Duane became downright hostile to his continuing in office. As significant as the falling away of some Republican support was the growing appreciation of McKean's position by the state's Federalists. By 1804 Federalists were openly praising his judicious use of the veto and commending him on his appreciation of proper judicial reform.[26]

The change in McKean's political support was noticeable as early as 1803 when, in Lancaster, a small group of McKean appointees, including William Barton, a county prothonotary, and Andrew Ellicott, who succeeded Tench Coxe as secretary of the Land Office, urged the development of a third party to support McKean against the criticism of the democrats.[27] They viewed McKean's efforts to blunt the radicalism of these Republican representatives as essential to the preservation of the state's institutions. To support McKean in his fight with a seemingly irresponsible legislature and to give aid and support to local and state candidates committed to him and his cause was the duty of every responsible Pennsylvanian. Some Federalists showed mild interest in the movement, but neither they nor the regular Republicans openly supported the tickets of the Lancaster third party, which enjoyed no real successes in the off-year elections.[28]

The time was not yet ripe for formal and public political realignments but an uneasiness with old political relationships was evident. The "wild extravagance & low intrigues" of the majority of Republican legislators made a "serious & painful impression" on the "respectable & considerate" Republicans outside the city. The "total destruction" of republicanism could be the only result of the "work of innovation, destruction, & new creation, by a few unprincipled, groveling, ambitious demogogues." James Hopkins, the Lancaster lawyer, suggested one remedy would be to "root out that cancer of republicanism, by such a choice of republican men [who] would insure an independent and cordial cooperation on the part of the legislature with the wise, patriotic & virtuous . . . Chief Magistrate." He concurred with Barton's and Ellicott's scheme to rally respectable men behind McKean in an effort to "rescue . . . republicanism in the State."[29] Upon his arrival in Lancaster in December 1803 Nathaniel Boileau found the third party movement to be "of much more consequences than [he] had imagined." It appeared to him that "all the officers of the Government," with one or two exceptions "were implicated." And that included McKean. Boileau at least assumed that the third party movement was seeking to entice Federalists to join in supporting McKean. Boileau assumed also that McKean's recent appointment of some "Old Tories & Apostate Whigs" to office signaled an understanding between McKean and the Federalists. He expressed his belief that if "the movement" and the "union & reconciliation" sought by McKean occurred, "true republicanism [would be] at an end in Pennsylvania." He told Montgomery County's Jonathan Roberts, Jr., that the Federalists had promised McKean the Presidency.[30]

A hardening of the new divisions occurred in February 1804 when William McCorkle founded his *Philadelphia Evening Post* and announced his intention of supporting McKean as "every good man must advocate the administration of so meritorious an officer." Observers correctly interpreted the new paper to be a rallying point for those opposing the Duane-Leib group within the Republican party. Within three months of the origin of the *Post* Leib and Duane gratuitously insulted McKean by refusing to toast his health during elaborate and closely orchestrated celebrations of the Louisiana Purchase by the Tammany Society and the Republican Greens. McCorkle's paper pounced on this omission to suggest that good men would not soon forget this calculated slight.[31]

Third party men recognized the need was not just to support McKean but to rally to Logan and others who could provide McKean additional punch in state and federal offices. Logan and others who were labeled the "Rising Sun" faction for their meeting at the Rising Sun Tavern in 1802, were intent on ousting the coalition bound to Leib and Duane and redirecting the party's ideological commitment into more conservative channels, and securing the bulk of patronage in the process. McKean did what he could to provide aid and offices for this group, and to wed them closely to his interests.

By January 1804 McKean had half convinced himself that the old bitterness between himself and the Federalists was dead, that he and the Federalists had a good deal in common. "My politics have never been a secret," he wrote Timothy Pickering in that month, "and I have never yet been able to discover from any Gentleman, under the name of Federalist, wherein he differs from me in the principles of Government," a statement that makes sense only if one interprets the phrase "Principles of Government" in a narrow sense. Though these sentiments were expressly designed to curry Federalist favor he was not yet committed to a complete party switch. He quickly rejected pleas from Federalists Uriah Tracy and Timothy Pickering to use his influence among Pennsylvania's legislators in opposition to the twelfth amendment. But it is demonstrable that he recognized the shifts in the state's political spectrum and was obviously maneuvering to retain a sufficient political base behind himself and his program to guarantee another successful campaign.³²

Jefferson, perplexed and alarmed at the strange goings-on in Pennsylvania, warned McKean in August 1804 not to be enticed into an alliance with Tories. He urged upon McKean the view that a small band of Republicans were "giving law to majorities by accepting the aid of the little band of federalists." "After the approbation of the Whigs," he told McKean, "the disapprobation of the Tories is the stock of my greatest confidence." If the sentiments seemed to McKean somewhat naive or irrelevant to the current political disorders in Pennsylvania— and Jefferson conceded that the "jumble of subdivision" in Pennsylvania left him confused—McKean accepted the general warning regarding Federalist designs. But he shared with Jefferson the added thought that one ought "never [to] confide in a Tory, nor in office-hunting, disappointed pretended & violent Whigs." He admitted that now "even the Tories eulogize me," but their strategy had long been clear to him; it was "borrowed from Greece and Rome." Federalists wished to render him suspect to the Whigs and Republicans, and to cause a diversion at the next gubernatorial election. Jefferson "need not fret over this current machination," McKean told him, "it will be frustrated." The governor warned Jefferson that the real danger lay with Duane and his followers, not the Federalists.³³

One device employed by McKean's opponents was to eliminate him or at least neutralize him by pushing him into a higher, federal post. McKean's success in the fall of 1802 had led to some speculation on his chances as a vice-presidential candidate. As the most visible and successful of the Republicans in a critical state, it was not out of the question to consider him a legitimate candidate for higher office. Even before his impressive win in the October 1802 election he had been approached by several congressmen during a visit to Washington and questioned about his willingness to take the post should it be offered. The thought was not altogether repugnant to him; he mentioned the overtures to members of his family, including Yrujo, who took the proposals seriously and assumed McKean did. Yrujo was of the opinion that McKean would be an excellent choice and could secure the nomination should he seek it.³⁴

The prospect of higher office for McKean was seized upon by the followers of Leib and Duane as a convenient means of removing his influence from state politics. They persuaded Dallas in October 1803 to approach him and to encourage him to seek the nomination. Dallas did not favor McKean's removal; indeed, he looked upon McKean as a vital element in the state's Republican party and an important guarantor of his own interests in the party. Perhaps more sensitive to McKean's feelings than others, perhaps more desirous of keeping him as a valuable protector for his party friends, perhaps fearful that his vaunted ambition would lead him into a politically embarrassing trap, Dallas made the request to McKean halfheartedly, hopeful that the governor would not take the bait. McKean, to Dallas' relief, rejected the overtures.[35]

On October 16 McKean wrote a long letter explaining his rejection of any suggestion that he seek a federal office. "What would be the . . . result of my acceptance of the [vice president] post?" he asked Dallas, then answered his own question: "Little, very little benefit to the people of America, but at least a doubtful situation to my fellow-citizens of Pennsylvania." He realized as did Dallas that he was the key to the success of at least the moderate and conservative branches of the Republican party. "What would be the fate of my friends, of those I have placed in office," he asked, "and of the liberty of the State at this most critical period, were I to resign the office?" "Who is there to control the wanton passions of men in general respectable, suddenly raised in power and frisking in the pasture of true liberty, yet not sufficiently secured proper barriers?" he went on. "Who will be my successor, possessing the same advantage from nativity in the State, education, experience, and from long public service in the most influential stations and employments; who can or will take the same liberty in vetoes . . . or otherwise, as I have done?" Who indeed?[36]

Even after McKean publicly and privately discouraged such speculation the issue did not die. In January 1804 he felt compelled to tell Jefferson that though "several Gentlemen of the Republican party have wished to use [his] name as a candidate for Vice President," he had "absolutely declined it on public & personal considerations." A month later he discovered that rumors were still coursing through Washington that he had created a third party cabal "composed principally of the officers of the Government... to oppose the re-election of... Jefferson as president, and to further [his own] election to that...office." McKean denounced the rumors as "an insidious and wicked fabrication," as indeed they seemed to be. He promised the President that state officers were loyal to him and would "use their utmost efforts to his re-election."[37]

In February, McKean wrote to Secretary of War Henry Dearborn to explain his position and to learn who persisted in spreading the "artful and abominable Lie" of his disaffection with Jefferson. Dearborn responded by assurring him that he knew the rumors to be "unfounded," as did the President. To McKean's disappointment, however, Dearborn refused to divulge the name of the author of the letter from which the rumors stemmed. Dearborn claimed to have simply heard the letter read, and he was "not permitted to know the name of the author."[38] What had begun in 1802 as legitimate speculation by McKean's friends regarding his fitness for the vice presidency, had by late 1803 degenerated into a scheme employed by his political enemies to first eliminate or neutralize his role in state affairs, then to drive a wedge between McKean and Jefferson. To his credit McKean followed the shifting emphasis closely and recognized the insincerity of many of the overtures and rumors. There is no demonstrable proof that he either overtly or covertly solicited the nomination for either the vice presidency or the presidency. He suffered no doubts of his ability to fill either station but, as he told Dallas, "the office of Governor of Pennsylvania satisifie[d] [his] ambition."[39]

Dallas, aware of growing political instability, vainly sought in January 1805 to impress McKean with the need for tact in his political dealings. While conceding that members of the legislature were "extravagant and unexpected," Dallas nonetheless deemed a reconciliation still possible. In light of the upcoming gubernatorial contest, such a reconciliation would be critical for McKean's chances. "You can overcome these nuisances," Dallas told McKean, "by the preeminence of your character, your station, your wisdom and your worth, but also by your indulgence and forebearance." It was sound advice.

But if McKean heeded Dallas' advice for a brief spell, events in February quickly undermined his restraint.[40] Nathaniel Boileau, Montgomery County's ambitious and restless representative, a leader among the more radical Republicans in the House, provided the irritant. Surreptitiously he published a memorial to the legislature calling for a convention to amend the state constitution and advocating a long list of possible changes, including proposals that senatorial and gubernatorial elections be more frequent, and that the governor's patronage powers be drastically curbed. But more critical would be changes to the judiciary where simplification and inexpensive provisions would replace current procedures. Boileau's memorial also called for judges to be appointed or elected for a specific term.[41]

McKean viewed the proposed convention with horror. He construed the memorial to be an outright attack upon republicanism as Pennsylvanians had heretofore understood it, the first salvo in a concerted struggle not only to destroy the state constitution he had labored so hard to build, but to eliminate the system of law on which it was based, as well as the legal profession which supported it. This then was no short-range political struggle over the loaves and fishes. This was a struggle to save republicanism itself, to guarantee that the goals of the American Revolution would survive.

When several legislators, including Simon Snyder, speaker of the House, visited McKean on March 21, to plead the case of one Henry Latscha for a political office, McKean refused Latscha on the grounds that his only qualification for office appeared to be his republicanism, and he had already appointed too many on that basis alone. Besides, he told his visitors, he had another man in mind for the post. At this point, at least according to McKean's later account of the meeting, he attempted to change the subject by referring to a letter expressing a retiring congressman's opposition to lawyers and "men of talents," and the correspondent's suggestion that such men were not fit for office. A fear of lawyers and highly educated officers of government was a common sentiment in the first three months of 1805, and several letters to that effect had appeared in the local press.

Referring to one such letter, this by John Stewart of York and Adams counties, McKean told the congressmen,

> I suppose we shall have him, and other such clodpoles (or, if they please, clodhoppers) of the same pernicious sentiments, returned as delegates to the projected convention! Can such men be qualified to legislate, or to form systems of government for so great a state as Pennsylvania? The memorial... for calling a convention, was a palpable libel, and the men, now attempting to destroy our happy form of government, were weak, mischievous, and wicked.... How can any man who had a regard for the truth, and is not grossly ignorant, sign his name to one, at least, of the assertions in the memorial: that "the governor of Pennsylvania had as great patronage as the king of England?"[42]

McKean went on to tell the men that "the present constitution [was] the production of as patriotic learned and enlightened men, as, perhaps ever assembled for a similar purpose." He asked them, "Shall a set of clodpoles, and ignoramuses overthrow it?...No....I will firmly resist....I fear not the want of aid and assistance from all wise and good men."[43]

The *Aurora* reported the incident in somewhat different form, one guaranteed to damage the governor in the eyes of "true Republicans." Here again, the *Aurora* reported, the governor had shown his true colors. He looked upon the common citizen as a Clodpole. He dismissed their legitimate aspirations with his vetoes and denigrated their worth by vile epithets. Now McKean could do little that was judged acceptable in the eyes of Duane.

One of the *Aurora's* most concerted and vitriolic attacks opened in April 1805 and centered around the Cabrera case, which came before the public in that month. In the summer of 1804 two checks were presented to the Bank of Pennsylvania in Yrujo's name, and cashed. Yrujo denied authorizing the transactions. On August 24, a free black man, Charles Lange, was arrested as he attempted to cash another check for three hundred dollars, purportedly signed by the Spanish minister. He confessed that he had been ordered to cash the check by his master and Yrujo's aide, Don Joseph Cabrera. Yrujo immediately asked state officials to detain Cabrera until it could be determined what to do with him. He sent Cabrera a note that McKean, at the urging of bank officials, had sought Yrujo's permission to turn Cabrera over to state authorities, and Yrujo had agreed. In accordance with the state's wishes then, Cabrera should report to debtor's prison where an apartment would be prepared for him. He was to rest assured that his salary would continue until a determination of his fate was made.

Yrujo played an interesting game. He told Cabrera that he was being confined by the state authorities at the urging of bank officers and McKean. But bank officials, convinced that this was a diplomatic matter, had clearly not ordered or urged Cabrera's arrest. McKean had ordered Cabrera's arrest and confinement at the instigation of Yrujo, not because of any personal desire to have the man punished by the state. McKean wrote to the sheriff on the day Lange implicated Cabrera to tell him that Cabrera was to be incarcerated despite his apparent diplomatic immunity. "By the law of nations . . . Cabrera is entitled to all the immunities appertaining to one of the train of envoy extraordinary and minister plenepotentiary of his Catholic Majesty," McKean told the sheriff, "and although he may not be amenable to our laws and tribunals, yet he may be secured with the consent of the minister of Spain until it shall be known whether his sovereign will direct, that he shall be sent to Spain for trial or delivered up to the justice of the state."

Cabrera's stay in prison quickly changed his mind about insisting on his diplomatic immunity. He proclaimed his innocence and his willingness to waive his immunity in exchange for a speedy state trial. Learning of this from Yrujo, McKean ordered his son to initiate proceedings against Cabrera. A grand jury subsequently indicted Cabrera for forgery and bail was set at two thousand dollars. However, unable to raise this amount, Cabrera demanded to be tried in Spain and insisted that Yrujo arrange it. When Yrujo dutifully informed McKean of this change of heart, McKean had his attorney

Marquis de Casa Yrujo. A Gilbert Stuart painting owned by Thomas R. McKean. Courtesy of Philadelphia Museum of Art

general enter a nolle prosequi on the bill against Cabrera. The issue then settled down to a contest between Cabrera, seeking to get out of jail either on a state directed habeas corpus writ or a recognition of his diplomatic immunity from arrest and confinement, and Yrujo, who sought to keep him confined until he could be returned to Spain. McKean acknowledged the state's impotence to press charges in light of the prisoner's diplomatic position, but was nonetheless willing to acquiesce in Yrujo's wishes to confine Cabrera until such time as he could face Spanish justice.[44]

On April 16 Yrujo informed McKean that his king was now content to have an American investigation determine the guilt or innocence of the prisoner, but once his guilt was proved the king would mete out the proper punishment. McKean immediately rejected the arrangement. Such a "solution" was no less repugant to him in 1805 than it had been when the French suggested a similar ploy in the Longchamps affair two decades before. McKean viewed both as destructive to the independence of Pennsylvania's courts. Cabrera had in the meantime applied to the President of the United States and to his secretary of state to have the federal government intervene in his behalf. An application was subsequently made to the United States Circuit Court for Cabrera's enlargement, and on April 22 his case was argued before Justices Richard Peters, and Bushrod Washington. Joseph Borden McKean argued the state's case, that the circuit court had no jurisdiction over Cabrera; it was a matter between Cabrera and the Spanish government. Cabrera's attorney, Samson Levy, insisted that the court could—and should—grant him a release on a writ of habeas corpus. The court found for the state and Cabrera remained incarcerated.

Cabrera's status changed on May 10, however, when Yrujo—having received orders from Don Pedro Cevallos, the Spanish foreign minister—informed McKean that Cabrera could be tried in Pennsylvania's courts. Cabrera appeared before the mayor's court in the June Sessions, 1805 and was convicted of forgery. The court sentenced him to two years at hard labor and fined him two thousand dollars. Less than two weeks after Cabrera's conviction McKean granted him a partial pardon by directing that he be excused from hard labor and from being fed and clothed according to jail regulations. Following Cabrera's full restitution to the bank for the funds it had lost from the forged checks, McKean granted him a full pardon.[45]

Duane scored McKean for his conduct in every phase of the Cabrera incident. He argued that McKean had illegally ordered Cabrera's arrest. Even though no formal charges were brought against Cabrera either by the bank or Yrujo, McKean had secured Cabrera's confinement. McKean had ignored the law of nations to favor a whim of his son-in-law, Duane charged; neither McKean nor Yrujo could strip the prisoner of his immunity, only the king could do so. McKean's mitigation of the Spaniard's sentence was labeled by Duane a naked usurpation of judicial powers. For his part, according to the *Aurora*, Yrujo had deliberately lied to Cabrera about the apartment being set up for him, and had, generally, treated the unfortunate Cabrera as one of his domestics rather than as a member of the Spanish diplomatic corps. A letter in the *Aurora* chided citizens of Pennsylvania for looking in the state constitution to see if McKean had the power to do what he had done in the Cabrera matter. "You look to the state constitution for his powers," wrote the correspondent, "but you forget there is a higher law, the common law of sovereigns.... The United Kingdom belongs to George the Third, so does Pennsylvania belong to Thomas the First." In England "everything is transacted in the name of the king, and for his benefit and that of his family," he concluded, "and so it is here."

The Cabrera developments were important in at least two respects. On the one hand they persuaded Duane to pull the gloves off in his campaign against McKean; it was only after the Cabrera case that one finds Duane launching ad hominem attacks against the governor. The case also elicited from Duane the observation that McKean may have committed an impeachable offense. From that point on their hatred of each other was implacable. McKean was unhappy with Duane even before the Cabrera case, but the Cabrera case did nothing to change his mind that Duane was an "incindiary diabolical news-publisher." He thought Duane considered himself "to be Superior to the governor of a State, or even the President of the United States."[46]

Even before Duane began his almost daily attacks on McKean for his roles in the Clodpole and Cabrera affairs, McKean received an important political boost. In mid-March the "Society of Constitutional Republicans" had been formed to oppose the proposed convention to revise the state constitution. With branches in each county the society hoped to persuade the good citizens of the state to petition the legislature to that end. Dallas, Logan, Peter Muhlenberg, and eleven others were chosen to oversee these efforts. Significantly, the society's literature appealed to all responsible citizens—Republicans and Federalists alike. The society did not officially endorse McKean as a candidate, but it was understood by all that such an organization would do whatever it could to support candidates sympathetic to its views regarding the convention.[47]

The *United States Gazette* warmly concurred that Federalists should oppose the convention and support anyone who agreed with that position. Past political differences paled in comparison to the current threat by the state's democrats. A warm contest developed between the proponents and opponents of the convention scheme as each faction strove to produce the largest number of petitions to the legislature. As a result of this activity Pennsylvania's Federalists were increasingly attracted to McKean as a possible gubernatorial candidate in 1805. With no Federalists candidate on the horizon capable of seriously challenging McKean or providing the same type of strong leadership he had exhibited against the democrats, and with McKean seemingly strong enough and willing enough to combat the "absurdities" of the Republicans in the General Assembly, McKean seemed a logical choice.[48]

Fifty Republican legislators, meeting in caucus on April 3, 1805, chose Simon Snyder, speaker of the House, rather than McKean as their gubernatorial choice. Oddly enough, Snyder was neither Duane's nor Michael Leib's first choice. Intent on ousting McKean, Duane and Leib had allowed themselves to be outmaneuvered, and they watched helplessly as the county Republicans determined the party's candidate and at the same time shifted the center of the party's power from Philadelphia to the counties. Nonetheless, left with the choice of Snyder or McKean, neither Duane nor Leib had any difficulty choosing their course of action. Duane's *Aurora* accelerated its attacks on McKean, his family, and his administration. He said what Cobbett had left unsaid in 1799.

McKean had apparently anticipated the move toward the German-speaking and suave Snyder and had taken steps prior to the April meeting to head off his nomination. John Binns, who would write hundreds of letters and pamphlets in Snyder's behalf, later recalled that McKean had given several of the legislators commissions as justices of the peace on condition they would not go to the caucus. If he did attempt such a ploy it had no marked success. The *Aurora* reported that forty-two favored Snyder, seven McKean, and one supported the candidacy of Samuel Maclay.

The very day that Snyder received his endorsement from the fifty Republicans in the legislature, thirty-four members of that body, including all eight Federalists, pledged support for McKean's candidacy. McKean's political fortunes received an additional boost when the Society of Constitutional Republicans voted at a meeting on March 21 to enlarge their program from that of merely opposing a convention to revise the constitution to one of actively encouraging the election of men holding compatible views, including McKean. The success of the society was attested to by the speed with which the supporters of Snyder emulated it in forming their own "Society of the Friends of the People." The creation of the two organizations marked the final split in Republican ranks and guaranteed that the battle for state supremacy would be fought between fragments of the same party.[49]

The Quids, as the third party was dubbed, were led by men who had actively supported McKean in the two previous campaigns, Tench Coxe, Albert Gallatin, Alexander Dallas, George Logan, and Israel Israel. They aggressively defended McKean's conduct in opposing the Assembly's more chimerical schemes, and denounced his opponents as revolutionists bent on destroying the constitution, property rights and religion. Basically, however, the Quids sought to establish themselves as the true Republicans and to tie their opponents into the dangerous scheme of tampering with the constitution.[50]

Duane proved as skillful in attacking McKean in 1805 as he had been in supporting him in 1799 and 1802. The battle as perceived by Duane was between representative democracy on the one hand and "reorganized Toryism" on the other. He made it plain that McKean had chosen to ally himself with the Tories and therefore must be opposed at all costs. While Duane, Leib, Snyder and other good Republicans had remained faithful to the principles of 1799, the governor had drifted from them, had become arbitrary, had defied the will of the people, vilified them, abused his rightful powers, and turned against those most responsible for his earlier successes. The "mantle of democracy was only assumed [by McKean] to gull the unsuspecting people, until he could once be securely seated in office," proclaimed the *Aurora*.[51] In July Duane published a toast: "Thomas McKean, heretofore supported as a 'substitute for a better,' may we soon have a better substitute."[52] Not even McKean's pardon of Cabrera on the stipulation that he leave the United States within twenty days and not return for a period of three years satisfied Duane. McKean's disregard for the laws of the state and his ready contempt of the law of nations, his willingness to see himself as the law, could not be erased by a single act. It was instructive, the readers of the *Aurora* were told, that the state's lawyers acquiesced in McKean's candidacy for the gubernatorial chair, for these "oracles of law and the idolators of the constitution" were often, like McKean, "in utter contempt and violation of both."[53]

The Federalist press initially maintained a respectable neutrality, insisting that the Quids, as the third party, were merely office seekers. As the campaign quickened, however, leading Federalists like William Lewis and William Hamilton of the *Lancaster Journal* conceded that McKean as a defender of the Constitution and law and order merited their formal support. The Quids, too, not initially interested in seeking Federalist endorsement—at least openly—saw the pitfalls of such a policy and eventually moved toward a coalition with the Federalists.[54]

As the election approached, the key to the contest seemed to be the ability of the Quids and their Federalist allies to convey the impression that the central issue was the constitution. A vote for McKean was said to be a vote for the current constitution, a vote for Snyder to destroy that enlightened document. McKean's constant admonition that "the charm of novelty should not be permitted so to fascinate as to give mere innovation the semblance of reform" struck a responsive chord. If the Federalists and Quids appreciated the wisdom of tying McKean closely to the constitution issue, the Democrats did not. As Professor Higginbotham has shown, it was not until too late that the Democrats realized that they had to disengage from such a trap, that they had to make McKean, his personality and his record, the central issue. And though they lashed out at him with renewed vigor, though they scored his policies, his friends, his relatives, and his family, they were too late.[55]

19. The Move to Impeach

McKean won his third term. But the exhileration of victory did not blind him to the realities of the election.[1] He understood the heavy debt he owed to Federalists, and he appreciated the fact that the coalition of moderate Republicans and Federalists responsible for his victory, already weak and fractious, was further threatened by developments in national affairs. Leibites were equally impressed by McKean's vulnerability. Indeed, Leib was confident that "with...proper discretion" his party could split the Federalists from their Quid allies and easily win the next election.[2] Furthermore, McKean's intimacy with the President was over. They had not corresponded since March 1805 and were not to do so again. And the state democratic leadership, although itself plagued by bickering and jealousy over who was to wield power and determine the course of party strategy, was solid in its opposition to McKean.

It was obvious the election had done nothing to abate the rancor within Pennsylvania's political community. Newspaper attacks on McKean were as heavy the month after the election as they had been in the month prior to it. The *Aurora* stated categorically that McKean had "succeeded by means corrupt and base."[3] If this were not enough to instill caution in McKean, he recognized that in the General Assembly those opposed to him and favorable to a constitutional convention were more numerous and determined than ever.

Conditions therefore demanded McKean's most subtle and deliberate considerations. In his own way McKean did make concessions to his fragile position; he issued no open challenge, at least. As a private citizen he turned to the courts to instigate libel proceedings against John Steele for circulating what McKean deemed to be a scurrilous pamphlet during the Republican nomination procedures. He brought similar charges against Thomas Leiper, Michael Leib, William Duane and others for accusing him of opposing the Louisiana Purchase, and for charging that he headed a "monstrous combination... against principles and people."[4] In his message to the legislature in December 1805 he was, on the surface at least, warm, and gracious. If criticism of the democrats appeared in his remarks it was in his implicit insinuations that they were weakening republican values and institutions.

He told the legislators that the eyes of all Americans were "anxiously fixed on the course of [their] deliberations and conduct," and that great hopes were held by all for their continuing to defend the principles of the Revolution and to uphold the standards of republicanism. He was content to repeat his call for a greater effort in the area of public education and public justice. A better public school system was essential if the state were to inculcate virtue and promote knowledge among its peoples, and strengthen the hope that true republican values would survive. A republican government "must be a type of the people themselves; and it will be good or bad, just as they are, or are not, virtuous and intelligent," he told the joint session of the legislature. A "pure, able, and efficient administration of justice" was of crucial importance for a healthy republic, McKean emphasized.

He reiterated his long-held conviction that the organization of the state's judiciary had "been long, and fairly condemned" but expressed his belief that there was no defect which the legislature could not quickly alleviate should it turn its attention to it. He outlined for the legislators his own plans for reform, now long-nurtured and familiar. Only the subdued tone was new in McKean's manner, and references to his recent re-election were conspicuously absent.

As gracious and controlled as McKean was in his address to the legislature, there were no tangible signs that he planned to trim his sails to accommodate the democrats. Two days before he spoke to the joint session of the Assembly he vetoed "An Act supplementary to the several acts of the Assembly for the establishing the judicial courts of this Commonwealth in conformity to the alteration and amendments in the constitution," a bill presented to him at the close of the previous session. In McKean's judgment the bill failed where its predecessors in the area of judicial reform had failed. It would increase the costs of justice substantially and at the same time oppress the already overworked justices. McKean patiently pointed out that the current four justices of the state's Supreme Court were required by law to hold court in all forty-two counties. Even if the judges stayed in each county for a week, the travel to and from the circuit courts would keep the judges away from Philadelphia for more than three-fourths of each year. The bill would thus compound the state's judicial problems by keeping the judges away from the busier and more demanding city courts. Also by dividing the state into two judicial districts (eastern and western) as the bill proposed to do, it would have political ramifications beyond those anticipated by its sponsors, for it would "revive the ideas of a political division, hitherto deemed to be so alarming and injurious."[5]

Privately McKean groused about the continuation of the democrats' efforts to oppose and frustrate him, referring to their tactics as a "conspiracy...hatched in hell and propagated by the imps of darkness." He wrote Dickinson that he had always been governed by two principles of government: not to govern too much, and never to use "compulsion where reason & persuasion will effect the purpose." Despite his moderation, he continued to be blindly opposed in the legislature and unfairly attacked in the press, he complained to Dickinson. He had finally resolved that "such wretches must be controlled by fear and by force."[6]

As usual, one of the first items on McKean's political calendar was to reward those who supported him and to chastise those who had not. He presented government printing contracts to editors William McCorkle, John Israel, John Snowden, Thomas Aitkinson, and Andrew and James Kennedy, who had championed his candidacy. McKean's friend and political ally, Francis Bailey, received two. Conspicuously absent from the recipients of the lucrative and much-sought contracts were Duane of the *Aurora* and William Dickson of the *Lancaster Intelligencer*. At the same time McKean sought and received the resignation of more than a dozen prothonotaries, registers, and justices of the peace who had opposed or been cool to his re-election. He refused to renew the commissions of a great many more, replacing them with Quids and Federalists who had exhibited vigor in his behalf. Moderate Republicans like Thomas Cooper and Joseph Reed received judicial posts, as did Federalists Bird Wilson and Jacob Rush. Reed was appointed prothonotary for the Supreme Court while Cooper, Wilson, and Rush became district presidents of the common pleas courts.

Rush's appointment came as no surprise to the still embittered John Adams, who told Benjamin Rush that McKean elevated Jacob because he was a "brother monarchist." "You and I remember the time when we heard your brother say that, in his opinion, the 'executive and senate ought to be hereditary' ", Adams reminisced with Benjamin Rush, "I have heard McKean say the same thing in the same words, and I know other substantial witnesses who can depose he freely expressed this opinion in many companies for several years." He added rather unconvincingly that he had "never thought McKean or [Jacob Rush] less friendly to our constitution for these speculative opinions;" however he wanted it clear that he had "never in [his] life [gone] to such a length as this."[7]

One of the principal targets of McKean's ire in late 1805 and early 1806 was the diminutive Samuel Bryan, comptroller general, who had initially harbored ambition to replace him as governor, then, when frustrated in that hope, worked assiduously to promote the interests of Snyder. McKean barely waited to

Thomas McKean, attributed to James Sharples. Courtesy of Independence National Historical Park Collection

learn the final results of his election before removing Bryan and replacing him with George Duffield, heretofore register general. Choosing to forget his own cavalier disregard and that of other Republicans for the Federalists who in 1799 and early 1800 had pleaded their cases before the public upon being removed by McKean, Bryan now took his own case to the citizens of Pennsylvania. He argued that he had been ousted solely on the whim of a capricious man. He assailed McKean for cutting off his salary just as his wife and son were on the verge of death. Bryan left the impression that McKean deliberately set out to hurt him at the very moment he was least able to defend himself or care for his family.[8]

Bryan asserted that McKean, not he, had acted improperly in office. On at least one occasion that Bryan could document McKean had knowingly broken the law. In 1801, according to Bryan, the survey general had applied to McKean on behalf of two Chester County militia colonels for a pair of stands of colors for their regiment. McKean had approved the request and a contract was subsequently entered into with a Mr. Clarke of Philadelphia. Clarke agreed to send the colors to Chester County, specifically to Boyd's Tavern, as soon as the paint was dry. In November of that year McKean, on his way to Lancaster, happened to see the colors at the stage office, presumably waiting to be sent on the next stage to Chester. In the meantime Clarke had written to Thomas McKean Thompson requesting his money from the state. McKean informed Thompson that the colors had been sent and the comptroller general should promptly see to it that Clarke received his money. Bryan refused to pay without a written voucher or a certificate personally signed by McKean establishing the fact that the contract had been carried out. McKean produced the certificate and Bryan paid the bill. Later Bryan, upset over his treatment at the hands of McKean, looked more closely into the matter and discovered that the colors had not been picked up in Chester until late in December, twenty-six days after McKean swore they had been delivered. Bryan charged McKean with violating the law.[9]

Bryan's public criticism of McKean, and complaints of other displaced and displeased office holders, amused the Federalists no end. Even the *Freeman's Journal* reminded the people of

Pennsylvania that the Republicans "threw everyone out of office once, yelling 'rotation in office,' now [they] are bitter when they are thrown out." A legislative committee led by Quids and Federalists sought to embarrass McKean's detractors by establishing Bryan's incompetence as comptroller general. They proposed to investigate charges against Bryan as well as to look into Bryan's accusations against McKean. At a committee hearing on January 9 Bryan detailed his allegations against the governor. Thomas McKean Thompson, who attended the hearing, repeatedly interrupted Bryan's testimony to cast aspersions on his veracity and character; then, following the hearing, he pursued him downstairs. There he struck Bryan several times after directing a number of "very opprobrious epithets" at the ex-comptroller general.[10]

The altercation between Bryan and Thompson was only the first of a series of predictable developments. The legislative committee investigating the allegations made against Bryan and by Bryan against McKean found that Bryan had been neglectful in his official duties. According to the committee's findings, Bryan's conduct had "not conform[ed] either to the letter or the spirit of the law or regulations during his tenure in office." The committee concluded that his charges against McKean had been "frivolous." The only reason that the committee did not press the House to bring formal charges against Bryan for maladministration in office was the fact that he no longer held the post. A move on the part of Republican legislators sympathetic to Bryan to censure Thompson for his conduct in assaulting Bryan was successfully blunted by a combination of moderate Republicans and Federalists. Still, Thompson and Bryan seemed determined to settle their differences on the field of honor, a fact that accounted in part for the General Assembly's sudden interest in passing a more stringent anti-dueling bill.

The *Aurora* was quite naturally delighted with this political windfall and took every advantage of Thompson's impetuosity to condemn McKean for his secretary's actions. As Thompson and Bryan negotiated a duel with more comic than tragic results, Duane, with Joseph McKean's attack on himself also fresh in his mind, told his readers that Thompson, much younger and larger than Bryan (four inches taller and fifty pounds heavier by Duane's calculations), illustrated the strong-armed tactics typically employed by the McKeans when crossed.[11] Within a month Duane was also accusing Thompson of attempted bribery. According to the *Aurora* and William Dickson's *Lancaster Intelligencer,* Henry Wertz, a democratic senator from Bedford County, was responsible for Duane's defeat as a candidate for the directorship of the board of the Bank of Pennsylvania. They claimed Wertz had voted against Duane because he had been offered the prothonotary office of his county by Thompson and McKean's personal secretary, John Hastings, should he cast his ballot against the editor. Thompson vehemently denied the allegations. Duane and Dickson expected as much from Thompson, but they appeared hopeful that Wertz would publicly confirm their account of the affair since it was apparently his testimony which first convinced them to level the charges against the governor. But Wertz remained silent. And McKean, characteristically the aggressor, brought formal proceedings against Dickson for his part in the accusations. Dickson was subsequently convicted, fined, and jailed.[12]

Unimpressed by Dickson's fate, Duane accelerated his attacks on McKean. He claimed that McKean had made overtures to him to the effect that in exchange for the editor's willingness to drop his long-standing charges against Joseph McKean, the state would drop charges currently pending against Duane. He also printed a toast to the governor: "General Arnold and Thomas McKean—both beans of one pod." One *Aurora* correspondent ("Try it") called for McKean's impeachment. Yrujo, already under severe attack from Jefferson and Madison for his conduct in Washington, also became the target of Duane's invective. "In no other country under heaven would the ambassador D'Yrujo be suffered to remain one hour," argued the *Aurora,* "but his insolence to the United States is of a piece with that of his family connexion to the State of Pennsylvania." "There can be very little doubt that the wily artifices of the Spanish marquis have had much influence on the arrogance of his father-in-law," wrote Duane, "Could the project of placing McKean on the presidential chair have been realized, we might have seen a system of government revived such as once prevailed in England." Duane labeled Yrujo "the little diable espagnol," and "a miserable poppinjay" who "would not dare to proceed so far as he had done, if he did not calculate upon an impunity in whatever course he might pursue."

By August McKean could take no more. He instituted a libel suit against Duane. Two days after McKean brought his charges, Yrujo, with Joseph McKean as his attorney, followed suit. McKean and Yrujo pressed to have the matters heard before the mayor's court where among the justices sat Moses Levy, a McKean appointee, and Andrew Pettit, a son-in-law, but Duane protested that he could not receive a fair trial before that tribunal and matters temporarily stalled.[13]

"Our wise, virtuous and above all temperate McKean has already begun to treat his quondam jacobinical friends in office with the same marked attention and civility which he paid to Federalists...immediately after his first election," wrote David Meredith, a reluctant supporter of McKean's in the previous gubernatorial election. "Little Sammy Bryan... is the first victim....It is said that the fun is not to stop there." And it did not. As displaced Republican officials mournfully pleaded their cases before the public McKean continued to replace his enemies and lukewarm friends with more eager recruits. Continuing a strategem begun in his first term, he named a number of his family and relatives to state posts. The most conspicuous example was the appointment of son-in-law George Buchanan of Baltimore as Lazaretto physician. But there were others. Andrew Pettit replaced John Shee as inspector of flour for the City and Port of Philadelphia. Cousin Andrew Henderson received a commission as prothonotary of the court of common pleas in Huntingdon County. William McKennan, brother-in-law to Thomas McKean Thompson, received a similar commission in Washington County. A distant relative, John Finney, was named justice of the peace for the townships of New London, London Britain, and Londonderry in Chester County.[14]

One of the most eagerly anticipated appointments was the replacement of Edward Shippen as the state's chief justice, for it was known that Joseph McKean desperately coveted the post. The *Aurora* assumed that he had the office locked up. Edward Burd, longtime prothonotary in the Supreme Court during McKean's tenure as chief justice, wrote that speculation on whether or not Joseph McKean would be named to the post by his father absorbed much of the time and attention of political activists in Philadelphia. Joseph and Tommy McKean went so far as to write letters to their father establishing Joseph's qualifications for the office. To Joseph's chagrin and the relief of most, McKean, who believed that current political exigencies required that the post "be conferred on one, not deemed a Republican," turned to the Federalist, William Tilghman.[15]

Tilghman proved to be an excellent choice; it is to McKean's credit that the two men he appointed to the highest judicial office in the state—Edward Shippen and Tilghman—were fine justices. Tilghman was a learned lawyer with an independent mind. Just how independent he was soon became clear to McKean when Tilghman refused to permit McKean to employ a familiar strategem in his assault upon Duane. Yrujo brought his charge against Duane several days after McKean initiated proceedings against the embattled editor because both men assumed that Duane would be put under bond for his good behavior as a result of McKean's accusations. In this way Yrujo would not have to submit the question of Duane's comments to a jury to determine whether or not they constituted libel; he merely had to prove that the editor had broken his bond. It was a ruse similar to that employed by McKean against Cobbett nearly a decade before. Unfortunately for McKean and Yrujo, Duane had not been put under bond before being released on a writ of habeas corpus, and Tilghman ruled that he need not have been. The ploy thus failed.[16]

The pleasure and relief engendered by Tilghman's appointment did not lead to a slackening of attacks on McKean's nepotism. It was said that he and his family wished to establish "a royal family," if not in Philadelphia, in the west. Tommy, Joseph, Yrujo, and Tom Thompson all were said to be desirous of an empire with McKean at its head. By August the *Aurora* was daily assailing McKean's relatives who had received political preferment, and it was widely acknowledged that Duane was laying the foundation for an impeachment effort against the governor.[17] By election day, 1806, the *Quid Mirror,* an anonymous pamphlet attacking McKean, his relatives, and his political allies, was circulating widely. Duane's scurrility paled in comparison. A passage on the inside cover noted that the editor had received the manuscript from an unknown author and disclaimed any responsibility for it. The pamphlet's purpose, according to the anonymous author, was to refute Dallas' contention that the Friends of the People were "without name, character, feeling or property." It was to prove that the Quids, not the democrats, really thirsted for office and in truth wished a monopoly on state and local offices. First the Quids had used the democratic party as "the ladder of ambition," the author asserted, but when this proved inconvenient, "Federalists were counted to become their horse-block."

The *Mirror's* image of McKean was sharp enough. He was accused of being "without even a commonplace acquaintance with subjects, out of the immediate sphere of the profession of law; without any mental quality above mediocrity, excepting that of mere memory." It went on to relate that his "origin was obscure," and his "initiatory study of morals and law, was coupled with the duties of an hostler." He has "been a democrat from interest," it said, and he had no real committment to republicanism. It concluded that "His ferocity...has no parallel but in that of Jeffries.... His gubernatorial career was commenced like an egotist, it has progressed in egotism, and it will and must end in contempt." He was currently a "Nero" who "considered the Commonwealth as his private estate." Joseph McKean fared no better. He was described as "a creature despised by all parties and without any merit on the score of service or talents." He was "the first born booby of McKean." "No one but his father, an ideot [sic] or a madman," the *Mirror* proclaimed, "could even have conceived the idea of his fitness for such a station [as the chief justice]." George Buchanan and Thomas McKean Thompson also received their share of barbs, as did Dallas, William Bache, David Jackson, Samuel Carver, George Logan, Israel Israel, and other supporters of McKean. It is unfortunate that such images must be seen in their true light, observed the *Mirror's* author, but, as it was said in relation to McKean's image, "If it should appear deformed to the beholder, the fault must not be attributed to the mirror, but to the man."[18]

Speculation as to the author of the *Mirror* became a favorite topic in Philadelphia's political circles. Duane and Leib were prominently mentioned, and at least Thomas McKean, Jr. was soon convinced that Leib was indeed the culprit. "I have been informed, and have every reason to believe that you are the author of a villainous anonimous [sic] publication, styled the "Quid Mirror," in which you have thought proper to traduce the characters of many gentlemen, my venerable Father among the number," he wrote to Leib on October 16, and he demanded satisfaction. Leib denied that he had authored the pamphlet and suggested that if the pamphlet were the only reason for the duel he could not accomodate him. He quickly added, however, that "if any other reasons exist," he would be happy to make the necessary arrangements for a meeting. Leib's denial did not impress young McKean. He encouraged his close friend and second, Richard Dennis, to proceed with arrangements for the duel.[19]

Meanwhile, the city elections of 1806 brought McKean more woes than those induced by the *Quid Mirror,* when a question arose over the validity of the election for sheriff of Philadelphia. The candidates in the hotly disputed contest were a Quid, and a republican friend of Michael Leib. Leib apparently sought to pressure McKean into appointing his friend, Frederick Wolbert: after the governor had named a committee to investigate the election returns, Leib persuaded the incumbent, John Barker (a friend of McKean's) to go to the governor with Wolbert and convince McKean to issue a commission of office to Wolbert. Whether or not, as Leib and Duane later contended, Barker was sent as an honest envoy of reconciliation between the two parties, or, more likely, as a ploy in another political strategem, it resulted in added recrimination on both sides. If the governor agreed to issue the commission to Wolbert, according to Barker's later version of the story, Duane and Leib "would bury the hatchet—they would present the olive branch, and . . . they would cease any further to persecute the governor or his family." Barker was seemingly sincerely interested in easing tensions between his friend McKean and his opponents, and he was convinced it was in McKean's interest, as it truly was, to recognize that a radical Republican would probably succeed McKean. Such a change would bode ill for McKean's friends and family currently holding office if the present antagonisms continued. This last idea was given by Leib who pushed it during a meeting between Barker and the two leaders of the "Jacobins." Although Duane remained silent during these meetings, Barker was persuaded that he acquiesced in Leib's proposals.

When Barker and Wolbert arrived at the Thompson residence in Lancaster where McKean was staying, McKean refused to see Wolbert. Barker thus later returned alone and repeated to McKean what Leib had suggested without mentioning the source of his information. Upon hearing the proposals, McKean made it plain that he knew the source to be Leib and Duane, and he expressed his determination to do his duty as he saw it even in the face of threats upon his life. When knowledge of Barker's visit to McKean became widespread and Barker was pressured by public opinion into disclosing the details surrounding the episode with McKean, Duane denied all and suggested that Barker merely hoped to obtain office for himself. The effect of the incident was simply to accelerate the confrontation between McKean and those he now termed the "Jacobins."[20]

In light of the political tumult outside the General Assembly it is not surprising that tension mounted within. In his opening remarks to the Assembly in December 1806 McKean wasted little time in identifying those issues rapidly undermining republican values and institutions in Pennsylvania. Following a perfuctory recitation of the need to increase the number of Supreme Court judges, to insure an impartial trial by jury in civil as well as criminal cases, and to revise the penal code, he launched into what he obviously now considered the most pressing of the legislature's tasks: to provide a proper curb to the licentiousness of the press. "Libeling (gross and malignant libeling) has become the crying sin of the nation and the times," he told the legislators. "It is not the licentiousness of a single press; nor the machination of a single party. . . . The crime is . . . the same whoever may be the criminal, and whoever may be the victim." It was "the general prostitution of the liberty of the press; the overwhelming torrent of political dissention; the indiscriminate demolition of public characters; and the barbarous inroads upon the peace and happiness of private individuals" that had convinced him to urge once again, this time more adamantly, that the legislature provide a cure.

McKean saw "the fatal consequences" of the scurrility in the press all around him. The press, he claimed, had lost its use both as an instructor and a censor. Citizen had been turned against citizen, respect for public officials had "fall[en] into derision." Good men would soon abandon public service. Each editor assailing the character of a citizen should be compelled to publish a defense, if asked by the victim, he argued. The law should require also that each printer and editor should register at "some public office in the proper county" to be "evidence of the fact of publication upon trials of law." Whenever a grand jury should present a press as a public nuisance, the printer and the editor should be bound in a recognizance, with sureties for their future good behavior and the court authorized to suppress it for a limited time. In short, McKean was asking the legislators to codify much of the common law practice that he had employed as a chief justice. He referred to the previous legislature's interest in a dueling bill and remarked that the crime of libeling was much like dueling in that "each depended for its indulgence and its impunity upon public taste and public opinion." "Duels are among the natural and usual effects of libels," McKean told the legislators, the one could be cured as the other was. He pressed them to act decisively and quickly in these matters, for republicanism tottered on the brink of failure.

He finished on a surprisingly soft note, expressing his hope that he could "repay the obligations which [he owed] his country, for its kindness, during a long and active life." "It cannot be... presumed, that I have not erred in judgement, on former occasions, nor do the infirmaties of age diminish the probability of future errors," he remarked, "but if a difference of opinion should rise between us... let both lament it as a misfortune; but neither impute it as a crime." It was one of the most deliberate attempts by McKean to reduce the tension between the executive and legislative branches of government, and perhaps at the same time bring a few of the Republicans who had drifted away from support of his administration back into line.[21]

McKean's efforts, however sincerely meant, seem to have had little effect on the legislators or, for that matter, on his opponents outside the legislature. A few expressions of regret and remorse over differences, and a short plea for mutual understanding could not erase the ill will built up over the last several years and given fresh force by his recent actions against Duane and in the Barker-Wolbert case. The *Aurora* mixed a bit of history to label McKean a Napoleon and compared his current administration with that of Prussia.[22]

As customary, a committee of the House prepared a response to McKean's address. The first draft of the committee's response made no mention of libeling or McKean's reaction to it; it merely conceded that differences between the governor and the House existed and expressed a belief that though they may "differ in modes or principles," the two branches ought to continue a reasonable and profitable exchange of ideas. On Monday, December 15, however, House members Engle and Leib presented a substitute reading, one that scathingly denounced not only McKean's unrepublican principles, particularly his practice of personally addressing the Assembly (a habit "discordant...with the economy and maxims of a republican government") but also decried his practice as a remnant of monarchy and argued that it had no place in Pennsylvania's modes of behavior. The report went on to score McKean for his views on freedom of the press, flinging back at him Jefferson's view of the press as delineated in his inaugural address. It caustically reminded the governor of the state constitution's prohibition against tampering with the free press. For the legislators to pursue McKean's admonitions to the ends he sought would force them to defy their own constitutional scruples, the report concluded. The House agreed to the substitute report, and it was sent along to the unhappy governor.

Even more scathing in its denunciation of McKean was Leib's report on McKean's specific proposals for legislation regarding libeling. Heading the committee assigned the task of putting into specific bills McKean's proposals, Leib, on January 13, brought in a report stating categorically that "the governor must have felt either a want of respect for the honor and integrity, or for the understanding of the General Assembly; or he could not have submitted projects to them which, if carried into effect, must implicate them in guilt or ignorance." The report charged that McKean's proposals flew directly in the face of the state constitution, that McKean persisted in making England and English law the "arbiter of conduct in Pennsylvania. . . . Are we to resort to the political vocabulary of kings to define the liberty of an American?" it asked.

It spared no reproach. Here we desire not a Star Chamber or a Jeffries, the author assured his colleagues in the House. Such might take root "in the regime of monarchy" but not in Pennsylvania. McKean's program would surely lead to "the deadly nightshade of the common law on libels," according to Leib. "The conflagration of the Alexandrean library by barbarians was not more fatal to toleration, than the project would be to the freedom of the press, and of the citizens." The report used McKean's call for libel legislation to review not only his patronage and executive policies but his own frequent recourse to the law in cases of libel. Leib's report noted that McKean had "availed himself of the current law to the fullest extent. . . . Already he had won damages of $50,000 against two defendants for distributing a political pamphlet," it reported, and it observed that McKean was "currently pressing charges against five more and asking damages from them totaling $200,000! . . . Whence, then, the necessity of any criminal law on this subject, when the common law is so fruitful in actions upon the case?" Leib asked his colleagues. The report concluded by strongly recommending that a committee be appointed to bring in a bill expressly declaring that no person shall hereafter be subject to a criminal prosecution on the charge of a libel, and that no citizen shall be held to answer for a libel upon the public character or public conduct of any citizen, excepting the author and printer.[23]

By January 1807 it was obvious that the governor and the legislature were on a collision course. Leib's committee report had all the markings of a call to impeach. Nearly blind with rage at the affrontery of Leib's reports, McKean fired off a letter to George Logan, bitterly assailing the "Catilinean Faction" and expressing his belief "that the Faction would set a church on fire, were it only, that they might roast Eggs in it." He no longer desired to placate them; he had "exhausted conciliation. . . . If they persist in their seditious measures," he told Logan, "I shall be reduced to the necessity of opposition

& hostility." According to McKean's estimation—and one suspects that he was as thorough in his estimation as he was in most of his practices—there were less than twenty leaders of the "Jacobins & Disorganizers" aligned against him. He readily conceded they were having a political impact far beyond their numbers. "One wicked man can effect more political if not private mischief, than a hundred well disposed persons can do good, in the present state of society," he lamented to the sympathetic Logan.[24]

By now McKean and the Leibites were eager each to attribute to the other the basest imputations. According to McKean the Jacobins were the harbinger of a leveling democracy, a movement guaranteed to destroy rather than enhance republican institutions. They were part of a "conspiracy hatched in hell and propagated by the imps of darkness." They sought power and patronage, not enlightened reforms; they sought the destruction of law for their own ends, not greater justice for all. Rather than thwarting the will of the people by his actions, McKean saw himself as the one effective safeguard of their rights and property against those who would destroy a law system perfected over the centuries and turn the state over to those incapable of sound and fair rule. He quite literally believed that the salvation of republicanism lay in his hands. Without his leadership Pennsylvanians would destroy themselves through their own chimerical schemes, or those of their ill-qualified and presumptious representatives in the Assembly.

To him the struggle was between the forces of progress and enlightenment and the forces of disorder, retrogression, and licentiousness, between those who wished to insure the permanence of Revolutionary goals and those seeking to corrupt those goals for selfish and short-range political benefits. The key to the struggle was, as it had always been, power and the patronage. Patronage accompanied power and supplemented it, and to this end McKean used every opportunity available to him to gather around him those he trusted, those who shared his concern for stability and tranquility. If this meant granting offices to his sons and sons-in-law, when they merited such positions, so be it. If it meant aligning with Federalists, so be that. Those who would employ a convention to change the government and tamper with justice must be stopped at any cost.

If McKean was myopic in denying the legitimacy of much of the democratic thrust within his state, concentrating instead on the opposition's selfish quest for power, Duane and Leib were equally blind to McKean's honest desire for justice and tranquility, preferring to interpret his actions as a frantic design to establish a royal family in America. They were willing to couch their own desires in less than candid terms while denying McKean the same prerogatives. This combination of principle and self-interest on both sides resulted in a situation whereby McKean's desire for a larger, more effective judicial system was seen by his enemies as a mere dodge to protect the selfish interests of lawyers and jurists; his willingness to abide by the will of the Spanish minister in the Cabrera case as a willful misuse of the law for the benefit of his own family; his nepotism as a means of creating a personal empire.

In reality, then, by 1807 Pennsylvania was witnessing a battle largely between strong-willed individuals and jealous factions, each seeking power or to husband power, a struggle for patronage, spoils, interest. Principles were often sacrificed for political advantage, programs were accepted or rejected on the basis of their impact upon "the enemy." Questions arose on the basis of their viability as political strategems. As early as 1805 the perspicacious Albert Gallatin had correctly foreseen much of the future in this respect. "McKean and Duane will be both implacable and immoveable [sic]," he wrote, "and the acts of the first and the continued proscriptions of the last will most probably and unfortunately defeat every attempt to reconcile."[25] Yet, principles were certainly involved. Each in his own way clung tenaciously to his view of republicanism and convinced himself that he was the guardian of its success. Certainly McKean, even as he protected himself and sought to wield power and influence for its own sake, believed deeply that he was doing it for the salvation of republicanism. If the American Revolution was to be successful, McKean would have to abort his enemies' schemes.

On January 12, 1807, the *Aurora* demanded that McKean be impeached. Two weeks later Leib directed the House's attention to the fact that the governor had not signed certain bills, that he had instead used a facsimile stamp. Because of this illegal act Leib would submit a resolution calling for a formal investigation by the House of McKean's conduct in office. Three days later, on January 30, true to his word, Leib introduced the resolution. Boileau and other Republicans sympathetic to most of Leib's policies to that point, balked at considering such a momentous question while the governor was reported to be ill. They managed to table the resolution after a forty-three to forty-three vote.[26]

The rumors concerning McKean's health were accurate. He was seriously ill throughout January and much of February, suffering severely from gout in both hands, one leg and a foot. By January 30 his condition was so alarming that Tom Thompson sent for Mrs. McKean, who in turn requested that the family doctor come to Lancaster.[27] He was kept posted on political developments and Thompson continued to process much of the governor's paperwork. He was in sufficient health by the third week in January to write a short note to his son Tommy providing some advice for a cousin who had been swindled and to express his hope that Poulson would reprint his 1797 charge to the grand jury on libel in the Cobbett proceedings, an act that he thought would have a salubrious effect on current practices. He also expressed a conviction that Leib "merits every punishment that can be honestly inflicted upon him." He took time to write to John Dickinson, now himself aged and ill, again bemoaning the lack of "first class citizens in the General Assembly." He told Dickinson that "for some years past" the state's representatives had not been selected from the first class of citizens and, as a consequence, they lacked manners and were defective in knowledge.[28] On the thirtieth of January, when Leib formally raised the issue of his impeachment, McKean's condition was grave. But he was not so ill in mid-February, nor so intimidated by the stirrings of an impeachment movement in the House, that he acquiesced in legislation he construed to be unwise. On February 16 he dictated a message to his secretary vetoing a Senate resolution calling for the publication of laws of a general nature in local newspapers. He defended his veto by pointing out that the resolution had the effect of uniting the functions of the executive and legislative branches in one person, which violated the separation doctrine of the state constitution. Exasperating as was the task, McKean patiently explained to the senators what he considered to be the resolution's flaws.²⁹

By late February McKean had recovered somewhat. The *Aurora* announced his recovery on the twenty-eighth of that month; less than a week later, on March 3, by a forty-three to thirty-eight vote, the House supported a move to name Leib to head a committee charged with considering impeachment resolutions against McKean. Throughout March the Leib committee collected testimony and evidence, not only on the question of the misuse of the facsimile stamp, but on five other charges as well.³⁰

How seriously McKean took the committee's actions is open to debate. Joseph McKean's actions suggest the governor deemed it essential that the committee's efforts be stalled. On March 17 Joseph asked the state Supreme Court to issue a warrant for the arrest of Leib for conspiring to force the governor to appoint Wolbert as sheriff of Philadelphia. Leib's attorney, Joseph Hopkinson, whose personal conflict with McKean had received wide publicity seven years before, insisted that as a member of the state legislature Leib was immune from arrest and that a warrant on behalf of the governor, whether or not designed to do so, would have the effect of truncating the committee's investigation into the governor's conduct. The court, he maintained, should not enter into such a conflict. Before the court could react to Hopkinson's argumentation, however, Joseph McKean withdrew his request and the court remained silent. Whatever McKean's part in the matter, Joseph McKean's move failed to improve the political climate or to intimidate Leib. Leibites asserted that "if the warrant had been granted, in less time than twice twenty-four hours we would have had seven hundred men at Lancaster . . . . The thunder and blitzen of the Northern Liberties, the wild Irish of Irish-town and all the butchers in Philadelphia would have turned out . . . . We would have pressed all the wagons and carriages in Philadelphia, and made the cartridges and cast the balls in the wagons coming up."³¹

Leib countered the action by suing Tommy McKean for sending him a challenge over the *Quid Mirror* matter, and for engaging Dennis to aid him. In May a court of quarter sessions, held in Philadelphia before Jacob Rush, brought indictments against both Tommy McKean and Dennis. The court refused to bring in a bill against Leib for his part in the affair. Convicted, McKean and Dennis submitted their claims to the "justice and impartiality of the Executive Magistrate," arguing that it was unfair to punish them for sending a challenge while ignoring Leib who accepted it. Such a "discrimination," they argued, "furnishes a precedent dangerous to the pure and equal administration of justice."[32] Tommy was no more intimidated than Leib. In late March he was observed strolling in front of the legislature with a substantial club clutched in his hand, a fair warning to legislators inside contemplating the impeachment resolution against his father. He tried desperately to provoke fights with at least two members of the Leib committee—and Leib himself—without success. Quite understandably, the *Aurora* kept the public abreast of these threatening gestures on the part of the McKean family.[33]

Five days before the committee brought in its report, McKean took a step guaranteed to diminish his backing in the House still further. He vetoed "An Act to prevent the Recorder of the City of Philadelphia from Practicing as an attorney or counsellor in any court of justices in this commonwealth or elsewhere." McKean knew as did every member of the legislature that the bill, sponsored by Leib, was directed at Moses Levy, who as a Quid and attorney for Joseph McKean in his long-pending case against Duane, was persona non grata to the democrats. If Levy remained as city recorder he would also oversee the mayor's court, before which the Duane cases would be argued. McKean complained that the bill reflected ignorance of the nature and duties of the recorder, that it deprived the recorder of his normal professional income and made no adequate substitution, and deprived the city of his services, for which he was compensated out of city funds. If this were not enough to justify negating the legislation, it was an ex post facto bill, designed to hurt the incumbent. Equally dangerous, it could easily be perverted into a precedent fatal to the executive powers of appointment. It would drive good men away from the office and destroy a pattern of more than one hundred years of beneficial service to the community. It denied the people of Philadelphia a say in the governance of their public interests. For all these reasons, McKean told the legislators, he could not stand idly by and watch it become part of the law of the Commonwealth. To his relief—and probably surprise—the General Assembly failed to pass the bill over his veto.³⁴

On March 30, two months after Leib had suggested a formal effort toward impeachment, Leib announced his committee's decision that McKean should be impeached on six counts. The first charge, "that the governor did premeditatedly, wantonly, unjustly and contrary to the true intent and meaning of the constitution, render void the election of a sheriff in the city and county of Philadelphia," included allegations that he had manipulated the vote, declared qualified voters unqualified, accepted numerous dubious votes, and allowed his son, the attorney general, the discretion of filling in the names of the election commissioners on signed blank commissions. The second charge, that he had usurped judicial prerogatives and interfered in favor of a convict to the detriment of the safety of the citizens of Philadelphia, concerned his role in the Cabrera case. The third accusation emanated from the appointment of his son-in-law, George Buchanan, as Lazaretto physician even though Buchanan was not a citizen of the state at the time of his appointment. The governor was further charged with "suffer[ing] his name to be stamped upon blank papers" and with superseding Dr. James Reynolds "contrary to law" as a member of the Board of Health. Finally, the Leib committee was satisfied that McKean had attempted to bribe Duane to drop his charge against Joseph McKean in return for Duane's dismissal from suits instigated by the state. This "compromise" offered to Duane by the governor and his allies was found by the committee to be "of a character truly dark and alarming."³⁵

The House accepted the Leib report on April 8. Boileau moved that the charges be referred to the succeeding legislature, probably because the term of the current body was rapidly drawing to an end. Efforts were made the following day by Federalists and Quids to postpone the issue indefinitely, but the ploy lost by four votes. By a mere two votes, forty-three to forty-one, the House then accepted Boileau's motion to turn the matter over to the next General Assembly.

Predictably, the *Aurora* covered the events in great detail and commented favorably upon the committee's efforts, while Quid organs like the *Freeman's Journal* belittled the committee's actions and cast aspersions on its leadership. The latter pointed out that the current speaker of the House, Simon Snyder, had run unsuccessfully against McKean and had been unhappily licking his political wounds since. It ridiculed Leib's eagerness to head the committee appointed "to persecute" the governor and scoffed at the testimony against the governor as politically inspired. It was instructive, wrote a correspondent in the *Freeman's Journal,* that McKean's enemies had waited until he "was attacked by disease . . . when his life was despaired of, and he was apparently stretched upon his bed of death," before launching their campaign to remove him.[36]

The day after the committee's report on his impeachment was accepted by the House, McKean vetoed a House resolution "denying the jurisdiction of the United States courts touching suits brought or that may be brought under the Act of Assembly . . . of April 3, 1792, directing the sale of vacant lands, lying north and west of the Rivers Ohio and Allegheny and Conewango Creek." He told members of the House he had examined the bill "with every possible deference to the legislative opinion, and not without some sentiment of good will towards the petitioners on whose prayer the resolution [was] founded" but found the bill unwise, and he could not accept it. It not only violated the principle of separation of powers but that of separation of state and national powers. The powers of the United States Supreme Court had been firmly established and it was clear to all thinking men that the cases under question fell within its jurisdiction. McKean returned the bill unsigned.

After Leib had brought in his committee's recommendations to impeach McKean, but before the House had acted formally upon them, McKean had vetoed still another pet project of the House, this time a bill "to extend the right of peremptory challenge to cases not hitherto provided for." McKean viewed the bill as unwise, for it failed to distinguish properly between capital and other offenders, and it was an experiment not limited by a specific duration. By multiplying the number of jurymen the bill would also "prejudice the public economy" as well as delay justice in the state. McKean was concerned too that it was an ex post facto law in that it would operate on indictments currently pending. He admitted that the privilege of peremptory challenges "in the case of misdemeanors ought to be just, ought to be reciprocal." But it "does not accord with my ideas of justice," he told the legislators, "that the assassin of public character, or private reputation, should have rights conferred on him, which are withheld from the injured and innocent victim, of his malice and revenge."[37]

Observers outside the General Assembly viewed with alarm the deepening split between the governor and the House. McKean's continuing defiance of the will of the legislators seemed a deliberate provocation to hasten his impeachment. "Poor Pennsylvania is still upon her broadside," wrote Benjamin Rush to John Adams. "Our governor, who is now the only anchor of our state, is in bad health and upon the eve of being impeached. . . . If not removed by death from office, he will probably be dismissed by the Senate." Rush, like a great many Pennsylvanians, did not think the Senate would "dare to acquit him" considering the political sentiment in the state. Still, the *Freeman's Journal* called for renewed exertions by the Constitutional Party in McKean's behalf. "If there ever was a time when it was necessary for the Constitutional Party to exert themselves, it is the present," wrote a correspondent to that paper. "When the whole body politic is in danger, it is childish to consume the time . . . in debating whether an egg should be broken at the large or small end."[38]

Meanwhile the democrats were busy preparing the people of the state, and national officers, for McKean's removal. Jefferson was kept apprised of developments through a number of sources, mostly unfriendly to McKean. Thomas Leiper, who once had expressed the opinion that McKean would hold a fee simple on the gubernatorial chair for the next ten years but now favored his dismissal, wrote to Jefferson to say "Our governor is a wicked mad man and all his officers are obliged to fall in with him or be turned out of office." Duane was even more graphic in describing McKean's failings to Jefferson. He reported that "Mr. McKean has completely succeeded in destroying poor Saml Bryan, who is now in this city with a numerous and young family . . . not fifty dollars in the world;

his furniture is left to pay the rent." He denounced McKean's intrigue in prosecuting John Steele, who had signed and circulated a memorial critical of McKean, even while the governor ignored the author of the offending petition.

Perhaps the most startling claim made by Duane to Jefferson was that the state militia would no longer follow McKean. No one had looked to the militia more ardently than McKean for the protection of republican values. From the outset of his gubernatorial career McKean had striven to strengthen and improve the state militia units. Yet in December Duane told the President that despite the worsening crisis in national and international affairs, militia personnel would refuse to turn out under McKean's command. They would turn out under their previous officers, and certainly they would mobilize if ordered to do so by the President, but "not with officers of McKean's nominations, in whom they could have no confidence," Duane reported. Duane left Jefferson with the impression that McKean's dismissal would not only improve the state political environment but would strengthen the nation's capacity to resist should war break out with France and England.[39]

None of this dissuaded McKean from carrying out his constitutional responsibilities as he saw them. He greeted the legislature in December as he had greeted the two previous legislatures, with veto messages. On December 3, 1807, McKean killed two bills from the previous session. The first, "An act to alter or amend . . . an act to provide for a settlement of public accounts," sought to enhance the powers of the treasurer in a way McKean thought "neither public policy, nor private justice, appears to warrant." By giving the treasurer new powers the bill in effect created a new office, and at the same time encroached upon the governor's prerogative to fill all offices in that department with personnel of his choice. But McKean saved his most forceful and eloquent effort for his veto of a bill designed to eliminate the use of any but American precedents in legal cases. Unquestionably it was one of his greatest state papers, a brilliant defense of the need for a broad understanding of the law to guarantee justice and liberty. "A difference of opinion, both in public and in private life," he began, "is nature to mankind; and an honest difference of opinion ought never to produce passion, prejudice, or reproach.

...Whenever it has been my misfortune to differ from the opinion of the Senate and the House," he went on, "I have not ventured to arraign the purity of their motives; although I may sometimes have been tempted on account of that difference, to question the correctness of my own judgment." Whenever he exercised his constitutional right to declare that he could not approve a resolution or bill, he told them, he did it "not to pronounce a sentence of condemnation upon others; but merely to assign reasons in vindication of [himself]." He thought the bill under scrutiny "instead of multiplying or assisting the memory of a judge, or informing the conscience of a jury" tended to limit those means. "Why confine our means of improvement, our source of information, in matters of jurisprudence, to the local boundaries of the United States," he asked, "while the professors of every other science, and the masters of every other art, may gather the fruits of human genius and knowledge, throughout the world, to enrich their studies, and to invigorate their judgements?"

"Shall the knowledge necessary to the administration of justice be permitted to enter our tribunals only in one direction, and at a single avenue?" McKean inquired. He discussed in some detail the relationship of British common law to the law of the state, indicating how intimately the two were intertwined. "Can it be denied," he asked, that "though a great, a wise, and a virtuous nation, that independent of foreign precedents and adjudications, we must be in these respects, more like a ship upon the ocean without a rudder or a compass?" He concluded that "a foreign code is here, in truth, the only evidence of the law . . . and the resolution that forbids an advocate, a judge, and jury to resort in court, to that code, forbids them, in effect, to learn and to understand the general rule, which is their duty to apply, at the very moment when its application is required."[40]

The conciliatory tone of the last veto message was carried over to his opening address to the General Assembly on the same day. He adroitly chose to put the current political squabbles in a different perspective. The state was obviously experiencing prosperity and progress, he declared. Although it was true that the need for judicial reforms remained, and one could also desire more and better schools, roads and other internal improvements, the real issue, the most pressing issue before them was not internal matters but the deepening crisis in international affairs. He sought to establish that those seeking radical reform, to protect their version of republicanism, would do well to concentrate first on reforming the state's militia system. In view of the impending crisis faced by Jefferson and the nation, Pennsylvania Republicans should channel their energy into achieving a formidable militia system.

Without specifically saying so, McKean left the impression that to continue with the impeachment and to maintain the focus on the state's internal disorder was to do so at the expense of far more important issues, issues quite capable of destroying the very republicanism the followers of Duane and Leib professed to cherish. It was an old, timeworn but effective ploy. While not backing away from either his program of judicial reform or his concept of the governor's proper role in Pennsylvania's political system, he provided the General Assembly with another list of priorities to consider.[41]

The soft, conciliatory tone of McKean's message and its emphasis on the nation's present crisis with foreign powers were not exclusively a calculated political ploy. McKean was sincerely disturbed by the crisis with Great Britain and the French over their violations of our maritime rights and he concurred with Jefferson's use of the embargo. But his deteriorating health and the aggressiveness of the "Jacobins" had brought home to him the very real threat to his political career. The possibility of his being successfully impeached, of ending his political career by being dismissed from office sobered him. He was now seventy-three, ill, tired; he recognized that he had made mistakes, he had judged at least some men badly. He wanted only to finish his term and retire, and he would do whatever was necessary to achieve that end. If it meant publicly confessing his failings, so be it.

Four days after McKean's opening remarks to the General Assembly, the House took up the question of his impeachment. It immediately became evident that the pro-impeachment forces were going to face serious difficulties in their quest. Two House members from Philadelphia County, John Sergeant and John Biddle, moved to postpone the issue until the second Monday in January, but this motion was quickly defeated forty-two to forty-two. A motion to refer the matter to a committee lost by the same vote. McKean's brilliant defense of the use of British legal precedents in American courts, and his December speech to the General Assembly, had had the desired effect. If they did not persuade some who had previously opposed him to change their votes, they clearly kept a number of House members, previously on the fence, from toppling over into the opposition's ranks. Pro-McKean members took advantage of a temporary majority in the third week of January to place on the House record a defense of McKean's actions by McKean himself.

McKean began his formal defense by asking for justice. "A long and dangerous sickness" had deprived him of an opportunity to peruse the journals of the House "or to have the least knowledge of the proceedings, in relation to an impeachment of [his] official conduct," until a month after the adjournment of the last session, he told House members. Since then a proper respect for the constitutional jurisdiction of the House had prevented him from publicly responding to the charges. These charges had now been "deliberately framed" and "openly discussed," however, and since they would soon "pass among the legislative records, into the hands of [his] constituents, and [his] posterity, with all its concomitant semblance of proof and asperity of animadversion," he now wished to respond formally to them. He waived the "discrimination" which might be owed him after more than forty years of public service. He demanded only the justice "extend[ed] in the case of every other citizen."

"I may have erred in judgment . . . I may have been mistaken in my general views of public policy and I may have been deceived by the objects of executive confidence, or benevolence," he told them, "but no act of my public life was ever done, from a corrupt motive, [or] without a deliberate opinion that the act *was lawful and proper* in itself." With that he launched into a spirited and highly effective defense of his actions. Like the proficient and skilled lawyer he was he marshaled his defense, documenting his actions, pointing to inconsistencies and flaws in the formal charges. None of the charges held up under McKean's concerted barrage. McKean might have been guilty of pride and arrogance, even political stupidity, but he was not guilty of crimes against the state. McKean concluded his defense by observing,

> Having travelled over a wide field of accusation and defence, I shall only add the expression of a sincere wish, to close my political life in peace with all men. It has been my lot, in tempestuous seasons of civil conflict, to oppose (what I honestly thought) the innovations of *anarchy,* as well as the encroachments of *tyranny;* but I must trust that (with all the acknowledged imperfections of my judgment) I have never been actuated in any private or public pursuit, by envy or malice; by the love of power, or the desire of wealth. Conceiving myself sometimes to be "a man more sinned against than sinning," the feelings of resentment, and the language of reproach, may for a moment, perhaps have been incautiously indulged; but I have never deliberately done unto others, what I would not in like circumstances, that others should do unto me; nor can I conceive any acts more honorable . . . than an atonement for errors, and a forgiveness of injuries.[42]

A rare combination of truth and nonsense. But whether truth or nonsense, McKean believed what he said. If McKean's argument did not fully convince many of the Republican House members, they were probably moved by his confessions of inadvertent sins. A more sober evaluation of the committee's charges, the tone and substance of McKean's refutation of those charges, and a changing political climate within the state, contributed to the failure of the impeachment movement. By February 1808 the democrats were content merely to assail the insertion of McKean's defense into the House record. They did not have the votes to impeach, and they knew it. McKean had survived his most trying hour.[43]

Conscious of his place in history and sobered by the virulence of the attack upon him, McKean had fought back intelligently, effectively, and on occasion, eloquently. Thomas McKean Thompson doubtless spoke for most of the governor's friends and admirers, and perhaps a few of his more sensitive critics when, following the failure of the impeachment proceedings, he wrote to Tommy McKean that "it is a subject of pride & exultation with the governor's friends here, that for nine years he has withstood the violent assaults of different factions, & has triumphed over all his enemies & that he goes out of office now in obedience to a constitutional provision."[44]

20. Look Back in Wonder

The final months of McKean's third gubernatorial term were uneventful. Confident of his survival by mid-February, he had Tommy distribute copies of his defense to friends and political allies in Philadelphia who had been particularly steadfast in their support of him. The fact that the "Jacobins in the General Assembly appear[ed] to be very sore and desperate" was a source of quiet pleasure for him. He wrote Tommy on February 13 that some of the "Jacobins appear[ed] to wish some notice from [him] lately" but he thought it impossible that they should "be forgiven without repentence." He was content to treat them "with dignified reserve," and to comfort himself with the fact that the great majority of people in Lancaster, and those passing through, "treat[ed] him with uncommon attention." Equally reassuring, his health had improved markedly; he now hoped to "return home a healthy, if not a young man."[1]

McKean's remaining gubernatorial duties were for the most part perfunctory ones. As was his custom, he granted pardons to a variety of petitioners, including one to his son and another to Richard Dennis for their part in the challenge to Michael Leib. He attached his signature to a steady stream of bills pouring from the General Assembly, but the deadlock in the Assembly which guaranteed McKean's political survival also insured an absence of controversial legislation. There were no vetoes and little furor over legislation throughout the summer and fall of 1808. He had the opportunity to name more than three dozen men to office in his last months as governor, but none of his appointments was controversial, and little attention was paid them. If he took interest in the gubernatorial campaign during the fall between James Ross, the Federalist, and Simon Snyder, he gave no outward sign of it.[2]

His final address to the General Assembly, in December 1808, focused almost exclusively on the response of the nation to foreign affairs. He conceded that Jefferson's embargo had hurt the state; Pennsylvanians had seen their profits severely reduced and a number of occupations hurt by the President's program. But he judged "these Inconveniences" not so great as "the Loss of private Property, which careless captures and arbitrary Confiscations would inevitably produce, and . . . unworthy of a Moment's Calculations." He praised Pennsylvanians for their courage and resolve in the face of the current difficulties, assuring them that their sacrifices would "animate and confirm the Virtue of her Sister States."

The present difficulties, McKean told the legislators, were reminiscent of an earlier crisis when sacrifices and virtue had also determined America's success. America in 1808, as two decades before, had to affirm both its independence and its republicanism. Great Britain again seemed determined to destroy American rights, to compromise its honor, to snuff out its republican institutions. Surely no sacrifice was too great to insure that the honor and independence of America be preserved, that the fruits of the American Revolution be passed on to future generations. He called upon his countrymen to join him in a "mutual Pledge of our Lives, our fortunes, and our Sacred Honor" to that end.

Past sacrifices and past giants were very much in McKean's mind in December 1808. He pressed the General Assembly to provide fitting monuments for two patriots of America's earlier struggles for independence, Anthony Wayne and Thomas Mifflin. His career, like theirs, was now finished, and it may be that in seeking to obtain memorials to their contributions he hoped to promote acclaim for his own. He alluded to his own public career and expressed his pleasure in having seen his country "progress... from a colonial to a national Character." He told the Legislators that his own "day of Exertion (of feeble Exertion at best) [was] past," but he contemplated the future "with a proud [and] an anxious Expectation." He then turned the state over to Simon Snyder.[3]

Not unexpectedly, the political influence of the "Royal Family" died with McKean's retirement. Several of McKean's most vocal supporters, anticipating Snyder's animosity, resigned before McKean left office. Most who remained were quickly removed. Thomas McKean Thompson, replaced on December 20, was the first of McKean's "family" to go. On January 9, Walter Franklin of Philadelphia succeeded Joseph McKean as attorney general. By the end of February only Thomas McKean, Jr., with his military commission, remained in "office." As frustrating as the eclipse of his political family must have been to McKean, more galling perhaps was the type of men who replaced them. Nathaniel Boileau, his nemesis in the Assembly, succeeded Thompson as secretary of the Commonwealth. William Dickson, author of the *Quid Mirror,* received the lucrative printing contracts for the state. Frederick Wolbert, a central figure in McKean's impeachment charges, was commissioned prothonotary of the court of common pleas for the City and County of Philadelphia. "Sammy" Bryan was named the register for the probate of wills for the City and County of Philadelphia.[4]

It seems only fitting that the McKean administration should have ended as it began, in the midst of controversy and threats of violence. Even as McKean was bidding farewell to the General Assembly, a Philadelphia court was weighing his libel charges (initiated in the late summer of 1805) against William Duane. Though Duane was found guilty on one count, the verdict failed to please the McKeans. The ex-governor managed to suppress any public comment on his disappointment but his son Joseph vented his frustration by attacking Duane's counsel. Charging that Duane's attorney, Richard Rush, had maliciously abused his father by constantly referring to his alleged use of the word "Clodpoles" to describe the people of Pennsylvania, Joseph McKean sought the help of Thomas Zantzinger in arranging a duel. Rush conceded that "the discussion, on the late trial, sometimes fell into irregularities on both sides," but he denied any premeditated malicious intent and refused to be drawn into a confrontation. There the matter ended despite a good deal of grumbling in the McKean camp.[5]

Retirement provided McKean the first opportunity in years to assess his land holdings and to view the total results of his lifelong drive to acquire an impressive estate. While Tommy helped him collect back rents and oversee the management of his Delaware lands, McKean sought to take stock of his vast Pennsylvania holdings, visiting those lands and tenants that he could, and requesting agents to provide this service when he could not. In September 1810 he offered eight hundred acres of his Delaware lands at "long credit...on payment of the interest annally [sic]." A year later he sold three hundred and fifty acres of his one thousand acres in Newcastle County for seven thousand dollars, a transaction which, he claimed, "added to [his] character and rank in life." Though his lands and rents appeared to produce more consternation than profits overall, he clung to more than ten thousand acres.[6]

Although satisfied with his economic station, McKean was deeply disappointed in the direction of the American republic. He saw the loss of earlier, laudable values all around him. In 1810 McKean asked his old friend from Wilmington, James Rogers, either to collect money owed him from George Ogle, John McBeath, and John Crow, one-time business associates of McKean, or sue them immediately. McKean was especially displeased with Crow. He calculated that by July 1810, ten years after Crow incurred the debt, the interest on the debt "amount[ed] to two third parts of the principal." For McKean the issue was more than a private matter. Recent visits to Newcastle had led him to observe that "the morals and manners of the People...[had] greatly depreciated....Insubordination, disre[s]pect for Magistrates and learned & worthy Characters appear[ed] to be common," according to McKean. Somehow he convinced himself that legal proceedings against John Crow would begin the rehabilitation of American values.[7] Nor was

Delaware alone in exhibiting a degeneration of ancient values; McKean found examples of this depressing condition "in all the States.... Can this be attributed to our Government, our laws, our Ministers of the Gospel, Schoolmasters, or what else?" he wondered. He was soon convinced that national politics mirrored the same degeneracy of timeworn values and practices.[8]

Nevertheless, McKean found it difficult to turn from politics. As an active participant in political matters for the greater part of his life, he found its attractions irresistible. The last years of Jefferson's administration and the early years of Madison's presidency particularly disappointed him. He considered both men more preoccupied with party concerns than with the quality of their patronage policies, an interesting assessment from a man long accused of being the ultimate spoilsman. Madison especially had appointed too many "low and designing men" for McKean's tastes. The increasing incompetence he observed in national politics was a product of such a slap-dash patronage system. It was also, according to McKean, another manifestation of the decline of American society. Vigilence against foreign enemies was wasted motion if a nation decayed from within by tolerating inferior personnel in leadership capacities.[9]

Continuing confusion and strife among the political leaders of the state created within McKean a certain ambivalence. On the one hand it confirmed his anxieties regarding the state of republicanism in the United States; on the other it created the possibility of his returning to the political wars. By the early months of 1811 McKean's former political adversary, Michael Leib, had become thoroughly disenchanted with Simon Snyder and his followers. The rift was a long-standing one; it dated back to the March 1808 caucus which nominated Snyder to succeed McKean. Disagreements over state matters were exacerbated by divisions over national concerns. By 1811 the followers of Snyder advocated the re-election of James Madison, whereas a faction of the Republican party of the state led by Leib opposed his renomination. Encouraged by some gentlemen in Lancaster and Philadelphia friendly to McKean, including Joseph Hiester, Leib began negotiations with the state's Quids and Federalists to back McKean for the gubernatorial post against Snyder.[10]

McKean affected disinterest. But in the same month that Hiester and Leib began tentative discussions regarding McKean's possible candidacy on a coalition ticket, McKean mentioned the gubernatorial race to his longtime friend and political ally, John Way of Allegheny County. "Many applications have been made to me by *Individuals* of all parties in the State to agree to be a Candidate for Governor at the next election," he wrote Way on July 16, "but as I enjoy such comfort, since I have been exempted from all professional and official duties as I never experienced during a long and protracted life, I cannot relinquish it." That is, he could not accept the nomination "without it was the desire of a majority of my fellow citizens." Then, in an obvious attempt to wring from Way some confirmation of his continuing popularity, he added rather pointedly that he had "heard nothing from the western counties" yet.[11]

The seventy-seven-year-old McKean may have been enthusiastic over his chances as a compromise candidate for the Leibites, Quids, and Federalists, but many of the Federalists who held the key to his nomination were not. They were split among those who favored McKean, those who preferred a candidate other than McKean, and still others who advocated the offering of no candidate against Snyder. This last group preferred to support no candidate rather than risk what they considered to be a certain defeat at the hands of the popular Snyder. Federalists opposed to McKean ultimately frustrated his selection as the nominee of that party, and with that the coalition proposed by Leib and Hiester collapsed.[12]

McKean surfaced only twice more as a political leader in state or city affairs. On October 30, 1812, he headed an electoral ticket supporting DeWitt Clinton. Earlier that year, in June, McKean had written a friend to say he had "[shaken] hands with the world three years ago, and we said farewell to each other.... Since my exemption from official and professional duties," he went on, "I have enjoyed a tranquillity never (during a long[,] protracted life) heretofore experienced." He thought "the toys and rattles of childhood would, in a few years, be probably as suitable to [him] as office, honor, or wealth." Four months later he agreed to head the unsuccessful Clintonian electoral ticket.[13]

McKean's hatred of the British, unabated since the Revolution, increased in the years prior to and during the War of 1812. Even when efforts were made to conclude an early peace, he had little optimism. If he distrusted British efforts in the last years of the Revolution to conclude a just peace, he had even less faith in their good will in 1814. He told John Adams in January 1814 that although "a glimmering of peace appears on the horizon... every preparation should be made for a continuance of the war.... When the British arms have been successful," he told Adams, "I have never found their rulers or ministers otherwise than haughty, rude, imperious, nay, insolent." His pessimism proved to be fully justified, and when the British burned Washington later in the year, he had to heed his own advice in making "every preparation for the continuance of the war." The opportunity to act publicly was provided by an exceptionally large meeting of citizens at the State House yard on August 26. The meeting was called to consider appropriate defense measures for Philadelphia and its environs. McKean, although now eighty, was elected to chair the meeting; in that capacity he helped to pass resolutions organizing resistance to any British threat to the city. Typically, he provided realistic, hard-headed advice. "We have nothing to do with the past," he told the gathering, "we must only think of the present."[14]

By November 1815 he could tell John Adams that he had nothing to do with politics "nor much with anything else in this world." But the old warrior was not yet comatose. In a poignant afterthought, he wrote, "but I hear and listen."[15]

Although McKean's public political activities ended after the War of 1812, he spent a good deal of time reflecting on his country's past, and on his own role in American history. Part of his growing concern with the past—and his nostalgia—was attributable to his renewed correspondence with his old political crony, John Adams. The intimate and candid correspondence between the two, terminated in the 1790s when Americans were sharply divided over the French Revolution and its implications for America, was renewed at the instigation of Adams in June 1812. Adams had been prompted to renew their correspondence by the news of George Clinton's death. Adams had long meant to write Clinton, he told McKean, now Clinton had "slipped from [his] reach." Adams wished to write to

McKean "lest [he] should glide away, where there [was] no pen and ink."[16]

Adams' subsequent comments and questions stimulated McKean to record some of his most valuable observations on the Revolutionary years. He confirmed and elaborated upon Adams' remark that a minority in both Delaware and Pennsylvania had been ardent Whigs during the Revolution, he provided Adams with fascinating anecdotes of the Stamp Act Congress, and he discussed the role of the Society for the Propagation of the Gospel in Foreign Parts in Delaware's Revolutionary struggle. They reviewed the impact of the French Revolution on American politics and explained away their own response to it and its aftermath. They touched, very lightly, on the current political scene. Each preferred to reminisce, to conjure up past glories, past giants. They agreed it had been a glorious past. "We have been spectators of such wonderful scenes within the last fifty years of our lives as perhaps were never seen before in the same space of time," McKean wrote Adams in July 1815. "Tempests, convulsion, wars & revolutions have succeeded each other with such rapidity & violence as to cause the utmost astonishment of the human mind."[17]

When Adams asked McKean the question he had so frequently posed to others: who could—and would—write the history of the American Revolution? McKean was adamant that he would not. This, despite the fact that he had "been spoken to, and even solicited by a great many of [his] acquaintances to undertake the American Revolution, beginning at the year 1760 or before." Benjamin Rush had been one of those pressing him to write down his observations. McKean was convinced that a history of the Revolution would "sell well," but as he told Adams, during his public life he had had neither the "leisure or inclination to write a history" and at his present age it was "out of the question." He was not sure that an accurate, comprehensive history of the Revolution would ever be produced.[18]

Adams' letters and those of others interested in America's Declaration of Independence led McKean to review his own role in that pivotal event. As early as 1796 he had expressed to Alexander Dallas his disappointment with accounts of the crucial days of July 1776. It will be recalled that he tried to clarify for Dallas who the signers of the Declaration had been, and when it had been signed. In the fall of 1813 he wrote a long account of America's separation from Great Britain for Caesar A. Rodney, who was interested in his uncle's part in those tumultuous events. In January 1814 McKean produced still another long account, this for Adams. In each of these letters McKean fell into errors of chronology, confusing the events of the fourth and the second of July. Still, it is from McKean's letters that we learn a great many particulars concerning the personnel of the Congress, and their reactions to the vital question of America's independence. His accounts still represent a vital link in the historian's chain of inquiry into America's most historically significant act. To McKean's chagrin—and that of subsequent historians—he could not recall the specifics of his own signing of that historic document.[19]

McKean's infatuation with the past, stimulated largely by Adams' questions and comments, moved him in August 1814 to write a short "history" of his own life. Writing in the third person, he sought to leave a record of his public career. The brief work, less than thirteen pages, carried McKean's career to the early years of the Revolution. Increasingly concerned with the loss of earlier, republican values among his fellow citizens, upset lest his country's history be forgotten or perverted, and fearful that he would, like most men "pass away unobserved, unheeded & unknown," McKean hoped his "history" would prove useful to others. He saw himself as a man who had "waded through many difficulties... and constantly retained... the confidence of his fellow citizens for fifty years in public stations of government," even though "assailed by the ambition, envy & malice of powerful individuals, or the flattery, or hatred of different factions & parties." He was convinced that his life, like the lives of others who "emerge[d] out of the general obscurity and are distinguished for their talents & virtues," was "suitable for the delineation of the historic pencil." Whether his initial enthusiasm for the project waned, or whether his health, which was no longer good, proved inadequate to the task, is difficult to ascertain. Whatever the case, the product of his labors is disappointing to the historian interested in assessing his life.[20]

It is interesting to note what McKean considered important in his early career from the vantage point of his eightieth year.

Clearly he did not judge genealogical specifics important. Nor did he provide detail on his illustrious career before the Delaware bar beyond saying that his practice was successful from the first. No mention was made of his celebrated defense of John Clowes in 1770, or of any of his triumphs before Pennsylvania's Supreme Court. Not unexpectedly, he centered his efforts on describing the variety of public posts he held, and on his role in the coming of the Revolution. Even here his autobiographical sketch holds some surprises, however. It will be remembered how much space he gave to his participation in the Stamp Act Congress.[21] But what catches the reader's eye is the obvious warmth with which McKean remembered his political position in the Three Lower Counties. Compared to the political environment he encountered in Pennsylvania after 1774, with its increasing emphasis on mass politics, and its rapidly changing conception of representation, Delaware offered McKean permanence and an almost blind deference to his will.

It was this permanence of power and deference given him by New Castle constituents before and during the Revolution which still loomed large in McKean's mind in 1814. And not too surprisingly, considering his tumultuous Pennsylvania years. In a sense his Delaware career represented the old politics, Pennsylvania the new. It was in Pennsylvania that McKean encountered most vividly the Revolution with its stress on individualism, the constituent powers of the people, more tightly controlled representatives, and an expanding concept of freedom. McKean's career after 1776 proved that he could function, even prosper politically, in the new environment, but his autobiographical sketch suggests he much preferred the old.

By the spring of 1817 McKean was gravely ill. More than three years earlier he had confessed to Adams that his eyes had grown markedly dimmer, his hearing duller, and he suffered from "other symptoms of age." In August 1814 he had settled his estate, designating that he be buried in "the most convenient cemetary or burying grounds." His funeral was to "be decent but not expensive." He asked that his family wear no mourning for him "unless such as was practiced by the Congress during the war between the United

States and Great Britain," as he had survived the usual term of existance.[22]

Still, he clung tenaciously to life. And even as he lay dying public figures sought to discover from him new facts about his career and the history of the nation. In May Jared Ingersoll, on behalf of James Wilkinson, who was preparing a fourth volume of his memoirs, sought from McKean "a precise statement of the circumstances of his having voted for the Declaration of Independence, and his name being omitted in the signatures of that instrument." Ingersoll was hopeful that Joseph could obtain the information he desired "without putting [his father] to inconvenience in his present weak state."[23]

Though Joseph wrote to his own son in the first week in June to tell him that his grandfather "hangs by a tender thread," McKean was lucid enough by the sixteenth to dictate a letter to the *Freeman's Journal* in an effort to provide the details desired by Ingersoll and others. He admitted that he did not "have . . . sufficient health and leisure to reply severally to each application . . . . If I am correct in my statement, it may be of use to future historians," he wrote, "if not, my errors can be readily corrected." Unfortunately, his account did contain errors, many of the same errors which appeared in his earlier letters to Dallas and Caesar A. Rodney. Indeed, he included in this last letter a long excerpt from his 1796 Dallas letter. He reiterated that only Pennsylvania and Delaware had not supported independence on July 1, and persisted in believing that the crucial vote on separation had come on July 4, rather than the second, and that it was on the fourth that Dickinson and Morris had absented themselves. He naturally maintained that it was on the fourth, too, that Rodney arrived from Delaware to cast with McKean for independence. He shed no light on when he signed Jefferson's historic document. He placed his name on a printed copy of the Declaration in 1781 when he edited the laws of Pennsylvania and included the Declaration in that edition, he maintained, but when he signed the parchment copy remains a mystery. The letter to the *Freeman's Journal* was McKean's last public statement.[24] On June 24, just before three o'clock in the afternoon, Thomas McKean died at the age of eighty-three.[25]

Remarkably enough, one of the most perceptive assessments of McKean's career, then or since, came from the pen of William Duane. He was sensitive as few people were to the contradictions in McKean's character. He recognized that the same "considerable share of energy" which explained his personal sacrifices to public service for well over half a century also accounted for an aggressive ambition "not to be resisted in public stations," and the ambivalence of the public towards his record of service. He saw, too, that the "decision of character" which prompted McKean's rigor in "[giving] the laws dignity by enforcing them," and which led to his generously (and privately) "rescu[ing] from public vengeance, and the inexorable law" persons who had "mistaken the path of true honor in forsaking their country to serve a tyrant" during the war, also led him at times precipitously and cavalierly to dismiss those with whom he disagreed. But Duane rightfully perceived that in the end McKean's merits far outweighed his failings, that his commitment to the public good was a more dominant force in his life than his quest for personal aggrandizement. As chief justice he had "pursued as much as human passions can admit" a policy of "equal and exact justice." He had "spurned the royal favor offered to him, preferring to such honors, and venal rewards, the prouder honors of devotion to his country and liberty." For all the political furor which had swirled around him, his values had remained "strictly republican" and he had diligently sought to foster republican values by expanding the opportunities of free public education to all. To McKean's credit, he recognized most of his own public mistakes and personal frailties and "no man more sincerely deplored such aberations [sic] than himself."[26]

Though Duane acknowledged the legacy of McKean's family and heritage in shaping his personality and career, he failed to fully appreciate the impact on McKean of the Revolution.[27] McKean himself indicated how critical the Revolution had been to him when he spoke to John Adams of the "Tempests, convulsions, wars & revolutions [which had] succeeded each other with such rapidity & violence as to cause the utmost astonishment of the human mind." Even in the decades prior to independence he had felt the impact of imperial squabbles.

The Stamp Act had given him his first opportunity to act on an intercolonial level. Thereafter he profited privately and professionally from the understandable importance of lawyers in the growing resistance movement, and from the steadily increasing power and articulation of the Presbyterian interests for whom he was a spokesman. In the end, the Revolution brought him political power and influence far beyond what his social station promised, and beyond that with which his "social betters" were comfortable.

Revolutionary forces brought forth men seeking power and those who saw in the rapidly changing conditions economic and social opportunities denied them in former times. Encouraged, too, were men willing to employ the appeal of the new political rhetoric even as they chose not to accept its literal implications. Men appeared who were anxious to establish republican institutions and values without fully appreciating the capacity of both to change and develop along radical lines. Out of the Revolutionary struggle also came men of unusual devotion to the cause of independence and the creation of a more virtuous and responsible citizenry, men willing to pay the price, whether in the counsels of government or on the battlefield, to achieve those ends. McKean was all of these. Like most of his contemporaries, he was at times self-serving, and at times completely devoted to the public good. Indeed, the line dividing the two was blurred to the participants even as it often is to today's historian. And the difficulty in defining the difference did not end with victory over the British. As conditions changed, so did the political, social, and economic issues dividing men. And so did an individual's assessment of the proper equilibrium between personal aggrandizement and the needs of society. McKean's various political "shifts" between 1777 and 1808, like those of many of his contemporaries, can not be understood apart from these changing perceptions.

Which is not to deny that the desire for honors and offices, the "loaves and fishes," played a role in such political "adjustments." But it was in McKean's case, at least, a secondary consideration. He joined the Constitutionalists in July 1777, when the balance of power was unclear; most of the prominent and influential men were in opposition, the fate of the new constitution was unknown, and the penalties for collaborating with the Constitutionalists were ill-defined. He joined the Federalist cause in 1787 before the new constitution was completed and while the balance between Federalist and anti-Federalist was judged to be dead even. His later association with the inchoate Republican party came when national and city politics were still firmly in Federalist hands. From his defense of John Clowes in 1770 to his opposition to the radical Republicans during his last term as governor, he strove to create a virtuous, flexible, but orderly society which put a premium on talent, experience and dedication to service, and which adequately rewarded a man's private and public efforts. As a practical man he allied with anyone who shared those goals, or offered the best means of achieving them.

It is understandable that Duane should comment upon the contradictions in McKean's career and personality, for few men had viewed McKean from such different perspectives at such different times as did the editor of the *Aurora*. McKean *was* a complex man, much more so than historians have generally conceded. Those who have described Pennsylvania and Delaware during the early republic have legitimately identified McKean's ample ambition but they have at the same time ignored how often his colleagues, particularly his Delaware colleagues, pleaded with him to assume onerous posts, and lamented their fate when, on rare occasions, he could not or would not do so. Much has been made of his undemocratic prejudices and his blind partisanship—and in respect to certain phases of McKean's life, they are fitting assessments—but too little notice has been given to how frequently he headed important popular committees and chaired meetings at the pleasure of both political factions. He has been described as almost pathological in his insistence upon deference in his political and judicial capacities, but too few historians have noted how he himself approached his superiors uncomfortably, combining a sense of awe at times with an aggressive irascibility that inevitably produced abrupt and haughty exchanges, at other times with an exaggerated obsequiousness.

McKean has been labeled a "provincial," yet for eight years he served in the national Congress and participated in some of its most critical committees touching on matters of foreign affairs. He read widely and carefully in foreign affairs, based several of his most crucial political shifts on foreign policy considerations, and claimed as his closest friends after 1780 several members of the foreign diplomatic corps in Philadelphia. He was said to have been a coldly practical man—and indeed he was in his survey of life and his assessment of America's republican experiment—but he was also attracted to novels, for as he told John Adams, they "universally make vice detested and punished, and virtue triumphant, which is not the case of history and real life." He was impetuous and hot-tempered, yet in his most difficult and crucial tests as a judge—witness the Longchamps case—he remained cool and judicious. He railed against Quakers for their neutrality and pacifism, and against Tories for their treason—and occasionally berated and mistreated them in his courtroom—even as he worked assiduously to establish a policy of moderation in matters of loyalty. He complained bitterly when lawyers coming before him failed to exhibit the knowledge and skills he thought essential—even such successful practitioners as William Lewis—but he ardently defended the craft against all attacks, public and private.

The contradictions are endless. He could be petty one moment, magnanimous the next. He was scrupulously thorough in his handling of state and judicial matters, yet he permitted his own vast estates to go largely unimproved and poorly administered. Born on the frontier and spending a good part of his judicial career serving frontier communities, McKean was never comfortable with or sympathetic to the people or the life style of Pennsylvania's backcountry. He demanded much of others, but even more of himself. All this is to say that, to contend that Thomas McKean was a one-dimensional man, a vain, office-hungry bureaucrat, is not only to do an injustice to his personality, but to his entire career as well.

McKean's role in saving Benjamin Franklin from removal in 1779 and his efforts in favor of independence in 1776 were rare instances when he played a pivotal part in establishing policy or direction in the Congress. But, as Professor Henderson has shown, the real achievement of the Continental Congress was its stability and durability. Even in the face of his heavy judicial burdens, McKean was among the Congress' most diligent and consistent participants during its most crucial years.

He brought the same tenacity and energy to his court. And if in the final analysis he plotted no radical legal course, or failed to drastically alter the institutional framework of Pennsylvania's legal and judicial systems, he did establish an efficient and independent court. He worked assiduously for a republic of law, a nation where all men would face the same law, a law impervious to thoughtless men and transient passions. And, for all his intemperance and bluster and occasional harshness, he did mollify to a degree much of the hostility towards Tories in the critical years of 1778-79. Though he hated the British imperial policies and British soldiers and railed against those in America supporting them, he was also convinced that in the end it was only British law which stood between Pennsylvanians and social anarchy. Thus, even as he labored assiduously to throw off the mantle of British dominance, cursed the designs of the British ministry and periodically commented on the impracticability and narrowness of certain British laws and practices, he sought to recreate the pageantry, ritual and apparel of the British courts, and to maintain the efficacy of British laws and precedents in his own state. Even when the immediate threat of Revolutionary chaos lessened, he hesitated to undermine society by proposing, or encouraging others to favor, the replacement of British laws and precedents with indigenous standards and practices.

Continuous upheavals during McKean's lifetime inexorably pushed Americans into new patterns of conduct and thought. But if McKean seized upon the new opportunities to secure honors and offices, he, like so many others, remained chary of the new. Much has been made of his early democratic, radical stance and his later seemingly deep-rooted conservatism. And there is no denying that his conservatism grew as his perception of the needs and goals of America changed, though his shifts appear more precipitant if one ignores the fact that many of the values and practices he advocated in 1775-76 were designed more to frustrate the British ministry than to reform radically American society. But many of the difficulties he faced as governor stemmed from his refusal to accept the new, the growing intolerance of pluralism, the increasing furor over nepotism, the propensity of the press to criticize public figures, or the mounting belief that the people's representatives should accurately mirror their constituents' wishes rather than their own considered opinion. Nor did he ever forsake his belief that a deference was owed to men like himself who through their own efforts, education and experience, had established their right to govern. Much of what Pennsylvanians interpreted as personal egomania and intransigence on his part was nothing more than his old-fashioned view of the proper conduct of a ruler. Thus a final contradiction: one of the Revolution's "new men" clinging tenaciously to time-worn political institutions and values.

Above all else, McKean was a fighter. What many took to be a congenital contentiousness, a blind adherence to his own set of standards, McKean saw as a personal and legitimate commitment to republicanism, a willingness to do battle with those who did not understand republicanism, or who, for their own reasons, sought to subvert it. He confessed that he had made mistakes, had on occasion unfairly deprecated the efforts of sincere and honest men,[28] but he was convinced overall that his contentiousness had served well the cause of American republicanism, whiggism and patriotism. Looking back on it from 1817 Duane concluded that McKean was right—a courageous assessment coming from a man who had suffered much at the hands of McKean. It is a judgment that will stand the test of time.

ABBREVIATIONS USED IN NOTES AND BIBLIOGRAPHY

ADA	*Poulson's American Daily Advertiser* (Philadelphia)
APS	American Philosophical Society, Philadelphia
Aurora	*Aurora and General Advertiser* (Philadelphia)
CCHS	Chester County Historical Society, West Chester, Pa.
FG	*Federal Gazette* (Philadelphia)
FJ	*Freeman's Journal* (Philadelphia)
GA	*General Advertiser* (Philadelphia)
GUS	*Gazette of the United States* (Philadelphia)
HJ	*Journal of the House of Representatives of the Commonwealth of Pennsylvania, 1799-1809* (Lancaster and Harrisburg, 1800-1810)
HR	Hall of Records, Dover, Del.
HSD	Historical Society of Delaware, Wilmington, Del.
HSP	Historical Society of Pennsylvania, Philadelphia
IG	*Independent Gazetteer* (Philadelphia)
JAH	*Journal of American History*
JCC	Worthington C. Ford, ed., *Journals of the Continental Congress, 1774-1789,* 15 vols. (Washington, 1904-1909)
LC	Library of Congress, Washington, D.C.
LJ	*Lancaster Journal* (Lancaster, Pa.)
LMCC	Edmund C. Burnett, ed., *Letters of Members of the Continental Congress,* 4 vols. (Washington, 1921-1928)
NG	*National Gazette* (Philadelphia)
NYHS	New York Historical Society
NYJ	*New York Journal* (New York)
NYPL	New York Public Library, New York City

Pa. Arch.	Samuel Hazard, et al., *Pennsylvania Archives,* 9 series (Philadelphia and Harrisburg, 1852-1935)
Pa. Hist.	*Pennsylvania History*
PC	*Pennsylvania Chronicle* (Philadelphia)
PCC	*Papers of the Continental Congress* (Washington, National Archives Microfilm Project)
PCR	*Colonial Records of Pennsylvania,* 15 vols. (Harrisburg, 1852)
PEP	*Pennsylvania Evening Post* (Philadelphia)
PG	*Pennsylvania Gazette* (Philadelphia)
PJ	*Pennsylvania Journal* (Philadelphia)
PMHB	*Pennsylvania Magazine of History and Biography*
PP	*Pennsylvania Packet* (Philadelphia)
PRD	Division of Public Records, Harrisburg, Pa.
PSQ	*Political Science Quarterly*
SEC	Pennsylvania Supreme Executive Council
SJ	*Journal of the...Senate of the Commonwealth of Pennsylvania, 1799-1809* (Lancaster and Harrisburg, 1800-1810)
USG	*United States Gazette* (Philadelphia)
WMQ	*The William and Mary Quarterly*

Notes

Preface

1. For a discussion of "republicanism" and a survey of recent historiography relating to it, see Robert E. Shalhope, "Towards a Republican Synthesis: The Emergence of an Understanding of Republicanism in American Historiography," *WMQ* 24 (1972): 49-80. See also W. Paul Adams, "Republicanism in Political Rhetoric Before 1776," *PSQ* 88 (1970): 397-421, and John R. Howe, *From the Revolution Through the Age of Jackson: Innocence and Empire in the Young Republic* (Englewood Cliffs, N.J., 1973).

2. See esp. Gordon S. Wood, *The Creation of the American Republic, 1776-1787* (Chapel Hill, 1969); and Caroline Robbins, "European Republicanism in the Century and a Half Before 1776," in *The Development of a Revolutionary Mentality* (Washington, D.C., 1972), pp. 31-51.

3. Richard Buel, Jr., "Democracy and the American Revolution: A Frame of Reference," *WMQ* 21 (1964): 165-90.

4. Consult Bernard Bailyn, *The Origins of American Politics* (New York, 1968), and his *The Ideological Origins of the American Revolution* (Cambridge, Mass., 1967), esp. pp. 144-59. For a view that the extralegal committees spawned by British legislation were "protorepublican" associations and served to demonstrate the viability of republican institutions, see Pauline Maier, "The Beginnings of American Republicanism, 1765-1776," in *The Development of a Revolutionary Mentality* (Washington, D.C., 1972), pp. 99-113, and "A Freeman," *Advices from Philadelphia,* dated July 23, 1774 (New York, 1774).

5. Wood, *The Creation of the American Republic,* chapt. 3; and Cecelia Kenyon, "Republicanism and Radicalism in the American Revolution: An Old Fashioned Interpretation," *WMQ* 19 (1962): 153-82. J.H. Plumb has argued that it was the fascination with virtue and the growing sense of despair with corruption in government, that made republicanism so

so attractive to Englishmen as well as Americans by mid-eighteenth century. See *The Development of a Revolutionary Mentality,* pp. 57-61.

6. Bailyn, *Ideological Origins,* chapts. 5 and 6.

7. Eric Foner, "Tom Paine's Republic: Radical Ideology and Social Change," in Alfred F. Young, ed., *The American Revolution: Explorations in the History of American Radicalism* (DeKalb, 1976), p. 206; John R. Howe, "Republican Thought and the Political Violence of the 1790's," *The American Quarterly* 19 (1967): 147-65. In truth, one of the reasons behind American fears of republics prior to 1776 was an appreciation of the inherent instability and fragility of republican forms of government. Thus, even as they admired the personal values and characteristics traditionally associated with republics, Americans seriously questioned the ability of republics to survive. See Maier, "The Beginnings of American Republicanism," pp. 99-102; and Stephen Lucas, *Portents of Rebellion: Rhetoric and Revolution in Philadelphia, 1765-1776* (Philadelphia, 1976), pp. 215-16.

8. *Aurora,* Apr. 25, 1799.

1. Ambivalent Legacies

1. Certificate signed by William Till, Oct. 7, 1754, Hampton L. Carson Collection, HSP; J. Thomas Scharf, *History of Delaware, 1609-1888,* 2 vols. (Philadelphia, 1888), I: 567; *Laws of the Government of New Castle, Kent and Sussex Upon Delaware* (Philadelphia, 1752), 20, 39-48; Thomas McKean, Autobiographical Sketch, p. 1, McKean Papers, HSP ("Autobiography").

2. Statement of Jacob Van Bebber and others, Oct. 19, 1756, New Castle County, Deed Book S, Vol. 1, Bk. 1, HR; George Ross to the Secretary of the Society for the Propagation of the Gospel (SPG), June 15, 1736, in William S. Perry, ed., *Historical Collections Relating to the American Colonial Church,* 5 vols., (New York, 1878), 5:75. A New Castle pastor looking out at his nearly destitute Irish parishioners "sit[ting] now in pews formerly possessed by those who were reputed Gentlemen," marveled that he had "lived to see . . . . so great a change."

3. Will of Susanna McCain (0387), Register of Wills, Chester County Clerks Office, West Chester; Chester County Tax Lists, 1693-1740, 9A: 4, Collection of the Genealogical Society of Pennsylvania, HSP; Inventory of Susanna McCain's Estate, Feb. 19, 1731 (0387), Register of Wills Office. Among the goods and animals passed on to her sons were "5 horses and one mair and colt," "twenty sheep with lames," eight cows, five calves, twenty-two swine, over a hundred bushels of barley. "almost as much wheat," a variety of farm implements, and, despite Mrs. McKean's illiteracy, "three bibles" and "several other books." It is not clear whether she brought servants with her from Ireland, or whether she secured them following her arrival, but in any case, by 1731 there were three bound servants in the McKean household, two females and a young lad.

Susanna McKean's husband may have died during the voyage or shortly after their arrival in America, but records do not reveal even that he accompanied her. He was the youngest of three sons born to James McKean of Balleymore, County of Antrim, Ireland. James was the second of three sons of William of Argyleshire, Scotland, who had emigrated to Londonderry, Ireland, in the last quarter of the seventeenth century. Known to have accompanied Susanna McKean to New London were sons John Creighton, William and Thomas, daughters Barbara and Margaret, plus an unidentified James McKean; a nephew, William Waugh; and Margaret's husband, John Henderson. Henderson and Creighton worked farms near that of Susanna McKean but neither of them held formal titles to their land, merely the "rights" to the acreage. Creighton (or Craghton) listed in his will property worth £80, another £80 in "current money," and a servant. See Register of Wills Office (0411), West Chester.

4. James T. Lemon, *The Best Poor Man's Country: A Geographical Study of Early Southeastern Pennsylvania* (Baltimore, 1972), *passim.*

5. Petitions for Tavern Licenses 3: 131-33, CCHS; J. Smith Futhey, *History of Chester County* (Philadelphia, 1881), 418; Harry Wilson to Charles W. Heathcote, Jan. 1, 1939, Historical Society of York County. A description of "Chatham," William McKean's tavern, appears in *PJ*, July 14, 1779.

6. "Autobiography," 2. Letty and William McKean's children included Robert, born 1732; Thomas, born 1734; and two younger children, William and Dorothea. Particulars on the Finney family can be found in Gregory B. Keen, "The Descendants of Joran Kyn, the Founder of Upland," *PMHB* 4 (1880): 234-39.

7. P.F. Thompson, ed., "Narrative of Thomas McKean Thompson," *PMHB* 52 (1928): 112 ("Narrative"); Charles Biddle, *Autobiography of Charles Biddle* (Philadelphia, 1883), p. 283.

8. Isaac Taylor to James Logan, Aug. 10, 1726, Taylor Papers, HSP; Logan to Taylor, Aug. 5, 1726, quoted in Futhey, *Chester County*, pp. 193-94. Susanna McKean's estate inventory listed 400 acres.

The McKeans also joined a group of dissidents seeking to build a new church in New London even before permission was obtained for such a building from the local presbytery. See W.R. Huston, *Historical Sketch of the New London Presbyterian Church, Chester County, Pennsylvania* (Philadelphia, n.d.), pp. 5, 7, 15.

9. Petitions for Tavern Licenses 4: 94-95, CCHS; Futhey, *Chester County*, p. 417.

10. Chester County Orphan's Court Records 4: 40, 45-46, 51, 86; 5:2; Chester County Clerk's Office, West Chester; James Logan, 1745, Estates Files, Register of Wills Office; Chester County Administrative Book B, Vol. 2, p. 85; Gilbert Cope Collection, Collections of the Genealogical Society of Pennsylvania, HSP; *Pa. Arch.*, ser. 3, 1:247; "*Simon Hadley v. McKean,*" Feb., 1750; "*Joseph McDowell v. McKean,*" Nov., 1750, Chester County Appearance Docket, 1742-1751, pp. 303, 306; Execution

Files, Prothonotary Office, West Chester; Chester County Common Pleas Docket, 1749-1754, pp. 213, 257, 286, 315-16; J. Hill Martin, *The Bench and Bar of Philadelphia* (Philadelphia, 1883), p. 241.

11. Biddle, *Autobiography*, p. 283; "Narrative": 111-12; *Aurora*, June 25, 1817. Similar contradictions can be found in his private life. He proved to be a warm and affectionate father who doted on his children and, later, his many grandchildren. His correspondence with his second wife, Sarah Armitage McKean, suggests he looked upon her as a companion, and as an individual in her own right. The abruptness and aloofness so apparent to the public were nowhere to be found in his relationships with his family and relatives.

12. David Finney to George Washington, Mar. 25, 1789, George Washington Papers: Applications for Office (copy courtesy of Professor Harold B. Hancock). "Autobiography," p. 3; *PG*, Nov. 24, 1743; Thomas C. Pears, "Ten Little Irish Lads," *The University [of Delaware] News*, Alumni Issue (June 1943), p. 5.

13. Born in the parish of Lect, County of Donegal, Ireland, in 1705, and educated at the University of Edinburgh where he earned an M.A. degree in 1732, Alison came to America three years later. He was installed by the New Castle Presbytery at New London to replace Samuel Gelston recently suspended for "immoral conduct." Alison was an ardent critic of the New Side Presbyterians' Log Colleges, and told his friend Ezra Stiles of New Haven that there "was not a College, nor even a good grammar school in the our [middle] Provinces... when [he] arrived" in 1735. He therefore undertook the "desperate cause of promoting Learning" in part in the hopes of producing learned and disciplined clergymen for the Old Sides. See Thomas C. Pears, "Francis Alison: Colonial Educator," *Delaware Notes* 17 (1944): 12; Pears, "Francis Alison," *Journal of the Presbyterian Historical Society* 28 (1950): 213-25; Robert DuBois, *A Discourse on the Origin and History of the Presbyterian Church and Congregation of New London in Chester County, Pennsylvania* (Philadelphia, 1845), p. 15; Francis Alison to Ezta Stiles, Dec. 12, 1767, in Franklin B. Dexter, ed., *Extracts from the Itineraries and other Miscellanies of Ezra Stiles* (New Haven, 1916), pp. 431-32.

14. Douglas Sloan, *The Scottish Enlightenment and the American College Ideal* (New York, 1971), chapt. 3; Lawrence Cremin, *American Education: The Colonial Experience, 1607-1783* (New York, 1970), pp. 325-26, 505; William T. Read, *Life and Correspondence of George Read* (Philadelphia, 1870), p. 336; Hugh H. Brackenridge, *Modern Chivalry*, edited by Claude N. Newlin (New York, 1937), p. 516; *PJ* Apr. 19, 1780.

15. See Caroline Robbins, "When It Is that Colonies May Turn Independent," *WMQ* 2 (1954): 215-51.

16. Alison, Sermon, Jan. 1756, quoted in Thomas C. Pears, "Presbyterians and American Freedom," *Journal of the Presbyterian Historical Society* 29 (1951): 79; See also James L. McAllister, "Francis Alison and

1. Ambivalent Legacies 413

John Witherspoon: Political Philosophers and Revolutionaries," *Journal of Presbyterian History* 5 (Spring 1976): 33-60.

17. *PJ*, Apr. 19, 1780; Alison to Ezra Stiles, Oct. 22, 1743, in Pears, "Francis Alison: Colonial Educator," p. 21.

18. Ibid. His comments here were directed at Newark but held true also of New London.

19. Pears, "Ten Little Irish Lads," pp. 5, 9; Allen Johnson and Dumas Malone, eds., *Dictionary of American Biography*, 20 vols., (New York, 1928-37), 6: 236-37; 15: 422-25; 18: 480-82; 20: 298-300; William B. Sprague, *Annals of the American Pulpit*, 9 vols. (New York, 1857-1869), 3: 178-82, 199-205, 215-20.

20. Robert Parke to his sister, Dec., 1725, in Charles A. Hanna, *The Scotch-Irish*, 2 vols. (New York, 1902), 2: 64-65; Robert Detweiler, "Ben Franklin's Dirty Pettifoggers," American Bar Association, *Journal* (Oct. 1973): 1165.

21. *PJ*, Sept. 23, 1772; "Diary of James Allen, Esq., of Philadelphia, Counsellor at Law, 1770-1778," *PMHB* (1880): 181.

22. Jackson Turner Main, *The Social Structure of Revolutionary America* (Princeton, N.J., 1965), pp. 102, 202-5; Edward Burd to Sarah Burd, Nov. 17, 1767, in L.B. Walker, ed., *The Burd Papers: Selections from Letters Written by Edward Burd, 1763-1828* (Philadelphia, 1899), p. 17; *PG*, Sept. 22, 1773; "A Marylander," in *PC*, Apr. 23, 1770; William Bradford to James Madison, Aug. 12, 1773, in William T. Hutchinson and William M. Rachal, eds., *James Madison Papers*, 6 vols. to date (Chicago, 1962-), 1: 91.

23. John Finney, a justice of the New Castle court of common pleas since 1738, was by 1750 also a justice of the court of oyer and terminer. Finney's father-in-law, Robert French, besides being a well-to-do merchant and respected political figure, had been, at least according to family legend, "a distinguished English barrister." See Keen, "The Descendants of Joran Kyn," pp. 234-39; Futhey, *Chester County*, p. 416; David Finney to George Washington, Mar. 25, 1789, George Washington Papers.

24. "Narrative," pp. 59-61.

25. "Autobiography," p. 2. For the duties of the offices, see *Laws* (1752), pp. 247-48.

26. Chester County Common Pleas Dockets, 1749-1754, *passim*.

27. Ibid., pp. 165, 210, 333, 359; Execution Files and Judgment Warrants, Prothonotary Office, West Chester; Chester County Appearance Docket, 1752-1756; *PG*, Jan. 15, 1750/1751; Harry Wilson to Charles W. Heathcote, Jan. 1, 1939, Hist. Society of York County. William McKean's brother-in-law, John Henderson, also fell on hard times and died in debt. Consult his will, Register of Wills Office, West Chester.

It may be significant that Thomas McKean named none of his own eleven children after his father, although he did name children after his mother and sister and brother. The fact is Thomas McKean seldom mentioned his father publicly after 1757 and he assumed responsibilities for his younger brother and sister long before his father's death in 1769.

28. Consult chapters 11 and 12 of this work for an elaboration of this theme.

29. For a contemporary's comments and stories touching on McKean's size and courage, see David Paul Brown, *The Forum,* 2 vols. (Philadelphia, 1856), 1: 341-42. It is worth noting, too, that when Francis Hopkinson attacked McKean under the pseudonym, "Jerry Switch," in 1774, he wrote: "When I see him in the morning, strutting his pavement in red slippers, plaid gown and starched cap, I am struck with a certain awe and fear of him." McKean stood well over six feet tall, while military records for the year 1758 suggest most Delaware men were less than five feet seven inches tall. See Misc. Papers, 1655-1805: The Three Lower Counties, pp. 257-59, HSP; *PJ,* Apr. 20, 1774.

30. See for example, William Cobbett, *Porcupine's Works,* 12 vols. (London, 1801), 7: 333 (Cobbett, *Works); Anonymous [William Dickson], *The Quid Mirror* (Philadelphia, 1806), pp. 3-5; *IG,* Oct. 15, 1782.

2. Delaware Lawyer

1. New Castle County, Oyer and Terminer Docket, 1746-1792; Sussex County, Oyer and Terminer Docket, 1757-1778, HR. Because the pagination of these dockets is inconsistent and sometimes absent altogether, page references will not appear in the citations unless the docket contains pages numbered consecutively.

2. *Laws* (1752), p. 49; *"The King* v. *John Neill,"* undated [probably 1757], loose note in Sussex County, Oyer and Terminer Docket, 1787-1817, HR. For background on Neill, see Scharf, *Delaware,* 1: 527.

3. Scharf, *Delaware,* 1: 563; G.S. Rowe, "The Legal Career of Thomas McKean, 1750-1775," *Delaware History* 16 (1974): 24n.

4. Robert Jenny to the Secretary of the SPG, July 30, 1748, in Perry, *Historical Collections* 5: 95; Read, *Read,* p. 33; Leonard W. Labaree, ed., *The Papers of Benjamin Franklin,* 20 vols. to date (New Haven, 1959-), 2: 298, Benjamin Chew to Richard Peters, Aug. 7, 1754, Misc. Papers: The Three Lower Counties, HSP.

5. George Ross to the Secretary of the SPG, Nov. 7, 1732, in Perry, *Historical Collections* 5: 64; *Laws of New Castle, Kent and Sussex Upon Delaware,* 2 vols. (Wilmington, 1763), 1: 89; Timoleon [James Tilton], *The Biographical History of Dionysius, Tyrant of Delaware* (Philadelphia, 1788), pp. 8, 98. One Anglican minister disgustedly reported to his superiors that "An Harange was made here T'other day, from the bench of Justices, exposing for Idiots who pay any Regard to Priests or Churches."

6. "Narrative," p. 76. In his "Autobiography" (p. 3) McKean wrote that "In a year [I] was in considerable practice."

7. George Ross to the Secretary of the SPG, Mar. 27, 1750, quoted in John A. Munroe, *Federalist Delaware, 1774-1815* (New Brunswick, 1954), p. 23; Ross to the Secretary, Mar. 6, 1741, Oct. 8, 1761, in Perry,

2. Delaware Lawyer 415

Historical Collections 5: 86, 105; Read, *Read,* p. 13; Andrew Burnaby, *Travels Through the Middle Settlements in North America in the Year 1759-1760* (Ithaca, 1960), p. 87.

8. See, for example, Edward Burd to his sister, Oct. 5, 1765, in J. Bennett Nolan, ed., *Neddie Burd's Reading Letters* (Reading, Pa., 1927), pp. 24-25. A list of fees can be found in *Laws* (1752), 247-48.

9. "Autobiography," p. 3.

10. *PG,* Sept. 5, 12, 19, 26, 1754.

11. Ibid.; *PJ,* Oct. 10, 1754.

12. Thomas McKean Thompson ("Narrative," p. 111) gives some credence to McKean's claims, but see McKean to George Washington, Apr. 27, 1789, McKean Papers, HSP; and McKean to John Bayard, Mar. 6, 1789, Sprague Collection, 3: 81, HSP.

13. Thomas McKean Thompson notes McKean's naivete in his "Narrative," p. 111.

14. J.H. Martin, *Bench and Bar,* p. 241. Also consult various New Castle and Chester County dockets cited in this chapter.

15. Chester County Common Pleas Docket, 1749-1754, pp. 333, 416; Execution Files and Judgment Warrants for 1753, Prothonotary Office, West Chester.

16. Chester County Administrative Book B, vol. 2, p. 85; Ann Logan's Will (1400), Register of Wills Office, West Chester; see also *Pa. Arch.,* ser. 3, 1: 247.

17. Chester County Appearance Dockets, 1752-1756, pp. 307, 335-36, 362, 399, 416, 513; Common Pleas Docket, 1754-1760, pp. 17, 26; 1749-1754, p. 365; Appearance Docket, 1757-1762, p. 232.

18. Execution Warrants for Nov., 1756, Prothonotary Office, West Chester; "Autobiography," p. 3; Certificate of entrance into the bar, dated April 17, 1758, Hampton L. Carson Collection, HSP.

19. Four times a year, in February, May, August, and November, McKean with other members of the Delaware and neighboring bars followed the circuit from Lewes to Dover to New Castle. Many practitioners continued on to Chester whenever the opportunity arose, to seek work in those courts or moved on to the courts in New Jersey and Maryland once the Delaware courts adjourned. Attorneys pleading before the court of oyer and terminer and Supreme Court in Delaware repeated the circuit in April and October.

20. McKean was practicing as early as 1756, but his commission was not formalized until June 29, 1757, Hampton L. Carson Collection, HSP; "Autobiography," p. 3.

21. On October 19, 1756, Robert McKean solicited letters of recommendation from Jacob Van Bebber and others in New Castle preparatory to going to London for ordination as an Anglican priest. He returned in December 1757. See chapter 4.

22. Rowe, "Legal Career of Thomas McKean," p. 32; Read, *Read,* pp. 48-49; John M. Coleman, *Thomas McKean: Forgotten Leader of the Revolution* (Rockaway, N.J., 1976), p. 34. In 1787 a writer calling himself

"Observator" (*IG*, Sept. 23, 1787) wrote of McKean: "The pomposity of his Honor the doctor of Law, alias Judge Jeff, alias I myself, continues to distend his... turgid countenance..." by stringing various titles "to the end of his name, like the tail of a boy's kite." He went on to say that "I have lately met with one which his *modesty* has not suffered him to *publish* in the newspapers; for the present he circulates it only by labeling it in his law-books, probably with a view to heighten himself in the opinion of the gentlemen of that profession.... It is proper that my fellow-citizens should know they are to respect this personage in future, as a MEMBER OF THE INNER TEMPLE, LONDON."

23. "Autobiography," p. 3. Commissions and notes in the Hampton L. Carson Collection, HSP, indicate that McKean was elected by a majority in October 1757, and re-elected unanimously in October 1758.

24. *PJ*, Aug. 3, 1758, July 11, 1771; "*Connor* v. *Wilds*," H.F. Brown Collection, Box 25, folder 5, HSD; "Narrative," p. 111. See also Richard Peters from McKean, Aug. 5, 1760, Peters Papers, 5: 68, HSP.

25. *PJ*, Jan. 10, 1771.

26. Thomas Montgomery, *A History of the University of Pennsylvania, 1740-1770* (Philadelphia, 1900), pp. 347-48, 363; Richard Peters to William Smith, May 28, 1763, in *PMHB* 10 (1886): 350. Three years before, the College had rewarded Robert McKean with a similar degree. One year after Thomas McKean's honor from the College McKean was commissioned along with his cousin David Finney and others, as a trustee of the New Castle Common. Part of his duty in that capacity was to oversee the educational needs of the community insofar as the revenues from the common could be directed towards educational services. Besides being a vitally interested supporter of the Newark Academy, McKean was one of the earliest advocates and board members of Wilmington Academy, a school established in the 1760s, and later recharted as a public grammar school serving New Castle County. When a portion of the New Castle Common was set aside by the Assembly in 1772 for the construction of a schoolhouse, McKean was among those named as trustees.

27. Based on a survey of various dockets and available biographical materials, including local histories and collective biographies. For the printed materials see John A. Munroe, *Federalist Delaware,* bibliography.

28. New Castle Common Pleas Docket, May Term, 1768, HR. The origins and functions of these special counsels in Delaware are obscure. Conceivably such attorneys were employed by the court to act as an impartial third party. Such referees were widely used in Pennsylvania and elsewhere. Perhaps, too, they were instances where lay judges called in outstanding members of the bar to seek clarification of difficult legal points. Maryland's county judges frequently did so. But the court appeared normally to follow this procedure as a matter of course when a defendant was without means of procuring his own legal counsel and in several such instances pleas were entered. Whether fees were paid to the attorney assigned to act as a public defender—if that is what he was—is not clear, but it is an important consideration. It has a bearing on whether

2. Delaware Lawyer

McKean was the most fee-conscious, the most public-spirited, the most able, or merely the most available of New Castle's attorneys. Whatever the reason, he was regularly assigned this role more often than any other member of the Delaware bar.

29. Rowe, "The Legal Career of Thomas McKean," pp. 45-46; "A Citizen of Philadelphia," *PG*, Sept. 22, 1773. It is of course difficult to determine just what part of the estates of men like David Finney, George Read, McKean, John Dickinson, and John Vining, or their wealth, was accrued directly as a result of their law practices.

30. Consult the New Castle Common Pleas Docket (esp. "*Rachel Isaac* v. *Thomas Givens*" and "The John Eliot, Jr." case), May Term, 1768; Common Pleas Docket, 1769; New Castle County, Oyer and Terminer Docket, 1746-1792, HR.

31. Charles Biddle once wrote, "Judge [Richard] Peters says all great and strange people we have in Pennsylvania are from Chester County. He kept a list of all he knew; at the head of it was [Thomas] McKean." It was not clear whether McKean owed his place on Peters' list to being great, or strange. See Biddle, *Autobiography*, p. 274.

32. Supreme Court Docket: Appearances, 1764-1768, pp. 50-51, 55, 63, 74, 85, RG-33, Box 2, PRD; Brown, *The Forum* 2: 399; Alexander Graydon, *Memories of His Own Time, with Reminiscences of the Men and Events of the Revolution*, John S. Littell, ed., (Philadelphia, 1846), pp. 119-120. John Dickinson may not have been listed as a practitioner before the Pennsylvania Supreme Court (see Coleman, *Thomas McKean*, p. 33) but the dockets show clearly that he practiced there. See also Stanley K. Johannesen, "John Dickinson and the American Revolution," *Historical Reflections* 2 (1975): 34.

33. New Castle County Deed Book S, vol. I, pt. 1: 180-81, 258-60, 290-93, 302-6; Deed Book T, vol. 1: 192-93, 194-95; Deed Book U, vol. 1: 104-5, 343, 536; Deed Book W, vol. 1: 109, 113; Deed Book Y, vol. 1, pt. 2: 695-96; *Pa. Arch.*, ser. 3, 11: 360; 24: 72, 726; Chester County Deed Book Q (Sept. 18, 1769), p. 196; Chester County Appearance Docket, 1752-1756, p. 513.

34. Rowe, "The Legal Career of Thomas McKean," pp. 45-46; Pennsylvania Supreme Court Docket: Appearances, 1769-1771, p. 79; 1772-1774, pp. 81-82, RG-33, Box 2, PRD; Daniel Boorstin, ed., *Delaware Cases, 1792-1830*, 2 vols., (St. Paul, 1943), 1: lxi-ii, lxiv, 154-55; Zechariah Chafee, Jr., "Review" of Boorstin's *Delaware Cases, 1792-1830*, in *Harvard Law Review* 57 (1944): 402. So far as the records show, three Delawareans joined the bar in the 1750s, four in the 1760s, eight (including David Hall) in the 1770s, twenty-seven (including Kensey Johns, John Vining, Jr., and William Killen, Jr.) in the 1780s, and eighteen more (among them C.A. Rodney, Nicholas Van Dyke, Jr., and Thomas McKean Thompson) in the 1790s. David Hall and John Parke of course were students of McKean.

35. McKean family Bible, McKean Papers, HSP; *PJ*, Jan. 3, 1754; June 12, 1755. Their wedding day, July 21, was Mary Borden's nineteenth birthday.

36. *PG*, Jan. 12; June 1, 1769. The following paragraphs rely heavily upon my "*Rex* v. *John Clowes, Jr.,* and the Shape of Politics in Pre-Revolutionary Sussex County," *Delaware History* (Fall-Winter 1977), pp. 215-35.

37. *PJ*, June 21, 1770. The judges' reply to the remonstrance, dated November Sessions, 1768, can be found in the 1770 Sussex Court of Quarter Sessions, HR. Judges Jacob Kollock, Benjamin Burton, Wrixam Lewis, Levin Crapper, Thomas Robinson, Anderson Parker, Parker Robinson, and John Wiltbank, signed the reply. John Rodney did not.

38. *PJ*, June 21, 1770; George Read to his wife, May 5, 1770, in Read, *Read*, p. 39. Read referred to Clowes as the "Wilkes or McDougal [l] of Sussex."

39. The law McKean alluded to was "An Act against speaking in derogation of the courts," *Laws of the State of Delaware...in Two Volumes* (New Castle, 1797), 1: 120.

40. *PJ*, Nov. 22, 1770; June 21, 1770. See also my "*Rex* v. *John Clowes, Jr.* and the Shape of Politics in Pre-Revolutionary Sussex County," *Delaware History* (Fall-Winter 1977), pp. 215-35.

41. *PJ*, Nov. 12, 1770; Jan. 10, 1771.

3. Liberty Under Attack

1. Compare the names found in *Votes and Proceedings of the House of Representatives of the Government of the Counties of New-Castle, Kent and Sussex Upon Delaware...* October, 1762 (Wilmington, 1762), p. 3, with those found in *Governor's Register, 1674-1851: State of Delaware* (Wilmington, 1926), 1: 13-17.

2. *Votes and Proceedings of the House of Representatives of the Government of the Counties of New-Castle, Kent and Sussex Upon Delaware, 1765-1770* (Dover, 1931), pp. 7, 175, 111, 153, 227; Read, *Read*, p. 38.

3. Charles Inglis to the Secretary of the SPG, May 10, 1760, in Perry, *Historical Collections* 5: 102; D.F. Wolcott, "Ryves Holt, of Lewes, Delaware, 1696-1763," *Delaware History* 8 (1958-1959): 7n.

4. Munroe, *Federalist Delaware,* pp. 72-73; *PG*, Sept. 10, 1777; *PP*, Sept. 7, 1779.

5. "Autobiography," pp. 4-5; Scharf, *Delaware* 1: 144; *Votes and Proceedings* (1762), pp. 11, 13, 15, 23, 32.

6. *Votes and Proceedings* (1762); McKean and Read, eds., *Laws of the Government of New Castle, Kent and Sussex Upon Delaware*, 2 vols. (Wilmington, 1763).

7. *Votes and Proceedings* (Oct. 1767), pp. 111, 120, 122; (Oct. 1768), pp. 153, 156; *PG*, Oct. 8, 1767; Munroe, *Federalist Delaware*, p. 42. In June 1767 McKean made an extended trip to New York under a charge from the Assembly to "carefully peruse all the Orders of Governors, Minutes of Council, surveys, patents, wills, records, and original papers, dated before the Year 1682. He was to transcribe all materials "in any wise related to the Titles of Lands of this Government." For five months

3. Liberty Under Attack 419

he sought out the records, transcribed them, compared them to the originals whenever possible, had them properly authenticated, and eventually bound them in a single folio. McKean's absence kept him from being elected to the Assembly for the first time since 1762. He was replaced by Thomas Dunn, who later became his brother-in-law (Dunn married a sister of McKean's second wife). McKean was given £113 by the Assembly to cover his New York costs.

8. Labaree, *The Papers of Benjamin Franklin* 11: 431ff; McKean, John Caton, and Benjamin Burton to Henry Wilmot, Oct. 20, 1764, Papers Relating to the Lower Counties, pp. 282-83, HSP.

9. G.S. Rowe, "Thomas McKean and the Coming of the Revolution," *PMHB* 96 (1972): 13ff.

10. Hezekiah Niles, ed., *Principles and Acts of the Revolution* (Baltimore, 1822), pp. 159-61. The people of Kent and Sussex chose to merely protest "the present distressful circumstances... occasioned, in some measure [as we apprehend], by several acts of Parliament." By contrast, New Castle, more bellicose, explicitly condemned the Stamp Act as illegal and vehemently proclaimed the "colonies' right of exclusion from parliamentary taxation."

11. "Autobiography," p. 10; Commissions can be found in the Hampton L. Carson Coll., HSP.

12. Joseph Galloway to Benjamin Franklin, Nov. 23, 1764; Charles Thomson to Franklin, Dec. 18, 1764, in Labaree, *The Papers of Benjamin Franklin* 11:, 467-68, 524; various letters cited in James Hutson, *Pennsylvania Politics, The Movement for Royal Government and Its Consequences, 1746-1770* (Princeton, 1972), p. 208.

13. C. Rodney to T. Rodney, Oct. 20, 1765, in George H. Ryden, ed., *Letters to and from Caesar Rodney, 1756-1784* (Philadelphia, 1933), p. 25; McKean to John Adams, Aug. 20, 1813, in Adams, *Works* 10:61.

14. Edmund S. and Helen M. Morgan, *The Stamp Act Crisis: Prologue to Revolution* (New York, 1965), p. 140; McKean to John Adams, Aug. 20, 1813, in Adams, *Works* 10: 60; McKean to Timothy Pickering, Jan. 13, 1804, McKean Papers, HSP.

15. C. Rodney to T. Rodney, Oct. 20, 1765, in Ryden, *Letters*, p. 26.

16. Henry Steele Commager, ed., *Documents of American History*, 6th ed., (New York, 1958), pp. 57-58.

17. "Autobiography," pp. 7-8; McKean to John Adams, Aug. 20, 1813, in Adams, *Works* 10: 60-61.

18. *New York Mercury*, Dec. 16, 1765; Morgans, *Stamp Act Crisis*, p. 147.

19. "Autobiography," pp. 7-8, 9.

20. Merrill Jensen, *The Founding of a Nation: A History of the American Revolution, 1763-1776* (New York, 1968), chapt. 5.

21. *PG*, Jan. 16, 1766; repeated in the *New York Gazette*, Jan. 9, 1766.

22. Benjamin Franklin to John Ross, Feb. 14, 1765, Labaree, *The Papers of Benjamin Franklin* 12: 68; John C. Miller, *Origins of the American Revolution* (Stanford, 1969), pp. 110-11.

23. Munroe, *Federalist Delaware*, p. 3; McKean, Benjamin Burton and John Caton to Henry Wilmot, Oct. 20, 1764, Papers Relating to the Lower Counties, pp. 282-83, HSP.

24. Richard Peters, Jr., to Jasper Yeates, Nov. 26, 1765, Yeates Papers, HSP.

25. *Purdie's Virginia Gazette,* Mar. 7, 1766; Morgans, *Stamp Act Crisis,* p. 225; *New York Gazette,* Nov. 20, 1765, quoted in Miller, *Origins,* p. 145; Anton-Hermann Chroust, "Lawyers in New Jersey during the Stamp Act," *American Journal of Legal History* 6 (1962): 286-97. It appears to this writer that Professor Chroust makes more of New Jersey's "lawyers' strike" than is warranted by the facts.

26. Thomas McKean to George Washington, Apr. 27, 1789, Hampton L. Carson Coll., HSP; Roberdeau Buchanan, *Life of the Honorable Thomas McKean* (Lancaster, 1890), p. 17; "Autobiography," p. 10.

27. *PJ*, Feb. 27, 1766; *PG*, Feb. 6, 1766; Jensen, *Founding of a Nation,* pp. 140-43. McKean thought his was the only court open in all the colonies but he was clearly mistaken. Benjamin Wynkoop of Pennsylvania noted in spite of "spirited peices [sic] lately published to rouse the People to compel the officers to immediately open [the courts] only those in Northampton, Pennsylvania, are functioning." See Wynkoop to Charles Ridgely, Feb. 7, 1766, in Leon De Valinger and Virginia E. Shaw, eds., *A Calendar of Ridgely Family Letters, 1742-1899,* in the *Delaware State Archives,* 2 vols. (Dover, 1948), 1:85.

28. Thomas McKean to George Washington, Apr. 27, 1789, Hampton L. Carson Coll., HSP. When McKean and Caesar Rodney appeared in the Delaware Assembly in May 1766, their first formal opportunity to report on their New York activities, they received the Assembly's plaudits. The extent to which the Assemblymen interpreted the resolutions emanating from the Congress to deny or seriously qualify parliamentary sovereignty over the colonies, or the extent to which they anticipated the implications and consequences of their attack on parliamentary power undoubtedly differed from indidivudal to individual. It is clear that few—including McKean—were committed either to revolution or to independence at this point.

29. *Votes and Proceedings* (1931), pp. 10, 50, 53, 54-55, 59-60, 121. DeBerdt's quote is on p. 60.

30. "Autobiography," p. 11. Cobbett (*Works* 11:107) later commented that McKean had been unhappy with the Declaratory Act, as well.

31. *Votes and Proceedings* (1931), pp. 168-69; *PC,* Apr. 10, 1769. "When it is considered, that your Majesty has a Negative upon our Laws, and the sole Execution of them, that our Governor is only during your Royal Pleasure, and all Honors and Distinctions are derived from the Crown," the petition schrewdly argued, "it is humbly hoped that the Dependence of this Colony on the Mother Country will appear to be sufficiently secured."

32. *PC,* Nov. 7, 1768, Apr. 10, 1769; *PJ,* Aug. 31, 1769; Read, *Read,* pp. 80-82. A writer in the *PC* observed that in their petition to the Crown

4. Conspiracy

the Delaware Counties had "harmonized" with their sister colonies. The agreement to participate in the boycott was part of this "harmonizing" process.

33. *PJ*, Nov. 30, Dec. 21, 1769; Nov. 22, 1770; Jan. 10, 1771.

34. Ibid., Nov. 22, 1770. I am thankful to Professor Harold B. Hancock for sharing with me copies of the Assembly minutes for October and November, 1770, prior to their publication. See also my *"Rex v. John Clowes, Jr., and the Shape of Politics in Pre-Revolutionary Sussex County," Delaware History* (Fall-Winter 1977), pp. 215-35.

4. Conspiracy

1. In the Hampton L. Carson Collection, HSP, there is a document showing that following the death of James Walker, James Hamilton appointed McKean collector of customs. Hamilton signed the commission September 10, 1771. Another document, dated September 13, suggests that McKean took the oath of office witnessed by George Read. On October 1, 1771, Henry Judson addressed a letter to McKean, "collector of his Majesty's Customs at New Castle," making his appointment official. For the arrangement between McKean and Hopkinson, see Hopkinson to McKean, Jan. 16, 1772, HR, and the letter from Hopkinson to McKean, Feb. 28, 1772, quoted in Coleman, *Thomas McKean*, p. 95.

2. See Alfred S. Martin, "The King's Customs: Philadelphia, 1763-1774," *WMQ* 5 (1948): esp. pp. 201, 213.

3. The relationship between McKean and Hopkinson began to cool shortly after these developments but what role the office played in their growing estrangement cannot be documented with any precision. For an unsigned attack upon McKean by Hopkinson in the press, see, *PJ*, Apr. 20, 1774. But see evidence that Hopkinson was wrong in accusing and attacking McKean, in ibid., Apr. 27, 1774 (supplement). See also "Autobiography," p. 10; George Hastings, *The Life and Works of Francis Hopkinson* (Chicago, 1928), pp. 167-68.

4. McKean to John Adams, Nov. 15, 1813, in Adams, *Works* 10:82. For criticism of McKean holding the post typical of the charges made throughout the 1799 gubernatorial campaign, see Cobbett, *Works* 11: 100, 102. If one accepts Cobbett's view that McKean was bought off by the customs post, one could also reconcile McKean's sudden support in the Assembly among members of the court party and his election to the speakership. Unfortunately such cause and effect relationships were seldom that clear in Delaware politics. It should be kept in mind that both David and John Finney were important naval officers for the port of New Castle (John Finney resigned in 1773) and they may have played some part in McKean's obtaining the post.

5. *Votes and Proceedings...Oct., 1773* (Wilmington, 1774), pp. 8, 10, 16.

6. *PCR* 10: 82-83; Charles Ridgely to C. Rodney, Mar. 12, 1770, in Ryden, *Letters*, pp. 34-35.

7. *Votes and Proceedings* (1773), pp. 16, 18, 19. McKinly was

something of a political aberration in this respect. See my "The Travail of John McKinly, First President of Delaware," *Delaware History* 17 (Spring-Summer, 1976): esp. 26-27. See also Gordon S. Wood, "The Democratization of Mind in the American Revolution," *Leadership in the American Revolution* (Washington, D.C., 1974), pp. 73-74.

8. *Votes and Proceedings* (1773), pp. 20, 25, 28, 30.

9. Ibid., pp. 22, 23, 25, 26, 28, 30; *PJ*, Jan. 10, 1771. See also *PJ* (Sept. 26, 1771) for events in Sussex.

10. *PG*. June 29, 1774; *PJ*, June 22, 1774.

11. *PG*, July 6, 1774; *PP*, July 4, 1774; G. Read to C. Rodney, June 29, 1774, in Leon DeValinger, "Rodney Letters," *Delaware History* 1 (1946): 102.

12. *PP*, Aug. 1, 1774; Peter Force, ed., *Am. Arch.*, 9 vols. (Washington, 1837-1853), ser. 4, 1: 658, 660; C.H.B. Turner, ed., *Records of Sussex County* (Philadelphia, 1909), p. 326; C. Rodney to G. Read, July 21, 1774, in Ryden, *Letters*, p. 41-42; Philip Davidson, *Propaganda and the American Revolution* (Chapel Hill, 1941), p. 199. McKean made the principal speech, the only one recorded that day. Davidson, the historian of American propaganda during the Revolution, considered McKean's speech at Lewes "one of the really fine speeches of his career."

13. Instructions to Rodney, Read and McKean, Aug. 2, 1774, in ibid, pp. 43, 44-47.

14. *PG*, Mar. 17, 1773. For a eulogy of Mary McKean, see Francis Hopkinson, *Miscellaneous Essays* 3 (Philadelphia, 1792), pt. 2: 161-63. In 1773 McKean's children included Joseph Borden, Robert, Elizabeth, Letitia, Mary and Ann.

15. *PG*, Sept. 9, 1774; McKean family Bible, McKean Papers, HSP; Sophie Seldon Rogers Collection of the Genealogical Collection of Pennsylvania, under "Armitage," HSP.

16. *JCC* 1: 25. Most members arrived at the State House on September 5.

17. Lyman H. Butterfield, ed., "Adams Diary and Autobiography," *The Adams Papers*, 4 vols. (Cambridge, 1964), 2: 114-15, 126-27, 134, 151 (*Diary and Autobiography*); Graydon, *Memoirs*, p. 117. McKean's estimate was low. Thirty members practiced law at one time or another.

18. See H. James Henderson, *Party Politics in the Continental Congress* (New York, 1974), esp. Chapts. 1-4.

19. *PP*, Sept. 26, 1774; *JCC* 1: 75-80. The vote is on p. 80.

20. Ibid., pp. 43-48, 49-51; Burnett, *LMCC* 1: 51-59; Edmund C. Burnett, *The Continental Congress* (New York, rep. 1964), p. 50; John A. Neuenschwander, *The Middle Colonies and the American Revolution* (Port Washington, New York, 1973), p. 47. There is no record of the alignment but Neuenschwander says "it is safe to conclude that on this question...Delaware voted with the Galloway-Duane clique." Perhaps he is right; the final vote was 6-5. But almost every single action of McKean's that can be documented both in this Congress and the subsequent one, indicates that he would have supported Adams and the eastern

4. Conspiracy

bloc on as vital an issue as this. For an elaboration of McKean's congressional career, see my "'A Valuable Acquisition in Congress:' Thomas McKean, Delegate from Delaware to the Continental Congress, 1774-1783," *Pennsylvania History* 38 (1971): 225-64. Rodney and Read probably outvoted McKean in this instance. Professor Neuenschwander is one of the few historians to recognize divisions in the Delaware delegation prior to January 1776.

21. T. Rodney to C. Rodney, Sept. 11, 1774, in Ryden, *Letters,* p. 46; Force, *Am. Arch.,* ser. 4, 2: 27-28; 3:1072.

22. McKean to J. Adams, Nov. 15, 1813, in Adams, *Works* 10: 80-81; Perry, *Historical Collections* 2:293; Charles Ridgely of Sussex was one of the leading lay members of the Church "sensible, of the necessity of Bishops in America & desir[ing] it." Charles Inglis to the Secretary of the SPG, Dec. 1, 1766, in ibid., 5:124.

23. G.W. Lamb, comp., "Clergymen Licensed to the American Colonies by the Bishops of London, 1745-1781," *Historical Magazine of the Protestant Episcopalian Church* 30 (1944): 139; William Pierson, "Historical Narrative," Medical Society of New Jersey, *Transactions,* (New Brunswick, 1865-1868), vols. 99-102: 67; Fred Rogers, "Robert McKean, First President of the Medical Society of New Jersey," *Journal of the Medical Society of New Jersey* (1953), p. 432; McKean Family Bible, McKean Papers, HSP. It would appear that McKean's fear of the Anglican Church increased after 1770.

24. Leonard Trinterud, *The Forming of an American Tradition* (New York, 1949), p. 244; Charles Inglis, "State of the Anglo-American Church in 1776," *The Documentary History of New York* 5 vols., (New York, 1848), 3: 1050-51.

25. John Hughes to B. Franklin, Sept. 8, 1765, in Labaree, *The Papers of Benjamin Franklin* 12: 264; Munroe, *Federalist Delaware,* p. 48; Theodore Thayer, *The Growth of Democracy, 1740-1776* (Harrisburg, 1953), p. 126; Joseph Montgomery, *A Sermon Preached at Christiana Bridge and New Castle, July 20, 1775* (Philadelphia, 1775). See also [Isaac Hunt], *A Letter from a Gentleman in Transilvania* (Philadelphia, 1764), p. 7 where the author refers to the "Pis-Brute-tarians... A Sect whose Principles have ever been diametrically opposed to Monarchy." Alexander MacKraby wrote in 1768 (*PMHB* 11 [1887] : 285) that "the Presbyterians should not be allowed to grow too great.... They are all of republican principles." A full-scale study of Delaware Presbyterians needs to be undertaken. In all probability it will be discovered that Delaware Presbyterians watched events in Pennsylvania very closely and exhibited similar self-interest.

26. McKean to Mrs. McKean, Mar. 16, 1775, McKean Papers, HSP; *JCC* 2: 12; *PG,* Mar. 22, 1775; *PP,* Mar. 20, 1775; C. Rodney to T. Rodney, Mar. 20, 1775, in Hancock, "Letters to and from Caesar Rodney," p. 64.

27. Ryden, *Letters,* p. 55-56. McKinly and Robinson, both cautious men, helped to write the instructions.

28. "Narrative," p. 77; McKean to J. Dickinson, Sept. 14, 1801, Dickinson Papers, R.R. Logan Collection, Box 5, HSP.

5. The Birth of a Republic

1. James H. Peeling, "The Public Life of Thomas McKean, 1734-1817" (Unpublished doctoral dissertation, Univ. Of Chicago, 1929), p. 31; Adams, *Works* 1: 57; *JCC* 6: 1063-64, 1066-68.

2. *JCC* 3:321, 335-36; 4:40, 113, 259; Burnett, *LMCC* 1:211, 231, 275. McKean was clerk to the committee. The committee's report appeared in the *PG*, Feb. 7, 1776.

3. McKean to G. Read, Jan. 19, 1776, in Burnett, *LMCC* 1:319.

4. *JCC* 3:259, 268-69, 276, 280-81, 291, 314-15, 480-82, 490-504; Burnett, *LMCC* 1:218-20; Neuenschwander, *The Middle Colonies,* pp. 134-35; *Diary and Autobiography,* 2:204, 206-7.

5. The best account of the factions within Congress is H. James Henderson's *Party Politics in the Continental Congress,* esp. chapter 2, "Congressional Factions and the Decision to Revolt."

6. Franklin B. Dexter, ed., *The Literary Diary of Ezra Stiles,* 2 vols. (New York, 1901), 1:635. The individual referred to was William Goddard, longtime editor of the *PJ*.

7. *Diary and Autobiography* 2: 178.

8. List of those over eighteen willing to bear arms in the Middle Ward of Philadelphia, dated May 1, 1775, and the roll of Little's Company, dated April 1775, in the Clymer MSS, HSP; William Duane, ed., *Passages from the Diary of Christopher Marshall, 1774-1777* (Philadelphia, 1839), pp. 24, 32.

9. McKean and C. Rodney to George Washington, June 29, 1775, in Ryden, *Letters,* p. 62; *PG,* Nov. 8, 1775; Burnett, *LMCC,* 3: 331, 336. The letter relating to apprentices and debtors went to a committee consisting of Thomas Paine, Richard Smith and McKean on Jan. 27, 1776. McKean moved to reconsider the committee's findings on Jan. 31.

10. Marshall, *Diary,* pp. 37, 42, 55-56; *Pa. Arch.,* ser. 8, 8:7327-30; *PG,* , Aug. 23, Nov. 1, 8, 1775. See also Richard A. Ryerson, "Leadership in Crisis: The Radical Committees of Philadelphia and the Coming of the Revolution in Pennsylvania, 1765-1776: A Study in the Revolutionary Process" (Unpublished doctoral dissertation, Johns Hopkins Univ., 1972).

11. *Pa. Arch.,* ser. 8, 8: 7334-36; McKean to J. Adams, Sept. 28, 1813, in Adams, *Works* 10:74. For a denial that the Quakers in fact controlled the politics of the Province, see David Freeman Hawke, *In the Midst of a Revolution* (Philadelphia, 1961), Chapt. 8. On the morning of the day that McKean joined Clymer to present the remonstrance to the Assembly, Mrs. McKean gave birth to a son. The boy lived only a few hours and was buried unnamed.

12. David Hawke, *In the Midst of a Revolution*, p. 18.

13. Edward Burd to James Burd, Mar. 15, 1776, in L.B. Walker, ed., *The Burd Papers: Selections from Letters Written by Edward Burd, 1763-1828* (Philadelphia, 1899), p. 82; Allen, "Diary," 186-87; Joseph Shippen to Edward Shippen, Feb. 29, 1776, Shippen Papers, 12:123, HSP.

5. *The Birth of a Republic* 425

14. McKean to J. Adams, Sept. 28, 1813, in Adams, *Works* 10:74. Also ibid., p. 87. McKean was in the mainstream of Philadelphia whiggism in this respect. Professor Stephen Lucas has correctly observed, "Whig leaders solicited only the support of ordinary Philadelphians, not their active participation." Lucas, *Portents of Rebellion: Rhetoric and Revolution in Philadelphia, 1765-1776* (Philadelphia, 1976), p. 260.

15. Marshall, *Diary*, pp. 77-78. See also Lucas, *Portents of Rebellion*, pp. 231, 235.

16. *JCC* 4: 343, 357-58.

17. David Hawke, *In the Midst of a Revolution*, p. 124, claims that North Carolina, New Jersey, Delaware and New York voted nay, and that Pennsylvania and Maryland abstained. Neuenschwander, *The Middle Colonies*, p. 194, agrees.

18. Burnett, *LMCC* 1: 445-46, 454.

19. *Diary and Autobiography* 2: 239; C. Rodney to T. Rodney, May 18, 1776, in Ryden, *Letters*, p. 81. Two of Delaware's representatives had to vote no if Hawke and Neuenschwander are correct on the vote. McKean's speech and activity on the fifteenth rule him out as a no vote. Rodney's comments came three days after the event and he had time to reassess his position.

20. Allen, "Diary," pp. 186-87; Jasper Yeates to James Burd, Mar. 7, 1776, Shippen Papers 7: 157, HSP.

21. Marshall, *Diary*, pp. 80, 82; *PG*, May 22, 1776; *PCR* 10:548.

22. Neuenschwander, *The Middle Colonies*, pp. 141-43; *PG*, May 22, 29, 1776.

23. *PG*, May 29, 1776; *PP*, May 27, 1776; *PJ*, Nov. 22, 1775; *Pa. Arch.*, Ser. 1, 1:94-95.

24. *PG*, June 5, 1776; Force, *Am. Arch.*, Ser.4, 5:689; Marshall, *Diary*, p. 85. McKean had continued to argue cases in Delaware's courts whenever time permitted and in the courts of Philadelphia county, especially the Supreme Court. Though younger attorneys like Miers Fisher, Nicholas Waln, Jasper Yeates, Joseph Reed and Edward Burd and more established practitioners such as Joseph Galloway continued to carry heavier dockets there than McKean, his business remained impressive throughout 1774 and 1775.

Of particular interest to McKean and David Finney during these months was their appeal of a case begun some sixteen years before. Finney had retained McKean in 1758 to argue a case involving family lands, part of what he considered his eventual inheritance. David French who, as we have seen, was the oldest son of Robert French, and a man who had studied law in England, died without issue and his substantial estate had fallen, by virtue of an order directed by the Delaware Supreme Court to the court of common pleas in Kent, to the family of David's sister, Ann French Ridgely, wife of Nicholas Ridgely. This, despite the desire on the part of most members of the French family, including Robert French, that the lands go instead to Elizabeth French Finney, wife of Dr. John Finney, and mother of David.

For years David Finney, through McKean his counsel, pressed to have the Delaware Supreme Court reverse its earlier order to the court of common pleas, arguing on the one hand that the superior court's ruling was based on a colonial law which had not received royal approval and which was contrary to common law, and on the other that the legal and equity powers of the Court permitted it to reverse itself in this matter without intervention of the legislature. Unfortunately for McKean and his client, John Vining, a step-son of Nicholas Ridgely, now held title to some of the lands in question. He not only held the prothonotaryship of the court of common pleas in Kent but he was currently chief justice of the Supreme Court, having succeeded the late Ryves Holt. If this were not disadvantage enough, Charles Ridgely, Nicholas' son, who now held most of the lands under dispute, had been president of the common pleas at the time of the original ruling. It was the contention of Finney and McKean that because of the vested interests of Vining and Ridgely, "the current of favor ran violently against the Plaintiffs in error in both courts." They appealed their case to the King in Council.

A month before they met in March 1774 to review the case, McKean and Finney had written to Benjamin Franklin in England, hopeful that he might use his considerable influence in their behalf. They had apparently discussed the details in depth with John Dickinson, for they pointed out to Franklin that Dickinson concurred wholeheartedly that their case was well founded in law and equity, and believed that the Supreme Court had both equity and legal powers to reverse itself. They had sent along a bill of exchange for £50 with the promise of more, Dickinson's assessment, as well as McKean's discussion of *Winthrop* v. *Lechmere* which he felt to be an excellent precedent for his own actions in *Finney* v. *Byrne*. In March 1774 McKean and Finney were still optimistic. Neither man could know that the case would never be resolved in England, or that theirs would be the very last appeal of record from the American colonies to the Privy Council. Joseph H. Smith, *Appeals to the Privy Council from the American Plantations* (New York, 1950), p. 653; David Finney to Benj. Franklin, Feb. 27, 1774; July 10, 1781; *Finney et al.*, v. *James Byrne;* opinion of Richard Jackson, Franklin Papers, APS 4: folio 10; 21: folio 76; 53: folio 13; 76: folio 14.

25. *PEP*, June 14, 1776.

26. Allen, "Diary," pp.185, 191; Hawke, *In the Midst of a Revolution,* p. 18.

27. Marshall, *Diary,* p. 67; *PP,* June 17, 1776.

28. *PCR* 10:548. The earliest reference to McKean as a colonel appears in April, but his battalion was formed either in November or December, 1775. See *PG,* Nov. 8, 1775; Jan. 10, 1776.

29. *PP,* June 17, 1776; *PMHB* 22 (1899): 469; Benjamin Rush to his wife, May 29, 1776, in Lyman H. Butterfield, ed., *The Letters of Benjamin Rush,* 2 vols. (Princeton, 1951), 1:99. Rush originally wrote in his own name, then crossed it out and wrote in McKean's instead. The by-stander

referred to here was Dr. James Clitheral of South Carolina, who was visiting Philadelphia and left an account of his visit.

30. *JCC* 5:436.

31. C. Rodney to John Haslet, May 17, 1776; C. Rodney to T. Rodney, May 22, 1776; T. Rodney to C. Rodney, May 26, 1776, in Ryden, *Letters,* pp. 79-81, 82-83, 84. Historicans have not concentrated on the popular movement in the Three Lower Counties but Rodney's remarks leave little doubt that he felt popular sentiment would force a convention if the Assembly did not act.

32. J. Adams to Samuel Chase, June 14, 1776, in Burnett, *LMCC* 1: 490.

33. Marshall, *Diary,* pp. 88-89; *PP,* June 17, 1776; *Pa. Arch.,* ser. 2, 3: 557, 559.

34. David Hawke (*In the Midst of a Revolution,* p. 172) makes the claim that Benjamin Franklin was the conference's first choice but his ill health prevented his election. For a more persuasive argument that McKean had earned the chairmanship, see Ryerson, "Leadership in Crisis," 545ff.

35. Ibid.

36. The ebb and flow of enthusiasm, at least among those on the leadership level, can best be followed in Ryerson, "Leadership in Crisis."

37. *Pa. Arch.,* ser. 2, 3:559-63, 575. McKean's later efforts at writing the Delaware constitution (September 1776) and his insistence there upon a strict religious oath suggests that he was among the Pennsylvanians in June who pressed for a similar oath. The question of the oath caused divisions among those attending the subsequent constitutional convention in Philadelphia.

38. Ibid., David Hawke (*In the Midst of a Revolution,* pp. 177-78) has remarked on McKean's astigmatism in not anticipating the ultimate implications of the work of the conference, and, to a degree, that is a valid assessment. But McKean's political myopia appears more obvious from hindsight. The conference accomplished at least two things which were utmost in McKean's mind in late June 1776: it threw its considerable weight behind the move toward independence, and it undercut the Pennsylvania Assembly which still loomed as a psychological if not a political barrier to Pennsylvania's acceptance of independence. But McKean's naivete—or assumptions—regarding the conference takes on a different color when his role in the later creation of a new Delaware constitution is assessed. It is clear that he was primarily interested in insuring the independence of America and, to that end, in replacing all office holders opposed to that goal. Nowhere prior to 1777 does he talk about a social revolution. When he did talk about "new men" he talked of men "distinguished for wisdom, integrity and a firm attachment to the liberties of the province as well as to the liberties of the United Colonies in general."

39. The best recreation of events in Congress on July 1 is David Hawke's, *A Transaction of Free Men: The Birth and Course of the Declaration of Independence* (New York, 1964).

40. McKean later became involved in several controversies arising from his own actions and those of Congress in July 1776. The first concerned when—and if—he sent for Caesar Rodney to come to Philadelphia to add his vote in favor of the independence of America. There is only McKean's statement that he was responsible for sending a servant at his own expense to alert Rodney of the need of his vote in Congress. Confusion also arose over when Rodney arrived to cast his vote. In letters to Alexander James Dallas, Caesar A. Rodney, John Adams, and the *FJ*, McKean correctly described the work of the Committee of the Whole on July 1 (at least insofar as discussing the question of independence and taking a straw-vote upon it), but neglected to note the critical vote for independence on the second. He constantly argued that the vote for independence occurred on the fourth, and that it was on the fourth that Rodney arrived. Rodney of course arrived on the second and the official vote on the question of America's separation from Britain took place on that day. McKean may well have sent for Rodney before the straw-vote on the first. McKean, like the other delegates in the City, knew that the vote would take place on that day and he did not have to hear the vote to know the fate of his own delegation. Finally, it should be noted that while McKean's memory regarding the role of the Pennsylvania and Delaware delegations on the critical question of independence was remarkably good, he did not remember South Carolina's negative or the failure of the New York delegation to vote. See McKean to Alexander James Dallas, Sept. 26, 1796, McKean Papers, HSP; McKean to C.A. Rodney, Sept. 22, 1813, McKean Papers; McKean to J. Adams, Jan., 1814, in Adams, *Works* 10: 87-89; public letter from McKean (written less than two weeks before his death), *Port Folio,* 4th (5th) ser., 4 (Sept. 1817): 246-48 (reprinted from the *FJ*.).

41. *JCC* 5: 507-18.

42. See the perceptive treatment of John Dickinson and his world, in Stanley K. Johannesen, "John Dickinson and the American Revolution," *Historical Reflections* 2 (1975): 29-49. George Read enjoyed much the same attitude towards life and his position in the Delaware community.

43. A careful examination of McKean's private and public statements between 1774 and 1776 shows clearly that he always insisted that, in the final analysis, responsible, virtuous leaders make the critical decisions for the revolutionary movement. Obviously he was willing to let more and more people participate in choosing those virtuous, responsible delegates during the crucial months of 1776, but that he advocated a leveling democracy is nowhere evident. For a general discussion of the whig attitude toward popular democracy, and for their concerns about republicanism generally, consult Lucas, *Portents of Rebellion,* pp. 189-90, 215-16, 260.

44. Consult letters cited in note 40 above.

6. The Shape of Republicanism

1. *JCC* 5: 519-20; *PP,* July 8, 1776; *PG,* July 10, 1776. McKean has played a conspicuous role in the historical controversy surrounding just

6. The Shape of Republicanism 429

when the Declaration of Independence was signed. That the signatures were added on July 4 received credence from such figures as Adams, Franklin and Jefferson in the years following that event. McKean, who had added to that mistaken belief in his letter to Dallas in 1796, was later the first to seriously challenge those insisting the signing took place on the fourth. In his letter to Caesar A. Rodney in 1813 he observed that "though in the printed journal of Congress for 1776, vol. 2, it would appear that the Declaration of Independence was signed on the 4th of July by the members, whose names are there inserted... the fact is not so for no person signed it on that day nor for many days after." In a much more publicized letter, one to John Adams on January 7, 1814, McKean reiterated his conviction that the document had not in fact been signed on the fourth. Adams sent the communication—he called it a curiosity—to Mercy Otis Warren, observing that "McKean is mistaken in a day or two.... The final vote of independence, after the last debate, was passed on the 2d or 3d of July, and the Declaration prepared and signed on the 4th." "What are we to think of history," he moaned, "when in less than forty years such diversities appear in the memories of living persons who were eyewitnesses."

Although guilty of numerous errors in his own account of the events following the first of July, McKean was vindicated in his suspicion that no formal signing took place on July 4, when, in 1884, Mellen Chamberlain unraveled much of the confusion surrounding the event. Unfortunately, not even Chamberlain could determine just when McKean had signed the document. It seems clear that McKean did not sign it prior to August 26, 1776, and that he had abundant opportunity to sign it between August 26, 1776, and 1781. McKean himself provided contradictory stories. He told Adams that he had signed the document upon his return to Philadelphia from Perth Amboy. In his last letter (June 16, 1817) he claimed to have signed a public edition of the document in 1781 while he was preparing an edition of the laws of Pennsylvania, but it is unlikely that we will ever know when he signed the parchment copy.

The fact that the signing did not take place until a lapse of time had occurred has convinced Daniel Boorstin, based on a reading of McKean's 1813 letter to C.A. Rodney, that "the purpose of the declaration as finally signed was to provide a kind of public loyalty-oath, a pledge of allegiance to the course already pursued." McKean had indeed remembered that "no persons should have a seat in Congress during that session until he should have signed the declaration, in order (as I have been given to understand) to prevent traitors or spies from worming themselves amongst us." See the following: McKean to J. Adams, Jan. 7, 1814, McKean Papers; McKean to C.A. Rodney, Sept. 22, 1813, McKean Papers; *Port Folio* "4th" [5th] ser., 4 (September, 1817): 246-48; J. Adams to Abigail Adams, July 3, 1776; J. Adams to Mercy Otis Warren, in Adams, *Works* 9:420; 10:87; Daniel Boorstin, *The Americans: The National Experience* (New York, 1965), pp. 378-79; Charles Warren, "Fourth of July Myths," *WMQ*, 2 (1945): 238-72; Mellen Chamberlain,

"Authentication of the Declaration of Independence," Massachusetts Historical Society, *Proceedings,* ser. 2 (Boston, 1885), 1: 273-98; Julian Boyd, ed., *The Papers of Thomas Jefferson,* 19 vols. to date, (Princeton, 1950-), 1: 299-308; *JCC* 5: 510-15; Peeling, "Thomas McKean," pp. 49-57; Roberdeau Buchanan, *The Life of the Honorable Thomas McKean,* 31ff.

2. *JCC* 5: 519-20; *PCR* 10: 639, 648; *PG,* July 10, 1776; McKean to Mrs. McKean, July 26, 1776, McKean Papers, HSP.

3. McKean to Mrs. McKean, Aug. 1 and 7, 1776.

4. Cobbett, *Works* 11: 46-47; McKean to Joseph Reed, Aug. 29, 1780, in William B. Reed, *Life and Correspondence of Joseph Reed,* 2 vols., (Philadelphia, 1847) 1: 250.

5. *Proceedings of the Convention of the Delaware State, Held at New Castle... Aug., 1776* (Wilmington, 1776), p. 4; McKean to the Council of Safety, Nov. 30, 1776, Gratz Coll., case 1, box 20, HSP; McKean to Mrs. McKean, Aug. 7, 1776; *In Convention for the State of Pennsylvania, Saturday, Aug. 10, 1776* (Philadelphia, 1776), p. 6; C. Rodney to T. Rodney, Aug. 3, 14, 21, 28, in Ryden, *Letters,* pp. 100, 103, 104, 105; *PG,* July 31, 1776.

6. C. Rodney to T. Rodney, Aug. 28, 1776, in Ryden, *Letters,* p. 105.

7. McKean to C.A. Rodney, Sept. 22, 1813, McKean Papers, HSP.

8. *Proceedings of the Convention of Delaware,* pp. 5-6; G. Read to C. Rodney, Aug. 30, 1776, in Ryden, *Letters,* p. 108. See also C. Rodney to J. Haslet, Sept. 12, 1776, in ibid., p. 116.

9. McKean to Mrs. McKean, Aug. 31, Sept. 2, 1776; *PG,* Sept. 11, 1776.

10. *Proceedings of the Convention of Delaware,* pp. 8-10; C. Rodney to T. Rodney, Sept. 11, 1776, in Ryden, *Letters,* p. 114.

11. *Proceedings of the Convention of Delaware,* pp. 11, 20; Timoleon [James Tilton], *The Biographical History of Dionysius, Tyrant of Delaware* (Philadelphia, 1788), pp. 6, 25-26.

12. G. Read to C. Rodney, Sept. 17, 1766; McKean to C. Rodney, Sept. 19, 1776, in Ryden, *Letters,* pp. 119, 123.

13. Ibid. The constitution is found in *Proceedings of the Convention of Delaware,* pp. 21-28, and *PG,* Oct. 2, 1776.

14. McKean to C. Rodney, Sept. 19, 1776, in Ryden, *Letters,* p. 123; J. Haslet to C. Rodney, Nov. 12, 1776, quoted in Munroe, *Federalist Delaware,* p. 84n; T. Rodney, "Notes on the Delaware Constitution" (1791?), HSD.

15. McKean to C. Rodney, Sept. 19, 1776, in Ryden, *Letters,* p. 123; *Proceedings of the Convention of Delaware,* pp. 20-21, 28.

16. McKean to Mrs. McKean, Oct. 31, 1776; McKean to G. Read, Feb. 2, 1778, in Read, *Read,* p. 298.

17. *PEP,* Sept. 10, 1776; *PG,* Sept. 18, 1776.

18. Despite their earlier differences over the course of the Revolution and the vote on independence, Dickinson apparently harbored no ill will towards McKean. In August Dickinson had written bitterly of the

Pennsylvania Presbyterians who had deserted him in the months prior to America's declaration of independence. He commented, too, on "The Jealousy of Some Gentlemen of Merit . . . desirous of drawing to themselves all the Weight that could be derived from that [religious] Body" and he named Joseph Reed and Benjamin Rush in particular. He did not mention McKean. See Dickinson to ?, Aug. 25, 1776, Dickinson Papers, Logan Coll., HSP. See also McKean to Thomas Sergeant, May 22, 1814, Soc. Coll., HSP.

19. Marshall, *Diary,* p. 110; *PP,* Oct. 22, 1776.

20. Marshall, *Diary,* p. 111.

21. *PP,* Oct. 22, 1776. It is doubtful that McKean concerned himself with the oaths; both before and after this meeting he pressed for stringent oaths.

22. *PP,* Dec. 18, 1776; *Pa. Arch.,* ser. 1, 5: 73-75, 94-95, 106.

23. *Pa. Arch.,* ser. 1, 5: 73-75, 94-95, 106.

24. This, despite the fact that McKean was still apparently working to have the new constitution reconsidered. It was later reported that he not only "bellow[ed] against it in Philadelphia [but] he and some others rode through some of the interior counties for the purpose of making converts to his opinion." *GUS,* Aug. 16, 28, 1799.

25. Matthius Slough to Jasper Yeates, Mar. 28, 1777, Prov. Del. Coll. 1: 57, HSP; Yeates to Colonel James Burd, Mar. 29, 1777, in Thomas Balch, ed., *Letters and Papers Relating Chiefly to the Provincial History of Pennsylvania* (Philadelphia, 1855), pp. 258-59.

26. *PG,* Mar. 26, 1777; Council to Joseph Reed, July 23, 1777, in *Pa. Arch.,* ser. 1, 10: 157; Joseph Reed to Council, July 23, 1777, in Reed, *Reed* 1: 301; John Roche, *Life of Joseph Reed* (New York, 1957), pp. 116-17. Both James Wilson and John Cadwalader urged Reed not to take the post and both hinted of the dire consequences if he should. See also Thomas R. Meehan, "The Pennsylvania Supreme Court in the Laws and the Commonwealth, 1776-1790" (Unpublished doctoral dissertation, University of Wisconsin, 1960), pp. 79-82.

27. McKean to Mrs. McKean, Dec. 8, 1776; *Minutes of the Council of the Delaware State, 1776-1792* (Wilmington, 1886), pp. 50, 59-60, 66, 77, 83; subscription list found in the Brown Coll., Box 25, folder 5, HSD. It is true that those who had turned him out a few months before still held reservations concerning his forwardness and preferred the moderation of a Dickinson and Evans. Yet it was clear to all by February few men of more moderate views than McKean would attend. Those who opposed returning McKean gained little by turning to Van Dyke and Sykes. Sykes was no more interested in defending his state's interests in Philadelphia than had been Evans or Dickinson in these months. His reluctance stemmed from a sense of inferiority, a recognition that he was not personally suited to the task. Van Dyke was a friend and close ally of McKean.

28. C. Rodney to T. Rodney, Aug. 28, 1776; G. Read to C. Rodney, Sept. 17, 1776, in Ryden, *Letters,* pp. 105, 119; *PP,* May 27, 1777; McKean to G. Read, Feb. 2, 1778, in Read, *Read,* p. 298.

29. McKean to ?, Feb. 25, 1777, Emmett Coll. New York Public Library (copy).

30. McKean to Mrs. McKean, May 21, 1777; McKean to C. Rodney, Mar. 7, 1777, in Hancock, "Letters to and from Caesar Rodney," p. 75.

31. *PP*, May 20, 1777; McKean to Mrs. McKean, May 21, 1777, McKean Papers, HSP.

32. Observe McKean's allusion to Cromwellian times. McKean drew a good many of his historical analogies from the English Civil War against Charles I. Note, too, the quotation of one Philadelphian to the effect that "The Scotch, in the Province of Pennsylvania, act and speak like their Ancestors. They covenanted against the tyranny of a Stewart, their own countryman; and they are determined with us never to become slaves of any Parliament or Potentate on earth . . . . They are here the very warmest advocates for liberty." This quote and the observation that many like McKean "looked back fondly to the days of Cromwell," can be found in Eric Foner, "Tom Paine's Republic: Radical Ideology and Social Change," in Alfred E. Young, ed., *The American Revolution: Explorations in the History of American Radicalism* (DeKalb, 1976), p. 203. See also Timothy Matlack to McKean, July 28, 1777, Hampton L. Carson Coll., HSP; McKean to John Dickinson, Aug. 15, 1777, McKean Papers, HSP.

33. See, for instance, Robert L. Brunhouse, *The Counter-Revolution in Pennsylvania*, pp. 34-35; John P. Roche, *Life of Joseph Reed*, p. 144; Meehan, "The Pennsylvania Supreme Court," 84-85. It is worth noting that Caesar Rodney, George Read, and, indeed, several other Delawareans in the two decades prior to the Revolution held more prestigious offices than did McKean. And a good many Pennsylvanians held more offices than he did in the two decades after 1776. Yet McKean's ambition has been portrayed in more vaulting terms. McKean's decision to take the chief justice position is seen as something insidious, something entirely personal. Joseph Reed, on the other hand, is characterized as a man of principle for refusing the post—even though he accepted the presidency of the state one year later. One suspects that it is because McKean held office for a good while in both Delaware and Pennsylvania that he is described as insatiably ambitious. The fact that he took a position in a government he had recently criticized also had its effect on later historians. All this is not to deny McKean's ambition—it cannot be denied; but in this respect he differs little from men surrounding him. I can find no instance where McKean seriously compromised himself merely to obtain office. The most difficult act of McKean's life in this respect is his quest of the customs post in 1771, but even here it is important to remember that Francis Hopkinson and George Read also sought the post and none questioned their integrity.

34. Opponents of McKean and a good many later historians have scoffed at McKean's observation that he took the chief justiceship in part because he was convinced that changes would soon be forthcoming in the state constitution. But in April 1778 he was still persuaded that such

changes would soon be forthcoming, and he called for those unhappy with the present constitution to do their duty to the state until the changes they sought could be achieved. See his *A Charge Delivered to the Grand Jury by the Honourable Thomas McKean, Esq., Chief Justice of Pennsylvania, at a Court of Oyer and Terminer, and General Goal Delivery, held at York, on the 21st Day of April 1778* . . . (Lancaster, 1778), p. 13, Historical Society of York County, York (also Evans no. 15876).

35. See in particular McKean's comments to C.A. Rodney, Sept. 22, 1813, McKean Papers, HSP. Professor David Hawke (*Honorable Treason: The Declaration of Independence and the Men Who Signed It* (New York, 1976, pp. 53, 54, 148, 161, 214) labels McKean a "politician." He defines a politician as a man driven by intrigue: "A sense of duty had not carried them into public life. Politics was not a hobby with them nor an adjunct to their lives. It was their life. It swallowed up their days. Wheeling and dealing spiced all their waking hours." This is not an accurate description of McKean in or out of Congress. Interestingly, George Read and Francis Hopkinson are not politicians, but merely "lawyers" in Hawke's scheme of things. For a more persuasive statement of the general philosophy of leadership held by men like McKean, see Gordon S. Wood, "The Democratization of Mind," *Leadership in the American Revolution* (Washington, D.C., 1974), p. 66.

36. *Pa. Arch.*, ser. 1, 5: 621; *PCR* 11: 254, 271, 304. Looking back from the perspective of the 1780s, Mrs. Samuel Shoemaker remembered that Pennsylvania in 1777 had had an "entirely Presbyterian Government & a distracted, unsettled one, too." Mrs. Samuel Shoemaker to her husband, Mar. 12, 1785, Shoemaker Papers 2: 189-90, HSP. See also Wayne L. Bockelman and Owen S. Ireland, "The Internal Revolution in Pennsylvania: An Ethnic-Religious Interpretation," *Pa. Hist.* 41 (1974): 125-60; James Leyburn, "Presbyterian Immigrants and the American Revolution," *Journal of Presbyterian History* 54 (Spring 1976): 9-32; Lucas, *Portents of Rebellion*, p. 120.

7. Establishing the Courts

1. *Statutes at Large of Pennsylvania from 1682-1801*, 16 vols., (Harrisburg, 1896-1908), 9: 29.

2. Allen, "Diary," p. 282; *PG*, July 30, 1777.

3. Matthias Slough to Jasper Yeates, Mar. 28, 1777, Yeates Papers, HSP; Graydon, *Memoirs*, p. 332; Jasper Yeates to Edward Burd, Feb. 15, 1778, Shippen Papers 3, HSP; John Montgomery to James Wilson, Apr. 21, 1777, Simon Gratz Coll., HSP.

4. Thomas R. Meehan, "Courts, Cases and Counselors in Revolutionary and Post-Revolutionary Pennsylvania," *PMHB* 91 (1967): 6-8.

5. Ibid., pp. 7-8; Burton A. Konkle, *The Life and Times of Thomas Smith, 1745-1797* (Philadelphia, 1904), pp. 68-80, 156; *Pa. Arch.*, ser. 1, 6: 12.

6. *PG*, Sept. 3, 1777; Marshall, *Diary*, p. 160; Robert Galbraith to

Thomas Wharton, Feb. 6, 1778, in *Pa. Arch.,* ser. 1, 6: 238.

7. Allen, "Diary," p. 196.

8. Henry J. Young, "Treason and its Punishment in Revolutionary Pennsylvania," *PMHB* 90 (1966): 288-89.

9. *Statutes at Large* 9: 45.

10. Meehan, "The Pennsylvania Supreme Court," p. 123.

11. *JCC* 8: 694-95.

12. *An Address to the Inhabitants of Pennsylvania By Those Freeman of the City of Philadelphia Who Are Now confined in the Masons' Lodge...*(Philadelphia, 1777), pp. 6-9, 12, 14-15, 31, 38; *PCR* 11: 283-84, 288-89; *PG*, Sept. 10, 1777.

13. "Diary of Robert Morton," *PMHB* 1 (1877): 4n; *PCR* 11: 301-2.

14. McKean to J. Adams, Sept. 19, 1777, McKean Papers, HSP.

15. *An Act to Empower the Supreme Executive Council to Provide for the Security...thereof in special cases...*(Philadelphia, 1777); *Proceedings of the General Assembly of the Commonwealth of Pennsylvania* (Philadelphia, 1777), pp. 88-89; Robert F. Oaks, "Philadelphians in Exile: The Problem of Loyalty During the Revolution," *PMHB* 96 (1972): 307. James Allen recorded in his diary that the Assembly's overturning of McKean's writs was "the very extreme of tyranny." (p. 293).

16. Council to Alexander Nesbitt, Sept. 16, 1777, *Pa. Arch.,* ser. I, 5: 628.

17. Morton, "Diary," p. 6; Enoch Story to Henry Drinker, Sept. 22, 1777, Society Coll., HSP; Jasper Yeates to James Burd, Dec. 26, 1777, in Balch, *Letters and Papers,* p. 265.

18. *Minutes of the Delaware Council,* p. 142.

19. McKean to C. Rodney, Sept. 25, 1777, in Ryden, *Letters,* p. 237.

20. McKean to C. Rodney, Oct. 15, 1777, in ibid., p. 241. See also Harold B. Hancock, *Liberty and Independence: The Delaware State During the American Revolution* (Wilmington, 1976), p. 92.

21. Read apparently arrived on Oct. 13, or shortly thereafter. See Read, *Read,* p. 276.

22. Edward Burd to Jasper Yeates, Nov. 16, 1777, Yeates Correspondence, HSP; McKean to G. Read, Feb. 12, 1778, in Read, *Read,* p. 298.

23. John Bayard to McKean, Feb. 27, 1778, McKean Papers, HSP.

24. *Minutes of the Second General Assembly of the Commonwealth of Pennsylvania...Oct. 27, 1777* (Lancaster, 1777), p. 74.

25. McKean, to Mrs. McKean, Apr. 9, 1778; Marshall, *Diary,* p. 176.

26. McKean, *A Charge to the Grand-Jury by the Honourable Thomas McKean, Esq., Chief Justice of Pennsylvania, at a Court of Oyer and Terminer, and General Gaol Delivery, held at York, for the County of York, on the 21st Day of April, 1778...*(Lancaster, 1778), pp. 4-5, 7, 9, 10-11, 13, 18. McKean repeated his charge to the Lancaster Court at the April 21 York court.

27. William Lyon to George Bryan, Feb. 2, 1778; Jonathan Dickinson Sergeant to Thomas Wharton, in *Pa. Arch.,* ser. 1, 6: 228, 496.

28. McKean to George Bryan, May 21, 1778 (copy), Emmett Coll.,

7. Establishing the Courts

NYPL; McKean to Bryan, May 27, 1778, in *Pa. Arch.*, ser. I, 6: 569-70.

29. McKean to W.A. Atlee, July 7, 1778, Atlee MSS, LC.

30. William Lewis to Timothy Matlack, July 14, 1778, in *Pa. Arch.*, ser. I, 6: 641.

31. McKean to W.A. Atlee, July 7, 1778, Atlee MSS, LC; *PEP*, July 9, 1778.

32. Jacob E. Cooke, "Tench Coxe: Tory Merchant," *PMHB*, 96 (1972): 85-87; *PP*, Dec. 12, 1778.

33. Andrew Robeson to Elizabeth Ferguson, July 12, 1778, *PMHB* 39, (1915): 293. For later views that McKean carried out a lenient policy behind the scenes while maintaining a rigid public image, see *Aurora*, Nov. 13, 1802; June 26, 1817.

34. Raymond C. Werner, ed., "Diary of Grace Grouden Galloway...," *PMHB* 58 (1934): 176, 180, 182-83, 186.

35. Reed, *Reed* 2: 34. Some running totals for 1778 and 1779 compiled from the *PEP*, can be found in Anne McCabe Ousterhout, "The Forgotten Antagonists: Pennsylvania Loyalists" (unpublished doctoral dissertation, Michigan State Univ., 1972), p. 188.

36. "*Respublica v. Abraham Carlisle,*" I *Dallas*, p. 35. McKean's notes are found in *Pa. Arch.*, ser. I, 7: 44-52.

37. Ibid., pp. 36-38.

38. Ibid., pp. 33-35.

39. "*Respublica v. John Roberts,*" in ibid., p. 39; C. Page Smith, *James Wilson: Founding Father, 1742-1798* (Chapel Hill, 1956), pp. 121-22; *PP*, Aug. 27, 1778. Elias Boudinot later argued Roberts' bail case, but he was overruled in his arguments by McKean.

40. *PP*, Nov. 7, 1778; "Civis," in ibid., Nov. 10, 1778; Philip Davidson, *Propaganda and the American Revolution*, p. 394.

41. *Pa. Arch.*, ser. I, 7: 52-53.

42. See Meehan, "The Pennsylvania Supreme Court," pp. 181-87; Henry J. Young, "Treason and its Punishment," 293, 295-96, 313.

43. Joseph Reed to Nathaniel Greene, Nov. 5, 1778, in Reed, *Reed* 2: 38.

44. For example, in 1779 one Joseph Judson was convicted of high treason in Delaware before, among other justices, David Finney, McKean's early preceptor. McKean's brother, William, sat on the jury that convicted him. The following sentence was pronounced: that Judson was to be taken to the "Gaol of the P[resent] County of New Castle from whence he came, & from thence to be drawn to the place of execution & there be hanged by the Neck, & then cut down alive, that his Entrails be taken out & be burned while he is yet alive, and that his head be cutt off, that his body be divided into Four Quarters, and that his Head & Quarters be at the disposal of the State." He was then reprieved. See Oyer and Terminer Docket, 1746-1792, New Castle County, p. 104. See also P.S. Clarkson and R.S. Jett, *Luther Martin of Maryland* (Baltimore, 1970), pp. 44, 47.

45. William Sargeant, *Loyalist Poetry of the Revolution* (Philadelphia,

1857), p. 19; Meehan, "The Pennsylvania Supreme Court," pp. 181-87. One expert on treason cases in early America has concluded that Roberts and Carlisle "had very fair trials before a court of moderate men who showed themselves willing to hear every argument of the learned counsel engaged to defend them. A jury of their peers found them guilty of acts clearly treasonable by known and established law." Bradley Chapin, *The American Law of Treason* (Seattle, 1964), pp. 57-58. For a harsher assessment, see Paul Lermack, "Peace Bonds and Criminal Justice in Colonial Philadelphia," *PMHB* C (1976), pp. 173-190, esp. p. 188.

8. The Origins of a Moderate, Independent Judiciary

1. Allen, "Diary, " p. 432.

2. J. Reed, to McKean, Apr. 20, 1779, *Pa. Arch.*, ser. I, 7: 328; *PG* Apr. 14, 1779; *PP*, Apr. 13, 1779; Marshall, *Diary,* p. 171.

3. "Journal of Samuel Rowland Fisher, of Philadelphia, 1779-1781," *PMHB* 41 (1971): 150, 186. But McKean did think him guilty. See McKean to Mrs. McKean, July 26, 1779, McKean Papers, HSP.

4. "Journal of Samuel Rowland Fisher," pp. 147-52, 280; J. Reed to McKean, Mar. 30, 1779; McKean to J. Reed, Mar. 31, 1779, *Pa. Arch.*, ser. I, 7: 274-75, 279.

5. J. Reed to McKean, May 9, 1780, in *Pa. Arch.*, ser. I, 8:234-35.

6. McKean to Mrs. McKean, Oct. 29, 1779; McKean to J. Reed, June 16, 1780, ibid., p. 331; J. Dickinson to the judges of the supreme court, Oct. 8, 1785, in ibid. 10: 523.

7. *Minutes of the Third General Assembly* (Philadelphia, 1779), pp. 71, 75, 81, 87, 90-91; Samuel Hazard, ed., *Register of Pennsylvania*, 16 vols., (Philadelphia, 1828-1836), 10: 114-15; *Statutes at Large* 10: 33-34, 37; IV *Dallas*, p. 402; Norman B. Wilkerson "Land Policy and Speculation in Pennsylvania, 1779-1800," (unpublished doctoral dissertation, Univ. of Pennsylvania, 1958), pp. 1-7.

8. Edward P. Cheyney, *History of the University of Pennsylvania, 1740-1940* (Philadelphia, 1940), pp. 119-20, 122; *PG*, Sept. 29, 1779; *PP*, Nov. 25, 1779; Robert Brunhouse, *The Counter-Revolution in Pennsylvania,* pp. 78, 253n. John Coleman (*Thomas McKean*, p. 233) argues that McKean opposed the charter revision but I find his arguments unconvincing and his citations fail to substantiate his claims. Perhaps one could argue that Wilson and Lewis looked to the Court because they knew McKean would support their views but there is no proof of this, or that McKean made any effort to help them. To argue that McKean would support a continuation of the charter because he supported the Penns in their land claims, as Coleman does, is to deny McKean's views on Presbyterianism, education, and his role in the passing of the earlier law to undermine the trustees and faculty at the College.

9. Brunhouse, *Counter-Revolution in Pennsylvania,* p. 79.

10. C. Page Smith, "The Attack on Fort Wilson," *PMHB* 38 (1954): 177-88. For a fresh view, see John K. Alexander, "The Fort Wilson

Incident of 1779: A Case Study of the Revolutionary Crowd," *WMQ* 31 (1974): 589-612.

11. Timothy Matlack to McKean, Oct. 4, 1779; McKean to J. Reed, Oct. 7, 1779; George Bryan to McKean, Oct. 10, 1779, in *Pa. Arch.*, ser. I, 7: 732, 735-36, 744; W.A. Atlee to Mrs. Atlee, Oct. 12, 1779, Atlee MSS, LC; *PG*, Nov. 17, 1779.

12. T.H. Hartley to Jasper Yeates, Dec. 25, 1779, Yeates Papers, cited in Meehan, "The Pennsylvania Supreme Court," p. 96.

13. Warner Mifflin to McKean, May 11, 1781, Cox-Parrish-Wharton Coll. 11: 79, HSP. I am endebted to Professor Jack Marietta for this citation.

14. "Journal of Samuel Rowland Fisher," pp. 279-80; John Pemberton Diary, 1777-1781. Pemberton Papers, Box 3, p. 160, HSP.

15. See, for instance, the case of Norris James, *IG*, Aug. 13, 21, 23, 28, 1787.

16. W. Mifflin to McKean, May 11, 1781, Cox-Parrish-Wharton Coll. 11: 79, HSP.

17. Suggestive of the new respect for channels was the handling of the Benedict Arnold case. News of his treachery came first to McKean and it was he who ordered a search for Arnold's personal papers and notified the council of the developments. Minutes of the Sup. Ex. Council, Sept. 27, 1780, in Reed, *Reed* 2: 272.

Pennsylvanians shared a common faith that the success of their republican experiment depended largely upon the establishment of balanced institutions of government. This stress on "constitutionalism" separated Pennsylvanians only when they disagreed over specifically how to separate each branch of government and just exactly how best to balance the various governmental institutions. See, for instance, the discussion in Kim T. Phillips, "William Duane, Philadelphia's Democratic Republicans, and the Origins of Modern Politics," *PMHB* 101 (1977): p. 378.

18. "Journal of Samuel Rowland Fisher," p. 275.

19. Ousterhout, "Forgotten Antagonists," p. 209; Reed, *Reed* 2: 262, 429ff; Brunhouse, *The Counter-Revolution in Pennsylvania*, p. 86.

20. I *Dallas*, pp. 46-48.

21. "Journal of Samuel Rowland Fisher," p. 330.

22. McKean to J. Reed, Dec. 12, 1780; Reed to McKean, Dec. 13, 1780, in *Pa. Arch.*, ser. I, 8: 649-50, 654-55.

23. McKean to J. Reed, Dec. 12, 1780; Reed to McKean, Dec. 15, 1780, in ibid., pp. 649, 657-58.

24. I *Dallas*, pp. 53-60. McKean "delivered a learned and circumstantial charge to the jury," it was said.

25. *Pa. Arch.*, ser. I, 8: 644-46. One wonders why Reed pressed the case. McKean had made it clear to him earlier that his judgment would not substantiate the state's position. Reed's action in other cases suggests he did not concur with McKean's assessment.

26. I *Dallas*, pp. 58-60.

27. "*Respublica* v. *Buffington*," ibid., p. 61; "*Respublica* v. *Buffington*," Bryan Papers, Box 1, case 63, HSP.

9. "A Valuable Acquisition in Congress"

1. Edmund C. Burnett, *The Continental Congress* (rep. New York, 1964), p. 319; McKean to G. Read, Feb. 12, 1778, in Read, *Read*, p. 298.

2. McKean to Mrs. McKean, May 11, June 9, 1778, McKean Papers, HSP; McKean to C. Rodney, Apr. 28, 1778, in Ryden, *Letters*, p. 265.

3. McKean to Mrs. McKean, June 17, 1778, McKean Papers, HSP; McKean to C. Rodney, Apr. 28, 1778, in Ryden, *Letters*, p. 265.

4. *JCC* 14: 1002, 1013-14; 16: 29-32, 61-63, 77, 357; 17: 519, 604. The report in McKean's hand can be found in *PCC*, Item 159, no. 22. While McKean was anxious to investigate several departments in 1778, he did not think an investigation of Thomas Mifflin, late quarter-master general, warranted.

5. *JCC* 10: 219, 300-301, 374, 392, 395, 496, 503; 11: 852-54, 592; McKean to G. Read, Apr. 3, 1778, in Read, *Read*, p. 309. Though McKean apparently favored pensions for the officers in the regular army he still favored the state militia over the army. On the question of half-pay measures, he did not favor state action but preferred instead to grant the federal government the initiative. See also Marcus Cunliffe, "Congressional Leadership in the American Revolution" *Leadership in the American Revolution* (Washington, D.C., 1974), p. 54.

6. McKean to G. Read, Apr. 3, 1778; Read to McKean, Mar. 4, 1778, in Read, *Read*, pp. 305, 308-9.

7. McKean to G. Read, Apr. 3, 1778, in ibid., pp. 308-9.

8. McKean to Thomas Collins, Feb. 3, 1781, McKean Papers, HSP; T. Rodney to Mrs. Rodney, Mar. 1, 1781, in Burnett, *LMCC* 6: 1; T. Rodney to C. Rodney, Mar. 2, 1781, in Ryden, *Letters*, p. 401.

9. *Biographical History of Dionysius*, p. 32.

10. McKean to G. Read, Feb. 12, Apr. 3, 1778, in Read, *Read*, pp. 298, 308-9.

11. John McKinly to G. Read, Aug. 28, 1778, in Read, *Read*, p. 313.

12. C. Rodney to Nicholas Van Dyke and McKean, Aug. 24, 1778, in Ryden, *Letters*, pp. 281-82; *JCC* 12: 912-13. Under the goad of McKinly, the Privy Council passed a resolution calling upon Delaware's congressional delegates to insist upon McKinly's release. Rodney still refrained from ordering McKean and Van Dyke to effect the exchange (support the exchange "as you think you can with propriety," he wrote). These developments have been treated in greater detail in my "The Travail of John McKinly, First President of Delaware," *Delaware History* 17 (Spring-Summer 1976): 21-36.

13. Testimony of George Noath, Dec. 23, 1778, in *PCC*, Item 159, no's 332-34.

14. Ibid., no.'s 293-94, 296-315.

15. *PP*, Dec. 31, 1778, Feb. 2, 1779; *PCC*, Item 159, no.'s 310, 316-17,

332-34, 336-38; Henry Laurens to Rawlins Lowndes, Dec. 16, 1778, in Burnett, *LMCC* 3: 537.

16. Gouveneur Morris to Joseph Reed, Apr. 9, 1779, in Burnett, *LMCC* 4: 152; see also ibid. 2: 523, 549-550; *JCC* 12: 1252-53.

17. *PP*, Dec. 29, 1778. For information on earlier conflicts with two army men, Robert Hooper and Casimir Pulaski, see *Minutes of the General Assembly of the Commonwealth of Pennsylvania . . . Sept. 3, 1777* (Lancaster, 1777), p. 96; *Pa. Arch.*, ser. I, 6: 77, 266-68; Nathaniel Greene to McKean, June 3, 1778; McKean to Greene, June 9, 1778, McKean Papers, HSP; Robert Hooper to G. Bryan, Aug. 31, 1778, in *Pa. Arch.*, ser. 2, 3: 236-37; *JCC* 10: 173, 176, 186, 194; 12: 974; Brunhouse, *Counter-Revolution in Pennsylvania*, p. 63.

18. *PCR* 11: 653, 659-60. "A Republican" addressed the Council thusly: "The General [Thompson] laughed at your impotent endeavors to mettle in matters whereof you have no cognizance since the Chief Justice, however guilty, could not be removed from office by you. The General further gave you to understand, that he would never set an example to betray the liberties of his fellow subjects, by obeying arbitrary mandates and orders contrary to law." *PJ*, Feb. 24, 1779.

19. PP, Dec. 31, 1778. See also Read, *Read*, pp. 119-35, esp. p. 132.

20. *PP*, Feb. 2, 1779.

21. Ibid., Feb. 25, 1779.

22. Ibid., Feb. 9, 1779; *FJ*, May 9, 1781.

23. H. James Henderson, *"Party Politics in the Continental Congress"* (New York, 1974), esp. pp. 70-99, 187-217.

24. *PEP*, Dec. 11, 1778.

25. I am much indebted to H. James Henderson, "Congressional Factionalism and the Attempt to Recall Franklin," *WMQ* 27 (1970): 246-67, in the following paragraphs.

26. G.S. Rowe, " 'A Valuable Acquisition in Congress:' Thomas McKean, Delegate from Delaware to the Continental Congress, 1774-1783," *Pa. Hist.* 38 (1971): 252n.

27. Henderson, "The Attempt to Recall Franklin," p. 255-56.

28. McKean to R.H. Lee, Mar. 25, 1780, in Burnett, *LMCC* 5: 94-95; McKean to J. Adams, Nov. 8, 1779, McKean Papers, HSP.

29. Ibid.

30. T. Rodney to C. Rodney, June 14, 1781, in Ryden, *Letters*, p. 414.

31. *JCC* 14: 542-43.

32. McKean to R. H. Lee, Mar. 25, 1780, in Burnett, *LMCC* 5: 94-95; R.H. Lee to Arthur Lee, Aug. 31, 1780, in J.C. Ballagh, ed., *Letters of Richard Henry Lee*, 2 vols. (New York, 1914), 2: 197.

33. *JCC* 13: 239-44; 14: 749-52, 851, 896-97, 924-26. Implicit in the developments regarding committee action was the recognition that the state—including McKean's court—was neither providing the effective administration Whigs sought nor the retribution upon those unfriendly to their cause that they expected. The people thus sought to provide

their own solutions. More than a dozen "enemies" were "arrested" and confined by the committeemen. It was three days after a major meeting on May 25 before the Council took steps to undercut the committees' powers by passing a resolve decrying the arrests and confinements by other than "the ordinary course of justice." President Reed promised effective response by the state and warned the people that to continue their activities would leave the state government open to severe criticism by its "common enemies." *PG*, May 25, 1779; *PEP*, May 29, June 5, 1779; *At A General Meeting of the Citizens of Philadelphia and Parts Adjacent on. . .the 25th of May, 1779* (Philadelphia, 1779); *Pa. Arch.*, ser. 2, 3: 263; *PCR* 12: 8-9. One call to "return to popular committee government" can be found in *An Address of the Committee of the City and Liberties of Philadelphia. . .*(Philadelphia, 1779). There is no evidence McKean advocated such a move.

34. *PJ*, July 14, 1779. For McKean's initial plans for his lands and his subsequent revisions of these hopes, see McKean to Mrs. McKean, July 12, 16, 20, 1779. McKean was very conscious of his deteriorating economic condition and kept a careful watch on the impact of inflation on his financial position. See his calculations for the year 1779 in McKean Papers, HSP.

35. *JCC* 14: 1013-14; 16: 29-32, 61-63, 77, 357; 17: 519, 604.

36. McKean to Mrs. McKean, May 4, July 26, 1779; *PEP*, June 29, 1779. It is difficult to assess McKean's role in the May 25 meeting. On the one hand Joseph Stansbury, the Loyalist, wrote of the meeting that

> And now the State-House yard was full,
> And orators, so grave and dull,
>   Appear'd upon the stage,
> But all was riot, noise, disgrace,
> And freedom's sons, o'er all the place,
>   In bloody frays engage.
>
> Each vagrant from the whipping-post,
> Or stranger stranded on the coast,
>   May here reform the State,
> And Peter, Mick, and Shad-row Jack,
> And Pompey-like McKean in black,
>   Decide a people's fate.

And yet McKean was not listed among those most dedicated to price controls, and committee action. See Roberdeau Buchanan, *The Life of the Honorable Thomas McKean*, p. 68; *The Independent & Constitutional Ticket, for a General Committee of the City of Philadelphia. . .*(Philadelphia, 1779). On McKean's private monetary contributions, see Reed, *Reed* 2: 262, 429ff; Brunhouse, *Counter-Revolution in Pennsylvania*, p. 86. McKean believed that a public sale of the vast Penn lands would bring in revenue enough "for another and yet another campaign." By opening the lands to foreigners as well as to the citizens of Pennsylvania, he thought "these strangers" would "thereby become neatly interested in the event of the war and in the prosperity of Pennsylvania in particular."

There should be no "condition of settlement, as contended for by some, there should rather, on the contrary. . . be a condition of forfeiture, in case of settlement during the war." Such a restriction would keep young men where the military needs were the greatest and prevent them from escaping to the back counties. "To limit the quantity of land to be granted," McKean concluded, "to any one person or family [would be] useless and impracticable." Unlike most of McKean's plans, this was poorly thought out. He seemed bent on allowing speculators free rein; indeed, his proposals would allow men to purchase great tracts of land under the guise of patriotism. There were no checks on those who would monopolize the new lands. See Reed to McKean, Aug. 25, 1780; McKean to Reed, Aug. 29, 1780, in Reed, *Reed* 2: 245-46, 249-50.

37. See E. James Ferguson, *The Power of the Purse* (Chapel Hill, 1961), esp. chapts. 6-7.

38. William Houston to McKean, Mar. 31, 1781; McKean to Samuel Adams, July 8, 1781, McKean Papers, HSP.

39. *JCC* 20: 764-66.

40. William Irvine to Col. Walter Stewart, Aug. 26, 1781, quoted in Ferguson, *The Power of the Purse,* p. 119; *PCC: Presidential Letterbook,* no.'s 16, 38; Joseph Harrison to Mrs. John Lawrence, June [July] 16, 1781, *PMHB* 14 (1890): 82.

41. T. Rodney to C. Rodney, July 10, 1781, in Ryden, *Letters,* p. 419.

42. McKean to George Washington, July 26, 1781; McKean to Lafayette, Aug. 3, 1781, McKean Papers, HSP. McKean's presidency can be reconstructed in large part from his papers in the McKean Papers, HSP, and the *PCC: Presidential Letterbook,* Item no. 16, and the *JCC.*

43. McKean to J. Dickinson, Dec. 25, 1780, June 23, 1800, McKean Papers, HSP.

44. *PCC: Presidential Letterbook,* Item no. 16.

45. "Autobiography of Peter DuPonceau," *PMHB* 63 (1939): 440; "Extracts from the Diary of Ann Rawle," ibid. 16 (1892): 103; Burnett, *LMCC,* 6: 252-53.

46. *JCC* 21: 1070-71.

10. The Changing Nature of Representation

1. McKean to J. Dickinson, June 23, 1800, McKean Papers, HSP; *Catalogue Colleqii Naeo-Caesariensis* (Trenton, 1789), p. 13.

2. On February 24, 1779, the Assembly voted 42 to 12 against McKean holding his two offices, but there was no follow-up and no official pressure applied to him to resign. *Journal of the Pennsylvania House of Representatives. . .1779* (Lancaster, 1779), pp. 320, 325. For criticisms in the press regarding McKean's pluralism, see "Simplex," and "Sidney," *PP,* Feb. 23, Apr. 24, 1779.

3. "Tenax," "Legality," *FJ,* July 18, 1781; F.N. Thorpe, ed., *The Federal and State Constitutions. . . ,* 7 vols., (Washington, 1909), 5: 3088.

4. *FJ,* July 25, Aug. 15, 1781.

5. William A. Atlee to McKean, July 18, 1781; John Evans to McKean, July 23, 1781, McKean Papers, HSP.
6. "Jurisperitus," *FJ*, July 25, 1781. See also ibid., Aug. 1, 1781.
7. Ibid., Aug. 1, 1781.
8. T. Rodney to McKean, Aug. 10, 1781, McKean Papers, HSP.
9. *FJ*, Aug. 22, 1781.
10. Rowe, "'A Valuable Acquisition in Congress'" pp. 229-30; McKean to J. Dickinson, Dec. 25, 1780, McKean Papers, HSP. For McKean's calculations on the amount owed him by Delaware, see McKean to the Speaker of the Assembly, Jan. 24, 1793, McKean Coll., HSD. He estimated that, with interest, the amount was more than £860 by 1793.
11. N. Van Dyke to T. Rodney, Oct. 15, 1781, Gratz Coll., Case 1, Box 12, HSP.
12. Samuel Patterson to McKean, Jan. 8, 1778, McKean Papers, HSP.
13. Samuel Patterson to C. Rodney, Aug. 17, 1778; Rodney to McKean, Apr. 18, 1778, in Ryden, *Letters*, pp. 261, 280.
14. *PP*, Sept. 7, 1779; "Autobiography," p. 4-5.
15. John Harvey Powell, "John Dickinson, President of the Delaware State, 1781-1782," *Delaware History* 1 (1946): 7-9, 24-25, 33-35.
16. *Minutes of the Delaware Council*, pp. 700, 709-10, 713, 715-17; Gordon Wood, *The Creation of the American Republic*, esp. pp. 369, 371.
17. J. Dickinson to C. Rodney, May 10, 1779; T. Rodney to C. Rodney, Feb. 9, 1782, in Ryden, *Letters*, pp. 301, 433.
18. McKean to J. Dickinson, Dec. 25, 1780; McKean to Thomas Collins, Feb. 3, 1781, McKean Papers, HSP.
19. See Rowe, "'A Valuable Acquisition in Congress,'" pp. 229-30.
20. A typical attack by "Valerius" can be found in *FJ*, Oct. 2, 1782.
21. *Minutes of the Delaware Council*, p. 760. James Tilton wrote, "The disgrace of being represented in Congress by foreigners had... become so generally impressed upon every man of the least delicacy that it was now not difficult to appoint residents of the State, instead of our delegates from abroad." *Biographical History of Dionysius*, p. 100. For Dickinson's rationale, see *PG*, Dec. 18 and 24, 1782.
22. "Valerius," *PJ*, Aug. 25, 1782. For a criticism of Wharton, see "A Watchman of Delaware," *PJ*, Apr. 6, 1782.
23. *Minutes of the Delaware Council*, p. 786. Delaware owed McKean £804 for services to 1783. Although the State apparently paid small sums towards that balance between 1788 and 1793, the amount owed was still £860 by 1793 owing to interest. See the accounts in the McKean Coll., HSD; McKean to Eleazer McComb, Dec. 1, 1785, (copy), Emmett Coll., NYPL.

McKean may have already made up his mind not to serve the Congress after 1782, for that year his work was episodic and uninspired, though compatible with the Read-Dickinson philosophy. His seeming concord with conservatives like Philemon Dickinson, Wharton and Pennsylvania Republicans is not to be construed as a change in his political orientation. The difference lay in Congress and the issues before it.

Conditions in 1782 differed appreciably from previous years. The radical bloc—James Lovell, William Whipple, Nathaniel Scudder, R.H. Lee, and Samuel Adams, among others—was no longer in attendance and its philosophy had not been replaced. New issues drove wedges into previous blocs so that past alliances had been dissipated and new ones not yet formed. McKean commented on the new harmony to his old friend, Samuel Adams, adding that only on the issue of the fisheries and western lands were there flashes of former bitterness.

Wharton's and Philemon Dickinson's dedication to Congress permitted McKean frequent absences, freedom from major assignments, and fewer ad hoc committees. A few issues did excite his imagination: he pressed for an act allowing General Washington to retaliate for acts of cruelty by the British to American citizens, and supported petitions for statehood from Vermont and Kentucky, although his enthusiasm for the Vermonters' cause was restrained. See Rowe, "'A Valuable Acquisition in Congress'" p. 261n; McKean to S. Adams, Oct. 13, 1782, McKean Papers, HSP; *JCC* 22: 107-8, 114, 158, 241, 423, 553; 23: 550, 552-53.

24. The details and developments of this case can be followed in the Rodney letters to Read, the letters exchanged between Caesar A. and Thomas Rodney, the correspondence between the Rodneys and McKean, and the letters from McKean to John Vining and Mrs. John Banning, found in various folders in the Rodney Collection, HSD. See also *Minutes of the Delaware Council,* pp. 1125, 1134, 1173, 1181, and W.B. Hamilton, *Thomas Rodney: Revolutionary & Builder of the West* (Durham, N.C., 1953), pp. 49-53. A deed in the Logan Papers (24: 82-83, HSP) suggests that McKean might have joined with several of Rodney's Philadelphia relatives to buy land once belonging to Caesar Rodney. Whether they purchased it for Thomas Rodney or in an effort to provide him with needed funds is not clear.

25. Richard S. Rodney, "The End of the Penns' Claim to Delaware, 1789-1814, Some Forgotten Lawsuits," *PMHB,* 61 (1937): 182; McKean to Edmund Physick, Dec. 14, 1789, John Penn to Physick, Apr. 7 and Oct. 1, 1790. Note also the notices in the McKean Papers, HSP, giving McKean power of attorney (dated Sept. 25, 1790) and the later request that McKean be a pall bearer for John Penn (Feb. 9, 1795). Two factors doubtless encouraged the Penns to turn to McKean. His opinion in 1779 had favored their claims in Pennsylvania, and McKean had remained friendly with one of the Penns' most important attorneys, Edward Shippen. Indeed, McKean had interceded in Shippen's behalf during the turbulent years of the Revolution.

26. John Penn to Physick, Oct. 1, 1790; McKean to Physick, Dec. 14, 1789, Penn-Physick Correspondence, HSP; Rodney, "The End of the Penns' Claim to Delaware," p. 190; John Penn to McKean, Sept. 25, 1790, McKean Papers, HSP.

27. John Penn to Edmund Physick, Oct. 11, 1792, Penn-Physick Correspondence, HSP, Rodney, "The End of the Penns' Claim to Delaware," pp. 184-188.

28. McKean and Physick, *A Calm Appeal to the People of Delaware* (Philadelphia, 1793).
29. McKean to J. Dickinson, July 23, 1792 and May 30, 1794, Dickinson Papers, R.R. Logan Coll., HSP.

11. New Directions

1. Elizabeth G. Brown, *British Statutes in American Law, 1776-1836* (Ann Arbor, 1964), pp. 9-10.
2. I *Dallas*, pp. 64-67. See also Joseph Hopkinson, *Considerations on the Abolition of the Common Law in the United States* (Philadelphia, 1809).
3. I *Dallas*, pp. 73-75.
4. *IG*, Oct. 1, 1782; *PG*, Jan. 1, 1783; John Harvey Powell, "John Dickinson, President of Pennsylvania," *Pa. Hist.* 28 (1961): 258ff.
5. J. Reed to William Bradford, May 2, 1784, in Reed, *Reed* 2: 413.
6. "Quidnunc," "Anti-Quibbler," *IG*, Oct. 1 and 8, 1782. See also *IG*, Sept. 28 and Oct. 2, 1782.
7. *IG*, Sept. 28 and Oct. 2, 1782.
8. *PG*, Oct. 16, 1782.
9. J. Reed To G. Bryan, Dec. 25, 1782, in Reed, *Reed* 2: 390; Benjamin Rush to John Montgomery, Oct. 15, 1782, in Butterfield, *Letters of Benjamin Rush* 1: 290.
10. *FJ*, Oct. 2, 1782; *IG*, Oct. 1, 1782; Jan. 11, 1783; Jacob Hiltzheimer, "Diary of Jacob Hiltzheimer," *PMHB* 16 (1892): 163-64.
11. "Tatler," "Mathematicus," *IG*, Oct. 12 and 15, 1782.
12. Ibid.
13. "Wilkes," "Koster," "Junius Wilkes," *IG*, Dec. 7, 1782.
14. "Candid," *IG*, Dec. 7, 1782.
15. *IG*, Dec. 3, 1782; Hiltzheimer, "Diary," pp. 52-53. In 1785, for instance, a correspondent in the *South Carolina Gazette and Public Advertiser* (Oct. 1, 1785) said that any judge who interfered with the freedom of the press should "consult the Chief Justice of Pennsylvania." Cited in Dwight Teeter, "The Printer and the Chief Justice," *Journalism Quarterly* (Summer 1968): 260.
16. Hiltzheimer, "Diary," p. 54. The Memorial is printed in the *IG*, Jan. 11, 1783. For an elaboration of McKean's views on juries and the rule of law, see my "Outlawry in Pennsylvania, 1782-1788 and the Achievement of an Independent State Judiciary," *The American Journal of Legal History* 20 (1976): 227-44.
17. *FJ*, Feb. 15, 1783; *IG*, Feb. 1, 1783; *PP*, Jan. 25, 1783.
18. See "Adrian" [Bryan], *FJ*, Jan. 15, 1783, answered by "Aristides" [John Witherspoon] who argued that the grand jury did not want to introduce the British concept of seditious libel "hitherto unknown" in America, ibid., Jan. 22, 1783. See also "Jurisperitus" [McKean], in *FJ*, Feb. 2 and 5, 1783, and *PP*, Jan. 25, 1783.
19. For a discussion of McKean's purchase of the Jacob Duche mansion, see Chapter 15. Duche was married to Francis Hopkinson's sister.

20. "One of the People," *PP*, Jan. 25, 1783. For more detailed and elaborate criticisms of McKean by Hopkinson, see Hopkinson, *Misc. Essays* 1: 297-315.

21. McKean to Mrs. McKean, Oct. 29, 1783, Nov. 10, 1785 and, Oct. 17, 1786; William Bradford to Mrs. Bradford, Nov. 4, 1783, May 9, 1785, and May 11, 1787, Bradford Papers, Wallace Collection, HSP.

22. McKean to G. Washington, Oct. 18, 1781, McKean Papers, HSP; John F. Meginnes, ed., *History of Lycoming County, Pennsylvania* (Chicago, 1892), p. 205; Meehan, "The Pennsylvania Supreme Court," p. 122.

23. McKean to Mrs. McKean, Apr. 28, 1778; William Atlee to Mrs. Atlee, Apr. 23, 1778, Atlee MSS, LC; *FJ*, Dec. 12, 1781; *Pa. Arch.*, ser. 4,3: 1030; Meehan, "The Pennsylvania Supreme Court," p. 361; *PP*, Jan. 3 and May 18, 1786; Yeates Legal Papers, esp. folder 2 (1779), folder 2 (1782), folder 4 (1786), folder 2 (1788).

24. McKean to Mrs. McKean, Oct. 27, 1786.

25. Hugh Henry Brackenridge, *Law Miscellanies* (1814), pp. 284-85, introduction; Alexander Addison, *Charges to Grand Juries of the Counties of the Fifth Circuit in the State of Pennsylvania* (Washington, 1800), p. 5.

26. A reference to the fact that the people did not want the Court to convene in the first place, or desired it to issue a death warrant without bothering with the proceedings of a formal trial. See G. Bryan to John Whitehill, June 10, 1785, Box 2, Case 63, Bryan Papers, HSP.

27. Pennsylvania, Oyer and Terminer Docket, 1778-1786, RG-33, p. 290 (Oct., 1785); G. Bryan to John Whitehill, June 10, 1785, Box 2 Case 63, Bryan Papers, HSP; Michael Huffnagle to James Irvine, May 27, 1785; Robert Galbraith to John Dickinson, May 25, 1785; in *Pa. Arch.*, ser. 1, 10: 466-67; J.W.F. White, "The Judiciary of Allegheny County," *PMHB* 7 (1883): 148; Hugh Henry Brackenridge, "The Trial of Mamachtaga," in Daniel Marder, ed., *A Hugh Henry Brackenridge Reader, 1770-1815* (Pittsburgh, 1970), pp. 355-64.

28. G. Washington to Thomas Smith, July 14, 1785, in John C. Fitzpatrick, ed., *The Writings of George Washington*, 39 vols., (Washington, 1931-1944), 28: 193; Smith to Washington, Nov. 17, 1785, in Burton A. Konkle, *The Life and Times of Thomas Smith, 1745-1809* (Philadelphia, 1904), p. 178; Norman B. Wilkerson, "Land Speculation in Pennsylvania," P. 63; "*Bonner v. Devebaugh*," III Binney, pp. 174, 187; "*Dick v. Cameron*," Addison, p. 337, M.P. Bothwell, "The Astonishing Croghans," *Western Pennsylvania Historical Magazine* 48 (1965): 138-42. Smith was doubtless urged on by the fact that James Wilson had offered to plead Washington's case if he could get away from his congressional obligations. See Washington to Smith, July 14, 1785, in Fitzpatrick, *Writings*, 195.

29. Boyd, *The Papers of Thomas Jefferson* 6: 476.

30. *JCC* 22: 354, 356, 389-92.

31. Boyd, *The Papers of Thomas Jefferson*, 6: 477-78, 480.

32. Matthew Smith to George Bryan, July 12, 1778, *Pa. Arch.*, ser. 1, :632; Thomas Hartley to McKean, Sept. 2, 1778, McKean Papers, HSP.

33. William Maclay to Joseph Reed, Apr. 2, 1780, *Pa. Arch.*, ser. 1, 8: 156; McKean and Jacob Rush to J. Dickinson, July 3, 1784; Deposition of John Armstrong, July 28, 1785, that of Thomas Brink, Aug. 12, 1784, in Robert J. Taylor, ed., *The Susquehannah Company Papers*, 11 vols. to date (Ithaca, 1956-), 8:2, 10-12, 29.

34. Petitions of Connecticut Prisoners at Easton to the SEC, Sept., 1784; John Franklin to William Samuel Johnson et al., Oct. 20, 1784, ibid., pp. 73-121.

35. Minutes of the Court at Sunbury, Nov. 8, 1784; John Franklin to Ebenezer Gray, Nov. 10, 1784, ibid., pp. 145-46, 151.

36. William Montgomery to McKean, May 20, 1786, in *Pa. Arch.*, ser. 1, 10: 766-67.

37. Ethan Allen to William Samuel Johnson, Aug. 15, 1785, in *Susquehannah Company Papers*, 8: 255-56. I am much in Professor Taylor's debt for my treatment here. See esp. ibid, 9: xv-xvi.

38. Timothy Pickering to Zebulon Butler, Apr. 2, 1787; Pickering to Obadiah Gore, Apr. 12, 1787, in ibid., pp. 88-89, 95-96. The quote is on p. 95; the Confirming Act on pp. 82-88.

39. Timothy Pickering to Samuel Hodgdon, May 29, 1787; John Franklin to the Speaker of the Pennsylvania General Assembly, Feb. 24, 1787, ibid., pp. 70, 140-41.

40. See McKean's warrant for the arrest of Franklin, Aug. 31, 1787, ibid., p. 174; *PCR* 15: 265.

41. Timothy Pickering to Samuel Hodgdon, Sept. 6, 1787; Timothy Pickering to John Swift, Oct. 9, 1787, in ibid. 9:181, 233; also 205; *Connecticut Courant*, Oct. 22, 1787.

42. McKean and Jacob Rush to Pickering, May 10, 1788; Pickering to Peter Muhlenberg, May 27, 1788; John Franklin to the Speaker of the Pennsylvania General Assembly, Sept. 17, 1788, ibid., pp. 373, 376, 494. See also pp. xlin, 366-67.

43. McKean had anticipated such a kidnapping. In October 1787 he wrote William Atlee, "John Franklin is still in close confinement, and his co-adjutors have pretended remorse & repentance—They are a cunning parcel of men, and I believe their overtures are designed to deceive, and that they intend to secure, if possible, either Colo: Pickering or some of the Judges of the Supreme Court, as hostages for Franklin, of which suspicion I have told Colo: Pickering, who is upon his guard." McKean to Atlee, Oct. 22, 1787, Atlee Papers, LC.

44. Legal opinion of McKean and G. Bryan, Aug. 7, 1788; Samuel Hodgdon to Pickering, Aug. 20, 1788; Indictment of Ira Manvil and Thirteen Others; Pickering to Hodgdon, Nov. 9, 1788, in *The Susquehanna Company Papers*, 9: 455-56, 475, 480-82, 516-17; *Pa. Arch.*, ser. 1, 11: 419-21. Franklin was indicted, arraigned and pleaded not guilty. The court agreed to delay his court appearance. Franklin's story is told by James E. Brady, "Wyoming: A Study of John Franklin and the Connecticut Settlement into Pennsylvania" (unpublished doctoral dissertation, Syracuse Univ., 1973).

45. *The Susquehannah Company Papers* 9:517. William Bradford, who accompanied McKean on the Wyoming circuit, wrote from there on November 14, 1788, that "Our Juridical expedition has been successful & I think must have considerable effect in establishing order & regard for Government there." He judged that "the Spirit of Opposition to the Laws seems in a great measure broken." Bradford to Thomas Houston, Nov. 14, 1788, Bradford Papers, Wallace Coll., HSP. At least one man thought that the Supreme Court and McKean should have taken a larger role in Wyoming developments. See Thomas Hartley to Bradford, Jan. 5, 1787, in *Pa. Arch.*, ser. 1, 11: 114-15.

12. The Achievement of an Independent Judiciary

1. Biddle, *Autobiography*, pp. 192-93. A survey of available dockets, and records appearing in the *Pa. Arch.*, as well as of the clemency files in the PRD, casts doubt on this conclusion. The Court did not appear to be more harsh or more vindictive after 1782. This chapter relies heavily upon my "Outlawry in Pennsylvania, 1782-1788, and the Achievement of an Independent Judiciary," *The American Journal of Legal History* 20 (1976): 227-44.

2. SEC, Forfeited Estates Files, RG-27, 1777-1790, Box 1, folder 2, PRD; Henry C. Mercer, "The Doans and their Times," *Collections of Papers Read Before the Bucks County Historical Society* (1908), 1: 271-82. George MacReynolds' *The New Doan Book* (1952) is excellent for the genealogical particulars. Stories of the Doans' involvement with Indians may be apocryphal but for their association with Blacks, see *Pa. Arch.*, ser. 1, 10: 584.

3. List by George Wall, Jr., July 30, 1778, SEC: Forfeited Estates File, box 1, folder 2: Joseph Hart to William Moore, Mar. 3, 1782; George Wall, Jr., to Joseph Hart, Apr. 22, 1782, in *Pa. Arch.*, ser. 1, 9: 507-8, 529-30; McKean and Bryan to Moore, Sept. 18, 1782, Hampton L. Carson Coll., HSP. The confessions of the Vickers can be found *Pa. Arch.*, ser. 1, 9: 609-17. Altogether some thirty-three robberies were attributed to the Doans and their recruits.

4. Pa., Sup. Ct. Dockets: Appearances, 1782-1783, pp. 226ff, PRD; Pa., Oyer and Terminer Dockets, 1778-1786, pp. 142ff, PRD.

5. Ibid., pp. 143-47. While the court awaited the response of the Doans and their accomplices to the writs of capias, it was able by virtue of several arrests to move against lesser members of the band late in 1782 and early 1783. Juries convicted Moses Winder, William Myers, Israel Doan, and John and Joshua Richards, and imposed on them a variety of minor punishments including branding, short jail terms, or fines. One accessory, John Tomlinson (or Thomlinson) was sentenced to die.

6. F. Pollack and F.W. Maitland, *History of English Law* (Boston, 1925), 1: 459-61, 525; 2: 578; William Holdsworth, *A History of English Law* (Boston, 1923), 3: 605. Generally the bill of indictment was presented in the King's Bench Division, but it could be presented elsewhere and removed to the King's Bench by certiorari. If the charge was treason

one capias to the sheriff of the country in which the case was initiated was sufficient; in other cases three were required (Hale, P.C., 2: 194). The accused's failure to surrender to the sheriff after five successive pronouncements at the county court terms led to a proclamation of outlawry by the county coroner. In London the judgment was given by the Recorder. A person could seek to remove the outlawry by surrendering himself and requesting a writ of error but even should he be successful he was called to stand trial for the charge in the indictment (ibid., p. 209; also 31 Eliz. 3: 400-401; 4 & 5 W. & M., c. 22; 14 & 15 Vict., c. 100, s. 24). The usual basis for a writ of error was the fact that a person had been out of the country when the writ of exigent was awarded but this option was specifically denied persons charged with treason (5 & 6 Ed. 6, c. 11, s. 7 & 8). In civil disputes the outlawry capias was merely a means of compelling appearances or, after judgment, of obtaining satisfaction. In cases of misdemeanor when the person refused to appear, it was viewed as a punishment for contempt of court (*R. v. Tippin*, 2 Salk. 494). For a general discussion of outlawry, see H. Erle Richards, "Is Outlawry Obsolete?" *The Law Quarterly Review* 71 (1902): esp. 298-303.

7. *Laws of the Province of Pennsylvania, passed by the Governor and General Assembly held at Philadelphia in the Years 1715, 1717, and 1718* (Philadelphia, 1718), pp. 308-16; *Votes and Proceedings of the House of Representatives... Oct., 18, 1707-June 16, 1726* (Philadelphia, 1753) pp. 211-13, 217, 220.

8. Meehan, "The Pennsylvania Supreme Court," p. 382.

9. Henry J. Young, "Treason and Punishment in Revolutionary Pennsylvania," *PMHB* 90: (1966): 287-313.

10. For the differences between attainders employed by the court and those used by the legislature and council, see ibid.

11. Charles Biddle, *Autobiography*, pp. 192-94; Johann David Shoepf, *Travels in the Confederation, 1783-1784* (New York, 1911), pp. 126-28. For the outline of the strategy to have McKean elected to the council where he was to become president and oversee the appointment of Reed to the bench, see *PG*, Jan. 15, 1783.

12. Note to John Dickinson, Sept. 11, 1783, recording sale of Joseph Doan's estate, SEC:FEF, box 1.

13. *Min. of the First Sess. of the Seventh Gen'l Assembly...* (Philadelphia, 1783), p. 895.

14. Ibid., pp. 904-5, 912-13, 926, 932; *Laws Enacted in the Third Sitting of the Seventh Gen'l Assembly...* (Philadelphia, 1783), 189-92.

15. *PG*, Sept. 3, 1783.

16. McKean to Mrs. McKean, Oct. 29, 1783, McKean papers, HSP; Deposition respecting the arrest of Joseph Doan, Sr., Sept. 25, 1783; Ephraim Douglas to John Armstrong, May 29, 1784, in *Pa. Arch.*, ser. 1, 10: 110-12, 504; Pa. Sup. Ct. Dockets: Appearances, Sept., 1783-Sept., 1785, pp. 215, 322; Pa., O. and T. Dockets, 1778-1786, pp. 173, 237-39; SEC: Clemency File, RG-27, box 5.

12. The Achievement of an Independent Judiciary 449

17. Pa., Sup. Ct. Dockets: Appearances, Sept., 1783-Sept., 1785, pp. 318-19.

18. Notes by J.H. Powell, R.R. Logan Papers, Lib. Co., Philadelphia, Bryan to James Irvin, Oct. 20, 1784, in *Pa. Arch.*, ser. 1, 10: 609.

19. "*Respublica* v. *Doan,*" I *Dallas,* pp. 86-88.

20. For evidence that McKean was considering stepping down from the Court in 1784, see Joseph Reed to William Bradford, May 2, 1784, in Reed, *Reed* 2:413.

21. Alfred Rosenthal, "The Marbois-Longchamps Affair," *PMHB* 63 (1939): 294-95; I *Dallas,* pp. 111-12; Luzerne to John Dickinson, May 19, 1784, *Pa. Arch.* ser. 1, 11: 462-64.

22. John Dickinson to Luzerne, May 20, 1784; same to same, May 21, 1784; Luzerne to Dickinson, May 22, 1784; Dickinson to Luzerne, May 22, 1784, *Pa. Arch.*, ser. 1, pp. 464-65, 466.

23. Rosenthal, "Marbois-Longchamps," pp. 294-95; Thomas Proctor to John Dickinson, May 27, 1784; Deposition of Escape, *Pa. Arch.*, ser. 1, pp. 277, 469, 471-74; *JCC*, 28: 314-15.

24. John Dickinson to the Judges, June 2, 1784; Van Berkel to Dickinson, May 28, 1784; Dickinson to Van Berkel, June 3, 1784, *Pa. Arch.* ser. 1, 11: 475, 478, 489.

25. Judges to John Dickinson, June 7, 1784, ibid., 484-85; Rosenthal, "Marbois-Longchamps," p. 300.

26. PCR 14: 135; I Dallas, pp. 86, 111-12, 113, 114, 115-18; Rosenthal, "Marbois-Longchamps," pp. 300-301; Smith, *James Wilson,* p. 195; *JCC* 28: 314-15.

27. Robert Brunhouse, *Counter-Revolution in Pennsylvania, pp. 166,* 184; *Laws Enacted in the Second Sitting of the Ninth Gen'l Assembly* . . . (Philadelphia, 1785), pp. 509-11.

28. McKean to J. Adams, Apr. 30, 1787, McKean Papers, HSP. See also the discussions relating to juries in chapter 11 and 16 of this work.

29. See Stanley K. Johannesen's perceptive discussion of Dickinson in his "John Dickinson and the American Revolution," *Historical Reflections* 2 (1975): esp. 47-48.

30. I *Dallas,* pp. 86-89.

31. The Court wrote, "There has never been a question seriously litigated in Westminster-Hall upon a writ of error to reverse an Outlawry in a capital case. Such a writ was never granted, but from justice, where there really was an error, or from a favor, where the King was *willing* the Outlawry should be reversed: they are grantable mere *ex gratia Regis,* and when granted, there never was any opposition made, and the courts reversed them upon slight and trivial objections, which could not have prevailed if opposed. . . . All was by consent of the King, and the reversal took place, though there was really *no error at all.*" Justices McKean, Bryan, and Rush to Dickinson, Jan. 15, 1785, Loggan Papers, XII, 39, HSP. For the Dawson particulars, see Meehan, "The Pennsylvania Supreme Court," pp. 173-75.

32. *PCR* 14: 387.

33. Ibid.: 388; *Minutes of the Second Sess. of the Ninth Gen'l Assembly*...(Philadelphia, 1785), p. 260.
34. Bryan to William A. Atlee, Mar. 29, 1785, Atlee MSS, LC.
35. *Minutes of the Second Sess. of the Ninth Gen'l Assembly*..., pp. 262, 281, 295-97.
36. PCR 15: 214; *Votes and Proceedings of the Twelfth Gen'l Assembly...of New Jersey...Oct., 1787* (Trenton, 1788), pp. 17-18. For the Doan petitions, dated Mar. 3, 27; Apr. 19; May 3, 28; July 27, 1786, see SEC: Clemency Files, box 7.
37. *PCR* 14: 558.
38. Pa., Sup. Ct. Dockets: Apparances, 1788-1789, p. 219; Pa., O. and T. Dockets Commencing April, 1787, p. 61: Sup. Ct. Notes, VII, 1262, HSP; Henry Wynkoop to McKean, Mar. 16, 1786, in *Pa. Arch.*, ser. 1, 10: 299.
39. MacReynolds, *New Doan Book*, pp. 447-48.
40. *PP*, Sept. 20, 1788.
41. Ibid., Sept. 22, 1788.
42. See the petitions dated June 7 and July 14, 1788, SEC: Clemency File, 1788, box 9; MacReynolds, *New Doan Book*, p. 449.
43. *PCR* 15: 497, 500-501, 525; McKean to William A. Atlee, Sept. 17, 1788, Atlee MSS, LC.
44. *Debates of the General Assembly of the Commonwealth of Pa.,* (Philadelphia, 1788), pp. 130, 159-62.
45. Several men assigned to this meeting later indicated that no meeting took place. Records of the Council, however, suggest that a meeting took place but that it apparently ended abruptly shortly after it began. *PCR* 15: 544.
46. Young, "Treason and Punishment in Revolutionary Pennsylvania," p. 309; Biddle, *Autobiography,* pp. 232-34. On September 25 McLene moved to have the House expunge from the official minutes all references to the committee assigned to meet with the Council. Fitzsimons opposed the move; he unsuccessfully urged the passing of a resolution specifically noting the Council's refusal to meet with the Assembly committee. *Debates of the Twelfth Gen'l Assembly...* , p. 206.
47. John M. Coleman has commented on the efforts prior to 1781 by McKean to establish an independent judiciary. See his "Thomas McKean and the Origins of an Independent Judiciary," *Pa. Hist.* 34 (1967): 111-30.
48. Unlike developments in several other states, the enhancement of the judiciary in Pennsylvania was accomplished without an attempt on the part of the Court formally to check either the Council or the Assembly, or to nullify laws passed by the legislature.

13. The Trials of Reform

1. McKean to William Atlee, Mar. 26, 1785, Atlee MSS, LC. Note the observation by "Adrian" (not George Bryan, in this instance) that "An idle curiosity led me, the other day, to the State-house, to see our Judges in their fire-new Scarlet Robes." *IG,* Apr. 16, 1785. McKean did not

13. The Trials of Reform

hesitate to emulate British pageantry or apparel in his courtroom; nor did he actively seek to replace British law and precedents with American equivalents. Indeed, in the case of the outlawry proceedings, to cite but one example, McKean contributed to the "Anglicization" of Pennsylvania law. But he was not reluctant to "adjust" British law to the American scene; nor did he refrain from criticizing certain aspects of British laws and customs.

2. McKean to Charles Biddle, Feb. 21, 1786, Brown Collection, HSD.

3. McKean to Benjamin Franklin, Jan. 28, 1786, John Nicholson Papers, Microfilm roll 12, PRD.

4. Hugh Henry Brackenridge, *Law Miscellanies* 19: 284-85; *IG*, July 31, 1784; Feb. 7, June 22 and 28, 1788; *GUS*, Aug. 14 and 15, 1797; *PG*, Aug. 21, 1797.

5. *IG*, Apr. 3, 1786.

6. *Laws Enacted by the 3rd Sess. of the 10th Gen'l Assembly* (Philadelphia, 1786), pp. 153-55; McKean to Mrs. McKean, Nov. 7, 1786, McKean Papers, HSP.

7. I *Dallas*, pp. 167-68.

8. George Washington to Robert Morris, Apr. 12, 1786, in Fitzpatrick, *Writings* 28: 407.

9. I *Dallas*, pp. 168-69. McKean stressed a case not mentioned by the bar (II *Salk*, p. 666) whereby a slave entering England had become free (according to Holt), but his sale in Virginia was legitimate. McKean observed how "solicitous" England had been "on the one hand to discountenace slavery in England, but, on the other hand, to do full justice to the sale, which, by the Lex Loci, was lawful in Virginia, where it was made."

10. I *Dallas*, pp. 469-70.

11. Ibid., pp. 471-72.

12. Ibid., pp. 472-79.

13. "Inimicus Tyrannis," *IG*, Mar. 14, 1787. See also I *Yeates*, pp. 368-69.

14. *PP*, Sept. 14, 1785; Brunhouse, *The Counter-Revolution*, p. 184; Harry Elmer Barnes, *The Evolution of Penology in Pennsylvania* (Indianapolis, 1927), pp. 86-87, 106-7.

15. McKean to John Dickinson, Feb. 13, 1784, R.R. Logan Coll., Box 4, HSP.

16. I *Dallas*, p. 125.

17. Scharf and Westcott, *History of Philadelphia* 1: 440, 443-44; McKean to Paul Hamilton, Sept. 1, 1800, Hampton L. Carson Coll., HSP. A list of those sentenced to hard labor between October 1787 and March 1788 can be found in Bryan Papers, Box 3, case 63, HSP.

18. See in particular, Hopkinson's criticism of a McKean speech welcoming Franklin on his return to America in 1785, in Hastings, *Hopkinson*, p. 388; Hopkinson, *Misc. Essays* 2: 69-75, and his comments on McKean's role in advocating reforms, in ibid.: 93-95.

19. For an inconsistent approach to McKean's part in a local election,

see *PP*, Oct. 7, 1785, and *Misc. Essays* 2:76-83. In this incident, Hopkinson first argued that the polls should be left open after the designated closing time to permit late voters, but when McKean did in fact allow the polls to stay open and a number of Constitutionalists took advantage of the situation to vote, Hopkinson denounced McKean's actions.

20. Francis Hopkinson to Thomas Jefferson, Sept. 28, 1785, quoted in Hastings, *Hopkinson*, p. 391.

21. Hopkinson, *Misc. Essays* 2:93-95. The court of errors and appeals was established as a court of last resort by an Act of Assembly on Feb. 28, 1780. McKean was commissioned with seven others on Nov. 20, 1780.

22. Hopkinson, *Misc. Essays* 2:95, 96-97, 99, 100, 103, 105. Hopkinson claimed that the justices helped to pen the bill.

23. Ibid., 106, 108-111.

24. Thomas R. Meehan, "'Not Made Out of Levity,' Evolution of Divorce in Early Pennsylvania," *PMHB* 93 (1968): 453-64; *Laws Enacted in the 2nd Sitting of the 9th Gen'l Assembly of the Commonwealth of Pennsylvania* (Philadelphia, 1785), pp. 664, 668.

25. *Pa. Arch.*, ser. 1, 11: 342-43; *Laws Enacted in the 2nd Sitting of the 13th Gen'l Assembly of the Commonwealth of Pennsylvania* (Philadelphia, 1789), pp. 14-15, 61. Rawle's quote is found in Meehan, "The Pennsylvania Supreme Court," p. 421.

26. For general criticism by Hopkinson concerning McKean's personal vindictiveness towards him which never reached the public ear, see Hopkinson to Clement Biddle, Sept. 11, 1786 and Hopkinson to Benjamin Franklin, Sept. 21, 1787, quoted in Hastings, *Hopkinson*, p. 321.

14. Federalist

1. Forrest McDonald, *We the People: The Economic Origins of the Constitution* (Chicago, 1958), pp. 174, 181.

2. Burton A. Konkle, *George Bryan and the Constitution of Pennsylvania, 1731-1791* (Philadelphia, 1922), pp. 300 and 303. McKean's private and public life during the Revolutionary and Confederation periods cannot be fit nicely into either Jackson T. Main's description of "Localists" or Douglas Arnold's "majoritarians"—both of which were said to encompass the Constitutionalists. Neither, for that matter, does McKean's career give much support to Robert Kelley's description of the republicanism which emerged in Pennsylvania during the Revolution. Compare McKean's position(s) (i.e., his republicanism) as described in this work with the assessments of political ideology and factions in Jackson T. Main, *Political Parties Before the Constitution* (Chapel Hill, 1973), esp. chapts 7, 12, 13; Douglas M. Arnold, "Political Ideology and the Internal Revolution in Pennsylvania, 1776-1790" (unpublished doctoral dissertation, Princeton Univ., 1976); and Robert Kelley, "Ideology and Political Culture from Jefferson to Nixon," *AHR* 82 (1977): 536-37.

3. McKean to John Adams, Apr. 30, 1787, McKean Papers, HSP; Adams to John M. Jackson, Dec. 30, 1817, in Adams, *Works* 10: 269.

4. McKean to William Atlee, Aug. 16, 1787 and Oct. 22, 1787, Atlee

MSS, LC; various invitations found in the McKean Papers, HSP. The results of the election can be found in *IG*, Oct. 15, 1787.

5. McKean to John Adams, Apr. 30, 1787, McKean Papers, HSP; McKean to William Atlee, Oct. 22, 1787, Atlee MSS, LC.

6. *IG*, Nov. 18, 1787.

7. Oswald Seidensticker, "Frederick A.C. Muhlenberg," *PMHB* 13 (1889): 202.

8. John B. McMaster and Frederick D. Stone, eds., *Pennsylvania and the Federal Constitution, 1787-1788* (Philadelphia, 1888), pp. 217-18, 219-30, 231-32, 235, 257, 364. See also R. Carter Pitman, ed., "Jasper Yeates' Notes on the Pennsylvania Ratifying Convention, 1787," *WMQ* 22 (1965): 312-14.

9. McMaster and Stone, *Pennsylvania and the Federal Constitution*, pp. 252, 271, 274, 282, 361, 363, 364, 365, 377; Pitman, "Jasper Yeates' Notes," 312; *IG*, Dec. 1, 13, 17, 18, 1787.

10. McMaster and Stone, *Pennsylvania and the Federal Constitution*, p. 425; *IG*, Dec. 14, 1787; Smith, *James Wilson*, p. 278.

11. McMaster and Stone, *Pennsylvania and the Federal Constitution*, pp. 378-79.

12. McDonald, *We the People*, pp. 163-82, esp. p. 175.

13. *IG*, Dec. 14 and 15, 1787.

14. "A Unitarian," ibid., Dec. 21, 1787.

15. Ibid., Jan. 9 and 14, 1788; John Montgomery to William Irvine, Jan. 19, 1788, Irvine Papers 9: 114, HSP.

16. *IG*, Jan. 9, 1788; Montgomery to Irvine, Jan. 19, 1788, Irvine Papers 9: 113, HSP.

17. Konkle, *George Bryan*, p. 322.

18. Walter Stewart to William Irvine, Feb. 20, 1788, Irvine Papers 9: 120, HSP.

19. William Bradford to Mrs. Bradford, May 27, 1788, Bradford Papers, Wallace Coll., HSP.

20. Benjamin Rush to Elias Boudinot, July 9, 1788, in Butterfield, *Letters of Benjamin Rush* 1: 473; Hopkinson, *Misc. Essays* 2: 349-401.

21. *IG*, July 11, 1788.

22. The observations of Wilson and McKean on the federal constitution were widely circulated, not only in the United States but in England as well. See Wilson and McKean, eds., *Commentaries on the Constitution of the United States* (London, 1793); also *The American Law Journal* 42 1st of new series (Philadelphia, 1813): 320-451.

23. I *Dallas*, pp. 319-20; Biddle, *Autobiography*, pp. 228-31; Bryan Papers, Box 3, case 63, HSP. For Oswald's account of the case and relevant documents, see *PP*, July 26, Aug. 20, Sept. 15, 1788.

24. McKean to William Atlee, Sept. 17, 1788, Atlee MSS, LC; McKean to Bryan, Oct. 11, 1788, Bryan Papers, Box 3, case 63, HSP. Hopkinson once wrote of Francis Bailey of the *FJ* and Oswald of the *IG* that "between the two, calumny and slander were carried to greater extent than was ever known, perhaps, in an civilized city." See Hopkinson, *Misc. Essays*

1:304n. See also I *Dallas,* pp. 324, 329; *PP,* July 26; *IG,* July 19, 1788; "Tacitus," ibid., July 22, 1788; "Public Justice", ibid., July 30, 1788; Biddle, *Autobiography,* p. 228. Biddle wrote that "I have no doubt but that Oswald would have been glad to have seen our judges hanged, especially the Chief Justice for whom he entertained an implacable hatred."

25. *Debates of the 12th Gen'l Assembly of the Commonwealth of Pennsylvania* (Philadelphia 1788), pp. 8, 20, 63-64, 65, 102-3.

26. McKean to William Atlee, Sept. 17, 1788, Atlee MSS, LC.

27. *Debates of the 12th Gen'l Assembly of the Commonwealth of Pennsylvania* (Philadelphia, 1788), pp. 135-37, 162-99, 311-13.

28. McKean to John Bayard, Mar. 6, 1789, Sprague Coll. 2: 81, HSP.

29. McKean to George Washington, Apr. 27, 1789, Hampton L. Carson Coll., HSP; Thomas Rodney to George Washington, Aug., 1789, Brown Collection, Box 22, folder 7, HSD; Fitzpatrick, *Writings* 31: 315; Smith, *James Wilson,* p. 304. David Finney, who also sought a federal post, did not mention McKean as a reference. Nor did McKean mention Finney.

30. *FG,* Sept. 3, 1789 and July 12, 1790; *PP,* July 9, 1790; Clement Biddle to George Joy, Sept. 8, 1789, Clement Biddle Letterbook, HSP; Biddle to William Rogers, July 7, 1790, ibid.; William Bradford to Elias Boudinot, June 17, 1790, Bradford Papers, Wallace Coll., HSP; *The Journal of William Maclay, United States Senator from Pennsylvania, 1789-1791* (New York, 1969), pp. 138-39; Roland M. Baumann, "'Heads I Win, Tails you Lose': The Public Creditors and the Assumption Issue in Pennsylvania, 1790-1802," *Pa. Hist.* 44 (1977): esp. 208, 212.

31. *PJ,* Feb. 3, 1779, June 23, 1784 and July 7, 1784; *PG,* Mar. 24, 1779 and Feb. 11, 1784.

32. *FG,* Oct. 12 and Dec. 11, 1789.

33. *Proceedings Relative to Calling the Conventions of 1776 and 1790. The Minutes of the Convention that formed the present Constitution of Pennsylvania, together with the Charter of William Penn, the Constitution of 1776 and 1790, and a View of the Proceedings of the Convention of 1776, and the Council Proceedings* (Harrisburg, 1825), pp. 165-66. For a later observation that as Speaker McKean refused to permit those in opposition to him to voice their opinions, see *GUS,* Aug. 28, 1799.

34. These arrangements had been worked out in a series of meetings between proponents and opponents of the new constitution prior to the convention.

35. McKean's views also permitted men from neighboring states to move to Pennsylvania and become politically active almost immediately. For complications arising from this provision, see chapter 18.

36. *Proceedings,* pp. 244, 248; C.A. Rodney to T. Rodney, Aug. 19, 1790, Rodney Coll., Box 4, folder 4, HSD.

37. *Proceedings,* p. 166. For the arrangements between Wilson and Findley, see Harry M. Tinkcom, *The Republicans and Federalists in Pennsylvania, 1790-1801* (Harrisburg, 1950), pp. 11-12.

38. C.A. Rodney to T. Rodney, Aug. 19, 1790, Rodney Coll., HSD;

15. Republican

McKean to John Adams, Apr. 30, 1787, McKean Papers, HSP.

39. *Proceedings,* pp. 177, 179, 265-66, 269, 375; Graydon, *Memoirs,* p. 320.

40. For two provocative studies of Adams' political thinking, see Gordon S. Wood, *The Creation of the American Republic, 1776-1787* (Chapel Hill, 1969), pp. 589ff; and Stephen G. Kurtz, "The Political Science of John Adams, A Guide to his Statecraft," *WMQ* 25: (1968): 605-13.

41. *Proceedings,* pp. 177, 179, 265-66, 269, 375.

42. McKean voted 92 times in the convention. Two of the votes were unanimous. Fifty-one times McKean was aligned with the majority, thirty-nine times with the minority. See *Aurora,* July 4, 1805; *Minutes of the Convention of the Commonwealth of Pennsylvania... Nov. 24, 1787* (Philadelphia, 1790), pp. 31, 33-34, 77, ff.

43. Edward Burd to Jasper Yeates, Dec. 10, 1789 and Oct. 13, 1789, in L.B. Walker, *The Burd Papers,* pp. 151-52.

44. *Proceedings,* pp. 296, 307.

45. On April 2, 1781, McKean was charged by the Assembly to compile the acts of the General Assembly passed between Sept. 30, 1775 and 1781. The work, known as McKean's Laws, was published in 1782 by Francis Bailey. McKean once remarked that it was during his work in this publication that he added his name to the Declaration of Independence, having discovered that it was not among the signatures there. See *The Acts of the Gen'l Assembly of the Commonwealth of Pennsylvania... passed between the 30th day of September, 1775 and the Revolution...* (Philadelphia, 1782).

46. Raymond Walters, *Alexander James Dallas: Lawyer, Politician, Financier* (Philadelphia, 1943), p. 23; Konkle, *George Bryan,* p. 295; David H. Flaherty, ed., *Essays in the History of Early American Law* (Chapel Hill, 1969), pp. 25-26.

47. I *Dallas,* pp. iii-iv.

48. Flaherty, *Essays in the History of Early American Law,* pp. 467-72. John Wilkes (1770), John Almon (1770), and John Horne (1777) were the victims of Mansfield's rulings in the libel cases.

49. McKean to William, Earl of Mansfield, Oct. 30, 1790, Hampton L. Carson Coll., HSP. Mansfield's quote is from Walters, *Dallas,* p. 23.

15. Republican

1. *FG,* Mar. 30, 1789; *IG,* Mar. 28 and Apr. 6, 1789.

2. "The Trifler," *Columbian Magazine,* 1788, quoted in J. Thomas Scharf and Thompson Westcott, *History of Philadelphia from 1609 to 1884,* 2 vols. (Philadelphia, 1884),2: 910. Significantly, "The Trifler" concluded that "each class closely imitates its immediate superior."

3. McKean to Mrs. McKean, July 12 and 26; Oct. 15, 1779. As early as Oct. 25, 1778, he had written that "It is high Time we are fixed." See also *PCR* 12: 578, 13:25; *Pa. Arch.,* ser. 1, 8:684. The property was also subject to a yearly ground rent of 232 and one-half bushels of wheat.

4. *GA*, Jan. 12, 1791; various commissions and papers in the McKean Papers, HSP; John H. Campbell, *History of the Friendly Sons of St. Patrick, and of the Hiberian Society for the Relief of Emigrants from Ireland* (Philadelphia, 1892), p. 330. He remained president of this last organization until his election as governor in 1799.

5. See Stephen J. Brobeck, "Changes in the Composition and Structure of Philadelphia's Elite Group, 1756-1790" (unpublished doctoral dissertation, Univ. of Pennsylvania, 1972), pp. 207-8; McKean family Bible, HSP; John W. Jordan, *Colonial Families of Philadelphia*, 2 vols. (New York, 1911), 1: 914-15.

6. *PG*, July 14, 1790; *PP*, July 9, 10, 1790; Tench Coxe to Alexander Hamilton, July 9, 10, 1790, in Syrett and Cooke, *Papers of Alexander Hamilton* 6:486-87, 490-91; Roland M. Baumann, "The Democratic-Republicans of Philadelphia: The Origins, 1776-1797" unpublished doctoral dissertation, Pennsylvania State Univ., 1970), p. 279.

7. *FG*, Feb. 16, 1790; *Memorial of the Public Creditors who are Citizens of Philadelphia* (Philadelphia, 1790); Syrett and Cooke, *Papers of Alexander Hamilton* 8:403. The Memorialists were concerned primarily with the interest rates promised in 1779 and 1780 and the failure of the government to pay them. They maintained that under the proposed plan domestic creditors would get only partial payment while foreigners' claims were to be "admitted in the fullest latitude, and funded on the broadest basis." Robert Morris presented the petition to the Congress on December 20. Three days later the Senate resolved that it would be inexpedient to alter the present funding bill as requested by the petition. The only Senator to vote for the petition was Morris.

8. Baumann, "The Democratic-Republicans of Philadelphia," p. 285; John C. Miller, *Alexander Hamilton: Portrait in Paradox* (New York, 1959), pp. 229-54; Syrett and Cooke, *Papers of Alexander Hamilton* 6:51-65. McKean made several contacts with Hamilton in 1788 ostensibly to seek his help in a legal matter, but one cannot help but think, in light of McKean's later advice to John Bayard (see chapter 14) that this was a deliberate attempt on McKean's part to bring himself to the attention of the New York Federalist. See ibid. 3:700; 5:238, 293.

9. Noble E. Cunningham, *The Jeffersonian Republicans: The Formation of Party Organization, 1789-1801* (Chapel Hill, 1957), pp. 35, 38. For a discussion of how each faction reached out to the people—their rhetoric and the forces shaping that rhetoric—consult Richard Buel, Jr., *Securing the Revolution: Ideology in American Politics, 1789-1815* (Ithaca, 1972), esp. chapt. 4.

10. *GA*, July 30 and Aug. 1, 1792; James Hutchinson to Albert Gallatin, Aug. 19, 1792, Gallatin Papers, NYHS.

11. *GA*, Aug. 10, 1792; *FG*, Aug. 1, 1792; *NG*, Aug. 4, 1792; James Hutchinson to Albert Gallatin, Aug. 19, 1792. Roland Baumann is one of the few historians treating this period who seems to have fully appreciated the basic neutrality of McKean in these years. See his "Democratic-Republicans in Philadelphia," p. 360. But see also Raymond

15. Republican

Walters' comment that "McKean was a Federalist, but he was on friendly terms with Dallas and other anti-Federalist leaders." Walters, *Dallas,* pp. 37-38.

12. *GA*, Aug. 4, 1792.

13. "Common Sense," ibid., Aug. 14, 1792; "Sidney," ibid., Aug. 9, 1792; *NG*, Sept. 29, 1792; Cunningham, *The Jeffersonian Republicans,* pp. 42-44; Tinkcom, *Republicans and Federalists,* p. 60. Richard Buel has argued that Republicans tended to employ more democratic rhetoric and encouraged more participation in the body politic by the common people because they did not view them as a threat to their position as did the Federalists. While McKean did not draft many of the public statements by the Republicans in 1792 and 1793, he lent his name to them. See Buel, *Securing the Revolution,* chapt. 4.

14. *GA*, Sept. 26 and 27, 1792; *IG*, Sept. 29, 1792. Only John Adams judged McKean to be "a sagacious politician." The fact is that while McKean proved effective in piecemeal political strategems, he was neither shrewd nor effective in pursuing long-range strategy. See John Adams to James Lloyd, Feb. 14, 1815, in Adams, *Works* 10:120.

15. Baumann, "The Democratic-Republicans of Philadelphia," chapt. 8, esp. p. 399; *GA*, Aug. 9; Nov. 6 and 23, 1792.

16. Hampton L. Carson, "The Case of the Sloop *Active,*" *PMHB* 16 (1892): 385-87; II *Dallas,* pp. 160-64; JCC 14: 1002; 16:32, 60, 62, 77, 357; 17:397. Earlier McKean had told the members of Pennsylvania's ratification convention that he had come to support the Constitution only after determining that it would not destroy the sovereignty of the states.

17. The best general account of the insurrection remains Leland D. Baldwin, *Whiskey Rebels: The Story of a Frontier Uprising* (Pittsburgh, 1968), but it should be supplemented by Jacob E. Cooke, "The Whiskey Insurrection: A Re-Evaluation," *Pa. Hist.* 30 (1963): 316-46. Reference to the threat to state sovereignty can be found in *The Journal of William Maclay,* pp. 376-77.

18. *Pa. Arch.,* ser. 2, 4:27; *GA*, Nov. 8, 1792.

19. Thomas Mifflin to the Judges of the Supreme Court, Oct. 5, 1792; McKean's charge to the Grand Jury, Nov. 8, 1792, in *Pa. Arch.,* ser. 2, 4:29, 35-36.

20. McKean to Jasper Yeates, June 22, 1793, Brown Coll., Box 25, HSD.

21. Baldwin, *Whiskey Rebels,* p. 95.

22. *GA*, July 25, 1794; *IG*, July 26, 1794; Tinkcom, *Republicans and Federalists,* p. 95.

23. *Pa. Arch.,* ser. 2, 4: 144-46. Washington hoped initially to rely on a Pennsylvania law of Sept. 22, 1783, authorizing calls of the militia on sudden emergencies, but Dallas pointed out that the law had been repealed.

24. Richard H. Kohn, "The Washington Administration's Decision to Crush the Whiskey Rebellion," *JAH* 59 (1972): 567-69; William Bradford

to Elias Boudinot, Aug. 1, 1794, Bradford Papers, Wallace Coll., HSP.

25. *Pa. Arch.*, ser. 2, 4:140, 145. McKean's full observation was "the judiciary power was equal to the task of quelling and punishing the riots, and that the employment of a military force at this period, would be as bad as anything that the Rioters had done—equally unconstitutional and illegal."

26. Kohn, "The Washington Administration," pp. 571-73; *Pa. Arch.*, ser. 2, 4: 82-83, 109-110.

27. Thomas Mifflin to McKean and William Irvine, Aug. 6, 1794, ibid., pp. 93-94.

28. William Irvine to A.J. Dallas, Aug. 17, 1794, ibid., p. 143.

29. H.H. Brackenridge, *Incidents of the Insurrection in the Western Part of Pennsylvania in the Year 1794* (Philadelphia, 1795), 1: 112-16; William Irvine to A.J. Dallas, Aug. 17, 1794, in *Pa. Arch.*, ser. 2, 4:143.

30. Ibid.: 155, 158-59, 165, 167.

31. Baldwin, *Whiskey Rebels*, pp. 193-95.

32. *Pa. Arch.*, ser. 2, 4:185-86; McKean to Jared Ingersoll, Aug. 29, 1794, in ibid., 183-84.

33. Brackenridge, *Incidents of the Insurrection* 2: 5; 3:153; Alexander Addison, ed., *Reports of Cases in the County Courts of the Fifth District and the High Court of Errors & Appeals, of the State of Pennsylvania* (Washington, 1800), p. 277. It took McKean and the commissioners a year to exact their revenge, but in the September Term, 1795, Jacob Cribs, Daniel Harold and eleven others were charged before the Westmoreland court with "intent to beat, wound, tar and feather" the commissioners. Nine were convicted.

34. *Pa. Arch.*, ser. 2, 4:186, 216; *IG*, Sept. 17, 1794; Baldwin, *Whiskey Rebels*, p. 209.

35. McKean to John Dickinson, July 23, 1793, Dickinson Papers, R.R. Logan Coll., HSP.

36. Joseph Galloway to McKean, Mar. 7, 1793, McKean Papers, HSP; Wilbur H. Siebert, *The Loyalists of Pennsylvania* (Columbus, Ohio, 1920), pp. 86-87. Galloway actually received a pardon but obviously felt that the public climate in Pennsylvania was not conducive to his return. See John High, "The Philadelphia Loyalists, 1763-1783" (unpublished doctoral dissertation, Temple Univ., 1975), pp. 273-74.

37. McKean to John Adams, June 13, 1812, in Adams, *Works* 10: 14; McKean to Jasper Yeates, June 22, 1793, Brown Coll., Box 25, HSD.

38. *GA*, May 24, 1793; Biddle, *Autobiography*, pp. 251-53.

39. Joseph Clay to McKean, July 6, 1793, Hampton L. Carson Coll., HSP. McKean associated closely with the French Minister on a social level and participated in a number of parties involving personnel from the French diplomatic community. Witness the numerous invitations in the McKean Papers, HSP.

40. The process by which men found their way into the Republican party by 1795 can be followed in Tinkcom, *Republicans and Federalists*, chapts. 1-9, and in Baumann, "The Democratic-Republicans of

Philadelphia." Neither claims that the Republicans were dominant in city and state politics by 1796, or that it was clear that they soon would be.

41. The social attachments, economic status and political aspirations of these men are treated in Brobeck, "Changes in the Composition and Structure of Philadelphia's Elite Group, 1756-1790." His observations are sound for the mid-1790s, as well. Richard Buel appears to take Republican rhetoric more seriously than I do. Much of the output by both parties in Pennsylvania seems to me calculated, insincere, but highly effective. See Richard Buel, *Securing the Revolution,* pp. 91-92.

42. For opposing views of the treaty which were quickly incorporated into the public debates, see William Bradford to Samuel Bayard, Mar. 30, 1795, Gratz Coll, HSP; A.J. Dallas to William Irvine, June 13, 1795, Irvine Papers, HSP. Scharf and Westcott *(History of Philadelphia* 1:475) claim that McKean was among a small number of Republicans calling for war against Britain in 1794, but there is no evidence of McKean's eagerness for war. It should be pointed out also that a good number of westerners who later became ardent Republicans looked upon the Jay's Treaty with favor—including John B. C. Lucas.

43. *IG,* July 23, 1795; John Beckley to DeWitt Clinton, July 24, 1795, quoted in Richard G. Miller, "Philadelphia, the Federalist City: A Study in Urban Politics, 1789-1800 (unpublished doctoral dissertation, Univ. of Nebraska, 1971), p. 144. Dr. Miller's book, based on this dissertation, did not come into my hands until this book was in press.

44. Scharf and Westcott, *History of Philadelphia* 1:481; *IG,* July 29, 1795; Robert Andrews to David Meredith, July 27, 1795, Meredith Papers, HSP.

45. *Aurora,* Oct. 24, 1796; John Adams to John Q. Adams, Dec. 5, 1796, quoted in Miller, "Philadelphia, the Federalist City," p. 186; McKean to J. Dickinson, Sept. 14, 1801, Dickinson Papers, R.R. Logan Coll., HSP. Other epithets applied by Adams to those in Pennsylvania like McKean opposing him can be found in Douglas Adair and John Schutz, eds., *The Spur of Fame: Dialogues of John Adams and Benjamin Rush, 1805-1813* (San Marino, 1966), pp. 135, 199, 219. The *GUS* (Jan. 24, 1797) wrote, "The foul and bitter dregs of our Society... including the scum as well as the bottom of the great European Cask, are Shaken and Stir'd up by the ambitious demogogues in our cities, as when they see fit."

46. McKean to John Dickinson, Sept. 14, 1801, Dickinson Papers, R.R. Logan Coll., HSP.

47. See John Howe, "Republican Thought and the Political Violence in the 1790's," *American Quarterly* 19 (1967): 147-65.

48. *GUS,* Nov. 4, 1796. Tardy returns from several counties led to a charge that the state government was manipulating the election returns. Mifflin sought the advice of McKean on whether he could delay announcing the results until a more representative return was available. When the Court encouraged him to wait, correspondents in the *GUS* charged Mifflin with failing to announce the winners within fourteen days of the election.

They also asserted that Mifflin, McKean, and Dallas "decided friends of party" had conspired to bring the "scandalous business" about. Background and details can be found in Tinkcom, *Republicans and Federalists,* pp. 169-72.

16. "The Democratic Judge"

1. McKean to John Dickinson, June 6, 1797 and Apr. 2, 1798, Dickinson Papers, R.R. Logan Coll., Box 5, HSP.
2. Ibid.
3. John Dickinson to McKean, Apr. 14, 1797, McKean Papers, HSP.
4. Cobbett, *Works* 6: 92-95. Scharf and Westcott report that McKean also presided at a Jan. 14, 1797 celebration in honor of Joshua Barney and his contributions to republicanism (*History of Philadelphia* 1:491).
5. John Dickinson to McKean, Oct. 13, 1797, McKean Papers, HSP.
6. McKean to Dickinson, Jan. 20, 1798, McKean Papers. The preface can be found in the Dickinson Papers, R.R. Logan Coll., Box 5, HSP. McKean's preface is essentially a biographical sketch of Dickinson, carefully worded to play down his refusal to sign the Declaration of Independence in 1776.
7. *The Letters of Fabius in 1788, On the Federal Constitution; and in 1797, On the Present Situation of Public Affairs* (Wilmington, 1797).
8. McKean to John Dickinson, Jan. 20, 1798, McKean Papers, HSP. One of McKean's most persistent critics throughout the 1790s in this respect was David Bruce. See, for instance, Harry R. Warfel, "David Bruce, Federalist Poet of Western Pennsylvania," *Western Pennsylvania Historical Magazine* 8 (1925): esp. 225.
9. McKean to John Dickinson, July 30, 1798, Logan Papers 12:79, HSP; Tinkcom, *Republicans and Federalists,* pp. 215-16.
10. Frederick Tolles, *George Logan of Philadelphia* (New York, 1953), pp. 153-55.
11. Deborah Norris Logan, *Memoir of Dr. George Logan of Stenton,* edited by Francis A. Logan (Philadelphia, 1899), pp. 55-57; Tolles, *George Logan,* pp. 155-56.
12. Ibid., pp. 156-57.
13. McKean to John Dickinson, June 24, 1798, McKean Papers, HSP.
14. *The Political Green-House for the Year 1798* (Hartford, 1799), p. 8.
15. McKean to Thomas Jefferson, Mar. 25, 1797, McKean Papers, HSP; Joseph Jaudennes to McKean, May 27, 1797. Mary Ridgely, a Delaware acquaintance of the McKeans, referred to Yrujo as "the little ugly mortal" but his portrait by Gilbert Stuart reveals a youthful, handsome, almost delicate man. When Henrietta Liston, wife of the British minister, met Yrujo in 1796 she described him as "a lively good humoured young man." See Scharf and Westcott, *History of Philadelphia* 2:913; Mary Ridgely to Henry M. Ridgely, Mar. 19, 1798, Ridgely Coll, HR; Bradford Perkins, "A Diplomat's Wife in Philadelphia: Letters of Henrietta Liston, 1796-1800," *WMQ* 2 (1954): 604. It was said that the two most vain men in

16. "The Democratic Judge"

Philadelphia were McKean and Yrujo. Sally, McKean's daughter, was probably the only person who controlled both.

Specifically, Yrujo was dismayed at what he deemed an unusual interest on the part of the British in Spain's western territory; he accused the British of actively conspiring to seize Spanish lands.

16. Cobbett, *Works* 6:273. The *Aurora* quote is from J.B. McMaster, *History of the People of the United States*, 5 vols. (New York, 1916), 2:352.

17. Mary Clark, *Peter Porcupine in America* (Philadelphia, 1939), pp. 114-15.

18. Cobbett, *Works* 7: 327-35, 337-38, 354-55, 356-58.

19. McKean Family Bible, McKean Papers, HSP.

20. *PG*, Apr. 11, 1798; *Claypoole's Am. Daily Advertiser*, Apr. 12, 1798; Cobbett, *Works* 9: 314-17. The *GUS* ignored the wedding.

21. Cobbett, *The Democratic Judge* (Philadelphia, 1798), pp. 51ff, esp. 77-78.

22. III *Dallas*, pp. 467-69, 473-74; III *Yeates*, p. 93. On Aug. 18, 1798, Cobbett was required to give bond for £2,000, and two sureties of £1,000 each.

23. Cobbett, *Works* 11: 137, 287; 10:190. See also III *Yeates*, pp. 100-101.

24. Davis and North sought to have their money returned through petitions both to the Assembly and the Supreme Court. They lost both pleas. *Journal of the 15th House of Representatives of the Commonwealth of Pennsylvania...* (Lancaster, 1804), pp. 597, 599; III *Yeates*, pp. 94-101; Cobbett, *Works* 11: 137, 287; 10:190.

25. James M. Smith, *Freedom's Fetters: The Alien and Sedition Laws and American Civil Liberties* (Ithaca, 1966), esp. chapts. 9, 10 and 11; Cobbett, *Works* 10: 97-98, 100.

26. Tinkcom, *Republicans and Federalists*, pp. 219-20. See also George M. Dallas, *Life and Writings of Alexander James Dallas* (Philadelphia, 1871), p. 225.

27. Walters, *Dallas*, p. 89, discusses Duane's and Leib's choice.

28. Oliver Wolcott to Frederick Wolcott, Apr. 2, 1799; Wolcott to Alexander Hamilton, Apr. 1, 1799, in George Gibbs, ed., *Memoirs of the Administration of Washington and Adams*, 2 vols., (New York, 1846), 2: 230-31.

29. McKean to John Dickinson, Jan. 20, 1798, McKean Papers, HSP.

30. Alexander Addison, ed., *Reports of Cases in the...Fifth District*, pp. 327-30. See also McKean to George Washington, Apr. 27, 1798, Hampton L. Carson Coll., HSP.

31. A.J. Dallas, *Reports of Cases Adjudged in the Courts...of Pennsylvania....* (Philadelphia, 1795), vol. 3.

32. For an example of his power outside the courtroom, see Elizabeth Meredith to David Meredith, July 2, 1796, Meredith Papers, HSP. Other examples can be found in Cobbett, *Works*, 10:97; T. Rodney to John

Dickinson, Apr. 15, 1798, quoted in Wilkerson, "Land Speculation in Pennsylvania," p. 307; Robert Morris to John Nicholson, Nov. 1, 1797, *PMHB* 6 (1882): 111. For his power as a trustee of the University of Pennsylvania, see David Rittenhouse to McKean, Dec. 26, 1795, Prov. Delegates Coll., 1:42, HSP and McKean to Joseph Priestley, Nov. 12, 1794, McKean Papers, HSP.

33. See the 1803 letter printed in the *Aurora*, Aug. 7, 1805, and McKean's letter to Dickinson, July 12, 1803, Dickinson Papers, R.R. Logan Coll., Box 5, HSP. In his letter to Dickinson McKean argued that he was reluctant to run and agreed to be a candidate only after a second visit by a delegation of Republicans, and only after they agreed that he would not have to exert his own efforts in his behalf.

34. Walters, *Dallas*, pp. 88-89.

35. *Aurora*, Apr. 25, 1799; John Beckley to William Irvine, Jan. 2, 1799, Irvine Papers, HSP; Tench Coxe to Albert Gallatin, Apr. 26, 1799, Gallatin Papers, NYHS. Coxe judged that the difference in the election would be McKean's more prominent reputation.

36. Cobbett, *Works* 10:190.

17. Republican Governor

1. *Aurora*, Oct. 4, 1799.

2. "An Address to the Freeman of Pennsylvania" (Germantown, 1799); "To the Electors of Pennsylvania...When a Candidate...." (Philadelphia, 1799).

3. Cobbett, *Works* 11: 21-23, 46-48, 99-107, 206; *Aurora*, June 5, 1799. See also *Pittsburgh Gazette*, Sept. 7, 1799; Russell J. Ferguson, *Early Western Pennsylvania Politics* (Pittsburgh, 1938), p. 152.

4. *Aurora*, Apr. 12, 16, 25, 30; May 6; July 8 and 30, 1799.

5. Ibid., Apr. 12, May 3, June 22, Aug. 6, 1799; "To the Citizens of the County of Philadelphia" (Philadelphia, 1799).

6. Ibid.; "To the Electors of Pennsylvania, Take Your Choice: McKean or James Ross?" (Philadelphia, 1799).

7. *Aurora*, May 15, 16, 21, June 24, Sept. 18, 1799; *Report of the Committee Appointed to Inquire into the Official Conduct of the Governor* (Lancaster, 1808); Sanford W. Higginbotham, *The Keystone in the Democratic Arch: Pennsylvania Politics, 1800-1816* (Harrisburg, 1952), p. 238; Scharf and Westcott, *History of Philadelphia* 1:497. Scharf and Westcott report that Joseph McKean assaulted John Fenno just a few days after he had joined those assailing Duane, this time for something Fenno had written about his father.

8. Tinkcom, *Republicans and Federalists*, p. 238; Letter of the Philadelphia Republican Committee, Sept. 25, 1799; C.A. Rodney to T. Rodney, Mar. 7, 1799, Rodney Coll., Box 5, folder 4, HSD.

9. *Aurora*, Dec. 21 and 24, 1799; *SJ*, 1799-1800, pp. 29-30; "A Setler," in Taylor, *The Susquehannah Company Papers* 10:478-79. Theodore Sedgwick said that the difference in the campaign was the role played by Dallas, Gallatin and Joseph Heister. He recommended that Federalists

17. Republican Governor

entice them into their ranks. Another observer, Henry M. Ridgely of Delaware, argued that the Germans of Cumberland County had been made to believe that McKean had disbanded the standing army and repealed the Alien and Sedition Acts. Alexander Addison agreed that chicanery had helped McKean. McKean garnered 37,255 votes out of a record total 69,898 cast. He carried but twelve counties to Ross' thirteen and, as expected, lost Philadelphia. An analysis of the returns indicates McKean's margin of victory was provided by the general antagonism to the federal "window tax," for his majority in three counties most plagued by discontent was 6,000. *Aurora,* Dec. 3, 1799; Ridgely to James Thomson, Nov. 16, 1800, Ridgely Papers, HR; *The Tree of Liberty,* Nov. 15, 1800.

10. *Aurora,* Dec. 20, 1799; Jan. 28, 1800.

11. Ibid., Nov. 8, 26, 27, 29, 1799; Jan. 11, 1800.

12. Rather lamely McKean answered the Senate's "premeditated insult" by arguing that the Senate was concerned with something that had occurred prior to his administration; thus it had no place in official business. "Regarding you . . . only in your representative character," he told them, "I have tho't it in some degree an official duty to suffer you to speak to me in terms, which as a private Gentleman, I would not have consented to hear." He maintained that it was the Senate's prerogative to respond only to the contents of his official message. Ibid., Nov. 12, 1799; Jan. 11, 1800; *Pa. Arch.,* ser. 4, 4:444-49. Support for McKean's position can be found in *Aurora,* Jan. 31, 1800.

13. *Pa. Arch.,* ser. 9, 3:1576; William Findley to Thomas Jefferson, March 1804, Jefferson Papers, LC.

14. Oliver Wolcott to Alexander Hamilton, Apr. 1, 1799, in Gibbs, *Memoirs* 2:231; McKean to Mrs. McKean, Jan. 9, 1800; McKean to John Dickinson, June 23, 1800, McKean Papers, HSP; McKean to Thomas Jefferson, Mar. 7, 1800, Jefferson Papers.

15. *JH, 1799-1800,* p. 69; *SJ, 1799-1800,* p. 35; McKean to Mrs. McKean, Jan. 19, 1800, Dec. 30, 1801, McKean Papers, HSP.

16. McKean to Thomas Jefferson, Mar. 7, 1800, Jefferson Papers; Jefferson to James Madison, Mar. 4, 1800, in Paul Ford, ed., *The Writings of Thomas Jefferson,* 12 vols. (New York, 1905), 7:433; Oliver Wolcott to Fisher Ames, Aug., 1800, in Gibbs, *Memoirs* 2:403. Wolcott wrote that "the moment the elections are determined, Governor McKean will be informed by express, and if the result is favorable to his views, the legislature will be instantly convened and electors appointed."

17. *Pa. Arch.,* ser. 4, 4:452-53, 454-56.

18. McKean to Thomas Jefferson, Dec. 15, 1800. McKean told Jefferson that James Ross in the United States Senate, and his brother-in-law, John Woods, Speaker of the Pennsylvania Senate, were behind the Federalist scheme. He also reported that a Federalist committee had been formed to keep the pressure on Federalist Senators to maintain their position. See Walters, *Dallas,* pp. 96-98, and the comment about Pennsylvania's possible disenfranchisement in William Meredith to David Meredith, Dec. 2, 1800, Meredith Papers, HSP.

19. McKean to Thomas Jefferson, Dec. 15, 1800, Jefferson Papers; Uriah Tracy to Oliver Wolcott, Aug. 7, 1800, in Gibbs, *Memoirs* 2:400. Tracy predicted that McKean would name the electors himself if the legislature did not soon do so.

20. McKean to Thomas Jefferson, Dec. 15, 1800; *Pa. Arch.*, ser. 4, 4:456-58. Federalists complained of McKean's calling the special session, saying that he thought himself "a law to himself." See the *LJ*, Jan. 10, 1801.

21. McKean to Thomas Jefferson, Jan. 10, 1801, Jefferson Papers.

22. McKean to Thomas Jefferson, Feb. 20, 1801, Jefferson Papers.

23. Jefferson to McKean, Mar. 9, 1801, in Ford, *Writings of Thomas Jefferson* 8: 13. See also McKean to Jefferson, Mar. 21, 1801, Jefferson Papers.

24. William Findley to Jefferson, Mar. 21, 1801; McKean to Jefferson, Jan. 27, 1801, Jefferson Papers, LC; McKean told Tench Coxe on June 14, 1801 that he simply wanted to appoint the best people possible to posts. See McKean to Coxe, June 14, 1801, Coxe Papers, HSP.

25. McKean to Thomas Jefferson, July 21, 1801, Jefferson Papers.

26. McKean to Thomas Jefferson, Aug. 10, 1801, Jefferson Papers.

27. William Irvine to McKean, Nov. 4, 1799, Irvine Papers, 14:99, HSP.

28. *Pa. Arch.*, ser. 9, 3:1576-77; McKean to John Dickinson, June 23, 1800, McKean Papers, HSP. Graydon who had married a daughter of Charles Pettit was related to McKean by marriage and thought, because of that, that his position was secure. See Biddle, *Autobiography*, p. 283.

29. *Pa. Arch.*, ser. 9, 3:1576, 1587; ser. 4, 4:444-49, esp. 447-49.

30. Charles L. Ogden to David Meredith, May 3, 1800, Meredith Papers, HSP; *Pa. Arch.*, ser. 9, 3:1584, 1609, 1624-25, 1641, 1645, 1737, 1877. Ronald P. Formisano's description of the "Patron-Client" patronage differs little from what colonial historians have long called "family politics:" providing for one's own friends and relatives. See his "Deferential-Participant Politics: The Early Republic's Political Culture, 1789-1840," *Am. Pol. Sci. Rev.* 68 (1974):479.

31. McKean to Thomas Jefferson, Mar. 7, 1800, Jan. 27, Mar. 21, 1801, June 10, 1802, Jefferson Papers; Jefferson to Don Joseph Yznardi, Mar. 26, 1801, in Ford, *Writings of Thomas Jefferson* 8:33-34; Jefferson to McKean, June 14, 1802; *Aurora*, July 30, 1802. Jefferson could not comply; he named someone else to the post after hearing of Robert's death and before McKean asked about Pettit's chances. Jefferson had his own political requests in the months and years that followed. Two of the most prominent requests involved John Beckley, the Republican propagandist, and Thomas Cooper, the editor. McKean found Beckley clerkships with the Philadelphia's Mayor's Court and the county's Orphans Court. Cooper received a judgeship.

32. *Pa. Arch.*, ser. 9, 3:1576, 1587, 1660; *Aurora*, Jan. 11, June 3, 1800; Ebenezer Hazard to Jedediah Morse, Dec. 24, 1799, Gratz Coll., case 8, box. 11, HSP.

33. McKean to Thomas Jefferson, Mar. 7, 1800, Jefferson Papers.

17. Republican Governor 465

34. Uriah Tracy to Oliver Wolcott, Aug. 7, 1800, in Gibbs, *Memoirs* 2:399; *LJ*, Feb. 14, 1801; *Pa. Arch.*, ser. 9, 3:1701.

35. *Aurora*, Jan. 4, 7; Feb. 14, 18; Mar. 25; Apr. 10, 1800.

36. For a letter from Duane seeking a patronage job from McKean and suggesting a failure to obtain patronage in Washington, see Duane to Thomas McKean Thompson, Mar. 26, 1802, Dreer Coll., HSP.

37. *Aurora*, Dec. 9, Mar. 17, 1801; *SJ, 1801-1802,* p. 397. The bill passed.

38. Jacob Alter to Matthew Carey, Feb. 18, 1801, Lee and Febriger Coll., HSP; *LJ*, Feb. 21, 1801.

39. *Aurora*, Feb. 23, 25, 27, 1801; Frederick Tolles, *George Logan,* pp. 219-21.

40. McKean to Thomas Jefferson, Feb. 20, 1801, Jefferson Papers; *Aurora*, Aug. 7, 1805.

41. McKean to Thomas Jefferson, Feb. 20, 1801, Jefferson Papers; William Findley to A.J. Dallas, Dec. 8, 1801, Dallas Papers, HSP.

42. *HJ, 1801-1802,* pp. 91-92, 94, 112, 115, 124, 174-75, 216-18, 238; *SJ, 1801-1802,* pp. 86, 88, 95, 106-107, 110-11, 142, 144, 251; *Pa. Arch.*, ser. 4, 4:484-86.

43. *Aurora*, Feb. 19, 1801; 4 *Dallas*, p. 229; 3 *Yeates*, pp. 300-17; McKean to Thomas Jefferson, Mar. 21, 1801, Jefferson Papers. Earlier, when Federalists had tried to remove him through court action, Dallas had resisted. He told McKean that he resisted out of consideration for the governor's "superior judgment," and that of "several legal friends" who urged him to fight the movement on constitutional grounds. He had been pleased by the state Supreme Court's unanimous dismissal of the suit, yet it was clear that the legislators wanted him to hold but one post. In the interest of harmony he stepped down. It was "with reluctance" that the governor accepted his resignation.

44. *Aurora*, Jan. 3, July 4, 1801; *LJ*, Mar. 25, 1801. In January the *Aurora* described Addison as having the "face of brass... [the] delicacy of a Hottentot, and the passion of a madman." Addison's most persistent and harsh critic, however, was Israel Israel's *The Tree of Liberty.* See Edward Everett, "Jeffersonian Democracy and *The Tree of Liberty,* 1800-1803," *West. Pa. Hist. Mag.* 32 (1949): esp. 32-34.

45. For this and the following paragraphs I have relied heavily upon Taylor, *The Susquehannah Company* Papers 10: Introduction.

46. Ibid.: xxxviii, xli; "A Setler," *Wilkesbarre Gazette,* Oct. 8, 1799, ibid., pp. 478-79; *Aurora,* Dec. 2, 10, 17, 1799; Jan. 1, 1800, July 16, 1801; Dumas Malone, *The Public Life of Thomas Cooper, 1783-1839* (New Haven, 1926), p. 155.

47. Tench Coxe to McKean, Oct. 3, 1800 and Dec. 8, 1800, in *Pa. Arch.*, ser. 2, 18: 740, 748, 752-53.

48. "Abridgement of the Intrusion Law by Thomas McKean..." (Philadelphia, 1800); Malone, *Cooper,* pp. 158, 160-61; *Aurora,* Mar. 11, 1802; Cooper to McKean, Oct. 20, 1802; The Commissioners to McKean, July 21, 1802, in *Pa. Arch.*, ser. 2, 18:492, 461-62; ser. 4, 4:505. Thomas

Cooper gave McKean some of the most candid advice he received regarding the Wyoming area. Cooper thought that some Wyoming men would have to be arrested, but it was imperative for McKean to remember the violent party was small and a policy of conciliation was the wisest. The use of force would enlarge the violent group, he told McKean, and turn the land into "a desart and a desart it would remain." Conciliation would also produce a valuable trade with the region as the people turned more and more towards Pennsylvania. The commissioners agreed with Cooper that Coxe was pushing "a mode of proceeding more strict and guarded than was consistent with prudence."

49. *Pa. Arch.,* ser. 4, 4:505ff.

50. *LJ,* Apr. 4, Oct. 10, 24, Dec. 12, 1801; *GUS,* Dec. 30, 1802; *Aurora,* Oct. 30, 1801.

51. Higginbotham, *Pennsylvania Politics,* chapt. 2; *Aurora,* Sept. 25, 1801, Jan. 14, Sept. 23, 25, 1802; *GUS,* Oct. 2, 1802; William Duane to Jefferson, June 10, 1801, "Duane Letters," Mass. Hist. Soc. *Proceedings,* ser., 2nd 20 (1906-1907): 265.

52. *Aurora,* Aug. 7, 1802. The call for a meeting to name a Federalist candidate can be found in *GUS,* Aug. 2, 1802.

53. William Duane to Jefferson, June 10, 1801, in "Duane Letters," p. 265.

54. For the political maneuvering in the 1802 election, see Higginbotham, *Pennsylvania Politics,* chapt. 2 and the *Aurora,* Sept. 18, 21, 1802; William Duane to Jefferson, Oct. 18, 1802, Jefferson Papers; Jefferson to McKean, July 24, 1801, Jefferson Papers. On Apr. 6, 1802, over fifty Republican members of the House announced their support for McKean. A series of city and county meetings followed suit. Muhlenberg, Dallas, Leiper, and Leib were chosen to head the McKean campaign effort.

55. Thomas Leiper to Thomas Jefferson, Sept. 19, 1802, Jefferson Papers. Leiper was the chairman of the Sept. 6 meeting supporting McKean.

56. *Aurora,* Oct. 15 and 30, 1802; *GUS,* Nov. 3 and 17, 1802; Higginbotham, *Pennsylvania Politics,* pp. 46-47; *Pa. Arch.,* ser. 4, 4:506-507; Wilkerson, "Land Policy and Speculation in Pennsylvania," pp. 231-35. Daniel Brodhead was dismissed by McKean from the Land Office after an investigation prompted by McKean implicated him in dubious practices.

18. Republicanism Under Attack

1. *Pa. Arch.,* ser. 4, 4:500-502, 506, 508. One Federalist response came in the *GUS,* Dec. 30, 1802. A Federalist writer in that paper wrote that Jefferson would "squeeze all the juice out of [McKean], and that by the time [we] get our hands on him, he will be reduced to an empty rind."

2. *Pa. Arch.,* ser. 4, 4:496-99.

3. Philip S. Foner, ed., *The Complete Writings of Thomas Paine,* 2 vols., (New York, 1969), 2:1003-6; McKean to John Adams, Apr. 30, 1787, McKean Papers, HSP; McKean to Timothy Pickering, Jan. 14, 1804, McKean Papers, HSP.

18. Republicanism Under Attack 467

4. *GUS*, Feb. 1, 2, 5, 1802. See also the excellent discussion of the Judiciary Act of 1801 in Linda K. Kerber, *Federalists in Dissent: Imagery and Ideology in Jeffersonian America* (Ithaca, 1970), chapt. 5.

5. *Pa. Arch.*, ser. 4, 4:519-21; Higginbotham, *Pennsylvania Politics*, 53.

6. *Pa. Arch.*, ser. 4, 4:522-25. For criticisms of McKean's veto, see *Aurora*, Jan.18, 1804.

7. *Pa. Arch.*, ser. 4, 4:521-22. The Senate overrode the veto, 20-2. It was at this point that McKean, upon receiving a book on inland navigation, suggested that he should give it to the legislature so that it could chart a better course. See McKean to Thomas McKean, Jr., Dec. 5, 1802. Also *HJ, 1803-1804*, pp. 17-20, 100; *SJ, 1803-1804*, pp. 68-69, 81-82.

8. *Pa. Arch.*, ser. 4, 4:516-17.

9. McKean to Thomas Jefferson, Feb. 7, 1803, Jefferson Papers; McKean to George Logan, Feb. 19, 1803, Dickinson Papers, R.R. Logan Coll., Box 5, HSP.

10. McKean to Thomas Jefferson, Feb. 7, 1803, Jefferson Papers.

11. Jefferson to McKean, Feb. 19, 1803, Jefferson Papers; Dumas Malone, *Jefferson the President: First Term, 1801-1805* (Boston, 1970), pp. 230-31.

12. "Respublica v. Dennie," 4 *Yeates*, pp. 266-68, 271. The final case was heard in 1805. Dennie was found not guilty.

13. *Pa. Arch.*, ser. 4, 4:482, 528, 531; *Aurora*, Mar. 22, 1803; Timothy Pickering to McKean, Dec 19, 1803; Uriah Tracy to McKean, Dec. 29, 1803, McKean Papers HSP.

14. McKean to Thomas Jefferson, Feb. 7, 1803; *LJ*, Jan. 1, 1803; *GUS*, Mar. 15, 1803; *SJ, 1802-1803*, pp. 30, 32, 40, 55-68, 152-75.

15. Higginbotham, *Pennsylvania Politics*, p. 56. A fourth justice, Republican Hugh Henry Brackenridge was not included in Passmore's charges. Passmore's complaints against the three justices stemmed from an insurance claim in 1801. After an arbitration panel had awarded him damages in a case involving a lost ship, two of the insurers, Andrew Bayard and McKean's son-in-law, Andrew Pettit, filed a protest. Stung by the delay caused by the protest, Passmore in September 1802 posted a notice at the City Tavern which criticized the insuror's actions and referred to Bayard as a "liar a rascal and a coward." Dallas, attorney for Bayard and Pettit, pressed the state Supreme Court to find Passmore in contempt, as the case was still pending before that tribunal. The Court gave Passmore ample opportunity to apologize and escape punishment but the obdurate merchant refused. The Court then sentenced him to thirty days in jail and a fifty-dollar fine for contempt. It was at this point that Passmore sought redress from the legislature, maintaining that the justices had acted arbitrarily and unconstitutionally.

16. *Aurora*, Mar. 31, Apr. 1, 5, 1804; *HJ, 1802-1803:* 393-94, 456, 492-93, 513-14, 518-19, 592, 597; *HJ, 1803-1804:* 227, 634, 670, 687-88; David Paul Brown, *The Forum*, 2 vols., (Philadelphia, 1856), 2: 345; McKean to Thomas McKean, Jr., Mar. 29, 1804; McKean to Jefferson, Feb. 18, 1805, Jefferson Papers; McKean to C.A. Rodney, Feb. 25, 1814, McKean Papers, HSP.

17. *Aurora,* Mar. 31, Apr. 1, 1803. Duane reported that Brackenridge had resigned but Brackenridge quickly corrected the editor. See ibid., Mar. 22, 1805.

18. *HJ, 1804-1805,* pp. 319, 461, 500, 529.

19. Foner, *The Complete Writings of Thomas Paine* 2:994, 1003; *Aurora,* Mar. 31, Apr. 1, 1803; Feb. 1, 1805; Higginbotham, *Pennsylvania Politics,* p. 82; *ADA,* Mar. 22, Apr. 15, 1805; [Jesse Higgins], *Sampson Against the Philistines, or the Reformation of Lawsuits,* 2nd. ed., (Philadelphia, 1805).

20. *Aurora,* Feb. 12, 1802, quoted in Higginbotham, *Pennsylvania Politics,* 79; Brackenridge, *Modern Chivalry,* pp. 447-48; T.I. Wharton, "Memoir of William Rawle," *Memoirs of the Historical Society of Pennsylvania* 4 (Philadelphia, 1840): 61; McKean to Dickinson, July 12, 1803, Dickinson Papers, R.R. Logan Coll., Box 5, HSP.

21. A.J. Dallas to Robert Smith, Apr. 11, 1805, in George M. Dallas, *Alexander James Dallas,* p. 117; McKean to Thomas McKean, Jr., Mar. 4, 1804, McKean Papers; *Pa. Arch.,* ser. 4, 4:534; *Aurora,* Mar. 22, 1804; *HJ, 1803-1804,* 702; *SJ, 1803-1804,* p. 509.

22. *Pa. Arch.,* ser. 4, 4:543-45, 547.

23. Ibid., pp. 565-66; *HJ, 1804-1805,* pp. 612-14, 643.

24. *Pa. Arch.,* ser. 4, 4:563-64; *HJ, 1804-1805,* pp. 574-84, 603-604.

25. McKean to Thomas McKean, Jr., Apr. 7, 1805, McKean Papers, HSP.

26. Ferguson, *Early Western Pennsylvania Politics,* pp. 179-80; Uriah Tracy to McKean, Dec. 29, 1803; Timothy Pickering to McKean, Dec. 19, 1803, McKean Papers, HSP.

27. McKean referred to the followers of Leib and Duane and the county members of the Republican party who generally supported them as democrats and this is the designation given them in this chapter.

28. Higginbotham, *Pennsylvania Politics,* p. 64. Duane erroneously thought McKean was a vital part of this. See *Aurora,* Aug. 7 and 8, 1805.

29. James Hopkins to A.J. Dallas, May 28, 1803, Dallas Papers, HSP.

30. Nathaniel Boileau to Jonathan Roberts, Jr., Dec. 10, 1803, Roberts Papers, HSP.

31. *Phil. Eve. Post,* Feb. 20 and Mar. 10, 1804. The paper later became the *FJ.* See also Higginbotham, *Pennsylvania Politics,* p. 68.

32. Timothy Pickering to McKean, Dec. 19, 1803; Uriah Tracy to McKean, Dec. 29, 1803; McKean to Pickering, Jan. 14, 1804; McKean to Jefferson, Jan. 8, 1804, Jefferson Papers.

33. Thomas Jefferson to McKean, Aug. 19, 1804; McKean to Jefferson, Feb. 18, 1805, Jefferson Papers; Jefferson to Thomas Leiper, June 11, 1804, in Ford, *Writings of Thomas Jefferson* 8:305.

34. *Aurora,* Apr. 15, 20, 1802; *LJ,* Nov. 1802; Yrujo to McKean, Nov. 20, 1803, McKean Papers, HSP. Duane wrote that "McKean is the man talked of as the future republican v.p. no other has been talked of, notwithstanding what has been said in the papers." Duane to Abraham Bishop, Aug. 28, 1802, "Duane Letters" 20:276.

35. A.J. Dallas to McKean, Oct. 13, 21, 1803. Dallas pointed out that he was working to allay the ferment in party circles.

36. McKean to A.J. Dallas, Oct. 16, 1803, McKean Papers, HSP.

37. McKean to Thomas Jefferson, Jan. 8, 1804, Jefferson Papers.

38. McKean to Henry Dearborn, Feb. 8, 1804; Dearborn to McKean, Feb. 20, 1804, Soc. Coll., HSP; Jefferson to McKean, Mar. 3, 1805, Jefferson Papers.

39. McKean to A.J. Dallas, Oct. 16, 1803, McKean Papers, HSP.

40. A.J. Dallas to McKean, Jan. 14, 1805, McKean Papers, HSP.

41. *Aurora*, Feb. 28, 1805. Boileau did not sign the memorial. Some speculated that Duane was the author. See Higginbotham, *Pennsylvania Politics*, p. 81.

42. Most of the pertinent details from McKean's point of view can be found in *The Address of the Society of Constitutional Republicans... To the Republicans of Pennsylvania* (Philadelphia, 1805), esp. pp. 23-28.

43. Ibid.; see also John Binns, *Recollections of John Binns* (Philadelphia, 1854), p. 177.

44. *ADA*, Apr. 23, 1805; *Aurora*, Apr. 23, 1805; *Relf's Phil. Gaz.*, May 22, 1805.

45. See esp. *Aurora*, Apr. 22, 29, 30, May 22, Sept. 6, 1805; Mayor's Court Docket, 1802-1808, pp. 184, 250.

46. *Aurora*, Apr. 26, 27, July 20, 23, 24, 27, 28, 29, Sept. 6, 1805; McKean to George Logan, Feb. 15, 1805, Logan Papers 5, HSP; McKean to Thomas Jefferson, Feb. 18, 1805, Jefferson Papers. McKean by this time concurred with the writer in the *LJ* who labeled Duane "Captain Daggerman." See *LJ*, June 30, 1804.

47. *FJ*, Mar. 5, 7, 1805; Higginbotham, *Pennsylvania Politics*, pp. 82-83.

48. Ibid., p. 95; Jasper Yeates to Edward Burd, Apr. 2, 1805, Shippen Papers, HSP; *LJ*, Apr. 6, 1805.

49. *Aurora*, Mar. 20 and Apr. 5, 1805; *LJ*, Apr. 6, 1805; Higginbotham, *Pennsylvania Politics*, pp. 87, 90; Binns, *Recollections*, p. 178.

50. *ADA*, Mar. 12 and Apr. 20, 1805; Benjamin Rush to John Adams, Sept. 21, 1805, in Butterfield, *Letters of Benjamin Rush*, 2:905.

51. *Aurora*, May 17, June 3, Oct. 8, 1805.

52. Ibid., May 11, 20, June 18, 24, July 9, Sept. 24, 1805.

53. Ibid., Apr. 26, May 8, July 23, 1805. For Duane's comments on Cabrera following his conviction by the Mayor's Court, see ibid., July 22, 1805.

54. Observe the comment by Federalist Horace Binney concerning his party's support of McKean: "We did our duty, however, not from love of McKean, but from scorn of his former politics." Charles C. Binney, *The Life of Horace Binney* (Philadelphia, 1903), p. 55. For Lewis' arguments and the response they elicited, see *LJ*, Sept. 27, 1805; *USG*, June 24, 25, 26, 30, Sept. 23, 1805.

55. Higginbotham, *Pennsylvania Politics*, pp. 96-101. One newspaper—*The Genius of Liberty and Fayette Advertiser*—put McKean's motto:

"The charm of novelty should not be permitted so to fascinate as to give mere innovation the semblance of reform" on its masthead. See Alston G. Field, "The Press in Western Pennsylvania to 1812," *West. Pa. Hist. Mag.* 20 (1937): 239.

19. The Move to Impeach

1. A late count revealed that Snyder was entitled to an additional 395 from Chester County which had earlier been given to a "Samuel Snyder." McKean's final margin of victory was thus less than 5,000 votes. He carried Philadelphia and seventeen counties. Snyder also carried seventeen counties. See *HJ, 1805-1806,* pp. 69-70; Higginbotham, *Pennsylvania Politics,* pp. 99-101.

2. Michael Leib to C.A. Rodney, Dec. 18, 1805, Rodney Coll., Box 5, folder 2, HSD.

3. *Aurora,* Nov. 26, 1805. Leib persuaded Jefferson to write a letter denying that he supported McKean in 1805. See Kim T. Phillips, "William Duane, Philadelphia's Democratic Republicans, and the Origins of Modern Politics," *PMHB,* 101 (1977): 382.

4. *Aurora,* Sept. 6, 1805, Jan. 1, 1806; G.M. Dallas, *Alexander James Dallas,* pp. 226ff.

5. *Pa. Arch.,* ser. 4, 4:569-74.

6. McKean to John Dickinson, Nov. 28, 1805, McKean Papers; Higginbotham, *Pennsylvania Politics,* p. 141.

7. *Pa. Arch.,* ser. 9, 3:2188, 2190, 2203, 2211, 2230-31; John Adams to Benjamin Rush, Mar. 26, 1806, in 1806, in *Spur of Fame,* p. 51.

8. *Pa. Arch.,* ser. 9, 3:2168; *Aurora,* Nov. 1, 1805.

9. *HJ, 1805-1806,* pp. 319-20.

10. Ibid., pp. 154-55; *Aurora,* Jan. 27, 1806; *FJ,* Apr. 25, 1806.

11. *HJ, 1805-1806,* pp. 157, 166, 311, 319, 323, 414, 572, 576, 621. On Mar. 22, 1806, the dueling bill passed and the Senate accepted it with amendments. For a discussion of the deliberations regarding the Bryan-Thompson duel, see "Benjamin Jordan" in *Aurora,* Jan. 27, 1806.

12. *Aurora,* Jan. 15, 27; Feb. 20, 22, 26, 1806. Duane accused Wertz also of supporting McKean's views on judicial reform in exchange for his commission. On Feb. 26, after Wertz's vote helped secure the passage of a bill favored by McKean, Duane commented that "The Governor and secretary *know the value of a vote* in the Senate."

13. Ibid., Jan. 15, 29, 30; Mar. 4; July 11, 21; Aug. 9, 12, 13; Aug. 13, 1806. For Yrujo's problems in Washington, see ibid., Feb. 15, 1806.

14. David Meredith to William Meredith, Oct. 19, 1805, Meredith Papers, HSP; *Pa. Arch.,* ser. 9, 3:2184, 2207, 2218, 2272.

15. *Aurora,* Jan. 1 and Mar. 1, 1806; McKean to Thomas McKean, Jr., Jan. 4, 1806, McKean Papers, HSP; Edward Burd to Jasper Yeates, Jan. 13, 1806, in L.B. Walker, *The Burd Papers,* p. 212; McKean to William Tilghman, Jan. 4, 1806; Biddle, *Autobiography,* p. 318; Brown, *The Forum,* 1:343-44. When the news of Shippen's retirement became known, Aaron Burr asked Charles Biddle to intercede with McKean in his behalf.

19. The Move to Impeach

Biddle mentioned Burr's interest to Joseph McKean, but the governor apparently never heard about it. William Duane expressed pleasure in Tilghman's selection and remarked that "the bar are highly delighted at their escape from the McKean dynasty on the bench."

David Paul Brown tells of a legislative committee who waited upon McKean to inform him of their opposition to Tilghman, introducing themselves as "representatives of the sovereign people." McKean purportedly responded, "Inform your constituents that I bow with submission to the will of the great democracy of Philadelphia; but by G—d, William Tilghman *shall be* chief justice of Pennsylvania."

16. Higginbotham, *Pennsylvania Politics,* p. 114; *Aurora,* Aug. 16 and 19, 1806; *USG,* Aug. 12, 1806.

17. *Aurora,* Jan. 15 and 30, 1806.

18. Anonymous [William Dickson], *The Quid Mirror* (Philadelphia, 1806), Introduction, pp. 3, 5, 15. Benjamin Rush wrote on Oct. 24, that the pamphlet had "produced several challenges and one assault and battery." Rush to John Adams, Oct. 24, 1806, in Butterfield, *Letters of Benjamin Rush* 2:934.

19. Thomas McKean, Jr., to Michael Leib, Oct. 16, 1806; Leib to Thomas McKean, Jr., Oct. 18, 1806; Thomas McKean, Jr., to Richard Dennis, Oct. 19, 1806, McKean Papers, HSP.

20. *FJ,* Dec. 4 and 5, 1806; Apr. 2, 1807; *HJ, 1807-1808,* pp. 348-49.

21. *Pa. Arch.,* ser. 4, 4:579-85.

22. *Aurora,* Dec. 20 and 24, 1806; Benjamin Rush to John Adams, Nov. 25, 1806, in Butterfield, *Letters of Benjamin Rush* 2:936.

23. *HJ, 1806-1807,* pp. 35, 64, 65, 66-68, 175-78, 181-86, 190.

24. McKean to George Logan, Dec. 20, 1806, Logan Papers 5, HSP.

25. Albert Gallatin to Jean Badollet, Oct. 25, 1805, Gallatin Papers, NYHS. A good many of America's leading politicians accepted the presence of a "conspiracy" against their interests at one time or other—including President Jefferson. See Buel, *Securing the Revolution,* chapts. 8, 11, 12.

26. *Aurora,* Jan. 12, 1807; *HJ, 1806-1807,* pp. 309-13, 499, 513-14.

27. Thomas McKean Thompson to Thomas McKean, Jr., Jan. 29 and 30, 1807, McKean Papers, HSP. See also same to same, Feb. 13, 1807, ibid.

28. McKean to Thomas McKean, Jr., Jan. 16, 1807, McKean Papers, HSP; McKean to John Dickinson, Jan. 12, 1807, Dickinson Papers, R.R. Logan Coll., Box 5, HSP.

29. *Pa. Arch.,* ser. 4, 4:601-2.

30. *HJ, 1806-1807,* pp. 513-14, 727-38; Higginbotham, *Pennsylvania Politics,* p. 126.

31. *Aurora,* Mar. 20 and 21, 1807.

32. The relevant letters and documents can be found in the McKean Papers, HSP.

33. *Aurora,* Apr. 11, 1807.

34. *Pa. Arch.,* ser. 4, 4:602-4.

35. *HJ, 1806-1807*, pp. 727-38.

36. *FJ*, Sept. 7, 1807.

37. *Pa. Arch.*, ser. 4, 4:604-7.

38. Benjamin Rush to John Adams, Apr. 3, 1807, in Butterfield, *Letters of Benjamin Rush* 2:938-39; *FJ*, Sept. 7, 1807.

39. Thomas Leiper to Thomas Jefferson, Aug. 20, 1807, Jefferson Papers; William Duane to Jefferson, n.d., received Dec. 5, 1807, "Duane Letters" 20:306. But see also McKean to Joseph Hiester, July 31, 1807, Gregg Coll., LC. Privately McKean admitted he was annoyed by the law which declared that officers were to be elected. With this provision neither "subordination nor discipline" could be maintained. "Besides," McKean wrote, "Youth between 18 & 21 years of age, day-labours, journey-mechanics, & artisans and aliens, who have resided six months only in the State . . . appear incompetent to make a proper choice of a General or Inspector of a Brigade."

40. But see Thomas Paine's counter arguments that Pennsylvania courts "have not yet arrived at the dignity of independence. . . . They hobble along by the stilts and crutches of English, and antiquated precedents. Their pleadings are . . . from English law books; many of which are tyrannical, and all of them now foreign to us." Foner, *The Complete Writings of Thomas Paine* 2:1003.

41. *Pa. Arch.*, ser. 4, 4:612-27; *HJ, 1807-1808*, pp. 43-44, 50-51, 113-14, 307-8, 321-434.

42. *HJ, 1807-1808*, pp. 428-29.

43. For Duane's view of McKean's defense, see *Aurora*, Feb. 20, 1808. Duane commented to the effect that Aaron Burr, Thomas McKean and John Randolph had "made a desperate push, and each in his fall from public confidence, carried with him his adherents, his sycophants, and his enthusiasts." He added that, like Lucifer, they will "never rise again."

44. Thomas McKean Thompson to Thomas McKean, Jr., Oct. 16, 1808, McKean Papers, HSP.

20. Look Back in Wonder

1. Thomas McKean to Thomas McKean, Jr., Feb. 13, 1808, McKean Papers, HSP.

2. *Pa. Arch.*, ser. 9, 4:2457, 2467; Thomas McKean Thompson to Thomas McKean, Jr., Oct. 17, 1808, McKean Papers, HSP. McKean did appoint Thomas McKean, Jr., as adjutant general of the state militia in his last months. This paragraph is not meant to imply that McKean no longer wielded influence in the legislature. He did, if only in a negative fashion. Charles Biddle (*Autobiography*, p. 328) observed that a German member of the Assembly argued against an insurance bill by proclaiming, "If you bass dis bill, old McKean will get his life insured, and so we shall never get rid of him." See also *Aurora*, Jan. 11, 1808.

3. *Pa. Arch.*, ser. 4, 4:649-51, 653-54.

4. Ibid., ser. 9, 4:2587-88, 2594, 2605, 2637. Some of the "Royal Family," such as Thomas McKean, Jr., could not be removed.

5. 1 *Binney,* 600-609; Joseph B. McKean to Thoms B. Zantzinger, Jan. 14, 16, 18, 1809, Dreer Coll., New Ser., in Boxes, HSP; Richard Rush to Thomas B. Zantzinger, Jan. 15 and 17, 1809, ibid.

6. McKean to Thomas McKean, Jr., Feb. 29, 1808, McKean Papers; *The American Watchman,* Sept. 8, 1810. McKean's will can be found in the McKean Papers, HSP; it is reprinted in Roberdeau Buchanan, *The Life of the Honorable Thomas McKean* (Lancaster, 1890), pp. 115-16.

7. McKean to James Rogers, July 24, 1810, McKean Coll., HSD; McKean to Rogers, Dec. 9, 1811, Hampton L. Carson, HSP.

8. Ibid.

9. McKean to John Adams, Aug. 20, 1813, in Adams, *Works* 10:61.

10. "Franklin," *Democratic Press,* Aug. 19, 1811. Additional details are provided by Higginbotham, *Pennsylvania Politics,* pp. 231-32.

11. McKean to John Way, July 16, 1811, Dreer Coll., New Ser. in Boxes, HSP.

12. Higginbotham, *Pennsylvania Politics,* p. 232.

13. *USG,* Oct. 8, 20, 21, 23, 1812; McKean to John Adams, June 13, 1812, in Adams, *Works* 10:14; Higginbotham, *Pennsylvania Politics,* p. 267.

14. McKean to John Adams, Jan., 1814, in ibid., p. 89; Scharf and Westcott, *History of Philadelphia* 2:571; Read, *Read,* p. 344.

15. McKean to John Adams, Nov. 20, 1815, in Adams, *Works* 10:178.

16. John Adams to McKean, June 2, 1812, in ibid., pp. 12-13.

17. McKean to John Adams, July 1, 1815, McKean Papers, HSP.

18. McKean to John Adams, Sept. 28, 1813; Jan., 1814.

19. See chapt. 6, note 1 above.

20. His discussion of his Delaware political career covered the years to 1779, but his concentrated treatment of the difficulties between America and Great Britain stopped short of the Declaration of Independence. One page of the manuscript is missing.

21. Consult chapt. 3.

22. McKean's will, McKean Papers, HSP.

23. Jared Ingersoll to Joseph B. McKean, May 8, 1817, Brown Coll., , Box 25, folder 2, HSD.

24. Joseph B. McKean to Samuel M. McKean, June 4, 1817, Brown Coll., Box 25, folder 2, HSD; *Port Folio,* 4th (5th) ser., IV (Sept., 1817), 246-48.

25. *ADA,* June 25, 1817; *Aurora,* June 25, 1817.

26. *Aurora,* June 25, 1817.

27. McKean's family was a source of some disappointment and pain to him. He took inordinate pride in the accomplishments of Joseph and in the happy marriages of his daughters, Elizabeth, Letitia, Ann and Sally, but one daughter, Sophia Dorothea, remained unmarried and two sons, Robert and Thomas, were unable to settle on a vocation well into their adult years. His fifth child and third daughter by Mary Borden died at the age of ten and his fifth and last child by Sarah Armitage did not survive her fourth year. McKean's first son by Sarah was stillborn. Throughout his first gubernatorial term the serious illnesses of Sally and

Sophia troubled him, as did the death of Sally Yrujo's first child. Son Robert died in 1802, daughters Ann in 1804, Elizabeth in 1811. The decision of the Yrujos to return to Spain in 1808 was a profound shock to McKean. He lamented the absence of Sally and her children daily.

28. Nor was McKean alone in this respect. It is instructive how often men like Alexander Hamilton, Thomas Jefferson, John Adams, Benjamin Franklin, William Duane, and others like them, attributed conspiratorial designs to their opponents. For one explanation, see John R. Howe, "Republican Thought and the Political Violence of the 1790's," *American Quarterly*, 19 (1967): 147-65; for another, Richard Buel, *Securing the Revolution*, chapts 8, 11, 12.

Bibliography

Several excellent bibliographies relevant to early Delaware and Pennsylvania have appeared in the last three decades, including those in Robert L. Brunhouse, *The Counter-Revolution in Pennsylvania, 1776-1790* (Harrisburg, 1942); Sanford W. Higginbotham, *The Keystone in the Democratic Arch: Pennsylvania Politics, 1800-1816* (Harrisburg, 1952); Joseph E. Illick, *Colonial Pennsylvania: A History* (New York, 1976); John A. Munroe, *Federalist Delaware, 1774-1815* (New Brunswick, 1954); Theodore Thayer, *Pennsylvania Politics and the Growth of Democracy, 1740-1776* (Harrisburg, 1953); Harry M. Tinkcom, *Republicans and Federalists in Pennsylvania, 1790-1801* (Harrisburg, 1950); and H. Clay and Mariam B. Reed, eds., *A Bibliography of Delaware Through 1960* (Newark, Del., 1960). The works of David H. Flaherty, ed., *Essays in the History of Early American Law* (Chapel Hill, 1969), and Lawrence Friedman, *A History of American Law* (New York, 1975), contain useful bibliographies relating to legal matters. A vast literature exists on the American Revolution and its aftermath. An excellent bibliographical essay is included in Jack P. Greene, ed., *The Reinterpretation of the American Revolution, 1763-1789* (New York, 1966), but one can profitably consult John Shy, ed., *The American Revolution.* "The Golden tree Bibliographies in American History Series" (New York, 1973). For an examination of the most important works touching upon republicanism in early American History, see Robert E. Shalhope, "Toward a Republican Synthesis: The Emergence of an Understanding of Republicanism in American Historiography," *WMQ* 29 (Jan., 1972): 49-80. No attempt has been made to duplicate these bibliographies. The footnotes in the present work contain full information on all sources used. Each source is given in full the first time it is cited. Following, then, is a select list of those materials I have found most useful.

A. UNPUBLISHED MANUSCRIPT COLLECTIONS

Alison, Francis. Manuscripts. Presbyterian Historical Society, Philadelphia
Atlee, William A. Papers, LC
Bradford, William. Papers. HSP
Brown, H.F. Collection, HSD
Bryan, George. Papers. HSP
Carson, Hampton L. Collection, HSP
Clemency Papers, PRD
Clymer, George. Papers, HSP
Colonial and Revolutionary Manuscripts, HSP
Coxe Papers, HSP
Dallas, Alexander J. Papers, HSP
Dreer, Ferdinand J. Collection, HSP
Emmett Collection, NYPL
Etting Papers, HSP
Franklin, Benjamin Papers, APS
Gallatin, Albert. Papers, NYHS
Governor's Papers (McKean Administration), PRD
Gratz, Simon. Collection, HSP
Gregg Collection, LC
Irvine, William. Papers, HSP
Jefferson, Thomas. Presidential Papers Microfilm Ed., LC
Lea and Febiger Collection, HSP
Legal Men of Pennsylvania Collection, HSP
Logan, Robert R. Collection, HSP
McKean, Thomas. Papers, HSP
McKean, Thomas. Papers, HSD
McKean, Thomas. Items, NYPL
McKean, Thomas. Items, LC
McKean, Thomas. Items, National Archives, Washington, D.C.
McKean, Thomas. Items, CCHS
Meredith Papers, HSP
Miscellaneous Collection, HSP
Nicholson, John. Papers, PRD
Papers Relating to the Continental Congress, Microfilm Edition, National Archives.
Parrish-Cox-Wharton Collection, HSP
Pemberton Papers HSP
Penn, John. Papers, HSP
Penn-Physick Correspondence, HSP
Pennsylvania Miscellaneous Collection, LC
Peters, Richard. Papers, HSP
Philadelphia Court Papers, HSP
Provincial Delegates Collection, HSP
Rawle Papers, HSP
Ridgely Papers, HR
Roberts Autograph Collection, Haverford College, Haverford, Pa.

Roberts, Jonathan. Papers, HSP
Rodney, Caesar A. Collection, HSD
Rodney, Thomas. Papers, HSD
Shippen Papers, HSP
Shoemaker Papers, HSP
Society Collection, HSP
Society for the Propagation of the Gospel Papers, Microfilm Edition, Courtesy of the University of Kansas
Sprague Collection, HSP
Stiles, Ezra. Manuscripts, Presbyterian Historical Society, Philadelphia
Supreme Court Notes, HSP
Taylor, Isaac. Papers, HSP
Yeates, Jasper. Correspondence, HSP
Yeates, Jasper. Legal Papers, HSP

B. UNPRINTED LOCAL RECORDS

Chester Co., Administrative Books. Chester Co. Clerks Office. West Chester, Pa.
Chester Co., Appearance Dockets, 1742-1751, 1752-1756, 1757-1762. Prothonotary Office, West Chester, Pa.
Chester Co., Common Pleas Dockets, 1749-1754, 1754-1760, 1760-1766. Prothonotary Office, West Chester, Pa.
Chester Co., Estate Files. Register of Wills. West Chester, Pa.
Chester Co., Execution and Judgment Files. Prothonotary Office, West Chester, Pa.
Chester, Co., Orphans Court Records. Chester Co. Clerks Office, West Chester, Pa.
Chester Co., Petitions for Tavern Licenses, vols. 1-4, CCHS
Chester Co., Tax Lists, 1693-1740, CCHS
Collections of the Genealogical Society of Pennsylvania, HSP
New Castle Co., Common Pleas Dockets, 1768, 1768/1769, 1769, HR
New Castle Co., Deed Books, HR
New Castle Co., Oyer and Terminer Dockets, 1746-1792, HR
Pennsylvania. Oyer and Terminer Dockets, 1778-1800, PRD
Pennsylvania. Supreme Court Dockets: Appearances, 1764-1768, 1769-1771, 1772-1774, 1774-1776, 1780-1782, 1783-1785, PRD
Pennsylvania. Supreme Court Execution files, PRD
Pennsylvania. Supreme Court Judgment Files, PRD
Pennsylvania. Supreme Court Minute Books, PRD
Pennsylvania. Supreme Court Narrative Papers, PRD
Pennsylvania. Supreme Court Verdicts, PRD
Pennsylvania. Supreme Executive Council, Clemency Files, PRD
Pennsylvania. Supreme Executive Council, Forfeited Estates File, PRD
Philadelphia. Common Pleas Dockets, 1796-1808. City Archives. Philadelphia
Philadelphia. Court Records, 1681-1800, HSP
Philadelphia. Mayor's Court Dockets, 1796-1808. City Archives. Philadelphia

Philadelphia. Quarter Sessions Dockets, 1796-1808, PRD
Sussex Co., Common Pleas Dockets, 1766-1770, HR
Sussex Co., Oyer and Terminer Dockets, 1754-1778, 1787-1817, HR

C. UNPUBLISHED DOCTORAL DISSERTATIONS

Arnold, Douglas. "Political Ideology and the Internal Revolution in Pennsylvania, 1776-1790." Princeton University, 1976.

Bauman, Roland. "The Democratic-Republicans of Philadelphia: The Origins, 1776-1797." Pennsylvania State University, 1970.

Boughner, Daniel T. "George Read and the Founding of the Delaware State, 1781-1798." Catholic University of America, 1970.

Brady, James E. "Wyoming: A Study of John Franklin and the Connecticut Settlement into Pennsylvania." Syracuse University, 1973.

Brobeck, Stephen J. "Changes in the Composition and Structure of Philadelphia's Elite Groups, 1756-1790." University of Pennsylvania, 1972.

Gatton, Douglas W. "A Study of the Roles of the State and Federal High Courts in the Law and Politics of Pennsylvania, 1787-1810." University of Illinois, 1973.

Henderson, Herbert James. "Political Factions in the Continental Congress." Columbia University, 1962.

High, John W. "The Philadelphia Loyalists, 1763-1783." Temple University, 1975.

Ingersoll, Elizabeth A. "Francis Alison: American *Philosophe,* 1705-1799." University of Delaware, 1974.

Keller, Kenneth W. "Diversity and Democracy: Ethnic Politics in Southeastern Pennsylvania, 1788-1799." Yale University, 1971.

McCoy, Drew. "The Republican Revolution: Political Economy in Jeffersonian America, 1776-1817." University of Virginia, 1976.

Meehan, Thomas R. "The Pennsylvania Supreme Court in the Laws and the Commonwealth, 1776-1790." University of Wisconsin, 1960.

Miller, Richard G. "Philadelphia, the Federalist City: A Study in Urban Politics, 1789-1800." University of Nebraska, 1971.

Ousterhout, Anne McCabe. "The Forgotten Antagonists: Pennsylvania Loyalists." Michigan State University, 1972.

Peeling, James H. "The Public Life of Thomas McKean, 1734-1817." University of Chicago, 1929.

Phillips, Kim T. "William Duane, Revolutionary Editor." University of California, Berkeley, 1968.

Rowe, Gail Stuart. "Power, Politics, and Public Service: The Life of Thomas McKean, 1734-1817." Stanford University, 1969.

Ryerson, Richard A. "Leadership in Crisis: The Radical Committees of Philadelphia and the Coming of the Revolution in Pennsylvania, 1765-1776: A Study in the Revolutionary Process." Johns Hopkins University, 1972.

Stumpf, Vernon O. "Colonel Eleazer Oswald: Politician and Editor." Duke University, 1968.

Wilkerson, Norman. "Land Policy and Speculation in Pennsylvania, 1779-1800." University of Pennsylvania, 1958.

D. NEWSPAPERS

American Daily Advertiser. Philadelphia.
American Watchman. Wilmington, Del.
Aurora and *General Advertiser.* Philadelphia.
Democratic Press. Philadelphia.
Freeman's Journal or the *North American Intelligencer.* Philadelphia.
Gazette of the United States. Philadelphia.
General Advertiser. Philadelphia.
Independent Gazetteer or the *Chronicle of Freedom.* Philadelphia.
Lancaster Intelligencer. Lancaster, Pa.
Lancaster Journal. Lancaster, Pa.
New York Gazette & Weekly Mercury. New York, N.Y.
New York Journal. New York, N.Y.
Oracle of Dauphin. Harrisburg, Pa.
Pennsylvania Chronicle, or the *York Weekly Advertiser.* York, Pa.
Pennsylvania Evening Post. Philadelphia.
Pennsylvania Gazette, Philadelphia.
Pennsylvania Journal or *Weekly Advertiser.* Philadelphia.
Pennsylvania Packet or *General Advertiser.* Philadelphia.
Pittsburgh Gazette. Pittsburgh.
Porcupine's Gazette. Philadelphia.
Poulson's American Daily Advertiser. Philadelphia.
Relf's Philadelphia Gazette. Philadelphia.
Republican Argus. Northumberland.
Tickler. Philadelphia.
United States Gazette. Philadelphia.

E. PUBLISHED WORKS BY MCKEAN

McKean, Thomas, and Edmund Physick. *A Calm Appeal to the People of Delaware.* Philadelphia. 1793.

McKean, Thomas. *A Charge Delivered to the Grand-Jury by the Honourable Thomas McKean, Esq., at a Court of Oyer and Terminer, and General Gaol Delivery . . . on the 21st Day of April, 1778 . . .* Lancaster, 1778.

McKean, Thomas, and James Wilson. *Commentaries on the Constitution of the United States.* London, 1793.

McKean, Thomas, and Caesar Rodney, eds., *Laws of New Castle, Kent and Sussex Counties Upon Delaware,* 2 vols. Wilmington, 1763.

McKean, Thomas. *The Acts of the General Assembly of the Commonwealth of Pennsylvania, carefully compared with the originals; and an Appendix containing the laws now in force, passed between the 30th day of September, 1775 and the Revolution . . .* Philadelphia, 1782.

McKean, Thomas, and George Read, eds., *Votes and Proceedings of the House of Representatives of the Governments of the Counties of*

New-Castle, Kent and Sussex Upon Delaware, for the Years 1765, 1766, 1767, 1768, 1769, 1770. Dover, 1931.

McKean, Thomas, and Caesar Rodney, eds., *Votes and Proceedings of the House of Representatives of the Governments of the Counties of New-Castle, Kent and Sussex Upon Delaware at a Session of the Assembly held in New Castle on the 20th Day of October, 1762.* Wilmington, 1763.

F. BOOKS, PRINTED RECORDS, AND COLLECTIONS

Most of the colonial and state records, pamphlets and broadsides cited in this work can be found in *Early American Imprints,* first series (Evans), 1639-1800, edited by Clifford K. Shipton (American Antiquarian Society); and second series (Shaw-Shoemaker), 1801-1819, edited by Clifford K. Shipton and James E. Mooney (American Antiquarian Society). Works not found in these collections or in the secondary studies listed earlier, or of *particular* value to this work are listed below.

Addison, Alexander, ed., *Reports of Cases in the County Courts of the Fifth District and the High Court of Errors & Appeals, of the State of Pennsylvania.* Washington, 1800.

Arbuckle, Robert D. *Pennsylvania Speculator and Patriot: The Entrepreneurial John Nicholson, 1757-1800.* University Park, Pa., and London, 1975.

Binney, Horace, ed., *Reports of Cases Adjudged in the Supreme Court of Pennsylvania,* 6 vols. Philadelphia, 1890-1891.

Brackenridge, Hugh Henry, *Modern Chivalry,* edited by Claude N. Newlin. New York, 1937.

Brown, David Paul, *The Forum,* 2 vols. Philadelphia, 1856.

Brown, Elizabeth G. *British Statutes in American Law, 1776-1836.* Ann Arbor, 1964.

Buchanan, Roberdeau, *The Life of the Honorable Thomas McKean.* Lancaster, 1890.

Buchanan, Roberdeau, *Genealogy of the McKean Family.* Lancaster, 1890.

Calhoon, Robert M. *The Loyalists in Revolutionary America, 1760-1781.* New York, 1973.

Chroust, Anton-Hermann, *The Rise of the Legal Profession in America,* 2 vols. Norman, Okla., 1965.

Cobbett, William, *Porcupine's Works,* 12 vols. London, 1801.

Coleman, John M. *Thomas McKean: Forgotten Leader of the Revolution.* Rockaway, N.J., 1975.

Cremin, Lawrence, *American Education: The Colonial Experience, 1607-1783.* New York, 1970.

Dallas, Alexander J., ed., *Reports of Cases in the Supreme Court of Pennsylvania,* 4 vols. Philadelphia, 1790-1807.

Eastman, Frank M. *Courts and Lawyers of Pennsylvania,* 4 vols. New York, 1922.

Ellis, Richard E., *The Jeffersonian Crisis: Courts and Politics in the Young Republic.* New York, 1971.

Friedenwald, Herbert, *The Declaration of Independence*. New York, 1904.
Futhey, J. Smith, *History of Chester County, Pennsylvania*. Philadelphia, 1881.
Gurr, T.R. *Why Men Rebel*. Princeton, 1970.
Hamilton, William B., *Thomas Rodney: Revolutionary & Builder of the West*. Durham, N.C., 1953.
Hancock, Harold B., *Liberty and Independence: The Delaware State During the American Revolution*. Wilmington, 1976.
Hastings, George E., *The Life and Works of Francis Hopkinson*. Chicago, 1928.
Hawke, David F., *A Transaction of Free Men: The Birth and Course of the Declaration of Independence*. New York, 1964.
Hawke, David F., *Benjamin Rush: Revolutionary Gadfly*. Indianapolis, 1973.
Hawke, David F., *In the Midst of a Revolution*. New York, 1960.
Hazelton, John, *The Declaration of Independence*. New York, 1906.
Henderson, H. James, *Party Politics in the Continental Congress*. New York, 1974.
Hutson, James H., *Pennsylvania Politics, 1746-1770: The Movement for Royal Government and its Consequences*. Princeton, 1972.
Hutson, James H. and Kurtz, Stephen G., eds., *Essays on the American Revolution*. New York, 1973.
Judson, C. Carroll, *Biographies of the Signers of the Declaration of Independence*. Philadelphia, 1839.
Konkle, Burton A., *George Bryan and the Constitution of Pennsylvania, 1731-1791*. Philadelphia, 1933.
Konkle, Burton A., *The Life and Times of Thomas Smith, 1745-1809*. Philadelphia, 1904.
Lemon, James T., *The Best Poor Man's Country: A Geographical Study of Early Southeastern Pennsylvania*. Baltimore and London, 1972.
Library of Congress Symposia on the American Revolution, *Leadership in the American Revolution*. Washington, 1974.
Library of Congress Symposia on the American Revolution, *The Development of a Revolutionary Mentality*. Washington, 1972.
Logan, Deborah Norris, *Memoir of Dr. George Logan of Stenton*. Philadelphia, 1899.
Lucas, Stephen E., *Portents of Rebellion: Rhetoric and Revolution in Philadelphia, 1765-1776* . Philadelphia, 1976.
MacReynolds, George, ed., *The New Doan Book*. Doylestown, Pa., 1952.
Martin, James K., *Men in Rebellion: Higher Governmental Leaders and the Coming of the Revolution*. New Brunswick, 1973.
McKean, Cornelius, *McKean Genealogies*. Des Moines, Iowa. 1902.
McKean, Frederick, *McKean Historical Notes*. Washington, 1906.
Miller, Richard C., *Philadelphia—The Federalist City: A Study of Urban Politics, 1789-1801*. Port Washington, N.Y., 1976.
Neuenschwander, John A., *The Middle Colonies and the Coming of the American Revolution*. Port Washington, N.Y., 1973.

Olton, Charles S., *Artisans for Independence: Philadelphia Mechanics and the American Revolution.* Syracuse, 1975.

Perry, William S., ed., *Historical Collections Relating to the American Colonial Church,* 5 vols. Hartford, 1870-1878.

Sanderson, John D. (group pseudonym), *Biographies of the Signers of the Declaration of Independence,* 5 vols. Philadelphia, 1828.

Sloan, Douglas, *The Scottish Enlightenment and the American College Ideal.* New York, 1971.

Smith, Joseph H., *Appeals to the Privy Council from the American Plantations.* New York, 1950.

Stevens, B.F., ed., *Facsimiles of Manuscripts in European Archives Relating to America, 1773-1783,* 25 vols. Wilmington, Dela., 1970.

Taylor, Robert J., ed., *The Susquehannah Company Papers,* 11 vols. Ithaca, N.Y., 1930-1971; vols. 1-4 edited by Julian Boyd.

Tolles, Frederick, *George Logan of Philadelphia.* New York, 1953.

Wharton, Francis, *State Trials of the United States During the Administration of Washington and Adams.* Philadelphia, 1849.

Weslager, C.A. *The Stamp Act Congress.* Cranbury, N.Y., 1976.

Wood, Gordon S., *The Creation of the American Republic, 1776-1787.* Chapel Hill, N.C., 1969.

Young, Alfred F., ed., *The American Revolution: Explorations in the History of American Radicalism.* DeKalb, 1976.

G. ARTICLES

Adams, W. Paul, "Republicanism in Political Rhetoric Before 1776," *PSQ* 85 (1970): 398-404.

Alexander, John K., "The Fort Wilson Incident of 1779: A Case Study of the Revolutionary Crowd," *WMQ* 31 (1974): 589-612.

Banning, Lance, "Republican Ideology and the Triumph of the Constitution, 1789 to 1793," *WMQ* 31 (1974): 167-88.

Bockelman, Wayne L. and Ireland, Owen S., "The Internal Revolution in Pennsylvania: An Ethnic-Religious Interpretation," *Pa. Hist.* 41 (1974): 125-60.

Carson, Hampton L., "The Case of the Sloop Active," *PMHB* 16 (1892): 385-98.

Chamberlain, Mellen, "The Authentication of the Declaration of Independence, July 4, 1776," Massachusetts Historical Society, *Proceedings,* ser. 2, 1 (1884-1885): 273-98.

Coleman, John M., "The Treason of Ralph Morden and Robert Land," *PMHB* 79 (1955): 439-51.

Coleman, John M., "Thomas McKean and the Origin of an Independent Judiciary," *Pa. Hist.* 34 (1967): 111-30.

Cooke, Jacob E., "Tench Coxe: Tory Merchant," *PMHB* 96 (1972): 48-88.

Cooke, Jacob E., "The Whiskey Insurrection: A Re-Evaluation," *Pa. Hist.* 30 (1963): 316-46.

Evans, Mary T., "Letters of Dr. John McKinly to his wife while a Prisoner of War, 1777-1778," *PMHB* 34 (1910): 9-20.

Hancock, Harold B., "County Committees and the Growth of Independence in the Three Lower Counties on the Delaware, 1765-1776," *Delaware History* 15 (1973): 269-94.

Henderson, H. James, "Congressional Factionalism and the Attempt to Recall Franklin," *WMQ* 27 (1970): 246-67.

Henderson, H. James, "Constitutionalists and Republicans in the Continental Congress, 1778-1786," *Pa. Hist.* 36 (1969): 119-44.

Hutson, James H., "The Partition Treaty and the Declaration of Independence," *JAH* 58 (1972): 877-96.

Keen, Gregory B., "The Descendants of Joran Kyn, the Founder of Upland," *PMHB* 4, (1880): 234-43.

Kohn, Richard H., "The Washington Administration's Decision to Crush the Whiskey Rebellion," *JAH* 59 (1972): 567-84.

Lermack, Paul, "Peace Bonds and Criminal Justice in Colonial Philadelphia," *PMHB* 100 (1976): 173-90.

Leyburn, James, "Presbyterian Immigrants and the American Revolution," *J. of Presbyterian Hist.* 54 (1976): 9-32.

McAllister, James L., "Francis Alison and John Witherspoon: Political Philosophers and Revolutionaries," *J. of Presbyterian Hist.* 54 (1976): 33-60.

McCoy, Drew R., "Republicanism and American Foreign Policy: James Madison and the Political Economy of Commercial Discrimination, 1789 to 1794," *WMQ* 31 (1974): 633-46.

Meehan, Thomas R., "Courts, Cases, and Counselors in Revolutionary and Post-Revolutionary Pennsylvania," *PMHB* 91 (1967): 3-34.

Meehan, Thomas R., "Not Made out of Levity: Evolution of Divorce in Early Pennsylvania," *PMHB* 93 (1968): 441-64.

Mercer, Henry C., "The Doans and Their Times," *Collections of Papers Read Before the Bucks County Historical Society* 1 (1908): 271-82.

Oaks, Robert F., "Philadelphians in Exile: The Problem of Loyalty During the American Revolution," *PMHB* 96 (1972): 298-325.

Pears, Thomas C., "Francis Alison," *J. of the Presbyterian Hist. Soc.* 27 (1950): 213-25.

Pears, Thomas C., "Francis Alison, Colonial Educator," *Delaware Notes* 17-21 (1944): 9-22.

Pears, Thomas C., "Presbyterians and American Freedom," *J. of the Presbyterian Hist. Soc.* 29 (1951): 77-95.

Pears, Thomas C., "Ten Little Irish Lads," *The University (of Delaware) News.* Alumni Issue, (1943), pp. 5-9.

Peeling, James H., "Governor McKean and the Pennsylvania Jacobins, 1799-1808," *PMHB* 54 (1930): 320-54.

Phillips, Kim T., "William Duane, Philadelphia's Democratic Republicans, and the Origins of Modern Politics," *PMHB* 101 (July 1977): 365-87.

Powell, John H., "John Dickinson as President of Delaware State, 1781-1782," *Delaware History* 1 (1946): 1-54.

Powell, John H., "John Dickinson as President of Pennsylvania," *Pa. Hist.* 28 (1966): 254-67.

Powell, John H., "The Declaration of Independence, July 1, 1776," *Delaware Notes* 22-26 (1950): 37-61.
Rodney, Richard S., "The End of the Penns' Claim to Delaware, 1789-1814, Some Forgotten Lawsuits," *PMHB* 61 (1937): 182-203.
Rogers, Fred B., "Robert McKean, First President of the Medical Society of New Jersey," *J. of the Med. Soc. of New Jersey,* (1953), pp. 432-37.
Rowe, G.S., "'A Valuable Acquisition in Congress:' Thomas McKean, Delegate From Delaware to the Continental Congress, 1774-1783," *Pa. Hist.* 38 (1971): 225-64.
Rowe, G.S., "Outlawry in Pennsylvania, 1782-1788, and the Achievement of an Independent Judiciary," *The American Journal of Legal History* 20 (1976): 227-44.
Rowe, G.S., "*Rex* v. *John Clowes, Jr.,* and the Shape of Politics in Pre-Revolutionary Sussex County," *Delaware History* (Fall-Winter 1977), pp. 215-35.
Rowe, G.S., "The Legal Career of Thomas McKean, 1750-1775," *Delaware History* 16 (1974): 22-46.
Rowe, G.S., "The Travail of John McKinly, First President of Delaware," *Delaware History,* 17 (1976): 21-36.
Rowe, G.S., "Thomas McKean and the Coming of the Revolution," *PMHB* 96 (1972): 3-47.
Ryerson, R.A., "Political Mobilization and the American Revolution: The Resistance in Philadelphia, 1765 to 1776," *WMQ* 31 (1974): 565-88.
Shaeffer, John N. "Public Consideration of the 1776 Pennsylvania Constitution," *PMHB* 98 (1974): 415-38.
Soler, William G., "John Dickinson's Attitude Toward the French, 1797-1801," *Delaware History* 6 (1954-1955): 294-98.
Surrency, Erwin C., "The Lawyer and the Revolution," *The American Journal of Legal History,* 8 (1964): 125-35.
Surrency, Erwin C., "When the Common Law was Unpopular in Pennsylvania," *Pennsylvania Bar Association Quarterly* 33 (1962): 291-300.
Teeter, Dwight L., "The Printer and the Chief Justice, Seditious Libel in 1782-1783," *Journalism Quarterly,* (1968), pp. 235-42, 260.
Thompson, J. Earl, Jr., "Slavery and Presbyterianism in the Revolutionary Era," *J. of Presbyterian Hist.* 54 (1976): 121-44.
Thompson, P.F., "Narrative of Thomas McKean Thompson," *PMHB* 52 (1928): 59-77, 111-29.
Wolcott, Daniel F., "Ryves Holt of Lewes, Delaware, 1696-1763," *Delaware History* 8 (1958-1959): 3-50.
Young, Henry J., "Treason and its Punishment in Revolutionary Pennsylvania," *PMHB* 90 (1966): 287-313.

Index

"Abigail Collicoe," 252
Abolition Society of Philadelphia, 230-31, 232
"A By Stander," 187
"A Calm Appeal to the People of Delaware," 176
Accounts and Claims Committee (Cont. Cong.), 65
"A Citizen of Philadelphia," 165
Active, the, case of, 271-73
Actual Settlers Bill, 194
Adams County (Pa.), 351
Adams, John, 39, 50, 57-58, 67, 69, 72-73, 78, 106, 154-55, 157-59, 242, 261, 283, 286, 287, 316, 363, 383, 396-98, 404
Adams-Lee congressional bloc, 227. *See also* Eastern bloc
Adams, Samuel, 154-55, 159, 161
Addison, Alexander, 327, 339-40, 463n*g*, 465n*44*
admiralty, court of (Cont. Cong.), 144; (Pa.), 271-72
"A Freeman," 310
"A Friend to the Army," 184
"A Hint to Grand Juries," 187
Aitkinson, Thomas, 363
Alexander, Gabriel, 4
Alien and Sedition Acts, 293-94, 303

Alison, Francis, 5-8, 10, 118, 412, 412n*13*
  values of, 12, 22, 26, 48, 57, 81-82, 100
Alison, Hannah, 57
Allegheny County (Pa.), 274-76, 322, 395
Allen, Andrew, 22, 73
Allen, Ethan, 197
Allen, James, 10, 73, 101-2, 434n*15*
Allen, Morrial, 19
Allen, William, 22
Alliance of 1778, 143, 155
Almon, John, 455n*48*
Amboy, Perth, 85-86
American common law, 181, 341
American Philosophical Society, 265
Angle, Margaret, 189
Anglican
  bishop, 60
  church, 60-61, 423n*22*
  clergy, 60
  faculty, 126
  mercantile faction, 33
anti-Federalists, 245-46, 249, 252, 270
"Anti-Quibbler," 182
Appeals to the Crown, 425-26n*24*
Armitage, Francis, 57

Armitage, James, 57
Armitage, Sarah, 57. *See also* McKean, Sarah Armitage
Armstrong, William, 32, 45, 57
army (Continental), 76, 123, 126, 144, 150-52, 182-84
Arnold, Benedict, 114, 147, 271, 437n*17*
Articles of Confederation, 144-45, 160, 195, 267
"Association," The Continental, 58. *See also* pages 85, 103
Associators, The (Pa.), 69, 76, 79, 86, 94
  Second Battalion, 69
  Fourth Battalion, 76-77, 85
  Fifth Battalion, 76
Atlee, Edwin A. 322
Atlee, William A., 104, 114, 128-29, 148, 165, 189, 211-12, 233, 243, 251, 255
Atlee, William R., 320
Attainders, Act of, 104, 111
  Bill of, 176
  cases of, 133, 138, 140
  writs of, 113-14, 121, 138, 205
Aurora, The (Phil.), 306, 323-24, 328, 340, 344, 351, 355, 357, 358, 360, 363, 367, 368, 369, 374, 377, 379-80, 382, 403

Bache, Benjamin, 285, 297, 370
Bailey, Francis, 363, 453n*24*, 455n*45*
Banning, Mrs. John, 443n*24*
Barker, John, 371-72, 374
Baron, Job, 203
Barton, William, 344-45
Bassett, Richard, 90-91
Bayard, John, 93, 109, 256, 456n*8*
Beckley, John, 284, 464n*31*
Bedford County (Pa.), 85, 111, 367
  courts of, 102
Belt, Francis, 230-32
benefit of clergy, 206
Berks County (Pa.), 271, 311
Bernard, Francis, 37, 55
Biddle, Charles, 3, 5, 218, 225, 228-29, 322, 417n*31*, 454n*24*, 470n*15*
Biddle, John, 386

Bingham family, 266
Bingham, William, 257, 325
Binney, Horace, 469n*54*
Binns, John, 357
Blacks, 180
Blackstone, William, 26, 216
Board of War, 98
Boggs, Dr. James, 21
Boileau, Nathaniel, 326, 341, 345, 350, 378, 381, 392, 469n*41*
Borden, Ann, 49. *See also* Hopkinson, Ann
Borden, Joseph, 26, 40
Borden, Mary (Mary McKean), 26, 57, 60, 62
Bordentown (N.J.), 26
Boston (Mass.), 49, 52, 54
boycott
  of British goods, 45, 56
  of legal offices, 95, 98, 102
Boyd, John, 218
Boyds Tavern (Chester Co., Pa.), 365
Bracken, James, 111
Brackenridge, Hugh Henry, 191, 193, 194, 279, 322, 340-41, 467n*15*, 468n*17*
Bradford, David, 278-79
Bradford, Thomas, 148-49
Bradford, William, 105, 138-39, 180, 188, 189, 212, 231, 251, 275-78
Bradley, Isaac, 88
Brice, John, 239
Brice, Sarah, 239
Brodhead, Daniel, 331, 466n*56*
Brown, Andrew, 253
Brownville (Pa.), 279-80
Bruce, David, 460n*8*
Bryan, George, 99, 133-34, 203, 208, 210, 218, 222, 251, 253-55, 320, 392
  "Fort Wilson" affair, 129
  Mamachtaga case, 190-91, 193
  Oswald case, 183, 188-89
Bryan, Samuel, 330, 363-65, 366-68, 470n*11*
Buchanan, Andrew, 266, 368
Buchanan, George, 321, 370, 381
Bucks County (Pa.), 138, 203, 206-7, 221, 293, 311

Index 487

Buffington, Joshua. *See Respublica v. Buffington*
Bulla, Sarah, 220
Bulla, Thomas, 207, 220
Burd, Edward, 109, 208, 261, 322, 368, 425n*24*
Burke, Thomas, 145, 156
Burlington (N.J.), 40
Burns Tavern (Phil.), 127
Burr, Aaron, 317-18, 470-71n*15*, 472n*43*
Burton, Benjamin, 27, 32, 47, 52, 418n*37*

Cabrera, Don Joseph, 351-56, 358, 371, 381, 469n*53*
Caldwell, Andrew, 26
Caldwell, Lillis, 20
Canada, 65-66, 219
"Candid," 186
Cannon, James, 72, 93
Cantwell, Richard, 89, 91
capias ad respondendum, 204, 207, 209. *See also* outlawry
Carlisle, Abraham, 115-16, 118-19
Carlisle (Pa.), 148, 250, 252, 281
Carpenters' Hall (Phil.) 57, 78
Carver, Samuel, 370
Chamberlain, Mellen, 429n*1*
chancery, courts of (New Castle), 11; (Pa.), 234-35
Chapman, John, 222
Chapman, Samuel. *See Respublica v. Chapman*
Chatham (Pa.), 3, 25
Chester County (Pa.), 2, 4, 26, 112, 118, 140, 181-82, 183, 191, 205-6, 208, 220, 312, 365, 368
 bar of, 104
 circuit courts in, 20
 courts, 10-11, 12, 19-20, 22, 25, 52, 102, 114, 429n*19*
 orphans court, 4, 20
Chew, Benjamin, 2, 22, 24-25, 33-34, 114, 282
Chew family, 266
"Cicero," 187
City Hall (Phil.), 113
City Tavern (Phil.) 57, 128
"Civis," 187

Clark, John, 218
Clarkson, Matthew, 257
Clayjon, William, 167
Clifford, Thomas, 180
Cling (or Kling), John, 183
Clinton, DeWitt, 395
Clinton, George, 396
Clinton, Gen. Henry, 143, 148
Clitheral, James, 427n*29*
"Clodpoles," 351, 393; affair 356
clothier-general department (Cont. Cong.), 144
Clowes, John, Jr., 27-28, 29, 31, 46-47, 52, 88-89, 146, 399, 403, 418n*38*
Clymer family, 266
Clymer, George, 69-70, 96, 258, 424n*11*
Cobbett, William, 291, 294-95, 297-98, 299-303, 306, 308-13, 357, 369
Cochran, John, 8
Cochranville (Pa.), 3
coercive acts, the, 52
College of New Jersey, 164
College of Philadelphia, 8, 22, 115, 126-27, 436n*8*
 trustees of, 127
Collins, Thomas, 146
commercial policy, 65, 67
Committee of Correspondence (Del.), 34, 45, 51-52; (Pa.), 269-70
Committee of Inspection (Del.), 50
Committee of Inspection and Observation (Pa.), 69-70, 74-78, 97; (Sussex Co., Del.), 88
Committee of Privates (Pa.), 76, 127
Committee of Safety (Del.), 91; (Lancaster Co., Pa.), 104; (Phil.), 80, 86, 91, 95
"Committee of Sixty," 278
Committee of the Whole (Del.), 45; (Cont. Cong.), 81; (Pa.), 259
Committee of Thirteen (Del.), 54; (Cont. Cong.), 155-56

Committee on Foreign Affairs (Cont. Cong.), 155
common law. See American common law; Great Britain
common pleas courts (Del.), 11, 23-24, 36, 43, 416n28;(Pa.),102, 343
Common Sense, 155
Compromise Act of 1799, 327-28
"Conferees," 269
confiscation legislation, 102, 104, 113, 124, 133
  cases of, 133
Connard, Edward, 204
Connard, Henry, 204
Connecticut, 44, 65, 158, 195-97, 198-200
Connor, Patrick, 21
Constitutionalists, 94-95, 99, 122, 124, 127, 161, 167-68, 178, 181, 182, 205, 215, 219, 241-42, 244, 258
Constitutional Party, 383
Constitution (Federal), 244-62
Continental "Association," 58. See also "Association"
Continental Congress (first), 41, 56-62, 70; (Second), 64, 87, 92, 94, 103-6, 109, 112, 121, 138, 142-64, 168, 211
  declares American independence, 80, 82-83
  in Pennsylvania politics, 71-73, 76-77
  in Wyoming controversy, 195
  journals of, 118
  military affairs, 84, 87
  non-exportation, 65
  non-importation, 65-67, 69
  office of the president, 163, 171
Convention, The (a brig), 271-72
Cooper, Jeremiah, 204
Cooper, Thomas, 328-29, 363, 464n31, 466n48
Cornwallis, Gen. Charles Lord, 163
"Correspondents," 269-70
Council of Censors (Pa.), 94
country party, 31, 45, 46
courthouse. See Philadelphia
court party, 27, 29, 46, 146
courts. See Delaware; Philadelphia, city courts; Pennsylvania; New Castle

Coxe, Tench, 113, 306, 312, 328, 331, 344, 357, 464n35, 466n48
Crapper, Levin, 27, 32, 46-47, 52, 418n37
Crapper, Manuel, 27
Crawford, William, 193
Creighton (or Craghton), John, 411n3
Cribs, Jacob, 458n33
Cromwell, Oliver, 99
Crow, John, 393
Cumberland County (Pa.), 246, 251, 281
currency, (Continental), 105, 159-60
customs
  office, 48, 308
  collector of, 48, 308

Dagworthy, John, 88-89
Dalby, Phillip, 230-32
Dalby v. *Belt*, 232
Dallas, Alexander James, 262, 268-70, 275, 278, 284, 286, 304-6, 312, 314, 316, 320-21, 326-27, 334, 348-50, 356-57, 370, 397, 400, 465n43, 466n54
Dallas family, 266
Dauphin County (Pa.), 320
Dawson, Daniel, 130
Dawson, David, 208, 217
Deane, Silas, 154, 156
  faction in Congress, 156-58
Dearborn, Henry, 349-50
DeBerdt, Dennys, 44, 143
Declaration of Independence, 80, 82, 84, 397-98, 400, 473n20
Declaration of Rights and Fundamental Rules of this State (Del.), 89-90
Declaration of Rights and Resolves, 58
Delaney, Sharp, 105, 221
Delaware River, 77, 325
Delaware (state) 57, 140, 162, 165, 168, 319, 397
  and Articles of Confederation, 144-45
  anti-lawyer tradition, 10
  Assembly, 33, 44-46, 48, 50-52, 54, 56, 61-62, 77-78, 90, 92, 97-98, 170, 173, 175-76

Index

attacked by British, 107
bar, 12-17, 19, 23, 26, 31, 33, 41-43
Committee of Correspondence, 51
congressional instructions, 62
congressional positions, 59, 64-67, 73-74, 81, 158, 169
constitutional convention (1776), 86-89, 92
Constitution of 1776, 89-92, 93, 427n*37*
counterfeiting in, 98
courts, 1, 12-15, 16-17, 20, 22, 24, 32, 34, 41-43, 75, 170, 415n*19*
defense of, 85
education in, 22, 98
elections in, 17, 29, 31-33, 46-48
judges, 1, 13, 15, 23, 32, 42-43
lawyers in, 14-16, 20, 27, 42-43, 416n*28*
Legislative Council, 90, 107
militia law, 98
politics in, 31-33, 48
Privy Council, 90
representations in Congress, 169
slavery in, 232
supreme court, 1, 12, 22, 28-29, 33
Democratic Judge, The, 300-301
Dennie, Joseph, 338, 467n*12*
Dennis, Richard, 371, 397-80, 391
Department of Marine (Cont. Cong.) 160-61
Department of Treasury (Cont. Cong.), 160
Department of War (Cont. Cong.), 160
Deshong, Peter, 112
Diana, The (a schooner), 62
Dickinson, John, 16, 20, 99, 158, 163, 176, 182, 234, 282, 295, 314, 320, 342, 362, 363, 378, 400, 417n*29, 32;* 426n*24,* 430-31n*18,* 431n*27*
  as lawyer, 22, 25
  as president of Delaware, 170-73
  correspondence with Marbois, 210-14
  drafts Articles of Confederation, 145
  foreign policy, 288-90
  in Delaware politics, 168-69
  in Second Continental Congress, 67, 71-72, 74, 81-82, 92-94
  Letters of Fabius, 291-93
  on outlawry, 196, 206-9, 215-25
  opposes royal movement in Pa., 34, 62
Dickinson, Philemon, 171-73, 443n*23*
Dickson, William, 363, 367, 392
"Dionysian faction," 146
Divesting Act (1779), 125
Doan, Aaron, 203, 207-9, 216, 219, 222, 224
Doan gang, 202-9, 215-27
Doan, Israel, 447n*5*
Doan, Joseph, Jr., 207, 220
Doan, Joseph, Sr., 204, 207
Doan, Levy (or Levi), 206, 220-21
Doan, Mablon, 204, 207
Doan, Moses, 203, 206-7
Dover (Del.), 91
Doz, Andrew, 123
Drinker, Henry, 24
Drum, Simon, 280-81
Duane, James, 58-59, 66, 72, 156
Duane, William, 304-6, 311-12, 324, 330-31, 334, 341, 344, 346, 347-48, 351, 355, 356, 358, 361, 363, 366-69, 371-72, 374-77, 380-81, 383, 386, 392, 401, 403, 406, 465n*36,* 468n*34,* 469n*46,* 471n*15,* 472n*43*
Ducke, Jacob, 265, 444n*19*
Dunn, Thomas, 419n*7*

East Bradford Township (Pa.), 140
Eastern bloc (Cont. Cong.), 58, 66-67, 154, 156, 159, 227
Easton (Pa.), 197
Edgar, James, 279
Edinburgh, University of, 6
education, 5-10, 22, 57, 81, 98, 324, 361, 412n*13,* 416n*26*
Ege, Michael, 189
ejectment, suits of, 24, 133, 179-80, 193, 198
Ellery, William, 156
Ellicott, Andrew, 344-45
Ellsworth, Oliver, 156
Elmslie, John, 130

embargo, 386, 391
embracery, 179-80
England. *See* Great Britain
Episcopalians. *See* Anglican
Epple's Tavern (Phil.), 250
Evans, John (Del.), 47, 51, 89, 91, 92, 431n27
Evans, John (Pa.), 104, 114, 128, 148, 165-66
Ewing, John, 8, 22, 123

"fair play" law, 189
"Fair Play Republic," 189
Fayette County (Pa.), 193, 203, 245, 279
Federal Constitutional Convention (Phil.), 244-45
Federalists, 241, 246, 327, 381, 395
   attack McKean, 307-10
   celebrate victory, 250-51, 252-53
   critical of McKean's patronage policies, 320-24
   form city slate for Fed. Const. Convention, 244
   in city politics, 257, 264, 266, 269-70
   on McKean as candidate, 356-59, 376
   oppose Republicans on state convention, 356
   seek to control electors, 316-18
   support McKean for governor, 366-81
Fell, John, 156
Fenno, John, 287, 462n7
Ferguson, Elizabeth, 113
Ferguson, Henry Hugh, 113
Findley, William, 222, 224, 246, 256, 260, 314, 316
Finney, David, 5, 10-13, 18-19, 24, 416n26, 417n29, 421n4, 425-26n24, 435n44, 454n29
Finney family, 3, 5, 11, 18
Finney, John (McKean's uncle), 11,' 18, 24, 413n23, 421n4

Finney, John (McKean's distant cousin), 368
Finney, Letitia (McKean's mother), 3
Finney, Robert, 3
First Troop of Philadelphia Cavalry, 266
Fisher, Jabez, 122
Fisher, Miers, 25, 105, 123, 425n24
Fisher, Samuel, 122-23
Fitzsimons, Thomas, 222, 224, 258, 450n46
Flying Camp, 85
"Fort Wilson" affair, 128-29, 131-32
France, 285, 291, 307
   aid from, 154-55, 163
   interests of, 157-58
   king of, 143, 283, 292
   ministers of, 285, 292
   revolution in, 283-85, 288-90, 396-97
   The Directory, 293-94
   treat with, 143, 155
Francis, Tench, 10-11
Franklin, Benjamin, 22, 34, 37, 219, 229, 237, 426n24, 427n34
   recalled, 154-55, 156-58, 404
Franklin, John, 197-99, 201, 327, 446n43
Franklin, Walter, 392
Franklin, William, 147
free press, 184, 186, 254, 444n15
Freeman's Journal, 164, 365, 381-82, 400
French Revolution. *See* France
French, Robert, 413n23, 425n24
Friends of Hibernia, The, 265
Fries, John, 311
funding bill, 267
funding program, 284

Gadsden, Chistopher, 66
Gallatin, Albert, 279, 357, 377
Galloway, Grace Grouden, 114
Galloway, Joseph, 11, 19, 22, 42, 58-59, 61, 114, 282, 283, 425n24, 485n36

Index

Gardner, Joseph, 182, 184
Garriques, Samuel, 122
Gaspee, The, 50, 55
Gates, Gen. Horatio, 167
Gazette of the United States, 287
Gelston, Samuel, 412n*13*
Genêt, Edmund, 283-84
George III, 45, 56, 59, 73
Georgia, 64-65, 81
Gerard (a sloop), 271-72
Gerard, Conrad Alexandre, 155
Germans, 36, 127-28, 310
  militiamen, 128
Gerry, Elbridge, 156
Glasgow, University of, 6
Goffney, James, 189
Golden, William, 18, 23
Graydon, Alexander, 261, 320, 464n*28*
Great Britain, 70, 79-80, 82, 85, 100, 138-39, 157, 178, 183, 221, 283-85, 292, 355, 391, 396
  acts of, 34, 48, 54-55, 56, 61
  common law of, 101, 103, 115, 179-80
  laws of, 178-79, 180-81, 186, 216, 341, 375
  ministers of, 285
  ministry of, 48, 62, 64, 66, 143
Greenburgh (Pa.), 280
Greene, Nathaniel, 119
Green Mountain Boys, 197
Griswold, Joseph, 134-37
Grouden, Laurence, 114
Grover, Nicholas, 203
Guardian, The, 6

Habeas Corpus Act, 106, 234
habeas corpus, writs of, 28, 97, 106, 107, 123, 129-30, 134, 136-37, 167, 230, 354, 369
Hadley, Simon, 5, 20
Hale, Lord, 99
Hall, David, Jr., 26, 29, 319, 417n*34*
Hall, David, Sr., 29, 32, 88
Hamilton, Alexander, 266-67, 273, 275, 282, 284, 456n*8*

Hamilton, William, 358
Hancock, John, 81
Hanna Town (Pa.), 193
Harold, Daniel, 458n*33*
Harris' Ferry (Harrisburg, Pa.), 109
Hart, Joseph, 203, 206-7
Hartley, T.H., 129
Haslet, John, 47, 51, 90, 92
Hastings, John, 367
Hemings, Sally, 338
Henderson, Andrew, 321, 368
Henderson, David, 11
Henderson, John, 411n*3*, 413n*27*
Henderson, William, 321
Henry, Patrick, 59
Henry, William, 270
Heusted, John, 321
Hiester, Joseph, 270-71, 394-95, 462-63n*9*
Higginbotham, Sanford W., 359
high court of errors and appeals, 304-5
Holden, Samuel, 155
Hole, Nicholas, 203
Holsey, Nathaniel, 207
Holt, Ryves, 1, 426n*24*
Hopkins, James, 345
Hopkinson, Ann (Borden), 188
Hopkinson, Francis, 48, 188, 235, 237-38, 240, 241, 244, 253, 322, 421n*1, 3;* 432n*33;* 452n*19, 26;* 453n*24*
Hopkinson, Joseph, 322-24, 379
Horne, John, 455n*48*
Houston, William, 161
Howe, John R. x, 287
Howe, Gen. William, 84, 109, 114, 143
Hubley, John, 320
Hunt, John, 105
Huntingdon County (Pa.), 368
Huntington, Samuel, 161-62
Hutcheson, Francis, 6, 7, 82
Hutchinson, James, 268-70, 284

Incompatibility Act, 326

Independent Gazetteer (Phil.), 182-83, 187, 230, 253-54
Indian Queen Tavern (Phil.), 95, 148
Indians, 194
Ingersoll, Jared, Jr., 400
Ingersoll, Jared, Sr., 140, 180, 275, 280, 321
Inglis, Charles, 26, 61
Inns of Court (London), 21
Intrusion Act, 328-29
Iris (a sloop), 294
Irish, the, 2, 23, 308-10, 410n2
Irvine, James, 218
Irvine, William, 277-78, 279, 281, 305, 320
Irwin, James, 208
Israel, Israel, 357, 370
Israel, John, 363
Izard, Ralph, 154, 156-57

Jackson, David, 370
Jackson, Paul, 8
"Jacobins," 372, 376, 390
James, Abel, 24, 114, 133-34
James Claims, 133-34
Jaudennes, Joseph, 295
Jay, John, 59, 66, 285
Jay Treaty, 285, 288-89, 291-93, 295, 307, 330
Jefferson, Thomas, 80-82, 158, 287, 291, 294, 315-21, 323, 325, 329, 336-38, 347-49, 360, 367, 374, 383-84, 391, 394
Jeffries, Judge, 184, 187, 375
"Jerry Switch" (Francis Hopkinson), 414n29
Johns, Kensey, 417n34
Johnson, Thomas, 67
Johnstone, George, 143
Jones, John, 92
Jones, William, 179
Judson, Henry, 421n1
Judson, Joseph, 435n44
"Junius Wilkes," 186
juries, role of, 194, 215, 249
justices of the peace, 36, 322, 333, 335-36, 341, 357, 363, 368

Keaney, Phillip, 21
Kebel's Reports, 20
Keith, Gov. William, 205
Kennedy, Andrew, 363
Kennedy, James, 363
Kent County, (Del.), 32, 36, 51, 55, 62, 77-78, 81, 89, 170
    delegation to Cont. Cong., 89, 91, 92
Killen, William, 319, 417n34
Kling (or Cling), John, 183
Kollock, Jacob, Jr., 32
Kollock, Jacob, Sr., 36, 418n37
Kollock, Phillip, 92
"Koster," 186
Kreamer, Laurence, 189

Lancaster (Pa.), 108-10, 128, 268, 272, 317, 344-45, 365, 372, 378-79, 390
Lancaster County (Pa.), 95, 104
    committee of safety, 104
    courts, 102, 114, 272
    grand jury, 110
Lancaster Intelligencer, 367
Lancaster Journal, 329, 358
Land Office (Pa.), 331, 466n56
land titles, 193
Lange, Charles, 351-52
Langworthy, Edward, 156
Latimer, George, 244
Latimer, James, 24, 47, 51
Latscha, Henry, 350
Latta, James, 8
Laurens, Henry, 142-43, 150, 155-56
law
    discussion of, 58
    study of, 10, 26, 110
"law of nations," 211-14, 352, 355, 358
lawyers, 10, 14, 23, 31, 41, 42, 57-58, 194. *See also* Delaware; Pennsylvania
    criticisms of, 10, 23, 190, 229-30, 341-42, 350
    opposition to Pa. Constitution of 1776, 95, 97, 102

Index

Lazaretto physician, 368, 381
Lea, John, 89, 91
Lee-Adams faction (Cont. Cong.), 156. *See also* Eastern bloc
Lee, Arthur, 154-55, 156-59
Lee, Richard Henry, 58-59, 66, 72, 78, 80-81, 155, 158
Lee, William, 154, 156-57
"Legality," 165-67
Leib, Michael, 304-6, 312, 320-21, 346, 348, 356, 358, 360, 370, 371-72, 374, 375, 377-81, 386, 391, 394-95, 466n54, 470n3
"Leibites," 360, 376
Leiper, Thomas, 331, 361, 383
levy court, 33
Levy, Moses, 368, 380
Levy, Samson, 208, 354
Lewes (Del.), 28, 55
Lewis, William, 112, 231, 253, 255-56, 258, 267, 271, 358, 469n54
   and College of Phil., 126-27
   and outlawry, 207-8, 222-25
   cases of, 115-16, 133-34, 140-41, 436n8
Lewis, Wrixam, 418n37
Lexington (Mass.), 64
libel, 185-86, 187, 254-56, 298-303, 332-33, 374-75, 378, 392-93, 444n18
Little, John, 69
Livingston, Robert R. 66, 183
Logan, Ann, 3, 19
Logan, George, 239, 293-95, 300, 303, 305-7, 310, 318, 325-26, 330, 337, 346, 356-57, 370, 375, 376
Logan, James, Jr., 19
Logan, James, Sr., 3-4, 19
Londonderry Township (Pa.), 3
London Grove Township (Pa.), 3
Longchamps, Charles Julian de, 209-11, 212, 214, 354, 404
Louis XVI. *See* France, king of
Louisiana Purchase, 346, 361
Lour, Margaret, 189

Loyalists. *See* Tories
Lucas, John B.C., 322, 327, 459n42
Luzerne, Chevalier Anne Cesar de la (Charles de la), 158, 210
Luzerne County (Pa.), 197-98, 199-201, 328, 342
Lycoming (Pa.), 189, 328

Maclay, Samuel, 357
Madison, James, 351-52, 394-95
Maitland, Frederick William, 204
Malin (first name unavailable), 116
Mamachtaga (an Indian), 191, 193, 227
Manlove, Boaz, 27, 29, 46-47, 146
Mansfield, Lord. *See* Murray, William
Marbois, Barbe de, 210-14
Marshall, Christopher, 72, 122
Marshall, John, 318
Maryland, 15-16, 81, 85, 145, 158, 160, 170, 231, 233
Mason, George, 249
Massachusetts, 34, 44, 50-52, 55, 64, 138, 158
"Mathematicus," 184
Matlack, Timothy, 76, 88, 93, 123, 128, 228-29
May 10-15 resolve (Cont. Cong.), 72-73, 77
McBeath, John, 393
McCall family, 266
McClenaghan, Blair, 285
McCorkle, William, 346, 363
McDowell, John, 183, 218
McDowell, Joseph, 5
McKean, Ann (McKean's daughter), 422n14, 473n26
McKean, Ann Logan (McKean's stepmother), 3. *See also* Logan, Ann
McKean, Barbara (McKean's aunt), 411n3
McKean, Elizabeth (McKean's daughter), 266, 422n14, 473n26
McKean, James (McKean's uncle?), 411n3
McKean, Joseph (McKean's son),

87, 89, 266, 306, 311-12, 321, 324, 327, 334, 352, 354, 366-70, 379-81, 392-93, 400, 422n*14*, 462n*7*, 471n*7*, 471n*15*, 473n*26*
McKean, Letitia (McKean's mother), 3, 411n*6*, 473n*26*
McKean, Letitia (McKean's daughter), 266, 422n*14*, 473n*26*
McKean, Margaret (McKean's aunt), 411n*3*
McKean, Mary (Mary Borden, McKean's first wife), 57, 60, 62, 417n*35*, 422n*14*
McKean, Mary (McKean's daughter), 422n*14*
McKean, Robert (McKean's brother), 5, 8, 20, 60-61, 411n*6*, 415n*27*, 416n*26*
McKean, Robert (McKean's son), 60, 284, 321-22, 422n*14*, 464n*31*, 473n*26*
McKean, Sarah Armitage (McKean's second wife), 57, 85-86, 87, 190, 300, 378, 412n*11*, 473n*26*
McKean, Sarah (McKean's daughter), 295, 300, 309, 473n*26*
McKean, Sophia Dorothea, 473n*26*
McKean, Susanna (McKean's grandmother), 2-4, 410n*3*, 411n*8*
McKean, Thomas (McKean's uncle), 2-3, 12, 118, 411n*3*
McKean, Thomas
   "A Calm Appeal to the People of Delaware," 176
   autobiographical sketch, 398-99
   character and personality, 57, 227, 249, 265-66, 280-81, 304-6, 401-6, 414n*29*, 415n*13*, 417n*31*, 432n*33*, 433n*35*, 452n*2*, 456n*14*
   congressional career, 57-69, 109-21, 142, 422n*20*, 442-43n*23*
      American commercial policy, 65-67
      Articles of Confederation, 144-46, 160
      coercive acts, 52-56

      declares America independent, 77, 81-83, 428n*40*, 429n*1*
      England, opposition to, 34-41, 45, 50-52, 54-55, 56; opposition to Church of, 60-61
      France, view of, 159-60
      Franklin's recall, 154-59
      Gaspee affair, 50-52
      McKinly (John) affair, 146-47
      Plan of Union, the, 58-59
      pluralism, 164-71, 405
      president of Congress, 162-63
      York, life in, 109-12
   Delaware political career, 31-86
      "A Freeman," 54
      Assembly career, 31-33, 34, 416n*23*, 418-19n*7*, 420n*30*
      attitudes towards Del. elections, 18-19
      courts and, 86-93
      customs office, 48-50
      offices, 11, 17-18, 21, 25, 36-37, 48-50, 92, 98, 432n*33*
      pluralism, 164-71, 432n*33*
      president of Delaware, 107-9
      Stamp Act, 34-37
      Stamp Act Congress, 37-41, 397, 399
      Townshend duties, reaction, 45
   education, 6-10
      aid to, 22, 98, 416n*26*
   family, 2-5, 57, 60-63, 87, 97-98, 266, 392-93, 411n*3*, *6;* 412n*11*, 413n*23*, *27;* 422n*14*, 424n*11*, 472n*4*, 473n*26*
   gubernatorial career, 306-89
      addresses to Pa. Assembly, 313, 314, 332-33, 362, 374, 387-88, 391-92
      assessment of first administration, 330-31
      Cabrera case, 351-56
      criticisms of Pa. Assembly, 336-37, 338, 340, 344, 362, 378
      election reforms sought, 315-18
      impeachment move against McKean, 374-89

Index   495

impeachment of Pa. judges, 340-41
judicial reforms, 333-34, 341, 362
libels, reacts to, 332-33, 337-38, 369, 372-73, 374-75, 392-93
nominated, 304-12
patronage policies, 318-25, 330, 363-67, 377
third party schemes, 341, 345-46, 347, 349, 357, 358-59, 361, 370-75, 376
vetoes, 334-36, 339, 342-44, 348, 362, 378, 380, 382, 384
honorary degrees, 22, 164
judicial career, 112, 114, 138-41
  Active case, 271-72
  appointed to chief justiceship, 99-100
  Carlisle (Abraham) case, 114-16, 436n45
  charge to grand jury, 110-11, 273
  Cobbett (William) case, 295-306
  Dallas *Reports,* 262-63
  divorces granted, 237-39
  Doan gang, 202-9, 215-25
  English law, reaction to, 178-81
  Fisher (Samuel) case, 122-23
  "Fort Wilson" affair, 127-30
  free press issues, 253-56, 295-303
  Griswold (Joseph) case, 134-38
  James Claims case, 133-34
  Logan (George) affair, 293-95
  Mamachtaga case, 191-92
  Marbois-Longchamps case, 209-14, 404
  Oswald (Eleazer) affair, 183-88
  penal reforms, supports, 234-36
  Penns' lands (Pa.), 124-26, 436n8, 440-41n36; (Del.), 175-76

Quakers, writs for, 105-7; cases of, 130-32
reforms supported, 227-40
Roberts (John) case, 116-20, 436n45
slavery, views of, 230-34, 451n9
theatre, oversees the, 239-40
Thompson (William) affair, 147-52
Washington (George) land case, 192-93
Whiskey rebellion, role in, 273-82
Wyoming controversy, 194-201, 327-29
law practice
  admitted to bar, 1-2, 10-13
  as lawyer, 14-26, 403, 414n6, 416-17n28, 425-26n24
  Clowes case, 26-29, 46-47, 52
  Middle Temple considered, 20-21
Pennsylvania political career
  as Associator, 69-77, 84-86
  College of Phil., reaction to, 126-27
  Committee of Safety, joins, 95
  constitutional convention, (1789-90), 259-62
  constitution of Pa. (1776), 93-95, 427n37, 431n24
  constitutional reforms, considers, 242-48
  criticisms of Pa. constitution, (1776), 75-76
  federal offices sought, 256-57
  France, view of, 159-60, 283-84, 291-93
  provincial conference (1776), 78-80, 427n38
  public securites holder, 250, 266-67
  ratification convention, 244-48
retirement
  autobiographical sketch of, 398-99

economic holdings, 393
reminiscences, 396-97
social status, 265-66
in Delaware, 12, 18, 21, 24-26, 46, 62, 265
in Pennsylvania, 241, 265-66
organizations joined, 265-66
purchase of Duche house, 265
McKean, Thomas, Jr. (McKean's son), 265, 370-71, 379-80, 389-92, 472n2, 4; 473n26
McKean, William (McKean's father), 2-5, 12, 19, 24-25, 411n3, 5, 6; 413n27
McKean, William (McKean's brother), 24, 232, 411n6, 435n44
McKennan, William, 321, 368
McKinly, John, xi, 18, 24, 51-52, 98, 107-8, 146-47, 152, 422n7, 423n27, 438n12
McLene, James, 218, 224
McSherry, Patrick, 189
McWilliams, Richard, 29
Medical Society of New Jersey, 8
Meehan, Thomas R., 120
Meredith, David, 368
Meredith, Samuel, 69
Middle Colonies, 65-66, 67, 74, 84-85, 100, 119
Middle Temple (London), 20-21
Middle Ward (Phil.), 69
Mifflin, Thomas, 231, 240, 273, 275-77, 279, 304-5, 311, 319-20, 392, 438n4, 459-60n48
Mifflin, Warner, 131
Miles, Samuel, 266, 306
Miles, Sarah, 266
military affairs, 69-77, 84-87, 107, 275, 384, 386
Mingo Creek, 274
misprision of treason. *See* treason
Moland, John, 10-11, 16, 19
Molder, Joshua, 116
Monongahela County (Pa.), 274
Monro, George, 24, 26
Monroe, James, 289, 291
Montgomery, Alexander, 26

Montgomery County (Pa.), 293, 311, 326, 345, 350
Montgomery, John, 251
Montgomery, Joseph, 61, 91
Montgomery, William, 197
Moore, Jacob, 88-90, 92
Morris family, 266
Morris, Gouveneur, 155-57
Morris Lessee v. *Vanderen*, 179-80
Morris, Robert, 81, 97, 128, 161, 163, 172, 183, 221, 231, 400, 456n7
Morton, Robert, 107
Muhlenberg, Frederick, 244, 330
Muhlenberg, Peter, 305-6, 310, 325-26, 330, 356
Murray, William (Lord Mansfield), 262-63, 455n49

Nationalists, 160-61, 172
Negro Betsy, 232
Neill, John, 15
Nesbitt, Alexander, 106
Neutrality, Proclamation of 1793, 283
Neville, John, 218, 275
Newark Academy, 22, 98, 416n26
Newark (Del.), 22, 98, 107-8, 413n18
New Castle (Del.), 11, 15-16, 18, 22, 28, 32-34, 46, 48, 51-52, 54-55, 61, 78, 87, 88, 89, 91, 97, 108, 170, 176, 266, 393
bar, 43
bench, 11, 14, 15, 42
common, 54, 175
courthouse, 1
courts, 11, 15, 22-23, 34, 43
customs office, 308
country party, 31, 45
elections, 18
grand jury, 43
New England, 66-67, 85, 156
New Hampshire, 158
New Jersey, 16, 26, 42, 60, 73-74, 84-85, 108, 158, 219, 222
Assembly, 26, 40

Index

New London Academy, 5-10, 22, 57, 81
New London Township (Pa.), 2, 7-8, 12
Newton (Pa.), 122, 220
New York City, 257
New York State, 26, 33, 34, 37, 39, 54, 58-59, 64-67, 73-74, 81, 84, 85, 158, 199
Nicholas, Francis, 182, 184
Nicholson, John, 228-29
Nicola, Lewis, 106
Noarth, George, 148
non-exportation policy, 65
non-importation agreements, 45, 56, 58, 65
non-jurors, 109-10
Northampton County (Pa.), 293, 311, 328
North Carolina, 64-65, 73, 81, 145, 158
Northumberland County (Pa.), 85, 328
notary, McKean as, 36
Noxon, William, 24

oaths of allegiance, 1, 80, 94, 113, 126
"Observator," 416n22
Oeller's Hotel (Phil.), 283, 289, 291
Ogden, Charles, 321
Ogden, Robert, 39, 41
Ogle, George, 393
Olmstead, Gideon, 271-73
One Hundred Dollar Act, 334, 342
Order of the Cincinnati, 265
orphans court, 4, 19, 20, 36
Oswald, Eleazer, 183-84, 186-87, 188, 207, 222, 250, 253-56, 453n24
Otis, James, 37
Ottenreed, William Frederick, 180
Otway, Thomas, 11, 19
outlawry, 203-9, 215-27
oyer and terminer, courts of (Del.), 14, 415n19; (Pa.), 110, 114, 116, 120, 122, 298, 413n23

Paca, William, 67, 156
Paine, Thomas, 155, 338, 341
Parke, John, 26, 417n34
Parker, Anderson, 418n37
Parkinson's Ferry, 277-78
Parliament, 38-39, 41, 58, 64, 67
Parrock, John, 133-34
Parrock, Sarah, 133-34
Passmore, Thomas, 339-40, 467n15
patronage, 318-25, 330, 363-67, 377
Patterson, Samuel, 97, 107, 169-70
Paul, Caleb, 203
Paul, Jacob, 220
Paul, James, 220
Paul, John, 203
Paxton (Paxtang), 109-10
peace commissioners, 143
Peale, Charles Willson, 105
Pemberton, Israel, 105, 117
penal reforms, 234-37
Penn, John, 25, 36, 50, 126, 282
Pennamites, 195-96
Penns' Lands, 124-25, 160, 167, 175-76, 282, 440-41n36
Pennsylvania Gazette, 18, 102
Pennsylvania Journal, 29
Pennsylvania Packet, 150-52
Pennsylvania
  Assembly (colonial), 34, 69, 70-73, 74-76, 79; (state), 101, 103, 107, 109, 121-23, 124-26, 131-32, 164-66, 196-98, 199-200, 205-6, 214-15, 218, 220-22, 224-26, 229, 234, 238, 255, 259, 280, 333-36
  chief justice of, 97, 99, 100-101, 106, 108, 113, 119, 128-29, 132, 142, 166
  congressional delegates, 151
  congressional position, 71, 81, 158
  constitutional convention of 1776, 93, 103

constitutional convention of 1789-1790, 259-62
Constitution of 1776, 93-94, 95, 98-100, 110, 167, 186
courts of, 75-76, 97, 101-2, 109-12, 120-21, 123, 129, 131, 138, 187, 196, 200-201
economic conditions, 159-60
education, 22
elections, 71
law, 117, 180-81, 196, 199
lawyers, 15-16, 17, 42
militia, 275, 384, 386
State House, 67, 81, 94, 112
Supreme Court, 20, 25, 75, 94, 102-5, 126, 129, 164, 176, 202-3, 205-6, 213-15, 218, 220-26
  criticism of, 229-30, 237-38, 338, 362, 399
  use of robes, 227-28
Wyoming claims, 195-201
Penrose, William, 306
pensions, army, 144, 438n5
Perth Amboy (N.J.), 85-86
"Peter Porcupine" (William Cobbett), 291, 300, 308-9
Peters, Richard, Jr., 11, 24-25, 297, 354-55, 417n*31*
Pettit, Andrew, 266, 321, 322, 368, 464n*31*, 467n*15*
Pettit, Charles, 257, 266-67, 285, 464n*28*
pettyfogging attorneys, 42
Philadelphia
  bar, 112
  captured by British, 109
  city courts, 102, 338, 380
  City Hall, 113
  City Tavern, 57, 128
  Coffee House, 148-49, 210
  College of, 22
  courthouse, 129
  grand jury, 102, 114, 183, 186, 188
  slavery in, 231, 233

State House, 67, 81, 94, 112, 396
Philadelphia Evening Post, 345
Philadelphia Gazette, 295
Philosophical Hall (Phil.), 74, 93
Physick, Edmund, 175-76, 319
Pickering, Timothy, 197-99, 201, 261, 297, 346
Pinckney, Charles, 317
Pittsburgh (Pa.), 191, 277, 310, 323, 330
Plan of Union, 58-59
Pleasants, Samuel, 105
Plumstead Township (Bucks County, Pa.), 202-3, 220
pluralism, 164-77, 182, 405
Polk, William, 88
Pollock, Frederick, 204
Poor Richard, 10
Porcupine's Gazette, 302, 308-9. See also Cobbett, William
Porter, Alexander, 22-23, 26, 51, 91-92
Portfolio, 338
Poulson, Zachariah, 378
Powel, Samuel, 269
Powell, John H., 208
Presbyterians, 2, 5, 22, 34, 36-37, 46, 60-61, 69, 91, 100, 126-27, 232, 402, 412n*13*, 423n*25*, 431n*18*, 433n*36*
  influence in College of Phil., 148-49
  views on slavery, 232, 239
Price, John, 19
probate of wills, 11
Proctor, Thomas, 183
Proprietary interests, 21, 34, 36, 50, 78, 124-25, 126
prothonotary office of New Castle, Del., 11
province-wide convention (Provincial Conference, Pa.), 70, 74, 78-80
public creditors, 257
Pugh, William, 24
Purchase of 1768, 194

Index 499

Purviance, Samuel, 24

Quakers, 23, 70, 103, 105, 106, 107, 126, 129, 130, 239, 310, 404
Qualifications Committee (Cont. Cong.), 65
quartermaster's office (Cont. Cong.), 144
quarter sessions, courts of (Del.), 36, 43, 418n37; (Pa.), 52, 75, 102, 304, 379
Quid Mirror, The, 369-71, 379, 392
"Quidnunc," 182
Quids, 357-59, 363, 366, 370

Randolph, Edmund, 275
Randolph, John, 472n43
Rawle, William, 240
Read, George, 8, 11, 67, 147, 151, 168, 170, 172, 175, 432n33
    and Articles of Confederation, 144-47
    and Declaration of Independence, 81-82
    as president of Delaware, 107-8
    in Delaware constitutional convention of 1776, 89-92
    in first Continental Congress, 56, 58-59, 62, 423n20
    law practice, 16, 19, 22-24, 417n29
    named to Committee of Correspondence (Del.) 51-52
    resists British, 43-45, 46-47
Reading (Pa.), 106, 111
Red Lion Hundred (Del.), 89
Reed, Joseph, 25, 69, 75, 115, 117, 119-20, 127-29, 139, 143, 215-16, 230, 425n24, 432n33, 440n33
    and issue of independent judiciary, 134-37
    president of Supreme Executive Council (Pa.), 121-25
    refuses chief justiceship, 97, 99, 431n26
    seeks chief justiceship, 181-83
Reed, Joseph, Jr., 363
Rench, James, 88-89
Report on the Public Credit, 267
Reports of Cases Ruled and Adjudged in the Courts of Pennsylvania before and since the Revolution, 262-63
Republican Greens, 346
republicanism, vii-x, 58, 61, 95, 100, 110, 152, 159, 161, 186, 200, 215-16, 254-55, 258, 287-89, 305, 309, 311-12, 318, 344-45, 350, 361, 423n25
Republicans (1776-1790), 126-27, 167-68, 173, 182, 215, 219, 241, 258; (1790-1817), 268-70, 284-86, 300-301, 331, 333, 375-76
    attack Federalists, 251
    control of presidential electors, 316-18
    discontent with McKean, 330-31
    divide over reforms, 334-36, 338
    foreign policy of, 285-86, 288-91, 293-95
    origins of, 265-66, 268-69, 284-85
    party splits, 351-54, 383, 394-95
    radicals oppose McKean, 356-57, 358, 375, 376, 385-89
    renominate McKean governor, 331
    seek gubernatorial candidate, 306
    seek new constitution, 258-59
    support McKean, 310-12
    support McKean's patronage, 323-24
Respublica v. Buffington, 140-41
Respublica v. Carlisle. See Carlisle, Abraham
Respublica v. Chapman, 138-40
Respublica v. Mesca, 180-81, 191
Respublica v. Negro Betsy, 232-33
Respublica v. Roberts. See Roberts, John

Restraining Act, 64, 65-66
Reynolds, James, 381
Rhode Island, 50-51, 158
Rice, Evan, 32, 45-46, 57
Richards, John, 447n5
Richards, Joshua, 447n5
Ridgely, Charles, 51, 60, 90-91, 423n22, 426n24
Ridgely, Nicholas, 426n24
"Rising Sun" faction, 346
Rising Sun Tavern, 346
Rittenhouse, David, 105, 224
Roberts, John, 117-19, 131
Roberts, Jonathan, Jr., 345
Robinson, Abraham, 89, 92
Robinson, Parker, 418n37
Robinson, Thomas, 27, 45, 47, 52, 56, 60, 146, 418n37, 420n28, 423n27, 432n33, 438n12
Rodney, Caesar, 29, 32, 34, 51-52, 54, 107, 143, 145, 147, 400, 432n33
   in Delaware constitutional convention of 1776, 86-88, 90-92
   in Delaware politics, 169-71
   in first Continental Congress, 56, 58-59, 62, 423n20, 428n40
   in second Continental Congress, 67, 73, 77, 81, 83
   in Stamp Act Congress, 36-38
   opposes British legislation, 44-46
Rodney, Caesar A., 173, 312, 319, 398, 400, 417n34, 443n24
Rodney, John, 418n37
Rodney, Thomas, 73, 90, 146, 167, 170-72, 173, 176, 257
Rogers, James, 393
Ross, George, 22, 115-17, 271-72
Ross, James, 278, 310-11, 312, 324, 330, 339, 391
Ross, John, 11, 20, 42
"Royal Refugees," 207
Ruggles, Timothy, 37, 39
Rush, Benjamin, 77, 252, 363, 383, 397, 431n18
Rush, Jacob, 211-12, 233, 255, 363, 379

Rush, Richard, 392-93
Rutledge, Edward, 59

Schuylkill River, 325
Scotch-Irish, 2, 5, 46, 232
Scotland, 2-3
Scottish Enlightment, 6
Scroggan (a slave owner), 233-34
Searle, Anthony, 61
Searle, James, 156
Second Battalion (Del.), 97
Second Battalion (Pa.), 69
Secret Committee (Cont. Cong.), 65, 155
seditious libel, 186-87. *See also* libel
"Senator," 165
Sergeant, John, 386
Sergeant, Jonathan Dickinson, 111, 115, 117, 138, 167, 212
Shays' Rebellion, 199, 201
Shee, John, 368
Shippen, Edward, 104, 114, 240, 273, 340, 344, 368, 443n25
Shippen, Joseph, 71
Short Introduction to Moral Philosophy (by Francis Hutcheson), 6, 82
Sinclair, George, 204
slavery, 56, 230-34
Smilie, John, 245-46
Smith, Isaac, 29, 47
Smith, James, 93
Smith, John, 191
Smith, Phillip, 203
Smith, Richard, 156
Smith, Samuel, 123
Smith, Thomas, 193, 340, 344
Snodgrass, James, 203
Snowden, John, 363
Snyder, Simon, 350, 356-58, 363, 382, 391-92, 394-95
Society for Promotion of Agriculture, 265
Society for Propagation of Gospel in Foreign Parts, 60

Index 501

Society of Constitutional Republicans, 356-57
Society of Friends of French Revolution, 283
Society of Friends of the People, 357, 370
South Carolina, 81, 158
  president of, 150
specialiter, 21
Spectator, The, 6
Stamp Act, 34, 36, 39, 41-44, 45, 56, 61, 402, 419n*10*
Stamp Act Congress, 36-41, 44, 397, 399
Stansbury, Joseph, 440n*36*
"Star-Chamber," 28
State House. *See* Philadelphia
Staughton (Va.), 106
Steele, John, 328, 361, 384
Steele, Robert, 204, 219-20
Stevens, James, 122
Stewart, John, 351
Stiles, Ezra, 8, 412n*13*
Stout, Jonathan, 21
Sugar Act, 38
Sunbury (Pa.), 102, 196, 197, 211
"Superintendent of Finance," 161
Supreme Court. *See* Pennsylvania
Supreme Executive Council (Pa.), 97-98, 102, 104-5, 107, 111-16, 118-21, 123, 125-27, 129, 131-32, 134-36, 140, 151, 164, 166, 181-83, 199-200, 203, 205-10, 217-18, 219-22, 225-26, 229, 238
Susquehannah Land Company, 195, 197-99
Susquehanna River, 189, 194
Susquehanna Valley, 2
Sussex County (Del.), 14, 20-22, 26, 28, 31-32, 36, 48, 51, 55, 60, 62, 77-78, 98
  constitutional delegation of 1776, 88-89, 91-92
  country party 31, 46
  court party, 27, 29, 46, 146
  courts, 20, 22, 52

election fraud in, 146
grand jury, 27-29, 47
Swanwick, John, 285
Swift, Mr., 180
Sykes, James, 431n*27*

tabellion (New Castle), 36
"Tacitus," 324
Talleyrand-Perigord, Charles Maurice de, 293
Tammany Society, 346
Tannehill, Adamson, 323
"Tatler, The," 184
tax, Parliament's right to, 38-39. *See also* Great Britain, acts of
Taylor, Isaac, 4
Taylor, John, 116
Taylor, Robert J., 446n*37*
"Tanax," 164, 166-67
Thomlinson (or Tomlinson), John, 447n*5*
Thompson, David, 22-24, 26
Thompson, Dorothea McKean, 89, 411n*6*
Thompson, John, 24, 89, 92, 232
Thompson, Thomas McKean (McKean's nephew), 3, 5, 62, 89, 321, 326, 341, 365-68, 370, 378, 388, 393
Thompson, William, 147-52, 439n*18*
Thomson, Charles, 8, 22, 81-82
Tilghman, William, 113, 369, 471n*15*
Till, William, 1
Tilton, James, 442n*21*
Tories, 65, 77, 87, 90-92, 100, 105, 112, 119-20, 124, 126-27, 146, 168, 170, 196, 404-5
Townshend duties, 45
Tracy, Uriah, 346, 464n*19*
treason. *See also* Attainders, Act of
  cases of, 115-18, 123, 133-34, 138-41
  charges of, 114-15, 122, 199, 201
  legislation, 103, 104, 109
  misprision of, 103-4

Tredyffrin Tavern, 12
Tredyffrin Township (Pa.), 3
Trenton Decree of 1782, 198
"Trial by Jury," 221

United Declaration of Thirteen Colonies, 82. *See also* Declaration of Independence
United Netherlands, 211
United States Gazette, 356
University of Edinburgh, 6
University of Glasgow, 6
University of Pennsylvania, 127, 169, 265. *See also* College of Philadelphia

"Valerius," 173
Van Berkel, O.J., 211-12
Van Dyke, Nicholas, 22, 23, 24, 26, 89, 92, 158, 169, 170, 417n*34*, 431n*27*, 438n*12*
Van Horne's *Lessee* v. *Dorrance,* 327
Van Leuvenigh, Zachariah, 232
Veiner, Elizabeth, 189
Vickers (Vickars), Jesse, 203, 206
Vickers (Vickars), Solomon, 203, 206
villeinage, 231-32
Vining, John, 1, 23, 32, 417n*29*, *34*; 426n*24*
Violet (a slave), 21
Virginia, 44, 50-51, 81, 145, 158, 160, 194, 230-31
Votes and Proceedings (Del.), 34, 51

Wall, George, Jr., 218
Wallace, Hugh, 147
Walls, William, Jr., 27
Waln, Nicholas, 425n*24*
Waples, Burton, 47
Washington, Bushrod, 354
Washington County (Pa.), 188-89, 190, 193-94, 203, 207, 274, 276, 278
Washington, George, 85, 156, 162-63, 189, 193-94, 227, 231, 256-57, 266, 270, 273, 275-76, 282-83, 285, 288-89, 329
Washington v. *James Scott et al.,* 193
Waugh, William, 411n*3*
Way, John, 395
Wayne, Anthony, 392
Wayne County (Pa.), 328
Weigert, John, 189
Wertz, Henry, 367, 470n*12*
West Bradford Township (Chester County), 140
West Caln Township (Chester County), 208
Westmoreland County (Pa.), 85, 203
Wharton et al. v. *Morris et al.,* 234
Wharton, Samuel, 171-73, 443n*23*
Wharton, Thomas, 98
wheelbarrow men, 235
Whipple, William, 155-56
White, Amos, 204
White, William, 221
White Clay Hundred (Del.), 97
Whitehill, John, 218, 246
Whitehill, Robert, 218
Wilderness, Elizabeth, 189
Wilds, Nathaniel, 21
"Wilkes," 186
Wilkes-Barre (Pa.), 194, 197-98, 201
Wilkes, John, 28, 52, 216, 455n*48*
Wilkinson, James, 400
Will, William, 183
Williamson, Hugh, 8
Willing, Thomas, 65-66
Wilmington Academy, 416n*26*
Wilmington (Del.), 292
Wilson, Bird, 363
Wilson, Elizabeth, 189
Wilson, James, 72, 96, 115-16, 117, 126-28, 212, 244-45, 246, 251, 253, 257-58, 260, 271, 275, 276, 431n*26*, 436n*8*
Wilson, Mathew, 8, 22
Wilson, William, 328

Wiltbank, John, 27, 52, 92, 418n37
Winder, Moses, 447n5
Wolbert, Frederick, 371-72, 374, 379, 392
Wolcott, Oliver, 463n16
Wolford, Job, 21
Wood, Gordon S., ix
Woods, George, 218
Woods, John, 463n18
writ of capias, 201, 204, 209, 216, 219-20. *See also* outlawry
writs of error, 216, 218
writs of exigent, 204
writs of habeas corpus. *See* habeas corpus, writs of
Wynkoop, Benjamin, 420n27
Wynkoop, Henry, 220
Wyoming Valley (Pa.), 65, 194-201, 276, 280, 327-29

Yeates, Jasper, 95, 129, 273, 278, 281, 330, 340, 344, 425n24
York (a servant), 189
York (Pa.), 109, 111, 142-43, 147, 162, 167, 169
York County (Pa.), 312, 351
Yorktown (Va.), 163, 170
Young, Henry J., 120
Young, Thomas, 72, 93
Yrujo, Don Carlos Martinez D' (Chevalier Charles de), 295-303, 309, 321, 347, 352-55, 367-69, 460-61n15

"Z," 221
Zantzinger, Thomas, 393